WHITE

WHITE

*The Biography of
Walter White, Mr. NAACP*

Kenneth Robert Janken

THE NEW PRESS
NEW YORK

Published in the United States by The New Press, New York, 2001
Distributed by W. W. Norton & Company, Inc., New York

The publisher is grateful to reproduce the following material:

"Ballad of Walter White," from *The Collected Poems of Langston Hughes*, by Langston Hughes, copyright © 1994 by the Estate of Langston Hughes. Used by permission of Alfred A. Knopf, a division of Random House, Inc. (and in the U.K. by permission of Harold Ober Associates Incorporated).

Part of chapter four previously appeared as Kenneth Robert Janken's Introduction to *Rope and Faggot: A Biography of Judge Lynch*, by Walter Francis White. Reprinted January 2001 by the University of Notre Dame Press. Used by permission of University of Notre Dame Press.

Part of chapter four previously appeared as "Civil Rights and Socializing in the Harlem Renaissance: Walter White and the Fictionalization of the 'New Negro' in Georgia," *Georgia Historical Quarterly* 80 (1996): 817–34.

Parts of chapters nine and ten previously appeared as "From Colonial Liberation to Cold War Liberalism: Walter White, the NAACP, and Foreign Affairs, 1941–1955," *Ethnic & Racial Studies* 21 (1998): 1074–95.

LIBRARY OF CONGRESS CATALOGING-IN-PUBLICATION DATA
Janken, Kenneth Robert, 1956–
   White : the biography of Walter White, Mr. NAACP / Kenneth Janken.
     p. cm.
   Includes bibliographical references and index.
   ISBN 1-56584-773-3 (hc.)
   1. White, Walter Francis, 1893–1955. 2. African Americans—Biography.
3. African American civil rights workers—Biography. 4. Civil rights workers—United States—Biography. 5. National Association for the Advancement of Colored People—Biography. 6. African Americans—Civil rights—United States—History—20th century. 7. Civil rights movements—United States—History—20th century. 8. United States—Race relations. I. Title: Biography of Walter White, Mr. NAACP. II. Title.
E185.97.W6 J36 2003
323'.092—dc21
[B]   2002141438

The New Press was established in 1990 as a not-for-profit alternative to the large, commercial publishing houses currently dominating the book publishing industry. The New Press operates in the public interest rather than for private gain, and is committed to publishing, in innovative ways, works of educational, cultural, and community value that are often deemed insufficiently profitable.

The New Press, 450 West 41st Street, 6th floor, New York, NY 10036
www.thenewpress.com

Printed in the United States of America

2   4   6   8   10   9   7   5   3   1

For my parents, Isabel M. Janken and A. Harold Janken,
and for my wife and children,
Patricia Puglisi, and Eric Janken and Sophia Janken

Contents

Acknowledgments

While the rhythm of researching and writing this book was subject to life's vicissitudes, one constant was the generosity of colleagues, friends, family, and institutions. I am thrilled to acknowledge the debts I have incurred.

I did most of the research for this biography in the truly voluminous papers of the National Association for the Advancement of Colored People, which are housed at the Library of Congress. University Publications of America has performed a monumental service to scholars and other people interested in the history of the NAACP by microfilming this collection. I was able to read them near home (at Duke University, whose library owns a copy of the microfilm), which accelerated this project.

I received several grants and fellowships that released me from teaching and enabled me to concentrate on Walter White. The University of North Carolina at Chapel Hill has been wonderfully supportive. I am grateful to the College of Arts and Sciences for a research and study leave in fall 1994. A grant from the Arts and Sciences Foundation in 1995 paid for the reproduction of documents and travel to out-of-state archives. The Institute for Research in Social Sciences provided a summer stipend in 1999. I was a fellow at the university's Institute for the Arts and Humanities during the fall 2001 semester, where I completed this book. A Fellowship for University Teachers from the National Endowment for the Humanities during the 1997–1998 academic year (grant no. FA-34572-97) made it possible for me to complete the lion's share of the research. I wrote most of this book at the National Humanities Center in Research Triangle Park, North Carolina, which awarded me a fellowship, endowed by the Rockefeller Foundation, for the academic year 2000–2001.

All of this financial support was facilitated by Julius Nyang'oro, chair of UNC's Department of African and Afro-American Studies. He unfailingly encouraged me to apply for grants and cheerfully released me from teaching. Debby Crowder, department administrative secretary, shepherded fellowship proposals through all the proper channels and handled the myriad administrative details involved in the search for funding; she also has a knack for finding elusive synonyms.

Several people who knew Walter White were kind enough to share their memories, and I have listed them in the bibliography. I especially want to thank Jane White Viazzi, Rose Palmer, Edwina Ford, and Cynthia White (née Cannon) for their accounts of life with him. They may not share my interpretation of Walter White in its entirety, but their reminiscences were invaluable to my understanding him.

Several scholars shared their own research with me, for which I thank them. In the early stages of this project, I benefited from August Meier's encyclopedic knowledge of the NAACP. Robert Zangrando read me the notes of his interviews with persons long deceased, who were intimately acquainted with Walter White. His spirit of cooperation defines what is best in the academic world. Other scholars who made their research available to me are William Jelani Cobb, Leon Fink, Michael Homel, Theodore Kornweibel, and William Tuttle. Kaye Lanning Minchew of the Troup County (Georgia) Archives tracked down documents confirming the White family's genealogical lore.

Several scholars either read parts of the manuscript or otherwise evaluated my ideas. First among them is David Levering Lewis, who took an interest in this biography from its inception. Over the years I have also been able to count on him for encouragement, speedy feedback, honest criticism, and sound advice. I would also like to thank: Beth Bates, Fitzhugh Brundage, William Jelani Cobb, Lee Formwalt, Kevin Gaines, Ray Gavins, Paula Giddings, Perry Hall, Trudier Harris-Lopez, Reginald Hildebrand, Gerald Horne, Charles Hamilton Houston, Jr., Michael Hunt, Tera Hunter, John Inscoe, Michael Lambert, Waldo Martin, Deborah McDowell, Tim McMillan, Gary Pomerantz, Barbara Savage, Mark Solomon, Patricia Sullivan, Michael West, and Komozi Woodard.

I am grateful too for the assistance of the staffs at the following institutions: Davis Library and the Southern Historical Collection of the University of North Carolina, Perkins Library at Duke University, Moorland-Spingarn Research Center at Howard University, Herbert Hoover Presidential Library, the Manuscript and Prints and Photographs Divisions of the Library of Congress, the Atlanta Historical Society, and the Beinecke Library of Yale University.

Combing through reels of microfilmed newspaper can be a mind-numbing job. Two University of North Carolina history graduate students, Rachael O'Toole and Sarah Thuesen, did not succumb, but rather provided valuable research assistance at important junctures.

Marc Favreau, my editor at The New Press, deployed with grace and accuracy his red pencil. His determination to excise the extraneous, ability to ask incisive questions, attention to argument, and uncanny skill in reorganizing the written word greatly improved this work. He inherited me from Joe Wood, his predecessor, who saw promise in this project before I had written a single chapter. Sadly, Joe's life was cut short in a hiking accident in 1999.

John and Brenda Blom, friends of long standing, opened their home—and their hearts—to me on my research trips to Washington, and my life is richer for knowing them. Because they live in Baltimore, I also credit them for hooking me on Chesapeake Bay crabs.

I have been fortunate to have been able to share this book with three very important people. Patricia Puglisi has lived with Walter White since he moved in with us in 1994; so too has our son Eric, who was born that year. Five years later, our daughter Sophia came into the world. Research and writing is for me mostly a solitary exercise. But in many ways, this book grew up around the kitchen table. My family respected my need sometimes to dominate the mealtime conversation with talk of this book. But neither were they shy in reminding me that they had interesting lives too, that they should have a claim on my attention. I am grateful to Eric for taking me outside to play baseball. Sophia's smile and humor dissolved even my worst frustrations caused by unproductive writing days.

I cannot reveal, and remain discreet, all that Patricia Puglisi has meant to this project and to my life. Suffice to say that it has been an awesome journey and one that I eagerly look forward to continuing forever.

Chapel Hill, North Carolina
November 2002

Now Walter White
Is mighty light.
Being a colored man
Who looks like white,
He can go down South
Where a lynching takes place
And the white folks never
Guess his race—
So he investigates
To his heart's desire
Whereas if he was brownskin
They'd set him on fire!
By being himself
Walter finds out
What them lynchers
Was all about.
But back to New York
Before going to press—
Cause if the crackers ever got him
There'd be one Negro less!
Yes, it's our good fortune
He was born so light
Cause it's swell to have a leader
That can pass for white.

> —Langston Hughes,
> "Ballad of Walter White" (1941)

Preface: The Man Called White

Although Walter White was Afro-America's most ubiquitous face during the three decades preceding the 1954 Supreme Court decision in *Brown* v. *Board of Education*, he is conspicuous in his absence from the ranks of biographical subjects. His white appearance (he had blond hair and blue eyes), his defense of integration and, at times, even assimilation, combined with his simultaneous devotion to the fight for full black equality, have made White a troubling subject for historians used to thinking about race in America in binary terms. This biography addresses questions crucial to African American history: how to understand and evaluate racial identity and authenticity; the tension between integrationism and various shades of nationalism; and the decisive impact of White's leadership style on the course of the civil rights movement.

As Langston Hughes's poem makes amply clear, Walter White was a "voluntary Negro," that is, an African American who appears to be white but chooses to live in the black world and identify with its experience(s). He used his anomalous condition to advantage. His popular writings on his complexion and "passing" exploded racial stereotypes and challenged the idea of race as an immutable category. At the same time, he exploited his position as a voluntary Negro; his exotic status paradoxically afforded him a social standing and a wealth of contacts that would have been denied him had he been white. White enjoyed masquerading alternately as white and as African American. He delighted in making fools of unsuspecting white supremacists and utilizing his ambiguous appearance to demonstrate the absurdity of racial categorization. His experiences run contrary to themes in contemporary scholarship and popular nonfiction, which emphasize the marginal position and fragmented sense of identity of "multiracial" Americans; White relished having a foot in each world and would have been dismayed to hear his life labeled "inauthentic." White's life history complicates accounts that move too quickly from racial identity to social marginalization.

From the beginning of his career, Walter White fought not only against segregation and discrimination, but also against manifestations of nationalism. Most well known is his 1934 conflict with W.E.B. Du Bois over the latter's endorsement of voluntary separation. White was an un-compromising champion of complete integration. He was proud of the institutions that African Americans had created, but he saw no particular virtue in preserving their exclusive racial character. For example, he prized the education he had received at historically black Atlanta University, yet he saw no danger in the school having a racially plural student body and faculty so long as it continued to teach within its founding tradition as a school to uplift emancipated blacks. As an advocate for African Americans who refused exclusive characterizations of that group, White's positions and actions cut across the dichotomies on which many contemporary debates about racial progress are framed.

A study of Walter White's life provides an excellent opportunity to explore conflicting approaches to reform in the black freedom struggle. Beginning in the years following World War I, his incognito investigations of racial pogroms and their subsequent publication in leading white liberal journals were central to turning public opinion against lynching. His was a style of work that depended upon rallying enlightened elites and favored a nascent civil rights bureaucracy over local and mass-oriented organizations. Certainly he achieved some stunning results. He orchestrated massive support in Congress for an antilynching law, which effort was defeated only by filibustering southern Democratic senators. When Marian Anderson was refused the use of Constitution Hall, White secured the Lincoln Memorial and assembled a sponsoring committee studded with New Deal officials for her Easter 1939 concert. He obtained a promise from President Truman to appoint a civil rights commission, which produced the landmark *To Secure These Rights* (1947).

Yet, though dominant, his was not the only style operating within the NAACP. In the thirties and forties, tireless organizers like Ella Baker crisscrossed the country building branches capable of mobilizing local people on a variety of issues like salary equalization for black teachers, police brutality, and employment discrimination. In those years other association officials, some with ties to the organized left, favored closer cooperation between the NAACP and workers who were trying to unionize. White saw these alternatives both as irrelevant to the strategic task of building a powerful civil rights lobby and as a personal challenge to his leadership. Walter White was the consummate "organization man," while people like Baker and NAACP attorney and legal strategist Charles Houston (and even Rayford Logan, who was on the association's periphery) were far less comfortable operating within a bureaucracy. His treatment of Ella Baker—who resigned in 1946—and of Ida B. Wells-Barnett before her (White ridiculed her lifework in Chicago) suggests both a hostility toward women in the movement's upper echelons and a distrust of women whose orientation was bottom-up organizing. White was victorious in this intra-organizational conflict, but at a great cost. When the civil rights movement entered a stage of mass activity beginning with the Montgomery bus boycott in 1955, the NAACP was woefully unprepared to participate.

Walter White's elite-oriented strategy was more successful in his forays into the world of culture. He was an energetic promoter of the Harlem Renaissance as well as an author of two of its novels. He believed that the primary obstacle to black progress was white ignorance and that cultural awareness was the principal solution. He helped to launch the careers of black artists and writers by connecting them with members of the white cultural establishment, with whom he was on intimate terms. White regularly chaperoned interested and well-placed whites on their voyeuristic tours of Harlem nightspots. He used the same strategy in the forties when he visited Hollywood. He consulted on scripts, helped to land Lena Horne her first major contract, and received pledges from the major studios to improve their treatment of blacks in film. He was both an effective self-promoter and a booster of the NAACP; his flair for publicity often took the association to places where diligence alone would not.

In life, White worked indefatigably to advance his program and the cause of civil rights, and a good fray was just part of the bargain. More than once he was reviled on the floor of the Senate, and presidential aides fulminated against him. The Communist Party took him to task with brio on one side, while the southern white liberals, whom White regularly courted during the antilynching crusade of the twenties and thirties, scolded him when they felt he had moved too fast. None of this bothered him in the least. If anything, he dusted himself off and strained to get back to work. He was the civil rights analog to baseball Hall of Famer Ernie Banks, who, though his teams suffered more losing seasons than winning ones, never lost his enthusiasm, and whose motto was "Let's play two!"

In fact, White delighted in the calumny, because he knew that there was no such thing as bad publicity; all of it, favorable and critical, was valuable advertising and brought him and the NAACP program to the nation's attention. What would distress him was public silence and indifference to the cause. To understand and assess the fight for civil rights in the first half of the twentieth century and its trajectory since, one must take full measure of Walter White, who had his hands in a multitude of projects and left his fingerprints everywhere.

WHITE

Chapter 1

Becoming Black

March 21, 1955, Walter White's last, began much like any other day for the executive secretary of the National Association for the Advancement of Colored People, and one of black America's best known faces. He awoke after a restless night, owing to chronic heart problems—brought on by excessive smoking and a lifetime of punishing travel in service to the cause—that had sidelined him for the past several weeks. But this day there was no keeping him away from the association's midtown New York offices. He had grown restless on his monthlong Caribbean holiday in February, where, instead of convalescing, he began to outline plans to pillory in the 1956 elections those liberal politicians "who today callously give us the brushoff."[1] He arrived shortly after noon and, as in thousands of days past, immersed himself in routine office matters. Roy Wilkins said that Walter "had seemed so very much his old self—chipper, cheerful, confident, even relaxed."[2] His last memo of the day, dictated around 3:00, suggested that the NAACP purchase tickets to a fund-raising banquet. It was not that he particularly cared for the cause, but Eleanor Roosevelt did, and he therefore thought it wise to take heed.[3] He puttered around the office until around 5:00, went home to his West Sixty-eighth Street town house, and dropped dead of a heart attack just before seven in the evening.

In its obituary the following day, the *New York Times* offered that "White, the nearest approach to a national leader of American Negroes since Booker T. Washington, was a Negro by choice."[4] In that epigram are the essential themes of Walter White's life and work: his will to be the preeminent Negro leader and determine the direction of the civil rights struggle, to counsel and influence presidents and other powerful politicians, to mediate between the worlds of the races—and of course his complexion, his straight blond hair and blue eyes. His appearance gave him the option—which he did not exercise—to pass for white, but it nevertheless stamped the way he looked at the world and the way the world looked at him.

Walter White reveled in the disorientation caused by his apparent whiteness. He loved to tell of the time he was on a train and an ostensibly cultured southern man assured him that he could tell if a Negro was trying to pass simply by looking at his fingernails; examining White's, the man told him that unlike his, blacks' fingernails had pink crescents at the cuticles. He recounted with glee the bafflement on prominent whites' faces when he unexpectedly revealed to them his racial identity. He derived great satisfaction from this masquerade, this putting one over on whites. At the same time he could make himself the punch line of the joke. His autobiography is titled *A Man Called White*. He enjoyed his work with Algernon Black, the leader of the Ethical Culture Society, with whom he served in the wake of the 1943 Harlem riot. White appreciated Black's comment that "the Black-White Committee is an ideal combination, especially since the man named 'Black' is white and the man named 'White' is black—or calls himself black."[5]

His complexion had a serious side to it as well—sometimes deadly serious. From 1918 to 1930 he investigated forty-one lynchings and eight race riots, frequently passing for white to gather information. His easy manner, Atlanta roots, and white appearance gave him sources in mobs and Ku Klux Klan circles that were the journalists' envy. On one occasion he was deputized and given permission to shoot blacks, and on others he worried about his personal safety should his incognito be exposed.[6]

African Americans' reactions to the way Walter White used his skin color to shape his public image ranged from amused to hostile. Several friends and acquaintances kidded him, saying he was passing for black. "Our very *deepest* personal and 'racial' thanks for your visit here," wrote one longtime friend after White spoke in her city. "Of course," she added, "you're not 'colored' but we accept your own label and thank you just the same—perhaps more."[7] At the other end, African Americans accused White of trading on his color to personal advantage, as seen in NAACP stalwart Joel Spingarn's keen observation "that hundreds of Negroes think you are really a white man whose natural desire is to associate with white men."[8]

In short, his fair complexion marked White almost from his birth on July 1, 1893, in Atlanta, Georgia. He was the fourth of seven children born to George W. White and Madeline Harrison, a postal carrier and former teacher, respectively. He was born into a family that had achieved some prominence in black Atlanta, owing to a confluence of three circumstances: the parents' light color, George White's occupation, and the family's religious affiliation.

Madeline White could trace her white ancestry at least back to Virginia in the 1830s. There, a female slave named Dilsia had six children by William Henry Harrison. When Harrison decided to run for president, he concluded that it would not be politic for him to have "bastard slave children," so he gave four of Dilsia's children to his brother. His brother sold them to Joseph Poythress, one of the earliest white settlers of La Grange, Georgia, who in 1840 was among that town's five largest slaveholders, with twenty-two males and fifteen females in chains.[9] In 1850, when Dilsia's children would have been in their early teens, Joseph Poythress's holdings expanded to include $18,000 in real property and ninety-five slaves. "Rich as Mrs. Poythress," a reference to his widow—he died in 1853—was a phrase common among La Grange residents.

Sometime between 1850 and 1860, a young medical doctor, Augustus Ware, himself a product of a well-to-do family, came to live in the Poythress household, headed by his sister Caroline, the widowed daughter-in-law of the late Joseph. It was here that Marie Harrison, one of Dilsia's children, caught his attention.[10] Ware was a fierce Confederate partisan; during the Civil War he volunteered his services as a surgeon but was rejected on health grounds. Instead, he instructed the country's only female militia—dubbed the "Nancy Harts"—in drilling, marching, and marksmanship.[11]

Ware had four children by Marie Harrison—the one born in 1863 being Madeline Harrison, Walter White's mother—and he installed her in a home downtown on Hamilton Street, around the time of emancipation. When Ware died in 1872, Marie Harrison remained in the home to raise the children. But they never married, Ware having also a lawful wife, whom he married the year Madeline was born—white, of course, and from an ancient Troup County family—by whom he had two, possibly three, children who carried his name and inherited his wealth and family connections.[12]

While it is possible that Ware's and Harrison's relationship eventually developed into a mutually affectionate one, the evidence strongly suggests that she was his concubine. It began under slavery, when Harrison had no right to refuse him. After emancipation, the relationship was facilitated by the fact that he and Marie lived on adjoining property and she may have continued to be his laundress. That it was practically completely hidden from Ware's white relations while being common knowledge to his black kin further suggests at least an element of coercion. What is certain is that Ware passed some of his substantial wealth and sponsorship to Marie and her children. With Ware's assistance, Nathaniel, Marie's only son to survive into adulthood, became a significant property owner in La Grange and a prominent contractor.[13]

The transfer of wealth may have helped Madeline to attend Clark University in Atlanta to become a teacher. The status that was conferred by the wealth almost certainly helped her, upon her return to La Grange, to marry in 1879 a similarly situated Marshall King. He was the son of a well-to-do antebellum free Negro and Reconstruction-era politician in Alabama. The marriage ended tragically that same year, when King suddenly died of a heart attack. (Indicative of the station King occupied is an obituary in the local paper—itself unusual for an African American—that stated that he was "held in high esteem by all classes of our community.") Despite her early widowhood, Madeline was assured of her position in the black elite, which usually was of mixed ancestry and whose material foundation was the transfer of wealth from a white planter to his black partner and their children.[14]

Little is known of Walter's father's background. He was born in Augusta in February 1857, enslaved like his future wife, the only child of poor and devoutly Christian parents.[15] There is circumstantial evidence that he knew the family of John Hope, the "voluntary Negro" who presided for many years over Morehouse College and later Atlanta University. If so, he would have had an early exposure to the genteel and racially integrated world of Augusta's mulatto elite, and it would also help to explain how Walter and all his siblings came to be comfortable crossing racial boundaries.[16] He completed eighth grade in Augusta, the highest level of public school available to blacks anywhere in Georgia before

1924, and in 1874 he enrolled in the college preparatory department of Atlanta University (AU). It was during this time that he and Madeline likely met. He graduated from Atlanta University's high school and completed one year of college before his parents died, forcing him to withdraw in 1879. George struggled to earn a living, first as a laborer and after 1882 as a postal worker.[17] How he heard that Madeline had become a widow is not known, but in October 1882 they married in La Grange and returned to Atlanta. The next year their first child, named George N., was born, followed over the next seventeen years by Alice, Olive, Walter, Ruby, Helen, and Madeline.[18]

Fair like his wife, George White brought to his union with Madeline the two other essentials to the family's success. First, as a federal employee he was—along with entrepreneurs catering to a predominantly white clientele, domestic workers for the most elite white families, and professionals—part of the upper stratum of Atlanta's black society in the last years of the nineteenth century.[19]

Second, a devout Christian, he was a deacon of the First Congregational Church, the city's premier black religious institution. Founded in 1867 by freed slaves in conjunction with the American Missionary Association, First Congregational early established itself as one of the leading Negro institutions in the city. Closely associated with its own founding both in time and personnel are the Storrs School, which provided elementary education and a variety of social services to the ex-slaves who poured into the city, and Atlanta University, whose first location was in fact the First Congregational Church.[20]

Walter's parents established for him and his siblings a world that was built upon the primacy of religion and education and a knowledge of the specialness of the institutions to which they were connected. The creed was Puritan, which George absorbed from the New England Congregationalists at AU, and the Sabbath routine was, according to Walter, invariable, interminable, and excruciating. Invariable in that the regimen never changed, even though the seasons did. Interminable in that after rising on Sunday morning at 6:30 for extended family prayers and breakfast, Walter and his siblings were packed off to First Congregational a half block from their home for Sunday school at 8:00, followed by a long service at 11:00. Excruciating, because all the kneeling rubbed Walter's knees raw. His father permitted no activity that would dishonor the Sabbath. Of course, household chores were forbidden, but so was studying and pleasure reading. His mother tempered the strict prohibitions with common sense, though, and when George was attending to the congregation's spiritual matters, she allowed her daughters to iron their clothes and otherwise prepare themselves for Monday's work world.[21]

If family rituals made young Walter restless, the First Congregational Church building must have awed him. The wooden pews were unforgiving, but the atmosphere in the sanctuary surely gave him pause to consider the importance of his religion in service to the Negro people and the connection between rectitude and rights. Dominating the church's interior are majestic stained-glass windows in which the spiritual and temporal worlds intersect. There depicted, among other people, are Jesus in the garden of Gethsemane; Abraham Lincoln, the Great Emancipator; and people prominent in the early efforts to educate the ex-slaves, including one of the founders of Atlanta University and the city's first female Congregational missionary. Kathleen Redding Adams, a contemporary of Walter White, explained that "those windows probably governed my life . . . "[22] The meaning of those windows extended far beyond the church into the surrounding Old Fourth Ward neighborhood.

The Old Fourth Ward contained within its borders more than a third of the city's 28,000 African Americans in 1890. It was an up-and-coming neighborhood; most blacks who relocated there came from other parts of the city's east side to live in a nicer house or to become owners. Upon their marriage George and Madeline rented a home in Houston Street, one of the neighborhood's principal thoroughfares. For nine years they saved, and in 1892 the Whites moved into a four-room, one-story house they built at 101 Houston Street, between Courtland and Piedmont. (Later, as the family grew, they moved this house to the back of their lot and constructed a two-story home in its place; they supplemented their income by renting out the old structure by the room.) Lucy Rucker Aiken, a childhood playmate of Walter White and the daughter of Henry Rucker, the collector of internal revenue under President McKinley, lived on Piedmont Avenue. She remembered that "most of the people I knew owned their homes; modest houses but not shacks by any means."[23]

In his autobiography Walter portrayed the neighborhood of his youth as "deteriorating," contrasting it with the orderly appearance of his home. This is misleading. The 1900 census shows that on White's block there was a mix of owners, renters, and boarders. The enumerator entered the occupations of very few people, but only a few were recorded as having been unemployed; on the block lived a "capitalist," a jeweler, a stenographer, a carpenter, and a bricklayer, as well as a janitor, cooks, laundresses, and day laborers. A predominantly black street, it was nevertheless racially mixed. His description of "down-at-heel" surroundings more accurately depicts "Darktown," a congested and destitute area several blocks east. But according to Mrs. Millie Jordan, the aunt of former mayor Maynard Jackson, the main body of the Old Fourth Ward "was the elite section of its day until . . . the twenties." On Walter's own street were bishops of the A.M.E. church and the president of Morris Brown College, which was on the same street before it moved to the west side.[24]

While Walter may have exaggerated the decay of his block, the White homestead likely did stand out. The interior was always painted, the exterior was in good repair, the fence whitewashed. Madeline kept pansies in the garden in front, which was ringed with brick. The front porch had a swing. Walter White's niece, Rose Palmer, remembers two houses in the neighborhood standing out: the Whites' and the Henry Ruckers'. Kathleen Redding Adams lived a few blocks away on Auburn Avenue, one of black Atlanta's principal commercial and residential arteries, and her father kept their home in excellent condition too. But in her memory, her home was not an island in a sea of disrepair; rather it was the source of good-natured teasing from prosperous friends. "My father," she recalled, "never said his house nor his home, but he always said, 'my residence.' So his friends used to tease him and our neighbors about the mansion; they called it 'the mansion.' And I can hear Bishop Holsey's daughter now, calling over the fence to my mother, 'Mrs. Ellen, Mrs. Ellen, what's he going to do to the mansion this year?' "[25]

The First Congregational Church also made its presence felt through the large number of people living in the neighborhood who were associated with AU. "I don't separate the two," said Kathleen Adams. "You say Atlanta University, you mean First Congregational Church. You say First Congregational Church, that means Atlanta University. . . . All the people who were living around me, the majority of the people living around me were Atlanta University graduates or Atlanta University students." It was common for AU students to board in homes in the Old Fourth Ward. At least one—Adrienne McNeil—boarded with George and Madeline. It was in their parlor that Alonzo Herndon, the ambitious owner of a downtown tonsorial establishment who used his savings to found in 1905 the Atlanta Life Insurance Company, courted "Miss Adrienne." (By all accounts, George White had strict house rules. When it came time to retire for the evening, he would come downstairs and say, "Miss Adrienne, do you know what time it is? I'm going to turn the lights out on you." Herndon's reply was, "Well, go ahead Mr. White, it will be better that way.") [26]

Once they graduated from Atlanta University, many went on to teach in the Old Fourth Ward's public school. Kathleen Adams remembered only three teachers at Gate City School, which Walter also attended, who were not graduated from AU. In the history of education for blacks in Atlanta, the Gate City Colored Public School (also known as Houston Street School) was unique. Founded in 1880, it became the first city school for black children to be staffed exclusively by black teachers and headed by an African American principal. The board of education expected the Houston Street faculty and staff to do what they were told, but the teachers and principal had other ideas. In 1885, principal Antoine Graves refused to join a parade when the remains of Jefferson Davis passed through Atlanta on their way to Richmond; he told the board that he could not honor a man who fought to keep blacks enslaved. The board fired him. [27]

Despite the inadequate facilities, overcrowding, and a funding formula that gave the majority of the city's education budget to white schools, the teachers at Houston Street cultivated an atmosphere in which success was assumed and students knew they were special. In this respect, Gate City was very much in the mold of exceptional black schools like M Street High in Washington, D.C. (motto: "I shall find a way or make one"), and the Avery Institute in Charleston, South Carolina. One need only take a glance at a pre-1900 photograph of Walter White and Lucy Rucker in their first-grade class to see that their parents expected great things of them. In this picture, taken in an era in which cameras were hardly the ubiquitous items they are today, Walter leads the class in a spelling exercise while Lucy looks on in rapt attention.

Walter grew up in a close family in which excellence was the standard. In the conduct of their personal lives and in family obligations, the parents expected much of the children. Walter's job was to accompany his father each weekday after school to collect the mail, a task he fondly remembered. He also was responsible for cleaning the cinders from the coal burner, a chore he liked a great deal less. He tried to fob the job off on one of his sisters; his mother caught him once, which was enough to keep him from shirking that responsibility again. Mostly things were done with good cheer, and Walter had a quick laugh, which he used to tease his sister Madeline, the baby of the family.[28] The ties nurtured at 101 Houston would last a lifetime, as the adult Walter returned to the family homestead when he traveled on business in the South, and in later years tried to spend holidays and vacations with his siblings. White wrote of his deep affection for his family to his friend Eleanor Roosevelt on the occasion of his mother's passing:

> You will probably remember that just about a year ago I took the liberty of bringing my mother with me when I came up to Hyde Park to see you.
>
> Last Sunday we buried Mother at Atlanta. She died quite suddenly from a heart attack. The last time I saw her she asked about you and again told me how much she had enjoyed meeting you. Your graciousness to her had given her renewed courage to face the trying lot which was hers, particularly in the illness of her youngest child at Oneonta who, a fortnight ago, finished four years flat on her back. [Walter enlisted the aid of New York Governor Lehman in getting the tuberculor Madeline into the state sanitorium at Oneonta.]
>
> Since Mother died I have had a new understanding of how remarkable a person she was. On a mail carrier's salary which never exceeded $125 a month she and Father established and maintained a Christian home with high ideals, acquired a little property, and put seven children through college. They did this in the face of all the prejudice which people like them encounter in a place like Atlanta. I am proud to be her son.[29]

George and Madeline sheltered their children as best they could from the friction and violence inherent in Jim Crow race relations. One time a white child caught Walter as he dared to drink from a whites-only water fountain. The boy pushed him from behind and then ran for the safety of his own block; Walter gave chase and threw a rock, hitting the child in the head. Walter ran home, arriving just before the white child's mother, who threatened to bring the full force of the law on him. Madeline defended her child's actions and forced the other woman to back down. But when they were alone, she beat her son with a switch, teaching Walter the lesson that black mothers since emancipation taught their children: do not openly defy racial etiquette for personal convenience.[30]

The streetcars were another site of friction and potential racial violence at the turn of the century, as not only was the seating segregated, but black riders were subject both to the whim of conductors, who could be rude and arbitrary, and to white passengers, who could also demand the very seat that a black occupied. Some families got around this by refusing to take public transportation. Lucy Rucker's father forbade the family from taking the streetcar; they would not pay the nickel fare if they could not get equal treatment. Consequently, Rucker and most of the Atlanta University students in the neighborhood walked the fifteen blocks to school rain or shine. Walter's niece Rose Palmer likewise heard family talk of the daily trek to AU.[31]

For Walter and his family, the indignity of the streetcars was compounded by their light complexion, which could lead to confusion, embarrassment, and heightened resentment. As he explained, if the female Whites boarded the streetcar and sat in the black section, they opened themselves up to "embarrassing stares and remarks" and insults from white male passengers who, believing them to be white, were aghast at the audacity of their sitting next to blacks, possibly even black men. Yet if they sat in the white section, they risked being censured by blacks who thought they were trying to pass; and if whites discovered them, they risked being put off the bus or being attacked. George White solved the family's problem by purchasing a horse-drawn surrey; it was Walter's job to maintain it and drive his mother to her social calls.[32]

In other ways too, the Whites sought to protect themselves from the humiliations of Jim Crow. Because of their position among Atlanta's black elite and because of their light complexion, they often were able to get courteous service in white-owned establishments. Madeline White shopped at Rich's, Atlanta's largest department store. Said Rose Palmer, her granddaughter, "Mr. Rich would greet my grandmother by name, Mrs. White." Kathleen Adams, whose father worked at a bank, shopped at all the downtown stores too, and was able to try on clothes. Other Negro elites had described their ability to open credit accounts at Rich's. But such was not always the case. While they could shop at Rich's, they could not eat in the store's restaurant or use the rest rooms, and in many places still they had to wait until all whites were served. Still, elite blacks like the White family had greater options, and Miles Amos, a pioneer black druggist in the fourth ward, recognized that while the black upper class could often command courteous treatment, things were worse for "the average Black person." [33]

Of course, hard as they tried, George and Madeline White could not prevent the facts of segregation and racial oppression from intruding in their and their children's lives—often violently, as in the case of the Atlanta riot of 1906. Beginning on the night of September 22, 1906, and continuing for two terrible days, white mobs roamed the streets of the Old Fourth Ward, the adjacent Five Points district, which was at the heart of downtown, the west side neighborhoods abutting Atlanta University and Morehouse College, and other African American residential areas in and around the city. They pulled black passengers off the streetcars and beat them to death. They set black-owned or -patronized restaurants and saloons on fire, incinerating their customers. Mobs chased African Americans and clubbed or stoned them or riddled them with bullets. They attacked a luxury hotel and a fashionable restaurant in hopes of surprising the black service staff. After three days of rioting, more than twenty-five African Americans were murdered, and hundreds more were injured.[34]

The proximate cause of the Atlanta riot was the race-baiting headlines in the city's principal dailies announcing spurious allegations of assaults on white women by black men. For several days previous, the papers stimulated white Atlantans' worst nightmares of sexually aggressive black men run amok. But what unloosed these psycho-sexual anxieties into a sustained spasm of antiblack violence was something more fundamental. In the early 1890s, Atlanta's commercial-civic elite, with strong ties to banking, investment, and industrial interests, seized control of the city government and worked tirelessly to build a New South commercial and industrial center. In addition to personal participation in the machinery of governance, this elite recognized the importance of communications media to establish and enrich their legitimacy, and they centered much of their activity on developing the daily press; the two most important papers were the *Constitution* and the *Journal*, but there were others as well.[35]

The process of building a New South city was messy. Industrialization led to sharpening class contradictions. Poor rural whites, drawn increasingly into the market economy either as producers of cash crops or as new arrivals to the world of the urban factory, took up cudgels in the 1880s and early 1890s against a mixed bag of enemies: railroads, banks, corrupt politicians, moral corruption. The most salient expression of their discontent was the populist movement. But their opposition to the exploitation by capital was flecked with racism. They viewed their challenge to the status quo as a whites-only affair. Many of the new white male urban proletarians, now dependent on wages for their livelihoods, viewed with alarm the erosion of the authority they enjoyed as heads of independent rural households. And while they blamed capital for their plight, they were also primed to lash out at blacks, especially black males, as the source of their troubles. The white working class attempted to preserve its position through such actions as hate strikes to prevent blacks from establishing themselves in industrial jobs, and assaulting African Americans in public places and on streetcars.

African Americans too struggled against the emergent New South. Black farmers formed the Colored Farmers Alliance, which championed the cause of Negro sharecroppers and occasionally found common ground with white populists to oppose lynch law, the convict-lease system, and the poll tax, among other measures. The last two decades of the nineteenth century also saw strikes by black laundresses protesting sagging wages. But black workers also employed less confrontational methods of resistance, such as the formation of mutual aid societies.[36]

The commercial-civic elite controlled the challenges to the emerging capitalist order by co-opting the poor whites. In exchange for their loyalty, the New South leaders extended racial privilege to white workers rather than political and economic power: the elites agreed to the continued exclusion of blacks from most industrial jobs and their elimination from civic life. They were assisted in the establishment of the new order by the acquiescence of Booker T. Washington, who represented that thin layer of black leaders composed of educators, business owners, and aspirants for patronage positions in federal service. Washington assumed his position as a preeminent black leader in 1895 by articulating what came to be known as the Atlanta Compromise. Washington committed African Americans to abstaining from politics, forswearing participation in labor disputes, and forfeiting civil rights. In return, the commercial-civic elite promised to give African Americans a fair chance to work themselves up from the bottom and to protect them from racial violence.[37]

Despite the Atlanta Compromise's evanescent promise of peaceful race relations in exchange for blacks' loyalty and faithfulness, African Americans continued to be targets of violence whenever poor whites chafed against the existing order. In 1906, Hoke Smith, a former cabinet secretary under President Cleveland, and Clark Howell, editor of the *Atlanta Constitution*, competed for the Democratic nomination for governor of Georgia in that party's all-white primary. Because Georgia was solidly Democratic, the victor of this contest was assured of winning the general election. Smith tried to garner the poor white vote by posing as a populist and advocating regulation of the railroads. He at first dodged the issue of black participation in politics. Howell, however, knew better how to capture the redneck vote: he accused his opponent of being soft on Negroes. Smith was put on the defensive, dropped his anticorporate platform, and began race-baiting. Throughout the summer primary campaign until the August election, each tried to top the other's increasingly hostile attacks on blacks. Smith's quick switch took him to victory, and howling of the imminent threat of "Negro domination," he swore to disfranchise blacks by constitutional amendment.

The shrillness of the campaign to deprive blacks of their political rights for all time was matched in intensity by rumors of black male sexual aggression. The editor of the *Atlanta Journal* made explicit the connection between black political activity and the crime of rape. He wrote that because they had been given the vote, African Americans made no distinction between political equality and social equality, which for whites was but a code word for interracial sex. Yet it was not so simple to return to a time before blacks participated in politics, for when the black male "cannot achieve social equality as he wishes with the instinct of a barbarian to destroy what he cannot attain to, he lies in wait" to assault white women.[38]

The newspaper's demagoguery hit its intended bull's-eye. It inflamed the racial animosity embedded in poor whites, even as they struggled against their impoverishment and abuse at the hands of the capitalists. The race-baiting surrounding the gubernatorial election once again diverted their rage at the emerging industrial order into a rampage against blacks. As one agitator told a gathering white mob, blacks (especially black men) were the instruments by which the capitalists exploited white workers and destroyed their way of life: "Tell me why this [the supposed epidemic of rape] goes on for one single day? I can tell you—for the negro's [sic] labor—to get more wealth for the South out of him. It is commercialism's will to trade on ravished white women!"[39]

There was, of course, no series of sexual assaults on white women by black men, and Atlanta's black community rejected this libelous explanation of the cause of the riot. Rather, they pointed to their reluctance to abide by the Jim Crow code of conduct that the white South tried to impose upon them. The indiscriminate and widespread attacks on African Americans of all classes and their property reveal that the mobs' intentions were to punish successful African Americans and ensure that none of the black population existed independent of white control. This certainly was how Walter White understood the actions of the mob, when he remembered its rampage up Houston Street.[40]

The recollections of the 1906 riot by most blacks who lived through it stress not only the mob's ferociousness but also the racial solidarity and manly resistance. Upon hearing of the violence, Lucy Rucker's father and brother ventured downtown to get more information only after she and her mother and sisters were safely settled in their home. W.E.B. Du Bois sat on the steps of Atlanta University's South Hall, shotgun lying across his lap, protecting his wife and child. John Hope, president of Morehouse College, did likewise at his campus. Helen Martin, Walter's younger sister, was seven years old in 1906; she remembers her father and brother returning from mail collection on the first night of the riot and standing guard against the mob, which was snaking its way down Houston Street.[41]

What Walter recalled of the riot is part of black Atlantans' collective memory. In various venues, stretching across two decades and including personal letters, a fictionalized account of the violence in his 1926 novel *Flight*, and autobiography, he emphasized four themes: white barbarity, incidents of personal heroism (such as his and his father's rescue of a doomed elderly black woman who was being chased by a mob), community self-defense, and a quickening racial consciousness.

White's recitation of much of what he saw during the riot remained consistent over the years, and other eyewitness testimony lends his credibility. But there are critical inconsistencies in his stories of his personal participation in the events of September 22, 1906. The Atlanta riot was for the young and fair-skinned Walter White a defining moment. For this reason it is important to examine his testimony and explore how he manipulated memory of the riot to inflate the value of his credentials as a race champion and to ease suspicion of him by the much darker majority of African Americans.

Walter White first related for the public his experiences in the 1906 riot through the voice of Mimi Daquin, the teenaged protagonist of

Flight, whose "cream-coloured skin, her Gallic name and her French ac-
cent gave her immunities she might not have possessed had she been
more distinctly Negro."[42] Mimi had moved to Atlanta's Old Fourth
Ward from New Orleans, whose racial barriers were far more permeable
than Atlanta and other southern cities. Her people, the Creoles of color,
placed emphasis in daily life on refinement and decorum. Mimi grew up
reading French classics. She worshiped in an integrated Catholic church
and was at ease in both black and white settings. She learned about (and
without sentiment objectively evaluated) her ancestors on both sides of
the color line. She understood herself to be neither black nor white.[43] In
Atlanta she scorned the black upper-class society into which her family
had moved. At the same time she learned to have nothing to do with
Atlanta's white world, though that meant giving up favorite pastimes like
attending the opera and the theater.

All that changed in an instant on September 22, 1906. Downtown
running an errand with her father on that evening, Mimi saw the mob
gather steam and beat to death a bootblack near Five Points. She saw a
white employer whisk two black employees to safety by rushing them in
his cart right through the mob. Both were scenes White recorded in his
autobiography. But on that day, "there flashed through her mind in letters that seared her brain the words, 'I too am a Negro!' " "Mimi dated
thereafter her consciousness of being coloured from September, nineteen
hundred and six. For her the old order had passed, she was now definitely
of a race set apart." In tone and substance, Mimi's awakening is no different than Walter's simple declaration in his autobiography that "I learn
what I am."[44]

The racial epiphany described in *Flight* and *A Man Called White* de-
serves closer examination. Several circumstances of his life encouraged
him to view race as "something that did exist but of which one was not
conscious except when it was impressed upon one," as he put it in *Flight*.
Most obviously was his complexion. So fair was his entire family that the
1900 census enumerator listed them as white, a mistake that was not so
glaring, given that whites also lived on Houston Street, as they did on
Auburn Avenue. There is no suggestion that the White family tried to
pass; indeed, the family was enmeshed in the city's principal African
American institutions. At the same time, Walter's maternal family history
must at least have suggested to him and his family that his connections
with whites were more than accidental and casual; the fact that Walter

lived in proximity to whites and on good terms with them may very well have fostered a feeling that race was incidental and not central to his existence.[45] And living in a reasonably prosperous neighborhood meant that he did not have to contend on a daily basis with the disabilities imposed upon most blacks.

Yet if he accurately described the context of his new self-awareness, he fabricated the single most-repeated incident of the Atlanta riot and the one that has been so closely associated with his own life: his armed defense of home and family against the approaching mob. It took its most developed and dramatic shape in the opening chapter of his memoir:

Late in the afternoon friends of my father's came to warn of more trouble that night. . . . There had never been a firearm in our house before that day. Father was reluctant even in those circumstances to violate the law, but he at last gave in at Mother's insistence.

We turned out the lights early, as did all our neighbors. No one removed his clothes or thought of sleep. . . .

Father told Mother to take my sisters, the youngest of them only six, to the rear of the house, which offered more protection from stones and bullets. My brother George was away, so Father and I, the only males in the house, took our places at the front windows of the parlor. . . . In a very few minutes the vanguard of the mob, some of them bearing torches, appeared. A voice which we recognized as that of the son of the grocer with whom we had traded for many years yelled, "That's where that nigger mail carrier lives! Let's burn it down! It's too nice for a nigger to live in!" In the eerie light Father turned his drawn face toward me. In a voice as quiet as though he were asking me to pass him the sugar at the breakfast table, he said, "Son, don't shoot until the first man puts his foot on the lawn and then—don't you miss!"

In the flickering light the mob swayed, paused, and began to flow toward us. In that instant there opened up within me a great awareness; I knew then who I was. . . .

The mob moved toward the lawn. I tried to aim my gun, wondering what it would feel like to kill a man. Suddenly there was a volley of shots. The mob hesitated, stopped. Some friends of my father's had barricaded themselves in a two-story brick building just below our house. It was they who had fired. . . . The mob broke up and retreated up Houston Street.

In the quiet that followed I put my gun aside and tried to relax. But a tension different from anything I had ever known possessed me. I was gripped by the knowledge of my identity, and in the depths of my soul I was vaguely aware that I was glad of it.[46]

Walter's first extant account of the mob menacing his home—just as terrifying but less embellished and therefore probably more accurate— came in a letter to the literary agent William Aspinwall Bradley, to whom he was explaining his credentials for writing about racial violence. The 1906 riot, Walter said, was his "definite introduction to the race problem in its harsher phases." The man who excited the mob to attack the home was not named as the grocer's son, but as "someone." And while "a group of colored men . . . who were very fond of my father fired upon the mob," White makes no reference at all to his armed defense of his home.[47]

The shotgun made its first appearance in a 1930 profile of White by Heywood Broun in *The Nation*. In this account, White shrank his age by a year, and the "someone" who shouted for an attack on the home now was the mob leader. Walter's father issued orders to protect the family, telling his son not to fire until the mob crossed the edge of the lawn and then "go on shooting as long as you can," which, while weighty, is not quite as dramatic as what White wrote in his memoirs. "I was twelve years old," Broun quotes White as saying. "After that night I never wanted to be a white man."[48] The article drew a skeptical response from his sister Alice: "Many thanks for the articles you sent. Read the one in *Nation* with much amusement. Where did the shot-gun come from?"[49]

Alice was not the only family member to question Walter's veracity. In 1934, he again recounted the Atlanta riot in a piece he submitted without luck to *Harper's*. Practically all was in place; his father's directions packed the drama of a Hollywood feature, though the mob leader had not yet metamorphosed into the neighborhood grocer's son.[50] Two days after he finished a very vivid first draft, he asked his youngest sister Madeline to get their mother's memories, because, inexplicably, "in the course of years, however, memory about certain specific details grows a bit vague."[51] Madeline's reply is not extant, but it must have contradicted practically all of Walter's account, for he asked her to question their mother again:

Dad did have guns and ammunition at the house. I remember Mother taking you, Helen, Ruby and Olive down under the old house. . . . My memory is quite definite on the matter of the guns but it is a little hazy on

whether we were watching at the parlor window downstairs or upstairs in
Mother's room. . . .

I hate to bother you again but I wish you would talk this over with
Mother and try to check up on my memory.[52]

Madeline replied that their mother remembered no firearms in the
house, and that the females were neither hidden in the back of the house
nor underneath the old house that was at the back of the lot; rather, the
females gazed at the mob from the upstairs bedroom window.[53] This did
not satisfy White, who must have thought that it impinged on his manhood if the females were not whisked to safety while he and his father
stood guard. Replied Walter, "Between you and me and the gatepost,
Mother's memory is not correct—that the family was at the bedroom
window. I will, however, have to make some sort of revision in the article
which, unfortunately, will materially lessen its effectiveness." Of course,
this he never did.[54]

The keys to understanding fully why Walter White fabricated the
armed defense of his house—when the truth of his involvement was both
heroic and horrific enough—lie properly in his adult efforts to raise his
national profile. He wanted to show whites that black men (including
himself) were just like white men in their determination to be brave pro-
tectors of the family, and he wanted to stifle the rumblings of his black
critics who questioned his race loyalty.[55]

But the concoctions were also his attempt to relieve the tensions of
class and color that he must have felt since childhood. In his "Why I Remain a Negro," a 1947 autobiographical essay for *The Saturday Review of
Literature* that formed the basis for the the first chapter of *A Man Called
White*, he let slip that "the Negroes resented our white skin, and the ethical standards which my parents maintained themselves and required of
their children."[56] Whether the source of the friction was envy of the
Whites by darker and poorer Negroes or Walter's own class prejudices,
his family's economic position and skin color set him apart and called his
membership in the black community into question, as when his longtime
friend from Atlanta, L. B. Palmer, said, "You are no more a Negro than
Roosevelt was a Dutchman. . . ."[57] His claims of extraordinary bravery
allowed him not only to affirm an affiliation with the race—the "one
drop" law did that—but also to demonstrate a vital connection to it.

If the violence of September 1906 annealed, however imperfectly,

Walter's racial identity, his education in the years following also tempered his personality. He was like many other children of the Old Fourth Ward who believed that their ties to the First Congregational Church and Atlanta University made them superior. All of George's and Madeline's children attended AU. Kathleen Adams said, "We didn't know anything except Atlanta University. . . . Atlanta University was the goal. . . . "[58] Lucy Rucker knew in her bones that AU made a person from her elite neighborhood complete:

> Atlanta University was a school you couldn't just walk into and make it a part of you. You had to have credentials and get into Atlanta University, and when you got in, you found why. Because everybody was high class out there. . . . They were just superior in almost every way.[59]

Just such an attitude guaranteed that Walter (and his brother George before him) would not consider going to Morehouse, and that Alice, Olive, Ruby, Helen, and Madeline would reject Spelman. Years later, Olive's daughter said she had so wanted to continue the family tradition and attend AU but could not because in 1929 it had transformed itself into a graduate institution.[60]

Among the features of the school that Walter found compelling was its interracial faculty and its commitment to eradicate the color line in student-faculty relations. Unlike other black colleges in Atlanta, students and faculty dined together, a dramatic suggestion of racial equality that cost AU its state appropriation in 1887. Students and teachers developed close relationships, more intimate than those of their counterparts at Spelman, according to Lucy Rucker Aiken. Edgar Webster was one of those teachers whose concern for his students' intellectual, social, and moral development was met with their full affection.[61] Webster, a New England missionary, headed the high school division and later the physical sciences department; he was a model of conciseness and precision and was always available to counsel his students. Years later Walter credited Webster and the other Yankee professors for cementing in him his militant belief in integration, for they "saved me from the defeatist belief that all whites are evil and bigoted in their attitude toward dark-skinned peoples."[62]

Walter entered Atlanta University's high school department in fall 1908, after completing Gate City School, there being no public education beyond eighth grade for black Atlantans. How he did at Gate City may never be known, for the school's records were destroyed in a fire. At AU, though, he showed himself to be an uninspired student. In his college preparatory classes—Latin, Greek, mathematics, ancient history, and natural sciences—he earned mostly *C*'s, with an occasional *B* and even a *D* or two. Only in composition and literature did he show exceptional promise, posting final grades of *B*+ and *A*, respectively. He exhibited almost no manual aptitude, achieving barely passing scores in carpentry, mechanical drawing, and other industrial subjects. His grades improved somewhat during his four years of college, and he even received an *A* in business law, but his college career, which ended upon his graduation in 1916, was certainly not academically distinguished.[63]

Instead, Walter sought an education outside the classroom, and he put his energies into extracurricular activities. Baseball was one of his childhood (and lifelong) passions, and he was the student manager of the AU team, his slight stature preventing him from taking the field. During his stint, the team—indeed all of the crimson-and-gray teams—suffered declining fortunes, owing to widespread cheating by opponents, who used ineligible players and even faculty members. But the disappointment caused by the club's mediocrity was salved by the fact that, of all the city's black colleges that fielded athletic teams—Atlanta Baptist, Morris Brown, and Clark were the others—only AU adhered to rigid rules that recognized "the scholar is greater than the athlete."[64] During his senior year he was on the football team—"playing not too good," is how he put it—and also served as class president.[65] The debate team also kept him busy that year, and though there is no record extant of the positions he took, it is safe to assume that his course work in elocution—he earned *B*'s is that subject—served him well. And then there were the faculty-chaperoned socials that took place after debate competition, where dancing was not allowed but precision marching was.[66]

In his last year of college, Walter took steps to prepare himself for life after graduation. The summer of 1915 he took a job selling insurance for the Standard Life Insurance Company, the largest black-owned business of its day. The territory of Atlanta being pretty well covered by veteran salesmen, he prospected in the smaller towns and rural areas outside the city. He developed his genial manner to the point where black folk trusted him enough to buy something from him. And, taking advantage of his ability to pass for white, he put his listening skills to use and heard the frank talk of rural southern whites about African Americans. It was good practice, and not only for a successful career in life insurance, for he would soon use these proficiencies to sell blacks on the NAACP and to gather intelligence on racial violence that would have been unavailable to a less discerning and darker person.

That summer, as White beat the countryside for customers, Leo Frank, a northern-bred Jewish factory supervisor, was kidnapped from an Atlanta prison and lynched, after his death sentence had been commuted to life imprisonment. The workers' and farmers' anxieties about and distrust of large capital were turned against Frank, who was a convenient representative of the ascending industrial order in the South; the white lower classes' spontaneous solutions to their dislocation, as in 1906, was directed not at a radical or even substantial economic and political restructuring, but at a minority—in this case Jews.[67] As he passed through rural Georgia, Walter heard venomous words from whites themselves, which must have been aimed not only at Jews but also at African Americans, who were showing their own displeasure at chronic poverty and racial violence by joining the Great Migration to the North.

Until that summer Walter appeared to be more concerned with extracurricular activities; he himself had noted the widely held opinion around this time that he was "too much interested in having a good time to do a responsible job satisfactorily."[68] His encounters with racism that summer convinced him that he must respond. When he returned to AU for his senior year, he decided to begin a chapter of the National Association for the Advancement of Colored People, founded in 1910. In September he wrote to W.E.B. Du Bois, who not only knew the White family but was the symbol of the NAACP. The coming year was to be his last at AU, and "before leaving it and becoming an alumnus I would like very much to be instrumental in the opening of a chapter here." More, White thought it fitting to establish a branch at the institution that gave the NAACP Du Bois and Augustus Dill. May Childs Nerney, the energetic national secretary of the association, wrote back with detailed instructions. But wary of chartering ephemeral branches, she was less than encouraging: "Be sure that you include a sufficient number of underclassmen to insure the carrying on of our work after you and the other seniors in the chapter have graduated," she wrote. "We strongly advise against your organizing a chapter unless you feel confident that it will grow and thrive." Whether Walter lost heart is not known, but there was no further correspondence on the subject, and no Atlanta University branch was chartered that academic year.[69]

The faulty connection was temporary. Walter graduated from AU and took a clerk's position at Standard Life and was soon promoted to cashier, which was high enough on the organizational chart to be listed on the company letterhead. His duties included handling cash and premium payments, overseeing accounts of the company's field agents, and selling insurance at night and on the weekends. He was headed up the company ladder and toward a prosperous career in the business world. His associates, either established business leaders or up-and-comers, were part of the city's new black elite, which was based in the segregated economy and which had supplanted the old elite based largely upon personal service to whites. They were race-conscious men, and, believing themselves uniquely fit to lead the community, they often sat around the office after work discussing the declining fortunes of Atlanta's black population.

They got their chance to do something in the fall of 1916, owing to two fortuitous circumstances. First, the Atlanta Board of Education voted to eliminate seventh grade from the public schools for blacks in order to finance a junior high school for whites. White and his cohorts had been unsure which of a host of grievances, including discriminatory treatment on the streetcars, to attack; but with their action, the school board handed them an issue around which black Atlantans had historically mobilized.[70] Second, when White and his colleagues resurrected efforts to found an NAACP branch, their labors were this time enthusiastically greeted by James Weldon Johnson, the veteran black activist and newly hired association field secretary.

The plan to eliminate the seventh grade was the third cut in three years. Two years previous, the board eliminated eighth grade for all students, leaving blacks with seven grades and whites with eleven. The year before that, in 1913, the board had voted to scrap both seventh and eighth grades from the black schools, substituting intead a regimen of vocational training. In that instance, protests by Lugenia Burns Hope of the Neighborhood Union, the Rev. Hugh H. Proctor of the First Congregational Church, and other black leaders forced the board to relent.[71]

"Things were at a low ebb during World War I, things were very low here," said Bazoline Usher, a former student of Du Bois at Atlanta University and a teacher at the Houston Street School.[72] White and his fellow insurance salesmen from Standard Life hoped to be the catalyst for a renewed struggle for equal rights in Atlanta. In December 1916, Walter asked the national headquarters of the NAACP for help. "Having felt the need for a long time of a chapter of the N.A.A.C.P. in Atlanta, the hotbed of discrimination and prejudice in this section of the country," he wrote,

> a few of the men of this city have decided to organize, if possible, a chapter here that will do some work towards the wiping out of some of the abuses practiced on the colored people. . . . We plan to gather a group of men and women, not necessarily radicals, but at the same time of the type that will dare to have thoughts and to act in such a manner as to work for the good of those of our people who cannot help themselves.[73]

Though Walter had addressed his letter to Roy Nash, the association's secretary, the quick response from national headquarters came from James Weldon Johnson. Nash, a white social worker, had replaced May Childs Nerney, whose increasingly rancorous relations with Du Bois unsettled the organization and raised concerns about disproportionate white influence and diminished black presence within the NAACP. Du Bois had wanted his old friend from Atlanta, John Hope, to take Nerney's place, but the white majority on the board was unwilling to alter the interracial formula for leadership that had been established at the association's founding: Du Bois, an African American, at the head of propaganda, and a white as the main organizer. But Du Bois's fears on this score were allayed when Johnson joined the association.[74] As it turned out, Nash was barely competent as an organizer, preferring to remain in his office and issue memoranda, while Johnson was the dynamic branch builder.

Realizing the importance of establishing branches in the South, Johnson immediately asked Walter for a list of men and women who would help start the Atlanta chapter and told him that he would soon visit the city as part of his southern tour. But White sent Johnson a roster of founding members that read like the register for an elite black men's social club. John Hope was enrolled, and so were six post office employees, perhaps as a result of Walter's father's connections. But the majority of founders were from the Standard Life Insurance Company, including secretary-treasurer Harry Pace and president Heman Perry. Johnson again urged White not to overlook women, but again White passed over the advice.

He was elected branch secretary, while the entire executive committee and the chapter's working committees were exclusively men who, Walter said, were familiar to Johnson and who would "form only a nucleus . . . [of] a large, prosperous and worth-while body, and only of the type who will have the courage of their convictions." (Years later, Johnson commented on the anomaly of Atlanta; when he made a speaking tour of the South in the winter of 1917, that branch was the only one that did not have a single woman participate in its organizational conference.)[75]

Even before the branch received its charter in 1917, White and the other executives got busy solidifying their base of support. In his first serious foray into race politics, White intuited well the outlook of the black middle-class males he sought to organize, and he utilized methods of leadership that became staples for the NAACP. Overlooking entirely the potential vigor that working-class African Americans could inject into a campaign, White sought instead to puncture the timidity of the elite. "You know," he reported to Johnson, "our folks generally like to wait and see if an enterprise is going to succeed, and if it does every one of them climbs aboard the bandwagon." With the addition of Atlanta University's George Towns, the physician William Penn, *Atlanta Independent* publisher Benjamin Davis, and the Methodist minister Lorenzo H. King (who would later move to Harlem and challenge White in the late-thirties world of New York politics), the middle class was becoming receptive to the branch's message.[76]

Having secured that initial support, the branch increased its influence with an attack on the school board's position. Clearly identifying itself and its constituency as belonging to the black elite, the branch employed uncompromising rhetoric and threats against the establishment should it not accede to its demands. On February 22, the executive committee got word that the board would consider the plan to eliminate the seventh grade in the black schools that afternoon. The committee assigned its older members, including John Hope, Ben Davis, Harry Pace, and Dr. Penn, to confront the board. Walter, the youngest and greenest of the group, stayed behind to write a report to Johnson. The branch was displaying its elite militance by going before the school board to represent "the thinking Negro and the tax-paying Negro." (He later reported approvingly that the delegation members were "representatives of the best element of the colored people.")[77]

The board backed down in the face of the "manly . . . straight-from-the-shoulder manner" of spokesman Dr. Penn. He told the board that there was no shortage of money, and that the board could find the funds for maintaining the seventh grade from the same place "they had gotten money to build fifty fine schools for whites." The delegation's argument won the sympathy of James Key, the future mayor, who voted to retain the seventh grade over the objection of Mayor Candler, the founder of Coca-Cola. "We certainly feel jubilant," White wrote to Johnson right after the delegation victoriously returned, "and if the N.A.A.C.P. does no more, it has earned its right for existence."[78]

This was a propitious beginning for the Atlanta branch. Membership soon climbed to 300, and the chapter continued its challenge to educational inequality while broadening its protests in other directions, including oblique threats to boycott the streetcar line should not treatment of African American passengers improve.[79] In March it issued demands for better schools, which included the elimination of double sessions; construction of safe facilities; a junior high school for industrial and commercial training for those "youth who cannot afford a college education"; and a high school. Despite pleas of municipal poverty, large sums of money were being expended on constructing white schools, the branch said. It called on its new members to be active in this campaign in order to demonstrate to the school board that the branch was no " 'flash-in-the-pan' outburst on the part of a few Negroes."[80]

Over the next six months, the branch focused on school overcrowding and double sessions. Since its initial victory, the school board had hardened its position. The board had bowed to white public opinion and refused to begin double sessions for white students, while at the same time refusing to end them for blacks. When another special committee argued without success before the school board, White wrote a letter to the editor of the *Atlanta Constitution* exposing the unfavorable conditions under which black students were forced to try to learn.

The letter was mild in tenor; indeed White identified himself as an officer of Standard Life and not as secretary of the Atlanta NAACP branch. He made no direct mention of eliminating school segregation, though he alluded to the injustice of the presence of a newly constructed school for whites, which had a student population of only 25 percent of capacity, that was located in the heart of the predominantly black west side. Still, White wrote, blacks did not begrudge whites their education; they only asked that their children be afforded the same opportunity as whites. He did address directly whites' fears of losing their black labor force. "The exodus of negroes [sic] from the south" during the Great Migration was an economic hazard to the region; they would continue to leave so long as they could not find better opportunity at home. If "the thinking white man . . . is sincere in his avowed good will toward the negro [sic]," he can show it by eliminating double sessions, White wrote.[81] The letter was published and received favorable editorial comment from Clark Howell, who stated the board ought to do the right thing by blacks.

To back up the branch's demands, White informed Johnson, in words far less compromising than the letter to the *Constitution*, that there were plans afoot for "a monster silent protest similar to the one held in New York, in order to make some tangible move toward the abolishing of double sessions." The march never occurred; White indicated one of the principal reasons was the branch's inability to reach the majority of blacks directly or indirectly through the city's black clergy, thus demonstrating a chief shortcoming in the upper-class orientation of the organization.[82]

What the branch did do, however, was to start a voter registration drive in the predominantly black third and fourth wards to defeat a school bond referendum, because city leaders had pledged that none of the money so raised would go to black schools. Though African Americans were disfranchised in most elections by the 1908 state constitution and the white primary, they could vote on bond issues if they paid their poll taxes. Passage of bonds in Atlanta required the assent of two-thirds of the registered voters; a large black turnout against the bonds or a boycott by blacks would prevent that. Twice, in July 1918 and April 1919, the city tried to get authorization to issue the bonds. Both referendums were defeated, owing in great measure to the branch drive, which more than doubled the number of black voters to 1,723 for the second election. It was not until 1921, when the city agreed to designate a share of the bond issue to the construction of a high school for blacks that a referendum passed; Booker T. Washington High School opened in 1924.[83]

During the first phases of the campaign for school equality in 1917, White expressed the exuberance that came to define his style of work. Political work was serious, but Walter was giddy with success and reveling in the drama that unfolded before him. He talked big, as when he threatened "other measures, that the white people of this town evidently think we haven't sense enough to use or back-bone enough to try to use." When Johnson visited Atlanta in March 1917 and spoke to an overflow crowd of 1,500 at the Odd Fellow's Building on Auburn Avenue, he suddenly asked White to say a few words; Walter bellowed that "we have got to show these white people that we aren't going to stand being pushed around any longer. As Patrick Henry said, so must we say, 'Give me liberty, or give me death!' " Yet he could also leaven his comments so that he would not sound so earnest; after writing a letter to Johnson that puffed up the branch's activities and accomplishments, he signed his name, identified himself as "Secretary, Atlanta Branch NAACP," and followed that with the parenthetical remark "Sounds big, doesn't it?"[84]

Johnson's visit set into motion events that would change Walter's life. Among those attending the branch conference following the public mass meeting were fifty of the city's most prominent black men. Johnson knew some of them; indeed, many would rise to prominence, including Louis Wright, who would become chairman of the NAACP board of directors. But of them all, it was Walter White, "a very young man who . . . became singled out in my mind." Johnson was "impressed with the degree of mental and physical energy he seemed to be able to bring into play and center on the job at hand."[85] Johnson returned to New York, was appointed acting secretary when Roy Nash resigned, and, when the opportunity presented itself, he proposed to the NAACP board that Walter White be plucked from Atlanta and brought to New York. "I feel that it is something that would give any young man of the race an unsurpassed opportunity for good work and a bright future," Johnson wrote to White.[86]

Yet for all his jauntiness and apparent devotion to the cause, Walter was reluctant throughout 1917 to make a career out of race advancement. He gave a broad indication that he was satisfied to sell life insurance while he weighed his options. For a time he thought he might apply for the segregated officer-training program at Camp Des Moines. But he would not do so unless the material and status benefits of such a move were clear: "If I can know absolutely the exact terms and conditions of such a project, I think I can arrange my work so as to attend this camp," he wrote to Roy Nash,

> but I do not intend to take any chances. I have my future pretty well mapped out and I do not intend to run the risk of losing all that I have attained since leaving school for any uncertainty.[87]

Indeed, in April 1916 Walter had been one of the founders of the Standard Loan and Realty Company, "a corporation organized and promoted by the young business men of Atlanta who are just taking their place in the business world," according to the *Atlanta Independent*. As one of fifteen directors, Walter likely had invested $1,000 in the new company. So his hesitation was understandable.[88]

When Johnson offered White the job of assistant secretary, he and Du Bois, who also desired Walter in the front office, had taken a big chance. These two venerable leaders recognized the value of Walter's energy—and, additionally, Du Bois could vouchsafe Walter's family background—but the NAACP board hesitated. Several of the members doubted the wisdom of hiring someone so young as Walter—he was twenty-four—not to mention someone so unknown and from the deep South. They also questioned whether the association should hire an African American as assistant secretary; they wanted someone who would eventually assume the secretary's position, and board policy had reserved that slot for a white person.[89]

Yet while Johnson and Du Bois were able to win over the board with their vision of the association's future, Walter stalled, again referring to his comfortable prospects with Standard Life: "You realize my chances for advancement," he wrote, pleading for more time to think. He then raised a series of other qualms: with the pay so low, where would he live? (He could have room and board for a reasonable $35 monthly, Johnson replied.) He worried about how relocating would affect his draft status; he did not want incur moving expenses only to be conscripted.[90]

Johnson's reply cut through White's hesitations and dodges: "That is a contingency which I think will have to be taken into account as all the other uncertainties of life."[91] Until now, Walter had shown flashes of excellence. Johnson was now asking him to assume responsibilities for race advancement commensurate with his abilities. White was persuaded. He packed his belongings and moved to Manhattan, beginning work on the last day of January 1918. Recalling more than a decade later (when he was under considerable fire from some quarters in the NAACP) the auspicious day he decided to make a career of civil rights, he still affirmed his choice: "As I look back upon the years which have intervened," he told his college mentor Edgar Webster, who had advised White to stay put at Atlanta Life and pursue a career in business, "I have the feeling that I did make a wise decision years ago in deciding to come to what was larger work than that which was offered to me in Atlanta."[92]

Chapter 2

Witness for
the Prosecution

Almost as soon as he arrived in New York City, Walter White was sent out across the South to investigate racial violence. Nineteen-eighteen promised to be as sanguinary as 1917: lynching was on the upswing and took especially macabre forms; the Great Migration, World War I, and organized labor's racially exclusionary policies resulted in antiblack pogroms in cities across the country; local southern governments, prodded by planters and other employers nervous about losing control over Negro labor, dragooned African Americans with "work or fight" laws. Between 1918 and 1926 White logged thousands of miles on the road, frequently traveling incognito as a white man, to document firsthand the mounting carnage. It was during these years, and especially between 1918 and 1920, that he built his reputation as a person of extreme courage and aplomb by making audacious forays into enemy territory—and sometimes into the homes of Klansmen—to reveal the truth about mob violence.

On February 13, 1918, less than two weeks after joining the national staff, White and James Weldon Johnson read in the paper during their morning commute of the lynching of Jim McIlherron the previous day—Lincoln's birthday—in Estill Springs, Tennessee. A mob of more than 1,000 watched as McIlherron was chained to a tree, doused with coal oil, poked with hot irons, castrated, and slowly roasted alive, before his body was thrown on a pyre. Shaken, White and Johnson arrived at headquarters and discussed with association secretary John Shillady what action to take. The usual practice was for the national office to send protests (and encourage association branches to do likewise) to the governor, other elected officials, and candidates for office, and to send out press releases to the daily papers and black weeklies. Occasionally the association sent an official investigator to the crime scene, and in one case it hired the Burns Detective Agency. Exposé was the NAACP's chief weapon; Johnson spent ten days in and around Memphis in the summer of 1917 looking into the lynching of Ell Pearson, and he succeeded in establishing a branch in that city. But these methods earned little sustained public attention and few tangible results.[1] White volunteered to go undercover in hopes of making a breakthrough in publicity. With the reluctant consent of Johnson, who feared for his protégé's safety, White "started a phase of work for the Association which neither it nor [he] had contemplated when [he] was employed."[2]

Five days after reading about McIlherron's lynching, White arrived in Estill Springs, midway between Chattanooga and Nashville. He had tucked into his back pocket press credentials from the *New York Evening Post*, NAACP stalwart Oswald Garrison Villard's paper; just in case he found himself in a jam, he hoped that a reporter's bona fides would extricate him.[3] Years after this reconnoiter he admitted the terror that washed over him on his long train ride to the scene. But his reports to the association's headquarters display not fear but a relish for the task. His cover was "a salesman for the Exelento Medicine Company of Atlanta selling hair-straightener, who is awaiting a fresh batch of samples which should have reached here on Saturday. It has worked beautifully so far." He then thumbed his nose one final time at both the white residents of this backwater and the danger he faced: "Give my regards to Mr. Johnson and tell him they haven't lynched his Corona [typewriter] yet."[4] Fooling the locals could be fun, and White delighted in it. His use of sarcasm and irony became a fixture of his investigative reports, as in the article he wrote for H. L. Mencken's *American Mercury*, called "I Investigate Lynchings." Putting one over on whites may have relieved White's apprehension at being in danger, but it also served a larger political purpose: ridiculing the mob helped African Americans and sympathetic whites to shake off its authority and grip of fear.

White showed in his reports a fine eye for detail and a keen ability for getting people to talk about themselves and their deeds. The excitement of the lynching had not worn off, though the town's residents were at first unwilling to share the details of the events with an itinerant salesman. "But by waiting for them to bring up the subject, which I knew would be inevitable, and by cautious questioning I got all the information I needed," he wrote home.[5] What he uncovered, sickening in their particulars, were the first elements in a comprehensive analysis of lynching.

Among the conditions that fueled the lynching of Jim McIlherron was Estill Springs's geographic isolation and the fundamentalist religious beliefs of its white residents. This settlement of 200 was in the middle of a cotton-growing area dominated by subsistence farms; about 15 percent of the county's 20,000 residents was African American. The town, which White judged stagnant, had a rail station and a three-block-long main street. The businesses were "purely local in nature." Its people were "leisurely of manner and slow of speech and comprehension." They were also devoutly religious, supporting two white Baptist, one white Methodist, and one Disciples of Christ congregations.[6] Christianity, White would conclude after investigating this and dozens more incidents of violence, allowed lynching to flourish, and "emotional, primitive religion" such as existed in Estill Springs, propelled the mob.[7]

Whites resented Jim McIlherron because of their jealousy of his family's prosperity and its refusal to bow to Jim Crow conventions. More, he had lived several years in Detroit and Chicago, which made him further suspect in the eyes of whites, who believed that the North "ruined" African Americans. So McIlherron was on his guard on February 8 when three young white men began to throw rocks at him on the town's main street; such harassment was a common way for white youth to pass the time. McIlherron and the whites argued. One of them threatened McIlherron, who then pulled a gun and shot into the group, killing two. Some of the assistant secretary's white informants conceded that McIlherron acted in self-defense.[8]

McIlherron fled to his minister's home for assistance in escaping; with the Rev. Lych's help, he made it as far as nearby McMinnville. Meanwhile, a mob had formed. Discovering Lych's role, it murdered him, and moved on to McMinn-ville, where it captured McIlherron and returned him by train to Estill Springs. Whites from a fifty-mile radius arrived by automobile, horse cart, and on foot, swelling by ten times the town's population, to witness the gruesome immolation of Jim McIlherron.[9]

After two days in Tennessee and a brief detour to Fayetteville, Georgia, to report on another lynching, White returned home to New York and to the office routine. But it was not too long before mob violence again called him into the field, this time to south Georgia. For one week, beginning May 17, mobs in Brooks and Lowndes counties terrorized black residents, killing at least eleven people in an orgy of ritualized violence.

Hampton Smith of the town of Barney, one of the largest landowners in the two counties, was reputed to be one of the cruelest. He could not retain workers, so he resorted to paying the fines of black convicts and forcing them to work for him. Sidney Johnson was one such unlucky soul who one day did not show up for work; Smith went to his home, and, finding him there, beat him. Johnson threatened to kill Smith, which he did a few days later; he then escaped to the nearby town of Valdosta. A mob formed. Local whites, already skittish at such signs of black independence as participation in the Great Migration, fabricated an African American conspiracy to murder Smith. They set out to murder eighteen blacks, "on the theory that the life of one white man was worth the lives of eighteen Negroes."[10] That day the mob seized two black men in Troupville, and pumped 700 bullets into them. The next day, Saturday, May 18, whites kidnapped Hayes Turner, whom they suspected of masterminding the putative conspiracy and who was being held for safekeeping by the sheriff; he was left hanging from a tree for two days, as "hundreds of automobiles, buggies and wagons bore sightseers to the spot while many more tramped there on foot." That same day, two other men, who had absolutely no connection to Sidney Johnson, were lynched.[11]

Mary Turner, nearly nine months pregnant, vowed to find out who killed her husband and swear out warrants for their arrests. The mob, enraged by this display of independence from a black woman, determined to teach her a lesson. On May 18 she was taken from home and hung upside down from a tree near Folsom's Bridge over the Little River, soaked with gasoline, and set ablaze. The fire died out, but Mary Turner still exhibited signs of life. Her womb was split open and the child she was carrying tumbled to the ground; it "gave two feeble cries and then its head was crushed by a member of the mob with his heel. Hundreds of bullets were then fired into the body of the woman, now mercifully dead, and the work was over."[12]

For the next several days, African Americans were seized in their homes and disappeared. Sidney Johnson was finally captured in Valdosta. He was shot to death. His corpse was castrated and then dragged by car through the main street of town and back to Barney, where it was tied to a tree and burned. Over the next three months, more than 500 African Americans fled Brooks and Lowndes counties, in spite of the fact that they were threatened with death if they attempted to do so. Between May and November, eight more African Americans were lynched.[13]

White spoke to people on both sides of the color line; he talked with local professionals, merchants, mob members, and ordinary townsfolk. His investigation yielded an eyewitness, Dr. George Spratling, a Negro physician, and the names of seventeen members of the mob, all of whom were prominent citizens of nearby Quitman.[14] White impersonated a reporter for the *New York Evening Post*—he never returned his press credentials after his trip to Estill Springs—to present his findings to Governor Hugh Dorsey of Georgia; his freelancing style and his unauthorized use of Oswald Garrison Villard's press credentials dismayed secretary Shillady, who tried to rein him in. But it was precisely this display of the derring-do that increasingly came to define his investigative work.[15] The undercover probes in Tennessee and Georgia highlighted an essential part of Walter White's personality that endeared him to African Americans: he could complete a dangerous assignment with flair, and in the process of shaming the white South, he could also make it look inept by infiltrating its inner sancta.

The assistant secretary's investigations in Tennessee and Georgia earned the NAACP more publicity than it had received for past investigations. Newspapers across the country, including the South, ran articles on both the atrocities and NAACP protests. The *San Antonio Express*, prompted by the sadism in Georgia, offered rewards of $1,000 for information leading to convictions of the lynchers, and the association's work around the murder of Mary Turner finally compelled President Woodrow Wilson directly and unequivocally to condemn lynching.[16] Even in the South the white public exhibited a growing discomfort with lynch law, though it did not always forthrightly condemn it.

But would the NAACP be able to utilize this sentiment to put an end to the crime and local, state, and federal governments' tolerance of it? The association tried mightily to cultivate this opinion, to develop citizens' pressure on local law enforcement to prevent lynching, but with decidedly mixed results. Yet an examination of NAACP collaboration with southern whites who opposed the Tennessee and Georgia lynchings illustrates the chronic difficulties the association had in forging alliances with white liberals.

Part of the challenge lay in the extreme social and political limitations of the NAACP's potential allies. The pages of *The Crisis*, the association's monthly magazine, reveal two prominent themes during 1918 and 1919: the alarming spread of racial violence and the labor movement's complicity in the racial oppression of African Americans.[17] Unions may have opposed mob justice in southern hamlets, but they often legitimized antiblack violence when it came to protecting their vested interests on the factory floor, and they continued to exclude African Americans from membership and oppose their aspirations on all fronts. This state of affairs was played out most acutely in East St. Louis, Illinois, when the Armour and Swift meatpacking companies—that city's dominant employers—threatened in 1917 to hire newly arrived African Americans in order to bust the local American Federation of Labor. White labor's anxiety over jobs and housing in this city with a swelling wartime population erupted in May and July, with some of the nation's worst urban violence. At least thirty-nine blacks and eight whites perished, as white gangs roamed the streets torching black neighborhoods and exchanging mementoes of the terror. W.E.B. Du Bois blamed the pogrom on organized labor's falling in line with capital's plan to divide black and white workers.

The southern liberals who spoke out against lynching displayed courage, of course, and risked being ostracized by their communities. Their most prominent organization was the Commission on Interracial Cooperation (CIC), founded by Will Alexander and Willis Weatherford after World War I and in reaction to the postwar resurgence of the Ku Klux Klan. But while interracial commission members were shocked by white violence, they were chained to a past in which "good Negroes" deferred to the "better class of whites" and the system of white supremacy was the natural order. They discouraged outspokenness among blacks. Other southern liberals—but not Alexander or Weatherford and likely not many CIC members—were convinced that lynching, while wrong, was sometimes an understandable—if not excusable—response by good white citizens to the plodding wheels of justice.[18]

The Southern liberals' wavering bedeviled the NAACP in these early years of the antilynching crusade. In 1917 the association had sent Lily Hammond, a white Georgian whose husband had formerly been head of

Paine College, a black Methodist institution, to tour the South and gauge support for a southern antilynching conference. The meeting never was organized, and the NAACP's major antilynching conference, finally held two years later, drew only tepid southern support.[19]

After the lynching of Jim McIlherron, the third in the state in a six-month period, some white southern elites began to worry at the potentially destabilizing effects of mob violence. Bolton Smith, a mortgage lender in Memphis, led prominent white Tennesseans in the formation of the Law and Order League to combat lynching. Mob justice, according to Smith, created its own set of problems that rattled the foundations of white supremacy. First, it was preventing African Americans from lining up wholeheartedly in support of World War I. Second, it discouraged "law-abiding" blacks from cooperating with whites in combating criminal activity within the race. Third, mob activity radicalized the black population across class lines and encouraged them to make common cause with vocal advocates of racial equality. Smith longed for the days when the Negro was "jolly, care-free, and good natured."[20]

The assistant secretary practically had to make a part-time job out of repudiating paternalistic whites who either longed for the mythic good old days of race relations or minimized the wave of violence washing over Afro-America. James Hardy Dillard, president of the Virginia-based Slater Fund, wrote a letter to the *New York Times* filled with unctuous pronouncements about southern whites' affection for their colored neighbors. Things were improving, claimed Dillard, for on a recent inspection tour of the South he had run into one or two white farmers who believed that "qualified" African Americans should be allowed to vote. Then came the widely stated but largely unproved assertion that most southern whites "disapproved" of lynching. Dillard extemporized on this last point in a missive to John Shillady. "The white population of the South is perhaps 25,000,000. As well as I can calculate from information, the lynchings that occurred in 1918 were participated in, in any way, by less than 3,000. Even if we say 5,000, this number is small in comparison. I am sure that 99% of the rest of the 25,000,000 are utterly opposed to lynching." White dismissed Dillard's chatter as "idle vaporing of little value."[21]

Yet if the young assistant secretary wanted to dismiss Bolton Smith and the Law and Order League and people like Dillard, his political instincts told him that the NAACP would have to find a way to work with this stratum of southern society. Despite the fact that some of the white racial moderates—such as Hamilton County, Tennessee, prosecutor George Chamlee, who would in the thirties appear as the defense counsel for the Scottsboro Boys—justified lynching as a legitimate response to "a dread of the claim of 'social equality' with its resulting degradation," the fact was that the Law and Order League backed both an antilynching bill in the Tennessee legislature and an early federal statute written by Leonidas C. Dyer, the Republican representative from St. Louis.[22] White and the association were to a great extent hamstrung; they knew that in many ways gaining the cooperation of Southern whites was essential to the elimination of lynching, and until the NAACP became stronger it would have to bend to the will of some paternalistic whites. This would become more clear in the wake of the Mary Turner lynching.

Events in Lowndes and Brooks counties had pricked the nation's conscience, and over the summer of 1918 there was talk in both the Senate and House of conducting hearings. A week after he returned from Georgia, White was dispatched to Washington, where he supervised four researchers who combed the nation's newspapers for information on wartime violence, with the hope that the data would be presented to a session of the House judiciary committee.[23] White meanwhile tried mightily to convince George Spratling, the black eyewitness to the lynchings, to testify at the hearings, even offering to pay his way and then help him and his family to relocate should it be inadvisable for him to return to Quitman.[24]

As the assistant secretary and his colleagues worked to put things in place, they were being displaced by a well-connected white racial moderate, C. P. Dam of Washington, D.C., a lawyer in private practice. Dam was made aware of the crime of lynching by his domestic servant, who had read White's article "The Work of a Mob" in *The Crisis*; he paid heed to her because she was "a very intelligent colored woman, a woman of high personal character, though she be colored."[25] He was, he said, so moved that he got in touch with his friend, Republican Senator William Kenyon of Iowa, to urge him to investigate. Kenyon agreed and, according to Dam, assigned him the job of assembling hearings. Once he received his commission, Dam contacted the NAACP for assistance and information.[26]

White was happy to cooperate with the Iowa senator's staff, especially if that was the most promising avenue for congressional hearings. At

Dam's request, White stopped in Washington to be debriefed on his
turn from a southern investigation. And he made certain to keep D[ ]
abreast via memoranda on all new developments in the Lowndes and
Brooks counties cases, including the difficulties he was having in convincing Dr. Spratling to leave Quitman and testify at the hearings. It appears
from this distance that in his eagerness to secure the cooperation of
prominent whites the assistant secretary disclosed more about NAACP
efforts than was necessary.[27]

Yet collaboration did not, in the association's mind, exclude independent action on the Mary Turner case or any other. And it likely never even
occurred to White and the association to subordinate their activity to a
man like Dam, who had just become aware that lynching was a problem.
Yet that was just what Dam was asking. Building upon White's extensive
discussions with Rep. Dyer, Archibald Grimke and James Cobb of the
District of Columbia branch conducted negotiations with Dyer and Representative Martin Madden, Republican from Illinois, to bring NAACP
testimony before the House.[28] Shillady had also contacted Senator
Kenyon without Dam's prior knowledge. From the NAACP's perspective, it did not matter whether the Senate or the House held the hearings,
so long as one of them did; and as the association only recently had become acquainted with Dam, there certainly was no compelling reason to
defer to him. Dam took exception. He protested that the NAACP's initiatives broke the agreement that he had with Senator Kenyon: "It was
agreed that I would take all details in my hands as far as possible," he
wrote to Shillady. "Unless you feel free to trust me in handling the matter
here in Washington I believe that there is great danger of not making satisfactory headway."[29]

The national staff was prepared at a minimum to mobilize black voters
to pressure their elected officials on the issue of lynching; they wanted to
reward potential friends in Congress and punish their enemies. They did
not want to leave the fate of antilynching measures exclusively to politicians and their aides. To Dam, this reasoning was beside the point;
African Americans had no place in the antilynching crusade: "I note what
you say about the interview with Congressman Madden and his expressed
wish that 'the colored people get behind this movement nationally.' Of
course the colored people are behind it, but such talk is buncombe. This
is a matter that must be settled, and settled right by the *White People*."[30]
Dam, of course, was not the only sympathetic white to counsel African

Americans to restrict their actions for civil rights. NAACP founder and board member Moorfield Storey had impeccable abolitionist credentials and argued several of the association's cases before the Supreme Court. Yet he advised White to keep a low profile in lobbying for a wartime anti-lynching bill and admonished the association not even to publicize the pending legislation.[31] Recognizing its limited ability to influence the pace and direction of change on Capitol Hill, the NAACP staff could do little but cede leadership in the legislative domain to paternalistic whites who were horrified by lynching yet unwilling to respect African Americans' political action. Not that these whites could do much better—neither Dam nor anyone else were able to jump-start congressional hearings. Still, for the time being, Walter White and his mentor James Weldon Johnson thought it better to concentrate organizational efforts on investigation and exposure of racial injustice.

As the episode was being sorted out, White was again sent to the South, this time to investigate several states' wartime "work or fight" laws. Enacted in Georgia and elsewhere in mid-1918, these statutes required men of draft age either to join the military or to work in specific jobs that local draft boards considered essential to the war effort. "Work or fight" laws were one of several devices at the disposal of both planters and white metropolitan elites. They were often used in conjunction with a military furlough program, in which black soldiers—whom military commanders in many cases did not want in uniform—were sent to work for large plantation owners. The statutes were frequently used interchangeably with vagrancy laws, under which unemployed African Americans were arrested, fined, and released into the custody of a white employer, for whom they would have to work off the fine.

Above all, the rural and urban white elite used these laws to alleviate the wartime labor shortage. Under the authority of the vagrancy laws, for example, police raided pool halls, roadhouses, and other places of African American amusement and arrested those who could furnish no proof of employment. White elites wanted to bind blacks to one employer and prevent them from switching jobs; then too, by cracking down on sites of entertainment, they attempted also to control blacks' leisure time. These laws helped to ensure that elites would have at hand a steady supply of labor. More, the laws were whites' response to the emergence of a New Negro: the war had sparked among African Americans both an international awareness and a determination to fight for economic advancement and political and civil rights. By impressing black soldiers into plantation labor, southern whites guaranteed that military duty and its associated privileges were reserved for white men.[32]

When White completed his report on the Mary Turner lynching, the association took up the "work or fight" laws with the U.S. Department of Labor, which in turn asked the NAACP to investigate. In mid-October, White packed his bags for what he thought would be a five-week journey through Georgia, Florida, Alabama, Louisiana, Arkansas, Tennessee, and North Carolina. This trip was to be different in that he would combine reporting with organizing and strengthening southern branches. White was able to make early headway on this project by tapping an extensive network of Standard Life Insurance agents that he oversaw when he was that company's cashier.[33]

In Atlanta, which was his base for the tour, he met Albion Holsey, the personal secretary to Robert R. Moton, Booker T. Washington's successor at Tuskegee. With some urgency Holsey asked White to place Alabama first on the list of places to investigate. The two men maintained a cordial relationship; over the years, Holsey sent White information of a confidential nature, which he, as a ranking executive of the officially accommodationist Tuskegee Institute, could not publicize. The assistant secretary found that conditions were much worse than he had imagined and that he would need almost two months in the field.[34]

White reported his findings in letters to Shillady and in " 'Work or Fight' in the South," which appeared in abbreviated form in *The New Republic*. He found "that in many instances colored women, too ill or weak to work, have been placed in fields" or domestic labor by white employers; this, he saw, was not limited to Alabama, but happened in Arkansas, Georgia, and Tennessee as well.[35] He reported an occurrence of an all-too-common dispute: A woman cook in the small town of Wetumpka, just outside Montgomery, Alabama, quit one Saturday evening when her employer, who happened to be the mayor, refused to pay her more. On Sunday morning the mayor arrested her. On Monday morning she appeared for trial before the mayor himself, who fined her fourteen dollars; the mayor then paid the fine and told her "to go on to the house and go to work and quit her foolishness."[36] In Tampa, Florida, White reported, eight poor black women were arrested on vagrancy charges and fined twenty-five dollars each; he conceded that their poverty may have forced them into vagrancy, but they were singled out "not because they were of the class that they were, but because of the fact that they were Negroes."[37]

Southern whites were also determined to redouble the suppression of African Americans after the war. "One indication of this," White wrote to the home office, "is the revival of the Ku Klux Klan, which white men have told me, indirectly, is to be used to handle the Negro soldier after the war when he comes back with some 'new' idea of democracy."[38] In Pelham, Georgia, a supervisor of twenty-five Standard Life agents who had in 1917 produced more than $900,000 in revenue, was told by a town official to find new work because he did not consider life insurance to be an "essential" occupation for blacks under "work or fight." A black worker at the Pelham Fertilizer Works sold life insurance for Standard on the side, supplementing his monthly income by between $150 and $175; the same official ordered him to quit this part-time job and work more hours at the plant. In Florida's citrus groves, workers who tried to switch employers for higher wages were threatened with conscription or imprisonment unless they returned to their original growers and at the same rate of pay. "I have become convinced on this trip as never before," White wrote home in a discouraging moment, "that the white man of the South is absolutely incapable of thinking or practicing Democracy, so far as any case where the Negro is concerned."[39]

Yet the investigation also had its promising moments. While the work or fight laws were executed more or less with impunity in rural areas, White helped to stimulate some successful resistance. The Jacksonville, Florida, city council passed a statute, but the African American population was so vigorous in its protest that the law was repealed. In Thomasville, Georgia, city officials tried to press black women into street-cleaning duty; White reported that a newly organized NAACP branch forced that practice to be dropped. His spying helped to bring an end to the dragooning of black women into the cotton fields of Pine Bluff, Arkansas, and white women's kitchens in Memphis.[40]

Returning to New York in mid-December to take over preparations for the association's annual meeting in January, White had spent perhaps three months of his first year on the road. He had made some significant breakthroughs. His lynching investigations had resulted in increased publicity for the NAACP in the daily press and a heightened public awareness of mob terror. He had placed an article in the prestigious *New Republic*, the first of many in influential journals of liberal opinion. And he established a modus operandi that combined sharp observational skills and a razor wit that punctured the arrogance of the white South. His second year on the job would bring much of the same.

For much of the winter and spring, White was in the South, investigating and organizing. Undercover in Shubuta, Mississippi, he exposed the truth of a quadruple lynching on a span over the Chicasawha River five days before Christmas 1918. According to meager press coverage, the four—two men and two women, ranging in ages from fifteen to twenty— were taken from the Shubuta jail, where they were being held on suspicion of ambushing a wealthy and retired white dentist. Not surprisingly, the local reporters acted as stenographers to the elite, and what White uncovered was far more sordid and gruesome. It was almost too much for local whites to stomach, for they were reluctant to talk about the affair and were almost impervious to White's interviewing skills. The assistant secretary also crossed over to the black side of town and convinced a Negro preacher who knew the facts of the lynching to talk with him; he also located a cousin of the two females, who was willing to talk about their involvement with the dead man.[41]

Richard Johnston was a dentist, but he was neither wealthy nor retired; a man of perhaps thirty-five years, he was an itinerant, unable to hold a steady job owing to alcoholism and business ineptitude. Despite the fact that he was married and had a child, he seduced black Maggie Howze, aged twenty, and her sixteen-year-old sister Alma, forcing them to move to his farm and impregnating them both. At the same time, Major Clark, a twenty-year-old black man who worked on Johnston's farm, began to show an interest in Maggie; when Johnston found out, he ordered Clark to leave her alone. The two men began to feud, and on December 10, Johnston was found murdered. There was no evidence of his killer's identity, though a rumor circulated among whites in Shubuta that he was killed by a white man who accused Johnston of having an affair with his wife. But a mob is not concerned with evidence, and it captured Clark, forcing a confession from him by placing his testicles in a vice. The Howze sisters, Major Clark, and his younger brother Andrew were arrested and held over for trial. But before it could take place, a mob, led by one of the town's prominent merchants and the district attorney, took them to the river and hanged them.[42]

When the peripatetic White arrived in a city or town to establish an NAACP branch or buttress an existing one, he wowed crowds with not only accounts of the heinous events, but also his abilities to pass and fool the whites, who were so certain about the inviolability of race. In Chattanooga, the Interdenominational Ministers Union was reluctant to sponsor his appearance, for which planning was practically nonexistent; still he was able to recruit a branch of between fifty and sixty people. His stop in Nashville catalyzed the new branch and netted sixty dues-paying members.[43] In Meridian, Mississippi, he arranged to have a branch started. He asserted that he "made the best speech [he had] ever made," in New Orleans, despite a case of food poisoning that nearly prevented him from standing up. Sharing the podium with him were practically all of the city's black clergy and the president of historically black Straight University. The local branch had advertised his appearance widely, broadcasting his exploits as a spy for the race, and he spoke before a standing-room-only audience. After he concluded his talk, 102 people became new dues-paying members, and the branch launched a campaign to increase their numbers to 5,000. A swing through Kentucky resulted in a branch in Paducah; in Louisville, White mediated an intra-branch dispute involving local finances.[44]

He returned again to the deep South to Sheffield, Alabama, for the trial of two whites charged with lynching two black men. White had never attended one before and thought it would be a good idea "to see just how the trials are conducted." Accompanied by association secretary John Shillady, the two men posed as white journalists and sat in the courtroom press section. White filed this report, parts of which appeared in the *New York Evening Post*:

> In no single person in the court room did there appear to be the slightest doubt of [the accused's] guilt, yet at the same time there was not the least doubt also, of his being acquitted. . . . In spite of the statement that the best element of the white people of the South are against lynching, the truthfulness of this statement is yet to be proved, for at the present time in communities such as Sheffield and Colbert County there is no chance whatever of securing a verdict of guilty against any white man, no matter how brutal his crime when he is accused of lynching a Negro.[45]

White was in Georgia investigating three more lynchings in July when the Red Summer exploded in Chicago. Much of white America was already on edge in 1919, providing important context for Chicago's riot. The Russian Revolution in October 1917 and the spread of labor and political unrest through much of Europe and into the United States alarmed the country's leaders. Politicians and industrialists jump-started a vicious campaign of anticommunism and xenophobia in an effort to quell incipient challenges to their rule. They blamed America's increasingly acute class conflict on foreign-born revolutionaries. Socialist and Communist meetings and newspaper offices were raided; noncitizens were rounded up and deported. Labor activists were arrested and charged with criminal syndicalism. The antiradical and nativist hysteria washed over the country's racial terrain, as whites perceived African Americans' attempts to improve their life circumstances as unpatriotic efforts to bring down the social order. "It seems that there is an air of expectancy of something which is about to happen—no one knows what," White wrote to Mary White Ovington. "Here in Atlanta today, every hardware store and pawnshop is crowded with white people buying revolvers, guns of every description and ammunition. Little or none is being sold to colored people." [46]

White explained the situation to the annual conference of the NAACP in Chicago in June, just a month before the riot. "We hear much in America today of the dangers of BOLSHEVISM. A far greater menace to our nation than Bolshevism is the wilful disregard of all laws by mobs and lynchers." [47] The month before he made this statement, white sailors and marines in Charleston, South Carolina, in a single night of violence, killed two blacks and wounded seventeen others. Less than a week later in Longview, Texas, whites would attack local African American leaders and try to assault the black section of town; they were jealous of local black merchants' and farmers' success at getting out from under the thumb of white storekeepers and cotton brokers. They would murder one African American, but in the process, blacks would repel their attack and leave four vigilantes dead. Within three weeks, white military personnel in the nation's capital, with police looking on and with the press publicizing their strategy and tactics in advance, would maraud through the black community for four days; five African Americans were killed, but the number would have been higher had the black community not armed and defended itself. An anonymous Washington woman, in a letter to *The Crisis*, captured the new mood among the race when now faced with white violence:

> The Washington riot gave me the thrill that comes once in a life time. . . .
> [A]t last our men had stood like men, struck back, were no longer dumb,
> driven cattle. . . .
>
> . . . [T]hank God for Washington colored men! All honor to them, for
> they first blazed the way and right swiftly did Chicago men follow. They
> put new hope, a new vision in their almost despairing women.[48]

White reported on the tinderbox conditions in Chicago.[49] Racial competition over jobs and housing, aggravated by the Great Migration, was the kindling that fueled the conflagration and helped it to spread across the city. (The Great Migration began around 1916. By the end of the decade, a half-million African Americans left the South for the urban North and Midwest; they were followed in the twenties by another million. They moved to what they hoped would be an increased opportunity in industrial jobs and to escape endemic violence, political disfranchisement, and social constriction.) In the summer of 1919, the Stockyards Labor Council, a federation of thirteen craft unions, was in the midst of an organizing drive in the meatpacking industry. The overwhelmingly white leadership understood that the council would have to emphasize organization among African Americans, who constituted a large plurality of workers in the industry.

Though black workers who had been resident in Chicago before the Great Migration had joined the union movement in roughly the same proportion as white workers, a large percentage of African American packinghouse workers were migrants who arrived after 1916. Most of these were highly suspicious of organized labor; in their experience in the South, unions were racist, worked to the detriment of black workers, and were in fact a white job trust. The migrants hung back, trying to see how the union would benefit them. In June and July the Stockyards Labor Council intensified its efforts, and wildcat strikes erupted in production departments that did not have 100 percent union membership. Despite the fact that there were white workers who refused to join the union, inevitably it was African American workers whom white unionists singled out; blacks were tagged as members of a "scab race." When the riot broke out, 41 percent of the clashes between blacks and whites occurred in the packinghouse district, an area where only whites lived and where African Americans traveled only to work.[50]

Chicago's African American population doubled in the second decade of the twentieth century to about 100,000, with most of the increase coming in the years after 1915. At the same time, resistance by white workers and real estate companies kept the South Side ghetto, home to about 90 percent of Chicago's black residents, from significantly expanding its borders. African Americans who attempted to move into better housing in less crowded adjacent neighborhoods faced bombs and threats of violence to drive them back across the color line. The Hyde Park–Kenwood Property Owners' Association, whose leadership were local realtors and members of the Chicago Real Estate Board, had been agitating for a year to "make Hyde Park white." Two months before the riot, White was in Chicago on an organizing drive, and he infiltrated one of the owners' group's meetings; he found it "inflammatory and incendiary." An African American woman, also passing for white, attended another of the meetings, where she heard plans for the forced removal of blacks in the neighborhood.[51]

What immediately detonated Chicago was a clash at the beach. With temperatures in the nineties, black and white Chicagoans flocked to Lake Michigan for some relief. On July 27, fights erupted on the Twenty-ninth Street beach, as a group of African American women and men challenged the traditional segregation of the waterfront and determined to swim in this "white" area. Meanwhile, a group of black teens, unaware of the altercation, floated a homemade raft from Twenty-sixth Street over the racial boundary line and into the "white" section; a white tough pelted them with bricks, striking and killing fourteen-year-old Eugene Williams. When the police refused to arrest the alleged assailant and instead took an African American into custody, bedlam took over. Rumors poured from the beach into Chicago's black and Irish neighborhoods. White gangs agitated for "cleaning up" the city. They invaded black neighborhoods to loot, burn, and murder, and set upon black workers commuting through white neighborhoods. African Americans were determined not to let whites attack them with impunity. They defended their neighborhoods and engaged in retaliatory violence, inflicting serious injury and casualties on white mobs. By the time the riot ended five days later, twenty-three African Americans lay dead (seven of them at the hands of police); fifteen whites also were killed. Over 500 Chicagoans of both races were injured.[52]

For the duration of the riot and several days after, most African Americans were stranded on the South Side, unable to get to work in the stockyards. More, the clashes had interrupted the delivery of groceries to the ghetto, and people were without food. The packinghouses took advantage of the situation to break the Stockyards Labor Council; trying to show that they were better friends to African Americans than were the unions, Swift, Armour, and other companies shipped provisions to black neighborhoods and arranged for the return to work of black workers under armed escort on August 4. The unions opposed this, claiming, rightly, that the companies were cynically trying to incite white violence against blacks and break the labor organizing drive. Because of the magnitude of labor's protest and continued violence in the neighborhoods surrounding the packinghouses, the planned return was delayed several days.[53]

White arrived in Chicago on August 6, after the worst clashes ended but while violence still menaced the city. He checked in and was briefed by two members of the local NAACP: Dr. Charles Bentley (a veteran race man, having been a member of Du Bois's Niagara Movement) and A. C. MacNeal (the former editor of the *Chicago Whip*, a militant black weekly). He also met with T. Arnold Hill and University of Chicago sociologist Robert Park, both of the Urban League. The next day was the planned back-to-work day for thousands of black workers. White provided this eyewitness account:

> I put on some old clothes and went out to the Stock yards as a riot was scheduled to take place then upon the colored workmen, some 3,000 of them going back to work. I spent three hours there and the only thing that prevented serious clashes was the presence of thousands of police and state troops. There was considerable hooting and muttering and the tension was very great, but the presence of troops with rifles and also several machine guns mounted on automobiles held the mobs in check.[54]

Later, just outside the black-owned Binga State Bank in the heart of the South Side ghetto, an African American man mistook White for a white man and fired a revolver at his head, barely missing him.[55]

Reconnoitering Chicago was only one item on the assistant secretary's mind. He also wanted to resuscitate the nearly moribund local branch. Since its formation as one of the association's first chapters, the Chicago branch had operated as a biracial oligarchy whose leading members were deeply distrustful of mass activity. It generally took no initiative on local affairs, preferring to wait for instructions from the national staff. Short of volunteer lawyers, it could press only a handful of discrimination cases in court, and it scored few victories in preventing city and state government from enacting legislation detrimental to African Americans. The branch was not in a position to tackle the critical problems in the Black Belt brought on by the Great Migration. In fact, by 1916, much of the local leadership had transferred its energy to the local Urban League chapter. Although the league stood for the gradual economic and social adjustment of African Americans to city life and not militant action for racial equality, it at least was dealing with the pressing issues facing the burgeoning black population. Just before the riots broke out, the local NAACP branch established a storefront presence in the South Side, but its program was both unclear and unfocused, with the association ceding leadership to other organizations.[56]

White's activities in Chicago foreshadow some of the leadership qualities that would define his work in the years to come. Within hours of participating in the near-riot in the stockyards, White measured the stakes in Chicago in a letter to Mary White Ovington. "It seemed and yet seems to me that the whole future of the Association in Chicago depends on our work in this crisis, as we are supposed to be a militant, aggressive organization. Enemies of ours are closely watching us to see if we can and will make good, and if we don't then we might as well close up shop."[57] His reports to the association's offices indicate that the enemies with whom he was concerned were not so much the racist property owners' associations, the sensationalist press, and the recalcitrant politicians, but African Americans and whites who were interested in race advancement but were not within the NAACP orbit. As a man of action he was anxious both to plant the flag of the NAACP and to dominate other race advancement and civil rights organizations. His orientation toward the Joint Emergency Committee (JEC) is instructive. Initiated by Shillady, who arrived in Chicago a few days before White, the JEC was composed of the NAACP, Urban League, YMCA, the black Cook County Bar Association, and the Ministers-Social Workers-Citizens Committee (later renamed the Peace and Protective Association). The JEC's principal function, according to Shillady, was to coordinate all aspects of the legal defense of African Americans arrested during the disturbances. Despite Chicago branch leader Bentley's reluctance to become involved in this work—he worried that some of the defendants might actually be felons—

Shillady was sure of the JEC's clarity of purpose and was content not to assume a leading role in it.[58]

White was not so certain of the JEC's activities, and he was aggressive in guarding what he perceived to be the association's turf. At his first meeting of the JEC, he "found that no definite program had been outlined," that work was carried out in a "slip-shod" manner, and that the NAACP, owing to the conservatism of its leadership, was "trailing with the crowd."[59] After another JEC meeting, he complained about its paralysis; Robert Park, he said, believed the organization's sole purpose was to "talk over things," to which the assistant secretary sharply replied that "there was an immediate need of action and if we were only to talk then we did not need a joint committee."[60] He met with John E. Haynes, the director of Negro economics for the U.S. Department of Labor and a founder of the National Urban League, and on his suggestion went to see an attorney named Barnett, because Haynes thought that the lawyer could be of help. White was highly annoyed to discover that

> his wife was Ida Wells-Barnett. Had I known it, I would not have gone. She launched into a tirade against every organization in Chicago because they have not come into her organization and allowed her to dictate to them. She is a troublemaker and is causing complications by starting a fund of her own to defend riot victims.[61]

From White's perspective, all that Wells-Barnett was concerned with was that she and her allies, and not the NAACP national office, get the credit for work done. At various times, he proposed that the national office not cooperate with her Peace and Protective Association, that the NAACP work to win over the city's ministers and " 'spike' the formation of another organization [with] national ambitions . . ." and that the NAACP "get up enough of an opposition here to put them out of the game." He proposed various ways in which the NAACP could circumvent the Wells-Barnett group, including making a national appeal for funds, which would diminish her prominence in the struggle.[62]

There is more than a little irony in White's shrill attack on Wells-Barnett. Proud and unyielding after nearly four decades as an antilynching crusader, Wells-Barnett had pioneered the type of investigation, agitation, and analysis that White had recently undertaken and for which he was just beginning to gain recognition. (White never acknowledged his debt to her.) His dismissive tone regarding her and her Chicago allies—they were "petty," "short-sighted," and "narrow"—is redolent of his aversion to engage independent-minded women leaders on equal terms. What White saw as her troublemaking was a style of work that insisted on promoting grassroots and local leadership and resisted the imposition of political strategy and tactics from national organizations. Her work was also predicated on uncompromising agitation with little concern for its affect on the sensibilities of white liberals. Quite beyond her still feeling the sting of being shunned from the founding leadership of the association, she believed the NAACP temporized on critical issues of racial equality for the sake of making itself acceptable to racial moderates. White's characterization of Wells-Barnett trivialized her and elided a principled debate over how best to build a civil rights response to racial violence and rampant inequality: by nurturing local organizing with indigenous leadership (with a strong female presence) or by building a professional (and male-dominated) race-reform bureaucracy? [63]

White achieved his objectives in this first sustained attempt at infighting. Soon the Peace and Protective Association withdrew from the JEC, which in October reconstituted itself as the Committee to Secure Equal Justice for Colored Riot Defendants and was now dominated by the NAACP. Importantly, by January 1920 this new committee secured acquittals or the dismissal of charges for fifty-eight of seventy-five blacks charged with serious offenses during the July disturbances. With White's able assistance it had forced the city to suspend and put on trial a police officer who had joined in the rioting.[64]

More important to White than tangible local civil rights victories, however, was the eclipsing of independent local leaders and the securing of hegemony of the NAACP. The decisive measure of victory was now the dominance of the association. In the future, whether in the campaigns for antilynching legislation or equity in New Deal relief or equal opportunity in the military, White would apply this standard and work mightily—and usually with mastery—either to subordinate other organizations to the NAACP program or to neutralize them in the field.

The Red Summer of 1919 erupted in a final violent spasm in rural Phillips County, Arkansas, in October. What happened in the towns of Helena and Elaine would have profound effects on the American system of criminal justice, on the National Association for the Advancement of Colored People, and on Walter White personally, who conducted one of his trademark undercover investigations and then orchestrated the association's response to this egregious miscarriage of justice. In August, black sharecroppers had organized the Progressive Farmers' and Housholders' Union of America and sought ways to both command a higher price for their cotton crop and compel their landlords to provide itemized statements of debits and credits at the annual settlement. Such organizing, of course, was a direct challenge to the widespread system of peonage then firmly entrenched in the Mississippi Delta. On the night of September 30, two white men, one of them a sheriff, fired upon a meeting of a union chapter in the hamlet of Hoop Spur. But as was the case earlier in the District of Columbia, Chicago, and elsewhere during the Red Summer, African Americans were prepared to fight back; union members returned the fire, killing one of the attackers. The next day, October 1, heavily armed white men from surrounding areas in Arkansas and from nearby Mississippi and Tennessee poured into the Phillips County towns of Helena and Elaine, engaging in firefights with armed black sharecroppers and massacring unarmed African Americans. That evening, Governor Charles Brough asked the secretary of war to send troops. Five hundred soldiers arrived the following day, with the governor at their head. They set about disarming and arresting blacks and turning their weapons over to civilian whites, who promptly ransacked black settlements. Blacks who succeeded in escaping to the canebrakes outside town were hunted down. Walter White estimated that at least twenty-five African Americans—and possibly more than 100—were murdered. Soldiers also participated in the carnage.[65]

To justify this bloodbath, local whites—amplified by the Arkansas and national press—claimed that the Progressive Farmers' and Householders' Union was plotting to massacre whites in Phillips County a few days hence, when the two white men fortuitously stumbled upon the organization's planning meeting. According to this tale, once discovered, the union had hastily implemented its plan. Governor Brough claimed that the riot was caused by agitation and propaganda in *The Crisis* and the *Chicago Defender*. A Committee of Seven, approved by the governor and with at least two local plantation owners among their number, took charge of the sweep of the black settlements. They had hundreds of blacks arrested, herded into a Helena stockade, and held incommunicado. They boasted to the press of confessions that proved the existence of an extensive plot, but as the assistant secretary reported, "When suspects were brought before this committee they were seated in a chair charged with electricity. If the Negroes did not talk as freely as the Committee wished, the current was turned on until they did so."[66]

In early November most of the defendants were put on trial in a town practically under martial law and in a courtroom saturated with the spirit of the mob. On the second of the month, two trials were held for a total of six men charged with first-degree murder. The Committee of Seven, the American Legion, the Rotary Club, and the Lions Club of Helena had promised to execute the defendants if the mob refrained from lynching them. The jury in the first case deliberated only eight minutes and returned a verdict of guilty against the lone defendant. In the second case, the jury took seven minutes to convict the remaining five men. The judge condemned all six to death in the electric chair. Over the course of that week, a total of twelve blacks received the death penalty, while eighty more were sentenced to prison terms of between one and twenty-one years.[67]

White felt compelled to visit Arkansas, despite the obvious and extreme personal danger should whites discover his true identity. Still, he petitioned his superiors: "I am exceedingly anxious to make the investigation personally and I do so with full realization of the past, and am assuming complete responsibility for any personal consequences which may possibly arise."[68] With that he packed his bags and, after trying unsuccessfully to meet with Attorney General A. Mitchell Palmer, caught a train for the battle front.[69]

White's account of his weeklong exploits in Arkansas is legendary, marking him as both a trickster and a man of extraordinary courage. As he testified in his 1948 autobiography, *A Man Called White*, he went to Arkansas posing as a reporter for the *Chicago Daily News*. (The paper's managing editor cooperated in the cover.) He secured an interview with Governor Brough, who, because White feigned ignorance on the Negro question, praised him as "able and experienced," invited him to tour Phillips County, and wrote him a letter of introduction that called him "one of the most brilliant newspapermen" the governor had ever met. He then spent several days in Helena, where he spoke only to white townsfolk—he avoided talking to blacks, lest they be punished for speaking to him once his report was published—tricking them into revealing the details of the recent massacre.[70]

As White walked through the downtown toward the county jail, where he was to meet with some of the Negro prisoners charged with conspiracy to massacre whites, he was approached by a black man who, in a whisper, told him he had an urgent message for him and to follow him. They turned a corner, crossed the railroad tracks, and stopped in a clump of woods. There the man told him he did not know who he was or why he was in town, but he had overheard whites " 'say they are going to get you. The way I figured it out is that if the white folks are so against you, you must be a friend of ours.' " The man also did not know why the whites wanted to harm him. The assistant secretary hightailed it to the railroad station by running up the tracks, barely catching the only train heading North, and boarding it from the side opposite the platform. The conductor, puzzled as to why anyone would purchase a ticket on the train rather than in the station, told White, "But you're leaving, mister, just when the fun is going to start. . . . There's a damned yellow nigger down here passing for white and the boys are going to get him." Barely escaping with his life and arriving in Memphis later that day, he heard reports that he had been lynched in Arkansas that afternoon.[71]

It is likely that White exaggerated the dramatic manner of his escape, much in the way he did his childhood experiences in the Atlanta riot and for the same reason: to promote himself as a fearless crusader for the race who does not so much as flinch in the face of personal danger. The extant record of his Arkansas travels is thin, the bulk of the NAACP's material on this phase of its work having been lost; but surviving documents reveal several inconsistencies between what White wrote at the time and what he later recalled having happened.

To be sure, Arkansas menaced White. As he acknowledged to Charles Bentley of the Chicago branch, who helped White acquire his cover, without his journalist's credentials he would not "have been able to have secured the facts or to have gotten out safely, as it was the most dangerous situation in which [he had] been."[72] While his position as a reporter for a Chicago paper gave him access to the governor, he did not advertise his cover to people in Helena; nor did he gather all of his information from gullible whites. Rather, as he reported soon after his return, he quietly dropped into Helena and visited the scenes of the recent troubles, talked with scores of Negroes, overheard the conversations of many whites, read the leading Arkansas newspapers, asked and got information and opinions and left the State without disclosing [his] identity and even being suspected of being a news writer.[73]

The first published account of his Arkansas exploits appeared in a 1929 article "I Investigate Lynchings," for H. L. Mencken's *American Mercury*. In this article, White took especial delight in ridiculing the stupidities of white supremacists:

Nothing contributes so much to the continued life of an investigator of lynchings and his tranquil possession of all his limbs as the obtuseness of the lynchers themselves. Like most boastful people who practice direct action when it involves no personal risk, they just can't help talk about their deeds to any person who manifests even the slightest interest in them.[74]

But in this piece he merely notes that he spoke with the governor and makes no mention at all of Brough's effusive praise for his journalistic acumen. The man who miraculously arrived to warn White is present in the 1929 piece, simply alerting him to imminent danger. But in later versions his appearance is even more dramatic, for the man's ignorance—he explicitly states he knows nothing about the assistant secretary or why whites would be after him—is in stunning contrast with the discovery of White's passing, knowledge which supposedly was so widespread among whites that the train conductor just arriving in Helena knew about it. And where in his 1929 recollection he simply made his way to the station, by 1948 he ran hidden along the right-of-way and arrived in the nick of time.

How close he came to being caught by the mob may never be known. It does appear as if a now unknown African American in Arkansas revealed White's identity, though it is not clear whether this happened while White was in the state or after he left; nor is it clear whether the disclosure was accidental or malicious. And the *Chicago Defender* in its coverage of the riot inadvertently revealed White to be a Negro, but again this was after the fact, and it had no repercussions on his ability to go undercover again, as he had feared.[75]

Nevertheless, it appears as if White embellished the circumstances of his departure from Arkansas. One would think that what he did in the state was courageous enough without exaggeration. Perhaps he did so because, as a consummate salesman, hyperbole was his stock-in-trade. But this version of events, like the one of his childhood epiphany that he was indeed a Negro, was first fabricated in 1929, around the time he became acting secretary of the NAACP and was attempting to establish his authority as a first-tier leader of African Americans. White must have felt that his actual displays of heroism were not adequate; while he may have enjoyed masquerading as white and duping whites, he was not sure that most African Americans would understand, and he felt that he needed something more to validate his leadership in their eyes.

In 1923 the U.S. Supreme Court issued *Moore* v. *Dempsey*, overturning the convictions of blacks in the Arkansas riot cases. The justices found that defendants were entitled not only to the appearances of a fair trial, but to the substance of one. "The whole proceeding," wrote Justice Oliver Wendell Holmes, "[was] a mask," a sham; the judge, jury, prosecutor, and public defender carried out the demands of the mob simply to forestall vigilante action. It was a stunning victory, amounting to a revolution in criminal procedure and guaranteeing defendants protection from mob domination of the courtroom. It was a "landmark decision under the Due Process Clause of the Fourteenth Amendment [that] paved the way for federal constitutional restrictions on the conduct of state criminal trials that are regarded today as commonplace."[76]

When the four-year campaign concluded, James Weldon Johnson, who in 1920 succeeded John Shillady as the NAACP secretary, gave his protégé full credit: "The Board will recall that it was the Assistant Secretary, Mr. White, who was sent to Arkansas immediately after the riots to make an investigation. The handling of the Arkansas cases at the National Office has been almost entirely in the hands of Mr. White who has performed the work with a great deal of intelligence and skill."[77] Over the course of the campaign, White had led fund-raising, coordinated branch protests, organized the legal team and smoothed out conflicts among counsel, and lobbied state and federal elected and appointed officials in behalf of the case.[78]

As 1919 closed out, Walter White was now a seasoned veteran of the movement for full equality. In the two years since he had joined the association's national staff, his undercover investigations had made him the star witness for the prosecution. The board of directors saw fit to reward him with a $500 pay increase, to the modest annual sum of $2,000—not what he could have made selling life insurance and developing property back in Atlanta, but enough to live on comfortably.[79] In the coming years, while he would continue his work incognito, he was ready to assume more responsibility within the association, both administratively and politically. As the NAACP began to focus its attentions on the passage of a federal antilynching bill, White would frequently find himself in Washington, lobbying representatives and senators and buttonholing cabinet members, perfecting a style of work that would mark the association for the next thirty years and amassing contacts in the government and press that would in time help to make him one of the country's most influential African Americans.

Chapter 3

Ambitions

With his keen investigative skills and light complexion, Walter White had proven to be the NAACP's secret weapon against white violence. He continued to use these attributes much to the association's advantage, breaking a series of major stories of various southern officials' complicity in heinous crimes against African Americans. Yet the assistant secretary had ambitions beyond playing *gotcha!* During the twenties the contours of White's life took shape along three main lines. He wanted prominence within the NAACP hierarchy, dominance for the association and himself within a national movement for civil rights, and recognition as a man of significant influence in America's political life. Under the tutelage of association secretary James Weldon Johnson, White cultivated his leadership methods and lobbying skills, beginning the decade by representing the NAACP at congressional hearings. Soon after, he was assisting Johnson to organize congressional support for the Dyer antilynching bill. By 1927, after some high-profile investigation and politicking, he was able to get the attention of the federal government, though neither he nor the association were able to make it consistently bend to their will. But as he built his reputation, White found that his complexion complicated his relations with other race advancement leaders both black and white, who looked upon him with varying degrees of respect, amusement, bemusement, and suspicion.

Through the first half of 1920, the association debated how best to

boost its presence in the South. As the June annual conference, set for Atlanta, approached, the membership and leadership debated the wisdom
of the location. On the one hand, the deep South was especially hostile to
the NAACP, as seen, for example, in the conviction and imprisonment of
the *Crisis* agent in Tchula, Mississippi, under a new state law prohibiting
the sale of literature that tended to incite African Americans. When the
national office protested, Mississippi officials stated that the agent was
treated with leniency, and that if someone from New York wanted to
come down, they would make an example of him.[1] Some feared that a
high-profile presence in Atlanta would lead to a repeat of the 1906 riot.
As James Weldon Johnson remembered, his predecessor John Shillady
confessed he would not go because, while he had the moral courage, he
had no physical courage; northern members who attended "did so feeling
that they were performing a rather heroic action." On the other hand, the
NAACP had to keep its appointment in the lion's den no matter the risks
if it had any hope at all of being a nationwide organization. Moreover, as
Du Bois pointed out, holding the festivities in the South would demonstrate that there were no differences in aim and desire between northern
and southern African Americans.[2] White aided the local organizing committee, but he labored outside of public view, the association's strategy
apparently to keep their secret weapon under wraps in the South for the
time being.[3] During much of 1920 White was most visible during his
barnstorming tours of the Northeast and Midwest to capitalize on his notoriety as an antilynching investigator.

In November 1920, election violence flared in Florida, and the assistant secretary dashed South, arriving on the scene on the Friday following the balloting. These elections held promise not so much because
either political party was responsive to blacks but because the establishment of women's suffrage held hope for a political mobilization, as thousands of African American females tried to exercise the franchise.
Southern political campaigns were not only citizenship rituals for white
men but also occasions to heap invective on black communities and re-
mind them of their subordinate status. In parts of Florida and other
southern states where blacks comprised a majority of the population,
whites, who were alarmed by the possibility of black women voting and
the general postwar assertiveness of African Americans, began a Ku Klux
Klan campaign of intimidation. The assistant secretary's investigation revealed that in Jacksonville the Klan marched through black neighbor-

hoods, daily papers agitated against black women having the balance of power in the coming election, and officials threatened to arrest any African American who was improperly registered yet tried to vote. Despite these tactics, thousands of Jacksonville blacks stood in line all day to cast ballots; local registrars' dilatoriness prevented more than 4,000 African Americans from entering the voting booth on election day.[4]

In the central Florida town of Ocoee, the situation was more extreme. Whites' hostility was intense. They regarded the assistant secretary with fierce suspicion and rebuffed his inquiries—until he let it be known that he might be interested in purchasing an orange grove.[5] Once he offered to do business with them, white Ocoeeans eagerly told him of their deeds, and he got his story: whites' fears of black political insurgence mixed with their resentment of some blacks' prosperity to create a volatile cocktail. After qualifying to vote in the county seat of Orlando, Moses Norman, a well-off African American orange-grove owner, tried to vote in Ocoee. The Klan, making good its preelection threat, beat Norman and confiscated his gun. Instead of going home, he went to see July Perry, a black man equally unpopular with whites because he owned his own home and was a foreman in a large grove owned by a northern white man. A mob formed, marched on the black section of town, and set fire to twenty homes, two churches, a school, and a fraternal lodge. Ocoee blacks organized a defense and shot four mob members, killing two. But black residents were outnumbered and overpowered; men, women, and children trying to flee the fires were either shot or forced back into the inferno. In an act that had by now become a gruesomely regular feature of mobbism, spectators clamored for charred souvenirs. One white participant told White that fifty-six blacks were known to have been killed. July Perry's arm was shot off. He was captured and taken to the county jail in Orlando; a second mob formed and convinced the sheriff to hand Perry over. He was taken outside the city limits and lynched.[6]

Upon his safe return to New York, the assistant secretary met with Representative Isaac Siegel, who chaired the House Committee on the Census, and arranged to have hearings held on the disenfranchisement of black voters. The committee would hear testimony on Siegel's proposed bill to reduce, in accordance with provisions of the Fourteenth Amendment, any state's congressional representation in proportion to the number of African Americans illegally barred from the voting booth.[7]

Over two days in late December, NAACP field secretary William

Pickens, Walter White, and James Weldon Johnson dueled with the southern representatives who dominated the proceedings. A steady stream of bluster, ignorance, and obfuscation was emitted from Representative William Larsen of Georgia when Pickens testified about registrars in South Carolina and Virginia refusing to register black women: "Mr. Chairman," Larsen said, "I would like to know if the members of this committee have to sit here and hear a commonwealth insulted by the witness. If so, I do not care to remain. . . . The nigger does not participate in the white primary. . . . Take Will May—that I happen to remember. He voted. He is a nigger, a pretty good nigger. I have nothing to say against him. . . . So the nigger was not discriminated against in his case." Representatives Carlos Bee of Texas, and Jacob Milligan of Missouri alternately harangued Pickens and denied that African Americans were blocked from the polls. Milligan even insisted that "the nigger women voting in the State of Missouri gathered around the polls on election day and kept the white women from voting."[8]

The southerners tried to pillory the assistant secretary when he took the witness chair immediately following Pickens. White's opening statement distilled his Ocoee investigation. Although the hearings were called in connection with reapportionment of the House, Representative Larsen chastised White for reporting only on southern violence and not bringing to the committee's attention instances of lawlessness in the North, such as the East St. Louis riots of 1917. But when, in answer to a specific query, White stated that many white southern communities were lawless, furnishing as evidence the 1919 Elaine, Arkansas, riot, and the lynching record since 1890, Louisiana Representative James Aswell stopped him. Larsen and Bee became a tag team, asking White questions in rapid succession and preventing him from replying. At one point, Larsen called White a liar, whereupon he was shunted aside altogether as the southern members of the committee testified to the good character of the white South, the absolute necessity of the white primary to the course of civilization, and the harm done by outsiders coming South and stirring up the black population.[9] James Weldon Johnson took the witness seat immediately following White. Larsen, Bee, and Aswell apparently had spent themselves sufficiently to do much mischief. Johnson was able, with a friendly assist from California Representative Henry Barbour, to present the association's case for the reduction of southern states' representation practically without interruption.[10]

Though no legislation emerged from the hearings, the association did succeed in flabbergasting the Bourbon South and thereby gaining black support there. Southern newspapers commented extensively on the hearings and were near unanimous in their denunciation of the association.[11] Nathan Young, who was at that time the president of Florida A&M College in Tallahassee and White's local contact for his foray to Ocoee, expressed his admiration in a letter to Johnson. "Evidently our organization has gotten under the skin of the Southerner and the more they rave, the more faith we have in the ultimate effectiveness of your work of bringing their evil doings into 'pitiless publicity.' " As to the charge that northern blacks agitated an otherwise passive southern black population, Young slyly noted: "Too bad about your New York Negroes—White of Ga., Pickens of Arkansas, Johnson from Fla."[12]

The hearings caught the attention of the executive branch. White followed his performance before the committee by meeting with Deputy Attorney General W. C. Herron, who promised a Department of Justice investigation of the Ku Klux Klan if the NAACP could provide evidence of that group's criminal acts. Heedless of the danger, White proposed to infiltrate the Klan; the association's board of directors, however, felt compelled to check his adventurousness and determined that it would "be unwise" for him to take on the task.[13]

From the evening of May 31 until June 1, Tulsa, Oklahoma, was rocked by a spasm of savagery; association executives sent White to investigate. Six hours after the *New York Evening Post* informed James Weldon Johnson of the riot, White was racing once more into the field incognito, and again carrying that paper's reporter's credentials.[14] He arrived on June 2; most of the shooting had abated, but whites continued to loot black Tulsa, and fires continued to burn. The assistant secretary filed newspaper stories and later wrote an article that appeared in *The Nation* for June 29.

The opening paragraph was chilling:

A hysterical white girl related that a nineteen-year-old colored boy attempted to assault her in the public elevator of a public office building of a thriving town of 100,000 in open daylight. Without pausing to find whether or not the story was true, without bothering with the slight detail of investigating the character of the woman who made the outcry (as a matter of fact, she was of exceedingly doubtful reputation), a mob of 100-

per-cent Americans set forth on a wild rampage that cost the lives of fifty white men; of between 150 and 200 colored men, women and children; the destruction by fire of $1,500,000 worth of property; the looting of many homes; and everlasting damage to the reputation of the city of Tulsa and the State of Oklahoma.[15]

The female told her story to police, who arrested Dick Rowland the next day, on May 31. That day, the *Tulsa Tribune* published an inflammatory story about the alleged incident, and by 4:00 a lynch mob began to gather. Black Tulsans responded without hesitation. A group of twenty-five armed African Americans marched to the city jail and offered to protect the jail from attack. The sheriff refused the offer and sent them home—though he did not disperse the crowd of 400 whites. About 9:00 in the evening, a rumor reached the black Greenwood neighborhood that the mob stormed the jail, and seventy-five African Americans mustered and returned to defend Rowland. The report was false, and the sheriff again persuaded them to return home. As they dispersed, a white man attempted to disarm one of the blacks, who resisted. A shot was fired—it is not clear by which side—and from then on the violence was unrelenting. When the first barrage ended, ten whites and two blacks lay dead. Gunfire continued until midnight, when the outnumbered black fighters retreated.

Around 5:00 the next morning, the white mob, which had mushroomed to more than 10,000, stormed Greenwood, armed with rifles, pistols, and machine guns. They toted oil, which they used to torch homes and businesses after looting them. Groups of deputized whites, charged with maintaining order, participated in the mayhem. Thousands of African Americans were interned and arrested, herded into Convention Hall and the fairgrounds; at least one, Dr. A. C. Jackson, whom the Mayo brothers described as the best black surgeon in the nation, was murdered by vigilantes even as he was being arrested by police. Whites, if they were at all interdicted, were disarmed and sent home. City police, fearing retaliation by blacks, commandeered private airplanes to surveil their movements; there were many credible reports of aerial bombings.

White identified himself in *The Nation* obliquely as someone who was "sworn in as a special deputy in Tulsa." In a statement published in the black *Washington Bee* upon his return from the scene of destruction, he said that he patrolled Tulsa as a deputy sheriff, which convinced him that what took place was unsurpassed "in sheer brutality and willful destruction of life and property."[16] But eight years elapsed before he explained all that he saw as he policed the city's streets. In his 1929 article for H. L. Mencken's *American Mercury*, "I Investigate Lynchings," he claimed that he fell in with a posse of whites. After he and fifty or sixty other men took an oath to uphold the laws and constitutions of the United States and Oklahoma, one of the men cheerily announced that he now had a license to kill blacks. Another of the men had a dim memory of a man named White who investigated racial violence but could not completely recall the relevant information. He menaced Walter with veiled references to Klan attacks on members of the "damned nigger Advancement Association." White suppressed his nerves, he said, returned the man's belligerence with a measure of hostility, and turned back the challenge.

Had the events of the tense overnight grown legendary with their retelling? It is likely that his presence in a posse had become more dramatic in memory. While the assistant secretary faithfully reported racial violence, he often took liberties in recording his own exploits. "I Investigate Lynchings" is further suspect because it was written partly to authenticate his racial loyalty at a time when he was about to assume the top position of the association. Still, his description of the mob members is certainly plausible. And for reasons of safety or to keep intact his ability to investigate racial violence, White could have determined that it was prudent not immediately to disclose his interactions with mob members. Whether White recorded the statements of deputized whites accurately or retold his confrontation with the pointedly hostile vigilante with fidelity will likely never be known with certainty, but it is doubtful.

Embellishment aside, the assistant secretary showed his mettle in Tulsa, as he would again in the future. But James Weldon Johnson and the NAACP Board of Directors—even White himself—grasped that courage, while essential, was not the sole trait of an effective leader. In his investigations, White cultivated only one dimension of a successful executive. He could spy on rednecks, and his bluff and bluster could make them howl; his moxie inspired others to embrace the cause. But he was deficient in the finer aspects of leadership, and his analytical abilities were weak. For all his travel he was still a provincial. There is no evidence from these years that he took an active part in the theoretical and strategic debates that engaged other African American leaders and intellectuals; he is silent, for example, on the discussion that brewed in *The Crisis* on African

Americans and socialist and radical thought.[17] To season him, White's mentor proposed another type of challenge: Johnson secured board approval for White to travel to Europe to promote the NAACP's antilynching campaign and attend the Second Pan-African Congress, to be held from August 27 to September 4, successively in London, Brussels, and Paris.

Launched in the aftermath of the Great War, the Pan-African Congress movement was inspired principally by W.E.B. Du Bois and bankrolled largely by the NAACP. Uniting organizations of blacks in Europe (principally France), the Americas, and Africa, the movement sought full equality for the race in the diaspora and self-determination for Europe's African colonies. Between 1919 and 1927, the congress convened four times, with sessions in London, Brussels, Paris, Lisbon, and New York. Unable to move the Western powers materially to improve the condition of their black minorities, to say nothing of divesting themselves of their colonies, the Pan-African Congress movement's importance lies elsewhere. It stimulated intercontinental race contacts, helped to lay the intellectual foundations for the post–World War II independence movements, and was an important political incubator for African Americans who rose to prominence between the two world wars.[18] Walter White, among others, was a beneficiary of this process.

White set sail for England on August 8 aboard the S.S. *Ryndam*, sharing a cabin with Du Bois.[19] No record survives of their voyage, but White, yappy, gregarious, and in nearly constant motion, must have strained Du Bois's patience. White thoroughly enjoyed his fresh adventure: "I spent all of the time eating, sleeping, reading and walking the deck," he enthusiastically wrote to Johnson. "The first few days I was very tired but I have never felt better in my life than now. The trip has worked wonders for me. I have gained tremendously in weight and am really ashamed of the amount of food I have consumed." White debarked at Plymouth, with a final destination of London, where he would iron out the details of the sessions there; Du Bois continued on to Boulogne and then to Paris, where he was to settle political disagreements between himself and the Francophone delegates that threatened to derail the congress.[20]

In London, White discovered that more than logistical details were involved. Sharp political disagreements divided the American and some

British participants. Du Bois had asked John Harris, organizing secretary of the Anti-Slavery and Aborigines Protection Society, to organize the meeting. Du Bois envisioned a large public gathering including participants from the Labour Party, the Church Missionary Society, and other concerned organizations. And though Du Bois held dear certain principles, including the unity of black people against the common oppressors, he would not dictate in advance the congress session's results. Jessie Fauset, literary editor of *The Crisis* and Du Bois's close collaborator, later explained in *The Crisis* Du Bois's orientation for the London gathering. "Men from strange and diverse lands came together. . . . Of necessity those first meetings had to be occasions for getting acquainted."[21]

But Harris balked; he desired only a small private gathering with "watertight" resolutions worked out in advance. More, Harris withheld support for the sessions to be held on the Continent. Harris was one of Britain's leading humanitarians, and during the war he denounced German colonial atrocities. But he was also one of the leading proponents of a trusteeship system that would allow Britain to continue to amass control over Africa under the guise of guiding Africans toward civilization while avoiding the stain of the label *spoils of war.* His paternalist bearing eventually placed him at odds with British blacks. He lost interest in the work of the Pan-African Congress and was replaced by Robert Broadhurst of the nationalist African Progress Union.[22]

White was present for this dispute, but he was unable to influence it. He could see that Harris, who wielded the most influence in policy circles of any of the British participants, could not be trusted. And he discerned that Broadhurst, while politically sincere, had not the executive ability to organize the conference. White asked Du Bois to come and set logistical and political matters straight.[23] Just before the opening session of the Pan-African Congress, Du Bois, with the assistant secretary in tow, conferred with Labour stalwarts Sidney Webb, Mrs. Philip Snowden, and the future Nobel laureate Norman Angell; despite Du Bois's erudition, he and White were unable to persuade the party to issue more than vague evasions on the topic of British colonialism. When the Congress recessed after the first day, Du Bois and White held a heated conference with representatives of the Anti-Slavery and Aborigines Protection Society. White, whose role in this meeting was to speak on the antilynching campaign, recorded what transpired in a letter to Johnson:

Dr. Du Bois most scathingly denounced so-called philanthropic organizations which believe in working for the natives in Africa and refuse, meanwhile, to work with Africans. This was exceedingly necessary, in view of the fact that the Anti-Slavery Society occupies the same position in England that the Tuskegee-Urban League group of whites in America—believing that the Negro should be developed up to a certain point as laborers and no farther.[24]

If Du Bois did not win any converts in the Anti-Slavery Society, he did win the day in the London sessions, with the Congress unequivocal in its criticism of American, British, and European imperialism.[25]

White delivered a speech on lynching also at the Paris session,[26] but except for these occasions he was peripheral to the proceedings. When on September 4 Du Bois gaveled the Pan-African Congress to a close, the assistant secretary remained in France reveling in Europe's grandeur. By the time he returned to London to develop antilynching publicity, he believed he had changed dramatically. "The experiences I have had have been wonderfully enlightening," he wrote home to Johnson.

The realization has come of how provincial I was two months ago. Not that I have progressed so amazingly but I am now able to see old problems in a way that is so much broader than before. I hope it will bear fruits in my being of increased value to the work at home.[27]

Obscured by White's uncharacteristically pedestrian formulation of the significance of his European sojourn is the full import of the Pan-African Congress movement on the civil rights movement in the United States. Among other African American participants were E. Franklin Frazier and Rayford Logan. Their pathbreaking scholarship and political writing in subsequent decades bore the marks of a movement that connected the history, present, and future of Afro-America with the struggles of Africans for self-determination. White himself and the NAACP would continue to work within an internationalist framework, as they maintained an interest in Caribbean affairs and placed the black American quest for equality during World War II and the postwar years in the world context of a fight by Africans and Asians to free themselves from European colonial domination.

When he returned to London, White did what he was fast becoming known for: charming VIP's and signing them up to work for the NAACP's program. Climbing to the upper reaches of British political life, he wooed Harold Laski, *Manchester Guardian* editor J. A. Hobson, female suffragist Mrs. Philip Snowden, and Norman Angell. Initially, none wanted anything to do with antilynching propaganda; they feared becoming involved in American domestic affairs, lest the United States government decide to tell Britain how to handle the Irish question. White countered their arguments and finally succeeded in getting them to call a public protest meeting and form an antilynching committee. He was also able, he reported, to secure promises from the Labourites to press their government to criticize lynching and the treatment of blacks by American organized labor.[28]

His meeting with H. G. Wells was especially gratifying for the breezy assistant secretary. White called upon him at his home, and the two men made their way to the exclusive Reform Club for lunch. Surrounded by the aristocratic opulence of his gentlemen-only surroundings, White engaged Wells in a discussion of lynching and the race problem in American generally. At first, Wells appeared not to be much interested in what the assistant secretary had to say. He had expected to meet an "elderly colored gentleman . . . and instead he saw a young man who was white." White became a much more compelling dining companion when he emphasized that he was in fact a Negro. After the meal, the two retired to the lounge where, amid the accoutrements of wealth, White, by dint of his great enthusiasm and ability to manipulate his interlocutor's impressions of himself as a Negro, convinced Wells to join an antilynching committee, put him in touch with other prominent folks, and tried to place articles on lynching with the *Saturday Evening Post.*[29]

White's class prejudices, which he shared with other African American elites, shone through as he related to NAACP chairman Mary White Ovington the details of his tête-à-tête. Wells had confessed his ignorance of—and unwittingly pled guilty to philistinism on—issues of race. White revealing himself as a Negro was all the more intriguing for Wells because, as Wells admitted, "most Englishmen, even the most intelligent, think of the American Negro in terms of the native Africans who come to London. They imagine him with a ring though his nose, a love for gaudy and ridiculous clothing and as one whose chief amusement is indulging in some cannibalistic orgy." White later remembered being disappointed by Wells, but at the time he simply volunteered to introduce him to the "proper persons," so that he might not get the "wrong angle." Though he did not share the extremes of Wells's racial fantasy, he held the same elitist premises that charged the lower classes with moral failure.[30]

European travel matured White. "I can already see the effects of your trip," Johnson wrote. "You have developed more in the last six weeks than you could have developed in a year without your experience abroad."[31] Lending validity to the adage about the finishing effects of world travel, White returned with a keen awareness in the transforming value of culture. Shortly after his return he put in a good deal of time with the cast of *Shuffle Along*, which staged a midnight revue to benefit the NAACP that raised more than $1,000. Soon, he was taking lunch with literary stars like Claude McKay, reviewing literature for *The Nation*, and immersing himself in the society and politics of the budding Harlem Renaissance. His activity would shortly open up to him the possibility of becoming a published author himself.

Closely related to his interest in a literary and artistic life was his interest in Gladys Powell, whom he wed on February 15, 1922. A month before the nuptials, Mary White Ovington confided a bit of gossip to Joel Spingarn:

> Did you know that Mr. White expects soon to marry his stenographer, Miss Powell? She is a statuesque creature, a bronze Galetia. Of all the girls she would have attracted me the least, but Mr. White thinks that being excitable himself he has incurred the proper contrast. He got his salary jacked up to $3000 [by] the board on the matrimonial prospect.[32]

Gladys was a counterbalance to the frenetic Walter. She was strikingly handsome, with a voice that was fine enough to land her a part in the opera *Deep River*, which ran in Philadelphia before moving to New York. By most accounts she was shy. White's personal secretary in the forties remembers her as aloof and snooty and bereft of friends, even in their 409 Edgecombe Avenue building, a center of Harlem life.[33]

At their apartment, first at 90 Edgecombe Avenue and then at 409, Walter and Gladys hosted luminaries of the Harlem Renaissance. Paul and Essie Robeson, concert singers Roland Hayes and Jules Bledsoe, the James Weldon Johnsons, Carl Van Vechten and Fania Marinoff—all were regular guests at the White residences. George Gershwin debuted his *Rhapsody in Blue* on the Whites' piano.[34] If the stars were not there for dinner, they came before or after a live performance and violated the Volstead Act. Outside the home Gladys accompanied Walter to one or another social affair, whether it was one of NAACP attorney (and Arthur Spingarn's law partner) Charles Studin's famous soirees or a dinner party at theater producer Courtenay Lemon's home. Gladys and Walter were not equal partners in this marriage; White appeared to want someone who would serve in a supporting role and help him penetrate the world of culture.

The assistant secretary demonstrated his developing political savvy in his work for the Dyer antilynching bill in 1921 and 1922. Republican Representative from St. Louis L. C. Dyer had first introduced his antilynching bill as a wartime measure in 1918. Whereas others in government called simply for investigations into lynching, Dyer's bill held states liable for failing to protect against lynchings, thereby opening the way for federal intervention. In 1921, Dyer reintroduced his bill with a new Congress and a new president. Republican Warren Harding, less than one month into office, called for Congress to consider investigating lynching. Dyer had continually sought help from the NAACP in passing this piece of legislation, and he was annoyed at the reluctance of the association's legal advisors—all of them white—to endorse it and make a finding that it was constitutional. But this was a time when Johnson, with White's assistance, was developing the NAACP's black secretariat and transferring power to it from the predominantly white board. Prevailing over the directors' hesitations, Johnson and White committed the association to an all-out effort to pass the Dyer bill.[35]

Although many Republican representatives supported the measure, Republican leaders in the House—and President Harding too, it turned out—were lukewarm. The association suspected that whatever enthusiasm there was for the bill was strongly connected with the party's desire to keep the black vote. Johnson spent three weeks in Washington in the fall of 1921, carefully lobbying representatives. In mid-November he was spelled by White, who soon feared that Republicans' resolve to see the bill through was weakening. One reason for this, White discovered, was the back-room dealings of black Republicans Henry Lincoln Johnson of Georgia and Perry Howard of Mississippi. They were affronted by the NAACP, which they believed leaned toward the Democrats, and they were determined to sabotage the association's efforts. The more politically sophisticated James Weldon Johnson quickly returned to lobbying legislators and quietly working against Henry Johnson and Howard. White, a man of far less political experience, indulged in bombast; he labeled the actions of his black Republican opponents as "treachery [by] our own people." The assistant secretary also seemed not to understand both the limits of the strength of the black vote and the ability of the NAACP to direct it, for he preferred initially to strong-arm representatives into voting for the bill by threatening a loss of black support in the 1922 elections. James Weldon Johnson clearly understood that *"the method is still tact and diplomacy and firm but friendly pressure*. Threats will at this moment do no particular good, and at no other time unless we are fully determined to carry them out." He instructed the national office to stick to this guideline until he determined that a switch was necessary, and then the association would "do it to the utmost." [36]

Johnson's orientation earned immediate dividends. White, Johnson, and the association's press official Herbert Seligmann had been working to build support for the bill among New York papers. On a lark, White approached Rollo Ogden, the new editor of the *New York Times*, for an editorial endorsement; Ogden was known to be sympathetic to the race, but none of the association officials had contacted him because they doubted his ability to persuade the *Times*'s publisher to modify his well-established southern sympathies. What White said to Ogden is unknown, but the editor pledged to back the bill. [37] The campaign reached a climax on January 25, when the Dyer bill was debated in the House. Before a packed gallery of African American spectators, a southern representative declared that lynching would never stop until " 'black rascals' keep their hands off white women and children." Pandemonium erupted in the audience, and Bourbon congressmen shouted from the House floor, "Sit down, niggers." But the spectators would not be silenced, as one person shouted back, "We are not niggers, you liar!" The next day, the antilynching bill passed the House by a wide margin. [38]

As the campaign shifted to the Senate, White took to heart his mentor's injunction to act diplomatically. Through the spring and summer of 1922, he canvassed the northeast, stimulating branch activity, lining up local elected officials behind Dyer, and urging state Republican Party conventions to embrace the pending legislation. Selected branches were encouraged to make it an election issue. But even here the tone was measured. For example, White took note of the hypocrisy of President Harding, who wanted legislation enabling the federal government to punish the murderers of aliens yet remained silent when it came to passing a federal antilynching law to protect the lives of black American citizens. But, said the assistant secretary, if the association could successfully spin Harding's stand against the killing of foreigners as a call to action on lynching, it would not attack the president.[39] The association demonstrated the size of the black vote in several states in November; though several supporters of the Dyer legislation lost in the general elections (for reasons unrelated to their antilynching stance), the association was confident that the next round of elections in 1924 would be tightly contested and that the Republicans would have to pay attention to the black vote. But given the opportunity after the November elections to say that African Americans would reward candidates who spoke or acted for the interests of the race while punishing those who did not, White instead chose to emphasize the prospects for united action rather than its achievement, because "unfortunately the Negro vote is not yet a sufficiently united body for us to rely upon except in this one instance of unity on the Dyer Bill." It would be another decade, during the fight to confirm Judge John Parker to the U.S. Supreme Court, before White would be comfortable in issuing such a threat. For now, the NAACP would have to be more circumspect in its words, and the Dyer bill went down to defeat in the short session after the elections.[40]

"Firm but friendly pressure" and diplomacy of a different order were required in the case of Detroit physician Ossian Sweet. In the fall of 1925 White was called to the Motor City to organize the legal and extralegal defense of the doctor, who, along with ten other family members and friends, was charged with murder and conspiracy in the shooting death of a member of a mob that had assembled outside his new home in a lower-middle-class white section of the city. White determined that the association had to take on not only segregationists and Ku Klux Klan sympathizers but also lukewarm white allies and differing factions within the black community. The legal proceedings ended victoriously. The first trial of all defendants resulted in a hung jury; in a second trial of only Ossian's brother Henry Sweet a jury returned a verdict of not guilty, and the charges were then dropped against the remaining defendants. Beyond the courtroom, the results of White's work would be a bonanza for the NAACP.

In 1917, the association had, in *Buchanan* v. *Warley*, won a landmark Supreme Court decision against municipal residential segregation laws.

But while it forbade cities from decreeing which race would live where—and it did not always do this, as Atlanta's ingenuity in skirting the High Court's verdict shows[41]—it did nothing to reduce the determination of whites to keep their neighborhoods racially homogenous. Friction over housing, which contributed, for example, to Chicago's Red Summer, only intensified in the postwar years, as African Americans continued to stream North to jobs and the promise of better lives.

The congestion of the Great Migration was intensely felt in Detroit, whose prewar black population of 8,000 swelled to 65,000 in 1925. As those African Americans who had the means attempted to move out of the city's ghetto to find decent housing, whites attempted to push them back. In June 1925 Dr. Alexander Turner purchased a home in a previously all-white neighborhood. On the day he and his family moved in, a mob of several thousand whites assaulted his dwelling. According to White's investigation, the mob forced the Turners' possessions back onto the moving van and to their previous residence; other reports state that the mob then broke every window in the home and tore the tiles from the roof. The assistant secretary believed that many whites sympathized with Turner and were prepared to support him, but after one day Turner surrendered and abandoned plans to stay. Perhaps emboldened by their quick victory, whites the next month ran Vollington Bristol, a mortician, from his new home on the boundary between white and black neighborhoods; in this encounter, several hundred shots were fired as the police looked on and then stepped in to arrest blacks. A few days later, the mob successfully repeated its performance in excluding John Fletcher. In each case, the mob, not surprisingly, was abetted by law enforcement; Ira Jayne, a well-connected Michigan jurist and NAACP board member said the police department was "honeycombed with Klansmen."[42]

In September, Dr. Sweet and his wife Gladys, a member of one of the city's oldest and most respected black families, purchased a home on Garland Avenue in the middle of a white neighborhood. Ironically, the previous owners were an interracial couple: Marie Smith was white, but her African American husband Ed, a real estate broker, passed. The Sweets had lived in Detroit since 1921, but had just returned from a year in Europe, where Ossian had studied pediatrics, gynecology, and radiology. When the Sweet ménage arrived on the eighth to take possession of their house, they were met by a mob, initially estimated at 5,000 and organized by the local property owners' association. Scared, the Sweets still moved and a cache of weapons. Tension [...] day, but on the ninth the mob [...] ny black unfortunates who hap- [...] me, windows were smashed, and [...] onium, Henry Sweet and at least [...] wd outside, killing one man and [...] red the house and arrested all the [...] days later the Sweets still had not [...] nd denied bail.[43]

[...] the Sweets' ordeal, the Detroit [...] ce to infiltrate the white commu- [...] r the defense counsel. Two days [...], the Board of Directors met and [...] troit with specific instructions. [...] the defendants (leaving him the [...] nd organize a fund-raising cam- [...] ld both support the Sweets and [...] t in 1925 was shaping up as a se- [...] mer in Chicago.[44]

He arrived in the Motor City late in the evening of September 14 and immediately seized control of practically all facets of the defense work. In his autobiography White remembered going to the jail directly from the train station to see the defendants, and with good reason too. The NAACP was not the only organization in town, and Marcus Garvey's Universal Negro Improvement Association's presence in Detroit worried White. And he was certain the large amount of money the NAACP was raising to defend the Sweets would attract charlatans. At the jail the Sweets signed an agreement to have the NAACP represent them.[45] As he had learned in Chicago six years previously, the first order of business was to secure the association's logistical control.

White then proceeded to reach out to the city's political leadership. In the days following the riot on Garland Avenue, Detroit's Mayor John W. Smith (a Catholic who was vigorously opposed by the Klan) pleaded for calm and pledged to appoint an interracial commission. He blamed the night of violence on KKK agitation but also implored African Americans to reduce racial tension by not exercising their right to live where they pleased. White breakfasted with Judge Jayne, the mayor's closest advisor, to discuss potential candidates for the commission, resulting in several friendly commissioners, including two NAACP branch officers and a "sincere and good" white man, also an association member.[46]

In a bold move, the assistant secretary extended his canvass of Detroit's establishment to include the prosecutor and the presiding judge, Frank Murphy. White began a long and warm friendship with Murphy, who would make a successful run for mayor in 1927 and governor in 1937 and then be nominated by Franklin Roosevelt for attorney general and then Supreme Court justice. It was the judge who initially advised White to hire a white lawyer to defend the Sweets.[47] Even the most enlightened among whites were against Sweet, so Murphy reasoned, and a white lawyer would help to win alienated public opinion to Sweet's cause.

White, swimming against the tide, wholeheartedly embraced this advice. Julian Perry, an African American lawyer whom Sweet initially called for assistance and who had previously represented him in some personal business matters, had appeared to represent the defendants, with two of his colleagues. But White thought little of the three, believing them to be not competent and interested primarily in getting their hands on the more than $1,100 that the local branch had been able raise in short order. The only black lawyer in Detroit for whom the assistant secretary had any regard was Hayes McKinney, a branch official. Before Charles Houston began to train African Americans in civil rights law at Howard University Law School in 1929, White had a dim view of black members of the bar, and there certainly was a basis for his belief that they were a motley lot: at the time, fewer than 10 percent of African American lawyers were graduated from top schools. While they could register a real estate transaction, they were generally not equipped to handle cases of the magnitude of the Sweet case. In the mid-twenties, using white litigators was the expedient approach. But it would be several more years until Houston had developed his first cadre of dedicated and qualified black civil rights attorneys. When they were ready in the early thirties, then White would encourage the switch to African American lawyers.[48]

White's position in the Sweet case sparked deep resentment among blacks in Detroit and elsewhere, as many believed that only a colored attorney ought to represent Sweet both as an expression of support for black professionals and because a Negro lawyer would better be able to understand the psychology of the defendant.[49] But White would not budge. He relieved the local leadership of the job of hiring counsel and instructed Mose Walker, the branch vice president, to keep Julian Perry and the other African American lawyers in check: "They have got to know that we are doing the employing in the case and we are going to pay the bill and it is not for them to dictate to us what we shall do."[50] The association's national legal committee, chaired by Arthur Spingarn and with the increasingly active participation of White, stated that if the defendants did not agree that the best attorney—read: white attorney—be retained, then the NAACP would back out of the case. This achieved the desired result, as Otis Sweet, another of Ossian's brothers, ceded all decisions about counsel to the NAACP.[51]

Pushing aside lingering objections to white lawyers, the NAACP moved to hire Clarence Darrow, the foremost defense attorney of his day, and assemble a dream team by partnering him with the eminent litigator Arthur Garfield Hays, who assisted Darrow at the Scopes trial earlier that year.[52] Hays recounted the first time he met the assistant secretary:

> My first personal connection with the N.A.A.C.P. was a good many years ago, with Clarence Darrow, and I shall never forget the occasion on which Darrow and I were visited by a committee headed by Spingarn, White, [Charles] Studin and Johnson. And after Arthur Spingarn had told the story of what happened to the Sweets in Detroit, fighting to defend themselves and being charged with murder, Darrow turned to Arthur Spingarn with his swarthy skin and dark hair and said: "I know the troubles of your race and I am deeply interested." Spingarn replied: "I don't happen to be a Negro." And Darrow turned to Studin and said: "You'll understand how I feel about this." And Studin said: "I am not a Negro, either." Then he turned to Walter White and said: "I won't make that mistake with you," and Walter said: "I am a Negro." Then we had some discussion with Walter White as to why he was so race-conscious and we found out that . . . although he is seven-eights white, he was just as race-conscious as any other Negro and he had decided to devote his life and his career to the question.[53]

The issue of representation and racial identity now decided, White turned his attention to schoomzing with all concerned. He was optimistic that his trademark congeniality would have maximum effect. Before the case came to trial, Judge Murphy made clear that the Sweets would receive a fair trial and that he would not allow prejudice to infect the proceedings. The judge, by all accounts a champion of the downtrodden, was contemplating a run for Detroit mayor in 1927 and planned to use this trial to take a positive stand against racism and contend for the African American vote. Murphy telegraphed his sympathies during jury selection too.

Each day blacks packed the courtroom. During one particularly tense moment, when a prospective juror admitted she was "very prejudiced," some spectators audibly voiced their disapproval. Murphy summoned White, who had no legal standing in the case, to the bench and then into his chambers and told him that any further outbursts would hurt the defense's case. White's and Murphy's interactions were not always so serious, either: "Today Judge Murphy called me up to the bench and asked me to have luncheon with him at the Detroit Athletic Club next week." He also worked the journalists. White sat at the press table, courtesy of the judge. Seated next to him was the *New York Times* reporter, a close friend of the arch-racist novelist Irvin Cobb. The assistant secretary appealed not to his journalist's ethos but to his baser instincts: the man wanted to move to the *New York World* and have his novel published, and White promised assistance on both accounts. "He's eating out of my hand," he reported. White also softened up Cash Asher of the *Detroit Free Press*, which had a hostile editorial line. "My flimsy connection with the *World*"—White knew the managing editor—"makes me a somewhat important figure in the eyes of the local newspaper men and they listen with respect thus far to my suggestion," he told James Weldon Johnson.[54]

White spent close to two months in Detroit and the Midwest during the trial, which began on November 4. He actively consulted about legal strategy with Darrow and Hays, spun news for the press corps, and raised money. The first week of November found him in Cleveland, Toledo, Chicago, and St. Paul. A group of Windy City black professionals begged him to return and guaranteed at least $1,000 if he did so. One of his speeches at the University of Minnesota was broadcast over the radio. He returned to Detroit with almost $2,700 in cash and more in pledges. In fact, the fund-raising was for more than the Sweet case. The NAACP had developed an ambitious plan to raise $50,000 to start a permanent legal defense fund, which initially would support Sweet as well as the challenge to the Texas white primary in *Nixon* v. *Herndon* and racially restrictive covenants in Washington, D.C. The left-wing Garland Fund subscribed for $5,000 with a promise of an additional $15,000 if the association could raise a total of $30,000. By February 1926, the fund exceeded $65,000 dollars, approximately 10 percent of which was raised by the Detroit branch.[53]

The flush state of the defense fund also brought White severe headaches. Try as it might, the association did not control all of the monies raised for the Sweets' defense. The Reverend Joseph Gomes of the Bethel A.M.E. Church led the City Wide Committee, which had raised nearly $3,000 for the cause. White approached Gomes to turn his funds over to the NAACP. He declined, and the best the assistant secretary could manage was to establish a joint committee to disburse the funds. What appears to be the source of Gomes's reluctance was a disagreement over the role of local black attorneys in the trial. Gomes believed that the black lawyers should be involved in the case and should be compensated; White urged Gomes not to pay them: "The very worst thing that could be done would be to have the City Wide Committee pay any more to the colored lawyers," he fulminated to Johnson. White believed that hiring Darrow "solves our problems," and he wanted the black lawyers to work pro bono, positions which he said were supported by Detroit's black community. As the second trial was set to commence, he sought to exclude two of the three lawyers from the defense table, while allowing a local white lawyer to be present.[56]

The assistant secretary's apparent faith in the inerrancy of the national office and the strategy of effecting change from the top prevented him from seeing the depth of feeling among African Americans. Robert Bagnall, the national office's director of branches and formerly of Detroit, reported "considerable talk about the NAACP not paying the colored lawyers the balance owing them while it has paid all the amounts due the white lawyers." Sympathizers tried to get word of the association's miserliness into print; the black weekly *Detroit Independent* spiked the story only because the editor was branch vice president Mose Walker's brother-in-law. The *Pittsburgh Courier* picked up the story and prepared to run it unless the association paid the lawyers. Faced with a public-relations fiasco, White acceded to Bagnall's advice and agreed to pay the attorneys.[57]

The *Courier*'s willingness to accept an article critical of the association was symptomatic of opposition to the NAACP's attempts to dominate the civil rights scene. That paper and the *Chicago Whip* complained loudly that the association was acting fraudulently, that on the pretense of raising money for the Sweet defense, it was in fact using it to develop other cases. The *Whip* accused the NAACP of hogging the Sweet case and undeservedly claiming credit for it. The *Courier* charged Johnson and Du Bois with corruption by diverting the legal defense funds for use by the NAACP. This was not true, of course, and there was no financial sleight of hand: from the beginning of the fund-raising campaign, the association had stated that money collected would go to developing challenges to all manner of legal injustices.[58] Yet White's imperious manner toward those African Americans who disagreed with the NAACP contributed to those individuals and organizations feeling provoked. At various times during his long career, he would find that his actions could invite loyalty or incite opposition. In the Sweet case, he found that he pretty much dominated the scene either by his charm or his iron determination to push through his plan of action.

After months of nearly constant travel, Walter was anxious to get home. He missed Gladys and daughter Jane, who was born in 1922, and he had family responsibilities. Their decision to have children upended the Walter White household. Both parents were self-centered, their daughter remembered—or focused, if one was inclined to be more generous. Walter was short-tempered around the house, especially about issues of order and neatness. He could be indulgent of his children (Walter Carl Darrow was born in 1927)—they had pets and trips to summer camp—and solicitous of their feelings, but only if such was his mood; he was not that way by nature. But Gladys too had a rigid code of behavior. And both parents were exceedingly mindful of impressions, which extended not only to dress and comportment but even to the way the children laughed.[59]

While Gladys performed most of the quotidian tasks of child rearing, Walter arranged for Jane's education, and he hustled to have a spot reserved for her in the Ethical Culture school at Central Park West and Sixty-third Street. She would be one of the few African American children there. Walter wanted Jane to break down racial barriers, as he did. Starting nearly two years early in his hunt for Jane's education, he lobbied hard for a full scholarship for her. He was engaged in vital work, he wrote to the school in justification of his request, and this entailed "considerable financial sacrifices." (His salary had risen to $3,300 in 1924 and $4,000 in 1925, lower than what he might have earned selling life insurance back in Atlanta, but comfortable enough for the Whites to afford a housekeeper and enjoy a middle-class life.) James Weldon Johnson and his brother-in-law, Harlem real estate mogul John B. Nail, agreed to sponsor Jane's application, though Nail and Johnson's wife Grace soon balked at the idea that Walter and Gladys needed full financial assistance. Nevertheless, he was successful in gaining full tuition assistance for Jane, who enrolled in 1927.[60]

Walter's push for Jane's elite education lets us peek behind his mind's curtain and see how he weighed financial matters. White worked hard, but he treated himself well. Friends and colleagues sprinkled him with gifts, whether it be clothes or the use of a vacation cottage. In these and other personal transactions, including his plea for the easing of the burden of a private education, one can see Walter's belief in entitlement: the perks he accrued were in his mind simply compensation for diligence in important work.[61]

Walter also drew comfort from close relationships with his siblings and parents. His mother and father were extraordinarily proud of him, bragged about him to all who would listen, eagerly awaited his letters, and waited for a visit when he was in the South on business. He helped his sister Olive's husband Alonzo Glenn get a promotion in the post office, which entailed moving the family to Cleveland.[62]

He was perhaps most intimate with his brother, George. Ten years his senior and a rising official in the American Missionary Association, George delighted in his kid brother's acclaim. He fed Walter anecdotes of life in the South—he toiled as principal at the Burrell Normal School in Florence, Alabama, until 1925, when he was elected the first black associate secretary of the AMA and then transferred to Chicago—which usually found their way into White's writing. Blond-haired and blue-eyed like his brother, George also wrestled with the impact of his Euro-American appearance on his career and self-image, and did not let Walter's celebrity prevent him from keeping his sibling honest. Examining a collection of caricatures of his brother, George thought one of them was "horrible, and your claim to have a negroid head—think of it! You went me one better—I don't think even my zeal for the race would make me claim that!"[63]

With his work on the Sweet case and his breakthrough investigation of a triple lynching in Aiken, South Carolina, later in 1926 that led to a series of front-page exposés in the *New York World* of racial violence and political corruption, Walter White was rapidly ascending the NAACP's organizational ladder and pushing his way onto the national political stage. When the lower Mississippi River overflowed its banks in spring 1927, the assistant secretary's investigation pierced the consciousness of the Republican administration in Washington, D.C.

The flood was not only a natural disaster, though it was that. After months of steady and heavy rain, the federally constructed dykes along the Mississippi crumbled south of Cairo, Illinois. Hundreds of thousands of acres of farm and city on either side of the river's banks were inundated, with a staggering loss of life, livestock, and property as the flood rumbled toward the Gulf of Mexico. The great flood was also a racial calamity, as a multitude of African American sharecroppers in and near the Mississippi Delta were displaced and then snared into peonage.

Five days after the flood waters pierced the levees near Cairo, they ruptured those near Greenville, Mississippi. When the embankments burst at Mounds Landing just north of the city, signaling imminent danger, refugees streamed to the levees in Greenville, virtually the only high ground in the surrounding area. Before too long, thousands of men, women, and children and their livestock crowded on this narrow strip of ground that hugged the river for eight miles. Supplies, when they reached the camp, were distributed unequally, according to Jim Crow custom. Blacks received no eating utensils and had no mess hall, so they had to eat with their fingers, either standing, sitting on the wet ground, or on their haunches. Canned fruit made its way only to whites, who feared that such delicacies would only spoil blacks; a butcher on the levees slaughtered up to eight cattle each day for the main refugee kitchen, but few African Americans received meat.[64]

The first reaction to the refugee crisis by Greenville's official emergency committee, headed by William Alexander Percy, the heir apparent of that family dynasty, was to evacuate the homeless downriver to Vicksburg, where they could either catch a train to other destinations or stay in Red Cross camps. Delta planters, however, vigorously opposed this plan, for they wanted to keep their labor close at hand, and they knew or strongly suspected that once gone, African Americans who had lost everything would not return. LeRoy Percy, the family scion and former U.S. senator with strong connections to Wall Street and elsewhere in the world of finance, overruled his son William. Henceforth, African American refugees were to be rounded up and kept in Greenville. The National Guard was ordered to police the levee and prevent blacks from leaving. Brutality against blacks increased exponentially.[65]

Despite the flood-imposed isolation, word leaked out about abuses in places like Greenville, and the NAACP board of directors in early May ordered Walter White to investigate. He left on May 14. James Weldon Johnson tried unsuccessfully to procure reporter's credentials from the *New York Times* and suggested to White that without this cover he might want to return. But he pressed on. He met a considerable number of African Americans in Memphis who had escaped from peonage and did not want to go back.[66] His report, which bore the alternate titles of "The Negro and the Flood" and "The Negro in the Flood," and which in condensed form was published in *The Nation*, was a scathing indictment of both flood relief and the Jim Crow South generally. The report opens with an anecdote about his trip from New York to Memphis. One of the passengers on his Pullman car was a well-to-do southern white woman who was appalled at some of the privileges that blacks in New York enjoyed. No matter what he and she talked about, she always returned to her obsession: "keeping niggers in their places." After visiting the flood-stricken South, White came to realize "even more fully than I had before how universal in the South is the opinion shared."[67]

White could not get to Greenville to see the mismanagement, but what he saw at some of the best-run camps shocked him. The four centers set up at the Vicksburg National Cemetery housed nearly 26,000 African Americans, three-fourths of whom worked on plantations, with the balance either small landowning farmers, tradesmen, professionals, or domestic workers in small Delta towns. General Curtis Green of the Mississippi National Guard, who commanded these four camps, was unfailingly courteous and assigned White a car and driver for unimpeded inspections. His gentlemanly yet direct manner impressed upon White how ingrained was the thinking of his Pullman companion.

> According to General Green, as the lands dry a plantation owner or his authorized manager or agent comes to the refugee camps after presenting proper identification, "picks out his niggers" and they are sent back to the plantation from which they came. General Green also told me how labor agents are kept from the camps "no man being allowed to talk to any other but *his own niggers.*" . . .

> . . . A number of Negroes vehemently and passionately said to me that they would rather be drowned in the flood than be forced to go back to the plantations from which they had come.[68]

White made his findings available to Secretary of Commerce Herbert Hoover, who was in charge of flood relief and who was contending for the Republican presidential nomination. They were also picked up by the *New York Times* and the *New York Herald Tribune*.[69] Hoover was mindful of the importance of blacks to his chances of becoming his party's standard-bearer in 1928, and his campaign worried about the fallout from reports that blistered the government's flood assistance. The journalist Will Irwin, who backed Hoover, visited the stricken areas and defended Hoover to African Americans. He also tried to silence Hoover's black critics. "I have managed to call off most of the dogs I know, except one Walker [sic] White. He is a negro [sic] who looks like white man and has set himself up as champion of his race. He has done some good work but he's a fanatic," Irwin wrote. He did not know the stature of the person with whom he was dealing. "White is literally the nigger in the woodpile and if anything can been done to placate or squelch him I think there will be no more trouble. . . . Perhaps if some of the big negroes [sic] would communicate with him they might tone him down."[70]

Hoover's response to Irwin and White as well as other questioners and critics was to deny the assistant secretary's findings. Guards, he said, were not restricting the movement of blacks into and out of the camps; as to White's evidence that federal authority was abetting peonage, Hoover claimed "no responsibility for the economic system which exists in the south or for matters which have taken place in previous years." But to address charges of abuse, Hoover said, he had "appointed a general investigating committee under Doctor [Robert Russa] Moton [Booker T. Washington's successor at Tuskegee] who are free to report what they like to any inquirer." Although among the committee's members was St. Louis NAACP official Sidney Redmond and Frances Williams, a YWCA leader who would soon become a staunch ally of White's, no one from the association's national office was chosen.[71] The Moton committee was window dressing with a dual purpose of buttressing black support for Hoover's presidential aspirations and neutralizing expected criticism from the NAACP. Claude Barnett, a committee member whose Associated Negro Press syndicated several articles praising Hoover's relief efforts, admitted as much. "Dr. Moton was desirous of your knowing we were trying to create a proper impression," Barnett informed Hoover.[72] With Hoover's decision to ignore the association, White would have nothing to do with his run for the presidency, though he would seriously consider joining Democrat Al Smith's campaign.

White's investigation came to an unexpectedly abrupt end. After little more than a week he became violently ill and returned to New York in serious condition. His physician, Louis Wright, who also was his longtime friend from Atlanta, diagnosed a partial obstruction of the bowel and ordered bed rest and a liquid diet; on May 26, Wright pronounced White out of danger and in no need of surgery.[73]

His star was rising higher in the race advancement firmament. Louis Marshall, a founder of the American Jewish Committee, who—as one of the country's leading constitutional lawyers put his expertise at the service of the NAACP—lionized White. Urging African Americans to follow the Jewish example and "give until it hurts," Marshall said, "I have never known of a man [who] faced martyrdom as he did and was only upheld by the feeling that he was doing his duty not only to his race but to the human family."[74]

But as the praise and recognition cascaded in, the assistant secretary seriously considered leaving the association for other lines of work. Perhaps the chronic danger depleted his reserves. Clearly the constant travel took its toll. And Gladys must have been unhappy both with his long absences and with the increased responsibilities that devolved upon a wife of a prominent and rising race man; she never was comfortable with being Mrs. Walter White.[75] He also wrestled with episodes of restlessness. For the remainder of his life he would periodically entertain career changes motivated by a mixture of desire for new experiences, a feeling that the association did not sufficiently appreciate his efforts, and a belief that he could achieve greater notoriety and influence independent of the NAACP.

When his close friend, the well-known classically trained tenor Roland Hayes asked him at the end of 1924 to become his American manager, White responded eagerly. He discussed it at length with Gladys, who was most receptive to the idea. "Needless to say," he wrote Hayes, "it is the first time she has ever become enthusiastic about any work other than that connected with the NAACP." He was going to talk the proposal over with literary critic Laurence Stallings, a southerner by birth who now wrote for the *New York World* and who was won to the cause of civil rights both by White's writings and by Hayes's singing. Not everyone was so enthralled with the proposal, however. "May I say as modestly as I can," White reported, "that in certain other quarters there is violent opposition. *Mirabile dictu*, Mr. Johnson doesn't welcome the idea of my leaving."[76] For the time being, the assistant secretary put the brakes on a change of jobs.

The decision to stay with the NAACP did not stop him from flirting with other prospects. Coincidentally, a few days after receiving Hayes's offer, White was waiting on a friend who was late for their luncheon date at the famed Al-gonquin Hotel when Frederick Allen of Harper & Brothers approached him. Knowing him only by reputation, Allen asked if he was Walter White. Their conversation began about Countee Cullen's poetry and then turned to Roland Hayes, and this segued into Allen proffering White a contract for a biography of Hayes. The assistant secretary was keen on the project; he wanted to tell his friend's story—the child of slaves reaches spectacular success in Europe but is still subject to discrimination in the North and Jim Crow in the South—"without the slightest bit of bitterness or venom." And having already written a novel, *The Fire in the Flint*, a biography "will give me a reputation in a different field of literature." The prospects came to naught despite White's ardor, because Hayes was suspicious of Frederick Allen's motives.[77]

In October 1926 White applied to the Guggenheim Foundation for a three-year fellowship to write novels and plays. This time he kept his plans secret, telling neither his mentor nor his close colleague in the association, Arthur Spingarn. Somehow Joel Spingarn got wind of White's plans and wrote him an alarmed letter: "I am much disturbed to hear of your decision to give up what I had thought was to be your life-work. Before you come to a final decision I wish that I might have a talk with you." The two met in mid-November 1926.[78]

A few days after White visited him at his West Seventy-second Street town house—he had moved back to the city for the winter from Troutbeck, his Hudson Valley estate in Amenia—Spingarn wrote to his wife Amy about their meeting. Much as he did not like it, White would leave the NAACP, at least temporarily: "His plan . . . is to . . . spend 2 or 3 years in Southern France writing. (This is *very* confidential.) His wife & child are to go along—so that's that."

What he wrote next was jaw-dropping:

I asked him frankly if he thought men of unmixed Negro blood capable of the highest achievement and character. At first he hedged, mentioned Bishop [John] Hurst [an NAACP founder and board member, African Methodist Episcopal prelate, and someone to whom White felt extremely close] and Roland Hayes and others whom we both admire (*are* they pure Negroes?), and gave all the other arguments that I as well as he and the rest of the NAACP have given for years. That was habit, perhaps we have used these arguments so long that we have to begin with them, at least in the presence of men of ill will. ("Let's stop joking, here comes a fool," old Dr. Johnson said; after all that may be the principle.) But finally he admitted that he had virtually never met a pure Negro whom he really could trust, that he didn't believe it was in them, that they *were* inferior, infinitely inferior now, whatever they might possibly become in future. So there's the conflict—nine-tenths white loathing the one-tenth black, one-tenth black hating the nine-tenths white. The passionate pro-Negro loyalty is a conflict, a whirlpool—and a mask.[79]

It is hard to square Spingarn's astonishing and unequivocal recounting of his and White's conversation that evening with White's professions on race matters. There is simply nothing in the record that suggests he subscribed to an equation of ability and character with racial patrimony. Certainly White perceived his complexion set him apart from the majority of African Americans, as did his darker compatriots. And in some instances, people he knew and worked with for years still disbelieved that he was black. L. B. Palmer, who along with White was a founder of the Atlanta branch of the association, pointedly asked him, "Why do you allow yourself to be called a Negro? You are no more a Negro than Roosevelt was a Dutchman or, if what Boas teaches is true, Marconi is a Negro." The educator N. B. Young, who at the time was president of Lincoln University in Missouri, gave White a sharp elbow in the ribs with his comment that "Jefferson City in its attitude toward your *alleged* people is more southern than some southern towns I know." Mary Talbert, the venerable leader of the National Association of Colored Women, worked closely with White on antilynching activities and seemed to place him in the camp of sympathetic whites when she gave him this advice as he prepared to leave for the Pan-African Congress in 1921:

Rest all you can. See all you can, but don't don't [sic] kill yourself, for these poor non-appreciative folks, *this race of mine*, I wonder sometimes if it pays to do all and so much when it is not appreciated by so many.[80]

Comments like these must have been a burr under White's saddle, and his reply was often testy, as in his riposte to Palmer: "Now, as to the announcement . . . that I am a Negro. In the first place, according to American standards I am a Negro and am tremendously proud of it."[81] His peers' reactions to his complexion likely created an inner tension whose outer expression was an exaggerated identification with the race, seen, for example, in his overstatements of his already stellar record of lynching investigations. But this is a far cry from loathing his black roots, which Spingarn attributes to White, who generally moved quite comfortably between racial worlds.

Most likely, White told Spingarn what he wanted to hear. Although the two men worked closely together in the association they were not of equal rank or stature. Spingarn proffered advice, career direction, and connections, especially in the publishing world, to which White aspired. In this particular instance, White was relying on Spingarn to recommend him for the Guggenheim fellowship. White was not above a trace of cravenness now and again if it would further his goals. His confession to Spingarn hints at a certain unsavory manipulative nature in White, but not any offensive racial prejudices.

What their conversation does reveal are the prejudices of even the most convinced white supporters of the fight for civil rights. The racial ambivalence Spingarn ascribed White may have expressed his own anxieties about African Americans. Certainly it would not be unheard of for even a strident advocate of racial equality—and Spingarn helped to breathe life into the NAACP with his program for a New Abolitionism— to harbor lingering racial prejudices. William English Walling, a Kentucky aristocrat who seemingly overcame congenital prejudice to marry a Russian Jew, join the Socialist Party, and become a founder of the NAACP, by most accounts got on easily with his black peers and colleagues in the association. Yet his wife Anna Strunsky revealed the limitations of his comfort with social equality. "He did not cringe viscerally when Dr. Du Bois, that great man, did us the honor of spending 2 or 3 weekends with us . . . and he went swimming with English and me," Strunsky said. But "English confessed to me that he felt he was '*swimming with a monkey.'* . . . But we had Negro visitors. Weldon Johnson for one whom English honored and loved to be with and Walter White as well [but] both of these men were white." [82] Even for someone as sensitive and perceptive as Joel Spingarn, the mask to which he refers may have been his own.

White won the prestigious Guggenheim fellowship, though for one year rather than the three he requested. He would leave in July 1927. He went with the good wishes and high hopes of many, including African Methodist Episcopal Bishop John Hurst, a man whom White once described as a second father:

> I cannot tell you how rejoiced I am over the recognition given you by the Guggenheim Foundation. I look upon it, not only as a recognition given to you alone, but to the organization which you have been upholding so intelligently and manfully.
>
> Bertha [the bishop's wife] and I have been talking about you; of the great progress you have made and the strong character you have developed, and above all, how well you fill your place in the world. We are proud of you. To us, this is but the beginning of larger things that await you. Bertha says that you are but a "kid," and to start now the larger world will feel your presence and know that you are in it. [83]

Once again he was heading to Europe, this time with Gladys, daughter Jane, and his second child, one-month-old Walter Carl Darrow White (about whom, more in the following chapter). White gathered his research notes on lynching and boxing—he planned a work of nonfiction on racial violence and a novel on the sweet science—and moved to southern France to make himself over as an author. [84]

Chapter 4

Socializing and Civil Rights in the Harlem Renaissance

The Harlem Renaissance was the ideal setting for Walter White to realize his ambition as an arbiter of culture and a champion of civil rights. Also called the New Negro movement, the Harlem Renaissance was staged large. Alain Locke, the Howard University philosophy professor and Harvard-trained aesthete, declared in 1925 that its participants, "the younger generation is vibrant with a new psychology; the new spirit is awake in the masses." A year later, Langston Hughes announced the mission for this younger generation of artists: "We build our temples for tomorrow, strong as we know how, and we stand on top of the mountain, free within ourselves." [1] Strategically perched near the peak, White surveyed the cultural-political topography, helped to plot the direction of the movement, and assisted an array of black artists in their ascent. All the while, White was going in overdrive: after a full day at the office, he spent hours at the center of the nightlife that was essential to the substance and aura of the New Negro movement. Indeed, he was much the small-town mayor: he knew everybody, called them by their first names, and initiated important visitors into the glories of Harlem's diversions. And he was writing up a storm, besides. In addition to occasional articles in *The Nation* and *The New Republic*, he authored three novels—*Fire in the Flint* (1924), *Flight* (1926), and the unpublished and until recently presumed lost *Blackjack*—and a searing book-length indictment of lynching, *Rope and Faggot* (1929).

White was not an originator of the Harlem Renaissance. That honor would have to go to others like Charles S. Johnson and James Weldon Johnson. In the aftermath of the racial holocaust of 1919, and the acceleration of African Americans' migration from the South to the urban North, the genius of the two Johnsons—Charles and James—lay in their proposition that racial friction would be allayed not mainly by a direct assault on discrimination but through the development of a black cultural movement. Or, as James Weldon Johnson put it to his protégé: "It has long been a cherished belief of mine that the development of Negro Art in the United States will not only mean a great deal for the Negro himself, but will provide the easiest and most effective approach to that whole question called the race question. It is the approach that offers the least friction." The watchwords of the Harlem Renaissance organizers would henceforth be, in the pithy phrase of historian David Levering Lewis, "civil rights by copyright."[2]

Between the Renaissance's 1917 beginning and 1935 ending (marked symbolically by the furious March night of rioting in Harlem), Johnson's vision was partially fulfilled. Even a truncated roster of writers, painters, musicians, and actors who emerged during the Harlem Renaissance is impressive: Marian Anderson, Gwendolyn Bennett, Countee Cullen, Aaron Douglas, Jessie Fauset, Rudolph Fisher, Roland Hayes, Langston Hughes, Zora Neale Hurston, Georgia Douglas Johnson, Nella Larsen, Claude McKay, and Paul Robeson. With the guidance of the NAACP's and the National Urban League's cultural arbiters—who were the principal conduits between the African American artists and the white publishers, promoters, and philanthropists, whose money fueled the Renaissance—this cohort of cultural producers "generated twenty-six novels, ten volumes of poetry, five Broadway plays, countless essays and short stories, three performed ballets and concerti, and a considerable output of canvas and sculpture."[3] But it was unrealistic to expect that an infinitesimal portion of the black population—no matter how talented— could resolve the race question, as James Weldon Johnson and others had hoped. The New Negro movement's art and literature, while it could uplift African Americans' spirit and had the potential to erase some whites' prejudice, simply could not do the heavy lifting of eradicating the nation's pervasive and race-based economic and social inequality by the country's business and political leaders.

But if the New Negro movement was not White's brainchild, he grasped its significance early and was one of its most energetic promoters, especially in the areas of attracting the interest and money of white bene-factors. And this field did not require a sophisticated awareness of art; one could be a lightweight so long as one knew the connoisseurs and could harness their expertise. Such abilities White had in abundance. He at-tempted to found a National Institute of Negro Letters, Music, and Art, and upon hearing that photography magnate George Eastman—who had endowed a conservatory in Rochester, New York, and had developed an interest in helping to found one for Negro music—White set out to con-vince him and other philanthropists of the efficacy of including in such a project drama and literature as well.[4] He turned to Alain Locke for assis-tance, who was electrified by White's scheme: "You have a wonderful proposition in the nest," he wrote. "Be motherly with it, I almost wish you were a hen."[5]

Locke's proposal was ambitious. It included provisions for teaching and research departments in music, drama, literature and folklore, design and painting, and sculpture and African crafts. Racially integrated juries would present annual medals that would not only act as incentives but would also be "something in the nature of an Academy award, with rec-ognized prestige." Its structure would be modeled after the NAACP, where the work of the foundation would be on an integrated basis while the executive posts would be filled "by men of the race." Locke concluded his proposal with a sentiment that White had come to embrace: more than any other activity, championing the arts and letters would lead white America to "a more sympathetic and revised estimate of the capacities of the Negro race as a group . . . "[6]

White loved the draft proposal and over the next year he marketed it domestically and internationally. Herman Lieber, an Indianapolis indus-trialist, was enchanted by the institute concept. He offered to approach George Eastman, with whom he had a close business relationship, with the idea, but he could of course guarantee no favorable result. He was certain that Eastman was "interested in the colored problem," and he suggested that White arrange for Roland Hayes to sing for Eastman in his home. But, alas, Lieber could spare no money for the endeavor.[7] Nor, apparently, could he provide access to Eastman, who silently disappears from the record. Yet White was hardly discouraged. Based on Locke's re-ports from abroad, where African American arts were in style, there seemed to be endless possibilities for publicity, especially concerning the mistreatment of blacks in the United States; White nudged theologian William Stuart Nelson, who had been expatriated in France for some years after World War I, to explore this angle. Work moved ahead steadily. Soon, the black fraternities and sororities agreed to provide funding for some of the institute's programs. But the American Fund for Public Service—the left-wing philanthropy also called the Garland Fund—decided not to fund the institute. This was an insurmountable obstacle, and White shelved the plan permanently in May 1924.[8]

But fostering the Harlem Renaissance involved more than soliciting philanthropic donations. The serious business of promotion also meant creating a buzz, which drew upon White's indefatigable capacity for socializing. Most Harlemites lived through the twenties quite unaware of the momentousness of the New Negro movement. The painter Aaron Douglas believed that "the man in the street . . . did not actually, consciously make a contribution; he made his contribution in an unconscious way." Langston Hughes somewhat more peevishly stated that "the ordinary Negroes hadn't heard of the Negro Renaissance. And if they had, it hadn't raised their wages any." But the success of the Renaissance project depended on the lubrication provided by all manner of diversions. Langston Hughes continued in the same tone about celebrity involvement in the Harlem Renaissance:

> It was a period when, at almost every Harlem upper-crust dance or party, one would be introduced to various distinguished white celebrities as guests. It was a period when almost any Harlem Negro of any social importance at all would be likely to say casually: "As I was remarking the other day to Heywood—," meaning Heywood Broun. Or: "As I said to George—," referring to George Gershwin.[9]

Certainly White was not shy about dropping names, and he derived infinite pleasure from his proximity to cultural trendsetters. Yet by so doing, he also assembled an enthusiastic audience for the New Negro writers and performers.

At one end of the spectrum of activities were the official dinners and receptions where New Negro writers, musicians, and artists gathered to mingle with patrons and publishers. The first of these took place in March 1924, when Charles Johnson, editor of the National Urban League's *Opportunity*, organized an evening at the downtown Civic Club

(Manhattan's only elite establishment that did not observe race or sex restrictions). Planned in honor of Jessie Fauset, whose just published *There Is Confusion* became the first novel of the Harlem Renaissance, the *Opportunity* dinner was, in Johnson's words, "one of the most significant and dramatic of the announcements of the renaissance. It marked the first public appearance of young creative writers in the company of the greatest of the nation's creative writers and philosophers."[10] More than one hundred guests heard Carl Van Doren of *Century* magazine and publisher Horace Liveright, both white, extol the potential of Negro arts and letters. Albert Barnes of Philadelphia, an eccentric who made his fortune in pharmaceuticals, spoke on his collection of African art; he sat next to— and had his ear bent by—Walter White. White spoke on the importance of a New Negro literature that spurned stereotype; Johnson thought the importance of White's remarks had "shown itself in frequent quotation since the night of the affair." Georgia Douglas Johnson and Gwendolyn Bennett read poetry. So too did Countee Cullen—whose verses were snapped up by *Harper's* editor Frederick Allen "as soon as he had finished reading them." In the aftermath of the dinner, White hastened to place a collection of Cullen's poetry with Liveright.[11]

Two weeks later, six hundred people assembled to wish W.E.B. Du Bois a belated fifty-sixth birthday. Arthur Spingarn reported on the festivities to absent brother Joel. It was a "complete success," he wrote, "a really remarkable group representing all worlds and interests in life and particularly good looking 'as regards the cullud folks.' " Heywood Broun was a no-show—surprisingly so, because he made a habit of attending these types of affairs—but he was one of the few not in attendance. The music was good, as was the poetry. The gaieties were somewhat dampened during the after-dinner speeches, however; they were "all execrable," Spingarn snapped. New York's lieutenant governor Herbert Lehman, who would later join the NAACP board, gave a speech that was "a cheap stereotype." Mary McLeod Bethune followed a set script. At 11:30 in the evening, Du Bois, breaking his self-imposed early-evening curfew, ascended the podium and "missed a great chance—the natural charm of his life." He chose to speak on his recent trip to Liberia.[12]

NAACP fund-raisers offered another venue to showcase black talent and let black and white elbows rub together. The association relied on the goodwill of African American entertainers, and the casts of both *Shuffle Along* (1921) and *Runnin' Wild* (1924) gave benefit performances, which fattened the association's coffers and allowed it to reach an otherwise difficult-to-reach strata of middle-class whites.[13] White relished hosting well-placed individuals at these events. He and Gladys invited the Mexican caricaturist Miguel Covarrubias to the annual spring dance in March 1931 at the Savoy Ballroom. Three bands, including Cab Calloway's and the Grand Central Red Caps orchestras, would knock out the tunes, and prizewinners would demonstrate the Lindy Hop. Walter bid Covarrubias meet at 409 Edgecombe at 10:30 in the evening "for a few blows at the Volstead Act before we go on to the dance."[14]

Uptown and downtown, parties abounded, all with seemingly endless opportunity for developing interracial goodwill. Charles Studin threw masterful parties. A college roommate of Arthur Spingarn's and a partner in his law firm, Studin took a keen interest in NAACP legal affairs. He also "had the most extraordinary parties of anybody in the city of New York," in Spingarn's estimation. Three times a week he would gather a diverse lot, sometimes pairing Bishop Spellman of the New York archdiocese with a contender for the heavyweight boxing crown. It was at one of these soirees in 1928 that White met Poppy Cannon. Born in South Africa in 1906 to Eastern European Jews, Lillian Poppy Gruskin was reared in Kittanning, Pennsylvania, outside Pittsburgh, and attended Vassar College. Her entrée into the world of race advancement and Afro-American culture came through her husband, Carl Cannon, a librarian with the New York Public Library, whose Harlem branch was an important center for the New Negro movement. Poppy claimed not to know who exactly Walter was, but they became friendly. Walter and Gladys spent weekends at the country home of Poppy and Carl, who had become the Yale University librarian, and generally the two couples got on well. In the early thirties, Walter and Poppy collaborated on a cookbook of African American cuisine, a project suggested by Mencken. Within a few years of their meeting, Walter and Poppy began an affair that continued, with hiatuses, through three of Poppy's marriages and until 1948, when they divorced their spouses and wed each other.[15]

White worked his contacts best when he entertained small groups. He and Gladys frequently hosted interracial gatherings for those elites who wanted to have fun. George Gershwin debuted *Rhapsody in Blue* at one of these.[16] White's social calendar for 1925 seemed to be especially busy. At one party, he told Roland Hayes, were Jules Bledsoe, Paul Robeson, James Weldon and Grace Johnson, Carl Van Vechten and Fania

Marinoff, Miguel Covarrubius, and Gershwin. "We had a gorgeous time and the only thing lacking was your presence. The affair being exceedingly informal, I believe you would have enjoyed it."[17] He fretted that he could not pull together a party for Grace Lewis, Sinclair's wife, when she was in town, though: "Gladys has been trying her best to get hold of some people for the evening when Gracie is to be in town but, unfortunately, we have had no success as yet. Larry Brown [Paul Robeson's accompanist] has gone South with William Lawrence (Roland Hayes' accompanist) to gather new Spirituals and work songs; Paul Robeson is in London; Roland Hayes is in Germany, and Julius Bledsoe is hard at work preparing for his recital at Town Hall on the 17th. By the way, he is a great artist and a chap you would adore."[18] The year ended with the Whites making a sweep of New Year's Eve parties; he had to miss the costume ball hosted by Aline and Arthur Garfield Hays because he had stayed at Alfred and Blanche Knopf's until 3:00 in the morning, but mostly because "we hadn't been able to decide on costumes or to fix them up."[19]

When White was not entertaining at their 90 Edgecombe Avenue apartment, he was showing whites the sights of Harlem. He took author Konrad Bercovici, who wrote a favorable review of *The Fire in the Flint*, to see the musical *Runnin' Wild*. White at first was reluctant to initiate him in this manner, fearing that he was simply a thrill-seeker, but he was pleasantly surprised at Bercovici's seriousness. Later, he took Bercovici and British novelist Rebecca West to Abyssinian Baptist Church and then out visiting; he promised them an exciting weekend at Villa Lewaro, millionairess A'Leila Walker's Hudson River estate. Another time these three were joined by Heywood Broun.[20] He even piqued the interest of Oswald Garrison Villard, who, after being unable to arrange an outing, chastised White, writing, "what a miserable foreflusher [*sic*], liar, and falsifier you are in the matter of your conducting me into the evil ways of Harlem night life!"[21]

White's goals from the beginning were to promote a literature and art that told a truth about African Americans and made no concessions to stereotype and to increase the number of African Americans who produced culture. "Writing about Negro life as it really exists," he argued, was a field "which is as yet practically untouched." He planned to correct this unfortunate situation.[22] His insistence on direct and unsparing art was influenced by H. L. Mencken, the newspaperman and tart critic of American culture, whom White met in late 1919 or early 1920. Taken by Mencken's disdain for mendacity, hypocrisy, and a Puritanism that was shocked by sex and desire yet remained silent, even complicit, in spectacles of lynching, White—like many of his contemporaries—draped himself in the Sage of Baltimore's satiric, ironic style. He wrote Mencken an appreciation of one of his most famous essays. "I am wondering if there isn't a good deal of innate meanness in my makeup when I so greatly enjoyed your philippic on 'The Sahara of Bozart.'" He eagerly anticipated the coming vitriol "by certain Bourbons who, by a miracle, might find out that other books have been written since the Bible and Pilgrim's Progress were published, and read your newest."[23]

Like Mencken, the architects of the Harlem Renaissance lashed their work to sturdy masts of aesthetic principles. Alain Locke's were refined. "The Howard University professor was a fanatic on culture," according to David Levering Lewis's finely etched profile, "and by 'culture' he meant all that was not common, vulgar, or racially distasteful." Faced with the charge of snobbery, Locke confessed that "culture will have to plead to a certain degree of this." Spending summers across the Atlantic, Locke conducted Countee Cullen and Langston Hughes on a grand tour of continental civilization in 1924, soaking up the Louvre, the Jeu de Paume, and Paul Guillaume's studio in Paris and later touring Venice. Exceedingly knowledgeable of European and African art, Locke sought out promising writers and artists and laid out feasts designed to refine their palates.[24] Likewise, W.E.B. Du Bois had definite tastes. After seeing some artists of the Harlem Renaissance become unmoored from the idea of art as a tool of racial advancement, he solemnly declared that "all art is propaganda and ever must be, despite the wailing of the purists. . . . I do not care a damn for any art that is not used for propaganda." If this sounded overly restrictive, he softened it with instructions to Negro readers and viewers to cultivate "that catholicity of temper which is going to enable the artist to have his widest chance for freedom."[25]

Walter White had neither the education of Locke or Du Bois, nor their wherewithal for making discriminating appraisals. His ideas about art were a hodgepodge, some borrowed from Du Bois's functional admonitions, some from Hughes's manifesto of artistic autonomy. He eschewed Du Bois's prudery, however, as well as some of the more lascivious prose by authors associated with Hughes. White's critical judgment was more often than not derivative, as seen in his plans for an article for Mencken's *American Mercury*. Tentatively titled "If White Had Been Black," his thesis was that "artistically, the world would probably be much further advanced if Negroes had been the masters and whites the slaves in the South. . . . The South has produced no great art save that of Joel Chandler Harris in his 'Uncle Remus' stories, and there he but acted as amanuensis for the illiterate Negro." It was a snappy argument, perfect in tone for Mencken's journal of opinion for the "well-fed" set who were "more interested in their own class than they are in the struggles and aspirations" of the working class and their advocates. The only problem was that White did not have the breadth of understanding to sustain such a charge, which was in fact bowdlerized from a more nuanced observation by James Weldon Johnson. In the preface to his *Book of American Negro Poetry*, Johnson sought to account for the apparent lack of literary production by a numerically much larger population of African Americans compared to that by black people in France, England, and Russia, which produced Dumas, Coleridge, and Pushkin, respectively. He explained that "the Negro in the United States is consuming all of his intellectual energy in this grueling race-struggle." In contrast to White's far more crude formulation, Johnson stated that southern whites' obsession with race was "in a general way" stunting their cultural growth; their creativity sought outlet only through "one narrow channel" of race.[26] One might very well suppose, Johnson asserted, that had blacks been the oppressors, they too would have been culturally crippled rather than carriers of enlightenment, for their creativity would have been similarly restricted by their racial obsessions.

Trying to prove his point, but doing so in a mechanical fashion, White polled influential people for their opinions. He asked Carl Van Doren, editor of the *Century* magazine, for his list of great white southerners; White believed that the list of creative spirits, including scientists and writers, was slim at best. White might be forgiven not knowing about a Georgia scientist who did pioneering work on anesthesia, but Van Doren sent back a roster that included obvious names like Edgar Allan Poe, Mark Twain, and Washington and Jefferson.[27]

Three months later he was "running down information on the influence of primitive African art on modern art," he wrote to Albert Barnes, an influential critic and holder of one of the most comprehensive collections of African art in the United States. Yet he still confessed to "meagre" knowledge. Trying to be authoritative, but not comprehending subtleties apparent to the authorities, White quoted approvingly certain scholars who attributed the power of African art to blacks' innate mentality; he then wrote a statement on the timelessness of "primitive" African art and asked Barnes to endorse it. Barnes scorched White; his sources were "the literary equivalents of prostitution." Rather than being primitive, African art followed a well-developed aesthetic. He urged White to excise fully half of his article. Even the revised article was, according to Barnes, " 'cheap,' 'futile' and 'exploitation.' "[28]

But if the greater portion of Walter White's theory was pedestrian, he understood better than most that works embodying the most pristine aesthetics exercised little influence unless they attracted a following. Thus, he directed his critical energy toward detecting talent and finding the largest audience for it. Rudolph Fisher, in the early twenties a radiology resident at Freedmen's Hospital in Washington, D.C., was one of the early beneficiaries of White's largesse. White had not heard of Fisher before he had read his short story "City of Refuge" in the *Atlantic Monthly*. From then on White made it a point to find promising black authors and extend them aid before they were published. He immediately offered assistance to Fisher, who then sent the assistant secretary some work-in-progress. White passed it to Mencken at the *American Mercury* and to Carl Van Doren just in case Mencken would not take it. "I was talking with him [Mencken] a few days ago, however," White wrote Fisher, "and he told me then that he had more material accepted and in type by and about Negroes and other non-Nordics than by the Nordics. He went on to say that 'Of course the damn Nordic is no good but we can't be too hard on him—we will soon have to be forming an organization for the protection of Nordics.' "[29]

White saw unlimited possibility in the selling of African American culture to both black and white worlds. Reporting on a conversation he had with two members of the newly formed Viking Press in 1925, he concluded that "the present keen interest in the Negro as an artist has its roots firmly fixed and that, instead of being a fad comparable to Couéism, Mah-Jong, and the present cross-word puzzle craze, it was a movement that was destined to develop and flower." That being the case, White did not hog the spotlight, but rather extended help to both neophytes like Fisher and established Harlem fixtures like Claude McKay.[30]

White's relationship with McKay proved to be one of his most exasperating. McKay, who was blunt and often tactless toward those who would help him, first appears in the record of White's literary activity in a fashion all too typical for him: he apologized for an article in the Garveyite *Negro World*, which linked him to unflattering references to White and James Weldon Johnson. McKay, at the time editor of the leftist *Liberator*, pleaded that he had been misquoted; but with his high-maintenance personality and sense of entitlement, it is at least plausible that he spoke freely of being "lionized at lunch" by "pseudo-intellectuals" of "the NAACP crowd." White generously reassured McKay of their friendship. He never believed what he read in Garvey's paper, he said, and, besides, he was acquainted with McKay well enough to know he was a man of integrity.[31]

While McKay displayed integrity in some parts of his life—he followed his socialist inclinations by abandoning the United States in 1922, first for Soviet Russia and then other European locales—what he mainly displayed to White was an outstretched hand and a prickliness born of having to ask for assistance from those whom he viewed with varying degrees of contempt. Having settled in Berlin after a stint in Moscow with the Communist International, McKay related to White all of the writing he had done on race and colonial issues for Soviet publications—which paid nothing. He then begged White for commissions. He would send an article to Du Bois if the *Crisis* paid anything. Would "any of your white friends want an article or two"? "You see I must have money to live on," he wrote.[32]

For the next several years, a cranky McKay shared tales of ill health and financial distress with White and sometimes berated him for not doing enough to help him. Yet on more than one occasion White arranged for him fiscal relief and offered publishing advice. McKay took the former while rejecting the latter. (Of course, McKay's ingratitude was not limited to Walter White. After receiving several donations and other assistance in the early twenties from Joel Spingarn, McKay dismissed him as a "bourgeois philanthropist"; compelled to beg once more in the mid-thirties, McKay, whom Max Eastman termed suspicious, tactless, and a "very hard person to help," offered an apology notable for its contentiousness and defense of past insults.)[33]

While financial woes figured prominently in McKay's transatlantic correspondence with the assistant secretary, his letters to White and others examine a central question of the Harlem Renaissance: to what extent would white patronage determine the style and content of blacks' art? "I do not think that the attitude of the whites towards writers of other races is quite correct," McKay protested to Joel Spingarn. "Many think that Negro art should be 'ragtimy'—wild & barbaric."[34] In one of their early exchanges, White had gotten wind of his friend's work-in-progress titled *Color Scheme*, the manuscript for which has yet to be found. "[Alain] Locke came in to see me a few days ago and told me something about it," White cagily informed McKay, "but in his usual indefinite manner which did not amount to much when boiled down to words of less than two syllables." Where White was poking fun at Locke's pomposity, McKay mined deeper significance. He saw deliberate obfuscation in Locke, Jean Toomer, and other writers, and he located this in "the long years the black race has lived in America without being allowed to express its own thoughts and feelings." Arguing against Toomer's "purple patches of mysticism" in *Cane* that he felt obscured black life as it really existed, McKay cautioned Renaissance writers not to allow themselves "to be patronized as Negro artists in America."[35]

In seeking a publisher for his novel, McKay was loath to trim his work to suit another's aesthetic judgments. When Knopf refused his manuscript, McKay criticized publishers for trying to limit black authors to portrayals of black life that suited a narrow range of whites' tastes. Patrons and publishers, McKay believed, may have been interested in the commercial value of books on black life, but they were not too keen on establishing a tradition of writing by African Americans. After all, Knopf had held on to his manuscript for several weeks, which McKay thought was designed to give the advantage to Carl Van Vechten's voyeuristic novel *Nigger Heaven*. The novelist, McKay told White, could write what he saw as life or "make himself the instrument of a group or body of opinion—the first is art the last is prostitution . . ." Knopf's rejection demonstrated to McKay "that the white literati cannot stand for a black author laughing at white folks' foibles." And he all but accused the NAACP of encouraging the literary prostitution by frowning on writing "that may run contrary to the aims of the NAACP."[36] McKay echoed Langston Hughes, who in "The Negro Artist and the Racial Mountain," declared the younger black writer's independence from both white patrons' tastes and the art-cum-racial uplift of the older generation of W.E.B. Du Bois.

While not unsympathetic to McKay's convictions, White's thoughts

and energy ran in a different direction. He seemed generally unconcerned by artists having to fit their works to patrons' or publishers' sensibilities. Rather, he believed burning artistic questions could be profitably
matched with marketing opportunities. Harper Bros. was to publish a
book of poetry by Countee Cullen in September 1925, White gushed to
McKay, and Langston Hughes had a volume accepted by Knopf. With
Rudolph Fisher's appearance in the *Atlantic Monthly* in February and May
1925, he had staked the claim as "by far the most promising short story
writer we have." White was positively effusive: "The Negro artist is really
in the ascendency just now. There is unlimited opportunity and I think
you would be amazed at the eagerness of magazine editors and book publishers to get hold of promising writers." His obligation to the New
Negro movement, as he saw it, was to get as many artists as much exposure as possible. "There are three or four first rate publishers who have
asked me to keep an eye open for likely material," and he recommended
that McKay place his work with the new Viking Press, for it was absolutely the "ideal place" for him. White was unperturbed when McKay
rejected the advice, and he suggested that McKay send his novel to Harcourt, which, for reasons he did not reveal, now superceded Viking as the
most suitable publisher.[37]

White eagerly lent a hand to emerging writers, shopping manuscripts
for Countee Cullen and Langston Hughes and providing secretarial assistance to Nella Larsen so that she could prepare the final draft of *Passing*. While proud to assist these fledgling writers, he likely took most
pride in promoting the career of the tenor Roland Hayes. The fellow
Georgians met in London in 1921 where the assistant secretary went for
political and cultural seasoning and Hayes was launching a concert career. The bond, apparently, was instant. When Hayes returned to the
United States for the 1924 concert season, White did his best to ensure it
was a triumphal one. He arranged for Hayes's promoter to reserve seats at
the February 5 recital for Heywood Broun and Ruth Hale; Raymond G.
Carroll, a syndicated columnist who appeared in the *Philadelphia Public-
Ledger* and the *New York Evening Post*; and Franklin P. Adams, a columnist
for the *New York World*. He arranged for Broun to spend a day with Hayes
before the concert; Broun then wrote an enthusiastic column on Hayes
and hosted a post-recital party in his honor. "I do not know whether I
made it strong enough yesterday but, while it is no more than you deserve, it means a very great deal to have Heywood Broun and Ruth Hale

give a party for you," White wrote, instructing Hayes to observe social niceties and compliment Broun to his editor.[38]

White believed Hayes's American tour was in part responsible for a surge of New Negro activity. "There has been a very decided renaissance—perhaps I should say nascence—of Negro art and Negro artists," he proudly reported to Hayes in mid-1924, now back in London. Jules Bledsoe, a native Texan who was studying medicine at Columbia, had a smashing concert debut at Aeolian Hall in April. Meeting with White several weeks after his recital, Bledsoe decided to quit medical school for an artistic career. The baritone was already booked for concerts for the 1925 season at the Metropolitan Opera House. Bledsoe, with White's encouragement and assistance, would stretch his artistic horizons, performing the role of Amonasro in *Aïda*, starring on stage in *Deep River, In Abraham's Bosom*, and an operatic production of *Emperor Jones*, and in the film *Show Boat*. Newcomer Marian Anderson was also getting positive notice, with a New York debut at Town Hall. The reviews were good, but White confessed disappointment. Her voice was fine, but her program selection betrayed a "certain shallowness"; she sang majestic arias and spirituals but followed them with songs White considered "banal." Her voice, he opined, was "marvelous . . . but she sings too mechanically and without any great depth of feeling." He hoped that in time and with experience she would develop into "the artist which she ought to be with that voice." White would have a hand in guiding her career too, including masterminding her Easter Sunday 1939 concert at the Lincoln Memorial, a quintessential moment in civil rights history.[39]

While White enjoyed positive relationships with the publishing industry, frequently deferring willingly to editors' opinions about New Negro authors in order to get them into print, his encounters with the music industry were edgy and contentious. In the twenties and thirties he clashed with the impresario Sol Hurok, who is generally—and wrongly—credited with discovering Marian Anderson, specifically over the manner in which he promoted the career of Jules Bledsoe and his exploitation of African American talent generally. Bledsoe signed with Hurok's management agency in 1924, but soon became dissatisfied. Hurok planned a domestic tour for Bledsoe that played only black churches and YMCAs. White interceded. He acknowledged the broad support that Bledsoe enjoyed with African American audiences, but he told Hurok "it is not our idea that Mr. Bledsoe should be booked . . . to sing simply before colored people." He and Gladys had presented Bledsoe in their Edgecombe Avenue apartment to white opinion makers Carl Van Vechten, Sinclair Lewis, and Heywood Broun, all of whom were interested in advancing Bledsoe's career. White also dropped the name of Otto Kahn, the financier and Metropolitan Opera board chairman who spoke enthusiastically of Bledsoe after having heard him sing at one of Van Vechten's parties. Despite White's best effort, Hurok continued to Jim Crow his client.[40] Bledsoe wanted out of his contract, but White was unable to find a way to abrogate it.[41]

Apparently Hurok's indifference to someone who was not yet an established concert attraction extended to his attitude to the struggle for black equality. Hurok did not mind profiting from Marian Anderson, whose voice and early activities were nurtured by African American communities, but in managing her career he discouraged her from supporting civil rights. In 1938 the NAACP had wanted Anderson to perform a benefit concert at Carnegie Hall for the association's burgeoning campaign against segregation in education, which would culminate in the Supreme Court's 1954 *Brown* decision. Hurok turned down the request; he proposed instead a ticket-sale scheme that would net the NAACP, the Urban League, the YMCA, and the Council on African Affairs a little more that $130 each. White complained that, "From what we know of Mr. Hurok's methods, he would use the pittance to the four organizations . . . as a means of refusing to do anything more substantial for Negro causes for a long time."[42]

White's interactions with the New Negro movement's cultural stars, an urge to join the center of Harlem's celebrity-studded nightlife, and ambition that could not be contained by one calling were some of the factors that led him to pursue a career as an author. Once he made the decision to try his hand at fiction, he approached the job with his customary explosive energy. And understanding that the volume of publicity was more important than whether it was positive or negative, he made certain his two published novels generated controversy.

"I wrote feverishly and incessantly for twelve days and parts of twelve nights, stopping only when complete fatigue made it physically and mentally impossible to write another word." Such was White's description of the creative process that resulted in the manuscript of *The Fire in the Flint*, his first novel about race relations, racial violence, and a nascent black consciousness in south Georgia. The book completed, he "dropped on a near-by couch" at "Riverbank," Mary White Ovington's cottage, where the novel was born, and slept for hours.[43] Refreshed, he set off to elbow his way onto the literary palisades, which he did by combining a knack for writing middlebrow prose with chutzpah redolent of Felix Krull.

The Fire in the Flint's straightforward plot moves at an energetic clip. Kenneth Harper, Atlanta University alumnus, talented northern-trained physician, and World War I veteran, returns from service in France to his home in fictional Central City in real South Georgia, there to start up a medical practice. He is determined to establish himself in short order not simply as a competent Negro doctor but as a surgeon and owner of a state-of-the-art clinic to serve the entire region of the state. Though he has lived in the relative freedom of the North and Europe (the latter especially was the stuff of contemporary mythology) Harper is determined not to buck Jim Crow. When his younger brother Bob, who withdrew from Atlanta University and returned to Central City to shoulder family obligations after their father's death, despairs of the increasingly antagonistic postwar race relations, Kenneth denies there are significant obstacles. "I'm going to solve my own problem, do as much good as I can, make as much money as I can! If every Negro in America did the same thing, there wouldn't be any 'race problem.' "[44] He would be like his father, a small construction contractor, who had accumulated enough wealth to provide for his family's comfortable existence. "Hope you ain't got none of them No'then ideas 'bout social equality while you was up there," one of the town's most prominent whites told Kenneth. "Jus' do like your daddy did, and you'll do a lot to keep the white folks' friendship." Kenneth escaped the pressures of caste by reading, and although W.E.B. Du Bois was the author he most admired, he hewed most closely to the Booker T. Washington nostrum that racism was something to be lived down, not talked down.[45]

Despite his best efforts, Kenneth is drawn inexorably into the web of racial conflict. When his sister Mamie is subjected to the importuning of some young rednecks on the town's main street, Bob is incensed and wants to act, but Kenneth demurs, preferring to speak in confidence with Roy Ewing, a representative of the "better class of whites." Ewing, while sympathetic to Mamie's plight, refuses to try to rein in the white boys, fearing that his actions would be detrimental to his business. Thus begins the erosion of Kenneth's faith in accommodationism. It is further eroded in a series of instances in which Kenneth provokes the whites' hostility by correctly diagnosing patients and countermanding treatment prescribed by Central City's white Dr. Bennett.

White belligerence toward Kenneth increases as he reluctantly champions the cause of the area's black sharecroppers. The previous incidents had opened Kenneth's mind to the futility of accommodationism. But it was his awkward love for the handsome, refined, intelligent, and acutely race-conscious Jane Phillips that moved him to put his oratorical and organizational skills behind the formation of the National Negro Farmers' Co-Operative and Protective League and help sharecroppers escape the crop-lien system. His involvement in this organization leads the Ku Klux Klan to watch him closely and causes most of the goodwill he had inherited from his father to vanish.

The last shred of Kenneth's faith in the better class of whites vaporizes when his sister Mamie is raped by the same gang of whites. Brother Bob grabs a pistol, storms up Lee Street, kills two of the offending whites, escapes out of town, but then kills himself when his capture by the pursuing mob is imminent. Cheated out of torturing and lynching him, the vigilantes riddle Bob's corpse with bullets, drag him back to town, and set him afire next to the Confederate memorial; children dash into the dying embers to retrieve souvenir charred bones.

In the final chapters, Kenneth's rage bursts like a ruptured appendix. "If by raising one finger I could save the whole white race from destruction," he told a white woman who pleaded with him to save her daughter's life, "and by not raising it could send them all straight down to hell, I'd die before I raised it! You've murdered my brother, my sister's body, my mother's mind, and my very soul!" Still, he relents and agrees to treat the girl at her home. On the way home from this midnight emergency, the Klan, which had been planning to attack Kenneth, seized the surprise opportunity of his leaving a white woman's house at night and lynches him, but not before he kept his oath that "before I go I'm going to take a few along with me!" [46]

Central City appears to be a composite picture of small-town South Georgia. White's prose drew upon his personal acquaintance with back roads Georgia as a traveling insurance salesman, and he modeled Kenneth Harper on his close friend and personal physician, Dr. Louis T. Wright.[47] Yet in his rendering of Central City, White likely drew literary inspiration from W.E.B. Du Bois's observations of Albany. The town's pace of life—"Drowsy, indolent during the first six days of the week" [48]— and its strict segregation of comparably debased white mill hands of "Factoryville" and residents of "Darktown" resemble nothing so much as W.E.B. Du Bois's commentary in *The Souls of Black Folk*:

> Albany is to-day a wide-streeted, placid, Southern town, . . . whites usu-ally to the north, and blacks to the south. Six days in the week the town looks decidedly too small for itself, and takes frequent and prolonged naps. But on Saturday suddenly the whole county disgorges itself upon the place, and a perfect flood of black peasantry pours through the streets, . . . [49]

Likewise, the sharecroppers' conditions, which White adumbrated as he tracked Kenneth Harper's racial awakening, recall Du Bois's chronicle of the misfortunes and resilience of blacks in Doughtery County. [50]

White tapped into a significant source of racial animus when he ex-plored white resentment over the Harpers' relative affluence that stoked the drive to lynch Bob and Kenneth. Their father, Joe Harper, had started out as a carpenter and slowly expanded his work to the point where he was a prosperous builder, having constructed most of the two-story buildings in Central City's business district. He flourished because he was honest and efficient, because he kept scrupulous books, and, most likely, because he had whites of some standing vouch for him. As soon as he died, however, the town's leading businessmen set to cheating his es-tate out of thousands of dollars. "Just yesterday," Bob complained to Kenneth, "Old Man Mygatt down to the bank got mad and told me I was an 'impudent young nigger that needed to be taught my place' because I called his hand on a note he claimed papa owed the bank. He knew I knew he was lying, and that's what made him so mad. They're already saying I'm not a 'good nigger' like papa was . . . " [51]

White also got right one of the more controversial scenes in *The Fire in the Flint*, the rape of Mamie Harper, who was assaulted just past down-town, right after she exited the dry-goods store. Claude McKay doubted this scene. "You make your rape take place right in the heart of a pretty populous city. . . . If you had sent her out walking on the Central City country road, brooding over her unhappy state in Georgia, have her wan-dering home through a field and then the attack—I think your case would have been far more effective. For if these things happen as you must and as I am bound to believe the world should see them in the true light—not in a melodramatic fashion." [52]

White replied to McKay that he had been engaged in a spirited debate with Carl Van Vechten and Sinclair Lewis on just this point. He conceded McKay's argument to a point. A sexual assault in a very public area would be unlikely, he wrote, if it was carried out by one man. "I quite agree that except a woman is drugged or beaten into unconsciousness, I don't believe that rape by one man is possible." But with more than one perpetrator, it is quite conceivable. Mamie's ordeal was not melodrama, but an accurate reflection of reality. Yet in an important sense McKay's reservations about the location of the rape was beside the point. White's statement that assaults on African American women were "so common, yet so carefully concealed" indicates his understanding that rape was not primarily a crime of opportunity but of power, that white rapists would violate black women wherever they wanted so long as they could assure themselves that there would be no reprisal. [53]

It was this last point, not the number of rapists or the site, that was the principal reason for White including Mamie's rape. In White's opinion, an attack on a black woman was one of the few things that would propel a black man to use retaliatory force; in *The Fire in the Flint*, Bob reacts to Mamie's distress by killing two of the perpetrators. It was a situation that recalled the rape of John Jones's little sister in Du Bois's "Of the Coming of John," one of the chapters in *Souls of Black Folk*. [54] How common this response was is not known, for while lynchings of blacks for supposed assaults on white women were publicized in banner headlines, stories of black men defending black women against white men's predations were routinely suppressed. Walter White believed this to be not unusual, and he recorded cases of this later in *Rope and Faggot*. Likewise, John Dittmer, in his study of African Americans in Progressive-era Georgia, documented incidents of this type. [55]

The way White told it, he showed the manuscript to John Farrar, who submitted it to George Doran Company without his knowledge; Doran initially was enthusiastic, then expressed reservations, and finally asked White to dilute his critique of the white South so as not to offend that region's white book-buying public. "I felt, however," he wrote to one correspondent, "that I had told the truth as I saw it and I informed them that I would destroy the manuscript before I would submit to emasculation which would kill the effectiveness of the novel. I withdrew the novel from that firm though they were willing to go ahead with their agreement. . . ." He then submitted it to Knopf, which was delighted to have it in its catalog.[56]

In fact, White took a dose of the medicine he prescribed for McKay, Cullen, and others and was far more accommodating than he let on. He of course would not concede the authenticity of his story when Doran raised objections. But he did not refuse to budge, either, and he looked for any number of ways to come to an agreement with Doran. He asked the Spingarn brothers, white southern liberal and Commission on Inter-racial Cooperation founder Will Alexander, and others to intercede in his behalf. He suggested that the book be published with prefatory material that would explain Doran's objections to the characterization of the white South.[57] His efforts failed to convince Doran to publish the novel, and contrary to White's assertions, it was the company that finally and unam-biguously rejected it.[58]

White appeared to be something like the protagonist in the Beatles song "Paperback Writer." And his flexibility is not hard to understand, given his pragmatic orientation toward the Harlem Renaissance and his desire to be a novelist. He begged Doran to change its mind because

> there is no firm that I want as publishers as much as I do Doran. As I said to you, Boni and Liveright will bring out in the spring a novel by Miss Jessie Fauset [*There Is Confusion*]. *The first novel in the field giving the reactions of the educated Negro is going to have a tremendous advantage. That is why I want Doran to publish the novel prior to any other of its kind.* Will you not, therefore, tell me specifically the things in the novel to which you object and also the things that you feel ought to be added.[59]

With Doran's rejection, though, White seems not to have missed a step. Ten days later he delivered the manuscript to Knopf. He spent a generous amount of time constructing a distribution network within the black community, including using NAACP branches to boost sales.[60] When Knopf accepted *The Fire in the Flint* for publication in December 1923, White's stock immediately soared in literary circles. He accepted congratulations from Eugene O'Neill, who wanted to turn the novel into a play, Konrad Bercovici, and Carl Van Doren, who commented shrewdly, "I am pleased to death at the news about your novel. You see not all publishers are idiots. If *The Fire in the Flint* sells well I shall decide that the public isn't all idiots either." [61]

It sold, but several well-meaning whites questioned whether *The Fire in the Flint* overstated its case. Here White saw an opportunity to engage whites who were sympathetic to the cause of black advancement in a dialogue. A typical letter came from Jacob Billikopf, the lawyer and civic reformer. "I am familiar with life in the South and your pictures of the various characters are absolutely true to life. I am just wondering whether the activities against the negro [*sic*] are not a bit overdrawn. I do not want some folk to come back at you with that accusation." White firmly but politely dissented from this future NAACP board member, pointing to a legion of examples of the barbarous treatment of African Americans. [62]

More skeptical was A. S. Frissell, a founder and official of the National Urban League. Frissell had registered a complaint with the novel's publisher, Alfred Knopf. The book was "untimely," he wrote. Although he conceded that "it is possible that there are individual cases similar to it," he believed "that the statistics show that the lynchings are decreasing throughout the country. I do not think this book will help it." [63] White replied, tactfully, that Frissell was deluded about the race problem.

> If I may be permitted to say so, your letter proves exactly the tragedy of the whole race problem in America—that one like yourself who has contributed so generously of his time to work for the Negro should feel that the story is overdrawn. My dear Mr. Frissell, I could furnish you with hundreds, even thousands, of cases far more terrible than anything that is pictured in my novel and the pitiable thing to me is that with your intimate knowledge of the whole question, you should be unaware of the fact that these things are so common. [64]

White was more direct in his criticism to an official at Knopf. Frissell's comments were stupid, White said, and he was "a man who is an ardent believer in 'sweetness and light,' believing that the only way to cure a cancer is by smearing vaseline on it." So White was delighted and surprised when Frissell recanted. "I was at a meeting of the officers of the National Urban League recently and I spoke about your book," Frissell wrote to White. "Nearly everyone there and perhaps all of them approved of it. Therefore, I think I was wrong—as I usually am—in the position I took in my note to Mr. Knopf. What more can I say?" [65]

Annie Bridgman, a leading colleague of White's brother George in the American Missionary Association, expressed pleasure with the novel, and, perhaps because she had heard about him from George, commented that his cheerful demeanor gave her hope about the race problem. In this respect, she continued, he was not at all like W.E.B. Du Bois, whose comments about whites in an article in the *American Mercury* as "damned fools" almost caused her to stop being friendly to African Americans. Du Bois was "too apt to tell only a half truth." Accepting her congratulations on his novel, he then empathized with her discomfort at reading Du Bois's words and acknowledged that many whites thought Du Bois bitter. But, he went on, what he wondered was "what peculiar factor there is in the makeup of the Negro which prevents him from being ten thousand times as bitter as he is."[66]

In the correspondence with Billikopf, Frissell, and Bridgman, one can see that Walter White thought his role as a novelist complemented his NAACP duties as an investigator and reporter of racial violence. Whether he corrected, chastised, or sympathized with the contradictory feelings of white progressives, the novelist and the NAACP functionary in White sought simultaneously to expose injustice and narrow the chasm between the races.

Members of the African American elite shared this orientation and believed that *The Fire in the Flint* went a long way toward achieving it. Two of the leading black newspapers wanted to serialize the novel; White refused the 1925 request of the *Baltimore Afro-American*, saying that it would cut into sales, but relented to the *Pittsburgh Courier* the next year. W.E.B. Du Bois, reviewing the novel in the *Crisis*, called it a "stirring story and a strong bit of propaganda against the white Klansman and the black pussy-foot." Charles S. Johnson, writing in the Urban League's *Opportunity*, compared it favorably with *Uncle Tom's Cabin* and *The Jungle*.[67]

Both Du Bois and Johnson commented too on White's lack of subtlety in character development, an opinion seconded by friendly white writers. Joel Spingarn thought *The Fire in the Flint* an "overwhelming story." But the novel's characters were wooden: "They simply do not live; and incident without character is melodrama, not drama."[68] Sinclair Lewis praised the book in a publicity blurb, predicting that it and E. M. Forster's *A Passage to India* "will prove much the most important books of this autumn." Privately, however, he offered White a passel of advice, mainly on character development. (Lewis's reading of White's book began a long friendship between the two men.) [69] H. G. Wells was the least ambivalent; he declined to endorse the book, saying that "it is a good second rate novel." [70] To these critiques, White was uncharacteristically modest. He acknowledged freely and with only a trace of defensiveness his rookie errors.

Critical press reviews were another matter, and some southern papers and writers, though not all, protested *The Fire in the Flint*'s appearance— loudly. The *Savannah Press* printed an editorial that branded the novel "unfair, unjust, and thoroughly reprehensible." A. S. Bernd, who self-consciously styled himself after H. L. Mencken and whose iconoclastic column appeared under the pseudonym Coleman Hill in the *Macon Telegraph*, reported favorably on White's novel. But the paper was besieged with letters from irate readers, and subscribers stopped taking it. When Lawrence Stallings, a Macon native now an editor at the *New York World*, favorably reviewed the book, the *Telegraph* pilloried him, warning him not to return home and to drop the claim that he was a "home boy." (On the other hand, Josephus Daniels, Jr., the son of the publisher of the *Raleigh News & Observer*, wrote an evenhanded review.) [71]

White took the criticism in stride, and he knew the public relations value of hostile reviews from the South. To be attacked by the defenders of Jim Crow was fine by White, for it meant his darts had hit bull's-eyes. "You need have no more fears about my getting too much praise on 'The Fire in the Flint,'" he wrote to Sinclair Lewis. "In the last few days, I have been getting editorials from southern newspapers and I am delighted at the denunciation which is coming to me." [72]

White worked like a fiend to promote *The Fire in the Flint*. He tried to adapt it for the theater—and telling all who would listen (confidentially, of course) that Paul Robeson was slated to play Kenneth Harper and Charles Gilpin would likely appear in another role. Ultimately both Eugene O'Neill and Courtney Lemon of the Theatre Guild declined to mount productions. From this distance it is unclear how real a possibility a stage version was; it may be that White's enthusiasm was part wish and part hype.

Yet White's enthusiasm could not be stymied as he tried to market himself to Broadway and Hollywood. Two years after *Fire in the Flint* was published, he heard that Cecil B. DeMille was interested in producing a film on black life. Feeling uniquely qualified to write the screenplay, White called upon some of his literary contacts, including playwright Jim

Tully, critic Laurence Stallings, and Richard Halliday at G.P. Putnam's. He so wanted to do the story for DeMille, he wrote to Tully, because "it would enable [him] to purchase some leisure to do one or two novels and a play or so, ideas for which are rattling in a not over capacious brain." [73] He begged Tully to speak with DeMille—he would "consider any reasonable offer." [74] But as with live productions of *Fire in the Flint*, White's plan came to naught. DeMille decided instead to produce a film version of *Porgy;* more distressing news followed when the Famous Players Theater declined to commission White to write a Negro play. [75] Thus ended his efforts to be a playwright or screenwriter. Less than two decades later, however, he would return to Hollywood—this time with more influence—to urge moviemakers to scuttle parts for mammies in favor of more dignified and race-proud roles.

Following the success of his first novel, White became more flinty regarding his writing. Alain Locke asked him to revise "The Color Line," his contribution to the 1924 special Harlem number of *Survey Graphic*, for inclusion in the landmark *The New Negro*. Locke strongly suggested that White include in his revisions points made by anthropologist Melville Herskovits in an article he had published in the *American Mercury*, also titled "The Color Line." White refused. White's article discussed not only white racial prejudice but also such African American responses to it as passing—far more prevalent, he said, than the *Survey's* white readership suspected—and intra-racial color prejudice, of both the blue-vein society and Garveyite varieties. White snarled at the suggestion that Herskovits had anything of value to add:

> I don't want you to think me hypersensitive or lacking in regard for Herskovits's brilliance, erudition, and powers of observation. I read his article and, frankly, I don't see that there is anything in it which would improve my Survey article. As a matter of fact, every one of us who is colored knows almost instinctively more about color lines within the race than almost any white man can ever know. You will forgive my frankness, I am sure, when I am dogmatic enough to say that I have never yet met a white person who thoroughly understood the psychology of race prejudice within the Negro race.

Locke backed off, and White's essay appeared without revision, save for the title, which was changed to "The Paradox of Color."[76]

White's prickliness was merely preparation for his reaction to the critical reception of his second novel, *Flight* (1926). He began work on it right after publication of *The Fire in the Flint*. As he wrote to Amy Spingarn, wife of Joel, "It will be about Negro and white characters but will be as different from 'The Fire in the Flint' as one can well be imagined. I tried it out on Mr. Arthur Spingarn Saturday night and he thinks there is a real story there."[77] Mimi Daquin, who is introduced to the reader at the age of fourteen, is a light-skinned Creole girl in New Orleans at the turn of the twentieth century. Like her father Jean, she is cultured and approaches life in the relaxed manner one would expect of elite *gens de coleur* from the Big Easy. From birth she was shielded from the unpleasant realities of racism by her parents and by her position near the top of a racially stratified Negro community. But her situation changes with her mother's death and her father's remarriage to the brown-skinned Mary Robertson, an acquisitive and ambitious woman from Chicago. Wearing Jean down, the Daquins move to Atlanta; Mimi and Jean feel anachronistic, while Mary enthusiastically partakes of the dull and avaricious activities of Atlanta's black bourgeoisie.

Mimi, however, is transformed by urban life. In a long passage reminiscent of White's autobiographical writings, Mimi becomes race conscious in the crucible of the 1906 Atlanta riot. Affirming various critics' assertions of the salvific capacity of Negro culture, White has Mimi embrace the blues and work songs sung by prisoners on the chain gang; she also frequents roadhouses with her love interest Carl, a rebellious son of the black bourgeoisie, who is sensitive but dissolute and ultimately weak willed. Forced to leave Atlanta around the age of twenty because she was carrying Carl's baby—she refuses to marry him because his initial reaction to her pregnancy was to demand that she have an abortion—Mimi settles first in Philadelphia and then in Harlem (after placing her child *Petit* Jean in an orphanage). She is plunged into poverty and the harsh life typical of black females in the urban North who were forced into personal-service occupations. But the hard edges of the migrant's life always were softened by the spiritual reservoir of African American culture—the dance, the music, the emotional storefront church services. Years after her self-exile, at a Harlem cabaret, her past catches up with her, as a wag from Atlanta espies her and blabs Mimi's secret to one of several Harlem gossip sheets.

Distraught and friendless, Mimi decides to pass. Finding employment in a dressmaker's shop, she works her way up from baster to international buyer and enjoys the high life in France and downtown Manhattan. Yet she can't help but notice that the white people with whom she comes into contact work too hard at play; for all their luxury and merrymaking, they are an unhappy lot, while poor blacks live joyously. Unable to continue living in a heartless—or soulless—white world, Mimi chooses to pass back to the Negro world. The novel closes with Mimi walking away from her Washington Square town house and affluent life and making plans to reclaim her son:

> "Free! Free! Free!" she whispered exultantly as with firm tread she went down the steps. "*Petit* Jean—my own people—and happiness!" was the song in her heart as she happily strode through the dawn, the rays of the morning sun dancing lightly upon the more brilliant gold of her hair. . . . [78]

Flight was widely anticipated, but according to the reviews, the author suffered from the sophomore jinx. Predictably, White's friend Carl Van Vechten was unstinting in his praise in the *New York Herald-Tribune* book page. But more typical were reviews in *The New Republic* and the *New York Times*. The former asserted that *Flight* was "neither a very consistent nor a very stirring story"; the latter allowed that "Mr. White makes his thesis convincing, but not his particular example; he demonstrates a factual truth but not an artistic one." The *Independent* was more blunt: "As a negro [*sic*] document, the book has value. As a novel it is heavy-footed and obvious." White's friend Sinclair Lewis liked the book, but he felt that the genre it represented would be unable to carry the New Negro movement. "It suddenly occurred to me that just possibly *all* of the astounding and extraordinarily interesting Negro fiction which is now appearing may be entirely off on the wrong foot," he wrote to Du Bois, who asked his opinion of the direction of black art. "For example, this problem of going over and passing for white must be one which will appeal to all of you. It must needs be much the same in your book or in Walter White's." [79]

White stewed at these reviews by whites; those by blacks riled him.

Jessie Fauset offered faint praise. "I think Flight is beautifully written," she wrote, "but I do not think it anywhere near as vivid or moving as 'The Fire In The Flint.' However I do consider it of great social importance and I'd be glad to say so in the Crisis and elsewhere." Written by Nora Waring, the *Crisis* review expressed qualified enthusiasm. But Frank Horne, a young poet of second rank, was positively dismissive in the July *Opportunity*. "At least the artist has attempted something worth-while," Horne razzed. "Mimi Daquin is a character worthy of a novel . . . and it irks no little to see her treated in a manner far inferior to her possibilities." With this scorching, White could no longer hold his tongue, and he set out to bully *Opportunity* editor Charles S. Johnson into either retracting it or permitting a rebuttal. White ridiculed Horne as a "likeable and intelligent" man who had no understanding of *Flight's* main themes and who too often split his infinitives. White called to task some New Negro writers who, he believed, in their supposed iconoclasm in fact became nihilistic in their attitudes toward other New Negro writers. He found it "discouraging" (read: infuriating) that a Negro journal would print such a negative piece. Johnson initially discounted White's letter as so much grousing, but he pressed his case. Johnson gave in, inviting Nella Larsen Imes to write a rejoinder. It appeared in the September issue, prompting a defense in October from Horne.[80]

But the last word was White's. In a final philippic in the December *Opportunity*, White declared "that hereafter I must write two versions of any book I want understood—one of them designed for readers of normal intelligence or better; the other supplied with maps, charts, graphs and pictures and written in words of not more than two syllables." White was cantankerous, but he succeeded in keeping his novel prominently before the reading public for six months; if he could not luxuriate in the kudos he desired, he could at least call attention to his project in the manner of a carnival barker. And for White himself, as for the larger New Negro project, an advertising barrage rather than aesthetic commendation may have been the more valuable outcome.[81]

Three years later, White wrote a coda to his tawdry behavior surrounding the critical reception of *Flight*. As a new decade was rung in, he received notice that his two novels had won a bronze medal in the Harmon Foundation's annual Negroes-only competition designed to honor distinguished achievement in the arts and literature. Recognition by well-placed whites, which this award represented, was one of the cornerstones of White's and other Harlem Renaissance impresarios' strategy of race advancement through the auspices of culture. By their reckoning, such validation was essential to the reshaping of popular white opinion about blacks, which in turn was fundamental to any substantial black progress. But White was miffed, both because he had not won the gold medal—none was given that year—and because he was not cited for his antilynching tome, *Rope and Faggot* (1929). He pouted to George E. Haynes, the African American head of the Harmon prize committee, and he whined to Joel Spingarn, who shamed him: "My feeling is that it would be wisest for you not to give another thought to the matter, both for your own sake and that of the dignity of letters. Prizes are of such slight importance except for the sake of advertisement and encouragement that the less said or thought about them the better. . . . It is best of all not to seek prizes at all, and second best, not to worry about the kind of prize one seeks and fails to get." White would not follow sensible advice, and he refused to attend the February 9 awards ceremony at Harlem's Mount Olivet Baptist Church.[82]

White's tantrum at the exclusion of *Rope and Faggot* from prize consideration was likely motivated by the dearness of that project to his future plans: it was to be the work that would launch a career as a full-time author. He had planned to write it on the Côte d'Azur during his Guggenheim fellowship year, which he was awarded in March 1927. Taking advantage of this opportunity, however, required a bit of rearranging. First, he had to postpone the start of the sabbatical from April to July, ostensibly so he could prepare for the association's annual conference, but also to give Gladys time to have their second child before journeying across the Atlantic.

Walter Carl Darrow White was born on June 8, and his arrival is curious for the muted reception by the father. Even in a time when expectant fathers were banished to the waiting room, Walter was unusually disengaged. No nervous pacing or handing out of cigars for Walter; instead, while Gladys was in labor, he read and critiqued the manuscript for Countee Cullen's anthology of poetry, *Caroling Dusk*. For weeks after the birth, when Walter would broadcast the good news, he would not utter the child's name, referring to him as "the boy" or his daughter Jane's brother. (Even twenty years later, in *A Man Called White*, he refers only to the birth of his nameless son.) This may be accounted for by the quandary of what to name the child. Four months before his birth, Walter confided to Sinclair Lewis, their good friends Clarence and Ruby Darrow told the

Whites that they would like the baby to be their namesake, "and, of course, Gladys and I were most happy to honor our son in this fashion." But when Gladys lobbied for naming the child after the father, Walter resisted. Gladys, he reported to family friend Carl Roberts, a Chicago physician, "was rather set on 'Walter Darrow White.' So far as I am concerned, I am a bit adverse to handicapping a child with his father's name. It is bad enough if the father doesn't amount to anything and worse if by any chance the father should ever do anything notable." When Walter sent birth announcements, the child's first name was Carl. Much to his dismay—"against my wishes," he wrote his brother George—Gladys, her parents, and his parents prevailed, and the newborn's name was finalized as Walter Carl Darrow White.[83]

At the time his son was born, White explained that the child was named for Carl Roberts. But it was widely believed—by daughter Jane, sister Ruby's husband, and Langston Hughes, and historians since—that the child's namesake was Carl Van Vechten, the white literary critic, novelist, and a New Negro movement patron. This was a burden of a different sort, for when Walter bestowed this honor on Van Vechten, he was persona non grata in most of Harlem, owing to his scandalous novel of the previous year, *Nigger Heaven*. Van Vechten began to insinuate himself in the Harlem Renaissance around 1924, when Walter and Gladys invited him to attend an NAACP fund-raising dance. He was smitten with Harlem's life and culture, its nightlife in particular: he was a regular in the clubs above Central Park, especially Small's Paradise. But he also established warm relationships with James Weldon Johnson, White, Hughes, and emerging novelist Nella Larsen, all of whom praised *Nigger Heaven*. He arranged Paul Robeson's first recital, at New York's Town Hall. His articles for *Vanity Fair* shared with white readers his passion and respect for African American art forms like the spirituals and the blues. His integrated parties at his West Side apartment brought together Harlem's writers, artists, and musicians and influential and flush whites.[84]

When the bestseller *Nigger Heaven* appeared, Van Vechten ("Carlo" to his friends) immediately became suspect. Had he taken advantage of Harlem's hospitality to write a potboiler chock-full of the most enduring stereotypes? Most of Harlem thought so. Just below the sympathetic *tsk-tsks* for the middle-class black characters who found themselves in difficult circumstances imposed by American race relations lurked what most whites considered to be the essential African American: ruled by passion, not reason, and prone to violence. But White (and James Weldon Johnson) dissented from W.E.B. Du Bois's verdict that *Nigger Heaven* was a "blow in the face." Van Vechten's novel, White believed, brought to the attention of white people the existence of a black middle class; a good portion of white racial prejudice, White said, stemmed from a conviction that all African Americans were poor and uneducated. *Nigger Heaven*, a blockbuster written by a white friend of the race, White told Du Bois, "will be read by people who will never read a line of what you or I or other Negroes may write" about the conditions of black life. It ought to be welcomed by African Americans for raising whites' awareness of the race issue. Wasn't this, after all, one of the components of "civil rights by copyright"? White's decision to stick by Van Vechten—and name his son Carl—may have been an act of friendly loyalty. But it also illuminates the importance White placed on cultivating and placating influential whites to the promotion of the Harlem Renaissance enterprise.[85]

Once Gladys recouped strength to travel, White, *en famille*, boarded the Cunard line's *Carmania* on July 23, 1927, bound for Havre. With his $2,500 Guggenheim stipend supplemented by three months paid leave from the association, the Whites settled in Villefranche-sur-Mer outside Nice, in a white stone villa on a hill overlooking the Mediterranean. Their home, he was pleasantly surprised to discover, had all the modern conveniences, including an indoor bathroom, hot and cold running water, and electricity. A Bon Marché grocery and Galleries Lafayette department store were twenty minutes away by tram. It was a bargain at the equivalent of fifty American dollars monthly. Assisted by William Aspinwall Bradley and W.E.B. Du Bois's French colleague Mme. Chapoteau, White secured the services of a "gorgeous" housekeeper, who also cooked what he considered to be gourmet fare. Their neighbors, a French painter and his wife, became good friends and, incidentally, solved the dilemma of what to call young White: they nicknamed him *"le petit pigeon,"* which morphed into Pidge, which stuck. (Slightly more than two decades later, estranged from his father because of his divorce and remarriage to Poppy Cannon, Pidge dropped his first name and became simply Carl Darrow White. Somewhat later, he dropped his surname altogether.) They remained in Villefranche for six months, but when the tourist season made the Côte d'Azur too expensive, the Whites relocated to Avignon. Here the assistant secretary felt he could keep in touch with the Anglophone authors—he kept company with Ford Madox Ford and

Somerset Maugham—while sampling a part of France that was not over-run with vacationing Americans and Brits or refugees from Mussolini's Italy. In both places, he worked steadily on *Rope and Faggot*.[86]

Subtitled "A Biography of Judge Lynch," *Rope and Faggot* is an out-standing example of partisan scholarship and is based upon White's first-hand investigations and a sampling of the relevant social scientific literature. The volume fulfilled two interrelated goals: it debunked southern whites' big lie that lynching punished black men for raping white women and protected the purity of the flower of the white race, and it delivered a penetrating critique of the southern culture that nourished this blood sport. In the tradition of Ida B. Wells-Barnett at the turn of the twentieth century, White marshaled statistics demonstrating that accusa-tions of rape or attempted rape accounted for less than 30 percent of lynchings. In those cases where the lynch victim did have sexual contact with a white female, White cast doubt on the veracity of the accusers. The assistant secretary identified four categories of girls or women likely to scream "rape": adolescents who were grappling with their nascent sex-uality; middle-aged women, whom he implied were open to sexual exper-imentation; wives trapped in long-term marriages to "unattractive" men; and "spinsters," who, again, he conjectured, sought some outlet for their sexual expression.[87] Brandishing evidence of white females of all classes crossing the color line for love—evidence that white supremacists them-selves broadcast in order to agitate whites to back antimiscegenation laws—White insisted that most interracial liaisons were consensual and not forced.

How to account for the fury and sadism with which the mob attacked lynch victims? Despite the popular notion that whites held darker peoples repugnant and repulsive, white southern males since the time of slavery had been attracted to black females. Through rape or concubinage, white men had been known to take advantage of black females, although to jus-tify their aggression they impugned them by claiming that black women were "naturally licentious."[88] The lynchers' savagery, including castra-tion, was born of the unarticulated suspicion that, despite protestations to the contrary, sexual attraction across the color line ran more than one way and "the absence of repulsion applies to both sexes of both races."[89] Through the act of lynching, the mobbist was projecting his own guilt about his sexual debauchery on a black scapegoat and also intimidating white women, who might likely find black men more attractive.[90] But,

White again emphasized, "the usual crime" was not usually the stimulus for the formation of the mob, although the cry of rape still circulated with alarming frequency because of whites' obsession with sex. At bottom, White asserted, whites employed lynching to keep blacks in their "place," and, more specifically, as a way to control the black labor force.[91]

As White showed in his chapter "The Economic Foundations of Lynch-Law," lynching first appeared in Virginia in the years immediately preceding the Revolutionary War, as a way for Patriots to mete out punishment to Loyalists. With established courts of law more than 200 miles distant, Thomas Lynch, a local person of considerable influence, established an extralegal tribunal to deal with the Patriots' opponents who, if convicted, were lashed and made to shout "long live liberty!" A similar method of summary judgment appeared in the western territories as they were being settled by Euro-Americans and before the establishment of a recognized authority. With the invention of the cotton gin and the renewed profitability and expansion of slavery in the early nineteenth century, lynch law, as it came to be known, became an important measure for the defense of slavery. Beginning around 1830, the planter class employed the rope and faggot with increasing frequency against white and black abolitionists and enslaved blacks suspected of having rebellious intentions. In the decade of the 1850s, what Walter White termed "obviously incomplete" data show that twenty-six blacks were killed by mobs for "killing their masters."[92]

The South produced one of its most gory chapters during the Reconstruction that followed the Civil War. An 1872 congressional investigation into Ku Klux Klan violence found that during a span of a few weeks in 1868 more than 2,000 African Americans were murdered by mobs in Louisiana; an incomplete count in Texas revealed that 1,035 were lynched between the end of the Civil War and 1868. Other southern states posted similarly gruesome statistics. These sanguinary efforts to return African Americans as close to slavery as possible had their effects. As historian Eric Foner noted, the violence, while widespread, was also focused on black politicians, community leaders, and activists; it was largely responsible for the overthrow of Reconstruction state governments and the final end of that experiment in multiracial democracy in 1877.[93] By the end of the century, most of the former Confederacy had disfranchised African Americans and was well on the way to constructing the edifice of legal segregation.

Lynching did not end with the vanquishing of African Americans from public life. Between 1890 and 1930, it was used with a high-level frequency to keep African Americans in their place by policing racial boundaries, punishing and terrorizing prosperous African Americans, and squelching hints of black opposition to the racial order. While many of the twentieth century's spectacular public lynchings involved charges of black males' sexual transgressions, such accusations were not always the proximate cause of mob action. Rather, rape was often used as an excuse for a lynching, as a way to enforce a white male consensus. But some of the mobs, such as the ones that murdered Mary Turner and about a dozen others near Valdosta, Georgia, in May 1918, openly avowed their intentions to control black labor. Countless other instances of murder, especially sparked by labor unrest, were carried out privately, without publicity.[94]

The impulse to lynch was embedded in small-town and rural Southern culture and economy, though the impetus appeared too in the industrial North. White states that "lynching often takes the place of the merry-go-round, the theatre, the symphony orchestra, and other diversions common to large communities."[95] The absence of cultural institutions like these was a manifestation of the authority of fundamentalist Christianity over life in the South. But, as the historian Grace Hale has shown, while the fundamentalist regime could keep these institutions out of large portions of the South, it could not stop modernity and its attendant culture of consumption, which profoundly affected the lynching industry. Affordable train fares, the diffusion of automobile ownership, a growing telephone network, and the widespread appearance of inexpensive photographs all contributed to the popularization of spectacle violence and its commodification. Notice of an impending lynching could be sent out in advance; participants and observers could organize special railroad excursions or car caravans; photographers could appear and quickly develop souvenir photos for those who wanted to send a postcard to family or friends or who were simply not lucky enough to procure a part of the victim's body. In the twentieth century, lynching became a shared cultural event—either in person or in retelling—that helped to define the identity of white southerners.[96]

From colonial times, Christianity, particularly the Southern Baptist and Methodist varieties, absorbed race prejudice into the core of its faith, offering defenses of slavery and refusing to emancipate enslaved blacks

who underwent religious conversions.[97] Southern fundamentalism became, in the words of French social scientist André Siegfried, whom
White quoted, "the religion of the Anglo-Saxon or 'superior' race."[98]
The convergence of fundamentalist dogma and racist ideology, which
supported the plantocracy, produced an overlap of the religious and terrorist leadership that enforced Jim Crow. Preachers populated the Ku
Klux Klan hierarchy; even those not associated with the Klan gave silent
assent to the mob and rarely spoke against it. Lynching was a salient feature of the Protestant Christian dictatorship in the South. Other features
included Know-Nothingism and the proliferation of antievolution
statutes that culminated in the 1925 Scopes monkey trial. So long as
white southerners filtered their views on race through the primitive beliefs and assertions of fundamentalism—and so long as the ministry continued to recruit men of at best mediocre intelligence—the assistant
secretary saw little hope for the benighted region.

Individual African Americans were not the only ones to pay the price
of lynching, White believed; the entire South paid a price as well. The
preachers and New South Democratic politicians enforced a rigid conformity in all controversial matters, of which the rope and faggot was an
extreme example. But its debilitating effects could also be found in the extraordinary difficulty white workers faced in organizing labor unions.
The southern press, when it was not eagerly announcing impending
lynchings, was simply incapable of performing its functions as watchdogs
and disseminators of critical information. As John Egerton, author of
Speak Now against the Day, has shown, a staggering number of southern
authors, intellectuals, artists, and musicians—African American and
white alike—fled the region's sterile climate in order to produce their
works of culture.[99]

Rope and Faggot builds upon the trailblazing work of Ida B. Wells-
Barnett. A pioneer of the antilynching crusade, Wells-Barnett had been
active for more than two decades before White began his work as an
NAACP investigator. Her principal writings on lynching offered a
scathing critique of white manliness and white civilization's colossal
struggle against black barbarity. It was Afro-America, she claimed, that
expressed manly qualities in its heroic gains in education and living standards. White men's concupiscence proved them unfit for civilization.
They squandered their vital energies raping or abetting the rape of black

women, finally turning their lust to dominate on black men, who expressed the finer qualities of civilization.[100]

That White did not acknowledge or even mention her pathbreaking work can be attributed to both the passage of time and the NAACP's disputes with Wells-Barnett. By the mid-twenties, when White was composing *Rope and Faggot*, Ida Wells-Barnett, who could be difficult to work with, was well past the acme of her lifework and was remembered only dimly—if at all—as a cranky and heroic fighter of the past. This historical indignity was compounded by White's personal—and the NAACP's collective—antagonism toward Wells-Barnett, dating to the association's founding and to divergent opinions about the direction of the antilynching crusade.[101]

The NAACP and Wells-Barnett differed on the role of women in the antilynching crusade. Because lynching called into question issues of black manhood and male power within the black community, "African American women's initiative against racial violence promoted gender anxiety," according to Patricia Schechter, one of Wells-Barnett's biographers. What African American women could do to stem the epidemic of mobbism was circumscribed by traditional notions of gender and respectability. Ida B. Wells-Barnett's brand of agitation usurped the leadership of the NAACP and other organizations and made them uncomfortable. The NAACP especially was moving away from a model of race advancement through agitation and toward one of institutionalizing the fight for equality by establishing a civil rights bureaucracy. The appropriate type of black women's antilynching work, in the opinion of White and the NAACP, was moral suasion. Though Wells-Barnett also believed in moral suasion, her approach was too confrontational for the NAACP and those who followed its lead. While the assistant secretary and others frowned upon Wells-Barnett's activism, the association supported and partially bankrolled the work of the "Anti-Lynching Crusaders," a network of black women whose program included fund-raising, education, and building relationships with white southern women.[102] In order to facilitate this last activity, the Anti-Lynching Crusaders excised from their analysis of mob violence the idea that interracial sexual contact, which was used as an excuse for the murder of black men, was in fact consensual; it was this dimension of the lynching epidemic that was at the heart of Wells-Barnett's argument.

White's pirating of Wells-Barnett's work also illuminates another of his less flattering characteristics. White had a penchant for appropriating without attribution the work of others. When the NAACP concentrated attention to international affairs in the forties and fifties, White solicited advice from W.E.B. Du Bois and Rayford Logan and then passed these along as his own; when Logan saw what White was doing, he vowed never to be robbed again.[103] But if White appears to be calculating—and in the cases of Du Bois, Logan, and Wells, he does—sometimes he appears simply petty. For example, just before the publication of *Rope and Faggot*, White had a conversation with Ernestine Rose, the librarian at the 135th Street branch of the New York Public Library, during which she invited him to help her organize a book fair in spring 1929; when White tried to enlist the aid of Henry Block, his editor at Knopf, he said that he had suggested the fair to Rose. In another instance, White, in a 1951 letter to Logan, claimed credit for stimulating an anticorruption campaign in Haiti. Here, as elsewhere, though, the advantage to be gained is so negligible or the claim so outlandish as to indicate not cunning but a nasty force of habit and a propensity to shade the truth with white lies.[104]

Viewed retrospectively, *Rope and Faggot* wears unevenly. The overview of the lynching industry, written in modulated tones, is for that very reason powerful. The chapter on sex is provocative. The extensive discussion of interracial love and families that acknowledge both their black and white members gave lie to the white supremacists' attempts to use rape as an excuse for lynching and to naturalize racism and segregation. White's discussion of southern white men's psychosexual anxieties as a cause of lynching still contains much explanatory power. The strongest sections deal with the economic and structural foundations of lynching. Here White identified the maintenance of the plantation economy and its attendant sharecropping and peonage systems as a principal stimulus for mob terror. As to the connection between the two, White wrote, "All of these reasons for the dominance of sex as a factor in lynching, with all their other complications, centre in one objective—economic ascendancy over Negro labour."[105] Stewart E. Tolnay and E. M. Beck, authors of the most ambitious and thorough sociological study of lynching, found that "although we have arrived at our respective destinations by traversing very different terrain, our conclusions overlap significantly with those reached much earlier by White. . . ."[106]

But the intervening years since *Rope and Faggot*'s publication have re-vealed the limitations of White's religious and cultural explanations of the lynching phenomenon. His reflections that the mob was suffused with the fundamentalist Protestant spirit and that its leadership often wore clerical garb are suggestive, and his recitation of examples of ritual brutality remain, as insightful as it is horrifying. Yet keen eye for detail notwithstanding, he did not develop these empirical observations into a thorough critique of the religious and communal meanings of ritual vio-lence. That task would fall to other scholars.

With the defeat of the South in the Civil War, "Lost Cause" mythol-ogy developed a strong fundamentalist foundation. According to sociolo-gist Orlando Patterson, white southerners came to believe they lost the war because they were insufficiently righteous or because God was test-ing and preparing them for a glory even greater than the antebellum past. The various symbols and stages of mob violence—the use of fire and the cross; the infliction of physical pain on the victim before death; the pref-erence for lynching sites laden with sacred connotations such as trees and bridges; the popularity of Sunday for the day of execution—exude reli-giosity. Lynching, wrote Patterson, is ritual sacrifice that "enacts and symbolically recreates a disrupted or threatened social world, and it re-solves, through the shedding of blood, a specific crisis of transition." [107] The popularization of photography and sound recordings made possible vicarious enjoyment of the event.[108] In other words, white southerners' communal response to the overthrow of slavery and the social and eco-nomic uncertainty created by African Americans' drive for equality was the establishment of the civil religion of the "Lost Cause" and the staging of human sacrifice. But "angry as he was at whites' religion," notes Donald Mathews, a historian of southern religions, Walter White "did not probe the internal punitiveness of a religion he identified with igno-rance and fanaticism to think about the sacred nature of the violence he documented in his work."[109]

H. L. Mencken tried to steer White in this analytical direction when he encouraged him to write for the *American Mercury* about the tech-nique of lynching, but Mencken deemed White's efforts to be "feeble and ineffective." They concentrated, said Mencken, not on the rituals but on lynching's historical contexts, ground White ably covered in *Rope and Faggot*. In both the book and the subsequent article, "The Technique of Lynching," the assistant secretary seemed to content himself with a general exposition of the problem of mob violence flavored with Mencken's distaste, expressed as irony, for Nordic civilization and narrow-minded Protestant fundamentalism.[110]

While these are not insignificant shortcomings, they do not detract from the book's contemporary and historical significance. *Rope and Faggot* was a powerful indictment of the lynching industry and it garnered excellent reviews. A few publications, perhaps discomfited by the subject matter, found fault with what they thought was overly excitable prose. University of Chicago sociologist Ellsworth Faris in *The New Republic* (May 8, 1929) kindly understood that "Mr. White cannot be reasonably expected to be calm." But Leon Whipple at *Survey* (October 1, 1929) obtusely made the point that his "controversial bent" led White "to make too much of beating down the straw men of exploded or eccentric doctrines" like pseudo-scientific racism and white males' jealousy of black men's virility (at a time when both ideas enjoyed much currency). However, most praised the author's care in stating his case. *Time* (June 24, 1929) hailed White for an "arresting exposition of a not-yet-vanished U.S. folkway." The review incited vicious protests from that magazine's readers. Robert E. Lee of Greenville, North Carolina, fulminated that "if anyone needed a coat of tar and feathers it's the author of 'Judge Lynch.' " Eldon Holdane of Atlanta declared that "down here we don't care if all the Negroes are lynched, or even burned or slit open with knives. The outrageous, damnable, unbearable spectacle of lawlessness of the Negro is infinitely greater than would be the entire extermination of the cursed race by the white man." White was delighted by this excoriation; he knew there was no such thing as bad publicity and he welcomed the wider exposure these denunciations brought.[111] Clarence Darrow emphasized in the *New York Herald Tribune* (April 21, 1929) that the facts came not from biased reports but from published accounts in the press near the vicinity of the lynching. Melville Herskovits generously praised the book in *The Nation* (May 15, 1929) for its "much considered presentation of the highest order" and its "healthy, sane, and desirable" point of view. *Modern Quarterly* editor V. F. Calverton told readers of the *New York World* (April 28, 1929) that "in every way it is a challenge to our civilization."

White's unvarnished analysis of the causes of lynching was clearer and more uncompromising than most of the sympathetic declarations by his white contemporaries. Even Arthur Raper's exhaustive *Tragedy of Lynching* (1933), usually identified as the starting point for recent histories of lynching, assigned blacks some culpability for lynching. Contrary to information presented by White and Wells-Barnett before him that mobs often singled out successful blacks for retribution, Raper believed that African Americans could do much to stamp out lynching by "demonstrating the ability, character, and good citizenship of the race" and by cooperating with "officials and influential white friends"[112]—favorite nostrums of Booker T. Washington. Will Alexander, head of the Commission for Interracial Cooperation and one of the most enlightened white southerners, refused to support the NAACP-backed federal Costigan-Wagner antilynching law; other southern white liberals, including prominent newspaper editors George Fort Milton and Virginius Dabney, likewise took Alexander's lead in opposing both lynching and the preferred legal remedy to the problem so far as African Americans were concerned.[113]

Rope and Faggot retains its significance too because it represents the perspective of African Americans in the fight against mob justice. White insisted on African Americans' humanity, equality, and potential. And neither the book nor its author shrank in the face of hostile white public opinion or shaded a conclusion to gain that public's acceptance. In presenting the harsh truth about lynching, Walter White showed himself to be a passionate, consistent, and articulate pursuer of racial justice.

White completed the manuscript of *Rope and Faggot* in late January 1928 in Avignon. With only a short detour to encourage the jazz duo Layton Turner and Clarence "Tandy" Johnston, who were wowing audiences in Paris and London, to make a substantial contribution to the NAACP, White began work on his third novel.[114] Titled *Blackjack*, it followed the life and career of pugilist Matthew "Blackjack" Fortune from his small Georgia hometown to Harlem. By the end of March he had written about 30,000 words, and he seemed to be happy with his progress. A reading of the extant manuscript indicates that White was overly optimistic about the novel's shape.[115]

But in early March a surprise letter from home knocked him off his authorial stride and caused him to put the novel aside. Charles Studin, Arthur Spingarn's law partner, was working for Al Smith's presidential campaign, and he asked White to return to New York in early April to head up the efforts to corral the Negro vote for the Democratic presidential aspirant. White was intrigued. Politics was like mother's milk to him, and a position in the Smith campaign in which he could leverage his NAACP ties might just lead to new career opportunities. There were several unknowns, of course, but White was inclined to pursue the matter further. He made arrangements for Gladys, Jane, and Pidge to remain in France, and cabled Studin that he would sail aboard the *France*, arriving in New York on April 10. Debarking, he took just enough time to drop his luggage at Louis Wright's West 139th Street apartment before heading to Studin's office.[116] His earlier experiences as an antilynching lobbyist and witness before congressional committees notwithstanding, Walter White was about to get his first full taste of national politics. He would fill his plate and then some.

Chapter 5

A Crooked Path
to Power

The suggestion that a major-party candidate for president was interested in securing the African American vote by pledging to fight for the race's equality was enough to pique the interest of several of the association's leaders. At the urging of his close political advisor and prominent social reformer Belle Moskowitz, who believed that the black vote—usually a lock for the Republicans—would be crucial for victory, Al Smith sent out feelers to prominent supporters in the field of race advancement. Moskowitz contacted Charles Studin, who in turn consulted his law partner Arthur Spingarn and James Weldon Johnson and then broached the subject with White in France. Would he be interested in heading up an independent effort to get out the black vote for Smith? "The powers that be" concluded that "the most advisable method of handling" the promotion of Smith among black voters "would be through placing a colored man on the firing line and have him develop the situation as the circumstances may warrant." White was Studin's and Moskowitz's first choice because "we shall need an aggressive, nationally known and representative man, who has not been heretofore tied up with the Democratic party."[1]

The offer was refreshing and tempting, the more so given the drubbing that African Americans had taken in national politics during the twenties. Warren Harding, who was elected president in 1920, was indifferent to African Americans' concerns. Two months before his victory he told James Weldon Johnson that, while he sympathized with the NAACP's demand for federal action to protect the franchise for blacks and abolish segregation in federal agencies and on interstate transportation, he would not say so publicly.[2]

Harding continued to neglect African Americans after he occupied the White House. In 1921, he endorsed a Treasury Department decision to build a Jim Crow veteran's hospital in Tuskegee, Alabama. The NAACP had opposed the construction of a segregated facility, especially one in the deep South, but when Harding ignored its objections, the association demanded that the hospital be staffed by blacks.[3] The president initially agreed, but as the project neared completion in 1923, he bowed to pressure from local whites who wanted to bar African Americans from professional employment at the hospital. When he reversed himself, Harding abandoned Robert Russa Moton, Booker T. Washington's successor at the Tuskegee Institute and one of the president's loyal black supporters; he also jeopardized African American support for the Republican Party in the next general election. Yet Harding was just continuing a trend begun by Theodore Roosevelt and William Howard Taft, his Republican predecessors, of turning the party lily-white and trying to break the Democratic monopoly on the southern white electorate.

Harding's reversal encouraged local whites to terrorize local blacks into submission. The KKK marched through the town of Tuskegee on July 4, wearing white sheets supplied from the hospital. Walter White went to Washington, D.C., to lodge complaints with the Justice Department, but was told by Bureau of Investigation director J. Edgar Hoover that the federal government could do nothing about such intimidation and threats.[4] As the assistant secretary delineated the issues in a letter to editors of New York papers, the reversal was "a revealing indication of the peculiar psychology of the Southern white man." Several years earlier, he wrote, Alabama had passed a law prohibiting white women from nursing black men. But now that a $65,000 monthly payroll was at stake, "race prejudice falls with a bang before the almighty dollar." Furthermore, "a friend of mine from Alabama has told me of another reason for the insistence by white Alabama that Negroes be not allowed to man this institution. . . . 'If niggers are put at the head of this hospital, they'll be responsible only to the United States government and we don't want any niggers in Alabama we can't control.' "[5] Only Harding's death in August

1923 opened up the possibility of eventually installing a black staff, as Calvin Coolidge took measures to keep the original promise.

But by the time the 1924 elections rolled around, the prospects for any African American influence on the political process looked bleaker than ever. The Republicans nominated Calvin Coolidge for a full term, and with financier Charles Dawes as a running mate, the party celebrated unfettered capitalism and opposed practically every reform proposal. The Democratic Party, bitterly divided between white ethnics in the urban Northeast and native white stock in the rural South and West, was extremely hostile to African Americans. The nominating convention's floor debate on the Ku Klux Klan erupted in fistfights, the meeting refused to condemn the Klan, and Texas delegates tried but were finally persuaded not to burn a cross. For a time it seemed as if the reconstituted Progressive Party would provide a political home for Afro-America. Wisconsin's Senator Robert La Follette, the Progressive presidential nominee, had a strong record of supporting economic equality, and his antimonopoly convictions certainly would have benefited African Americans. But at the party convention in Cleveland, not even the presence of NAACP founder William English Walling, Socialist Norman Thomas, Communist Robert Minor, and association field secretary William Pickens (the only African American present) could persuade the assembly to go on record against the Klan and Jim Crow.[6] Still, prominent African Americans backed La Follette in a losing presidential bid, as Coolidge reoccupied the White House.

The next quadrennium brought no relief to the effacement of African Americans in the political process. Democrats and Republicans continued to shun blacks. The American Federation of Labor continued to alternate between indifference and hostility. And the progressive remnants, with the exception of the Workers (Communist) Party, maintained a deafening silence on race. A salient feature of *The Crisis* during these years was the series of editorials upbraiding the supposed friends of the Negro for their derelictions.

It was, therefore, with some pleasurable anticipation that the assistant secretary and other NAACP officials greeted the Smith campaign's overtures. Here, apparently, was a sign that African Americans' long exile from the political process might be ending. White could work for Smith without reservation, he told Studin, because he believed Smith was the best man available for the presidency. As he assayed the political terrain, the assistant secretary saw a double opportunity in the proposed venture. First, a victory for Smith, who was Catholic, would strike a blow against bigotry, inasmuch as his enemies were blacks' enemies. Second, it would be an "excellent opportunity to appeal to Negroes to end their chronic Republicanism and having their votes counted before ever they are cast."[7]

But the assistant secretary's enthusiasm was tempered by personal and political realities that made his acceptance of Studin's offer far from certain. If Smith won, White could very well end up playing Booker Washington to Smith's Theodore Roosevelt. Being a dispenser of patronage had obvious appeal. But would a Smith defeat, White wondered, compromise his ability to support his family? "If I were single I would be willing to take a chance," he wrote to John Hurst, an association founder and board member, A.M.E. bishop, and paternal figure to White. "If Gladys and I had no children we could weather any storm which might arise. But, have I the right to jeopardize the future of Jane and Walter?"[8] Then there were the potentially negative political consequences of White's acceptance. Even if the assistant secretary resigned from the association to take the post, his value to Smith's campaign was his affiliation with the NAACP, which would in reality be abandoning its traditional nonpartisan stance; would such a switch harm the association?

Between his return to the United States in March and the Democratic Party's Houston nominating convention in July, White and the NAACP leadership wrestled with the merits and drawbacks of organizing for Smith. At the beginning of this process, the assistant secretary developed a plan of action for "The National Negro Independent 'Al Smith' Association." On this organization's letterhead would appear the names of prominent African Americans, including Edward Morris, national head of the Negro Odd Fellows; James Weldon Johnson; William Lewis of Boston, a former assistant United States attorney general and supporter of Booker T. Washington; and John Hurst. Drawing upon the assistance of influential and friendly whites like Clarence Darrow and Frank Murphy (the Detroit judge who presided over the Sweet trial), the organization would establish state affiliates and blitz contested cities with reasons blacks should support Smith for president. The propaganda and speakers' campaign would focus on the futility of blind allegiance to the Republican Party and on the need to effect a united front with Democratic-leaning white ethnics, who also were targets of the Ku Klux Klan and race-baiting politicians like Cole Blease and Tom Heflin.[9]

Adjunct to these initial plans was a sophisticated "Analysis of Possible Effect of Negro Vote in the 1928 Election." Predating by two decades Henry Lee Moon's seminal *The Balance of Power*, the assistant secretary's position paper demonstrated the potential for the African American vote to determine the next president. Several of the states that Smith needed in order to win the presidency had only a small proportion of black voters, but its importance was magnified by an evenly divided white electorate. The committee for Al Smith, therefore, could have maximum impact by concentrating its efforts in urban areas where the contest promised to be close and blacks could provide Smith with the margin of victory. The assistant secretary's position paper demonstrated an astute grasp of the workings of the political system.[10]

As spring turned to summer, a divided NAACP board debated whether to send White into the Smith campaign. Moorfield Storey, the venerable NAACP president and legendary attorney, was most enthusiastic about the possibility. Supporting Smith would win the NAACP some Democratic support, which—while not wholehearted—would at least be a basis for asking for further assistance. Contrariwise, the NAACP would condemn itself to political ineffectuality if it remained on the sidelines. Nor would neutrality win concessions from the Republicans, for Hoover had no intention of recognizing African Americans' rights. White's refusal would be interpreted not just by the Democrats but "by both parties as evidence of cowardice."[11]

Bishop Hurst inclined toward Storey, as did the assistant secretary. White had told Hurst that Du Bois opposed an endorsement of Smith because partisanship would harm the association; on the other hand, White continued, Charles Studin advised the assistant secretary to resign his position before joining Smith, thereby leaving the NAACP still officially neutral. Hurst conceded the legitimacy of both Du Bois's and Studin's points, but begged to disagree with them. The NAACP was founded for the "the purpose of giving political freedom to the Negro and equality with all the other races, social or otherwise." White's resignation from the association would not fool anyone, and it was better to face the issue of the NAACP's political action head-on. He reported to White that Carl Murphy, the publisher of the influential *Baltimore Afro-American*, would support his involvement with Smith. Both

Du Bois's and Studin's positions, Hurst concluded, were "a step backward."[12]

James Weldon Johnson was "quite definitely opposed" to the proposal. He and two other NAACP officials had worked for several months to persuade Smith to adopt a friendly stance toward African Americans. Smith's advisors had promised to deliver such a position, but the candidate had yet to speak out. In the meantime, there had been a lynching in Texas, black visitors to the Houston Democratic Party convention had been segregated in cages, and Smith had chosen for his running mate a segregationist, Senator Joseph Robinson of Arkansas. With the mixed signals coming from the Smith camp, Johnson did not believe that the NAACP could afford to abandon nonpartisanship. On the contrary, he felt that taking sides in this election would do "irretrievable harm" to the NAACP.[13]

In the end, White did not put on the hat of the Negroes for the Al Smith organization. Johnson and White had authored a statement for Smith's approval that decried disfranchisement, lynching, and discrimination in access to public school facilities, and committed him to combating them. The single paragraph, which did not explicitly mention segregation, delicately balanced the NAACP's demand for equal rights with an acknowledgment of the political reality that an open condemnation of Jim Crow would draw the ire of southern Democrats. But Smith feared antagonizing the South more than he desired racial reconciliation, and he would not sign the statement. Given the candidate's demurral, White could not embrace him. As he explained to Moorfield Storey,

> Had I no Association connections I might be willing to take a chance and support Smith without assurances but as I am known to colored people almost wholly because of my connection with the NAACP, the Association would be the target for venomous attacks if I went into it, and especially if Robinson made one of his Anti-Negro speeches.[14]

But matters did not end there. Johnson had indicated that neither he nor the association objected to White publicly endorsing Smith, and the assistant secretary became one of the campaign's unofficial advisors. Though he had come to believe that "Smith [does not know] very much about Negroes," he held some of his principal advisors, including Belle Moskowitz and Herbert Lehman (a future governor of New York,

NAACP board member, and personal friend of White) in the highest regard. Operating on the assumption that the candidate would still make some overtures to Negro voters, White engaged in some behind-the-scenes politicking to place African Americans friendly to the NAACP in the Smith campaign. He counseled Boston lawyer and former U.S. assistant attorney general William H. Lewis to take the job of organizing colored voters, endorsed *Baltimore Afro-American* publisher Carl Murphy for the campaign's publicity director (at a weekly salary of $150), recommended New York City's black civil service commissioner Ferdinand Q. Morton for the executive committee chairmanship, and lobbied for a spot for Bishop Hurst.[15]

The denouement of the assistant secretary's involvement in the 1928 presidential elections came in two parts. In October, White joined Du Bois, Johnson, and a cross section of nationally prominent black Republicans and Democrats in "accus[ing] the political leaders of this campaign of permitting without protest, public and repeated assertions on the platform, in the press, and by word of mouth, that color and race constitute in themselves an imputation of guilt and crime."[16] Then, in the last weeks of the contest, the assistant secretary wrote the election's obituary. In the first number of *Harlem: A Forum of Negro Life*, edited by Wallace Thurman, appeared White's essay "For Whom Shall the Negro Vote?" The 1928 presidential race resulted in several positive developments, he thought, despite the two major parties' race-baiting. In New York, for example, Tammany Hall's publicly announced indifference to the Negro voters in Harlem motivated blacks "who had self-respect, but who also had been cursed with slothfulness"; a movement of independent black voters was forming to control the political destiny of areas where African Americans were numerous. With blacks locked out of presidential politics, African Americans needed to turn their attention and power—he claimed blacks held the balance of power in ten states—to local elections. "The Negro must continue to make his ballot an uncertain quantity," he wrote. "The choice of members of both Houses of Congress and of state legislatures, and of county and city officials mean much more to minority groups than who shall sit in the White House."[17]

The strategy hinted at by White was put more succinctly by Du Bois in a December *Crisis* article summarizing the election results. With the refusal of the two major political parties to address issues of concern to the majority of Americans, there was a promise of a new political alignment; there was a substantial "number of other groups [than Negroes] who find themselves politically homeless: the women, the liberal white South, organized Labor, the Pacifists, and the Farmers are all politically dressed up with nowhere to go."[18]

The difficulty of implementing this broad coalition became evident in late December at the National Interracial Conference in Washington, D.C. Initiated in 1926 by the Federal Council of Churches, and with Walter White on the executive committee, the meeting was sponsored by sixteen progressive, liberal, and moderate organizations, including the Fellowship of Reconciliation, the American Friends Service Committee, the National Urban League, the southern white liberal Commission on Interracial Cooperation, the YMCA, and the YWCA. Delegates and speakers at the conference spread further across the spectrum, with representatives from various government agencies like the Department of Labor, settlement organizations, the American Federation of Labor, and philanthropies.[19]

All present desired better race relations, and all deplored the disgraceful conditions of African Americans in public health, education, access to recreation and public facilities, and similar spheres of society. But when the NAACP proposed the remedy of giving black citizens political power, the consensus shattered. As Du Bois noted, he listened to the debate on improving education in the South "with mounting astonishment"; the continuation of segregated schools was a given in this debate, yet the issue of black control over these separate institutions never arose. The discussion's participants assumed that schools would be improved not by African Americans' civic initiatives but by philanthropic ones. White paternalism crimped the development of a broad coalition to counter the anticipated effects of a Hoover administration. As it did during the antilynching campaign just after WWI—and as it would again during the antilynching campaign in the thirties—white liberalism cringed at black political independence and insisted that African Americans follow its leadership and conform to its limited notions of racial, social, and political reform.

Perhaps a more impenetrable obstacle was erected by organized labor. AFL spokesperson John Frey offered a "casuistic defense of exclusion of Negroes from labor unions," according to the assistant secretary's article on the conference in *The Nation*. Barring African Americans from unions was a practical exigency, Frey offered; it prevented the clash of white and black workers' economic interests from weakening the labor movement! Liberal paternalism and the House of Labor's narrow craft selfishness were twin burdens Walter White and the NAACP were forced to shoulder as they skirmished with the Hoover administration.[20]

In its first year, the Hoover administration and the NAACP engaged in a low-intensity clash over Republicans' attempts to oust black Mississippi party boss Perry Howard under the pretext of combating corruption. Neither White nor other association leaders cared much for Howard's politics—he stymied the NAACP's efforts in the campaign for the Dyer antilynching bill and on other occasions—and they knew of his corruption. But Howard was no worse than white GOP leaders, and the NAACP charged that the attacks on Howard were simply a way to eliminate an African American presence in the Republican Party.[21] This encounter was merely prologue to the all-out battle in 1930 over Hoover's nomination of John J. Parker to the Supreme Court.

On March 21, 1930, President Hoover nominated Parker, a North Carolina Republican and sitting judge on the Fourth Circuit Court of Appeals, to replace the late associate justice Edward Sanford. Walter White had for some time been looking for the issue over which to lead a full-scale fight against the president, and with an open seat on the High Court, he planned to fight whomever Hoover named.[22] The day the president's choice was announced, White wrote to A. M. Rivera, a dentist in Greensboro, North Carolina, asking for any information on the nominee. "We want to be in a position to work against his confirmation in the Senate if there is any reason for such action. Of course," he added, "if he is all right and is looked upon favorably by the colored people of North Carolina, we will not act." Two days later, Dr. Rivera replied that Parker, when he was candidate for governor in 1920, announced that he favored the continued disfranchisement of African Americans. Two days after receiving Dr. Rivera's statement, on March 28, White alerted NAACP branches in the North, West, and border states that the defeat of John J. Parker was a now the association's priority campaign.[23]

Even for an organization that led national campaigns in the past, it was a daring proposition, requiring an immediate and vigorous response in a short space of time; it was a sprint, not a distance run. Lucille Black, the NAACP membership secretary in the national office, remembered that the idea for the campaign originated entirely with White. Members of the national staff, she recalled, "sat there with our fingers crossed because

Walter was, we felt, getting a little far out on the limb when he was claiming what the Negro communities would do if this appointment was made, you know, and how they would react to it."[24]

White had good reason for his audaciousness. The previous September he had been appointed acting secretary when James Weldon Johnson took a year's leave to attend an international meeting in Japan on Pacific relations and pursue creative writing on a Rosenwald fellowship. White did not yet enjoy the association's complete confidence; Arthur Spingarn recalled that the board of directors was "very doubtful about Walter," primarily because they believed him to be fiscally irresponsible. "The doubt was Walter's vagueness on financial matters," Spingarn said.

> Walter was just an impossibly generous person. You were afraid to tell Walter that perhaps you didn't have a certain book, he was always broke, but if you didn't have that book, the next day he'd go down and buy it and send it to you. I remember we had a dinner with a man who gave us $10,000—one of the richest men in the country, and Walter insisted on paying for the dinner. He always did. He was just incurably generous and always broke. . . . I don't think Walter ever sent in an itemized statement. I don't mean to say that he was a dishonest man, he was just careless and vague about financial matters and that worried us.[25]

To guard against White's well-known tendency toward financial and political spontaneity, the board of directors established a Committee on Administration (COA), composed of the chairman of the board (Mary White Ovington), the treasurer (Joel Spingarn), the editor of *The Crisis* (Du Bois), the chairman of the legal committee (Arthur Spingarn), and the president of the Philadelphia branch (Isadore Martin). It would meet weekly, and, unlike Johnson, who was answerable only to the board, White would report to the COA. (The committee was conceived as a temporary body to oversee White during Johnson's absence. But when Johnson did not return and the board removed the word "acting" from White's title in 1931, the COA remained and initially provided White's opponents with a check on his power.)[26]

Additionally, the acting secretary inherited an organization that was, if not destabilized, riding over some rough patches and facing challenges on several fronts. Some of the staff were unhappy; a few months earlier, field secretary William Pickens was reprimanded by the board of directors for requesting an extra month of paid vacation and then not waiting for approval before taking it. After White assumed his new position, Pickens and director of branches Robert Bagnall proposed that their and White's salaries be augmented to compensate them for the additional work created by Johnson's leave. But they complained when they received less of a raise than did the acting secretary. Mary White Ovington, chairman of the board, weary of association work, wrote to White that she wanted to shed as much responsibility as she possibly could. The association, never fiscally comfortable, faced a precarious budgetary cycle because Johnson had been the expert fund-raiser and Louis Marshall, the outstanding attorney and prodigious fund-raiser among Jews for the NAACP, had recently passed away.[27]

White needed to take some serious initiatives to keep the association moving forward and earn the full confidence of the board and the membership. Among his first actions was to persuade Harvard University law professor and future Supreme Court justice Felix Frankfurter to join the NAACP board. Frankfurter was "very much disinclined" to take part in NAACP activities, which answer White, with his trademark personableness and perseverance, was disinclined to accept. After some hesitation, Frankfurter allowed as he would be willing to render assistance to the NAACP's program of legal redress whenever the association needed his expertise. This was the opening White looked for. As he related his conversation to the COA, he told Frankfurter that if he was willing to do that much "he might as well go the whole way and accept Board membership." White and Frankfurter split the difference, and he joined the association's national legal committee.[28]

The acting secretary simultaneously took measures to ensure the financial health of the association. He would continue to court major philanthropics and wealthy whites, with whom James Weldon Johnson had had much luck in the past. Working through Jacob Billikopf, the late Louis Marshall's son-in-law, Henry Moskowitz, and settlement house worker Lillian Wald, White mapped the geography of American Jewish munificence. In March 1930 he secured from William Rosenwald, the son of Julius, a pledge of $3,000, paid out in three annual installments, provided White could secure four similar pledges by the first of June; the acting secretary exceeded this goal, enlisting six patrons, including New York lieutenant governor Herbert Lehman, the financier Felix Warburg and his wife, Samuel Fels of the Fels-Naptha soap company, Harold

Guinsburg of Viking Press, and Edsel Ford, the only gentile in the group. (The son of the notorious anti-Semite Henry Ford, Edsel became familiar with the NAACP through Mary White Ovington, whose summer home in Maine was next to his.)[29] He continued to court the foundations and made sure the Rosenwald and Garland funds maintained or increased their support.

Yet White also knew that the association could thrive only with substantial support from African Americans, and well-heeled blacks at that. He inquired of the possibility that William Rosenwald might adjust the conditions for his annual gift, suggesting that he also match pledges of between $250 and $1,000 to attract the interest of well-to-do blacks who might be unable to contribute larger amounts.[30] He also saw the need to seek the support of ordinary African Americans, and he challenged Bagnall and Pickens to intensify their fund-raising activities. "I wonder if we can't revive the friendly rivalry we had a few years ago to see which of us could get the greatest number of $2.50, $5, $10, $25, $50 and larger memberships out of each meeting we address and, most important, how much of it we could get in cash," White wrote, as he promised to increase the number of local meetings he addressed.[31]

He also hired Pittsburgh's Daisy Lampkin as a regional field secretary. For the longest time fieldwork had meant organizing and visiting branches and arranging speakers. This needed to continue, White believed, but such activity was also a drain on the national budget. Lampkin had extensive experience as a fund-raiser for several race uplift organizations and was prepared to reinvigorate the association's fieldwork. In particular she looked forward to unleashing the power of women: "Where the women are weak in leadership, the whole movement lags," she wrote. White endorsed both her financial and gender emphases. The acting secretary wanted to focus field secretary reports so that they "dwell not so much on the number of meetings addressed and letters sent out as on actual cash raised at meetings and pledges secured."[32] If this appears to be a departure from a policy that emphasized propaganda to one of raising money for the national office—something White was accused of in the forties by Ella Baker—it is also true that the acting secretary was trying to revitalize stagnant branches. It would soon become customary for the national office to demand a substantial local commitment before it would become involved in a local campaign. The NAACP was not a social services agency, White believed; rather it was in the business of helping blacks organize themselves to fight for equality.

It was in these multiple contexts that the acting secretary took quick and decisive action on the Parker nomination. After alerting the branches, the acting secretary adumbrated a plan. He fired scattershot written protests to about half of the senators, prepared to testify at the confirmation hearings, moved to solidify African American support for the association's position, and sought allies among white liberals and progressives.

White appeared before the Senate Judiciary Committee on April 5. The difficulty he and the association faced was that practically no regard was given to blacks' objections to Parker. What did worry some of the senators was the negative reaction of the American Federation of Labor, which took exception to Parker's rulings upholding the legality of so-called yellow-dog contracts, in which workers as a condition of their employment were compelled to sign statements that they would not join labor unions. As White remembered it in his autobiography, William Green, the head of the Negrophobe AFL, avoided altogether the nominee's position on disfranchisement, when he testified. (He also declined to exchange pleasantries with the acting secretary.) White, who was the penultimate witness, made only a brief appearance, which elicited only mild interest from committee members. When the hearings ended, not one witness echoed the acting secretary's concerns, though the Socialist Party's Norman Thomas submitted a written statement that denounced Parker for being both antilabor and antiblack and explicitly supported the NAACP.[33]

But upon reflection, White saw that the fight did not have to stop after the Senate's vote to confirm or reject Parker, and certainly did not end with the Judiciary Committee's report. Two days after his testimony, he doubted that the nomination could be stopped; liberal forces had not "bestir[red] themselves," he wrote to friendly journalist Ernest Gruening. But hope lay in threatening with defeat senators who were to stand for reelection in November 1930 should they vote to confirm Parker. Here was the germ of the campaign that would flower in the months to come. The implications of this course of action were significant. Neither the acting secretary nor other association staffers would spend any significant time in Washington lobbying senators; rather, White, Pickens, Bagnall, Daisy

Lampkin, and Du Bois would preach to the hustings, ensuring that branches pressured their senators to vote against Parker.[34]

Ludwell Denny, the Washington bureau chief for the Scripps-Howard newspaper chain and a journalist with whom the acting secretary cultivated strong bonds, affirmed these tactics, telling White that the association's conduct of the campaign was "raising hell in Washington." That President Hoover worried about the NAACP's organizing could be surmised from a visit that two Justice Department officials made to James Cobb, a member of the NAACP legal committee from Washington, D.C.; they wanted to know what it would take for the association to drop its opposition. White came to believe that the NAACP, and not organized labor, was driving the mounting dissatisfaction with Hoover's choice for the High Court. Without too much difficulty, he secured the support of most African American leaders, including Robert Moton of Tuskegee, President Hoover's closest black advisor, and Oscar De Priest, the Republican representative from Chicago. He approvingly quoted the regionally influential Raleigh (North Carolina) *News & Observer* as saying that "a political cloud no larger than a man's hand a week ago has reached the proportions of a storm since the National Association for the Advancement of Colored People got actively into the fight." His confidence in the association's puissance had good basis, as Parker's supporters increasingly shifted from defending his labor record to defending him on race issues.[35]

Even without the collaboration of organized labor, the acting secretary was able to put a kink in the Parker nomination by reaching out to white liberals and progressives. But their cooperation was by no means a given, and White's success demonstrates both his considerable interpersonal and political skills and the anemic state of white racial liberalism, which affliction would bedevil him for the next quarter-century. Clara Cox was a member of the North Carolina affiliate of the Commission on Interracial Cooperation (CIC), and she objected to the NAACP's agitation against Parker. To her, African Americans were making steady progress, though she allowed as it might be proceeding rather slowly; the association's activities threatened these advances and alienated whites who might otherwise be influenced by the CIC's chief activity in the state of preaching the Golden Rule. African Americans, she said, had little difficulty voting in the Old North State, though there was substantial resistance to their active and extensive participation in the political process.

Yet just because Judge Parker endorsed suffrage restrictions was no reason to extrapolate that he was an enemy of African Americans. On the contrary, Cox reported, she knew Parker well, and she could assure the acting secretary that he was fair-minded.[36]

To stanch the initial opposition to his nomination of Parker, Hoover turned to his coreligionists in the Society of Friends. Robert Grey Taylor of the Quaker's Committee on Race Relations told Hoover that the Friends could not support Parker so long as he refused to answer the NAACP's questions. Two days after this meeting, Parker invited Taylor to his office to work on a statement concerning the judge's racial views that he hoped would allay the Quakers' objections. In the resulting letter Parker made a vague promise impartially to uphold the Constitution and denied any racial prejudice. The statement repudiated neither Parker's 1920 statement favoring disfranchisement nor the Republican's lily-whitism, but its saccharin phrases and Parker's genial personality were enough to hook Taylor; he emerged from the meeting enchanted with Parker and stated his intentions to dissolve the Quakers' opposition.[37]

The acting secretary was disturbed by this turn of events, and he rushed to Washington the following day to meet with Taylor and other members of the Committee on Race Relations. All save Helen Bryan, who would play a prominent role a few years hence in the NAACP's drive for a federal antilynching law, were prepared to accept "at face value" Parker's statements that his speeches on disfranchisement during his race for the governor were made in the heat of the campaign and that he would respect the rights of all people. White argued vigorously; accepting Parker's letter, he said, would be disastrous and a retreat from "the high ethical stand" that the Quakers had taken. After three hours, he prevailed, forestalling an endorsement that "would have been almost disastrous in the fight against Parker."[38]

With White's success at keeping the Quakers in line, the drive against Parker's confirmation gained momentum while the judge's position steadily deteriorated. The acting secretary headed to the Midwest, speaking to branches and mass meetings in Chicago, Detroit, and Cleveland, from which hundreds of telegrams were sent to their respective senators. While White pressured senators on their home turf, the Friends in Washington cornered senators in their offices, and the newly reenergized Robert Taylor spent an entire day lobbying them via telephone just before the confirmation vote. White credited newspapermen Ernest

Gruening and Ludwell Denny with an assist for keeping him informed daily of senators' latest thinking and vacillations and providing confidential information about Parker's supporters. So armed, the NAACP could squeeze wavering legislators and, in one critical instance, foil a plan for the Senate to meet in executive session, which would have kept secret the vote on Parker. With a roll call vote assured, the NAACP-led coalition mustered enough votes to block John Parker's ascension to the Supreme Court. After a Senate debate, in which many opponents denounced his labor record and Robert Wagner from New York linked his anti-worker history to his support for white supremacy, the full Senate on May 7 voted 41–39 against confirmation. Nationally, the press declared the American Federation of Labor to be ineffectual and either scorned or praised the NAACP for its leadership of the campaign.[39]

Walter White gave credit for the successful campaign to the association's branches, which, he said, were exemplary both in taking the initiative and in responding to directives from the national office. Daisy Lampkin had a slightly different perspective on national-local relations. Some branches were fully engaged in the national political fight. In the midst of the Parker affair, the Indianapolis branch launched a membership drive; it was "on its toes" and was "using the Parker Victory" as a selling point. In this instance, the association's "glorious victory" was being shared by an active branch. In Cleveland too the NAACP's support from other organizations and individuals had never been higher, and it enjoyed greater prestige than ever before.[40]

Yet even as the acting secretary and the national organization were basking in praise, Lampkin warned, many branches remained on the sidelines. The association in Toledo seemed to have nothing to do with the campaign. More indicative of the activists' disposition was their bristling at the national office's demand for money, in this case an insistence that the women's auxiliary hand over the proceeds of a whist tournament, for which the women had plans. "Sometimes," Lampkin chided the acting secretary, "we lose more by letting the people think that all we want is money, rather than giving them a chance to carry out their own plans." The conundrum, to Lampkin, was that quite often the branches' plans were inchoate and they were unable to utilize the favorable conditions created by the Parker campaign. Writing of efforts in several Indiana and Ohio localities, Lampkin offered this analysis: "It is true everyone is interested in the Parker fight, but it is equally true that there is a diffusion, and only when special effort is put forth, as I am doing down here, are we going to get large results."[41]

Synchronizing the branches and the national office and stimulating and sustaining independent local activity were two important goals the acting secretary hoped to achieve when the NAACP extended its anti-Parker campaign to work for the defeat of pro-Parker senators in the 1930 elections. In May the national office announced that it would work against Henry Allen of Kansas, and in July it officially opposed Roscoe McCulloch of Ohio. Robert Bagnall, national director of branches, stumped throughout the Sunflower state; though Allen won the party primary, the association, in coalition with labor and disgruntled farmers, turned him out in the general election. White concentrated on Ohio, a state with a larger African American population and a more developed NAACP infrastructure in the form of a state conference of branches.[42]

Opinion within the association was divided on whether to oppose McCulloch. Some of the association's leaders in Ohio favored maintaining nonpartisanship as a practical matter. Jesse Heslip, a Toledo attorney who would later serve on the association's legal committee, argued that blacks were unaccustomed to voting for Democrats and that despite his support for Parker, McCulloch would win the majority of their votes. Wendell Dabney of the Cincinnati branch agreed with Heslip's assessment and for that reason proposed a "gum shoe campaign" against McCulloch. A silent campaign would have several beneficial effects. It had the potential to prevent a coalescing of white voters for McCulloch. And in the event of his expected victory, the NAACP would have a "splendid alibi," while the association would still be able to claim credit should the Republican be upset. Harry Davis, a Cleveland civil service commissioner and NAACP board member, also weighed in against a campaign. He believed McCulloch was not that bad and pointed to his support of the Dyer antilynching bill when he was a representative; his opponent, Democrat Robert Bulkley, would have voted for Parker too, he believed. On a practical level, Davis pointed to Ohio's Republican tradition and worried that a defeat would damage the NAACP's hard-won prestige.[43]

The acting secretary was ranged on the other side of the argument. Taking a stand against McCulloch was vital to the future credibility of the association. "The future attitude, especially in Washington, towards the Negro and, specifically, towards the NAACP will in large measure depend upon whether or not we make good on statements made during the

Parker fight that we would vote for those who voted against Parker and oppose those senators who voted for confirmation." While he was not unsympathetic to the dilemmas of black Republican leaders like Harry Davis who wanted to tread cautiously, he believed the calls for nonpartisanship came primarily from branch leaders who were connected to the Republican Party and who were trying to aid their own partisan activities. Daisy Lampkin moved beyond various leaders' hesitations by pointing out that "it seems to be taken for granted . . . that the Negroes of Ohio are expected to oppose him [McCulloch]. There seems to be no question in their minds as to this." Despite continued misgivings within the association about becoming involved in a political campaign, the Ohio conference of branches was given approval to oppose McCulloch; though the campaign was run primarily by state officials, it had significant support from White, Du Bois, and others on the national staff.[44]

Of course, despite his assurance that the association's activities would be strictly anti-McCulloch, the acting secretary recognized the untenability of this position. In the midst of the campaign, he accepted an invitation to meet with Robert Bulkley, the Democratic candidate, and inched toward supporting him. He continued to protest to the black press that the NAACP was anti-McCulloch, but, he reasoned, "if in advising Negroes to vote against McCulloch we are able to make public a statement by Bulkley of his attitude if elected, we will doubly insure the effectiveness of what we do against McCulloch." White found himself favorably impressed with Bulkley's stands on African Americans—he promised to support a federal antilynching law, equal school funding, and enforcement of the Fourteenth and Fifteenth Amendments—and his friendly disposition to the cause of labor, both of which made the acting secretary stump enthusiastically for him.[45]

On hearing that the Republicans were set to dispatch prominent African Americans to Ohio to campaign for McCulloch, White proposed to send a "friendly letter" to Moton, Perry Howard, and former Booker T. Washington personal secretary Emmet Scott explaining the exact reasons for the NAACP's position and "drop[ping] a gentle but firm hint that the NAACP does not expect them to try to pull McCulloch's chestnuts out of the fire." Then he hit the campaign trail in the closing weeks, crisscrossing Ohio to help give the NAACP work a higher profile. At a Cincinnati rally sponsored jointly by the Baptist Alliance and Interdenominational Ministerial Alliance, several ministers were moved to declare their support for the acting secretary, but when a local black Republican operative rose to contradict White, the audience became indignant at the "paid political hireling" and moved to adjourn. The acting secretary was also enthusiastically received on his Lincoln League–sponsored swing through the eastern half of the state, despite black Republicans' attempts to disrupt his speeches.[46]

The climax came in Columbus at the last rally two days before the November 4 election. According to eyewitness Geraldyne Freeland, a group of African Americans in the pay of the Republican senatorial campaign planned to heckle White and in the ensuing confusion to turn it into a rally for McCulloch. But when White heard that their leader, the Reverend J. C. Olden, was in the crowd, he invited him to the stage and read the speech that Olden had just given to a rally of his supporters. (The speech had been copied down by Freedland, a local NAACP official who had herself infiltrated that meeting.) White's rendition was accompanied by mordant commentary, which thoroughly deflated Olden. According to Freeland, pandemonium reigned, and afterward the audience thronged the acting secretary: "The crowd was wild to touch him, to speak to him, to do homage to him. When we came out of the entrance . . . a cheer rolled up and down the street like thunder: 'WHAT'S THE MATTER WITH WALTER WHITE. HE'S ALL RIGHT. WHO'S ALL RIGHT. *WALTER WHITE*.' "[47]

Bulkley squeaked by with an 80,000-vote margin of victory, which the acting secretary claimed African Americans provided. This was only partially accurate. An analysis by Harry Davis indicated that the large black electorate in Cleveland still went for McCulloch, while Bulkley benefited from organized labor and voters who wanted an end to Prohibition or who blamed Republicans for the 1929 Depression.[48] But because it came out on the winning side, the NAACP could justly claim credit.

This foray into electoral politics was, in the words of one historian, "a precursor to the New Deal coalition." In the drive to defeat Parker and his supporters, two members of that coalition—African Americans and organized labor—worked separately for a common goal; the AFL, with the exception of the Brotherhood of Sleeping Car Porters, did not even recognize blacks' claims. With the demonstrated power of the NAACP would come labor's cooperation on such future issues as federal anti-lynching legislation and the organization of African American workers in the automobile industry, for example. In these endeavors the NAACP would gain the sympathetic attention of northern New Dealers, like Senator Robert Wagner of New York. But, as shall be demonstrated shortly, the alliance would never be completely cemented, as organized labor resisted the NAACP's attempts to subject unions to the antidiscrimination laws it was fighting to have Congress enact. Still, shaky though the later New Deal coalition was, the anti-McCulloch campaign pointed to the future, and it also signaled increased NAACP involvement in politics.[49]

For the acting secretary personally, the election in Ohio was a highwater mark of his career. He developed better access to the legislative branch of government and cultivated closer ties with the fourth estate. His bold declarations and their translation into action won him a measure of confidence from the board of directors, which would, after another four months of apprenticeship, officially anoint White secretary of the association. He earned increased visibility and public recognition as a race leader of central importance. He began to receive laudatory letters like the following, which was delivered after he spoke in Toledo: "For those of us Negroes who struggle in the wilderness, insisting on the great advance and achievements of the Negro and the high places he commands, it is a boon to be able—at least now and then—to point to an example; to be able to say 'behold—here in the flesh is what we are talking about!' "[50]

Walter White's reaction to an incident on a Memphis-bound train in March 1931 led him to squander nearly entirely the considerable political cachet he had so meticulously accumulated. Scottsboro still survives in American memory. On the twenty-fifth of that month as the train steamed through the Alabama countryside, a group of African American youths, tramping in search of work, scuffled with a similarly situated group of whites. The blacks, feeling that they had as much right as anyone else to hop a freight car, refused to give ground when the white vagrants tried to enforce Jim Crow. A fight ensued, and the whites, who lost, fled the train and complained to the nearest railroad official. When the train pulled into the Paint Rock, Alabama, depot, law officers were there to roust the black hoboes. They arrested nine teenage males and, much to everyone's surprise, two white women, prostitutes who were riding the rails. Fearing their own arrest under the Mann Act, the two claimed they had been raped by the nine teens, including one, Willie

Roberson, whose body was so infected by syphilis as to make him sexually dysfunctional. As the small-town crowd outside the jail grew and became more menacing, the sheriff contacted the governor; 100 national guardsmen were dispatched to the scene, the prisoners were spirited away to the county seat of Scottsboro, and white Alabama congratulated itself on preventing a lynching. Twelve days later the nine, forever after dubbed the "Scottsboro Boys," were convicted of rape, and eight were condemned to death.

The NAACP as a whole was slow to respond to this miscarriage of justice—*dithered* might be a more apt descriptor. The branch nearest Scottsboro was in Chattanooga, and it was barely functional. Nevertheless, local NAACP leader P. A. Stephens secured, under the auspices of the Interdenominational Ministerial Alliance, counsel for the defendants. Chattanooga attorney Stephen Roddy arrived in Scottsboro inebriated and barely in time to meet with his clients before their trial. To the secretary, however, this was of little consequence. Only two things mattered, White told Stephens: that Roddy ensure that a proper trial transcript was prepared and sent to New York for the NAACP legal committee's inspection, and that Stephens maintain contact with the nine and make sure they did not enter into any agreements with the Communist Party's International Labor Defense (ILD) until the NAACP had decided whether or not to defend them. A month passed before the association entered the case, but by then the situation was far more complicated, as the Communist Party (CP or CPUSA) had established itself as the leading defender of the accused.[51]

Since the early twenties, the CP had worked to attract African American support for its revolutionary program. It had demonstrated admirable commitment—it was practically alone among white liberals, progressives, and radicals in its practice of militant interracialism and its demand for racial equality—but had enjoyed limited success. Scottsboro presented the CP with a cause célèbre on the order of Sacco and Vanzetti. Through its national and international contacts, its disregard for respectability, and its combination of mass pressure and legal acumen, the Communists offered the black freedom struggle unprecedented world exposure and an alternative to the NAACP. The NAACP had a venerable record of defending Afro-America's legal rights, especially in the judicial arena, having secured Supreme Court victories against residential segregation laws, the grandfather clause, and the white primary. But the pace of reform was slow, and, buffeted by the Great Depression, African Americans were desperate for more rapid change and open to radical paths. Patience, especially when it could be construed as indifference, was not a virtue, all the more so when the association justified its apparent inactivity by resting on its past record.

At its first meeting following the incident, the board of directors, unaware of—or perhaps oblivious to—black America's mounting indignation and desire to do something to protest the arrests and verdicts, contented itself with taking note of the sham nature of the legal proceedings; it voted to send an investigator to Alabama, but expressly decided not to send the secretary. Inexplicably, White made the trip anyway, but by then more than two additional weeks had slipped away. When he finally met with the Scottsboro defendants and their parents in Birmingham's Kilby Prison, it was already May. The CP had given the case a high profile, the defendants and their parents were inclined to continue their relationship with the party, and Walter White had his work cut out for him to convince them otherwise.[52]

The secretary handicapped himself from the beginning by betraying prejudices against blacks who were not from the middle class; he tried not at all to conceal his contempt for the defendants and their parents. To more than one correspondent, he broadcast his estimate of the "ignorance and stupidity of the boys' parents." The defendants were "illiterate," which to him meant they were easily manipulated by flattery and flamboyance. And searching for an explanation for their resistance to his considerable powers of persuasion, the secretary dismissed them as "the type of Negro who would believe anything said by a white man, no matter how absurd, in preference to what might be said by the finest and most trustworthy Negro alive." (The CP's lawyers who met with the defendants were white.) It was apparent that the secretary neither fully comprehended the black working class nor felt comfortable in their presence. After the meetings, and while the defendants and their parents vacillated on whether the NAACP or the CP would represent them in appealing the verdicts, the secretary, with more than a hint of frustration, blamed the board for the entanglement with the Communists. "Our chief mistake lies in my not coming down here at the very beginning as I wanted to. All this mess would then have been obviated."[53]

"This mess" was both an avalanche of criticism of the NAACP and a nasty free-for-all with the Communists that only increased with time.

When the NAACP finally withdrew from the case a year later, after it became clear it could not dislodge the CPUSA, the association had taken a beating in public opinion. The black press criticized the association's indifference to the defendants' fates and criticized the NAACP for anti-CP invective, which increasingly became its chief activity in this case. The *Baltimore Afro-American* called for the NAACP to end its obstructionism and work out an agreement with the ILD. The *Washington World* lamented the association's recent actions. "The spirit of the NAACP seems to be changed," stated editor Eugene Davidson, an important figure in black Washington.

> The association has done a great deal of good in the past. It has been our leading organ for fighting our enemies. But it has outlived its usefulness if it now feels that fighting the spread of communism is more important than fighting white Southerners who will lynch, massacre and slaughter and expect to get away with it.

The *Pittsburgh Courier* and the *Chicago Defender* echoed these sentiments.[54]

To these charges, the secretary responded testily and evasively. Roddy's presence at the defense table, alcoholic though it may have been, was sufficient proof that the NAACP had been interested in the case from the beginning. More, White insisted, the black press had no right to call into question the association's commitment to Scottsboro, given its twenty-two-year history of struggle. The NAACP was silent, White said, because it needed to make sure of the facts of the case. He now believed the defendants were innocent, but he hedged his bet with the statement that even if they were guilty they deserved a better defense. In any event, he claimed that he *had* acted by securing the services of Roderick Beddow, one of the best criminal lawyers in Alabama. All would work out, he implied, if only the association was allowed to continue its quiet work and the CP was muzzled.[55]

When dissent bubbled up from within the association's ranks, the secretary bristled. He tried to contain himself when association members demanded that White account for his queer silence. To the branches he replied that the reasons for the silence were "obvious" and "we shall make public in due course, when it is wise for us to do so, the part which we are taking in these cases."[56] But his even temper failed him when William

Pickens and Roy Wilkins, the former newspaperman from the *Kansas City Call* who had only recently been installed as White's second-in-command, in separate instances called into question the NAACP's passivity on the case. In an unguarded moment and unaware that the NAACP was planning to enter the case, Pickens wrote a letter enclosing a check to the CP's *Daily Worker* stating, "This is one occasion for every Negro who has intelligence enough to read, to send aid to you and the ILD." The board unanimously condemned him for disloyalty, Mary White Ovington sharply called him to task, and the secretary quickly denounced his remarks and demanded that he retract them and repudiate the CP.[57]

The comments by Wilkins, whom White ardently recruited to join the national staff, cut the secretary the deepest. With White on the road performing triage on the NAACP's reputation, Wilkins had been the one initially to field the criticism from the black press. Because the association had provided no news of its activities vis-à-vis Scottsboro, Wilkins told his boss, he was reduced to rewriting the Communists' own news releases for redistribution as NAACP press releases. White, said Wilkins, needed to do away with fact-based reporting of Scottsboro and move toward a crusading type of journalism typical of past NAACP campaigns. Feeling under siege, White rebuked Wilkins, practically accusing him of betrayal.[58]

If White's justifications for the NAACP's indolence on Scottsboro appear to be prevarication, the CP's explanations—that White and the NAACP were capitalist tools and wanted to see the defendants get the electric chair—are at least as mendacious. The outlandishness of these statements derive from the Communists' gross miscalculation that worldwide capitalism was entering its penultimate stage—or "third period," as the Communist International termed it. In this phase of ever-increasing capitalist destabilization, the working class and its allies (including, in this country, African Americans) would grow more revolutionary. The chief obstacles to this radicalization were, in the CP's estimation, the labor aristocracy, which was entrenched in the American Federation of Labor, and so-called petit bourgeois nationalists like Walter White and others in the NAACP. As the capitalists' principal social prop among African Americans, the NAACP had to be thoroughly exposed.[59] Rather than reflecting the secretary's desire to do the capitalists' bidding, the NAACP's calamitous showing in Scottsboro indicated White's smugness, his reliance on a flawed strategy, and animosity toward the CP based not on ideological antipathy but on more quotidian considerations.[60]

It was axiomatic to White that the NAACP had written the script for civil rights victory and any deviation from it would be disastrous. He was content to let the Scottsboro cases wend their ways through the legal system. White tried to persuade the ILD to accept Clarence Darrow and Arthur Garfield Hays as counsel for the appeal process; the plan was aborted when the eminent attorneys refused to sever their ties with the NAACP unless the ILD attorneys did likewise. But even before this outcome was clear, the secretary, without consulting the ILD, announced that the appeal would be based on *Moore* v. *Dempsey*, the association's successful appeal of the 1919 Arkansas riot cases. Street demonstrations, incendiary agitation, mass pressure directed at Alabama officials, polemics—mainstays of the CP's extralegal activity—were, in the secretary's opinion, not only ephemeral and disruptive, they were also historically irrelevant. As he explained it to James Weldon Johnson, if the CP lost the appeal, people would blame them for botching the legal work, which was the NAACP's specialty. But if the party won, White said, people would recognize that the victory was possible only because of the association's triumph in 1919. Credit would accrue to the NAACP if it only stood pat, save for raising money for the defense fund. Johnson, who, unlike his former protégé, was not complacent, shot back that hardly anyone remembered, let alone understood, the NAACP's legal arguments in those cases anymore, so credit was not likely to be forthcoming. If the NAACP wanted accolades, it would have to work for them; victory was not inevitable, and the NAACP's competitors would not fall by the wayside.[61]

The secretary's desire to keep a low profile in the Scottsboro case flowed from a strategic belief that the best way to achieve results was to rely on the reasonableness of liberal whites, especially the southern variety; as an investigator for the American Civil Liberties Union, which was trying to effect an entente cordiale between the NAACP and the ILD, put it, White preferred "working quietly with as little publicity as possible, through liberal contacts in the south wherever possible."[62] But southern liberals were not a homogenous cohort. There were dedicated and consistent fighters for Negro rights, people like Howard "Buck" Kester, the theologian, Socialist Party activist, and Southern Tenant Farmers Union organizer. But most white liberals, while they were disconcerted by the Scottsboro verdicts, did not see Scottsboro's miscarriage of justice as a systemic problem, and they demanded that any protest be moderate, polite, and defer to the Jim Crow order. Central to their worldview was the belief that although white supremacy imposed some inconveniences on some African Americans, communism presented a signal danger to whites' way of life. As the secretary tried to persuade southern liberals to join him in the Scottsboro campaign, he was faced with the fact that they were willing to allow the defendants to die so long as the CP was involved in their cases.

In the early stages of the appeals process, some southern liberals were willing to support a commutation of the sentences; none, apparently, considered that the defendants were innocent and should be freed.[63] Somewhat later, but before the U.S. Supreme Court had reversed the convictions, Will Alexander of the CIC thought he could convince his milieu to support mercy, but only conditionally: "I shall go ahead laying the plans for as powerful an appeal as can be made for executive clemency, and I think there is a good chance for success if it is not complicated by the communists."[64] In a report to the secretary on his visit to Alabama, William Pickens related a damning conversation he had on this topic. "[Stephen] Roddy [the original defense attorney] told me confidentially that Judge Hawkins [who presided over the trial] told him before the hearings yesterday that the CHIEF ISSUE now is the REDS,—that if they were out of it, it might be simpler; that he (the trial judge) did not really think the boys should be put to death, but that the Communists are more of an issue than are the FACTS of the case. God, what a mess, and what a savage confession!"[65] Buck Kester echoed this assessment. Proclaiming the defendants' innocence, Kester nevertheless concluded that the best that one could hope for under the circumstances was a 12–15 year sentence, with a later possibility of pardon. Enlightened white opinion was pleased enough that the boys had not been lynched; it was not likely to concede anything more so long as the CP was in the picture.[66]

Dispiriting as this must have been to the secretary, he continued to try to cultivate the thin soil of southern liberal humanity. White believed he faced a Hobson's choice. He was not anticommunist on principle, but embracing it was a condition of promoting an alliance with the "better class of Alabamians" and other southerners, as Roderick Beddow, White's impeccable choice for Scottsboro defense counsel, put it. And from the secretary's and others' perspective, there were few alternative allies. Organized labor continued its hostility, and northern liberals their indifference. (As late as 1939, a prominent financial backer of the association, Godfrey Cabot, excoriated Walter White for his belief that the Scottsboro nine were innocent. In Cabot's view, this was a "preposterous statement" and an "attempt to beatify two negroes [*sic*] of a decidedly low type." White's statements, tepid as they were, placed the NAACP "in a somewhat similar position to that of the Sacco-Vanzetti sympathizers."[67]) This strategy would bedevil the secretary throughout the thirties in the NAACP's campaign for federal antilynching legislation. He was only able to modify it when labor modulated its views, and African Americans began to shake off en masse their somnolence in the forties.

White's combat with the Communists is frequently taken as a sign of hard-shelled conservatism. With Scottsboro coinciding with the onset of a full-scale debate within the NAACP over whether it should augment its traditional drive for constitutional rights with direct-action tactics (discussed in detail in the following chapter), the secretary is made out to be hidebound and backward looking. But White's anticommunism was grounded in pragmatic considerations, not in ideology; he was anti–Communist Party but not anticommunist. Even this opposition was contingent, judging from the evolution of his position since he joined the association's national staff.

Race came first for White, as it did for most black activists of the day. In a friendly exchange with W. A. Domingo, a Harlem radical who cooperated closely with the CP but never joined it, White explained his reluctance to embrace socialism: "I am quite convinced," he wrote, "that the Negro both in America and in other parts of the world has got to keep his head and not rush blindly into any panacea which looks favorable. Certain it is that whatever the form of government or whatever arrangement of society there may be, the Negro must take under consideration under any regime the fact that race prejudice in the long run is more ingrained than prejudices for and against any economic system."[68]

The economic crisis in the thirties stimulated White's colleagues critically to engage radical ideas. W.E.B. Du Bois probed the applicability of Marxism and the class struggle in his essay "Marxism and the Negro Problem." In two prominent articles for the *Journal of Negro Education*, Ralph Bunche attacked what he saw as the limitations of race-advancement movements that were based on the reform of the capitalist system. James Weldon Johnson's *Negro Americans, What Now?* seriously weighed the strategic value of communism for African Americans, as did a host of editors of black newspapers.[69] But Walter White, much in the manner he framed aesthetic discussions during the Harlem Renaissance or other social or political questions, looked at communism and the Communist Party far more narrowly: What was its effect on the NAACP? For example, at a time when J. Edgar Hoover's Bureau of Investigation (BI) was subjecting the NAACP to intense scrutiny, White was willing to provide it vague bits of information in order to throw the bureau off the NAACP's trail. In October 1919, he voluntarily reported to the BI's radical division his "belief that a well known white radical" was agitating among black New Yorkers for them to hold "a monster demonstration" to "demand their 'rights.' " He went on to define the NAACP as the responsible alternative to radical chaos. There is no evidence that the BI "turned" White into a regular source of intelligence.[70]

But for most of the twenties and early thirties, White was unconcerned by the Communists. If anything, he welcomed their presence because they spiced up the literary and cultural scene in New York. The growing affinity of Claude McKay, Countee Cullen, and Langston Hughes for the CP did not stop him from maintaining close relations with them. He still tried to raise living expenses for McKay, sought a producer for one of Cullen's plays, and encouraged Hughes to join the NAACP campaign against lynching—even after Hughes did a hatchet job on White in a Soviet publication.[71]

But he was also friendly with Robert Minor, the white Texan in charge of the party's Negro work, and his wife Lydia Gibson. The Minors and the Whites spent time in each other's homes. On a political level, the Minors felt comfortable enough in the mid-twenties asking White to recommend "alert, intelligent, race-conscious people of the working class point of view" for study in the Soviet Union. For his part, White kept the Minors up to date on important NAACP campaigns.[72]

Things remained more or less cordial between the NAACP and the Communists into 1930. The association still focused much of its energy on the legal system, and in particular on defending African Americans who were unjustly accused of crimes or who received obviously unfair trials. The International Labor Defense, which by 1930 was taking over much of the party's Negro work, was championing similar cases. In May 1930, six Communists—two white men, two black men, and two white women—were arrested in Atlanta on charges of inciting an insurrection.

The NAACP was among the first organizations the ILD contacted for assistance in defending the Atlanta Six. After some debate, the NAACP declined, yet neither White nor the other association officers avoided the ILD, despite the best advice of white southern liberals like Will Alexander. White apparently saw the wisdom of the ILD's opinion that "the indignation these cases has arouzed [sic], not among radical alone, but among liberal elements, and with 'old fashioned Americans,' is sufficient to assure you that it does not come within narrow limits which might take some case outside the interest of the NAACP." The NAACP, itself strapped for cash, contributed $200, or approximately 10 percent of the total cost, to the defense fund. When friends of the association asked what the NAACP was doing about the Atlanta Six, White invited them to contribute money to the ILD too.[73]

But relations between the NAACP and the CP soon deteriorated, and the reasons do not lay only or mainly in the association's botched handling of the Scottsboro case. Rather, their most energetic disputes centered around money—$100,000 to be exact. In late 1929 the NAACP applied to the left-wing American Fund for Public Service, or Garland Fund, for grants; it proposed to use the funds to launch a campaign against educational inequality, a campaign that in fact culminated in *Brown* v. *Board of Education.* Garland Fund board member Roger Baldwin, who was also a leading member of the American Civil Liberties Union, seriously doubted the viability of the association's plan. He preferred to place philanthropic dollars in the hands of the Communist-led American Negro Labor Congress (ANLC) for the purpose of organizing black workers. But at the end of May 1930, the committee charged with allocating the foundation's funds to race-advancement work decided to make the award to the NAACP, despite the best efforts of Clarina Michelson, the Communists' representative on that body.[74] Prior to the end of May, the CP was both restrained and selective in its criticism of the NAACP. The overwhelming majority of articles on blacks were silent on the association and singled out for vituperation A. Philip Randolph and the Brotherhood of Sleeping Car Porters, with whom the ANLC had an active dispute. Only articles signed by James Ford, a party leader in Negro work, and articles about his work singled out NAACP leaders like James Weldon Johnson, W.E.B. Du Bois, and William Pickens as "lackeys to imperialism" and "Negro Capitalists and reformists."[75]

As both James Weldon Johnson and Walter White made clear, they did not disagree with the ANLC's program, which covered workers' rights, discrimination within organized labor, civil rights, and solidarity with Africa and the Caribbean. Its principles were fine, said the NAACP leaders, though they were overgeneral. But the ANLC had no track record to speak of and proposed no specific strategies or tactics, while in each programmatic area the NAACP had a wealth of experiences. Nor was the secretary particularly averse to the strategic revolutionary goal of the Communists. As Walter White put it in a defense of the NAACP's work:

> We all want to see the millennium, but millennia don't just happen. It takes many years of preparation and of hard, unremitting work to bring about the millennium or anything approximating it. Consider, for example, Russia. It is a well known fact that only a small percentage of Russians resident in Russia today are members of the Communist Party. I point to that as a somewhat analogous situation to that of the Negro in America, in that all forward looking movements are minority movements.[76]

Reviewing the NAACP's activity, White and Johnson felt that, given the American Federation of Labor's racism, a concentration on labor issues— and the association had given support to Randolph's Pullman porters union—was the area least likely to see a breakthrough.[77]

It appears that the Communist Party began its polemics against the NAACP not when Scottsboro erupted in March 1931, but nearly a year earlier when the association was awarded $100,000.[78] But despite the attacks, some of which were quite outlandish, the NAACP retained a neutral public stance. In September 1930, White testified at length before a House of Representatives special committee on Communist activity among African Americans. As committee members tried to bait him, White maintained that the NAACP was neither pro- nor anticommunist, that Communists were welcome to join the association so long as they adhered to the program, that the ANLC, while sharply critical of the NAACP, did not set itself up in opposition to it. Even when the CP lobbed salvos at the NAACP at the beginnings of Scottsboro, the association's board of directors and national staff believed it unwise to "enter into any dispute with the Communists."[79]

White's apparent openness turned to alarm, however, when the black press and black mass opinion took notice of the CP's energetic response to Scottsboro and the NAACP's lethargy, which the secretary preferred to think of as deliberate and timely, but not necessarily speedy, action. The CP had gotten a jump on the NAACP, which, in the words of an ACLU official friendly with him, had "gotten sadly under your skin. . . . [Y]ou are good and sore and can't help showing it."[80] More, White believed, the Communists' campaign of disruption, which appealed to large numbers of African Americans whose hope for justice within the system was completely spent, threatened the NAACP's financial health. Significantly, White did not worry that white liberals would stop sending the NAACP money if the association came into proximity of the Communists. Rather the threat of insolvency appeared when Communists were arrested, because they appealed for bail money to the Garland Fund, which then diverted funds originally promised to the NAACP. Thus, his polemics, like the typical "The Negro and the Communists," which appeared in *Harper's* in December 1931. For the next several years, White kept up a steady attack on the Communist Party, all with a leitmotif that they coveted the $100,000 grant from the Garland Fund.[81]

But if the secretary was correct in identifying the CP's covetousness as the factor driving the organizations' mutual animosity, the CP had legitimate complaints against the NAACP too. Black churches were likely the most fecund spots to raise money for race-advancement causes, and the NAACP actively worked to deny the CP a hearing there. At the same time, White treated the clergy, which largely supported him, and their flock as the association's cash reserves. In August 1931, the NAACP planned a "Scottsboro Defense Fund Sunday," during which it would collect donations from churches. But at the secretary's direction, collections were to go to the association's general fund rather than the Scottsboro defense fund; the church appeal was to name Scottsboro as "an outstanding instance of the work of the Association," as opposed to a case for which the NAACP was actively soliciting donations.[82]

Upon its withdrawal from the case in January 1932, the NAACP claimed that it had collected about $7,000 for the defense from branches and individuals and other organizations and that it had expended about $100 more than it had taken in. But one must look at this sum skeptically, as it refers only to dedicated donations. The actual amount of Scottsboro-related donations was likely much higher; the secretary intimated as much when, in the cash-strapped year of 1932, the association gave $1,000 to the ILD lawyer who handled the appeal to the Supreme Court.

If White thought this might earn some relief from CP attacks, the CP believed the time was long past for reciprocation; the Communists issued a statement that "the International Labor Defense accepts this $1,000 as only part payment of the money collected by the NAACP under the pretext of defending the Scottsboro boys." The record appears to support charges of financial deceit. Three years after the association withdrew, the NAACP still was sitting on funds it had raised for Scottsboro.[83]

Finally realizing that it could neither dislodge the CP nor come close to winning a public relations war with them, the NAACP withdrew from the Scottsboro case in January 1932. Its nine-month involvement had been an unqualified disaster. The impact of its legal maneuvering, for which it had become justly famous, was ephemeral.[84] Most of the NAACP work on the case consisted of attacks on the CP and ILD, for which the association's reputation rightly suffered. The secretary still enjoyed support from the board of directors, especially those members who were branch presidents and who were involved in the organization's legal work, like Arthur Spingarn and Charles Studin. (Other board members liked him personally, even if they had some criticism of his work style.)[85]

But rumbling in the near distance was a storm of dissatisfaction with the new secretary's leadership. A portion could be attributed to the recent debacle, and he was keenly aware of the need for him to score a major victory in order to erase all memory of Scottsboro.[86] But other sources of discontent had nothing to do with the case—at least not directly. Some members of the national staff as well as important workers in the national office disliked what they saw as the secretary's imperiousness. And emanating from certain quarters of the association's membership was the conviction that the NAACP needed to respond more directly, effectively, and creatively to African Americans' ever worsening straits brought on by the Great Depression. In short, challenges arose from all sides. The next several years would be steeped in tumult. And they would be complicated by personal misfortunes that would strike Walter White.

Chapter 6

A Hard Decade

On January 4, 1931, James Weldon Johnson, recently retired from the NAACP and soon to become the first Adam K. Spence Professor of Creative Literature at Fisk University, took his place at the lectern to address the NAACP's winter mass rally, a gathering that traditionally capped the association's annual business meeting. In pro forma fashion he reflected on the association's growth since its formation more than two decades earlier. Then, its program was considered radical, and it frightened most favorably disposed whites. Now, however, the NAACP not only had taken root among African Americans across the nation, it had fostered a climate that attracted whites. But under conditions of heightened economic and social distress brought on by the Depression, success brought with it a bevy of criticism; as some in the black political class stumbled toward a kind of nationalism and professed shades of exclusive racial self-reliance, the prominent role of the Spingarn brothers, Mary White Ovington, and other progressive whites came under sharp scrutiny. It was being alleged in Harlem circles, Johnson said, that he retired because Joel Spingarn had been elected association president. The same mills were also churning out rumors that he was dissatisfied with the performance of his successor, Walter White, who doggedly pursued the integrationist program. So troubling was this gossip that Johnson felt compelled to refute them. Reports of dissension within the NAACP had the ulterior purpose of injecting "a poisonous racial chauvinism into the association";

certainly African Americans had to cultivate racial pride, but forsaking the friendship of whites like Clarence Darrow, Moorfield Storey, or Florence Kelley was counterproductive. As for Walter White, Johnson professed only admiration for him and the job he and the national staff had done in his absence.[1]

Johnson's imprimatur may have stopped the rumors, but his statement did little to arrest the discontent within the ranks of the national staff. Du Bois's nationalist pronouncements in favor of self-segregation and group economic uplift would rattle the NAACP's windows a few years hence. For now, the static was caused by the new secretary's propensity to micro-manage office affairs, in bold relief to Johnson's style of setting a direction and allowing staff to develop a plan of implementation. Overlooking lower Manhattan from an upper floor of a loft building at 69 Fifth Avenue, near Fourteenth Street, the association's headquarters was a hive of activity. The largest portion of the office was taken up by an unpartitioned space that accommodated more than a dozen clerical employees. Here was handled, under the watchful eye of office manager Richetta Randolph, both the association's routine tasks, including the mimeograph and carbon-paper reproduction of a steady stream of press releases, and the materials and the periodic, frantic letter blitzes of legislators designed to influence votes on vital proposals, like the various antilynching bills. Behind this spacious work area were the executives' offices. Everyone knew not to disturb W.E.B. Du Bois in *The Crisis* office; he rarely passed out more than a curt greeting to the staff upon entering or leaving. The other leading administrators—White, assistant secretary Roy Wilkins, field secretary William Pickens, department of branches secretary Robert Bagnall, publicity director Herbert Seligmann—also were ensconced in comfortable offices. Each had his own secretary and clerical assistants, who occupied anterooms to their respective bosses. When the NAACP hired Charles Houston to form the legal department in 1933, the 5,500-square-foot space would become more crowded with attorneys and clerical workers.[2]

While lean by corporate standards, the NAACP's headquarters were larger than most advocacy groups' of its day; with the addition of its legal apparatus, it was almost certainly heftier than the Urban League's. Administrative activities were critical not only for raising the name recognition of the NAACP. They were essential to the fortification of the association's growing bureaucracy. For the past decade and more, the

NAACP had developed itself as an organization of civil rights profession-als. The executives, Walter White in particular, increasingly stressed both the primacy of the national office's activities and the branches' fi-nancial obligations to headquarters. In this context, the morale of the na-tional staff—executive, administrative, clerical—directly affected the implementation of the association's program. But in the early years of Walter White's regime, his leadership style threatened to suffocate the esprit de corps that his predecessor had nurtured.

Richetta Randolph's claustrophobia was palpable. "I am so disap-pointed by your letter this morning," she wrote to Johnson in October 1930, when he had requested six additional weeks of leave, at the end of which he would surprise the staff with his resignation. "Six weeks more! It seems I have existed here in the office these twelve months just because I knew that at the end of them you would be back. . . . Lots of things I have simply 'endured' just because I knew it wouldn't be so always. Now—six weeks more! It sounds like six years."[3]

White's sins, though venial, demoralized the staff and were cataloged in a series of memoranda and private letters. "Mr. White has tried to su-pervise everything in connection with the work," Ms. Randolph com-plained. "He included in this supervision of the outer office to a large extent, going over the time cards, checking up on the clerks, which is without question my part of the work." He demanded the clerical staff "rigidly adhere" to the policy of punching the time clock and began to deduct pay for both tardiness and failure to follow the rule. He forbade personal telephone calls, though one of his trusted assistants informed him that office workers were not abusing phone privileges. He even tried to regulate the toilet habits of the largely female clerical pool. At the same time, White was not above playing politics with employment, as when he hired and kept on an incompetent messenger, simply because he had promised officials at his children's private school that he would do so. During the first few years of his stewardship of the NAACP, White, in Queeg-like fashion, displayed both unseemly suspicion and a boorish lack of appreciation for the work of the office staff, even going so far as to threaten them with meager pay raises should they not "demonstrate the proper spirit."[4]

White's bureaucratic hand grabbed national staff officials too. He tried to regulate Robert Bagnall's working hours and loudly disapproved of youth secretary Juanita Jackson making a weekend visit to her family home in Baltimore. Publicity director Herbert Seligmann came under particular scrutiny for sending out letters to editors without showing them to White, despite the fact that the secretary's demand was neither past practice nor enforced on other staff executives. The new secretary dismissed Seligmann's complaints, accusing him of "lacking in team spirit." The publicity director soon found the office climate unbearable and quit on the last day of 1932.[5] Seligmann was the only immediate casualty of White's imperiousness, as the office staff preferred to remain loyal to the secretary—highly irritated, perhaps, but employed. But the association's executives watched with mounting anxiety as White attempted to accumulate authority in his hands.

Foremost among those sounding the alarums was W.E.B. Du Bois. Although Du Bois had heartily endorsed White's recruitment to the national staff in 1918, he soon took a dislike to the native Atlantan a quarter century his junior. The two were, of course, of opposite temperaments: the cerebral, worldly, aristocratic, stiffly formal Du Bois was annoyed by White, the informal, gregarious, middlebrow, action-oriented organizer. Du Bois knew White's prominent family in Atlanta, and though he had not, as many suppose, taught him at Atlanta University, White may have been his Latin student at the preparatory high school attached to AU. Was the editor offended by what he may have perceived as an absence of deference from the social leveler White? White's disinterest in the swirling theoretical debate on art and literature in the Harlem Renaissance disqualified him in the editor's eyes from ever being the association's chief executive; his eagerness to promote what Du Bois considered the salacious prose of Carl Van Vechten and Claude McKay and satisfy the cultural voyeurism of well-placed whites only reinforced Du Bois's impression of White as uncouth and unsophisticated or, alternately, a yappy, ankle-biting small dog.

Du Bois's pronounced personal distaste for White, though, was only a circumstance that aggravated discord. It overlay the increasingly acute competition for declining revenues and between different strategies for building the NAACP and the fight for racial equality. Ultimately, it compounded organizational friction, where goodwill would have been salubrious and helped find ground for compromise. But it was not the cause of the intra-association strife.

As *The Crisis* heaved along, buffeted by the same financial exigencies that affected the entire association and all of Negro America, the editor tried any number of ways to ensure the publication's fiscal health. In February 1930 he tried to lure Roy Wilkins, whom he believed to be energetic and enterprising, from the editorship of the *Kansas City Call* to join *The Crisis* staff as a business manager. (After some thought, Wilkins declined Du Bois's offer; the salary—$2,500 with the possibility of an equal amount in performance-based bonuses—was insufficient, and anyway he was exploring other avenues to advance his career.)[6] He was unable to make the publication pay for itself, and for the rest of the year, the editor insisted on cash infusions from the association. But prying funds from Walter White's hands proved nearly impossible. The secretary resisted Du Bois's proposal that between 30 and 50 percent of new members' dues be dedicated to keeping *The Crisis* afloat. White protested to the Rosenwald Foundation when it appeared to him that a donation to the association's general fund was reduced by an amount equal to that donated to the magazine. As the NAACP prepared its proposal to the Garland Fund for $100,000 to finance the challenge to segregated education, the secretary deleted *The Crisis* from the budget.[7]

Then, at the July board meeting, Du Bois asked the NAACP to take over the publication's finances while he continued to maintain editorial control. After he left the room to allow for full and frank discussion, the board, at Joel Spingarn's behest and with Walter White's endorsement, approved a takeover, with the caveat that *The Crisis* be tethered more tightly to the association. The resolution specified an editorial board of four on which White would sit. When the board returned from its summer break, it heard from Du Bois, who agreed to more oversight but who wanted to exclude White and include Du Bois ally Lillian Alexander on an editorial board of five. White won this round: he secured spots on *The Crisis* board for himself and Seligmann and kept Alexander off. It appeared as if the curtain was beginning to descend on two decades of Du Bois's virtual independence in the propaganda department.[8]

The editor's impressions of White's coarseness likely were not shared by other association executives. Nevertheless, Du Bois could count on support from Bagnall, Seligmann, Pickens, and even the newly arrived Wilkins, who in mid-1931 had taken White's old job of assistant secretary. They believed that White lacked integrity and operated on a double standard in regard to finances. In January 1931, when it became all but certain that White would be named Johnson's permanent replacement, Du Bois moved to restrict the powers of the secretary's office. When

Pickens was disciplined in 1929 for taking unauthorized leave, the board passed a resolution stating that the secretary was the "executive officer of this Association, and that all employees and all officers receiving a salary from the Association shall be subject to his authority." This was fine so long as Johnson was the secretary. But now that White's ascendance to the post was imminent, Du Bois warned Arthur Spingarn, the situation would be unbearable; the resolution now was "drastic" and even included him, threatening his much cherished editorial and political independence. He proposed the resolution be amended to circumscribe the secretary's supervisory powers over the other salaried executives. Bagnall backed these "minimum regulations which would permit harmonious relations in the new appointment of a Secretary," and he intimated that other executives did too. The February board meeting repealed the earlier resolution.[9]

The first sign that the fault line was poised to quake the organization came in mid-December. Despite Joel Spingarn's best efforts to husband the association's finances, austerity was the watchword for deflationary times. The board's budget committee, supplied with data by Walter White, recommended cuts in all salaries of between 5 and 10 percent and that *The Crisis's* operations be completely taken over by the association.[10] The secretary unfairly charged that neither the field nor *The Crisis* staffs were doing enough to raise funds and in any case were not bringing in enough to justify their remunerations. Du Bois, Seligmann, Pickens, Bagnall, and Wilkins erupted. In a collective letter to the board, they accused the secretary, abetted by board chair Ovington, of supplying false information to the budget committee and of lying about their performance to cover his own wastefulness. "The Secretary has absolute domination of these expenditures and practically reports to nobody," they wrote. "It would be possible, in our opinion, to save more by reasonable limitations of money wasted than by decreasing salaries or dismissing officials." The secretary's lack of integrity threatened to doom the association, they said. "Unless Mr. White is going to be more honest and straight-forward with his colleagues, more truthful in his statement of facts, more conscientious in his expenditures of money . . . the chief question before this organization is how long he can remain in his present position and keep the NAACP from utter disaster." Then came the final swipe: "We have all had considerable and varied experiences, but in our several careers, we have never met a man like Walter White who under an outward and charming manner has succeeded within a short time in alienating and antagonizing every one of his co-workers, including all the clerks in the office."[11]

The blow could not have come at a worse moment, as political fallout from Scottsboro and a series of personal traumas pressed in on White's world and took their toll on his mental well-being. The event that shook him to his foundations was the agonizing death of his father in November in Atlanta. On the sixteenth of that month, a Monday, Walter awoke to an airmail special delivery letter from his brother-in-law Eugene Martin informing him that his father had been hit by a car four days earlier. The letter was terse, and did not tell the entire story. While walking home from his daughter Olive Westmoreland's home, George White paused at the corner of Houston and Piedmont, only a few blocks from his house. Checking traffic, and carrying Olive's homemade pies back home for himself, his wife, and his daughter Madeline, Walter's father stepped from the curb and was run over by a reckless driver. When he was late returning home, Madeline searched for him and discovered him lying in the street. While she ran to summon the family physician, help arrived to transport him to Grady hospital. Madeline returned to find him missing. With Olive's husband Will, she went to the ward reserved for Negroes, only to be told he was not there. Because George White was as light-complected as his sons, Will and Madeline crossed the street to inquire at the white ward, where they found him. When hospital staff realized that George White was a Negro, they removed him to the Jim Crow section—dingy, dilapidated, ill-equipped. Five days after receiving Martin's notice, when it became fairly certain that his father would not survive, Walter and his brother George returned home to be with their father. After more than two weeks of slipping in and out of consciousness, the elder White's seventy-four-year-old body gave out, and he expired on the twenty-ninth.[12]

Writing of the incident two years later in an article for *Harper's* that remained unpublished, the humiliation of his father's death still burned. Describing the scene when Will Westmoreland entered the examination room and identified his father-in-law, White wrote:

> An expression of horror and incredulity swept over the attendants.
>
> "What!" one them exclaimed, "have we got a nigger over here on the white side?"

Gingerly but speedily and somewhat roughly they bundled him up, hove him onto a stretcher, and carted him across the street in a rainstorm. . . .

The shame of segregation didn't end with the physical surroundings. In the women's ward across the hall from his father was a servant to a white family. Her employer, "a sallow, stringy, sharp-voiced white woman," visited one day, and she happened to glance at Walter's father, from whom life was ebbing. "He may be a nigger," White reported she said in a grating voice, "but he's the whitest nigger I ever seen!" A particular source of irony and irritation were the white gospel singers patrolling the Negro ward to comfort the dying and their survivors.[13]

Segregated medical care, often with disastrous results, was the norm in the South. Just weeks before his father's tragedy, Juliette Derricotte, the dean of women at Fisk University, was involved in an automobile accident in Dalton, Georgia, near Chattanooga. She likely would have survived had she immediately been hospitalized, but the local hospital refused to admit blacks. It was some time before an African American physician arrived to assist her, and when she was finally transported to Chattanooga and admitted to a segregated hospital, she was beyond healing. White filed a report about her death, facts of which he gathered while he was in Atlanta attending to his father, but he might just as well have been writing of his own father:

> [T]he barbarity of race segregation in the South is shown in all its brutal ugliness by the willingness to let cultured respected and leading colored women die for lack of hospital facilities which are available to a white person no matter how low in the social scale. . . .
> . . . If there is such a thing as murder, the segregation system of the south murdered Miss Derricotte.[14]

Juliette Derricotte, George White, Bessie Smith, Charles Drew, all victims of automobile accidents—these stories of the callous disregard for the life, health, and bodies of black folk have been encrypted in African American lore about the iniquity of Jim Crow medical care. Yet in some of these and similar cases—Charles Drew's most prominently—the literal truth has been encrusted by a compelling rumor. (Drew, the single person most responsible for pioneering the technology of banking blood, is said to have died after being refused emergency treatment, including—ironically—blood transfusions, in a rural North Carolina hospital that did not admit blacks. In fact, Drew received all available medical help, but to no avail.) As historian Spencie Love explains, "People pass on a rumor because it conveys an experiential truth that has deep meaning for them," in this case the criminal negligence of medical and civil authorities toward African Americans in dire need.[15]

To this category must be added Walter White's account of his father's death. While the general outline of George White's demise is undisputed—he was run over, initially treated in the white ward of Grady Hospital but was discovered to be a Negro and then transferred to the Jim Crow ward, where he languished in squalid conditions—White invented two key facts in the recounting in his autobiography. First, neither his sister Madeline nor his brother-in-law Will Westmoreland—the only two family members present in the white emergency room—remembered any medical personnel using the word *nigger* to describe George White's presence in the room. Against Walter's insistence that this did in fact happen, Madeline replied that "Will stated that the first time he had heard the remark about the 'Nigger' in the white ward was when I asked him about it. As for me personally I . . . did not hear any such remark at the hospital."[16] Second, Walter places himself at his father's side within a few hours of the accident, rather than more than a week later. Immediately following his father's transfer, White wrote, he arrived at the hospital to find that he had regained consciousness.[17]

There are several good reasons why Walter would want to embellish his personal tragedy. Nearest the surface was his desire to tell the white readers of *Harper's* of the violence of segregation. "My approach to the article," he wrote Madeline, "is not as a story so much about Dad as it is a picture of what a Negro father of high ideals for himself and family has to undergo in the South, and no matter how exemplary his life and character have been, he also can be made the victim of mob violence as quickly as that of the most worthless Negro." Leaving aside the bald class bias of his statement, White believed that piling on more shocking details of his father's ignominious death would bring segregation into clearer relief. And as he admitted to his brother George, "much of the punch of the article depends on this particular episode."[18]

Then too the secretary was trying to bolster his leadership credentials, the association's internecine conflict having ended in July with Du Bois's resignation. This phase will be considered in full later, but this much should be now noted: Fearing the Du Bois–inspired campaign to "get" him that called into question his racial credentials, White clearly hoped his article would demonstrate that even blacks with the one mighty drop suffer—even to the point of death—from the rankest discrimination. Hence, it was not enough that his father die in a Jim Crow ward; White needed for him to be cursed on his way there too.[19]

But his placing himself practically at the scene of the accident reveals a man tortured by the demise of his father. The accident was the third, and most calamitous, personal crisis in little more than two years for the secretary. In October 1929, his father suffered two apparent heart episodes. His sister Olive reported that only his strong constitution enabled him to live. While there was no doubt of Walter's love for his family, there was a feeling among some members that he was not paying enough attention to them. He was delinquent in pitching in for an expensive Christmas present for his father, and some of the siblings were at least slightly annoyed. Nor was he keeping abreast of all his sisters. Shaken by his father's mortality, Walter took his family to Atlanta for Christmas—in nearly eight years of marriage, Gladys had never met her parents-in-law—and tried to become more attentive.[20]

In May 1930, Walter received another blow when John Hurst, a bishop in the African Methodist Episcopal Church, passed away. An association founder and board member, the Baltimore-based Hurst during his career oversaw A.M.E. affairs and denominational colleges in Florida, Georgia, and South Carolina. Hurst, whom Du Bois had once described as an "efficient man of affairs," and his wife "Miss Bertha," were two of White's biggest boosters. When White came up against political dilemmas—how to deal with a race man from a competing perspective or whether to become involved in the Al Smith presidential campaign, for example—he could always count on Hurst's honest appraisal. The bishop made himself available to do anything at all to promote White's *Fire in the Flint*. Perhaps more importantly, Hurst gave unstintingly of his encouragement, as in this typical communication:

Bertha and I have been talking about you; of the great progress you have made and the strong character you have developed, and above all, how well you fill your place in the world. We are proud of you. To us, this is but the beginning of larger things that await you. Bertha says that you are but a "kid," and to start now the larger world will feel your presence and know that you are in it.[21]

While his own father was undeniably proud of him and took joy in his son's family, Walter's personal affection for Hurst was intertwined with political bonds, and the two conducted a wide-ranging relationship characterized by a personal ease and intimacy that was strikingly absent in the infrequent communications with his father, who closed his laconic letters with "sincerely." White had named John and Bertha Hurst godparents for his daughter Jane. When he fulfilled Hurst's dying request to deliver his funeral eulogy, White spoke with deep grief. "He was as dear to me as my own father and I can say no more than that. I knew always that I could turn to him for comfort when life seemed harsh and hopeless. I could always turn to him for counsel when in doubt. . . . It is probably a selfish thought, but I can not help the feeling that I personally have lost him who was one of the truest and best beloved friends I have ever known."[22]

This grief grew into despair with the death of White's father a year later. Did he feel remorse at having apparently neglected his Atlanta family? It would appear to be the reason why, years after the tragedy, White placed himself at his father's side from the earliest moments after his accident. Positioning himself thusly was his attempt to assuage the guilt he likely felt at having waited nearly a week before deciding to go home. And if the shedding of blood is redemptive, White's imagining the scene so that he appears in close proximity to the scene of his death may be his way of bringing himself closer to his father and making personal sense out of his immense loss.

Walter left Atlanta shortly after his father's funeral, having made time for a family portrait, into which a photograph of the deceased would be inserted. He arrived in New York on December 6, on the Crescent Limited; sometime during the night a thief had entered his Pullman berth and stolen his wallet, money clip, and other valuable effects. His disorientation was palpable. His first stop was not home or NAACP headquarters, but Poppy Cannon's eastside apartment. The strain of the previous days showed on her face, she said. He went to see her, he reportedly told her, because, after the treatment whites meted out to his father, he feared he would end up hating all white people. He may have had on his mind not only how a white person had ended his father's life but also how that person had placed enormous financial burdens on his mother, his siblings, and himself; he would soon find out that the driver of the car, a physician, offered the paltry sum of $200, to be paid out over six months. It would now be up to the children to ensure their mother's financial health. These conditions too must have pressed in on Walter. In a cathartic instant, he fell into her arms and wept.[23] But in that moment White placed his marriage and career in jeopardy.

He returned to the office to find some measure of sympathy. Joel Spingarn recognized that personal trauma only made the roiling office controversies more unpleasant—"I am doubly sorry," he wrote, "that this should come when you have so many other things to cause you worry." Langston Hughes sent his condolences from North Carolina, where he was on tour reading his poetry. Hughes gave White a boost with the news that he was "showing your picture every day to the youth of the race as one of our biggest men. That's part of my road show."[24]

But then came the challenge of Du Bois's and the other executives' collective letter. Walter put aside his personal turmoil, became once again the secretary, and made plans to counter the mutiny. Ovington and Joel Spingarn, whatever their misgivings about the secretary, were prepared to stick by him. A day after Du Bois and the others had indicted the secretary, Ovington, who was distressed by White's disinclination to consult her, nevertheless confided in Arthur Spingarn that Du Bois "has been growing increasingly incompetent. As a choice between him and Walter White, Walter is worth ten times as much to us." Joel Spingarn was dismayed by the collective missive. He told the editor that another board member, to whom he had shown the letter, had responded that Du Bois was "just a badly brought up child who needs a spanking," and he implored his friend to drop the charges against the secretary.[25]

Du Bois characteristically refused to budge: "I will not retract or change a single word in the statement I signed & read before the Board," he asserted to Spingarn. But his confreres scattered for cover once it was apparent that their quick thrust would not result in White's elimination. Wilkins was the first to cave, scribbling a note to the secretary the morning after the board meeting that he was "simply sick over the part I took in that awful mess," and offering to resign. Pickens showed up at the office just after Wilkins had recanted. He wrote an apology that obfuscated his role in the affair. So murky was his repentance that he had to write a postscript that read, "To make sure you get me: What I mean is: That I withdraw my signature to any parts of the statement that even seem to reflect on your honor or honesty as a person." He then wrote to Du Bois to extricate himself: he didn't mean to leave Du Bois holding the bag, but "it was understood that the statement would be made by all the men, or not at all." And when Wilkins withdrew his name, he felt compelled to do so too. Seligmann abjectly called his actions "cruel and indefensible," and Bagnall begged Du Bois to remove his name from the bill of particulars.[26]

With the withdrawal of charges by four of the five complainants, Spingarn believed there was no longer any corpus delicti. He heaved a sigh of relief and engineered a compromise. Allegations of mismanagement against the secretary—but not personal accusations—would be scrutinized by an independent audit rather than by a special board committee, but so too would *Crisis* expenditures. Edna Lonigan, whose specialty was examining philanthropic and civic organizations, would peer into association finances, structure, and practices and submit a report in three months' time, thus holding out hope to White and Du Bois that the other would be held responsible for the organization's woes.[27]

Penury only sharpened the conflict between the secretary and the editor and made the relations between the two men more volatile, but it was anchored in diverging conceptions of building and sustaining a movement for Negro advancement. For W.E.B. Du Bois, *The Crisis*—or other, similar journals—had to be at the center of the movement. Always insistent on placing Afro-America in an international context, *The Crisis* kept black Americans abreast of world developments and informed of all manner of efforts to change the world. He provided insightful analysis of Marxism and its application to African Americans, analyzed the socialist experiment in the Soviet Union, criticized the labor movement, and called government to task. In his view, it was important but hardly sufficient for *The Crisis* to publicize NAACP activities; the worldview Du Bois presented to readers every month was a guide to action, essential to sustaining the movement, he believed.

But for White, Ovington, and other NAACP leaders, propaganda, while not entirely expendable, was of secondary importance compared to beefing up the association's practical activities. They recognized that at one time *The Crisis* was the most visible face of the NAACP and that its influence far outstripped that of the rest of the association. But times had changed, and the association was a recognized force in American politics. What was needed from *The Crisis*, they thought, was not more theory and propaganda but an approach that was "popular," a magazine that promoted the NAACP's activities. Ovington said as much when she said Du Bois was "not fitted" to be editor any longer; White made his position clear when he deleted the journal from the grant proposal he submitted to the Garland Fund. What the NAACP needed, and urgently needed, White believed, was a solid legal and lobbying campaign to defend and extend the constitutional rights of African Americans and a vehicle for publicizing this effort.[28]

The secretary had tried to gain some leverage over *The Crisis* earlier when he was appointed to the oversight committee. But the auditor's report dealt him a setback. The board decided to continue to fund *The Crisis* and reconstitute a committee to guide it—without the secretary, a fact that greatly pleased the editor. Du Bois was invited to take a more active role in the running of the organization through participation in the Committee on Administration. The report then dissected the secretary's style of work to date. He was called to task for treating the branches as cash cows; it was incumbent upon the association to develop all-sided relationships with local officers. The auditor also rebuked White for the morale problems created by his draconian budget measures. Rather than the immediate resort to layoffs, the organization's paid administrative and clerical staff would be more energized if other measures were implemented, including asking for higher productivity rather than salary reductions, and then salary reductions rather than letting people go. Then came the windmill punch: while he was enforcing austerity on others, the secretary spent extravagantly on himself when he traveled. White refused to economize, as seen in his use of "taxicabs, valet and laundry service, and continuously high expenses for rooms and meals." Charges of profligacy unnerved White. High overhead was the price of productivity, he argued. Taxis boosted his efficiency, he needed clean and quiet accommodations, and he had to take his meals in pleasant surroundings. None of this convinced board member John Haynes Holmes, who believed that the secretary, though hardworking, had gotten away from living and working simply, qualities upon which the association had been built. Accusations that he was a spendthrift, utilized ethically gray areas to develop a financial cushion, and took undue advantage of the generosity of better-situated acquaintances would dog White for the rest of his career. For now, they caused him to soften his management style.[29]

Buried in the audit's mélange of administrative recommendations was a declarative statement on the urgent need for the NAACP to develop an economic program. Du Bois was not the only one who recognized that the Depression had drastically altered the terrain on which the battles for equality would be fought, who divined that the economic crisis presented not only severe financial shortfalls but also potential windfalls in terms of the willingness of African Americans to become active. He was simply the most articulate on this count. While ordinary African Americans were gladdened by the NAACP's planned assault on segregation in higher education, it was not the sort of issue that would stimulate them to take their places on the ramparts. Even if they were so prepared, the association's emphasis on litigation cleared no space for them. On the other hand, different approaches were showing promise for their ability to harness mass discontent. The CP was drawing sympathetic notice for its Scottsboro work and organizing among sharecroppers. Black workers were showing signs of stirring, and both the CP and noncommunist black activists helped to reach out to them.[30] Even some of the secretary's close allies saw the need to retool the association. Board member Louis Wright, White's personal physician and longtime friend from Atlanta, worried that, especially after the Scottsboro fiasco, "the Association seems to be losing ground with the average man in the street because the work lacks inspiration." Echoing this concern, Joel Spingarn proposed the convening of a second Amenia conference primarily of emerging race leaders to thrash out a new program for the new era. (The first, held in 1916, likewise galvanized a generation of race leaders.) Planned initially for summer 1932 at his upstate New York estate, the Depression forced its postponement for a year. The invitation to meet ushered in a two-year period during which time ideas blossomed for reorganizing the NAACP and reshaping its program.[31]

Debate and reflection were unusually robust at the 1932 annual meeting in Washington, D.C. With the campaign to punish pro-Parker senators still active, delegates continued to discuss the proper role of the NAACP in politics. While there were still some holdovers from previous years who wanted to either abstain from the electoral arena or remain loyal to the party of Lincoln, a consensus was forming to support independent political activism. From the delegates, the secretary sensed a growing militant, progressive, independent mood among African Americans and declared that the time was nigh for the organized black vote to hold the balance of power in several states across the nation.[32]

But what line of attack would African Americans pursue? Du Bois offered a penetrating critique of "What Is Wrong with the NAACP." He defended the association's historical actions in such areas as centralizing decision making in a few hands in the national office and concentrating on legal redress and other issues of concern primarily to the "Talented Tenth." But he agitated for change based upon new world conditions. He pressed his attack on the secretary's leadership on two fronts. First, he said that while paid association officers were hardly living extravagantly, some (that is, White) had forgotten that their incomes were far above what the majority of African Americans earned and that they aspired to use their positions to accumulate wealth. Second, it would no longer be sufficient to make the fight against segregation and Jim Crow justice the association's exclusive focus. Focusing primarily on abolishing the color line was too reactive and would not address the myriad new problems created by the Depression and the sharpening class struggle. The NAACP had to expand its program explicitly to confront the ever-more acute problems of black workers and must work to place the struggle of African Americans in an international context.[33]

Though White usually did not think broadly or programmatically, preferring instead to remain focused on the campaign or task at hand, he enthusiastically echoed Du Bois, so compelling was the editor's argument. Savaged by the Depression, African Americans were open to alternatives to capitalism, White said. They were paying close attention to the Soviet experiment. They were taking off their blinders and seeking out a new world in which the exploitation of black, brown, and yellow people would cease and in which the world's great wealth would be distributed for the good of the majority. White's was an implicit endorsement of a nascent clamor for change within the association.[34]

The national office initiated campaigns to improve the economic lot of black workers. Working with the San Francisco branch, the Los Angeles chapter of the National Urban League, the National Bar Association, and two organizations of black workers in Las Vegas, the NAACP demanded the federal government stop the exclusion of African Americans from the Boulder Dam construction project. In the waning days of the Hoover administration, this coalition won a marginal victory, increasing the number of black workers on the job to forty in October from five the previous month. While Hoover did his best to ignore the association's protests, they paid dividends in the succeeding Roosevelt administration when interior secretary Harold Ickes promised to end discrimination on his department's public-works projects.[35] Similarly, when the secretary became aware of the abysmal conditions on the Mississippi levee construction projects, he urged quick action. Helen Boardman, whom White asked to investigate the situation, found vicious abuse: African American workers were paid about ten cents per hour and were returning between 50–75 percent of their wages to contractors in the form of inflated prices at company commissaries; beatings for insignificant infractions were common; and work camps were unsanitary. White ordered the investigation to "form the basis for a vigorous campaign for jobs for blacks which will strike a major chord of interest today." Branches were to demand jobs for Negroes on all public-works projects. He succeeded, in conjunction with the American Federation of Labor, in getting Robert Wagner, the Democratic senator from New York, to sponsor a resolution to investigate the labor practices on the construction projects. While Hoover was recalcitrant, the Roosevelt administration responded by rewriting and enforcing new regulations governing the running of labor camps.[36]

The pressure to reform the NAACP and expand its purview continued to build throughout 1933, driven largely by an influx of younger black professionals, many of them influenced intellectually by Marxism or excited by the practical radical activity of the Communists' International Labor Defense. But the drive to embrace an economic program and champion issues of concern to black workers was difficult to sustain, because of both the inertia of many local leaders and the halfhearted commitment to change by the secretary and his aides. The 1933 annual convention was a pivotal moment in the effort to remake the NAACP.

For the second consecutive year, the convention was more than an occasion to celebrate the association's accomplishments and rally the troops. In Chicago, the site of the meeting, the NAACP's reputation continued to wane while the Communists' waxed.[37] The opening speech by Earl Dickerson of the host branch set the tone. Welcoming delegates to the Windy City, Dickerson stated that most people thought of the NAACP as a collection of cases; when particularly grievous acts of discrimination occurred, the association dispatched its attorneys to represent those aggrieved. But, he maintained, the law was designed to protect the status quo, and by emphasizing litigation the NAACP had allowed itself to be defined by the parameters of the law. It had fallen into a program of handling individual cases rather than overtly challenging the system. The association, he proposed, needed to reform and become less reactive, less conservative, less legalistic.[38]

A roundtable discussion on tactics entitled "Shifting Lines of Attack to Meet the Needs of the Day" sharpened the issues. Irvin Mollison of the Chicago branch sharply criticized the NAACP as too conservative and too worried about what its white friends would think of militant action. He was joined in these comments by C. L. Dellums, active in both the San Francisco–area NAACP and the national leadership of the Brotherhood of Sleeping Car Porters. They were denounced by several rearguard branch leaders. C. A. MacPherson of the Birmingham branch, who let his fear of being branded radical by his city's white moderates determine what timid actions he might take, said that those who were not willing to follow the NAACP's leadership were unthinking; the ordinary person was in no position to decide in which campaigns the NAACP ought to engage. A. T. Walden of Atlanta simply begged NAACP activists not to go over to the ILD. Roy Wilkins, who moderated the discussion, smugly dismissed the radicals' criticisms altogether by claiming, "No single speaker has proposed a concrete method by which a program could be carried to and executed by the masses."[39]

Between these two factions was "the great undecided middle group," so called by Charles Houston, who located himself there. Many considered him part of the radical cohort, but Houston, soon to become the NAACP's first paid attorney, always tempered his leftist sympathies with a pragmatic streak. Rather than allow himself to be limited by being identified as belonging to one camp, Houston sought the common ground on which the radicals and the middle could come together. Principles were important to Houston, but they were not useful if all one did was polish them; they had to guide practical work. Most opportunities for direct action on working-class issues presented themselves on the local level, he told the delegates. The Toledo branch, for example, had successfully conducted a "don't buy where you can't work" boycott that resulted in the hiring of African Americans in retail establishments throughout the city. Blame for a branch's sloth needed to be placed squarely on the branch, and not on the national office, as had Dellums. Houston invited radicals to become involved in the branches, to win them to their program. He cautioned black professionals not to build local branches that would fight for their narrow economic or social interests or that would entice the masses to join only to pull their chestnuts out of the fire. Rather, he encouraged them to build branches that implemented an "uncompromising program of fight and struggle for the Negro's rights."[40]

The secretary also recognized the power of mass action and multi-class participation in the association and had at times tried without much success to stimulate branches to direct action. But unlike his close friend Houston, he was far less willing to encourage a transformation of the NAACP. White tended to dismiss the criticisms of the traditional program of reactive litigation simply because the critics did not have a fully germinated alternative. Although in the run-up to the convention White promised association members and leaders alike a pivotal gathering, by the meeting's end he was much more conservative. In his speech closing the convention, White praised the debate—for its cathartic effect. And with two of the most influential critics of the NAACP's direction—Joel Spingarn and Du Bois—absent from the convention, he signaled his intention to hew closely to the current program and strategy. He tweaked the dissenters: "Those who, for example, have recently been intrigued by such phrases as 'mass action' were reminded by other delegates that the NAACP had been using mass action for twenty-three years," citing as proof the victories he coordinated in the Arkansas riot and Sweet cases and the Parker campaign. White obscured the fact that these instances of direct action were not equivalent to the critics' demands for a program suited to the cataclysmic economic and political crisis shaking the country; he essentially thanked the delegates for their input and returned to business as usual.[41]

Annual convention completed, the struggle over the association's program and direction shifted venue to Troutbeck, Joel Spingarn's Hudson River Valley estate in Amenia, Dutchess County, New York. For more than a year the NAACP had been unable to hold Spingarn's attention, and sensing this was the case with Du Bois and a coterie of younger black intellectuals and activists, he had proposed the second Amenia conference as a way to resuscitate their flagging stake in the association. The continued drift of the organization led Spingarn to resign as chairman of the association in March.[42] As he wrote to Mary White Ovington, whom he had succeeded as chair in 1932 when she was caught in the cross fire between the secretary and *The Crisis* editor:

I have lost interest in the Association as it is now run, I do not approve of the spirit that motivates it, and I not feel like allowing my name to be used to represent that spirit. If I were a lawyer like my brother, I should find some difficult and interesting question involved in every one of our successive "cases," and I should hardly miss the cement of a programme. But as it is, I am not interested in a succession of cases. When I joined the Association we had what was a thrilling programme, revolutionary for its time, and one that gave us a little hope of solving the whole problem. Now we have only cases, no programme, and no hope. Every effort I have made to try to put this hope into our work by framing a programme has been ignored or thwarted by the Secretary or by the Board. You said, "The branches want dramatic cases, not programmes," as if that were not the reason why so many of them were moribund,—or as if a programme were an academic thesis instead of an instrument of hope and enthusiasm![43]

Tectonic plates shifted underneath Walter White when Spingarn resigned. Though Spingarn had at times been critical of White's management of the association, he had always understood the secretary's value to the organization and had supported his leadership against challenges from Du Bois and others. White foresaw dicey times ahead should Spingarn pull back from the NAACP, and he begged him not to resign as chairman.[44]

Yet it was the secretary's own indifference to calls for change that provoked Spingarn's action in the first place. When active preparations commenced in April, Spingarn, White, and Du Bois were deputized to make the arrangements. Du Bois, who had left New York to take a visiting professorship at Atlanta University (soon to become permanent), offered White whatever assistance he could provide from a distance. But "Walter did nothing," the editor reported. White had a different take on the organizing, but he unintentionally confirmed Spingarn's and Du Bois's conclusion. Distraught at the thought of Spingarn's departure, he wrote James Weldon Johnson, now ensconced at Fisk University and removed from the minutiae of association politics. "[S]ome member, or members of the Board told Joel that I was not particularly keen about the Amenia Conference," White wrote to his mentor. This, he suspected, was a major factor in Spingarn's resignation. Why Spingarn would believe such a statement was a puzzle, he wrote. "We have been so damned busy here at the office trying to keep our heads above water" that he could not possibly have said something to offend the president. Yet his treading water was precisely a source of Spingarn's frustrations; while White concentrated on successive cases, he was steadfastly refusing to examine the association's program.[45]

Nearly a month passed before the secretary began to show signs of interest in the Amenia conference. Du Bois forwarded a list of possible participants to Spingarn, who in consultation with White and Wilkins selected a portion while leaving the rest to Du Bois. As host, Spingarn exercised his prerogative to set the number of invitees at thirty-two, including Roy Wilkins, despite Du Bois's observation that he could be left off "without the slightest hurt to intelligent discussion." But then the secretary got to the business of organizing the three-day conference, arranging for the delivery of food and the tents and cots in which conferees would meet, eat, and sleep.[46]

With a median age of thirty, the gathering exemplified the maturing generation of the race's leaders. Howard University was well represented: the poet Sterling Brown, Ralph Bunche, Abram Harris, Emmet Dorsey, and Charles Houston all attended. So did E. Franklin Frazier, who would soon leave Fisk University and join them. They all had to varying degrees been pushing the movement to embrace a class analysis and a program inclusive of black workers. Bunche and Harris in particular were heavily influenced by Marxism. YWCA staffers Frances Williams and Marion Cuthbert, who would play critical roles in the campaign for a federal antilynching law in the coming years (and who would provide critical support for the secretary), and Juanita Jackson of the Jackson civil rights dynasty in Baltimore, offered a perspective from black women. Attorney Louis Redding from Delaware, who two decades later would represent plaintiffs in a school desegregation suit that would be heard by the U.S. Supreme Court as part of the *Brown* case, also attended. Rayford Logan, one of Du Bois's closest collaborators and a promising historian, was under doctor's orders not to travel; William Hastie, the future federal judge and Walter White confidant, likewise did not attend.[47]

The long August weekend was organized around formal plenaries and committee meetings punctuated by informal discussion, organized play, fishing, and roaming the grounds of Troutbeck. Further to promote the frank exchange of ideas, the proceedings were not recorded. The combination of faux rustic surroundings, intense and wide-ranging discussion, and the chance to meet and engage the race's rising stars had an intoxicating, liberating effect on the participants. Frances Williams bubbled over at her meeting Houston, Bunche, and Frazier—they "were worth crossing a continent to know." Emmet Dorsey, who of all the attendees was closest to the Communists, raved about Amenia; no stranger to radical meetings, Dorsey told White that Amenia was the best conference he had ever attended. Louis Redding was deeply agitated by the proceedings, so aware was he of the momentousness of the gathering.[48]

Redding, whose summary letter to Roy Wilkins provides an account of the conference that is both candid and thorough, reported that participants arrived with the "judgment that the older policies for Negro advancement had failed and were inappropriate" to the situation of deep economic crisis and social dislocation. He, like many others, hoped the weekend's brainstorming would lead to a "resolute decision to junk the old policies, followed by a clear-cut outlining of basically new philosophies, or policies. Such new policies I hoped would be adaptable to the Negro masses rather than considerate only of the 'talented tenth.' " But what he found as the sessions progressed was a falling away from this position as several unnamed participants found themselves more concerned with their personal safety in the current economic order. Nevertheless, several fecund ideas filtered through the gauze of self-preservation.[49]

First, the conference findings, strongly influenced by Marxism, placed the race problem firmly within the context of the crisis of overproduction. "The primary problem is economic," the final document bluntly put it. Industry's drive for profit led to the exploitation of American workers, none more so than Negro laborers, and resulted in their impoverishment. "[T]he whole system of private property and private profit is being called into question." Surveying the extant tools for the black proletariat's and the race's liberation, the conferees found them sadly inadequate. Working from the assumption that "the welfare of white and black labor are one and inseparable," they found that the organizations "working among and for Negroes have conspicuously failed" to strike the necessary alliance between them. If anything, the record of organized labor was more dismal, with the labor movement expressing outright hostility to black workers.[50]

The conferees rejected fascism, a political movement that in 1933 was gaining currency among workers in Germany and held power in Italy, because it would cement the subordinate position of African Americans in the social structure. They considered the Communist solution, apparently with some sympathy for the goal of the elimination of class exploitation, but rejected it as unrealizable so long as white workers continued their chauvinist position on the race question and so long as black workers continued to look for solidarity not with white workers but with white philanthropy. For the time being, at any rate, class solidarity across race lines was a wish and not within the realm of possibility. Recognizing this, conference participants came to back E. Franklin Frazier's adumbration of a revolutionary nationalism, whose purpose was twofold. Racial cohesion was a fungible ideology that could maneuver the masses into a position to wage a class struggle; and by promoting economic independence, nationalism was a first step to compelling white workers to ally with blacks.[51]

The conference recommended a continuations committee be established to explore the ramifications of this outline for the NAACP's work. This group, temporarily chaired by Charles Houston but driven by Abram Harris, subsequently was constituted as the Committee on Future Plan and Program. It labored steadily over the coming months to develop a new document to be adopted at the 1934 annual convention. (Adoption was delayed a year.) The proposed program credited the NAACP with fighting for the rights of black workers, including its persistent protest against the exclusionary policies of the American Federation of Labor and its support for black railroad workers; but it stated that the association's labor and economic program had always been an adjunct to its principal activity of pursuing the race's civil rights and liberties. At bottom, the NAACP's traditional program rested on the faulty principles of eighteenth-century liberalism, which guaranteed an individual's political and property rights but which assumed the great mass of people to be propertyless workers and condemned them to poverty and exploitation. Thus, the acquisition of full citizenship rights such as the NAACP traditionally advocated would in all likelihood not have changed the essential status of African Americans as landless wage laborers. The impoverishment of black proletarians as a consequence of the Great Depression was simply a more acute manifestation of what was occurring to white workers, and there would be no fundamental alteration in the race's position until there could be effected an interracial class solidarity. The NAACP could no longer meet the needs of African Americans by maintaining itself as an organization with a powerful central executive staff engaged in lobbying and political agitation and a collection of branches engaged in sporadic agitation. Rather, the association had to establish regional workers' and farmers' councils to: conduct education and agitation among black workers and farmers; foster an interracial industrial union movement that would also struggle to rectify the special grievances of African Americans through, for example, a fight against lynching and the complete elimination of Jim Crow in public and in the labor movement; establish a cooperative movement to provide immediate relief from economic distress but which would not be racially separatist in character; intensify its involvement in politics, including helping to establish a third party to advance the "interests of American workers as a whole and the special interests of the Negro."[52]

The secretary could see that such a radical transformation would likely mean that he would be out of a job. Du Bois had already proposed that all paid executives be laid off as part of a reorganization; though this plan to rid the organization of White was set aside, the secretary sensed that he would not be asked to oversee the change. So quite aside from his objections to the political viability of the Amenia resolutions and the future plan—and his criticisms of the futility of emphasizing uniting with white workers was well founded—the secretary had a personal stake in making certain the new plan was not implemented. He would spend the next two years stymieing it.

White's plan to turn back the challenge posed by those, including Communists, seeking a thoroughgoing reordering of America's social and economic system pivoted on the efficacy of his legalistic strategy. The blueprint for this approach was contained in the $100,000 grant from the Garland Fund to challenge segregated education in the South, but it also included the association's traditional vigorous criminal defense of African Americans whose cases involved significant issues of constitutional rights. Two such cases—one of each type—presented themselves just as criticism of the secretary and the old program were approaching a crescendo.

In March 1933, Thomas Hocutt, a twenty-four-year-old black resident of Durham, North Carolina, and assistant headwaiter at the Washington Duke Hotel on the campus of Duke University, submitted his application for the University of North Carolina School of Pharmacy, the only such public school in the state. When he was denied admission on the grounds that he could attend only the five state institutions reserved for African Americans, the North Carolina College for Negroes in his hometown among them—which he had attended—Hocutt filed suit. His lawyers applied to Walter White for assistance. The secretary, who was

anxious to display the superiority of the legal strategy for civil rights—
and to check the muscular Communist Party in Scottsboro's aftermath—
leapt at the opportunity and referred it to Charles Houston for
immediate action. Houston assigned his cousin William Hastie, who
would soon become one of the secretary's close collaborators and a
prominent jurist, to try the case.[53]

Hastie had to contend with opinion on both sides of the color line
that, while there was merit in blacks' complaints of exclusion from publicly funded professional education, the depth of economic crisis was no
time to press for redress. Of the voices of caution, none was louder than
that belonging to James Shepard, the most prominent African American
educator in the state and the head of the North Carolina College. Three
years earlier he had defended John Parker's nomination to the Supreme
Court. He was not now about to do anything to jeopardize his institution's position or the status of the segregated system of education in the
state. He withheld Thomas Hocutt's college transcript, a document that
every applicant had to supply in order to be admitted to the pharmacy
school.

At trial, Hastie could not surmount Shepard's obstructions. His witnesses testified to Hocutt's scholastic competence; the state's lawyers argued that Hocutt was woefully unprepared and that the entire case was
brought to advance a secret agenda of social equality and miscegenation.
The judge in the case said that without proof of Hocutt's grades he was
unable to order his admission, and the case was thrown out on this tech-
nicality. But on a related point, he gave the NAACP cause for hope. He
could have, he said, ordered the university to review Hocutt's application
fairly and without regard to his race. But Hocutt's attorneys had asked for
more than that, and that was as far as he could rule.

Despite the adverse ruling, the secretary was elated. Hastie's conduct
of the case had remarkably turned around public opinion. Local white
barristers, jurists, law professors from Duke University and the University of North Carolina, leading white Durhamites, Durham's African
American community—all now pledged enthusiastic support for the
NAACP's legal quest, the secretary informed the board. He predicted the
eclipse of old-line leaders like Shepard.[54]

Capitalizing on the momentum of this moral victory, White toured
North Carolina and Virginia in mid-May. In Chapel Hill, university
president and great advocate of human rights for African Americans

Frank Porter Graham lent White a sympathetic ear. The secretary returned energized, he wrote to James Weldon Johnson. Events in the Tar
Heel State had convinced him that

> we have a golden opportunity right now to make progress hitherto impos-
> sible in the matter of education. We cannot say it to the Garland Fund
> Board, what with the Communist members, but everywhere I went in the
> south the white people are afraid of the effect of Communist propaganda
> on the Negro. As a result, they are willing now more than ever before to
> consider the program of the NAACP and to make concessions to it if for
> no other reason than that in their opinion it is the lesser of two evils.

He saw potential to challenge Jim Crow in several areas, including filing
suits against the racial differential in teacher pay, and to increase the
number of dues-paying members.[55]

Contemporaneous with the Hocutt suit, Charles Houston fought the
extradition of George Crawford, an accused murderer, from Boston to
Virginia. At issue was the exclusion of African Americans from grand and
trial juries in Virginia, which Houston argued was a violation of
Crawford's right to a fair trial. In a major victory for the NAACP, a
United States District Court judge blocked the extradition. An appeals
court judge reinstated the order, however, and Crawford was sent back to
Loudon County to face trial. In a decisive moment, the secretary decided
that now was the time for the NAACP to abandon its long tradition of
using only white attorneys, and Houston became the first black NAACP
lawyer to try one of its cases. With the secretary in the courtroom for the
four-day trial (the better to help direct the legal strategy) Houston put up
the best defense possible given that a shaky alibi, damning testimony
from Loudon blacks, and the sudden surfacing of evidence of Crawford's
guilt caused his case to disintegrate before he had called his first witness.
He could not now win an acquittal, he realized, but with his skill and
comportment he so astonished the jury that they spared Crawford elec-
trocution. Judge, jury, and journalists expressed admiration for the legal
perspicacity of the NAACP.[56]

As in Hocutt, the secretary from the beginning was acutely aware that
a successful pursuit of victory in the Crawford case was the only restora-
tive for an organization so shaken in stature by the Communist Party. Before agreeing to represent Crawford, White insisted that the defendant

sign an exclusive agreement with the NAACP. "More and more the Communists are trying every possible way to 'demand' that they be permitted to 'cooperate' or to assume control of and dictatorial powers over every case in which the Association is interested," he wrote to Arthur Spingarn with more than a hint of defensiveness. He was pleased by press coverage of the case that highlighted the NAACP's prominent role and quoted him as saying that the CP would be unable to "snatch" it away, as it did in Scottsboro. (White still clung to the fiction that the NAACP ever was in the leadership of Scottsboro.) His vigilance paid off handsomely this time, as he was able, with some effort, to protect his left flank; the only articles critical of White's management of the case were Martha Gruening's in the radical *New Masses*, Gruening's and Helen Boardman's in *The Nation*, and Du Bois's short but dyspeptic postscript in the insubordinate *Crisis*.[57]

To the secretary's mind, the verdict was quite beside the point when assessing the effectiveness of the NAACP program. But ear to ground, he heard vibrations of dissatisfaction from members and other African Americans. How could White declare a murder conviction a victory? "Don't get the wrong slant on the Crawford case," he cautioned Daisy Lampkin. His guilt, which took the defense team quite by surprise, if anything magnified what the NAACP had accomplished and was a "vindication of the Association's methods. For here was a Negro guilty of killing in the South not one white woman but two of them, and . . . who was tried in the South by all-Negro counsel, saved from the electric chair, and the trial ended with unbounded respect for and a new concept of the Negro among all classes of both white and colored people." As a corollary, the association had forged an energetic and intelligent cadre of black attorneys, including Houston, Leon Ransom, Edward Lovett, James Tyson, Louis Redding, and others. Soon to be augmented by Howard University law student Thurgood Marshall, this nucleus would, over the next two decades, try some of the most significant cases that would lead to the demolition of Jim Crow with the *Brown* decision. Of only slightly less importance to White, five southern states, as a result of the extradition fight, began to impanel blacks for jury duty. Finally, the work on the case yielded cordial relations with influential southern white liberals, including Richmond newspaper editors Virginius Dabney and Douglas Southall Freeman.[58]

But if White could contain criticism in the Crawford case, challenges to his stewardship of the association were not isolated. They ignited like prairie fires and were just as difficult to stamp out. As Abram Harris's mission to reformulate the NAACP program gathered momentum, Du Bois lit a couple of new matches in the brush. In the January 1934 issue of *The Crisis* the editor published his incendiary essay "Segregation." His argument was blunt: "The thinking colored people of the United States must stop being stampeded by the word segregation. The opposition to racial segregation is not or should not be any distaste or unwillingness of colored people to work with each other, to co-operate with each other, to live with each other." Du Bois drew a distinction between segregation—a condition that accurately described all manner of public intercourse in which blacks could take justifiable pride, including schools, churches, and voluntary associations—and discrimination, which he defined as the imposition of racially based inequalities. At a time when the white majority showed no inclination toward racial inclusiveness, Du Bois exhorted black workers and farmers voluntarily to segregate themselves and establish a group economy. "It must be remembered," he wrote, "that in the last quarter of a century, the advance of the colored people has been mainly in the lines where they themselves working by and for themselves, have accomplished the greatest advance." [59]

Du Bois's bomb couldn't have come at a more sensitive time, White told him. Franklin Roosevelt's New Deal had in its first year been notoriously unresponsive to the needs of African Americans; to take just one case in point, the experimental Subsistence Homestead Colony in Arthurdale, West Virginia, which was championed by First Lady Eleanor Roosevelt, had voted to bar black farmers from membership. The secretary had only recently been able to prevail upon her to force a policy revision. Now, however, agitators to keep Arthurdale's racial status quo were using Du Bois's editorial to justify blacks' exclusion. The secretary wanted Du Bois to print in the February *Crisis* his article defending the NAACP's traditional program, stating his unequivocal animus to segregation, and rebutting the editor's mischief; it was imperative to have his article in print before he met Mrs. Roosevelt again. The editor returned White's statement, claiming that it was replete with errors but offering to run it in the March issue, alongside other responses and only as an individual opinion. [60]

For the next several months the two jousted over just what was the NAACP's historical position on segregation, with board members alternately spectating and partaking. Du Bois insisted that the NAACP had never categorically condemned segregation, and had even compromised with it. He cited as proof the association's endorsement of officer training on a segregated basis during WWI as the only way for African Americans to earn a commission, and its demand for black control over the segregated veterans' hospital at Tuskegee. For his part, the secretary conceded that while the association had never taken a formal vote on the matter, it had always vigorously opposed segregation. This facet of their dispute set the board off to find an acceptable definition of segregation—did the term imply only the involuntary type? and would the NAACP be unalterably opposed to every manifestation of it?—that was in fact a diversion from the principal issue.

And that issue was Du Bois's attempts to portray Walter White's certain opposition to the "Segregation" editorial as a manifestation of racial self-hatred; Du Bois thus hoped to neutralize White's grab for control of the organization. Joel Spingarn, who as both assimilated Jew and white conservator of the most established civil rights organization of the day, was supremely sensitive to shades of Negro opinion, cautioned White. Whether one liked it or not—and neither assimilated Jew nor borderline assimilated African American cared at all for it—cultural nationalism, which tended toward separation, was a "strong contemporary trend" among the black intelligentsia, and the secretary would be well advised not to be dismissive in his opposition. Spingarn recognized that White's complexion rendered his opposition to nationalism suspect in the eyes of other African Americans; he also understood the psychic scars inflicted upon the secretary by the warring between the assimilationist and nationalist impulses swirling around and within him. "Confidentially, may I advise you to act carefully when dealing with this whole question, as you are at somewhat a disadvantage?" counseled Spingarn. "I am not suggesting that you hide your opinions in any way, but that you realize that hundreds of Negroes think you are really a white man whose natural desire is to associate with white men. Many have said this to me about you, and all I suggest is that your opposition to segregation must not seem to spring from a desire to associate with white people."[61]

White denied any conflict, as he typically did when he was accused of racial disloyalty or ambivalence. He was not at all troubled by some blacks thinking his commitment to integration stemmed from a desire to associate with whites. Had that really been the case, he wrote to

Spingarn, he would long ago have passed over to the white world. As it was, he chose his friends "not on the basis of their race but wholly on mutual points of interest," as if a common history of subjection and struggle was of no influence at all in shaping personal preferences. His public response to Du Bois, published in the March *Crisis* as "On Segregation," did nothing to calm persistent questions about his racial affinities. Negro group solidarity to the point of voluntary separation, he wrote, "means spiritual atrophy." The all-rounded well-being of the race—and that of whites—demanded integration. It was not only White's political enemies who could interpret such a statement as a desire to "be white." His words are redolent of the very ones his friend Langston Hughes criticized as racial abnegation in his 1926 salvo "The Negro Artist and the Racial Mountain."[62]

Du Bois attempted to make the secretary fall on his own sword. In the same March *Crisis* that contained White's position on segregation, Du Bois blistered White for trying to force African Americans' way into the white subsistence homestead colonies championed by Eleanor Roosevelt. The salience of race in America's history and present made it impossible for the colonies to be racially integrated. The white colonies would never admit blacks, "except as servants and casual laborers." Protest, no matter how vigorous, was not only futile, it was an embarrassment to the race. Under the prevailing conditions of exclusion, he cut with a surgeon's skill:

> . . . it would be nothing less than idiotic for colored people themselves to refuse to accept or neglect to ask for subsistence homestead colonies of their own. They would have a chance to select the character of people with whom they wanted to live; they would have a chance of making these settlements model settlements of which anybody would be proud, and they would do more in the long run to break down the Color Line than they could by any futile and helpless denunciation of race prejudice. It seems almost impossible that honest, clear-thinking American Negroes can not see this patent fact.[63]

If the editor had successfully pared away White's objections to "Segregation," he blundered and turned the knife on himself in the April issue, nakedly playing the "race card." The secretary's arguments had logic, wrote Du Bois, but they were "quite beside the point." What was the point? "In the first place, Walter White is white."

He has more white companions and friends than colored. He goes where he will in New York City and naturally meets no Color Line, for the simple and sufficient reason that he isn't "colored"; he feels his new freedom in bitter contrast to what he was born to in Georgia. This is perfectly natural and he does what anyone else of his complexion would do.

But it is fantastic to assume that this has anything to do with the color problem in the United States. It naturally makes Mr. White an extreme opponent of any segregation based on a myth of race. But this argument does not apply to [persons of a darker hue]. Moreover, Mr. White knows this. He moved once into a white apartment house and it went black on him. He now lives in a colored apartment house with attendant limitation. . . .

. . . [I]f association and contact with Negroes is distasteful to you, what is it to white people? Remember that the white people of America will certainly never want us until we want ourselves.[64]

Joel Spingarn was disappointed by the editor's descent into demagogy. Du Bois had hit "below the belt, all the more since you know that Pickens and most Negro editors [all of whom were darker than White] feel exactly as he does about segregation." Letters flooded association headquarters demanding an end to the fisticuffs. Four additional board members—Ovington, James Weldon Johnson, Isadore Martin of Philadelphia, one of the most active African Americans on the board, and Carl Murphy, editor of the *Baltimore Afro-American*—rallied to the secretary's defense. After some fine-tuning, the board passed a resolution affirming the association's traditional stand against segregation, and when Du Bois questioned the board's action, it responded by censuring the editor and forbidding paid NAACP officers to criticize the association. Silencing of his voice was something the editor would not abide, and he resigned as *Crisis* editor and a member of the board effective July 1934.[65]

The secretary had been bloodied—but he had prevailed.[66] With Du Bois gone, White took control of *The Crisis*, appointing his subordinate Roy Wilkins acting editor. He took steps to consolidate his position on the board; when Joel Spingarn stepped down as chairman, White's friend and supporter Louis Wright took his place. The secretary began to attend meetings of the board's nominating committee as a way to influence its proceedings.

Neither the moral victories inherent in the Hocutt and Crawford cases nor the tangible victory in a 1934 suit to force the admission of Donald Murray to the University of Maryland School of Law, however, could placate advocates of a new program from pressing their case. Allowing hardly a moment for the secretary to reorient himself following Du Bois's apopemptic, Abram Harris and others began to assail White with demands for change. As White prepared for the floor debate that would crop up at the 1934 Oklahoma City annual convention, Frances Williams gently told him that some of the membership's ire was due to shortcomings in his interpersonal skills. Leading the NAACP in the post–Du Bois area was "a very big job." He could avoid a lot of their criticism that the association was unconcerned with workers by "trying not to be so sophisticated. Your Manhattan airs don't go well in the provinces. Be like you are at home—very simple & easy to know."[67] When the promised new program was not ready in time for the 1934 annual convention, delegates insisted that the process take no longer than one more year.

Responding to this mandate, the board at its July meeting appointed a committee to finalize the new program, on which no member of the executive staff sat. The secretary was peeved by the decision. How could the board exclude from so crucial a committee the very persons who were most knowledgeable about the association's work nationwide and who would be responsible for implementing it? The board, he felt, was disconnected from the association, perhaps fatigued by the sustained battle with the former editor. In contrast to the vibrant annual convention, he vented to Spingarn in a "Dear Joel" letter marked "personal," the board meeting had given him a "sense of unreality and of bewilderment, as though I were in a somewhat unreal world." When it was his turn to speak, "Certain members of the Board talked during the report and I had a definite feeling of lack of interest on the part of practically every member of the Board present."[68]

Spingarn corrected the oversight, adding himself and the secretary as members ex officio to the committee composed of Harris, Ovington, James Weldon Johnson, Sterling Brown, Louis Wright, and Rachel Davis Du Bois, a pioneering white educator of what would later be called multiculturalism who was close to but no relation of the former editor. Spingarn also agreed that the board had been neglecting the association's work. Yet in his kindly, slightly paternalistic fashion, Spingarn cautioned White not to take board members' faux pas personally. "I have been troubled by the state of your health and nervous system as a result of such worry. No statesman or executive can survive unless he has a very bad memory for criticisms, irritations, and defeat."[69]

But the secretary survived—indeed thrived and consolidated his leadership in the association—in large part because of his sharp memory. Once on the future program committee, White prepared to fashion it to his own purpose of guiding an institutionalized, bureaucratized, and developed organization in the quest for civil rights primarily through legalism and lobbying. To the secretary, the thrust of the preliminary program was perfectly fine. In fact, he was prepared to accept it almost in its entirety.

But White believed that the politics of the new program were largely irrelevant. As he and Harris debated the draft, White insisted that what mattered was money. You want to shift the organization to agitation on economic issues? he rhetorically asked Harris. "I would like to suggest that your committee recommend that the Association attempt to raise a special fund of at least $5,000 annually," was his reply. He also made his views known to Ovington, as the committee continued to finalize its work. "Some very interesting recommendations are going to be made . . . but, as you readily see, the job is that of getting money to put any program into effect." Harris, whose mandate was to write a program that would make the NAACP relevant to the most pressing struggles of the African American people, would not rise to the secretary's bait. Where White saw the solution to the NAACP's programmatic quandaries as a bureaucratic one, Harris saw an issue of political will. "You raised the question of the additional cost that this program will entail if put into operation and seem to think that the Committee ought to tell you how the money is going to be raised. . . . [M]y attitude in the whole matter is simply this: . . . The question as to how you are going to get the money to put these proposals into operation is a matter for you and your associates to decide, that is, if you are convinced that they will give the Association the correct orientation in facing current problems."[70]

For committee member Ovington, the program was too much of a departure for her comfort, despite her sympathy for its aims. The program preached class struggle. She agreed with this, but few blacks did, while "every Negro stands for our platform. (They don't all say so but they do in their hearts.)" Should the association switch tactics it would lose its traditional base. Other prominent association members had pause too. Bill

Hastie and Charlie Houston embraced elements of the program. But it was difficult to change an established organization's direction, more difficult than building a new organization from the beginning. While they thought that economic questions had to take on increased importance and visibility, these would be not central but part of a many-sided program, "for the time being at least." Some board members had reservations too, but on the motion of James Weldon Johnson, the board adopted it.[71]

As the association moved toward its June 1935 annual convention in St. Louis, internal debate intensified, and the secretary worked feverishly to annex the new program to his legalistic disposition. One of the proposed resolutions—vetoed by White—called for NAACP support for the founding of the left-wing National Negro Congress, of whose odyssey more will be written in the next chapter. The Chicago branch was primed to struggle for more grassroots political activity. J. L. LeFlore of the Mobile, Alabama, branch demanded a "swing to the left." Bridling this wave of militancy, the secretary warned that if African Americans were not given their rights, they would secure them through violence. But among an important portion of the NAACP leadership, enthusiasm for the new program was dissipating. Ovington worried about its practical effect.[72] Joel Spingarn, who officially kicked off the search for a program with his call for the Amenia Conference, now pleaded caution. Said he to the assembled delegates:

> Of course, it is very easy for the colored people of the country to say, "Well, let's take the easiest way. Here is an economic doctrine that promises everything. Let's adopt it." I agree with Dr. Du Bois that if the colored people become Communists they will merely serve as the shock troops to be slaughtered and that even if the victory is won, they won't be there to enjoy it. I hope they will learn something from the unfortunate experience of the Jewish people, of whom perhaps one or two per cent are Communists. Yet in the mind of every American every Communist is a Jew and every Jew is a Communist, with certain tragic results for the whole race.[73]

While White spoke militantly, he had to temper his remarks; his rhetoric had to be such as to keep the emerging left wing within the NAACP, but he also had to placate the association's traditional, more cautious base. Significantly, he lobbied Eleanor Roosevelt to provide a high-ranking member of the administration as a featured speaker. It was important, he wrote, to demonstrate the NAACP's influence in the White House. Otherwise, there was no telling what direction the African American freedom struggle might take. With Harry Hopkins and Harold Ickes unable to make it, Josephine Roche, an assistant treasury secretary, took the podium to laud the NAACP. And when the convention adopted the new program, two major modifications strengthened White's hand and reassured those most queasy with unbound radical change. First, there was no commitment on the part of the association to establish workers' councils. Second, the secretary was vested with unprecedented responsibility for implementing the program. With explicit control over all aspects of the association's activities, White's authority was now virtually supreme within the NAACP, as Joel Spingarn, who had the most reservations about his leadership, finally decided to defer to him.[74]

The secretary's balancing act apparently worked. White would not be able completely to ignore the future plan and program by any means, but he would exercise his administrative prerogatives to pursue legal remedies to the problems of Afro-America. "I agree with you wholeheartedly in what you say about the root of our racial evils being in segregated schools and disfranchisement and in the basic economic aspects of our problem," he wrote to Will Jones, a syndicated columnist who appeared in the *Baltimore Afro-American* and who had digested for the secretary the current of criticism of the NAACP. He dismissed as "academic" Marxists like Ben Stolberg, who desired to see the NAACP orient itself toward the class struggle. Such an approach, while dramatic, amounted to "ballyhoo." But of this trio of evils, White would focus on the first two.[75]

At the same time, he was able to keep the trust of influential portions of the left. Charles Houston continued his ties with the ILD's lawyers, yet he remained a supporter of the secretary; his leftist sympathies and common sense kept White from making any number of blunders in his drive to master the CPUSA. Howard "Buck" Kester, the white southern socialist and cofounder of the Southern Tenant Farmers Union, was convinced White set the appropriate course at the annual convention. "I believe in you more to-day than I ever did," he wrote to White, with whom he was close and friendly but not uncritical. Kester told White that he wrote positively to a fellow leftist who expressed the suspicious mien of that crowd about the NAACP's direction.

I am ready to state now, however, that in my opinion the NAACP did move to the left at the Convention, that it is attempting to do so continuously and that it is increasingly becoming the sort of organization we might wish it to become. I think I am in a little better position to understand the situation than I was a year ago and I am considerably more hopeful than I was then. I think Walter White is less inclined to follow the bourgeoise [*sic*] group he seemed to follow so closely sometime ago. He seems genuinely concerned for the NAACP to identify itself increasingly with the working class and its organizations.[76]

Kester's endorsement is important both as a barometer of the left's feelings toward White and because their two organizations would enjoy a symbiotic relationship in the fight against peonage and lynching, with the NAACP working the legal side of the street.

The year 1935 was the last one for more than a decade that Walter White would have to stare down opposition within the NAACP. Certainly there would be strong currents of opposition to his leadership and to legalism from without. On the left, the National Negro Congress, headed by professional gadfly John P. Davis, tried, without success, to muscle its way into the NAACP's antilynching crusade. There would also continue to be sharp discussion about how the NAACP ought to deal with organized labor, given the association's endorsement of the Congress of Industrial Organization. From the center, White would be hammered by white southern liberals for being too aggressive on the antilynching campaign. But there would be no challenge of his leadership within the association. Ovington's reluctance to launch the legal campaign against segregated education in 1934—because the prospects for immediate victories seemed remote and because the secretary was in need of "a few laurels . . . at just this moment"—was a distant memory.[77] At the 1937 convention he was awarded the Spingarn Medal, the association's highest honor. In a *This Is Your Life* moment, Frank Murphy, now the attorney general of the United States, and James Weldon Johnson mounted the podium to praise the secretary's wise stewardship of the association.

When, two years later, Joel Spingarn died, control of the association devolved irreversibly on the secretary and, as Elliott Rudwick and August Meier point out, on a paid African American staff. From the time that Louis Wright had succeeded Spingarn as chairman in 1935, board members had been increasingly content to let White run the organization. That same year the legal department, whose oversight fell to the secretary, was established to supercede the old volunteer legal committee, which was largely composed of white attorneys.[78] With Spingarn's passing, White had lost an important mentor, someone who spoke frankly to him of his shortcomings, yet who nevertheless championed him. According to Joel's brother Arthur, who was himself a warm friend, the secretary did not fully appreciate the efforts Joel made on his behalf, and the death notice he wrote was oddly stiff and formal, as if he was impatient for the obsequies to end. In paying tribute to the late pillar of the association, Walter White noted that a great many women and men of Spingarn's caliber were joining to continue his life's work—only this time, White stated significantly, they were for the most part lawyers.[79]

Chapter 7

Walter, Eleanor, and Franklin: The Federal Antilynching Campaign, 1933–1940

One of the ways that African Americans experienced the country's sustained economic free fall was an uptick in lynchings. After dropping to around ten mob murders annually in the late twenties, African Americans felt a spike in 1930, with more than thirty in the first nine months alone. The secretary blamed the recrudescence on the Depression's social dislocation. As White had recently demonstrated in *Rope and Faggot* (1929), the principal cause of racial violence was the attempt of the planter class to control black labor. The planters sought to soften the ravages of the economic crisis on their wealth by squeezing more tightly African American sharecroppers. Usually awash in debt even when the agricultural economy prospered, black farmers were now clobbered by a tidal wave of red ink. African Americans resisted being driven into peonage, and the resulting friction resulted in higher incidents of mob murder. Or, as White mused to James Weldon Johnson, "lynchings usually go up in number when the price of cotton goes down." The reaction of southern politicians to the defeat of the Parker nomination played its part in spreading racial violence as well, as evidenced in a new saturnalia of demagoguery from Cole Blease and Tom Heflin. Their toxic rantings about white supremacy and the protection of white womanhood simply encouraged ordinary whites to participate in or acquiesce to the mob as it did its bloody work.[1]

The stain of mob violence spread beyond the South, however. On the night of August 7, 1930, in the east-central Indiana town of Marion, mid-way between Fort Wayne and Indianapolis, a young white couple who had slipped away to the local "lover's lane" were robbed; in the ensuing struggle, the man was murdered. Three black youths, eighteen-year-old Abe Smith, nineteen-year-old Thomas Shipp, and sixteen-year-old James Cameron, were apprehended for the crime. They had in fact been committing robberies that evening at gunpoint. Before long, false rumor roared through the town: the couple were engaged to be married and were paused by the roadside discussing their wedding plans (they were not); and the woman was raped (she was not). That evening a mob of be-tween fifty and a hundred stormed the jail, kidnapped Smith and Shipp, beat them to death, and hung them by a tree in the public square before a crowd of between 10,000 and 15,000 persons; their bodies remained sus-pended from the tree until 10:00 the next morning. Miraculously, Cameron was set free.[2]

Visiting the scene of the crime openly this time, Walter White turned up the following facts. The state's governor refused to call out the na-tional guard. The sheriff, who had been elected with strong support from the Ku Klux Klan, left unlocked three steel doors that could have pro-tected the victims; he refused to fire into the crowd to disperse it, because, he said, he feared such action would incite it! This despite Indiana's anti-lynching law that allowed law officers no such discretion when they are protecting the lives of potential lynching victims. White forwarded to the governor a list of twenty-seven mob members. A few of the accused were put on trial the following year, but sympathy for them ran strong; it proved difficult to impanel an impartial jury, and they were acquitted. White and Indiana NAACP leader Katherine Bailey nevertheless counted even a trial a victory; they were convinced that nothing would have happened without the association's pressure.[3]

As the secretary's actions demonstrated, the NAACP continued its longstanding commitment to investigating lynchings. But the association had no strategic plan for fighting lynching, and White was now disin-clined to believe that exposure of these heinous crimes by itself would mobilize African Americans. "The brother is still asleep," he sighed to James Weldon Johnson about the difficulty of rousing to antilynching ac-tion African Americans in the South, "and the vast majority of them don't care how many lynchings take place as long as they themselves are not in-cinerated."[4] With this hint of resignation, and under pressure from radicals within, White decided to shelve the antilynching work in favor of taking up issues around which African Americans were beginning to stir. In the first days of the Roosevelt administration, Addie Hunton, an association board member who was also one of the few black officials in the Women's International League for Peace and Freedom (WILPF), approached the secretary about striking an alliance to push for federal antilynching legislation. After some reflection, White declined actively to pursue this course. First of all, "interest has shifted to a purely economic field" and all of Afro-America's, and therefore the NAACP's, "energies and enthusiasms are being given to a supreme effort" to establish for blacks a secure position within the New Deal's recovery efforts.[5]

But a new wave of terrorism forced White to reconsider abandoning the antilynching campaign. In August, two black men, Dan Pippen and A. T. Harden, were arrested and placed in jail in Birmingham, Alabama; a week later they were transferred without explanation to a jail in Tuscaloosa. Shortly after, the prisoners were returned to Birmingham along a little-traveled road. At the small town of Woodstock, two carloads of lynchers stopped the sheriff, pulled Pippen and Harden from the car, and murdered them. With a little poking around, it became evident to Charles Houston that local law enforcement officials were not merely negligent but were an active part of a conspiracy to kill the two men. Not wanting to lose out to the CPUSA in Alabama again—the association was still smarting from Scottsboro—White and Houston initiated a coalition with the ILD and the American Civil Liberties Union to demand federal action. (Their quick action was the cause for Houston's optimism that the NAACP would finally have a presence in the state.) Attorney General Cummings met with Houston but rejected his argument that the federal government had the authority to act in cases where local officials clearly were negligent, thus indicating something less than a keen attitude on the part of the executive branch.[6]

Then in October, in Princess Anne, Maryland, just outside of the nation's capital, George Armwood, a mentally retarded black man whom the authorities suspected for the rape of an elderly white woman, was taken from jail two days after his arrest. Incited by a drunken former jailer, a mob had pulled down a telephone pole and used it to batter down the jail doors; a crowd of more than 2,000 whites watched the spectacle. Armwood was beaten to death, after which his body was dragged by automobile through the streets, mutilated, and burned. Although state and local law enforcement officials knew of eight mob leaders, no action was taken against them. Despite the Maryland attorney general's stated desire to punish the lynchers, police officials and prosecutors, who are elected, feared that any such action would jeopardize their careers.[7]

In response, White instructed the legal committee to draft a bill to introduce in Congress. He secured a pledge from Senator Edward Costigan of Colorado to introduce the bill on the first day of that house's second session in January 1934. After a fruitless search for a representative from Maryland or another border state to introduce the bill in the House, White decided to seek his fortune entirely in the Senate and enlisted Robert Wagner of New York as cosponsor.[8]

The guts of the Costigan-Wagner bill was federal oversight of the prosecution of lynching. Lynching would remain an ordinary crime under a state's jurisdiction, provided local authorities faithfully discharged their obligations to protect people in their custody who were in danger of being lynched and worked diligently to apprehend and bring to trial those accused of participating in a mob. Federal authority would be brought to bear only when local and state officials were found negligent. Derelict officials could be placed on trial and the counties where lynchings occurred could be subject to a substantial fine.

Taking a page from the NAACP's drive for the Dyer bill in the twenties, the push for Costigan-Wagner, as it came to be called, would be extensive, intensive, and on a grand scale. White charged branches with the immediate formation of local antilynching committees, including sympathetic organizations like the YWCA and the WILPF; the organization of protest marches, rallies, and newspaper and radio coverage; and fund-raising. Meanwhile, the secretary would initiate a broad united front that would include a formidable array of intellectuals, white southern radicals, liberals, and moderates, and—at arm's length—even Communists.[9]

Bringing all progressive forces under one big tent, White orchestrated a two-day Senate hearing on the Costigan-Wagner bill; limited to the bill's proponents, the hearings were by design a large-scale publicity event. The secretary produced a racially integrated and geographically balanced list of some three dozen witnesses. Notably absent was any representative from organized labor: the secretary had invited AFL president William Green to testify, but Green dodged the invitation by telling White that he had ordered the federation's legislative committee to look at the chances for the bill's passage. James Ford and Bernard Ades—two Communists representing the League of Struggle for Negro Rights and the ILD, respectively—testified on the last day, ostensibly to support the bill but in fact to criticize what they perceived to be its shortcomings. Serendipitously, an anonymous donor used her influence—and her money—to have the NBC radio network broadcast the entire proceedings nationwide.[10]

The tour de force presented the NAACP's strongest possible case for antilynching legislation and highlighted the breadth of support for it. Karl Lewellyn, one of the country's foremost professors of law; Arthur Spingarn; and Arthur Garfield Hays, who represented the American Civil Liberties Union, provided ample forensic evidence of the bill's legality.[11] Marc Connelly, author of the black-themed play *Green Pastures* and director of the Dramatists' Guild, represented the Writers League against Lynching, an assembly of more than 200 writers.[12] Charles Houston called attention to the disgrace the rope and faggot brought upon the United States internationally. There was not a single country thinking of waging war against the United States that was not counting upon the discontent of African Americans, who with good reason were not at all enthusiastic about defending the country and were looking with evident interest at the Communist Party.[13]

During his turn at the witness table, White guided the senators and the radio audience through African Americans' gruesome odyssey of racial violence and their practically fruitless search for justice. Under conditions of economic dislocation lynch mobs could easily "extend their activities to Communists, Socialists, the foreign-born and members of whatsoever groups which happen to incur popular disfavor. . . ." He presented statements by a dozen governors, including Florida's, in opposition to lynching, and editorials in support of the bill from twenty-four newspapers, many of them from the South. Should lynching not stop, the secretary warned, African Americans' only alternative was revolt. "No longer is the Negro the carefree, happy-go-lucky, laughing individual pictured by minstrel shows and vaudeville comedians," he stated to senators who likely had little or no contact with the race.

> Swift, deep currents of unrest, of bitter resentment against the lynching mob and every other form of proscription surge through the life of those who form one tenth of America's population. . . . [L]ynching will

inevitably result in a deepening of this resentment which America would do well to consider.[14]

Houston's and White's pleas were impassioned, but hardly surprising. What must have caught the senators' and the nation's attention was the impressive display of support for an antilynching bill by white southerners, male and female. Elizabeth Yates Webb taught history at Vassar College, but she was born and reared in Shelby, North Carolina, and was the daughter of former representative and current U.S. district court judge E. Y. Webb and the niece of former governor O. Max Gardner. Her southernness lent verisimilitude to her stand against mob rule. To be sure, antilynching sentiment was still a "submerged element," as she put it, but not for long. The pervasiveness of the states-rights heritage notwithstanding, the spirit was catching on, among both educated southern white thirtysomethings and the current generation of college students.[15]

Albert Barnett, native Alabamian, Southern Methodist minister, and ten-year professor of Bible and history at Nashville's Scarritt College, shouldered the task of organizing the southern white antilynching sentiment. Closely associated with Buck Kester's religious-tinged radicalism, Barnett was unleashed by the prospects of a federal antilynching bill and pledged his full cooperation. He testified at the hearings, paid his own expenses, and brought with him eight other witnesses from Nashville. But it was his organizing in Nashville and southwide that made him especially valuable to the Costigan-Wagner campaign. Disgusted by the ministers who preached against lynching yet covertly abetted the mob, Barnett set out to organize genuine opinion against lynching. He assembled support for the bill from a committee of Methodist ministers, the General Board of Christian Education, the General Board of Missions, and the interdenominational Nashville Ministerial Alliance. He and a local rabbi held a mass rally not simply to denounce lynching in principle—there had already been enough of that—but also to endorse the proposed federal legislation. He hoped, he said, to develop a regional effort, especially through the Southern Methodist church, whose women members were vocal against mob terror.[16]

The secretary had organized a public-relations road show that convincingly demonstrated popular support for federal legislation even in the South, a region popularly thought of as a backwater of states rights and Confederate sympathy. He believed that the only way to move the bill through the Congress was to batter the argument that the South was solidly against the legislation and thereby either free or compel a critical number of Dixie lawmakers to vote for it. Armed with this fresh perspective, the Senate Judiciary Committee easily reported out the Costigan-Wagner bill two months after the hearings; for the moment it appeared as if the NAACP's efforts would enjoy a different fate than when the Dyer bill stalled in the Senate.

Notwithstanding Barnett's diligent efforts, the endorsement of the daughter of bona fide Southern aristocracy, and the sympathetic backing of a few state chairwomen of the influential Association of Southern Women for the Prevention of Lynching (ASWPL), southern white liberals' and moderates' expressions of solidarity with the NAACP's antilynching campaign were far more conditional than Walter White let on at the hearings. For while enlightened southern opinion generally agreed on the need to eliminate the crime of lynching, it nevertheless entertained substantial resistance to the NAACP's strategy and tactics.

As he hatched his plans for Costigan-Wagner, the secretary had expected more from the ASWPL. It was founded in 1930 by a small group of southern white women in response to a lynching in east Texas. The mob was agitated by false rumors that George Hughes had raped a white woman; in reality, the charges were merely pretext, the root issue being a heated dispute over wages. The ASWPL, led by Jessie Daniel Ames, set itself the task of using the "moral and social leverage of organized women to prevent lynchings in the rural and small-town South."[17] White quickly discovered that the ASWPL, despite its program, was hardly sympathetic to the NAACP's antilynching work. In December 1933, the Georgia affiliate of the ASWPL had praised President Roosevelt's tough stand against mob rule, which he took during a nationally broadcast radio address. When the ASWPL held its annual meeting the next month, it called for active federal-state cooperation to eliminate lynching. Yet it remained silent, largely at Ames's insistence, on federal legislation. The secretary wrote Ames, congratulating her on the steps her organization had already taken but inviting her to endorse Costigan-Wagner. If White was guilty of addressing Ames without the deference she would have expected both as a longtime toiler in the vineyard and as a southern white woman—he was, after all, famously breezy and informal in his approach to most political leaders—Ames was in her own way condescending. Thus was set into motion a political relationship more oppositional than cooperative.[18]

Ames's objection to Costigan-Wagner was one part organizing strategy and leadership philosophy and one part racial paternalism. The ASWPL's success in preventing lynchings—and it had some dramatic triumphs—came from its relentlessly local focus. In 1934 the ASWPL began a drive to get sheriffs to sign a statement that lynching was never justified, that lynchers should be prosecuted, and that they pledged to stop the crime before it took place. By 1941, more than 1,300 law enforcement officers had signed the statement, and in one year alone, peace officers had prevented forty lynchings. In several instances, alert local ASWPL leaders, even in the deep South, caught wind of incipient lynchings; they contacted news agencies, hounded governors, and harangued jailers and were able to either fend off mobs or persuade them to disband. The antilynching association's members, many of whom had mob participants in their families, drew their authority from the "ingenious use of southern folkways and institutions together with the modes of influence available to them as middle-class women." Drawing upon the tested tactics of moral reform and uplift in the private spheres of life that had worked so effectively for earlier female reform movements, the ASWPL believed that it could restrain the lynch mob and even exert influence over the lynchers. Ames feared that her organization would lose the credibility it had carefully built up by becoming involved in an overtly political movement, especially one that cut against the grain of local and states-rights tradition.[19]

But Ames's insistence on a local orientation was more than a matter of expediency. In reality it meant a racially exclusive approach. Lynching sickened her, she said, and in the tradition of other southern paternalists, its eradication was the moral business of whites. Her organization admitted no African Americans. Despite insistent calls for federal intervention by southern black women, Ames steadfastly maintained that she knew what was best for them. And though she stated often enough that lynching was part of a matrix of economic, political, and social problems, she did not propose the dismantling of segregation and only in the forties recognized the need for black suffrage. Ames's preference for a regional solution to lynching was a claim for white racial supremacy and an erasure of African Americans from the antilynching crusade.

Ames's and the ASWPL's first response to White's overtures were matched by the timidity and passive opposition of the Commission on Interracial Cooperation. Even before his decision to reemphasize antilynching legislation, White, who worked harmoniously with Will Alexander, the head of the CIC, had recognized that the "Interracial Commission is ever too prone to compromise."[20] But when Albert Barnett told him that several key Southern Methodist women activists who were undecided about federal legislation were going to take their cue from Alexander, the secretary was only more convinced of the necessity of getting the doyen of white southern liberalism on board. White believed he had won Alexander's support when he agreed to appear at the hearings, but when the final dates were set for February 20–21, Alexander begged off, citing a scheduling conflict. The statement he sent in absentia, rather than endorsing the specific remedy before the committee that most African Americans agreed ought to be tried, was a Milquetoast endorsement of general federal action. Will Alexander, among the best and most sincere of his ilk, simply could not rid himself of notions that the enlightened white South was ordained to improve conditions for African Americans, who in turn would have to wait patiently. "[T]he majority of thoughtful people in the south are not yet ready to commit themselves to the principle of federal legislation," he informed the secretary—though what he really meant was thoughtful *white* people—and he would not stray too far from that opinion.[21]

The secretary fared no better at the hands of the South's influential newspaper editors, with the notable exception of H. L. Mencken, whose endorsement of the Costigan-Wagner bill in the *Baltimore Sun* was as clear as his acid-dipped barbs, aimed at the mobs and their evangelical defenders, were sharp. Julian Harris, editor of the *Atlanta Constitution*, was typical. He shared a Pulitzer Prize with his wife Julia for a 1925 editorial campaign against the KKK when they co-owned the Columbus (Georgia) *Sun Enquirer*; but he flinched when it came to "outside" criticism of the South. Explaining to the secretary why he favored some unspecified federal law only rather than the very specific Costigan-Wagner bill, Harris said he favored states rights and believed that northern and federal intrusion created unnecessary friction. "Outside interference upset the apple cart in the case of Leo Frank, and I think it did much harm in the Scottsboro cases." Though he assured the secretary that he personally shared none of these feelings, he made it plain that his editorial crusading had its limits.[22]

White's dialogue with George Fort Milton, editor of the *Chattanooga News*, was more thoughtful but produced the same results. In 1930, Milton had headed the biracial Southern Commission on the Study of Lynching (SCSL), organized by Will Alexander in response to the recent spate of lynchings. After fifteen months of investigation, the SCSL produced *Lynchings and What They Mean*, which was notable not so much for its findings—they echoed the secretary's *Rope and Faggot*—but for the fact that white southerners were embracing (though not acknowledging) the NAACP's analysis. Revealing the limitations of even the most forthright and nondefensive southerner, Milton and the SCSL reserved the adjustment of the lynching problem to the South, particularly the white South. Milton's objections were at first primarily technical. He did not think a federal statute would pressure states to prevent mob violence or prosecute lynchers because state and federal juries would be drawn from the same pool. His demurral pained him, he said, because he knew that the CPUSA was heaping invective on the association and he wanted to do nothing, even inadvertently, that would further pro-communist sympathies among African Americans. White thanked Milton for "one of the finest, frankest and most honest [letters] I have ever received and I want you to know how grateful I am to you for it." But he took issue with the editor's position. Federal judges and prosecutors were not beholden to the white electorate, as were local authorities, and they were, in his vast investigative experience, often able to cultivate respect for the law. Trying to take advantage of Milton's anticommunism, the secretary wrote to him that passage of the bill would surely strengthen the NAACP as a bulwark against the CP, while its defeat might very well have the opposite effect. All of this was of no avail, however. After consulting with fellow white liberals Will Alexander and Douglas Southall Freeman, editor of the *Richmond News Leader*, he decided to stand pat. He concurred with both men that the white South needed at least one more chance to correct its own errors.[23]

The white southern liberals' self-made quandary irritated the secretary. He had managed to build a distinguished coalition, including influential interracial organizations like the YWCA and the Federal Council of Churches. Unlike the 1922 campaign for the Dyer bill, the association would not have to fight alone. But the southerners' cowardliness threatened to deny White the broad and deep southern support he needed to convince President Roosevelt that Costigan-Wagner was worth supporting. He searched for a way to penalize them, but could do little beyond quoting their own words about the dangers of lynching before the Senate hearings, thus raising questions about their absence.[24]

The secretary had spent important time courting the support of Eleanor Roosevelt. At first he proposed that she appear before the Senate committee; she considered the idea but then declined, telling New Deal administrator and head of the American Friends Service Committee Clarence Pickett that she feared stirring up popular antagonism and thus doing more harm than good. White then met with ER at the beginning of March, at which time she told him the startling news that the president had "told her to inform [White] that he was going to do everything he could to get the bill passed at this session. He is working quietly in order to avoid raising too much opposition to the bill." This glint of interest by the president must have surprised White because FDR was known not to challenge southern politicians on behalf of African Americans for fear of them blocking other aspects of his recovery program.[25]

Meanwhile, the Senate Judiciary Committee favorably reported the legislation and sent it to the full Senate for consideration. By late April and early May, when the Congress began to think of adjournment, the secretary counted enough votes in both houses to enact the bill. But the Senate's agenda-setting southern members were firmly against allowing it to be considered, and they would not allow it on the legislative calendar. Its last, best chance was for the president to tell Senate Democrats he considered the bill a legislative priority. White put his considerable lobbying skills to work; with the intercession of ER, whom he had persuaded that victory was a distinct possibility, White went to work on the president.

ER apparently tried to soften up her husband; to his objections that the South would be solidly opposed to an antilynching measure, she presented him with the list of southern endorsers and a raft of southern newspaper editorials favoring federal action. FDR, however, remained unconvinced. On the first Wednesday in May, she wrote the secretary a sympathetic note indicating her willingness to advance the cause:

> The President talked to me rather at length today about the lynching bill. As I do not think you will either like or agree with everything that he thinks, I would like an opportunity of telling you about it, and would also like you to talk to the President if you feel you want to. There-

fore, will you let me know if you are going to be in Washington before long?

White packed his bags and his potent combination of personal charm and focused political instinct, and on the following Sunday he was ushered onto the White House veranda for evening tea.[26]

Because she invited him, the secretary first met with ER, who was accompanied by the president's mother. FDR was delayed in his return from sailing on the Potomac. When he joined the others on the porch, he, in his usual manner, avoided a topic he was reluctant to discuss by telling a hefty assortment of anecdotes and stories. ER directed his attention to the antilynching bill. For each of his objections—Senate Majority Leader Joe Robinson of Arkansas believed the bill to be unconstitutional; the county-penalty provision was too draconian; and so forth—the secretary had a rehearsed rebuttal. Sensing that he had been conspired against, the president good-naturedly stopped his stonewalling. "Over teacups we discussed every phase of the bill and the situation generally," White happily reported to Daisy Lampkin. The president promised White that he would consult with Senator Wagner to spur passage and that he would tell Senate Democrats that he wanted the bill passed. But, he said, he would do nothing to stop an anticipated filibuster; he could not challenge his party's southern leadership, he believed, without jeopardizing the rest of his legislative program. The secretary left the meeting in fine fettle, believing victory was within his grasp.[27]

The high degree of optimism was not warranted. A cabal of four senators from the deep South states in which more than 35 percent of the lynchings since 1882 had taken place were blocking consideration of the bill. The NAACP's new angle of attack was to publicize these senators' actions as defending the right to lynch, but it had little effect on moving the legislative process along. Rather, there was growing sentiment on the part of other southern senators for a filibuster. To make matters more desperate, the *New York Times* reported that FDR was once again expressing doubts about Costigan-Wagner's constitutionality. The NAACP was hearing from sympathetic Republican senators that they were prepared to vote for the bill, but they were not about to rescue the president from the southern Democrats by pushing it to the front of the Senate's agenda.[28]

Once again, White turned to ER. Would she please place before the president some critical pieces of information that would almost certainly help him to make up his mind? Would she please call to his attention the worsening racial situation in the deep South? He applied pressure in other ways. Utilizing his extensive press contacts, White persuaded a reporter from the Scripps-Howard chain to ask FDR at a press conference whether he favored Costigan-Wagner being brought up for a vote. Now, FDR answered "yes." The president repeated his desires in a meeting with Costigan and Wagner; the senators chose to leave White out of the meeting, though, fearing his presence would inflame presidential secretary Marvin McIntyre, whose southern inclinations were well known. The president went a bit further in early June, communicating to the secretary through his wife. White immediately relayed her urgent message to Senator Costigan: "If the sponsors of the bill will go at once to Senator Robinson and say to him that, if, in a lull, the anti-lynching bill can be brought up for a vote, the President authorizes the sponsors to say that the president will be glad to see the bill pass and wishes it passed." But a third-hand statement, delivered after a tumultuous public silence and without the president having placed the bill on his legislative priority list, was bound to have little effect. Senator Robinson ignored the request, and Senators Costigan and Wagner admitted defeat. They removed their antilynching bill from consideration until the new Congress met in January 1935.[29]

The secretary had achieved a good deal in this first phase of the fight for Costigan-Wagner: extensive publicity, especially via radio; closer ties with reform-minded organizations; entrée to the White House and a developing bond with Eleanor Roosevelt; inroads with some southern white liberal groups; and a developing rapport with Washington journalists and congressional aides. But a dissection of the campaign so far revealed several areas in need of improvement. The secretary spent the summer and fall of 1934 and early 1935 broadening the antilynching coalition, drawing the association's membership actively into the campaign through direct action, and continuing his efforts to win over white southern liberals, or at least to neutralize them.

One part of the campaign that the secretary sought to enhance was the participation of Jews, because the early phases passed without significant Jewish support. That this was the case may occasion surprise, given the prominent part played by Jewish figures like the Spingarn brothers in association business, the participation of Jews of means in past fund-raising drives, and especially because of the secretary's longtime connections with Louis Marshall and his son-in-law Jacob Billikopf, who were both active in Jewish-American affairs. But despite the efforts of these individuals—and the mythological "Black-Jewish alliance"—the Jewish participants in NAACP affairs and the black civil rights movement in the thirties were the exception; and they did so as individuals and not as representatives of organizations, which were largely unconcerned with blacks. Generally speaking, Jewish officialdom—the aforementioned leaders notwithstanding—aimed to keep a low profile; by not drawing attention to themselves, they hoped to tamp down the cyclical flare-ups of anti-Semitism and ease the way for their assimilation into American society.[30] Such an alliance would come in the next decade, would be suffused with tensions, and would be based more on self-interest and shared goals than on idealism. As the fight approached a crescendo in April 1934, White had lamented to Billikopf that he had been unable to make contact with any of the "influential Jewish groups" save Stephen Wise's American Jewish Congress. White tried to put over the argument that it was in Jews' interest to back antilynching legislation, inasmuch as some of its provisions would afford protection to those subjected to anti-Semitic violence. But his request for help in raising $1,000, a sum he thought sufficient to push Costigan-Wagner over the top, went unfilled.[31]

As the coalition geared up for the bill's reintroduction, it broached the issue of attracting Jewish interest and financial support. White's approach to several Jewish clerics yielded some interest but no significant funds at first. The rabbi of New York's Park Avenue Synagogue and member of the social justice committee of the Rabbinical Assembly of America assured the secretary of full moral support—but because the organization was impoverished, the NAACP should expect no contribution. In December, the American Jewish Congress pledged a paltry $25 and the American Jewish Committee donated an anemic $100. After these initial contacts, White received endorsements from Jewish labor leaders, the National Organization of Jewish War Veterans, and the National Federation of Temple Sisterhoods, representing 55,000 members. But Jewish participation remained marginal.[32]

The secretary also took measures to pressure labor, whose earlier silence was enormous. In October, the San Francisco branch of the NAACP picketed the annual convention of the American Federation of Labor, protesting not only its indifference to lynching but also its discrimination against black workers. In response, the AFL passed a resolution in favor of the Costigan-Wagner bill. (Its treatment of black workers, however, continued to be a source of conflict between the two organizations for many years.) The secretary was assisted in this project by the AFL's energetic and sympathetic Washington lobbyist, Mike Flynn. It was Flynn's contention that the NAACP needed to administer "strong-arm tactics" when it came time to introduce the antilynching bill in the House. Because southern Democrats controlled the House Judiciary Committee, Flynn said, the NAACP ought to see about having large numbers of representatives file separate bills and thus overwhelm the reactionaries. And Flynn was not shy in suggesting that NAACP branches and local labor bodies in areas with large black constituencies should unite to pressure their representatives to declare their stand on antilynching legislation. Later, when the AFL wanted the NAACP's support for wages and hours legislation, Flynn suggested that White approach William Green and ask for his endorsement of a constitutional amendment mandating the "safeguard of human rights and liberties," which instantly would do away with objections that antilynching legislation was unconstitutional. On this aspect of the NAACP's program at least, Walter White succeeded in bridging the chasm between African Americans and organized labor.[33]

The October 1935 lynching of Claude Neal in Florida and the executive branch's seeming indifference to the heinousness of this public spectacle convinced the secretary of the efficacy of direct action and other tactics, both as a way to get the administration's attention and to involve the association's members in its program. On October 19, Claude Neal, a twenty-three-year-old African American, was arrested in the Florida panhandle town of Marianna for the murder of Lola Cannidy, age twenty, a white woman. Cannidy was the daughter of the farm owner for whom Neal and his family worked; living across the road from each other, Neal and Cannidy had been friends since childhood, and for some time had been having an affair. On the eighteenth, Cannidy arranged to meet Neal for the purpose of breaking off their relationship; when she told him that she did not want to see him anymore and then threatened to tell the town's white men on him, which meant certain death, Neal murdered her.

To keep him from the mob that was gathering, local officials moved Neal several times, finally placing him in a jail about 150 miles away in

Brewton, Alabama. That was not far enough. A mob stormed the jail, took custody of Neal, and transported him back to Marianna. News of the impending lynching spread with brushfire speed. The *Eagle* of Dothan, Alabama, just over the Florida border, announced in its pages that Neal would be put to death just outside town. (The paper was mistaken; Neal was lynched in Florida.) The Dothan radio station broadcast a notice that "all white people" were invited to see Neal die. The sheriff of neighboring Washington County, Florida, announced on the afternoon of the lynching that Neal would be lynched that evening. The Associated Press telephoned Walter White with this information. Immediately upon hearing this, White telegraphed the governor and asked him to call out the National Guard to protect Neal. He demurred, saying he could not comply unless the sheriff made the request. That night, on the schedule announced by the sheriff, after hours of ghastly torture at the hands of a hundred white men, between 3,000 and 7,000 spectators from eleven southern states, including women and children, watched as a woman came out from the Cannidy house and stabbed Claude Neal through the heart. As in previous spectacle lynchings, parts of Neal's mutilated body were placed on display throughout Marianna.[34]

When Attorney General Homer Cummings rejected White's plea for the prosecution of the lynchers based on the 1932 Lindbergh Kidnap Act, which made it a federal crime to abduct someone across state lines for "ransom, reward, or otherwise," the secretary burrowed deeper into the politics of lobbying to pressure the administration and Congress to pass an antilynching measure. First he lodged a complaint with Eleanor Roosevelt: Cummings's cravenness was stimulating a growing cynicism on the part of African Americans about the administration's stand on lynching. Would she please urge the president to say something? And would she not consider headlining the "monster rally" the NAACP was organizing in January to coincide with the opening of Congress? ER was anxious to assist. She forwarded White's letter to her husband with "FDR—I would like to do it" at the bottom. But she was not entirely a free agent. When FDR asked her not to speak at the protest because "this is dynamite," she regretfully declined, though she assured the secretary she would continue to discuss the legislation with the president. A few weeks later, she wrote the secretary that "I talked with the President yesterday about your letter [questioning FDR's commitment to antilynching legislation] and he said that he hoped very much to get the Costigan-Wagner Bill passed in the coming session."[35]

The secretary cut other angles to cultivate ER's support and budge the president. White received a letter from retired Representative L. C. Dyer telling him that he had been duped, that antilynching legislation would never pass so long as the Democrats controlled Congress, and that the NAACP ought to tell black voters the truth. In his reply, White claimed that it would be foolish for African Americans "to be blindly partisan so far as Democrats are concerned as it was for them to be blindly Republican"; the NAACP was "still maintaining its principle of political independence." White forwarded the correspondence to ER, informing her that doubts about the Democratic Congress were becoming fashionable among "thoughtful colored and white people." He, however, would continue to "cling to [his] belief that you and the President will be able through vigorous action" to ensure Costigan-Wagner's passage. But he did not know how long he could continue to hold these views and remain credible.[36]

When the president omitted Costigan-Wagner from his legislative agenda in his January address to Congress, White was bitterly disappointed. In a letter to ER he told of a torrent of messages expressing anger and disappointment at the president; he had, he told ER, counseled patience, telling them that perhaps the president would issue a separate statement. He wanted to know: was he foolishly optimistic? Two days later the secretary sent ER clippings from the black press that criticized the NAACP, White personally, and FDR for the speech, along with an ominous warning that negative sentiment "is going to grow speedily unless some forthright action is taken soon, I fear." The threat of black desertion of FDR was enough to get his attention and squeeze out a small expression of support. "I talked to the President about both your letters this morning," ER wrote White. "He wants me to say that he has talked to the leaders on the lynching question and his sentence on crime in his address to Congress touched on that because lynching is a crime. However, he, himself, will write you more fully a little later on."[37]

The secretary explored a new publicity avenue when he organized the "Art Commentary on Lynching," an exhibit of thirty-eight artists, including ten African Americans, that opened for a two-week run in February in Manhattan. The exhibit's profile was raised by the inclusion of pieces by recognized artists. Isamu Noguchi provided *Death (Lynching Figure)*, a metal sculpture based on a photograph supplied him by the secretary. Thomas Hart Benton showed his modernist painting *A Lynching*. *This Is Her First Lynching*, a drawing by Reginald Marsh, one of the original *New Yorker* cartoonists, depicted a packed mob excitedly watching a spectacle; in the foreground is a woman holding her child above the crowd for an unobstructed view of all the gory action. Most of the work by black artists—Richmond Barthé's *The Mother* is an excellent example—focus on the victimization of black men and are suffused with the religious themes of the crucifixion of Jesus and the shedding of blood.[38]

White hoped that by filtering the brutality of lynching through the gauze of fine art he would be able to reach an important segment of the population: well-heeled northern liberals who preferred not to contemplate it. In his efforts to reach this stratum, White found that once again he was in competition with the Communist Party. According to the influential Harlem weekly, the *Amsterdam News*, the CP-backed League of Struggle for Negro Rights and the John Reed Club tried to "take the project away" from the NAACP by demanding to become sponsoring organizations. When they did not succeed, they planned an alternative exhibit. The secretary tread cautiously as he organized a group of "distinguished Americans" to sponsor the show. He asked his old friend Langston Hughes, who had moved to the left, if he would not like to become a patron. But in a moment of uncertainty, White stuttered out a reference to the competing exhibits: "I want to say, however, that if you think to do so would be at all embarrassing to you or that you may run the risk of being criticized by the Communists, I will understand perfectly if you choose not to serve." With his sharp wit, Hughes tweaked the secretary: "You yourself give me so many reasons in your letter for not being a patron of your lynching exhibit, that I guess I had better not be one—although I would rather like to be as a personal gesture toward that united front against oppression and hunger of which I hope the NAACP will someday become a part."[39]

Another "distinguished American" the secretary wanted to enlist was Eleanor Roosevelt. When White telegrammed her a week before the opening, she replied that she was "glad" to oblige. A few days later, however, the eponymous owner of the Jacques Seligmann Galleries, faced with the prospect of CP protesters, canceled the Art Commentary.[40] As the secretary scrambled to find another location—the Arthur U. Newton

Galleries agreed—the imbroglio both heightened interest in the show and caused ER to have second thoughts. In a letter to White that demonstrated her political calculation, her distress at not being able to be more demonstratively helpful, and her desire to be of service to him, ER wrote:

> [T]his morning I went into talk to my husband about it. . . .
>
> My husband said it was quite all right for me to go, but if some reporter took the occasion to describe some horrible picture, it would cause more southern opposition. . . .
>
> I do not want to do anything which will harm the ultimate objective even though we might think for the moment that it was helpful and even though you may feel that it would make some of your race feel more kindly toward us. Therefore, I really think that it would be safer if I came without any publicity or did not come at all. Will you kindly telephone me at my New York house at seven o'clock on Friday night? . . . You can then tell me how you feel.[41]

Ultimately, ER decided to limit her participation to a visit "for few minutes. Cannot make statement nor see reporters. You can say I have been there after I leave."[42]

In contrast to the self-assurance he showed in lobbying official Washington and working in the world of culture, White was far more cautious when it came to applying mass pressure. Protest rallies were standard issue in the NAACP armory, and he encouraged branches to be active in organizing them; he was particularly insistent that deep South branches sponsor mass meetings in conjunction with local YWCA chapters and Federal Council of Churches affiliates. Picketing and marching were not the usual stock-in-trade, however, and the secretary had an undeveloped political instinct for their use. When Roy Wilkins proposed that the District of Columbia branch set up a picket line to protest both Cummings's response to the Claude Neal lynching and his refusal to place lynching on the agenda of a national conference on crime he was organizing for December, the secretary initially faltered. Unsure whether this was a good action to take, White consulted two of his important contacts in the Washington press corps, Ludwell Denny and Lowell Mellett, who discouraged the plan because they believed demonstrations had been overdone and were no longer likely to garner publicity. Wilkins countered his boss's doubts, arguing effectively that publicity in the white press was only one reason to demonstrate. The protest would also build the branch's esprit de corps and would almost certainly be covered by the Negro papers. Thus persuaded, the secretary became an enthusiastic backer of the picket.[43]

Wilkins took charge of the preparatory work, but he quickly lost interest when the D.C. branch, which had a history of friction with the national office, was slow to initiate plans. While Wilkins made other plans for the day of protest, December 11, White visited the Washington branch leaders and smoothed out the wrinkles, reported to Wilkins that the membership was "all excited" and were "going through with it," and invited him to return to the capital to lead the pickets. Wilkins declined, saying he was now too busy and only returned when the secretary ordered him to. As it turned out, the action was a rousing success. Over two days, seventy pickets, "half girls," made for a "very impressive" and disciplined display, said eyewitness Charles Houston. Wilkins's and three branch leaders' arrests for parading without a permit on the first day made the front page of the *Washington News* and received favorable coverage in New York City. Wilkins characteristically took all the credit, forgetting that he had nearly bailed out. President Roosevelt, feeling the pressure from the street as well as from White via ER, denounced lynching in certain terms in his speech before the crime conference. The simultaneous use of mass protest and insider lobbying proved to be a powerful cocktail.[44]

As public sentiment was again building for passage of an antilynching law, southern white liberals remained a burr under the secretary's saddle. Will Alexander continued his quiet campaign against the NAACP's efforts. He now said that legislation was of no use in ending lynching, and that education was the only way; at the same time, and somewhat contradictorily, he maintained that there was no correlation between the NAACP's agitation for the bill in 1934 and a corresponding reduction in lynchings. Speaking derisively of White to Katherine Gardner of the Federal Council of Churches, Alexander complained that White had failed to consult him in the early stages of the campaign. To cap things off, Alexander played a bit of mischief by telling White's allies that the bill would never pass because, he had heard from southern newspaperman Mark Ethridge, FDR opposed it. (White then spent valuable time confirming with ER that Ethridge was mistaken.)[45]

His luck was little better with other white liberals, despite his trying to put them on the spot. In vain he argued that their fear of a solid South was baseless, with black southerners, important white southern men, and large portions of the ASWPL favoring the Costigan-Wagner bill. George Fort Milton was the most helpful of the bunch; he agreed to testify that lynching was horrible and not to mention his opposition to the Costigan-Wagner bill unless asked. Virginius Dabney swayed with the wind. At first agreeing to alter his opposition to the bill and indicating he would editorialize in its favor, Dabney once again backed off. At a time when black blood was still being shed in the South, Dabney had "some misgivings concerning the effects of the measure upon interracial relationships. . . ." Jessie Daniel Ames continued to believe that the bill was a "joker." [46]

Senators Costigan and Wagner introduced their bill once more in January. Although it was favorably reported out by the Judiciary Committee and had enough support to pass the Senate, southern Democrats prepared to filibuster. The secretary joined with the United Mine Workers, who were formidable in southern Illinois, to pressure that state's wavering senator. He also urged the Chicago branch to organize mass rallies to the same end. Roy Wilkins had earlier chided White's emphasis on lobbying and advocated mass action as the way to pressure legislators; not particularly concerned with consistency, the assistant secretary now was convinced that grassroots activity was useless, and that what was critical was lining up support from millionaire bankers and industrialists. The secretary scrutinized this advice and then calculated that the critical move was to get FDR to prevent a filibuster before it started. [47]

Getting FDR's attention, however, was becoming more difficult, as his staff, which was more favorably disposed to southern politicians, tried to filter out African American perspectives from the president's attention. With much urgency, White approached ER [48] FDR, timid in race issues as ever, ignored his wife's advice and remained silent throughout the southern filibuster that commenced in late April. In action redolent of the campaign for the Dyer bill more than a decade earlier, the secretary raced to Washington to direct a strategy to defeat the stall. Richetta Randolph captured the mood in a letter to her old boss, James Weldon Johnson: "Work here in the office in connection with the bill carries us back to 1922. Yesterday we did about two days work in two hours—material that had to be rushed to Washington to Mr. White." The secretary had at his disposal a large contingent of volunteer lobbyists, including officials from the Women's International League for Peace and Freedom; the Washington representative of the YWCA; John P. Davis, a founder of the Joint Committee for National Recovery and who would soon help to establish the National Negro Congress; Ted Berry and Virginia McGuire, presidents of the Cincinnati and District of Columbia NAACP branches, respectively; "a white woman visiting from Minnesota, and two young colored women from North Carolina."[49]

Just before the filibuster began, Ab Young was kidnapped in Tennessee, transported across the border to Slayden, Mississippi, and lynched; he was the third victim of the year, and his was the second interstate lynching in five months. Despite evidence of intensified racial violence and increasing public support for federal antilynching legislation, the filibuster was conducted in the gutter. For eight days, the NAACP and sympathetic senators staved off attempts of the filibusterers to adjourn the Senate, thereby displacing the Costigan-Wagner bill. Outside Congress, students at several southern black colleges planned May Day demonstrations to protest the stall. Charles Houston observed that "any time Negroes can tie up the United States Senate and the affairs of the country for eight straight days, the Negro is really coming of age politically." But a week was all the majority of senators was willing to fight for the rights and safety of African Americans; even as the Costigan-Wagner bill was being suffocated, FDR was rallying support for landmark New Deal legislation, including the Social Security Act and the National Labor Relations Act, both of which—perhaps not coincidentally—excluded from their protection large numbers of African Americans.[50]

The secretary proclaimed a moral victory and exercised his outrage by resigning his presidential appointment to the Virgin Islands Advisory Commission, telling FDR that he could not "continue to remain even a small part of your official family" and be loyal to the cause of the NAACP. His actions earned the secretary even more ill will from Bourbon-leaning members of FDR's staff. His press secretary, Stephen Early, wrote a "personal and confidential" memo to ER's personal secretary Malvina Schneider in an attempt to cut off White's access to the White House. "The memorandum is sent at this time because Walter White has been bombarding the President with telegrams and letters. . . . Frankly, some of his messages to the President have been decidedly insulting. . . . Walter White, before President Roosevelt came to the White House, because of his activities, has been one of the worst and most continuous of trouble makers."[51]

But even in his vexation, White did not fire scattershot. Hugo Black, senator from Alabama, was an eager filibusterer, and during the debate he stirred passions against the bill, demagogically implying that Senator Costigan was simply fronting for the NAACP and resurrecting the specter of Negro domination. But White's previous, though limited, dealings with Black convinced him that he was more substantial than the Senate's usual gang of race-baiters. In 1931, Will Alexander, who was terribly concerned by the Communist Party's presence in the South, told the secretary that Black, for similar reasons, was possibly interested in intervening on behalf of the Scottsboro defendants. (This did not come to fruition, however, as Black purposefully kept his distance from the case.) When Senator Wagner introduced a resolution to investigate abuses of black laborers on Mississippi-levee construction projects in 1932, White, through backdoor channels, interested Black in supporting it.[52]

Because he staked a large measure of his antilynching strategy on persuading southern white moderates, his feel for this stratum was usually accurate, as it was this time. Hugo Black was much in the mold of his friend Alexander. According to his biographer, Black grew up with a basic sense of fairness, decency, and courtesy regarding African Americans. As a young prosecutor, he pursued racially explosive issues like police brutality against black citizens in Bessemer, Alabama, and he later was known to try white men accused of murdering blacks.[53]

Hugo Black had limits to his sense of justice, as did practically all of the South's white liberals of the day. His biographer states that he "disregarded race as much as a public official in Birmingham at the time could," and that "guilt [and not race] was Black's criterion in deciding whom to prosecute."[54] His attitude, while exceptional among white southerners, assumed that he knew what was best for African Americans. Like Alexander, Ames, and liberal southern journalists, Black believed that it was whites who were to determine what constituted fairness for African Americans. Throughout his time in the Senate he was unwilling to introduce or back legislation that explicitly remedied racial discrimination.[55]

At the same time, the politically ambitious Black pandered to popular prejudice to advance his career and improve his fiscal position. In 1923 he joined the Ku Klux Klan, later rationalizing his decision as a matter of political pragmatism: the Klan controlled the votes in Alabama. After he reached Washington in 1927, he offered on the Senate floor a defense, albeit mild and oblique, of black disfranchisement, a rather more vigorous support for nativism, and public approval of antimiscegenation laws.[56]

In examining what really amounted to thin shoots of hope sprouting from Black's record and seeing that they were tangled with uglier and perhaps more sturdy ones, the secretary nevertheless perceived an opportunity to engage Black in the aftermath of the filibuster. His criticism was frank but measured. Using as a departure point the pronounced anticommunism that Will Alexander and Hugo Black shared, the secretary told the senator that he had "unwittingly" handed the CP a propaganda bonanza. He had no doubt that the filibuster would become Exhibit A in the Communists' case to show African Americans that they stood no chance of gaining justice from the federal government. And he concluded his letter with the assurance that "what I have said, or may say in future, is not born of any feeling of ill will towards you for your statements on the floor of the Senate concerning the Association and myself. I merely ask you to consider this thoughtfully and carefully."[57]

There is no record of Black's reaction, though in practice the senator once again opposed antilynching legislation when it came up in 1937. But when later that year Black was nominated to the Supreme Court and confirmed in rapid fashion, White, despite his reservations, assented, based on the opinion of "persons in a position to know" that he would be a sympathetic justice. This time the secretary was right, as Black became both a personal friend and a consistent champion of civil rights on the High Court. But White's approval, as will be shown in the next chapter, was not simply wishful thinking. It was based on his estimate of the best way to bring FDR's New Deal into sympathy with African Americans, and for this he faced rather pointed opposition within the association.[58]

Nineteen thirty-six brought more moral victories only. Bolstered by a $5,000 gift to the antilynching fund from James Ryan, the heir to the fortune of a Virginia-born industrialist, White planned a comprehensive program to force congressional action on lynching and the status of blacks in the New Deal and presidential action to open up the military to African Americans and urge the end of the white primary. On the second day of the new year, the secretary had a private meeting with FDR, who expressed sympathy but predicted that such legislation was unlikely to be passed. White was frankly skeptical when Roosevelt proposed that instead of Costigan-Wagner, White promote a Senate bill instructing the Department of Justice to investigate the previous year's nineteen lynchings. He questioned the probative value of a toothless investigation by a plainly unenthusiastic attorney general.[59]

Still, one ignored presidential suggestions at his own peril. And faced with the strong possibility of another filibuster of Costigan-Wagner, the secretary modified FDR's suggestion to suit his purposes; he brought to the president's attention a proposed resolution from Indiana's Frederick Van Nuys authorizing a Senate investigation. FDR "read it in a most interested fashion and indicated that it met with his approval," White wrote Van Nuys. But despite the continued private encouragement delivered via ER and the secretary being given carte blanche by Judiciary Committee chairman Henry Ashurst to name the subcommittee for hearings on the resolution, it languished in an election year.[60]

Simultaneously, the secretary tried to force House Democrats to dislodge antilynching legislation. Plotting strategy with Joe Gavagan, who represented Harlem, White pushed for the convening of the Democratic caucus to make antilynching legislation a priority. The secretary's role in organizing a meeting of what was an official legislative body was transparent. Party rules mandated a caucus be called when twenty-five House members signed a petition for one. White all but carried the petition onto the House floor to cajole sympathetic and wavering representatives into signing.[61]

White's influence and the power of the black vote were the reasons a caucus was called at all. Several House members wrote to White that they supported antilynching legislation and that they attended the caucus. John Dingell of Michigan showed up, making a special trip to Washington from his Detroit home, though he was quite put out: "As a friend of the colored people," he lectured White, "I want to say that some of your recent activities have been antagonistic rather than helpful and for the sake of the cause I would urge you to desist." But White was not powerful enough to maneuver around the southern leadership. The caucus was convened but promptly adjourned for lack of a quorum; when the secretary tried to find out who attended and who stayed away, he could get no answer. Said Lowell Mellett, "Everybody passes the buck. Nobody admits having list of those present. Sorry."[62]

Again in 1937, White, acting the part of a congressional chief of staff, pushed Gavagan's bill in the House. In dramatic fashion the two succeeded in getting the bill discharged from the Judiciary Committee, where it had been bottled up by chairman Hatton Sumners of Texas; by a vote of 277–120, the Gavagan bill passed the House.

As the bill was coming up for final consideration in the House, a gruesome lynching occurred in Duck Hill, Mississippi: two men were taken from jail with the collusion of the sheriff and burned to death with acetylene torches. When the bill came before the Senate, Champ Clark of Missouri posted photos of the murder on the Senate bulletin board with the caption "There Have Been *No* Arrests, *No* Indictments, and *No* Convictions of Any One of the Lynchers. This was *NOT* a rape case." Clark's courageous action brought national publicity and rattled the cages of southern senators. But it could not force a vote on the bill. In November 1937, White and Senator Wagner—Costigan had retired, and his place as sponsor was taken by Van Nuys—agreed to withdraw the bill from consideration in favor of New Deal farm legislation the president desired to see passed with the understanding that it could be brought up in the next session, which convened in January 1938.

When it was brought up again, it was immediately filibustered. For six weeks, Bourbon senators fulminated against Walter White, race mixing, and interracial sex. James Byrnes of South Carolina fingered the secretary as the bill's inspirer:

> One Negro, whose name has heretofore been mentioned in the debate—Walter White . . . —has ordered this bill to pass. . . .
>
> What legislation will he next demand of the Congress of the United States? . . . I do not know; but I know he will make other demands.

Theodore Bilbo of Mississippi, in deep dudgeon as usual, pronounced in the Senate well that "the underlying motive of the Ethiopian who has inspired this proposed legislation . . . and desires its enactment into law with a zeal and frenzy equal if not paramount to the lust and lasciviousness of the rape fiend in his diabolical effort to despoil the womanhood of the Caucasian race, is to realize the consummation of his dream and ever-abiding hope and most fervent prayer to become social and politically equal to the white man." Bilbo's feral oratory was extreme but not unusual. He and the company he kept—Byrnes, Cotton Ed Smith, and Tom Connally, among others—owed their political longevity to such racial demagogy, which found favor among the bitter, poor, and exploited (but also racist) whites.[63]

Their vitriol was entirely out of proportion to Americans' opinions about lynching and federal legislation. Even in the South a majority of white southerners supported some sort of intervention. Again, the filibuster garnered maximum publicity, with White landing on the cover of *Time*. (Some notoriety was unwelcome. After his portrait graced the magazine, White suddenly found that his recurring reservation at the Hay-Adams House was no longer honored.) But as the remark by Byrnes illustrates, the professional southern politicians' fears no longer revolved exclusively around federal intervention against the crime of lynching. Rather, their querulousness reflected both their worry that northern Democrats were less willing than in the past to cede management of race relations to the South and their fear of black political activity in the South. But in contrast to the unity of the southern reactionaries, southern white progressives, having once moved closer than ever to supporting antilynching legislation, were now divided. Richmond newspaper editors Virginius Dabney and Douglas Southall Freeman blamed the filibuster for delaying FDR's recovery efforts, but the *Atlanta Constitution* called the Wagner-Van Nuys bill demagogic. Jessie Daniel Ames cheered on the efforts of majority leader Tom Connally of Texas, while Claude Pepper, one of the Senate's leading liberals, lent his voice to the filibuster. On February 21, when it was clear the filibuster could not be stopped, the bill was withdrawn, the Senate turned its face away from racial justice and busily began work on a relief appropriations bill.[64]

Senators were not the only people exhausted by the campaign for the Wagner-Van Nuys bill. Nineteen thirty-eight was the acme of the fight for a federal antilynching law, and when one did not materialize, progressives renewed their calls, first raised after the 1935 filibuster, for the secretary to acknowledge the political reality that no such bill would pass Congress and to cash in his winnings. White ignored this advice and, brandishing an unexpected presidential endorsement of the old Van Nuys resolution, tried once more. But in January 1939, James Ryan decided not to renew his hefty contribution to the antilynching fund, and in July the association board of directors downgraded the campaign.[65]

The NAACP's crusade for an antilynching law was undeniably responsible for the growth and development of a strong public opinion against lynching. During the thirties even white southerners abandoned a defense of lynching both in the abstract and in specific cases. The association had developed a high profile in official Washington. Yet if these accomplishments were not fully formed until 1939, they were well on their way to maturity years earlier. Why, then, did the secretary continue to insist on the primacy of the antilynching campaign when some of the most astute political observers and strategists within and close to the NAACP—including Charles Houston, Mary White Ovington, and Elizabeth Eastman of the YWCA, who was as loyal and committed an ally in the campaign as any—counseled him that the association had reaped maximum benefits from the fight by 1936?[66]

Two intertwined circumstances go far to explain the secretary's stubbornness in the face of evidence that a bill never would pass. First, having found success influencing lawmakers, adumbrating tactics for a legislative floor fight, and establishing a sincere relationship with Eleanor Roosevelt, the secretary overestimated the extent of the utility of these strategic elements. The secretary had a warm relationship with Costigan, whom he called "Chief," as did other members of the senator's staff. Senator Wagner's door was always open to him. He directed strategy from a back room in Representative Gavagan's office. At each new legislative session, the secretary selected the representatives who introduced the bills that were largely crafted by NAACP lawyers. Senators and representatives across the country answered his queries and assured him of their support. His entrée to the White House was unprecedented for an African American, even Booker T. Washington. When he was blocked, as he often was, by FDR's staff, he could count on ER to represent—often even advocate—his views to her husband. The secretary developed another avenue to the president through Irvin and Elizabeth McDuffie, FDR's valet and ER's personal maid, respectively.[67]

But White confused his influence and access to power, which was considerable and important, with power itself. At different times he blamed the organization's inability to break Senate logjams on the NAACP's depleted treasury. "It is heartbreaking to be so close to victory and then not be able to win because of lack of just a little money," he wrote to Rabbi Stephen Wise. Yet it was not penury but the obstinacy of the southern congressional Democratic delegations and Franklin Roosevelt's refusal to buck them that kept the bills from passing. But the secretary, probably because of his warm personal and political relationship with ER, quixotically believed that with the next letter to her she would deliver her husband's mandate to his party to support antilynching legislation.

Of course, FDR never proffered his endorsement. But if Roosevelt could not jettison the Bourbons in his party, the secretary now would not break with the president in any meaningful way. He had been unenthusiastic about Roosevelt the candidate in 1932—with John Nance Garner of Texas on the ticket, White thought FDR might prove just as bad as Herbert Hoover—and had cast his ballot for Socialist Norman Thomas. Reinforcing his disaffection with FDR were his unsuccessful efforts, despite interventions by Herbert Lehman, New York's new governor, and Joel Spingarn, FDR's Hudson River Valley neighbor, to make an appointment to meet him before he assumed office; as he told Spingarn, he wanted the president-elect to "turn towards ourselves instead of towards professional politicians when issues involving the Negro arose during his administration." But the ready access he had to non-southern congressional Democrats and the perceived openness of the new administration to African American concerns dampened White's suspiciousness and eventually won him over. Harold Ickes, for example, who had been an NAACP official in Chicago, was now interior secretary; he and labor secretary Frances Perkins were listening to White and taking at least half-measures to correct abuses of African Americans in public-works projects. The president appointed advisors on "Negro affairs" in practically every New Deal agency. And Eleanor Roosevelt consulted White and even gave him the telephone number to her New York residence.[68]

Fairly quickly, the secretary had a great deal invested in supporting FDR. His resignation from the administration's Virgin Islands Advisory Commission in 1935 was symbolic and involved no significant repercussions. When Hugo Black's past membership in the Ku Klux Klan surfaced during his confirmation hearings, the secretary refused to oppose his nomination to the Supreme Court; White used specious logic in his defense, claiming that unlike in the Parker nomination the Senate rushed to confirm Black without asking interested organizations and citizens for their comments. Given that Black's membership on the High Court was an accomplished fact, it was better that he not start his appointment with a hostile attitude toward the NAACP. Board member John Haynes Holmes accused White of being "under the Roosevelt spell." That some of Black's foes—large corporations and the reactionary Hearst newspaper chain—were also enemies of the NAACP was no reason to support the nomination, Holmes said. The NAACP, Holmes complained, was letting its actions be determined by the administration's supporters and opponents. White denied this, but he would make no move to disassociate himself from presidential actions that might prove disastrous to the NAACP program. When FDR maintained his silence during the 1938 filibuster, White begged him to say something, but pointedly deleted from an earlier draft of the letter was an accusation that FDR's nonaction amounted to a betrayal of the Negro people and a threat that blacks would turn their backs on him.[69]

Paradoxically, while several of the secretary's associates were urging him to reorient the NAACP toward the important New Deal issues of economic and social dislocation, the left-wing National Negro Congress (NNC) was recognizing the appeal of an antilynching campaign for their overall program. The NNC tried to both effect a united front with the NAACP and develop a mass protest movement for antilynching legislation, which actions provided White further incentive to push what was increasingly his campaign. He felt compelled to neutralize the left by intensifying his legislative and lobbying activities.

Organizing for the NNC began with a May 1935 conference at Howard University that strongly endorsed Abram Harris's labor-oriented program developed after the Amenia Conference. One of the meeting's sponsors was that school's Social Science Department, headed by Ralph Bunche and populated with fellow radicals Harris and Emmett Dorsey. The cosponsor was the Joint Committee on National Recovery, effectively a two-person operation composed of John P. Davis and Robert Weaver, energetic young intellectuals who gathered the data and crunched the numbers exposing the deleterious effects of New Deal programs on African American workers—especially the N.R.A. wage differentials for industries that employed large numbers of blacks. Davis was the driving force of the Joint Committee, the Howard conference, and the formal debut of the NNC in February 1936. A political chameleon, he was at one time identified with the Republican Party but now was affiliated with the CP. In the same way that Walter White dealt with Harris and his supporters, the NAACP bankrolled the Joint Committee in order to make maximum use of solid research, and to control the growing radical impulse among African Americans.

But where Abram Harris chose not to become involved in the implementation of his program, John P. Davis was a committed organizer. The CP had repudiated its "third period" tactics of polemics and confrontation with reform organizations, including the NAACP, which they felt retarded the revolutionizing of the masses; believing social revolution was no longer imminent, it tried to work with reformers in a popular front. Davis tried to make it easy for White to cooperate with the NNC. Davis invited White to speak on lynching at the NNC's official founding in Chicago; he tried to tempt the secretary with the promise of a large audience and a radio broadcast of his speech and offered him office space and secretarial assistance should he want to combine his visit with a regional NAACP conference. Because it was not entirely clear to White or the board what political forces were behind the formation of the NNC, he declined the invitation; the board sent Roy Wilkins, but only as an observer.[70]

Charles Houston, who did not share White's or Wilkins's hamhanded disposition toward the left, provided the secretary with some much-needed intelligence. His first impressions were not particularly favorable. The NNC had no fixed agenda, and the buildup to the meeting was disorganized. Those paying more attention, he sniffed, were "emotional beings who go off in sympathy for anything labeled Negro progress," and "second-string folk and the risers" who were scared not to go for fear they might miss out on something important. He was also getting some strong hints that Davis was drawing financial aid from the CP.[71]

This was enough for the secretary to give up on the NNC. He wrote to A. Philip Randolph, who brought his Brotherhood of Sleeping Car Porters into the NNC's tent and became the group's first president, that he hoped the "Congress is not permitted to be 'sold down the river' to any political group. I have heard many disturbing rumors that there is danger of this." But Houston's opinion changed after the February founding. Several people whom he respected had told him that the meeting was in fact quite representative and that it was strongest on labor issues. If the NNC did nothing in the next year but work on implementing its "very fine" resolutions it would do a "striking job," Houston reported. Houston encouraged cooperation between the two organizations, with the NAACP supplying its legal expertise in support of a black labor movement.[72]

The secretary was quite willing to have John P. Davis's organization do some heavy lifting for the antilynching campaign, such as circulate petitions, raise money, and speak at rallies sponsored by very broad coalitions. He was happy too to have other Communists participate in lobbying senators for the Van Nuys resolution—provided they did so quietly and did not emphasize their organizational ties. And, apparently, the NNC was a willing bird dog, hoping thereby to ingratiate itself with White and his considerable network. But for organizational and political reasons, the secretary steadfastly refused to hold leadership meetings with the NNC or take any action that would accord the NNC any respect or stature in the NAACP's campaign.[73]

White believed that the presence of a radical threat within the anti-lynching coalition would alarm the president and cause him to act affirmatively on the issue. In pleading for her help, the secretary wrote ER of the potentially ominous formation of the NNC. The sessions, he informed ER, continually criticized the NAACP for promising federal action on lynching but failing to show meaningful results. Though still not certain the CP was a major sponsor of the NNC, he told her, "the spirit of unrest and revolt which it represented is not in the main an artificially stimulated one but is instead an expression of a widespread dissatisfaction which cannot and should not be ignored." Eleanor Roosevelt highlighted sections of the letter dealing with left-wing sentiment among African Americans and instructed her husband to read them.[74]

At the same time, White worried that too close an association with the left would damage his credibility with the administration and in Congress. For example, Davis had waded into the controversy within the House of Labor, unhesitatingly backing the breakaway Congress of Industrial Organizations over the stodgy and racially recalcitrant American Federation of Labor. As the YWCA's Elizabeth Eastman, White's close ally in Washington and upon whom he relied for counsel, warned, "John Davis can well upset our whole legislative applecart. We must still rely on both of the labor groups in Congress, as you know, and cannot jeopardize all our legislative program by seeming to have taken sides. This difficulty confronts many of us who believe in a strong labor movement as a whole. In Congress the A. F. of L. is too strong to be alienated, as you realize from your own experiences on the bill."[75]

More than anything, however, the secretary feared losing to the left the association's substantial progressive following. Several association stalwarts, including William Hastie, board member Marion Cuthbert (who was also elected to a position in the NNC), Roy Wilkins, and several branch officials had called for close cooperation between the NAACP and the NNC.[76] White's warnings to Eleanor Roosevelt about the growth of radical sentiment was not simply a ploy to force FDR's hand. Rather, the secretary had to work hard to keep elements of his coalition in his camp. The NNC's insistence on a mass campaign for an antilynching bill was gaining appeal among those who had been working hardest with White. He was taken by surprise after the filibuster in 1938 when the NNC, realizing its patience would not end in a payoff, called for a mass conference on lynching. Representatives of the Labor Non-Partisan League, the United Mine Workers, and the CIO were to attend. The national YWCA thought seriously of lending its support. And Charles Houston appeared to be in favor of it. When Davis decided to go ahead with his plans in spite of White's urging delay, the secretary acted decisively to derail the conference. He not only refused an invitation to speak, he publicized the fact that the NAACP would not be participating and was not a sponsor. Elizabeth Eastman kept the YWCA and other progressive women's organizations from sending even an observer. The conference turned out to be small, with only 100 people in attendance, mostly members of the National Negro Congress.[77]

The center—White's center—had held. Antilynching legislation was off the agenda of Congress and of the association, but his persistence at both ends of Pennsylvania Avenue and his efforts to fend off a more radical antilynching campaign still had paid off handsomely. The secretary preserved his legislative influence and access to the White House, and the association maintained its position as an important member of the New Deal coalition.

Chapter 8

Radicals, Liberals, and Labor:
The NAACP in the New Deal
and the Great Depression

It was not that Walter White was unmoved by the plummeting economic status of African Americans in the Great Depression. If for no other reason—and there were others—the secretary was alarmed at the plummeting living standard of his race because the membership dues of blacks supplied a substantial portion of the association's budget. Rather, his disinclination to become enmeshed in economic issues and New Deal politics and policies had to do primarily with practical considerations. First of all, for most of its existence, the NAACP had ceded leadership on labor issues to others, especially the National Urban League. In one of its periodic declarations, this one in 1924, the association's board of directors said that although organized labor "does not come under the scope of the Association's activities," the NAACP ought to apply for a Garland Fund grant to make an "exhaustive investigation of the situation of the Negro workman in industry." Thus, the organization limited its work on labor to fact-finding and education, which mission was reflected in the extensive coverage of labor issues in *The Crisis*.[1]

Which is not to say that the association had no contact with the labor movement in the twenties and early thirties. In 1920 White took up the complaint of the Association of Colored Railway Trainmen, who charged southern rail lines with pay discrimination. Some of the roads had reclassified all black employees (whether brakemen, switchmen, conductors, or baggage men) as porters and paid them porters' wages. When, in January

1920, White appeared before the Railway Administration and won back pay, white trainmen in the South began a campaign of intimidation and violence to eliminate black workers. Through White's and the NAACP's efforts, some white trainmen were arrested on state and federal charges. The NAACP was an early supporter of the Brotherhood of Sleeping Car Porters, the most significant manifestation of black organized labor, for which efforts White was made an honorary union member.[2]

These sorts of activities were well within the scope of the NAACP's traditional approach to race advancement, involving methods with which White was familiar: investigation, education, lobbying, and, in the case of the trainmen's complaint, litigation. And while Walter White, as seen in the antilynching crusade and the Harlem Renaissance, was innovative and willing to experiment, he also unhesitatingly paid homage to precedent. Lobbying paid great dividends in the fight for the Dyer bill, and he would repeat these methods in the fight for Costigan-Wagner; litigation worked famously in the Arkansas peonage cases and from then on he championed this approach.

But White's limited forays directly into organized labor's province made painfully little headway, and he was loath to try it very often. In 1929, White was approached by Frank Crosswaith, the black Socialist labor organizer, and Norman Thomas, head of the Socialist Party, concerning the case of a linoleum layer in Manhattan by the name of J. H. Jones. When his shop was organized by the International Upholsterers Union, Jones, who was black, was refused membership on account of his race; the company then had to let him go, despite the fact that he was one of its best workers. And because the union controlled all shops in the city, Jones was unable to find work. White agreed to take up the case and appealed both to William Green, head of the AFL, and to Upholsterers' head William Kohn. Green's representative in New York contacted White and told him the union had erred in not admitting Jones, but would not force the issue. Kohn at first gave White the runaround and then turned hostile. He told White that Jones had never applied for membership—a statement that Jones vigorously disputed. When Jones reapplied, the local union refused him. When White pressed the case, Kohn accused him of "making an issue of the question of race, creed or color."[3]

When the NAACP decided, in applying for a major grant from the left-wing Garland Fund, explicitly to disavow direct support for labor organizing, it did so for reasons of efficacy. Taking up the demands and concerns of black *workers* was best left to organizations like the Brotherhood of Sleeping Car Porters, and the secretary encouraged A. Philip Randolph also to approach the Garland Fund. And when Walter White argued against a competing application from the CP-backed American Negro Labor Congress and urged the philanthropy to support the NAACP's program of litigation on educational issues instead, his reasoning was practical. White and James Weldon Johnson liked the ANLC's program. But, they argued, it had no record of accomplishment, only slogans. And while the association's labor record was stellar by comparison, it too was woefully thin. If the aim was to organize black workers into unions, the NAACP argued, then no organization outside the labor movement—including the NAACP and ANLC—stood any chance of forcing the AFL to reform its practices. They could offer indirect support in various forms—the association and the American Civil Liberties Union had provided legal help, for example—but "[t]o put money into the salaries of union organizers and into the rent of union headquarters, at this stage, would be like pouring money down a sink."[4]

The NAACP's programmatic decision not to involve itself in direct support of organizing black workers in favor of campaigning for a federal antilynching law and, beginning in 1933, fighting for educational equality left open to others the defense of African Americans' standard of living and associated bread-and-butter issues. Among the many black critics of what they considered to be abdication of leadership by the NAACP, few were more spirited than Harvard students Robert Weaver, a doctoral candidate in economics, and John P. Davis of the law school. In 1933, the two formed the Negro Industrial League (NIL), whose purpose was to track the spate of New Deal business codes and fight against those provisions that discriminated against black workers.

Raised in the security of black Washington's established middle class and products of the outstanding Dunbar High School, an anomaly in the world of Jim Crow education, Weaver's and Davis's social and racial consciences were sharpened by the onslaught of the Great Depression. With fellow Dunbar graduate William Hastie, also at Harvard Law, and Ralph Bunche, a graduate student in political science, they gathered in the late-night hours, playing poker and dissecting the black establishment's ineffectuality. They critiqued the remnants of black Republican machinery, which survived because of its power to dispense patronage to favored members of the black community. And they expressed dismay at the NAACP's seemingly exclusive focus on lynching.[5]

The New Deal, with its emphasis on federal supremacy, presented the possibility for meaningful action to revolutionize African Americans' position in the nation's economy and polity. But if in the development of the New Deal the black leadership did not forcefully represent the interests of black labor, Davis and Weaver feared, then recovery efforts would surely codify existing discrimination. Such was the case with the cotton reduction program, a prominent initiative of the Agricultural Adjustment Administration (AAA), one of the first New Deal alphabet agencies. Relief under this program was monopolized and inequitably distributed by landlords, who frequently reduced the acreage of cotton by evicting their black tenant farmers. The NAACP issued protests but otherwise took little action to forestall the disastrous policies of the AAA.[6]

Weaver and Davis were determined not to let the same thing happen in the area of industrial recovery. When they returned to Washington in the summer of 1933, they set up the NIL—in reality a two-man operation—in donated office space with a donated typewriter and supplies. Somehow, they monitored the ever-mounting pile of releases from the National Recovery Administration (NRA), analyzed proposed codes, and testified at hundreds of hearings about the deleterious effects of various codes, especially the ones sanctioning lower pay for black workers. In an effort to expand the reach of the NIL and establish a united front to fight for racial equality in the New Deal, in the late summer Davis proposed the formation of the Joint Committee on National Recovery (JCNR). The National Urban League declined the invitation, believing that Davis and Weaver were poaching on its preserve, but thirteen other organizations joined to make the codes more friendly to blacks, including the NAACP, the A.M.E. and A.M.E. Zion churches, the YWCA, the National Negro Business League, the Elks, and the National Association of Colored Women. The Rosenwald Fund provided seed money for the committee, and the NAACP agreed to chip in a monthly salary for Davis, who became the JCNR's executive secretary; other organizations contributed much smaller amounts.[7]

Over the next two years, the JCNR—and really this meant John P. Davis, because tenuous finances forced Weaver to find other work before he joined Interior Secretary Harold Ickes's staff late in the year—haunted congressional hearings and combated attempts by southern businesses to codify a lower wage for African American workers. Critiquing employers' rationales for the lower wage—blacks' maintenance costs were lower, higher wages would make black laborers unmanageable, black workers were less efficient and unproductive—the JCNR persuaded the Roosevelt administration to reject these myths, stand for a unitary pay scale, and encourage black-white cooperation. (Southern capitalists were able to get the NRA to enact a lower regional wage scale, which allowed them to reclassify jobs that were predominantly held by African Americans and thus indirectly achieve a lower wage for blacks.)[8]

After the formation of the JCNR, Weaver and Davis followed different trajectories. At the urging of and with financing from the Rosenwald Fund, President Roosevelt named the first of a series of advisors on Negro affairs of federal departments and agencies. His appointment of Clark Foreman, a liberal white Georgian, as the custodian for black issues in the interior department, caused a firestorm of protest from African Americans. Walter White, for instance, believed the president should have appointed an African American. Acknowledging the legitimacy of this sentiment, Foreman tapped Weaver to join his staff. He soon inherited the entire operation of the office of Negro affairs. Weaver saw the possibilities inherent in the New Deal and was anxious to become a part of it.[9]

John Davis, however, continued to be a gadfly. One historian of African American radicalism in the thirties points out that Davis "became increasingly committed to the role of critic outside the system." In the words of Patricia Sullivan, Davis "typified the new political leadership that emerged from the dual impact of the Depression and the federal initiatives of the New Deal." He was "dynamic and improvisational." By late 1934, he had shed whatever Republican residue remained, began to see racial discrimination as an integral part of the capitalist system, and embraced the Communist Party program. In 1935, he was instrumental in the establishment of the National Negro Congress.[10]

Davis's leftist ties were of some concern to White, but it was his improvisational style, his lack of institutional pedigree, and his position outside the civil rights bureaucracy that the secretary found particularly troublesome and that led to his wary attitude toward the JCNR. While the secretary almost certainly appreciated Davis's enthusiasm—after all, he himself was a dynamo—his free agency made him suspect. White was the consummate organization man, and energy and initiative were subordinate to plan. The strategy that the secretary championed in the recovery program, as in the antilynching campaign, was to lobby, testify, and negotiate on Capitol Hill and in the White House. Organized branch protests, monster rallies, picket lines—all were subsidiary actions and were designed primarily for publicity purposes. As the head of an important civil rights bureaucracy, White paid attention to his organization's demands, but he was nearly equally consumed by derivative questions: When to deliver the message in a modulated voice? Will relations with one government official alienate another? Will an alliance with leftists be salutary or combustible? These were questions that were of little concern to John P. Davis—not because he was sympathetic to the Communist program, but because he was unencumbered by a developed organization. In this regard he was similar to Ida B. Wells before him and Rayford Logan, his contemporary and another independent-minded intellectual. Logan, in 1933 a professor of history at Atlanta University and self-described "Bad Negro," was not a Communist, but he did not hesitate to work with the CP in Atlanta even when such an alliance earned him disfavor with the city's establishment. He was a strident critic of the New Deal's inequalities, had no qualms about calling into question the progressive credentials of the New Deal Negro advisors, and did not shrink from castigating Walter White and the NAACP for inordinate attention to decorum. Logan—and Davis too, as head of the JCNR—functioned quite effectively as the conscience of the fight for black equality. But because they forsook the stability of an institution, did not want to be bound by it, they had limited potential to influence the direction of the movement.

At the same time as he distrusted what he considered John Davis's strategic folly, the secretary welcomed his solid research and propaganda skills. As he was wont to do in other circumstances, White invited Davis to work closely with the NAACP and under its direction. He hoped thereby to take advantage of the JCNR's investigations while taming Davis's extracurricular attempts to organize a movement that was oriented toward effecting an alliance between Negro and white workers. At first, the secretary thought of the JCNR as an adjunct to the NAACP's nascent attention to African Americans' economic distress. He told George E. Haynes of the Federal Council of Churches, another of the JCNR's sponsoring organizations, that the NAACP would participate in its work for perhaps six months and only until it had completed a thorough study of the NRA codes. White said that one board member whom he did not name but who was Abram Harris, the principal proponent of a new program that concentrated on economics and black workers, was prepared to annex the JCNR permanently to the association; but, wrote the secretary to Haynes, such proposals were premature. And turning a political question—would closer NAACP ties to the JCNR, given the latter's activist ambitions, be a liability or an asset?—into a logistical one, White told Harris that his proposal was woefully incomplete because he hadn't come forth with a method of financing the closer alignment. As he had with the larger intra-association debate over the future program, White shepherded the discussion down a cul-de-sac.[11]

But as advocates of a new program became more vocal and numerous within the association, the secretary faced the possibility of closer cooperation with the JCNR. In September 1934, the board of directors formed a committee composed of White, Harris, and William Hastie to explore the possibility of taking over the work of the Joint Committee. The following month, the board agreed to take that action. Wanting to assume the committee's research functions, the board offered to pay Davis a monthly salary of $100, for which he would also help to establish the NAACP's programmatic work on labor, the economy, and recovery. The agreement between the two parties explicitly recognized that the association "shall have the privilege of access to and utilization of materials and information in the files of the Joint Committee on National Recovery."[12]

Davis proved an able publicist for the NAACP, writing detailed articles for *The Crisis* on blacks in the New Deal recovery effort. But when it came to lobbying congressional representatives and other federal officials, White shunted Davis aside, showing once again his hegemonic tendencies. As black organizations geared up for another round of congressional hearings in March 1935 on racial discrimination in New Deal agencies, Pervical Prattis, editor of the *Pittsburgh Courier*, suggested that White cooperate with the National Urban League. Writing to Charles Houston, White sneered at the idea. While it was possible to work profitably with local affiliates of the Urban League, on a national level NUL head T. Arnold Hill "would try to grab off the whole thing for the Urban League and hog the show." The secretary suggested that Houston and Davis plan for the hearings, including making suggestions for their scope and potential witnesses. But for the task of contacting witnesses and friendly New Dealers like Harold Ickes and Harry Hopkins, he told Houston, "you and I had best see most of these instead of John." [13]

John P. Davis was irrepressible, however, and the secretary found that he could not control him. By the end of 1935, the NAACP had gotten most of the mileage it was going to get from the JCNR, whose activity Davis was seeking to expand. In making plans for the Howard University conference on the Negro and the New Deal, which was the prelude to the National Negro Congress and which was bankrolled in large part by the NAACP, Davis approached African Americans from across the political spectrum, but he gave prominence to left-leaning blacks, including James Ford, the highest-ranking African American in the CPUSA. The NUL, the NAACP, black fraternal organizations, the decimated Garvey movement—even W.E.B. Du Bois—came under criticism and intense scrutiny for having "abandoned the black workers to pursue middle class goals," according to one historian of black radicalism in the thirties. The secretary was highly annoyed; although he had been using the JCNR for his own purposes, he had no intention of letting Davis use him or the association. "Incidentally, John has not helped himself with the people who have been financing the Joint Committee by his putting Communists, or near-Communists in the key positions on the program, nor by his having the closing session restricted to Socialist and Communist answers to the problems as though there were no other answers," he vented to Charles Houston. "The feeling, as I gather it, is that John has simply proved again that he is inclined to use anybody and anything." When the agreement between the NAACP and the JCNR expired, White chose not to renew it, the NAACP withdrew its funding, and the JCNR expired, virtually rolling its forces into the NNC.[14]

This is not to say that Walter White had no ideological proclivities. His diligence in lobbying, cultivating enduring relationships with lawmakers and donors, and schmoozing occupants of the White House were supremely adroit measures, but they also reflected a faith that at bottom capitalism and its political system could be made to work for African Americans. He publicized his clear channels to Eleanor Roosevelt, key New Dealers, and later Harry Truman as proof of his belief. Where W.E.B. Du Bois had developed a cogent and sharp critique of American capitalism and American democracy, and where A. Philip Randolph and Charles Houston tempered their leftist sympathies with the conclusion that, alas, it was simply not practical to follow them consistently, the secretary appeared not to share in these. During the Depression years and for some time after, though, White's predilections remained background assumptions. His polemics against the NNC and the CPUSA were conducted primarily on practical grounds of whose program would work.

It was the secretary's bedrock conviction that organized labor was at best an unreliable ally. The past is prologue, White might have told the leading lights from the Howard conference and the National Negro Congress. With some notable exceptions, organized labor meant *white* organized labor, which had little interest in African American workers, except to the extent that black laborers could help them in their battles with employers. He did endorse a truly inclusive program of industrial unionism, but he had little faith in and saw little tangible evidence of organized labor making consistent headway in this regard. "Our sympathy would be with organized labor if only organized labor would permit this," White observed cryptically.[15] His beliefs were born out even as the labor movement tried to organize its way out of the thirties economic crisis with the benefit of the New Deal.

Section 7a of the National Labor Relations Act of 1934 (also known as the Wagner-Connery Act) was organized labor's bonanza. Formally recognizing workers' rights to join unions and bargain collectively with employers, the provision unleashed a tsunami of organizing activities, especially among unskilled workers in mass-production industries like steel. Within a year of the enactment of this legislation, advocates of a "new labor movement" that embraced industrial unionism (organizing all workers in a given industry in one union) would break away from the aristocratic, narrow craft-unionism of the American Federation of Labor and form the Congress of Industrial Organizations (CIO). Section 7a, like other facets of the New Deal, strengthened the hands of the interventionist state. In exchange for the government's protection of the right to organize, the CIO shed any pretense of embracing an ideology and program of class conflict and accepted the legitimacy of capitalism—one historian of the period termed it "moral capitalism"—and the American political system.[16]

As originally written, Wagner-Connery contained no provision outlawing racial discrimination by unions. The secretary, who had developed a solid relationship with Robert Wagner through the antilynching campaign, immediately approached the senator to correct this critical defect; he suggested language that would allow the establishment of closed shops—meaning that a worker's employment was contingent upon his or her joining the union upon being hired—only if the union did not bar membership on account of race, creed, or color. Wagner agreed, but the AFL, his other constituency, opposed the amendment, ostensibly because they were against federal oversight of any aspect of their business but in reality because most AFL unions planned to continue their exclusionary practices. Because the House of Labor exercised more political clout than the NAACP, Wagner, despite his friendship and warm regards for White, acceded to the AFL's demands and omitted the antidiscrimination provision from the legislation. Even for someone as progressive as Wagner, organized labor's interests were integral to the country's economic recovery, while black labor's were peripheral and expendable. With Wagner's assent, White asked James Couzens of Michigan to offer an antidiscriminatory amendment to the bill from the Senate floor, but Couzens, whose constituency included members of the UAW, declined.[17]

For the rest of the decade, amending the Wagner-Connery Act was a programmatic staple of NAACP conventions. But in 1940, the association made a serious effort to introduce such a correction, only to run once again into a powerful reaction by labor. The secretary had decided to ask Representative Tom Hennings of St. Louis, who had been favorably disposed to antilynching legislation, to sponsor the measure. He was a logical choice, given that more than a third of his constituency was African American. Hennings, however, was cautious; before he would commit, he asked the secretary to find out how many of his constituents were union members and to which organizations they belonged. When White informed him that between 60 and 65 percent of the state's union membership, most of whom were white, lived in his district, he declined to attach his name to the bill.[18]

Outside the legislative arena, African Americans fared little better with organized labor during the Depression. The AFL meted out its usual blend of indifference and hostility, as seen, for example, in an explosive dispute in the Tampa, Florida, shipyards.[19] In June 1938 the War Department had awarded a $7 million contract for four ships to the Tampa Shipbuilding and Engineering Company. Previously a nonunion operation, the company's practice had been to hire blacks and whites in roughly equal numbers, but the defense contract now required it to maintain a closed shop with several designated AFL unions. The principal one, the

International Brotherhood of Boilermakers, Iron Ship Builders and Helpers, excluded blacks from membership.

That same month, thirteen workers—twelve black and one white—organized a strike that led to the formation of an integrated local of the Laborers Union to represent all 1,200 shipyard workers. This local concluded a verbal agreement with the company to continue the policy of racial parity in hiring. Shortly after, a white laborer objected to the integrated local; bowing to pressure, the Laborers international Jim Crowed the black members and installed a racist white business manager to oversee the newly segregated local. At the same time, the company came to terms with the Boilermakers. As work on the four ships progressed and the job required more skilled and semiskilled help, the black workers lost their jobs to white skilled help; whereas at the beginning of the job, 600 blacks were employed, by September 1939 that figure had declined to 118, with all but two of them in unskilled positions. The Ku Klux Klan, taking advantage of the workplace racial tensions, initiated a campaign of violence in the shipyard.

The secretary, who investigated the situation in July 1939, said that he "found the Tampa situation to be a perfect illustration of double-crossing of Negro workers by labor unions." He sent his findings to Eleanor Roosevelt, asking her to intercede with the president and the Department of Justice. FDR refused to become involved, and the attorney general, believing that no laws were broken, declined to pursue the matter. William Green of the AFL ordered an investigation at the secretary's behest. But Green's emissary neither talked with black workers and union officials nor even told them he was looking into the matter. Green seemed satisfied with this, because he transmitted to the secretary statements from white AFL officials in Tampa threatening violence unless black workers called off the investigation. For good measure, the AFL president accused White of consorting with Communists when he was in Florida. For more than two years after the secretary first heard of the conflict, organized labor and the federal government had successfully stonewalled a redress of black workers' grievances.

The secretary heard more conciliatory rhetoric from the CIO. In 1937, White lodged a vigorous complaint with United Auto Workers president Homer Martin over reports that the union was establishing Jim Crow units as part of its organizing drive at Ford and were excluding blacks at unionized Chrysler plants from the seniority lists. Martin's immediate denial of the charges and his statement of commitment to full protection of black workers was widely circulated by the NAACP. When later that year White heard that the AFL and the CIO were discussing ways to patch their differences and merge—something that did not happen for nearly two decades—CIO head John L. Lewis assured him that a ban on union racial discrimination was a cardinal condition for any consolidation. Lewis also supported White's efforts to amend the National Labor Relations Act to deny any union that practiced racial discrimination the right to represent workers in collective bargaining.[20]

But the practice of its constituent unions did not always match the CIO leader's pronouncements. For all the intense debate within the NAACP and black America generally about whether to join the CIO movement, that organization was largely silent on the need to foster an interracial labor movement. The UAW, long perceived to be the most racially egalitarian of the new industrial unions, is a case in point. It knew that it could not organize the industry without organizing the Ford Motor Company, which because of its employment practices enjoyed a friendly, if paternalistic, relationship with Detroit's black community. But the UAW was startlingly inattentive to the concerns of African American workers about discrimination in employment and promotion. Black workers were also excluded from union social affairs. Not surprisingly, when the wave of sit-down strikes washed over Detroit and environs in 1937, only a handful of black workers participated, the majority of them leaving the plant until the strikes were settled.[21]

The union's indifference and refusal to confront its white members' prejudice nearly cost the CIO the NAACP's support. The association's 1937 annual conference in Detroit almost repudiated the previous year's endorsement of the new union movement. Detroit branch officials, many of whom enjoyed patronage relationships with Ford, and members were implacably opposed to the appearance of Homer Martin, president of the UAW. Pro-union speakers were heckled—and cheered too, exposing a black community of two minds about organized labor. The convention's resolution on labor instead criticized discrimination by unions. Unable to overcome the opposition, the secretary in his speech closing the conference maintained silence on unions. Despite pro-CIO remarks in ensuing months by prominent blacks like journalist George Schuyler and

Howard University president Mordecai Johnson, black auto workers maintained their distance from the UAW.[22]

The National Negro Congress had begun its life by proclaiming that the elimination of capitalism and the establishment of the alliance of African Americans with the labor movement were prerequisites of black liberation. In its first year the NNC came to an agreement with the Steel Workers Organizing Committee, under which the NNC led the union drive among black workers. The NNC's energetic organization of African American steelworkers denied the companies the opportunity to utilize black workers as strikebreakers; the NNC provided a crucial ingredient to the highly successful drive to force the industry to recognize the United Steel Workers. Black radicals found smaller-scale success in the textile industry and among West Coast dockworkers, but they were unable to replicate their initial breakthrough. Despite the CIO's official antidiscrimination position, Philip Murray, the head of the steelworkers, had announced that his priority was the organization of white laborers. And for the remainder of the thirties, the auto workers' and tobacco workers' unions largely ignored NNC overtures. Far from embracing African American workers as equal members of a multinational and multiracial proletariat, even the best of new union movement put blacks in a position of having to prove their worthiness to be organized.[23]

In part, organized labor's racial obstinacy forced the black radicals of the NNC to adjust their program of multiracial class solidarity as the path toward social transformation. And in part this modulation was driven by the CPUSA's "popular front" strategy, which dropped talk of revolutionary aims and emphasized instead the unity of liberal and progressive organizations around a program of reform. Following the trajectory of the CPUSA in the labor and other movements, members of NNC became "bird dogs" for the CIO. In return for doing organized labor's heavy lifting among African Americans, the NNC now sought not the revolutionary transformation of the social order, but a very traditional quid pro quo: the support by labor for a legislative agenda beneficial to blacks. In particular, the NNC now began to emphasize the campaign for a federal antilynching law. "Ironically, having failed to convince the NAACP to direct its program to the organization of Black workers, the radicals now set out to use the organization of Black workers to bring about the NAACP's program," concluded Keith Griffler, a historian of

African American radicalism in the thirties. "[John P.] Davis, as practical radical, only differed from the NAACP leadership, evidently, in operating on the premise that securing these transitional changes required the assistance of the trade union movement."[24]

The NNC's shift, far more than any ideological reckoning, aroused Walter White's suspicions. The secretary was smug enough in his belief that African Americans were guests and not residents in the House of Labor not to be terribly bothered by black radicals issuing what he considered millennial manifestos. In fact, White thought, the NNC might even be a useful foil as he tried to wring concessions from the Roosevelt administration. But when the NNC tried to insinuate itself with the NAACP, the secretary acted to preserve the association's supremacy over its program and moved to isolate its competitor.

If the secretary enjoyed little Depression-era success with labor, his orchestration of soprano Marian Anderson's Easter Sunday 1939 concert at the Lincoln Memorial embedded the cause of civil rights in the American mind, and the litany of events would become basic race-relations catechism. Because of her race, Marian Anderson was denied use of Constitution Hall, a facility owned by the Daughters of the American Revolution (DAR), for her annual Howard University–sponsored spring concert. A protest ensued, and the injustice was brought to the attention of Eleanor Roosevelt. After trying without success to change the DAR's policy, ER publicly resigned her membership in that staid organization, and with her intercession, Anderson gave a concert at the Lincoln Memorial on Easter Sunday. Her performances of "America the Beautiful" and "My Country 'Tis of Thee" stirred the racially integrated audience of 75,000. Against the backdrop of Congress's dismal civil rights record, the continuation of gruesome racial murder, and America's tone-deafness to victims of Hitler's persecutions, the concert was a stark reminder of both the nation's hypocrisy and the hopes of millions of African Americans.[25]

Popular memory of the concert generally highlights the personal integrity of Eleanor Roosevelt. It is certainly true that ER's very public resignation from the DAR focused national attention on concert plans and that her friendships with African American leaders like the secretary and Mary McLeod Bethune facilitated planning for the extravaganza. But lost in this account is that the DAR had been a hidebound and reactionary organization for more than a decade before ER resigned. Liberal-minded women were run out. The organization adopted a blacklist, including among its ninety organizations the NAACP, the Federal Council of Churches, the ACLU, and the U.S. Department of Labor, and individuals like W.E.B. Du Bois and Jane Addams. Lost too is the fact that, although she herself supported the concert, ER was not on the sponsoring committee and did not attend, preferring to maintain a low profile and not squander her political capital. It was Walter White, the publicity impresario and skilled politicker, who set the conditions for the unforgettable civil rights moment.

In early January, Howard University asked the DAR, whose Constitution Hall was the largest concert venue in the District of Columbia, to reserve April 9 for Anderson's concert. Three days later, the auditorium's manager informed Howard that the date was booked and reminded the school of the hall's policy of barring appearances by black performers. Animated by its own tradition of activism and the New Deal optimism that affected much of the civil rights bureaucracy, Howard University fought the DAR's obvious injustice. It first turned to Anderson's manager, Sol Hurok.

Angered that his client was denied a booking, Hurok fumed but otherwise counseled caution and patient negotiation to get the DAR to allow the concert. When he saw the futility of this approach, he proposed that Anderson sing in the park across the street from the hall, an idea that the secretary ridiculed as "undignified and too much like a small boy thumbing his nose at the back of a larger boy who has beaten him up."[26] White saw in Hurok's concert-in-the-park idea a proposal that would bring attention narrowly to Marian Anderson (and Hurok) without adequately addressing racial discrimination.

White began a campaign to support Anderson and expose the hypocrisy of a particularly malignant form of Americanism. He got the NAACP to award her the coveted Spingarn medal and arranged to have Eleanor Roosevelt present it to her at the annual meeting of the NAACP in July. With the assistance of a reporter from *Time*, he lined up support for her from a dozen of the foremost whites in the world of high and popular culture, including symphony conductors Arturo Toscanini and Leopold Stowkowski, baritone Lawrence Tibbett, soprano Lily Pons, and singer-actor Nelson Eddy. A steady campaign of publicity, the founding of the Marian Anderson Citizens' Committee, and protest and picketing of the District of Columbia school board, which refused Anderson use of its large Central High School auditorium, followed in short order. With the secretary's assent, ER then brought national attention to the incident by announcing in her syndicated "My Day" column her resignation from the DAR.

The secretary proved his ability to think big when it came to deciding where Marian Anderson would in fact sing. With options dwindling, in mid-March White proposed the Lincoln Memorial as the proper venue.[27]

One week before the scheduled date of April 9, Harold Ickes announced that the Interior Department had granted permission for the concert. White hastily but efficiently assembled a sponsoring committee, with the Georgia-born New York representative Caroline O'Day as its chairwoman. By Easter Sunday, more than 300 prominent Americans had signed up, including Hugo Black and two other Supreme Court justices; Secretary of the Treasury Henry Morganthau; Attorney General Frank Murphy, White's old friend from the Sweet trial in Detroit; Senators Wagner, La Follette, Taft, Capper, and Borah; Mary McLeod Bethune; and actors Tallulah Bankhead, Fredric March, and Katharine Hepburn. Many of these were among the 200 dignataries who sat on stage during the concert.

As the 5:00 hour of the concert approached, 75,000 people crammed the Mall in integrated splendor from the Lincoln Memorial back toward the Washington Monument and on both sides of the reflecting pools. When a late-night sleet that he feared would keep the crowd away failed to materialize, the secretary's anxiety transformed into elation. After brief introductory remarks by Ickes, Marian Anderson took the stage. White's prediction that the irony of singing "America" would not be lost was accurate and lasting. At the event's conclusion the crowd pressed forward to greet the fur-clad Anderson and threatened a stampede; White stepped forward to calm the audience's enthusiasm, thus averting a potential disaster.

In the concert's aftermath, White used his influence to consecrate the historic performance with a mural of the event to be installed in the Interior Department. But he put the brakes on further protest against the DAR. That organization was already exposed as a group of "pathetic old ladies," he wrote to Houston, and he thought that a picket against them might stir up sympathy where none existed. In so doing, he honored a request by Eleanor Roosevelt, who urged White "to use your influence against this and to leave well enough alone." In engineering the Easter Sunday spectacle, White bequeathed a "format for mass politics" that became a movement staple in the various incarnations of the March on Washington.[28]

The threat of a different type of event at the Lincoln Memorial—the 1941 March on Washington—focused the secretary's attention once again on labor and economic issues. This episode was organized against the backdrop of the United States' imminent entry into World War II and the shift to a wartime economy; it mobilized a broad swath of the African American population, much of which was beyond the control of the NAACP and to varying degrees in conflict with it. Unlike previous explosions of activity, the March on Washington Movement (MOWM) and other responses to the war buildup ran too deep within Afro-America for the secretary to ignore or try to squelch. Though the methods of the MOWM were more confrontational than those preferred by Walter White, he was determined to embrace them, at least temporarily, and figure out a way to get out in front and address the labor and economic problems of black Americans. The demands of the MOWM and other initiatives led to some of the most tangible accomplishments of the New Deal era.

With the advent of the world war Afro-America, sensing an opportunity to democratize American race relations, debated what its attitude should be toward the impending conflagration. Prior to America's entry in the war, the dominant strain of thought among blacks was isolationist: why fight a war to eradicate fascism in Europe when African Americans lived under it in the South? Against this grain, though, was Rayford Logan, whose 1935 newspaper article "The Negro Studies War Some More" welcomed a global conflict. "I, for one, am convinced that it is the best thing that can happen for [the world's] 200,000,000 black men," he brazenly declared. Expressing a common sentiment, shared even by Walter White, Logan said that African Americans were suffering intensely, "even under the New Deal and even under a President whose personal attitude on the race question is loftier than that of most of his predecessors." Africa's inferior position had been officially enshrined in the charter of the League of Nations, which all but precluded that continent's independence. A conflagration pitting the Euro-American powers against one another would pierce the worldwide united front of the white race that subordinated black people. Africans might be able to utilize the conflict to liberate themselves, and African Americans would be in a position to demand their full human rights as the price for their support of the war effort.[29]

By late 1939, African American public opinion began to move toward Logan's. The *Pittsburgh Courier*, one of the country's leading black papers, formed the Committee for the Participation of Negroes in the National Defense Program (CPNNDP), an alliance of African American college fraternities and sororities, and veterans', professional, and benevolent associations, and headed by Logan. The committee called for the proportional representation of blacks at all levels of the armed forces, which were being bolstered in preparation for hostilities; though it grudgingly conceded the continued existence of a segregated military, the CPNNDP opposed the restriction of African Americans to support units and their exclusion from the commissioned ranks. The *Courier* committee also demanded that African Americans have unfettered access to federally funded education and vocational training for jobs in defense industries. In particular, it sought black advisors and staff on all relevant government bodies, the banning of discrimination by state agencies that received federal monies for defense purposes, and legislation barring labor unions from excluding blacks from training or apprenticeship programs. With outlets in twenty-five states and the District of Columbia, the CPNNDP maintained an active protest and lobbying agenda. In its first year of existence it scored an impressive victory when Logan wrote, New York representative Hamilton Fish introduced, and Congress passed an amendment to a military appropriations bill that outlawed racial discrimination in the selection and training of military personnel.[30]

White and the NAACP were slow to embrace a campaign for inclusion in the burgeoning national defense program. One reason was that from its inception, the separate-but-equal framework controlled the debate initiated by the *Courier* and its committee. In the hopes of making meaningful inroads in the military establishment for African Americans, Logan and the CPNNDP reluctantly acquiesced to the realities of a Jim Crow army. The secretary believed this position was a poor substitute for the demand for a complete abolition of segregation. But because all of the relevant proposed legislation—even that sponsored by Senator Wagner, whom the secretary felt the NAACP could not oppose—likewise assumed a continuation of segregation, the association was hamstrung. Roy Wilkins recognized the price the NAACP paid for its disengagement and not "beating the tom tom of public opinion over the country."[31]

What shook the secretary out of his torpor was the labor movement. On the one hand, the CIO was finally drawing practical conclusions from its knowledge that it could not organize in mass production industries without the support of black workers. As the UAW-CIO pressed once again to organize Ford in Detroit, it again encountered an unconvinced African American labor force. When the union struck in early 1941, concentrating on the mammoth Ford Rouge industrial complex, black employees crossed the picket lines. Racially charged skirmishes threatened to escalate into full-scale battles. Ford skillfully exploited the tensions. Fearing collapse of the strike, the UAW reached out to the NAACP. The youth auxiliary of the Detroit branch, which, in marked contrast to the conservative NAACP adults, had for the previous five years taken an interest in labor issues, endorsed the union, and worked to keep black Ford workers from crossing the picket lines. The secretary gave a boost to the youth and pro-labor elements in the branch when he telegraphed the branch secretary, urging him to take "an unequivocal position that Negroes refrain from strike-breaking and cooperate fully with the union." As tensions appeared to reach their zenith, the secretary flew to the Motor City, arriving on April 7, to meet with union officials, race leaders, and journalists.[32]

As the secretary told it in his memoirs, he was wildly successful. Debarking the plane, he convinced reluctant branch leaders to back the strike; from there he circled the Ford Rouge plant in a sound truck and walked the picket line, directly addressing black workers inside the plant. He was on hand to suggest the formation of interracial groups of pickets to demonstrate to those blacks still working the union's commitment to minority rights. After a few hours, he said, his efforts began to pay off, as hundreds of African American workers streaked out of the Rouge, setting the stage for a vote in which the UAW would be certified as the workers' bargaining agent.[33]

The idea that the secretary, by agitating at the plant gates, turned black workers' sentiment toward the union and thereby guaranteed a UAW victory is a dramatic contrivance. First, it ignores that a small cadre of black union organizers and the NAACP youth council in Detroit had worked doggedly to reverse the black community's suspicion of the union. Second, his account overlooks the almost complete ineffectiveness of his plant-gate agitprop; of the hundreds of black strikebreakers still in the plant, no more than a handful left. Nevertheless, White's efforts were important for encouraging the local branch to become pro-union and for effecting on a national level an alliance between one of the most important CIO unions and the NAACP. With the backing of the UAW, the secretary believed, the association would be able to address labor and economic issues with more authority while also enjoying the CIO's backing on key civil rights issues such as a federal antilynching law.[34]

By the end of 1940, black laborers were forcing their way into the secretary's consciousness, as he discovered on a four-week tour of the Pacific coast in November. The initial purpose of the trip was to reconnoiter Hollywood. He was the guest of honor at a luncheon hosted by film producer Walter Wanger, at which White discussed with industry leaders the social costs of Hollywood limiting blacks to comic roles or roles as servants, and the need to revise this attitude. He was in best trim as he made a pitch to those gathered to contribute money to the NAACP. Wanger and the Hollywood representative of the American Jewish Committee further assisted the secretary in setting up a series of private dinners with other Hollywood moguls. He would return to Tinseltown to much fanfare in 1942.[35]

If the secretary took great satisfaction in Hollywood social life, he also noted an increase in instances of discrimination against blacks in the defense programs, which energized the Pacific Coast NAACP branches. He instructed them to continue to collect information on discrimination, interview employers, and publicize vocational classes and apprentice programs. He proposed several avenues of action for the NAACP: on a general level, he planned to approach Sidney Hillman, the first president of the Amalgamated Clothing Workers of America and presently on the Advisory Commission of the Council on National Defense, David Dubinsky of the International Ladies Garment Workers Union, and Philip Murray of the CIO to find ways of breaking down discrimination. He had strong reasons to suspect that these leaders, whose unions had constitutional bans on racial discrimination, would work with the NAACP on seeking nondiscrimination clauses in all government contracts, amending the Wagner-Connery Act, and helping to organize congressional hearings.[36]

Then in November the Hampton Institute hosted a conference on Negroes in the national defense program. More than 2,000 people flocked to the opening session, and more than 200 people took part in the three days of meetings, which demanded an end to discrimination and exclusion in the civilian and military aspects of national defense. While Roy Wilkins represented the NAACP in the secretary's absence, the association sadly tailed the interests and efforts of other black activists, so much so that Rayford Logan called White and the association to task for being "asleep at the switch." [37]

Still, the association's national efforts slogged along. Against the better judgment of his closest advisors, the secretary declined invitations to ally with organizations like the CPNNDP. Though Charles Houston joined the *Courier* committee and participated in its activities, White, as he so often did, placed a premium on working in conjunction with other race organizations only when the association could be assured a preeminent role. While the CPNNDP racked up endorsements and pressured a Senate committee chaired by Harry Truman for hearings on African Americans in the national defense program, White—attempting to outflank his competitors—initiated actions that could only be described as ineffective. He enlisted A. Philip Randolph and T. Arnold Hill of the Urban League—and pointedly excluded Logan—to meet with the president and push for the complete integration of the military and defense efforts. FDR was predictably vague, but two weeks after the meeting his office released a statement that falsely claimed that White, Randolph, and Hill had agreed to accept concessions within the framework of segregation. The secretary prevailed upon members of the Truman committee to block the proposed hearings, but he was unable to have the Senate consider alternate hearings that he himself had suggested. Unable to implement with any consistency an association program or wrest control of the movement from others, the secretary came under severe scrutiny and criticism by the black press. [38]

Thus when A. Philip Randolph issued the call in January 1941 for a massive demonstration to take place in Washington in July to demand an end to discrimination in employment in the defense industry he had Walter White's full attention. The NAACP's own version of mass action in late January was a flop—only twenty-five branches around the country held protest meetings. After watching his own national campaign splutter for several more weeks, White accepted Randolph's invitation to join the

MOWM. (Randolph also invited, in addition to White, several moderates to join the leadership body, including Lester Granger of the Urban League and Channing Tobias, head of Negro work for the YMCA; somewhat later, Rayford Logan also joined, bolstering the radical voice.) The association was an early financial backer of the movement and encouraged all branches to join local MOWM committees or initiate one.[39]

Of all the black leaders only A. Philip Randolph possessed the audacity and authority to issue a realistic call for mass protest based upon the idea that African Americans would never desegregate the defense program so long as they stuck with old tactics. The Communists were bold enough to make such a declaration, but they lacked the influence and organization to pull it off; Walter White could stage a protest at the Lincoln Memorial against the Daughters of the American Revolution, but he had not the chutzpah to march so directly against FDR.

Organizing hit a bump in May when Randolph insisted the march be all-black in character. Since resigning as president of the National Negro Congress the previous year and alleging CP domination of that organization, Randolph had made it a point of principle to exclude Communists from organizations he led. At his insistence the Brotherhood of Sleeping Car Porters barred Communists from holding office. And with the March on Washington, he resolved to exclude whites to prevent it "from being penetrated by certain elements that will discredit it and take away from it its Negro character." With some fancy footwork, he explained that he wasn't excluding whites because they were white—"No sane Negro" would think of excluding Caucasians of good will like Mary White Ovington and Norman Thomas, he said—"but it would be quite unwise to let the gates down to all white people. We would be swamped with Communists who would use the March for ulterior purposes."[40]

His reasoning brought no comfort to several people in the interracial NAACP, including its firmly integrationist secretary. When Gertrude Stone, the white secretary of the District of Columbia branch, was informed by that city's MOWM committee that they had sent her an invitation to participate in march planning in error, she complained to White. William Hastie, soon to become the civilian aide for Negro affairs to the secretary of defense, and a future federal judge, introduced a motion in the branch to withhold an endorsement of the MOWM. The resolution passed, despite the branch's enthusiasm for the goals of eradicating racial discrimination in the national defense program. Charles

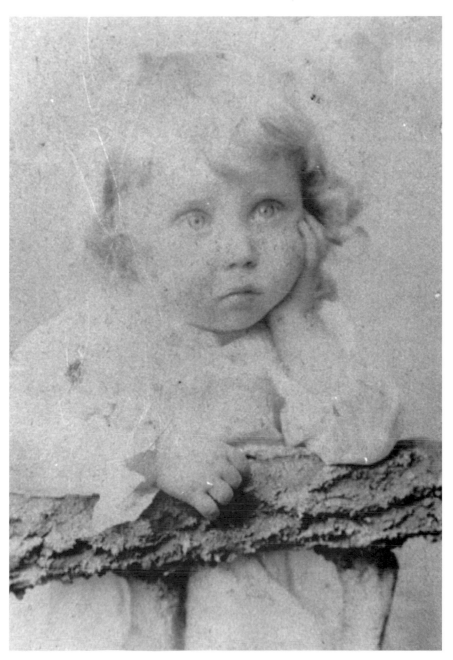

Walter White, age three. *Courtesy Rose M. Palmer*

Walter White at chalkboard, demonstrating first-grade spelling lesson. Lucy Aiken (née Rucker) is on right.
Courtesy Rose M. Palmer

The White family home on Houston Street in Atlanta. This house assumed a central importance in Walter's recounting of the 1906 Atlanta race riot and his own awakening race consciousness.
Courtesy Rose M. Palmer

Walter and sister Ruby,
undated photograph.
Courtesy Rose M. Palmer

Atlanta University, class of 1916. Walter White is on the right. *Courtesy Rose M.*
Palmer

The White family. This formal portrait was taken in 1931, after George White's fatal traffic accident. A space was left in the portrait, into which a photograph of the deceased was inserted. (Sitting, left to right): Helen, Walter, Madeline (mother), George (father), Ruby. (Standing, left to right): Madeline, George, Alice, Olive. *Courtesy Rose M. Palmer*

Gladys White.
Courtesy Rose M. Palmer

Walter White, surrounded from left to right by children Walter Carl Darrow ("Pidge") and Jane, and wife Gladys, circa 1930s. *Courtesy Rose M. Palmer*

Walter White and Poppy Cannon, 1949. Taken in Japan during the *Round the World Town Hall of the Air* tour, this photograph adorned the newlyweds' first Christmas card. *Library of Congress, Prints & Photographs Division, Visual Materials from the NAACP Records*

Founding executive board of the Atlanta branch of the NAACP, 1917. White is seated on far right. John Hope is standing, second from right. *Library of Congress, Prints & Photographs Division, Visual Materials from the NAACP Records*

Walter White's leadership of the NAACP was facilitated and challenged by a host of influential persons. James Weldon Johnson, Joel Spingarn, and Arthur Spingarn took the young White under their wings, while W.E.B. Du Bois, who was initially favorably disposed to him, became increasingly alarmed at White's imperious style. Mary White Ovington, an NAACP founder, believed White was trying to shunt her aside. White found himself in conflict with Ida B. Wells-Barnett and Ella Baker over the strategy and tactics for building a civil rights movement.

NAACP annual convention, Philadelphia, 1924. James Weldon Johnson is in back row, third from left. Mary White Ovington is in front row, fourth from left. Du Bois is to her right, with White next to him. *Library of Congress, Prints & Photographs Division, Visual Materials from the NAACP Records*

Joel Spingarn. *Library of Congress, Prints & Photographs Division, Visual Materials from the NAACP Records*

Arthur Spingarn. *Library of Congress, Prints & Photographs Division, Visual Materials from the NAACP Records*

W.E.B. Du Bois.
*Library of Congress, Prints & Photographs Division,
Visual Materials from the NAACP Records*

Ida B. Wells-Barnett.
*Library of Congress,
Prints & Photographs
Division, Visual Materials
from the NAACP Records*

Ella Baker.
*Library of Congress, Prints & Photographs Division,
Visual Materials from the NAACP Records*

Second Amenia Conference, August 1933. (Back row, left to right): Charles Houston (second), Roy Wilkins (third). (Third row, left to right): Ralph Bunche, Du Bois, E. Franklin Frazier (fifth), Mary White Ovington (seventh), Walter White (far right). (Second row): Joel Spingarn (sixth from left). *Library of Congress, Prints & Photographs Division, Visual Materials from the NAACP Records*

NAACP lawyers at the trial of George Crawford, Loudon County, Virginia, 1933. White, Charles Houston, James G. Tyson, Leon A. Ransom, and Edward P. Lovett. This was the first NAACP case tried by African American attorneys. *Library of Congress, Prints & Photographs Division, Visual Materials from the NAACP Records*

A mob of between 10,000 and 15,000 watched the lynching of eighteen-year-old Abe Smith and nineteen-year-old Thomas Shipp on August 7, 1930, in Marion, Indiana. *Library of Congress, Prints & Photographs Division, Visual Materials from the NAACP Records*

Howard University students protest the decision of the attorney general not to place lynching on the agenda of the National Crime Conference, December 1934. *Library of Congress, Prints & Photographs Division, Visual Materials from the NAACP Records*

White (left) and Charles Houston (right) in the Mississippi Delta, 1936, investigating charges of peonage on federal flood-control projects. *Library of Congress, Prints & Photographs Division, Visual Materials from the NAACP Records*

Culture and politics: Walter White was in the thick of promoting the value of culture to the cause of civil rights.

Langston Hughes, Charles S. Johnson, E. Franklin Frazier, Rudolph Fisher, Hubert Delany on a Harlem rooftop, circa 1926. *Moorland-Spingarn Research Center, Howard University*

Marian Anderson and Walter White, undated photograph. *Library of Congress, Prints & Photographs Division, Visual Materials from the NAACP Records*

Walter White, Hattie McDaniel, and Los Angeles Mayor Fletcher Bowren, circa 1940s. *Library of Congress, Prints & Photographs Division, Visual Materials from the NAACP Records*

The National Emergency Committee against Mob Violence, formed in response to the riot in Columbia, Tennessee, in February 1946, meets with President Truman. On White's initiative, the committee successfully prevailed upon Truman to name a presidential committee on civil rights, which in 1947 issued *To Secure These Rights*. White is to the right of Truman; Channing Tobias is on far right. *Library of Congress, Prints & Photographs Division, Visual Materials from the NAACP Records*

Facing page: Walter White on his inspection tour of the Pacific Theater of Operations, between December 1944 and April 1945.
Library of Congress, Prints & Photographs Division, Visual Materials from the NAACP Records

Seated left to right: NAACP board member James McLendon, Eleanor Roosevelt, Thurgood Marshall. Standing: Walter White, Roy Wilkins, 1947. *Library of Congress, Prints & Photographs Division, Visual Materials from the NAACP Records*

Houston took issue with Randolph too. African Americans would be unable to win "the battle for integration and citizenship" alone; rather, he said, their success would come in proportion to their ability to attract others to their cause. Beside his ideological objections, Houston pointed out the obvious flaw in Randolph's reasoning: Communists were not only white, but also black.[41]

The BSCP president diffused these objections by downplaying the anti-CP purpose of the ban and repackaging it as a strategy for racial unity. In a letter to Hastie, the secretary did his best to explain in neutral tones the rationale for a policy with which he disagreed but over which he knew he had no control: "Entirely aside from the possible danger of the Comrades trying to capture the march or to create the impression that they were running it from behind the scene was this consideration—that Negroes themselves are using this means of saying to the government what they as Negroes think and feel about discrimination in the defense program." Faced with the alternative of staying on the perimeter as the MOWM continued to gather momentum, the NAACP dissenters decided instead to climb aboard, and Randolph's pronouncement settled the matter. The NAACP left no doubt that it supported the march by announcing that it was cutting short by one day its annual meeting in Houston in late June so that delegates could then travel to Washington. "The action was taken also to indicate the NAACP's full support of the March for Jobs and to make plain to heads of the government the unity of colored people . . ." stated the association.[42]

Steadily, Randolph increased his attendance projections, and Roosevelt took worried notice. When at the beginning of June Randolph wrote to FDR, members of his administration, New Deal officials, and heads of AFL and CIO unions and asked them to address the rally, the president took steps to halt it. On June 10, Eleanor Roosevelt pleaded with Randolph to cancel the protest. "I have talked over your letter with the President and I feel very strongly that your group is making a very grave mistake at the present time to allow this march to take place," she wrote. Distemper was the rule in official Washington, she said, and tensions on the streets were likewise high. An outbreak of violence or ruckus—even the threat of one—endangered all the progress hitherto achieved under the New Deal. "You know that I am deeply concerned about the rights of Negro people, but I think one must face situations as they are and not as one wishes them to be. I think this is a very serious decision for you to take." At the urging of her husband, she sent a copy of her letter to the assistant secretary of war "in the hopes that everything possible is being done to prevent this march on Washington." She proposed instead a high-level meeting between the president and some of his aides and Randolph and the secretary to work out some sort of compromise.[43]

ER's missive had the effect of exposing a cleavage within the civil rights leadership. At a meeting of the MOWM directorate called primarily to plot a response to the administration's machinations, Lester Granger and Channing Tobias urged a moderation of demands and an easing of the pressure on FDR. On the first point and in response to Randolph's statement that the "paramount purpose of this March was to stop and abolish discrimination and . . . to cause the President to issue an executive order to abolish discrimination in Army service and in the Government," Granger guardedly implied that these were impossible. He insisted that the committee should "plan for those things that can be achieved." Tobias didn't even like the word "demand"—it was a "CP-copyrighted word. Can we subsitute a word so as not to be dubbed 'red'?" Tobias also admonished the MOWM representatives who were to meet with the president not to insist on immediate executive action. It would be sufficient, he said, if FDR gave unspecified "assurances" that he would remedy the situation. The secretary, who more than the other leaders in the room knew about presidential assurances, rebutted Tobias: "Don't kid yourself. The President's promises are not more than water, and soon forgotten because it is politically expedient." Nor should leaders agree to a postponement or cancellation of the march without a firm commitment from FDR to act, because without an executive order, people will travel to Washington anyway, providing the CP an opportunity to "grab the group."[44]

Over the next ten days, Randolph and White and New York Mayor Fiorello La Guardia, who represented the president but who had the trust of the MOWM, met with FDR and some of his advisors. On June 18, Randolph and White offered to call off the march in exchange for an executive order banning discrimination in defense industries. FDR asked for patience, but he was unwilling to issue an order, though he endorsed an antidiscrimination appeal to war industries. The two black leaders held firm, and the two sides adjourned, with Roosevelt charging La Guardia with the task of reaching an agreement. Five days later they recovened. The mayor and Aubrey Williams, a white progressive who headed the National Youth Administration, represented the president; Walter White was in Houston presiding over the NAACP annual meeting, so Randolph was joined by national MOWM assistant director Eugene Davidson of Washington, Thurman Dodson of the Washington MOWM committee, and Rayford Logan. La Guardia stated Roosevelt's readiness to end discrimination in defense industries and establish a Fair Employment Practices Committee to enforce it. Davidson wanted an additional ban on discrimination in government service. With this standoff, the two sides recessed to consult others not present. Randolph telephoned White, who told him he would accept the draft order as presented. The president told La Guardia that Davidson's proposal was a deal-breaker. Davidson proposed a compromise: the preamble of the order would make mention of official opposition to discrimination in government, but such mention would be omitted from the scope of the ban. This sleight of hand satisfied both sides, and late in the afternoon of June 23, Franklin Roosevelt agreed to sign Executive Order 8802. (It was issued two days later.) In exchange, A. Philip Randolph canceled—he said postponed—the March on Washington.[45]

Roosevelt's concession was a substantial, though partial, victory. The youth division of New York's MOWM committee denounced the order's incompleteness and insisted that the march be rescheduled since all demands hadn't been met. Flush with victory, delegates to the NAACP annual conference thought it better to press their advantage and claim that E.O. 8802 was a good first step—but not more than that. White offered his warm and personal thanks to Eleanor Roosevelt for her crucial efforts. But before the assembled delegates, he expressed a distinct lack of pleasure in the "exceedingly limited" scope of the president's directive. Still, White saw the ability to force FDR into any action and to have him appoint African Americans to two of the five seats on the FEPC as confirmation of the NAACP's credible threat to mobilize tens of thousands of people to protest in the streets and simultaneously to engage in hard-nosed negotiation.[46]

What the secretary failed to appreciate was that the accumulation of affirmative presidential actions—in October 1940, FDR promoted Benjamin O. Davis, Jr., to the rank of general and committed the military to increasing the number of African American officers and soldiers—was the result of much more than the combination of tactics in proper proportion. White—and Randolph too—seemed to be unaware that their efforts in the defense program were strategically canny moves that took advantage of the binds in which FDR was beginning to find himself. Thus, the secretary's previous ineptness in forcing executive and congressional action was obviated by Roosevelt's estimation that it would be politically expedient to offer some concessions. His October 1940 actions were preceded by opinion polls showing Republican candidate Wendell Willkie gaining popularity and the endorsement of him by CIO head John L. Lewis.[47] Likewise, two days before FDR signed E.O. 8802, Germany invaded the Soviet Union, presaging a possible collapse of the Allied cause and forcing him to accelerate war preparations. In assessing the reasons for the MOWM's victory, Rayford Logan, a student of history and social movements, articulated what White, the practical (and sometimes myopic) politician, missed: "When he [the President] leans in one direction at any given time, he does so because that particular group's arguments are buttressed by other factors that transcend the interests of any one group and involve the very safety of the nation itself."[48]

Soon after Roosevelt's edict White began to back away from further cooperation with Randolph and the MOWM. In June 1942, the secretary addressed mass rallies sponsored by the MOWM at Madison Square Garden, Griffith Stadium (home of the Washington Senators baseball team), and the Coliseum in Chicago. The mood at all three was militant and uncompromising: there was talk of finally descending on the nation's capital and launching a campaign of civil disobedience directed at Jim Crow transportation facilities.[49] Publicly, the secretary explained the end of the cooperative relationship as a difference over tactics and methods. The MOWM had become unduly fixated on mass protest, he wrote in notes for a speech. "Huge demonstrations . . . [are] absolutely necessary . . . [b]ut alone they are not enough," he told an MOWM-sponsored mass meeting. They must be backed up by lobbying and voting—the "unspectacular, unrewarding, day-to-day work." He downplayed rumors of competition between him and Randolph. He had too much respect for the BSCP president to try to undermine him.[50]

Though the secretary may have believed that confrontational tactics would ill serve the drive for civil rights, White's private correspondence makes clear that his main concern was maintaining the NAACP's supremacy over all phases of the movement's work. Roy Wilkins warned his boss about the "traditional NAACP attitude, namely, that these people are of no importance, and the movement is bound to fail, and that we cannot be damaged or our prestige or membership hurt." The secretary agreed that the MOWM was a competitor worth keeping an eye on, and he confessed worry about "some people believing that the March-On-Washington Movement should replace the NAACP." White chided Randolph for trying to establish a permanent MOWM, and deliberately moved to isolate the BSCP president in the defense program.[51] In that respect, the cooperative attitude he displayed with Randolph was transitory, an interlude between competitive phases, which were fundamental.

In both its rewards and its disappointments, the Depression decade taught Walter White that he could not substitute his own schematic for the actual course of a movement for civil rights. As African Americans' participation became more generalized, the secretary learned that he ignored labor and economic issues at his own peril. To his credit, he was far more quick to make adjustments in regards to the New Deal than he was, say, in Scottsboro. He also learned that at a time of intensified activity, other organizations would develop with which he would have to deal. Unlike the aftermath of the Chicago riot of 1919, for example, where he could breeze by other organizations and impose a strategy that other black groups were compelled to follow, White found himself in the new position of having to work with others on terms not of his design.

As the United States barreled toward WWII, the arena of race advancement expanded exponentially. As in the previous one, this war mobilization ushered in a period of race conflict, with riots erupting in Detroit and Harlem; the secretary would be called on to help broker a peace. The fight for civil rights became bound more intimately than ever to international affairs and foreign policy, and in the wake of the war, African Americans would demand their say in the shaping of the peace. White would strain himself to influence the process. With the revving up of the entertainment industry to both promote patriotism and project a global image of a democratic United States, the secretary espied a unique opportunity in Hollywood to rehabilitate the popular image of black America. In these and other endeavors he would frequently find himself in unfamiliar situations, and though he would never have admitted it, more than once he was in over his head. The New Deal years, however, prepared him to swim rather than sink—and to cling to the principal of fighting for the supremacy of the NAACP.

Chapter 9

Live from the War Zones: Hollywood, Harlem, Europe, and the Pacific

The March on Washington Movement, the work of the *Courier* committee, and the belated entry of the NAACP into the fight for equality in the nation's defense program all aroused African Americans across the country. As soon as the Fair Employment Practices Committee opened for business, black workers flooded it with complaints; over its five-year life, the FEPC logged an average of 5,000 annually. From the beginning, the NAACP assisted individuals to file complaints and helped prepare witnesses for the committee's first public hearings in Los Angeles, Chicago, and New York in 1941 and 1942. Branches across the country conducted probes into employer and union discrimination in defense industries, especially aviation companies. Although the association employed their traditional tactics of investigation and publicity most frequently, branches did not shy away from other actions, including litigation in the deep South.[1]

The NAACP was a chief beneficiary of this burst of energy. In 1941, seventy-one branches were organized, the most since 1926; in 1942 ninety new branches were chartered. Of the established branches, Detroit's was the largest, with almost 5,400 members in 1941, followed by Baltimore with more than 4,500. The next year, the Motor City's membership had swollen to more than 12,000, while Baltimore's grew to 7,800. In 1941, thirteen branches had more than 1,000 members; that number was twenty-four the following year. Much of this growth was in the Northeast and Midwest, but branches in deep South locales like Monroe, Louisiana, and Albany, Georgia, conducted public membership drives and signed up thousands of members despite the threat of financial ruin and physical harm to those who dared to participate.[2]

The association felt the pains of its own rapid growth. During the thirties White had devoted his attention principally to lobbying Congress and Franklin and Eleanor Roosevelt for antilynching legislation and equity in the disbursement of New Deal largesse. While he was developing a solid presence in national politics, he relegated organization building to a position of tertiary importance. Ella Baker, who in the sixties was the principal inspirer of the Student Non-Violent Coordinating Committee, joined the NAACP executive staff in 1941 as an assistant field secretary, and found some disturbing trends hidden by the exponential membership growth. Most members did little more with the NAACP than pay dues. Baker wanted to develop ways to encourage members also to participate actively in local activities.[3]

Oversight of branch operations was weed-choked, thought Roy Wilkins. Having operated for nearly a decade in the secretary's shadow and not having realized the level of pecuniary stability he wished, Wilkins added neglect of the field to his list of complaints and advertised an intention to leave the association. White averted this particular crisis, but only by massaging his subordinate's ego. The secretary told Wilkins that though he might earn a higher salary as the new editor of the *Amsterdam News*, he would never attain the stature or prestige that he could at 69 Fifth Avenue. (In the course of this pep talk, the secretary revealed that he had declined New York Mayor Fiorello La Guardia's offer of a remunerative position as a commissioner of an unnamed city agency and Mark Ethridge's proffer of a seat on the FEPC at an annual salary of $9,000, a raise of nearly $4,000 over his NAACP pay.)[4]

With the warning flags thus raised, the secretary took a more active interest in the branches. For much of October and November, White was on the road, speaking at branch meetings and helping to revive dormant branches. Concentrating on Maryland, Virginia, and North Carolina, he paid special attention to organizing African American public school teachers. The previous year Thurgood Marshall, Oliver Hill from Richmond, and other attorneys from the NAACP's legal cadre had won *Alston v. School Board of City of Norfolk*, which mandated equal pay for African American educators. Having established the principle of salary equalization, the teachers had to extract it from recalcitrant school boards. In Richmond, for example, black teachers were willing to eliminate the differential over five years, but the board wanted a twelve-year process. It took the teachers an additional year of organizing and protesting to compel city leaders to meet their demands. The script was the same practically everywhere.[5]

The secretary's attention on teachers underscored the association's growing emphasis on dismantling Jim Crow by confronting it in public education. With a portion of the $100,000 grant by the Garland Fund—Depression conditions forced the philanthropy in 1933 to all but suspend the appropriation before it had even disbursed a quarter of the amount—the NAACP had commenced the first of a series of legal challenges to segregated education. Because association leaders understood that an immediate demand for integration would find few friends in the courts, they initially targeted the exclusion of African Americans from state-operated professional schools and proposed as a remedy that the offending states either close those schools entirely or open separate and equal institutions for African Americans. The NAACP hoped to make the cost of maintaining such an arrangement prohibitive, thus forcing states to integrate their schools. Victories in Maryland's high court in *Murray* v. *Pearson* (1934) and at the Supreme Court in *Missouri ex. rel Gaines* v. *Canada* (1938) established precedents for blacks' equal access to education and a foundation for the *Brown* decision.

Next in the fight against unequal public education would come the campaign for teacher-salary equalization. From the standpoint of legal strategy it was a complementary move. As Charles Houston pointed out, because a direct attack was still too risky, as southern states would vigorously dispute this charge and predominantly white juries were not likely to be sympathetic.[6]

Legal considerations aside, however, the salary cases made sense from the perspective of building a robust organization. With the historical emphasis on education among African Americans, teachers were among a community's most respected members. But if they enjoyed an exalted status, the fact that they were dependent upon white school boards for their livelihoods often doused their ardor for civil rights. Such was especially the case with education leaders, including many in positions of authority at the historically black public colleges. White had hoped that in the wake of the *Gaines* decision, these educators, whom he said were among "the weaker-kneed brethren," would cease their "chiseling or pussyfooting." But he was disappointed to learn that, despite their grumbling about how southern states would surely circumvent the High Court's edict in *Gaines* and erect inferior Jim Crow institutions, they were resigned to accept whatever stale crumbs were tossed their way. The secretary chastised them for not molding public opinion, but tailing it.[7]

By taking on an issue immediately dear to black teachers, White hoped to sever them from their more conservative leadership, bring them into the NAACP, and thereby encourage other community members to join. And because finances were never far from his mind, the secretary hoped that teachers—among the race's more solvent citizens—would reciprocate the NAACP's efforts by making generous contributions. His calculations were not off. The salary-equalization suits were wildly popular, especially throughout Maryland and Virginia. Teachers formed the core of many branches in the South, and they frequently took leadership positions. According to historian Adam Fairclough, even in Mississippi, teachers preferred the NAACP's direct pursuit of pay equality to gradualist approaches of groups like the Commission for Interracial Cooperation. In Louisiana, Texas, and Virginia, state organizations of black teachers financed these suits.[8]

Local swells of teacher and community activism around education matched comfortably with the association's challenge of segregated schools nationally, and because of this fit the secretary put concentrated attention into assisting the branches concerned. But in most instances, the surge in African American political activity manifested itself in decidedly local ways—against discrimination by a single local employer, for example—and did not immediately or obviously amplify the NAACP's national plans. In these cases, White preferred to let the branches coast along, even when others on the staff and even local leaders favored national intervention. He did not see as a serious problem the observation by E. Frederic Morrow, who was charged with servicing established branches, that there was a high level of dissatisfaction in the field. Branches complained that they were not receiving sufficient attention from the national office, Morrow reported. The annual conventions were practically the only occasion for local activists to exchange ideas and successful strategies and tactics and place their work in a nationwide framework. But in contrast to the gatherings in the early thirties when the secretary had no sinecure and had to defend and articulate a program, the conventions since the late thirties had been primarily opportunities for the national office to parade its influential contacts in government before the membership.[9] Ella Baker and youth director Madison Jones on their several organizing tours witnessed the quickening of African Americans' dissatisfaction and believed that the national office's resources could help sustain what amounted to sporadic activity. But they were especially concerned about the fiefdoms that controlled several influential branches. These cliques, they believed, retarded the association's potential to organize black protest.[10]

To the secretary these and similar instances were more irritants than serious threats to the organization. Branch building was important to Walter White. But unlike Ella Baker, who believed strong and active branches would encourage—indeed, demand—African Americans to take part in their own fight, the secretary conceived of them primarily as expressions of the clout of the national office; among his favorite turns of phrase when he addressed politicians or other influentials was his reminder to his interlocutors that he was speaking in behalf of several tens of thousands of NAACP members. Even in a period of heightened unrest and increased flow of activity, Walter White maintained as he had in the past his *profession de foi* that the association's success depended on good public relations and a high national profile.[11]

Reciting this creed, the secretary turned his attention to Hollywood, where image *was* substance. With few exceptions, the film industry was closed to African Americans before the war. For every Hattie McDaniel, Stepin Fetchit, Clarence Muse, and Butterfly McQueen who made comfortable livings on contract with the major studios, hundreds of actors measured their screen careers in hours and earned a daily wage of a few dollars and a box lunch. Except for Paul Robeson, the New Negroes not only had not conquered Hollywood, they had not even established much of a toehold. African Americans before the war were limited to roles as "Old Negroes"—buffoons, servants, craven characters—stereotypes for which that arbiter of highbrow culture Alain Locke had long ago written an obituary in his seminal essay announcing the Harlem Renaissance. Otherwise, celluloid was lily-white, and unlike literature and the theater, which did tackle racial issues, Hollywood studios created a "structured absence" of African Americans, who were thus erased from a medium of growing importance for American culture—and, through film export, foreign cultures too.[12]

The reasons for this sorry state were varied. Cardinal among them was that the democratic and egalitarian critique of scientific racism and other chauvinistic ideologies that gained legitimacy in the New Deal had not yet penetrated Hollywood, except among the anti-Nazi Jews. Then too studios would not make movies that threatened their profits; each had white southern in-house consultants who advised them that films with characters who departed from traditional racial stereotypes would not be distributed in Dixie. As the culture czars preferred consensus to risk and entertainment to enlightenment, serious treatment of race was either nonexistent or left in the cutting room.

But with winds of war came winds of change. The federal government, which initially focused its domestic wartime propaganda on disseminating information, by 1942 had established a Hollywood bureau for its Office of War Information (OWI) and took an interest in the progressive portrayal of blacks. (The OWI was charged with coordinating the United States' foreign and domestic propaganda.) The administration realized that African Americans were more likely to support the war effort if the national culture portrayed the race in humane terms.

The secretary believed he could direct this irruption of conscience toward revolutionizing Hollywood's depiction of African Americans and opening industry opportunities to them. White, who as the person in charge of an aspiring bureaucracy with quite limited means often found himself in the role of the Great and Powerful Oz, was well aware of the power of the moving picture. In a comment characteristic of both his enthusiasm and his tendency to undervalue the unspectacular but essential work of quotidian organizing, White allowed that he considered "the matter of treatment of the Negro in the motion pictures of such importance that it takes rank over some other phases of our work."[13] And so it happened that the secretary, lured also by the prospects of frequent repasts with stars and studio executives and possessed of a restless but as yet unformed desire to make it in Tinseltown, headed for Hollywood in 1942.

But even before this junket the secretary had been sending out feelers. He knew by the favorable response to his antilynching appeal from Eddie Cantor, who became a star doing blackface comedy, that the considerable immigrant Jewish presence in Hollywood was receptive to the NAACP's pleas for justice.[14] In 1938 mogul David O. Selznick had asked White to be a consultant for his production of *Gone With the Wind;* a Jew whose keen feelings for the sufferings of his German coreligionists led him to sympathize with an oppressed race in the United States, Selznick wanted to make sure that neither the script nor the final product demeaned African Americans. White informed the producer of a palpable anxiety throughout Afro-America about the effects of the film; he suggested Selznick read Du Bois's *Black Reconstruction* and hire an African American to check the production for factual and interpretive errors. Selznick agreed, but when White saw the final cut he was heartsick. The secretary recognized the producer's good intentions, but he blamed *Gone With the Wind* for a renewed interest in the Negrophobic film *Birth of a Nation* and a dramatic rise in the popularity of the Ku Klux Klan. Selznick, distressed by the secretary's correlation of his masterpiece with a recrudescence of night riders, asked White what he could do to prove his sincerity. Without hesitation, the secretary said: give money. So prompted, Selznick began an annual donation of $100. White could not have been happy with such miserly almsgiving, but if he protested to Selznick or others, there is no record. Over the next decade, White would be asked to vet scripts and offer "expert" advice by producers, writers, and the OWI.[15]

White's wartime trips to Hollywood—two intensive visits in 1942 and a third in 1943—were guided by Wendell Willkie, the 1940 Republican presidential candidate, whom the secretary met just after his failed election bid. During the campaign White had been impressed with Willkie—but not enough to abandon his support for FDR. And he had refused to meet with the candidate before the election because he knew interested parties would construe it as an endorsement. When they finally made each other's acquaintance, Willkie arranged for the secretary to be introduced to film producer Walter Wanger, who then did much of the advance work for White's 1940 Hollywood tour. Willkie, a wealthy lawyer by profession, was a liberal, an internationalist with anticolonial impulses, and now chairman of the board of Twentieth Century-Fox. According to the plan, the two would take a series of meetings with producers, directors, and actors and actresses and explain to them the national and global stakes in rehabilitating African Americans' image. Additionally equipped with a letter of introduction from Eleanor Roosevelt, the secretary sought his fortune in Hollywood.[16]

For the nine days in February that the secretary was in Hollywood, he haunted the movie lots and studio offices and took up residence at the comfortable Roosevelt Hotel. His cold calls yielded meetings with stars, which puffed White up considerably. "Jimmy Cagney," White wrote with great importance to Roy Wilkins, who was holding down the fort in New York, was to host a luncheon for him at MGM in Culver City. He also had the time to schmooze with Melvyn Douglas and Jean Muir, a reprisal of their gustatory affair of 1940. Though it must have been great fun, not even the secretary could fool himself that these meetings amounted to much except to celebrity watchers. "It's the producers we've got to crack," he somewhat sheepishly acknowledged to Wilkins. But for a week and more, they had ignored the secretary, despite his dropping Willkie's name. "The movie moguls are just beginning to become dimly aware that war, anti-Semitism and world collapse affect Hollywood, too," he continued. "They still live in a dream world where they feel it necessary to prove themselves big shots by saying they are so busy they can't 'see you until a week from next Tuesday at 4:13½ P.M.' "[17]

On his last day in California, Willkie rescued White, setting up a "feverish" day of eating and meetings at the Biltmore Hotel with producers Darryl Zanuck (practically the only influential non-Jewish producer) and Walter Wanger, and a few others whom the secretary did not know and whose names he neglected to collect in the excitement. The Twentieth Century-Fox chairman said that White had legitimate grievances about the portrayal of blacks that needed to be met. The secretary respectfully disagreed with Zanuck's suggestion that the NAACP fund a Negro censor in the Production Code Administration who would purge scripts of racist language. (Hattie McDaniel had already demanded the expurgation of *nigger* from *Gone With the Wind*.) In White's opinion, the cinematic problem wasn't "so much that of deletion as it is of getting the moving pictures to present the Negro as a normal human being and an integral part of human life and activity." Zanuck was stunned by the secretary's pronouncement—or pretended to be. "Zanuck, after we had talked for a few minutes, marched up and down puffing a cigar and stopped to declaim, 'I make one-sixth of the pictures made in Hollywood and I never thought of this until you presented the facts.' " Out of this impromptu gathering, Zanuck and Wanger agreed to arrange a conference for White with all major film producers and one with the Screen Writers and Screen Actors Guilds; these would take place in July, when the secretary returned to Los Angeles for the annual NAACP convention. At a meeting upon his return to New York, responsible officers in the New York headquarters of Warner Brothers, Metro-Goldwyn-Mayer, and

Paramount expressed their complete agreement with the NAACP "and pledged themselves to do all in their power to effect as rapid a change as possible in the treatment of Negroes in moving pictures."[18]

He returned to Hollywood that summer in a triumphant mood. With his help Lena Horne, who he hoped would help to redefine screen roles for blacks, negotiated a breakthrough contract with MGM. Crowning the visit was a luncheon at the Cafe de Paris hosted by Zanuck and Wanger. Seventy of the town's biggest producers and industry executives gathered to hear the secretary exhort them to broaden their depiction of blacks in film; he assured them he was not after propaganda and "that he did not expect Negroes to be treated always as heroes but simply as human beings, or as other persons would be treated under the same circumstances." Zanuck later told his colleagues that he was moved by the secretary's "simple and direct" statement of the problem and that he had "committed myself to this program and hope very much that you will also find ways of helping to put this into effect as early as possible."[19]

The wartime exigency of national unity had resulted in the marginal improvement of the treatment of blacks in film. There was, for example, the dignified role for Eddie Anderson, who played a student wrongly accused of vehicular homicide in *In This Our Life;* and a crowd scene at the Statue of Liberty in *Sabateur* included a Negro extra. There were other upticks too. But as the editor of the *Los Angeles Tribune*, a black weekly, pointed out, the association, in contrast to its prominent and legally binding victories against segregation in court, achieved only dubious results when it appealed to whites' morality, as it had done with the movie moguls.[20]

The editor's point was made evident not long after Zanuck's and Wanger's guests had eaten their last bit of dessert. MGM had produced a film biography of Andrew Johnson under the working title *The Man on America's Conscience* and later changed to *Tennessee Johnson*. White was sent a clipping from the *Daily Worker*, which criticized the project as a whitewash of Johnson, a vilification of Thaddeus Stevens, an unjust and inaccurate indictment of Reconstruction, and a rehabilitation of the Confederacy. Before he passed judgment on the film, he sent the clipping to Louis B. Mayer, along with a request to review the script. Mayer's paternalistic response told White how pleased he was that the secretary had done the right thing by reporting the CP's criticism. He further told White how "fond" he was of him. But he never got around to addressing the secretary's concerns about the film. Through Lowell Mellett, FDR's former press aide who now ran the OWI, the secretary was able to read the script, and his criticism mirrored what the CP had said.[21]

Nevertheless, the OWI recommended theatrical release of the film. As one official put it, MGM was trying to produce a film that promoted national unity and reconciliation and stressed the importance of avoiding extremist solutions to protracted social problems. In the case of Reconstruction, that meant writing African Americans' deeds, thoughts, and accomplishments out of the script. In Mayer's view, the fact that the main agitation against the film came from Communists was further proof of the moderate and laudable content of the movie. Mayer's and Mellett's response was another instance of the limitations of liberalism on the race question. The spirit of the war moved them to appeal for the fair treatment and portrayal of African Americans in film, but they believed change needed to be gradual and moderate.[22]

If the secretary had charmed producers, directors, and white stars, many of Hollywood's African American actors were downright hostile to his presence. They were furious that he came to town and tried to change the movies without consulting them. The Mammy stereotype and clownish roles had provided a steady income for Hattie McDaniel, Butterfly McQueen, Stepin Fetchit, Clarence Muse, and a handful of others. Fearing the secretary's attempt to clean up the industry would result in their loss of livelihoods, they were gleeful when his first foray produced pious sentiment and little else. White disagreed, believing that his agitation would lead to expanded acting opportunities. But more to the point, he scorned his critics. Realistically, he said, he didn't expect thanks for his work, but he did expect those actors, who would ultimately benefit from his negotiations "without their having to lift a finger," would remain gratefully silent.[23]

Veteran black actors also accused the secretary of trying to "whiten" the African American screen image. Clarence Muse, who at one time headed the NAACP branch in Los Angeles, was the first to air this in an article for the *Pittsburgh Courier*. Behind the secretary's supposed goal of a more rounded film depiction of African American life, Muse said, was his real goal of presenting a view of blacks that was simply more palatable to whites:

There should be only a few Black-skinned Negroes, more browns and even more Mulattoes. The boys with their hair straightened will give a better social picture and all the pictures should have the Negro Lawyer, Doctor and Architect and, above all, don't have them too black. . . . In other words, this business is being "white-washed."[24]

Antipathy toward White only intensified when he returned to Los Angeles for a conference sponsored by the left-leaning Hollywood Writers' Mobilization. In the run-up to the conference his pronouncement against films with all-black casts—he said they "would not materially affect the much bigger objective . . . namely, picturization of the Negro as a normal and integral part of the life of America and of the world"—hardly endeared him to those actors for whom such productions were their best chance for employment. Once in California, he maintained a physical distance from the race; his stated objective was to spend time with producers and representatives of the overwhelmingly white writers' and directors' guilds. More, he refused to meet with his opponents, dismissing them with the fillip that he was "not in the least bothered with the criticisms and attacks of Clarence Muse and others . . ." In so doing, he rejected the advice of the film critic from the left-wing New York daily *PM*, who counseled the secretary to find some common ground with the black actors, who had formed their own Fair Play Committee to lobby for better parts. And he accepted without comment the worst sort of pigment mongering by a prominent black Angeleno businessman, who told White not to meet with Muse, McDaniel, and others because, "Naturally, a person physically large (or small), dark, limited in background and appearance can not appear in parts designed for ingenues, gigolos or dashing heroes; therefore, it is possible that a sort of jealousy or inferiority complex is associated with the whole matter, especially when we take into consideration your friendliness with Lena Horne—certainly not of the type mentioned above."[25]

White further disturbed black film actors with his 1945 proposal to establish an NAACP bureau in Hollywood. What the secretary viewed as an opportunity to influence the industry, established entertainers saw as interference in their ability to earn a living. Hattie McDaniel quipped that the secretary, having only one-eighth Negro blood, had no right to speak for African Americans. But White was guilty only of a desire to hobnob with moguls and celebrities, bad judgment, and a notable lack of grace—not a preference for light skin. He was backed up in his Hollywood efforts by the major black dailies. The *Baltimore Afro-American*

ridiculed the "rebellion of the so-called 'Uncle Toms' and 'Aunt Dinahs'
against Walter White . . . with a whole phalanx of featured players hop-
ping all over Mr. White." The *Chicago Defender* lambasted "a clique of
Hollywood Negro actors," while opining that McDaniel, Muse, Louise
Beavers, and others "are not capable of acting as judges of what is good
and what is bad in Hollywood because they have fallen victim to the poi-
son of Hollywood stereotypes."[26]

But nestled in the secretary's plans to shake up the studios' portrayal of
blacks was a germ of a scheme to install himself as the shomer of scripts
and projects. As early as 1942, White had considered transferring to Hollywood for up to six months. He lobbied hard with Walter Wanger at
Universal Pictures to produce a film of the life of Felix Eboué, the black
governor general of French Equatorial Africa who resisted Hitler's inva-
sion of the continent and declared his allegiance to the Free French. He
promoted the idea to a Twentieth Century-Fox executive that he make
himself available to read and discuss scripts and ideas with writers and
producers. He angled for a job on the team that would produce a proposed biopic of George Washington Carver.[27]

The *Pittsburgh Courier's* critic Billy Rowe intuited an ulterior motive
in the secretary's proposing an NAACP bureau in Hollywood. While acknowledging the benefits of having a lobby with the power and reputation of the NAACP to push for the reform of the black screen image, he
feared that "Walter White is trying to stick his thumb into the motion
picture pie and pull out a plum." Carlton Moss, who defended White
against charges of being "color struck," also believed White was ingrati-
ating himself in Hollywood. He *"loved* to know big people . . . and he
loved to curry attention with names." And the moguls responded positively, not because of the secretary's flattery, he said, but because they saw
him as a reformer whose proposed measures would forestall more drastic
changes in the way they did business.[28]

Carlton Moss's observations suggest some reasons why White's and
the NAACP's wartime Hollywood activities brought only minor respite
from the unrelieved dreariness of the movie industry's characterization of
African Americans. The secretary relied on influence-peddling, lobbying, and goodwill of the studio heads whose first allegiance was to the
profitability of their companies. As he had in the past, White mistook his
access to powerful persons for access to power itself.

But it is doubtful that a different approach would have yielded measurably greater results. The interests of African Americans and those of immigrant Jews who dominated the Hollywood studio system over-lapped but were hardly identical. The moguls were willing to eliminate the most inflammatory Negrophobic stereotypes from the silver screen. David O. Selznick did just that when he transformed the black rapist in Margaret Mitchell's *Gone With the Wind* into a white beast in the film ver-sion, and sent a black man to save Scarlett. By thus making a stand for fair play for an oppressed minority, Hollywood's immigrant Jews were dis-playing their Americanness and demonstrating for all to see that they were assimilating and assimilable. But they were not concerned with pre-senting fully-drawn black characters. Far from it. Whether on-screen in blackface like Al Jolson and Eddie Cantor or off-camera and producing blockbusters like *Gone With the Wind*, the immigrant Jewish cultural agenda was to use prevalent white stereotypes of African Americans in order to enter America's melting pot. Jolson sheds his old-world heritage by becoming the Jazz Singer and performing "Mammy." Selznick pro-duces a movie that makes Hattie McDaniel famous as a mammy. George Gershwin, Jerome Kern, and Irving Berlin borrow jazz, the blues, and spirituals to produce classic American film scores. With the major stu-dios—and only Twentieth Century-Fox was not dominated by Jews—convinced that the road to Americanization lay in the appropriation of black culture and symbols while simultaneously excluding African Amer-icans from serious consideration, the concessions Walter White won were probably near the maximum one could achieve.[29]

The secretary's Hollywood reveries were interrupted by a wave of vio-lence in the spring and summer of 1943 against black workers, civilians, and soldiers, reminding him of a restless and impatient militance in Afro-America that could not be satisfied by a new or revised script. Mobile, Al-abama, a city congested with black and white migrants come to work in the shipyards and further swollen by the presence of military personnel, had been tense since the previous year, when a white bus driver shot and killed a debarking black soldier. In late May, in response to the repeated demands of African American workers at Alabama Dry Dock and Ship-building Company to be promoted into skilled classifications, twelve of their number were upgraded to welders; the next day, thousands of white workers rampaged, attacking their black coworkers with pipes and other weapons; the assault ended only when army troops from a nearby base restored order. The CIO union that represented shipyard workers opposed the violence, but otherwise did little to address the grievances of their black members.[30]

In Detroit, black and white migration likewise racheted up racial frictions during the early war years. The previous year, white Detroiters rioted to prevent black workers from moving into the new Sojourner Truth housing project, which was built in a predominantly white neighborhood; abetted by a resurgent Ku Klux Klan, whites wanted the development as their exclusive enclave. Also in 1943, a series of hate strikes hit the automobile industry, as white workers refused to work next to blacks. The wildcatting crescendoed when 25,000 white Packard workers, encouraged by the company—which wanted to undermine the UAW—walked off the job in late May and early June. Unlike the union in Mobile, however, the UAW remained true to its pledge of interracial solidarity. It supported the immediate occupancy of Sojourner Truth by blacks, ordered a halt to the Packard strike, and directed white workers to work next to any qualified union member regardless of race.[31]

The Packard strike took place just as the NAACP opened its annual meeting in Detroit. In his spirited and combative keynote address the secretary agitated against the privations African Americans suffered in housing and employment, made more acute by the war and epitomized by the unholy alliance between Packard and its racist employees. The secretary explained the international stakes of African Americans' wartime struggle for civil rights. "Tokio and Berlin tonight rejoice at the effective and unexpected aid given them by" the Packard company leadership. Not only did the hate strike have the potential to deprive the military the weaponry to fight the Axis powers, but such naked displays of white supremacy "would be broadcast throughout the Pacific to colored peoples there to turn them further towards Japan and against ourselves."[32]

But there was another dimension to this international context. As had W.E.B. Du Bois in World War I, Walter White linked the fight for African Americans' civil rights with the Africans' and Asians' struggle for liberation from colonialism. White scoffed at those who claimed that militance disrupted the war effort and called for forbearance. Neither enemy nor fair-weather friend would succeed in placing the NAACP on the defensive; African Americans were asking for "simple justice . . . not

alone for himself, but for all other disadvantaged peoples of the earth."
He demanded that African Americans and "other colored peoples
throughout the world" have the right to exercise their full participation in
the planning of a democratic world when the war was finally won. The
seeds of a third world war would be sown should the peace instead be
built upon "white rule and white exploitation."[33]

Less than three weeks after this fiery speech, Walter White returned
to Detroit—at the peak of a three-day riot. On June 20, scattered fights
between blacks and whites at Belle Isle, the city's main amusement center,
mushroomed into a festival of violence against African Americans. Especially troubling was the unbridled police violence: of the twenty-five
African Americans killed in the disturbance, three-fourths were shot by
law officers. Alarmed at the ferocity of the outbreak, the secretary
boarded a plane and with Thurgood Marshall launched an investigation
and planned to defend black victims of official brutality. The secretary's
report identified overcrowding; the avariciousness of the real estate industry, which segregated blacks in order to support higher housing
prices; auto-industry agitation to turn white workers against black and divide the UAW along race lines; renewed activity by the Ku Klux Klan and
other white supremacist organizations; and "wilful inefficiency" and the
police's rampant racism as major factors in precipitating the riot. Similar
conditions existed in all cities throughout the country. A mitigating factor, which did not appear everywhere, was the presence in Detroit of a
strong interracial union movement. As both White and the UAW were
quick to point out, union appeals against "lawlessness and racial hatred"
during the three days of rioting prevented violence in any of the unionized auto factories.[34]

The firestorm erupted next in Harlem. On the evening of August 1, a
black soldier intervened in a police officer's altercation with a black
woman. The soldier allegedly grabbed the officer's billy club, struck him,
and began to walk away; the officer fired his handgun at the soldier,
wounding him in the shoulder. Rumors that the soldier had been killed
blazed through Harlem. As the secretary reported for *The New Republic*,
"Blind, unreasoning fury swept the community with the speed of lighten-
ing." Angry African Americans smashed shop windows along 125th
Street. Significantly, looting, which White blamed on poverty-stricken
Harlemites, did not occur until much later; ordinary people were inflamed by pent-up injustice and were beyond greed, said White. Harlem

residents attacked whites who had driven into the area, unaware of the explosion of discontent.[35]

According to the chain of events recounted in his autobiography, White had turned in for the evening when he was awakened by an NAACP staffer with news of the riot. Immediately after, Mayor La Guardia telephoned and asked the secretary to meet him at the West 123rd Street police station. Accompanied by Roy Wilkins, he hailed a cab in front of their apartment building. They were able to make the trip of about twenty blocks to the precinct, White remembered, because Wilkins's brown skin allowed for safe passage. At the mayor's suggestion, he and White toured the riot zone, exhorting people to stop the violence and go home. Popular wrath, however, outstripped this tandem effort, and White offered to mobilize Harlem celebrities like Duke Ellington, Cab Calloway, and Joe Louis to appeal for calm. These three, unfortunately, were out of town, but on hand were Adam Clayton Powell and another minister; the city's parole commissioner; and Ferdinand Smith, a Communist and president of the National Maritime Union. Boarding city-owned sound trucks, these prominent black New Yorkers cruised Harlem's streets broadcasting that the rumor of the black soldier's death was not true and urging people to go home. Several times during the night, Mayor La Guardia spoke to New Yorkers on the radio, demanding a cessation to the riot but not condemning Harlem's citizenry as a whole.[36]

By 9:00 the next morning, twelve hours after its start, Harlem's rage had spent itself. Six persons—all African Americans—were killed, and 185 people received treatment for injuries. Property damage was estimated at $5 million. The secretary was quick to praise the measured and compassionate response of the mayor and the police, which he believed was in stark contrast to the naked official retaliation in Detroit. He condemned the resort to violence; the rioters' acts were "criminal and unforgivable," he wrote in *The New Republic*. But his reprobation was tempered by his despair at the underlying causes of the riot: African Americans' grinding poverty, woefully congested housing and inadequate recreation facilities, continued exclusion from defense industries, and especially the "unchecked, unpunished, and often unrebuked shooting, maiming, and insulting of Negro troops, particularly in the Southern states."[37]

The Harlem riot was an outward expression of Afro-America's inflamed consciousness. Unlike the violence in Detroit and earlier outbursts like East St. Louis (1917) and Chicago (1919), which were spawned by competition between blacks and whites for employment, housing, and other essential services, the Harlem uprising focused on white property, and was undergirded by "resentment over relative deprivation caused by rising expectations [brought on by the war and] blocked opportunities." It was a classic answer to Langston Hughes's poetic question, "What happens to a dream deferred?"[38]

The riot had profound consequences on black leadership too. Mary McLeod Bethune, close friend of Eleanor Roosevelt and a reliably conservative African American voice, compared Harlem's rioters to the participants in the Boston Tea Party; they were simply responding to FDR's call to defend the Four Freedoms and fight international fascism. "They are a part of a people's war," she wrote. "The little people want 'out.' Just as the Colonists at the Boston Tea Party wanted 'out' from under tyranny and oppression and taxation without representation, the Chinese want 'out,' the Indians want 'out,' and colored Americans want 'out.' "[39]

Similarly the racial disturbances of 1943 were a powerful check on the secretary's own prejudices and preferences. While his old class biases still leaked out—"the Bigger Thomases of New York," he called rioters in *The New Republic*, in contrast to the "decent" folk[40]—he nevertheless had to concede that the riot was a clear, if undesirable, form of protest. He was surprised at the harsh laughter and profanity that greeted his attempts to disperse rioters, but in the disturbances' wake he too would display less patience and declared his unwillingness to accept palliatives. His ken of the global stakes of the Negroes' fight for freedom deepened, and he would with increasing frequency wave the banner that upheld an alliance between African Americans in their fight for civil rights and the colonial peoples of Asia and Africa fighting for national liberation.

If the secretary was now explicitly hitching the black freedom struggle to the radical position of a postwar world without colonies, he nevertheless still believed in the power of his traditional methods—high-profile publicity and symbolic actions by persons in power—for bringing about change. In April 1942, less than a year after the proclamation of the Atlantic Charter by Britain and the United States, which seemingly committed both to a postwar world without colonial domination, the secretary dashed off a confidential letter to leading black Americans concerning the plan he was brewing to support Indian independence. His attention to India was consonant with the American public's growing interest in the subcontinent. In the aftermath of Pearl Harbor, the press increased its criticism of Britain's determination to hold on to its Asian empire as an obstacle to the successful prosecution of the war. The black newspapers and journals in particular had long been supporters of Gandhi and the Indian National Congress. Many leading Americans, including Sumner Welles and President Roosevelt himself, advocated Indian self-determination.[41] White informed his correspondents, who included W.E.B. Du Bois, A. Philip Randolph, and black newspapermen and college presidents, that as part of his plan he had met with Lord Halifax, Britain's ambassador to the United States and former colonial governor of India. Their discussion had focused on the basis on which Britain's south Asian colonial population could be mobilized to support the Allied war effort. Much to Lord Halifax's bemusement, White told him that he had asked President Roosevelt to declare his support for Indian independence, link his concern for people of color in Asia with a concern for black America, and appoint a distinguished commission (that included a prominent and phenotypical African American) to travel to India to reassure Indians of American support for their cause.[42]

Before World War II the NAACP had exhibited only limited interest in the international dimensions of race, and whatever actions it took generally were a result of individual initiative. The Pan-African Congress movement that blossomed in the anglophone parts of the diaspora in the decade after the first world war was largely the creation of W.E.B. Du Bois. While the association was the movement's nominal patron in the United States, Du Bois in fact acted independently and without the association's oversight. Few in the NAACP grasped the relationship of African Americans to people of color around the world; besides, vital domestic issues claimed the association's limited resources.

In the immediate post–World War I years, though, the NAACP was one of several competing black rights organizations, and it had not yet established its paramountcy. Other formations, especially Marcus Garvey's Universal Negro Improvement Association (UNIA), captured the pan-African imagination with its call for international race unity. In the twenties the NAACP and the Pan-African Congress movement sought to ameliorate the problems of colonialism by agitating for reforms of the colonial system and by including African Americans and Africans in the decision-making processes that affected them. In contrast, for the UNIA, whose program was far more compelling to the masses of black Americans, the connection between African Americans and foreign affairs was direct and immediate: the lives of blacks in the United States would not improve until Africa was redeemed. In the decade following the war, black America's interest in foreign affairs was nurtured largely by Garveyism.[43]

Italy's aggression against Ethiopia in 1935 reminded the NAACP once again of the importance of foreign affairs to the black struggle against discrimination. *The Crisis* frequently carried articles about what was at stake in Ethiopia.[44] But with an ambitious agenda, including a campaign for a federal antilynching law and the desegregation of public education, the NAACP was unable to take the lead in mobilizing public opinion against Mussolini and worked primarily in the background, vainly trying to influence American policy.

It was not only time constraints that prevented a vigorous NAACP presence in the Ethiopian crisis. The association maintained a low profile in this affair primarily because the secretary believed the politics and leadership styles of the principals in the Ethiopian solidarity movement were suspect. One such group was the Communist Party. He also had to contend with the prominence of black nationalists who, in their actions and propaganda, actively opposed White's and the association's integrationist politics. Furthermore, most pro-Ethiopian activity took the form of mass protest, with which the secretary was uncomfortable.[45]

So while the NAACP ceded mass leadership to figures like Adam Clayton Powell, Jr., and the popular nationalist street agitators in Harlem and Chicago, White mustered a delegation of prominent African Americans to meet with President Roosevelt and otherwise tried to influence official policy. While he included the moderate and conservative voices of Representative Arthur Mitchell, Mary McLeod Bethune, and representatives from black fraternal, sororal, and professional organizations, he excluded mass-oriented and radical figures like Powell and A. Philip Randolph.[46] But the government was determined not to get involved in the Italo-Ethiopian crisis, the meeting with the president never materialized, and by 1936 the NAACP's efforts petered out.

Between 1942 and 1944, under the influence of official wartime antiimperialist rhetoric and the activities of third-world, and especially Indian, nationalists, White's worldview broadened and his anticolonial sentiments became more pronounced. He envisioned Roosevelt calling a meeting of leaders of Asian nations and liberation movements that would explicitly guarantee the principle of self-determination for that continent and the Pacific. He desperately thought that the president needed to make a statement that "the era of white domination of colored peoples is ended and that the peoples of these countries can be assured that there will be no post-war economic or other penetration."[47]

But almost from the moment of his meeting with Lord Halifax, the White House staff stonewalled the secretary's attempts to meet the president. White even asked Eleanor Roosevelt for assistance—something he had done with success in the past—but she either declined to help or could not convince her husband to meet him.[48] Despite the enthusiasm of New Dealers like Sumner Welles and Henry Wallace, Roosevelt decided that support for decolonization was not politically feasible. Though he personally was opposed to imperialism, as a practical matter Roosevelt felt that he could not interfere in something that was "strictly speaking, none of my business."[49] The British arrests of Mohandas Gandhi, Jawaharlal Nehru, and other Indian nationalist leaders in August 1942, and the president's lack of public response, further emboldened White. He canceled plans to broadcast a message to the Japanese people at the request of the OWI. His short speech was to have emphasized the growing numbers in America who were working to eradicate racism and turn the war into a genuine war against colonialism; in changing his mind, he told government officials that "arrests leave me with nothing convincing to say." He then wired Roosevelt, demanding that he speak out against the arrests: "One billion brown and yellow peoples in the Pacific," he said, "will without question consider ruthless treatment of Indian leaders and people typical of what white peoples will do to colored peoples if United Nations win."[50]

White also ran into what he saw as a thick layer of public opinion that opposed decolonization, which he summarized in a June 1942 memorandum for his records.[51] He wrote that Allied setbacks early in the war, especially in the Pacific, had temporarily silenced American racists, who, like all Americans, were worried about the war's outcome and wanted to drum up as much support as possible from the colonial world. But recent Allied advances created feelings that the war would not be protracted; consequently, the racists were beginning to reassert themselves. "Already lines are being sharply drawn for a knock-down, drag-out fight between the Westbrook Peglers [a right-wing columnist for the *New York Post*] and those who are decent and wise enough to know that no lasting peace will ever be fashioned until the colored people of the world who form a majority are no longer exploited because of color."

White saw some hope in the pronouncements of Henry Wallace, who talked of the war as one of a free world against a slave world, a "people's revolution," and a conflict with the aim of overthrowing the doctrine of racial superiority. But Wallace and the NAACP were in the minority, and White cited editorial opinion from across the nation stating that this was in fact a war for the spoils of empire. That political climate could lead to "a nation-wide, and perhaps world-wide wave against colored peoples of terrifying proportions and bitterness." White then adumbrated a line of action:

> We of the NAACP have an enormous task to perform. It is that of awakening the world to the fact that military victory over Germany and Japan which brings in its wake a racial hysteria of this sort will, as surely as the sun rises, prepare the ground for World War III, which will come as soon as we have recovered from this conflict. That is why the outburst now of the editorial fuehrers are more sinister than they at first glance appear to be.

The only way to avoid a racial conflagration was to remove the dependent peoples from the struggle for empire and proclaim their equality by supporting their demands for decolonization.

The secretary countered such ominous public opinion in the manner with which he was most comfortable and which had in the past, he felt, afforded him the greatest success: a well-publicized personal investigation of the European, North African, and Pacific war theaters. He planned to follow this with a book, which eventually became *A Rising Wind* (1945). His scheming to get access to the highly restricted war zones is vintage Walter White. He turned aside an opportunity to write syndicated dispatches for the black press in favor of more notoriety—and lucre—from *Time*, *Life*, and the *New York Post*. He tried, through ER, to get the president to endorse his trip or at least to remove logistical and political obstacles in the way of the successful completion of his mission, and without prior approval, he used Supreme Court Justice Hugo Black as a reference. Although Eleanor Roosevelt told White that neither she nor her husband could comply with his request, he told Lord Halifax that his planned trip to England was with the president's knowledge and cooperation.[52]

Some War Department officials, however, initially opposed White's visit and were "anxious to prevent it," Lord Halifax informed the British Foreign Office. The secretary's visit, they feared, would increase agitation for the end of discrimination and segregation in the American armed services. Other military leaders believed that a better way to avoid negative publicity was to extend him a high level of hospitality and give him unfettered access to all but the most sensitive areas. The head of the U.S. army's office of public relations, Major General A. D. Surles, was not overly worried that the secretary would be incediary. White was a "fair but sharply critical writer." Even though he would bring to light the military's shortcomings in race relations, his reports would on balance likely be favorable and would be credible among African Americans. In the end, other domestic political considerations—increasing blacks' morale and ensuring the African American vote for FDR—trumped the military's preferences for Jim Crow, and the government allowed the secretary to travel abroad. The army even assigned White a car, driver, and escort and ordered officers in all geographic areas to let him inspect whatever and talk with whomever he wished.[53] Having thus overcome the hesitation of the United States military brass, the secretary tucked his press credentials in his flak jacket and boarded a Britain-bound plane in the first week of January 1944. He planned to be gone three and a half months, with subsequent stops in North Africa, the Middle East, and Italy.[54]

Neither the Foreign Office, the India office, the Colonial Office, nor the Ministry of Information were expecting him, the result of a communication breakdown with London's embassy in Washington. His surprise arrival only increased His Majesty's Government's own apprehensions about Walter White. They were alarmed by his pronounced anti-imperialism, especially his recent comment about an Indian official that "it appears that Negroes are not the only ones who are cursed with Uncle Toms." Proving that the British could exhibit a white supremacy every bit as crude as the American variety, a Foreign Office functionary wrote of White's arrival: "he is the nigger in the woodpile . . . of some race conscious folk in the U.S." Whatever else White wanted to do, British officials were determined to prevent him from traveling to India and meeting with Gandhi and other jailed nationalists.[55]

But after meeting with the secretary, British officials decided that rather than holding him at a distance they would heed Lord Halifax's advice that "it would be worth while to take some trouble with him." [56] In the course of his first encounter with White, an official in the British Ministry of Information discovered what the secretary's friends and associates had always known: Walter White loved an adventure and socializing with important people, and sometimes allowed a moment's excitement to distract him from the main objectives. As Robin Cruikshank, with a heavy dollop of imperial condescension, observed to his colleague in the British Foreign Office:

> One small but significant touch. Since he has been in London White has heard two Air Raid alerts, accompanied by a very moderate amount of gun fire, but this has impressed him quite beyond expectation. "Ah," said he, shaking his silver head, "that brings home the terrible reality of war in a way you could never know in New York." I think there is a key to the solving of the White problem here: he is an imaginative and impressionable character, and if our people can show him stirring and remarkable things when he goes about the Empire it will do much more good than arguing over his race theories. We have a hard nut to crack, but he is well worth taking a lot of trouble over. . . . [57]

In fact, White was plenty dazzled by the luminaries he met and was eager to relate to provincial Yanks all the strange and wonderful sights he saw. His letters to NAACP headquarters are a mixture of eyewitness journalism and banal commentary. He was feted at the Cafe Royale in Picadilly Circus; General John Lee, head of Supply of Service, hosted a dinner party in his honor—complete with cocktails and hors d'oeuvres—in his flat. He had to get used to the "eerie experience" of sitting through a blackout, and he acquainted folks back home with Britishisms such as *torch* ("flashlight"), *Jerry* ("German soldier"), and *tube* ("subway"). Names dropped like autumn leaves. One day he had to see a Colonel Lawrence in the public relations office, he told the NAACP staff. "On entering his office we greeted each other ebulliently when I found that Col. Lawrence is my very good friend, Jock Lawrence from Hollywood who I met through Walter Wanger when Wendell Willkie and I went out there two years ago." In another letter, he told of the excitement of boarding a flying fortress and participating in a bombing mission. But, an incredulous

Foreign Office official reported, "what he did not succeed in doing was in getting interviews with the Secretary of State, the Prime Minister or (he even suggested it!) The King." [58]

Only a couple of White's *Post* articles were published, the balance falling victim to the military censor, and only two of his regular "People & Places" columns for the *Chicago Defender* discussed what he discovered in England—one on British perceptions of American politics and another on his admiration for the Brits' stiff upper lips. [59]

The full story of his inspection appeared in early 1945 as *A Rising Wind*. As the title implies, White insisted that the war against fascism was promoting a democratic spirit among white American soldiers and ordinary Britons, which boded well for a postwar world without colonies. The book is laced with anecdotes of white southern GIs abandoning Jim Crow etiquette as the experience of being under enemy fire led them to embrace Afro-Americans' humanity. White sincerely hoped that these tangible expressions of solidarity were America's future. But he was no Pollyanna, and he was the angry black soldiers' amanuensis. The word *enemy* had a double meaning for black GIs, he reported: the Nazis and white American soldiers. African American troops resented the separate and unequal recreation facilities and having towns declared off-limits to them. They bristled at being confined to support units. At one stop on his tour, in Oran, Algeria, he sat on stage at an amphitheater and faced between 5,000 and 6,000 sullen black combat-trained soldiers who fumed at having been utilized only as stevedores.

He regularly expressed amazement at the British population's friendly attitude toward black American troops and their resistance to adopting American racial segregation. In this sense, the British Foreign Office received a free pass on its mistreatment of its colonial subjects. But his soft-pedaling of imperial wrongdoing had less to do with the information ministry throwing dust in his eyes than with a desire to promote an alternative to the harsh reality of American Jim Crow; in pursuing this rhetorical strategy, the secretary was following a distinguished line of black authors who praised black-white relations in Europe to induce the reform of racial practices in the United States. [60]

But by no means did imperialism escape his scrutiny. He was indignant at the treatment of Arabs in Morocco. With his keen eye for detail and his full enjoyment of playing the role of the "voluntary Negro," White lampooned the colonial mentality. At a dinner party in London, he stopped his hosts' hypocritical denunciation of American race relations by discussing his planned visit to India. He wanted to meet with Lord Wavell, he stated, but there would be difficulties should the two try to dine at a certain exclusive club in Calcutta. When the other dinner guests asked what could possibly stand in the way of two men dining at the un-named club, White told them that the establishment "boasts that no per-son of colored blood has ever crossed its threshold. And I am a Negro." As he then related, "There was no further discussion that evening of the race question." He also revealed a bizarre luncheon with the Virginia-born Lady Astor, who arrived more than a half hour late and greeted the secretary by blurting out, "You *are* an idiot, calling yourself a Negro when you're whiter than I am, with blue eyes and blond hair!" After listening to her complain about the "near-white ones who cause the trouble," White concluded that for all her polish, Lady Astor was really quite dim—and quite representative of the British ruling elite: "[I]n nothing she said was there any hint of a newer world in which there would be much change from the old one. . . . [O]ne knew she was convinced that control of the destinies of the world would remain in the hands of those who held the reins before."[61]

White's analysis of the stakes of the war and African America's and the third world's place in the postwar world reflected a sharpening and popu-lar militancy. If he was deceived at all, it was by his own hand and con-cerned the impact of his findings on American military policy. Shortly before his departure from London, White met with General Eisenhower and his second-in-command Lieutenant General Lee, at which the secre-tary presented his finding that the source of racial friction and violence was racist military officers determined "in various ways to force accep-tance of patterns of racial behavior like those of Mississippi." He pro-posed specific recommendations to rectify the situation and boost black troops' morale, including the establishment of a biracial and impartial board to review court-martial records of black troops (the secretary had documented the willingness of the military justice system to mete out dis-proportionately severe justice to black soldiers and to convict them of trumped-up charges); forbidding officers from declaring locations off-limits on the basis of race; the integration of recreational facilities; the ac-tivation of black combat troops; and the formation of integrated military police patrols. White said that Eisenhower approved of his recommenda-tions. And General Lee was effusive in his praise for the secretary's effort, proclaiming his visit "invaluable" for the promotion of black soldiers' morale and declaring his contributions to interracial understanding "fundamental." But how much effect White's labors had on the military can be more accurately measured by the conclusions of the army's own investigation that was sparked by his report:

> That investigation of the allegations contained in Mr. White's report reveals no condition of serious consequence concerning racial relations in this Theater.
>
> That there is no evidence of discrimination against the colored troops.
>
> That the existing instructions issued from this headquarters on the racial subject are adequate.[62]

The secretary returned home in March, planning to rest but briefly and resume globe-trotting in the Pacific war theatre. The board of directors had other ideas, however. Some members believed that White ought not to go abroad again. They were likely echoing criticism articulated before the secretary's European voyage. Carl Murphy, board member from Baltimore and publisher of the *Afro-American*, thought White's ventures were primarily a way to promote his career as a reporter and author. "Walter ought to devote his time to the work of the Association and quit using the facilities and time of the Association for his journalistic chores," he told the board. Board chairman Louis Wright, White's longtime friend and personal physician, thought the secretary of the NAACP should not be abroad when there was so much planning to do for the struggle for civil rights in the imminent postwar; he suggested that other association officials go to the Pacific in White's stead. Arthur Spingarn, whose position carried the day, argued that the secretary remain in the States until after the November election; there were bound to be important questions concerning the presidential and congressional contests that required his input, and besides, summer and fall were the worst seasons for travel in the tropics.[63]

In the hiatus between inspections, the secretary was venerated by civil rights warhorses and helped to plot electoral strategy. In late May, 750 guests packed the Roosevelt Hotel in Manhattan to mark Walter White's twenty-fifth anniversary with the NAACP. (The tribute was in fact more than a year tardy, White having become assistant secretary in January

1918.) Arthur Spingarn, like several others, reminisced about the secretary's early years and aimed some good-natured pokes at White's well-known foibles, including a legendary informality that sometimes infuriated prominent people: "I don't think that Walter knows there are more than six people in the United States who have last names," he said. "I remember someone telling me that a certain prominent man was a cold fish and I asked him why. 'Well,' he said, 'he and Walter talked for almost half an hour before they called each other by their first names.' " Edwin Embree of the Rosenwald Fund captured the interplay of the secretary's personality and his presence as a force for equality:

> I have never doubted that you have a hearty ego! Your frank delight in it is one of your most attractive traits. But even your healthy self-esteem can scarcely gauge the value of the work you have done or the high place you have as a human being and as a symbol in American life. An increasing number of people are recognizing that your contribution is not so much to the well being of Negroes, as to the preservation of American democracy.

Arthur Garfield Hays retold the story of the first time Clarence Darrow met the secretary. After mistakenly proffering his sympathies for the plight of "your people" to two white attorneys, the venerable lawyer then mistook the secretary for white.[64]

Eleanor Roosevelt, the marquee speaker, better than anyone that evening spoke to the difficult conditions inherent in working for progressive causes and the aplomb with which the secretary acquitted himself:

> I know perhaps better than most people how disheartening it is to work as Mr. White has worked and stand up under defeat over and over again and pick the pieces up and start again and always hope that each defeat means some victory and a step forward. I think that takes great courage, and for that reason tonight I want to congratulate Mr. White, not on the personal courage which he showed when he was young, but on the courage which it takes to accept temporary defeats in order that you may eventually win and never to acknowledge that you really are defeated.[65]

After the gentle roasting, President Mordecai Johnson of Howard University mounted the rostrum and urged those present to give until it hurt and then give some more; his cajoling raised $20,000 for the NAACP Legal Defense and Education Fund.

How the Negro would vote was more uncertain in 1944 than in the previous two presidential elections, and black advancement organizations pressed this advantage. In June, representatives of twenty-five organizations met at the invitation of the NAACP to update the "Declaration of Negro Voters," originally adopted the previous November. Although conceding that black voters had recently been voting Democrat, the document pointed out a fact that must have alarmed that party: in the off-year elections of 1943, African American voters in New York City had been essential in electing Ben Davis, a black Communist, to the city council and Hubert Delany, a black radical Republican, to the bench, while their counterparts in Kentucky helped to put a Republican in the governor's mansion. Especially in light of these manifestations of political independence, the declaration stated, party hacks would not determine for whom African Americans would vote, black votes were not for sale, and party platforms had to move well beyond "meaningless generalities." The twenty-five organizations, with a combined membership of more than six million African Americans, ticked off six minimum demands that parties would have to support to earn black votes: the right to vote in every state, unrestricted by poll taxes, white primaries, lily-white party conventions, gerrymandered districts, or other artifice; abolition of the poll tax by an act of Congress rather than by the cumbersome process of constitutional amendment; federal antilynching legislation; unsegregated integration of the armed forces; a permanent FEPC; and a foreign policy of international cooperation.[66]

The secretary was picked to deliver the declaration to the Republican National Convention in Chicago later that month. With Wendell Willkie out of the picture and the nomination of New York Governor Thomas Dewey on the agenda, the GOP was not likely to address the issues raised by the statement. The secretary called the Republicans advocates of "cautious donothingness." He was not surprised, he told the readers of his *Defender* column, but he "left Chicago depressed with the thought that in July we will have to go back there and look into the faces of a Democratic platform committee, studded with such handsome, intelligent faces as that of the senior Senator from Mississippi, the Honorable Theodore G. Bilbo."[67]

It was worse than the secretary imagined. In the weeks leading up to the Democratic convention, rumors abounded that FDR, seeking an unprecedented fourth term, would bow to the pressure of his party's southern wing, drop Henry Wallace as his running mate, and tap instead James Byrnes, the arch-segregationist from South Carolina with a long résumé of government service. Wallace, who had previously served as FDR's agriculture secretary, had broadened his support significantly from his base in rural America to include urban-industrial areas. Immediately after the Detroit riot, Wallace visited the city and proclaimed racial justice and tolerance as the critical issues facing the United States in the postwar era. He also applauded organized labor and boldly stated that racial and anti-labor violence only benefited reactionary and powerful forces in the country. As a result, he was the overwhelming favorite of the CIO, progressives in the New Deal, and African Americans.[68]

The secretary was in a fighting mood. Before an audience of 40,000 persons attending the closing session of the NAACP's annual convention in Chicago, he blistered the Democratic leaders' plans to remove Wallace as a betrayal of blacks, the professed democratic war aims, and the cause of national liberation of the darker world:

> On this 952nd day of America's participation in a war to save the world from the military aggression and racial bigotry of Germany and Japan, the United Nations with a comparable master race theory of its own moves on to victory. The growing certainty of that victory intensifies determination to permit no fundamental change in the attitude of "white" nations toward the "colored" peoples of the earth.

He ripped both Republicans and Democrats, but he was particularly alarmed by the plans to replace Wallace with a southerner. Despite African Americans' affection for ER, he claimed that they needed to be prepared "to submit to the temporary defeat of seeing Tweedledum replace Tweedledee . . . [W]e cannot run the risk—so desperate is our plight—of an anti-Negro figure as heir apparent to the most powerful position in the world today."[69]

The Chicago dailies were alarmed at the secretary's radicalism. But when White pressed his case privately to Eleanor Roosevelt, he made certain to tell her that the crowd "was most vociferous in its applause of the section of the speech dealing with the southern conspiracy to replace Mr. Wallace. . . ." And he assured her that other black leaders shared his sentiments. "On returning to New York I was deluged with telephone calls from influential Negroes like Dr. Channing H. Tobias who were alarmed at the report that Mr. Byrnes was favored by the high command of the Democratic Party. . . . Every person with whom I have talked is convinced that his nomination would cause ninety percent of Negroes to vote the Republican ticket or abstain from voting."[70]

Wallace's disappearance from the ticket was preordained by party leaders—Roosevelt had decided not to make known whom he preferred as a running mate and to let the convention decide—but his replacement was not. Byrnes withdrew his name from consideration and Harry Truman, an unknown quantity in the struggle for democracy and civil rights, was named FDR's running mate. White wrote in the *Defender* that "the 1944 Democratic convention marked the coming of age politically of the Negro" because the threat of a defection of black voters to the Republican Party was the "decisive factor" in the rejection of Byrnes.[71] But this was so much whistling in the dark, as his frank correspondence with Eleanor Roosevelt shows.

ER, ever sympathetic to White and the cause, was not nearly so assured, and she doubted that the NAACP or the black vote was responsible for scratching Byrnes's nomination:

I read your speech [to the NAACP convention in Chicago] with very deep interest. I am always torn in my mind as to whether the voicing of bitterness, and some of this speech is bitter of necessity, is going to help solve our extremely difficult questions both in the present and in the future.

I entirely understand why you and the other leaders of the colored race feel as they do. Both the President and I were as disturbed as you were by the reports which we received that Justice Byrnes was under consideration and showing considerable strength. I was very glad that he withdrew but I was never quite sure that he was not being used just as a red herring to prevent Wallace from increasing his strength and to make Senator Truman the candidate.

As to the value of any possible NAACP victory in the nomination affair, ER had this to say: "The liberals will have to learn to elect a majority of delegates beforehand and not trust to anything that is done at the last minute."

Then in a startlingly candid statement that revealed both her weariness and a warm friendship with Walter White, she confessed that, "To tell the truth, from a personal standpoint and not for publication, a defeat will not be an unmixed sorrow for me." [72]

The secretary seemed to accept her explanation that rumors of Byrnes's nomination were a gambit to deny Wallace. And in his private correspondence with ER, he shelved his public posturing about the political maturation of African Americans. Except for the fact that black voters were determined not to be appendages to any political party, White was particularly gloomy. "Most of all, I am disturbed by the despair among Negroes who feel that there is little for them to hope for from either party. Their sole ray of hope is that between now and election day the Administration, and in particular the President, will by act and word demonstrate that the fight for liberalism is not only going to be continued but will be stepped up." [73]

Here, then, was the bind in which Walter White and the NAACP found themselves. Publicly the secretary preached black political independence, as when he facetiously advocated a Wallace-Willkie ticket. The former, he said, agitated for workers to seize power from the northern and southern Democratic party-machine politicians, and the latter's liberal internationalism stood in bold contrast to the "congenital decrepitude of the Republican party." [74] But privately he was unwilling to abandon Roosevelt and worked to corral the African American vote once again for him.

It soon became apparent that neither White nor the NAACP board in plenary had stomachs for autonomous action. At a special board meeting, directors like Alfred Baker Lewis, a member of the Socialist Party with a wide anticommunist streak, favored business as usual. The association ought to limit itself to compiling and publishing voting records of congressional candidates while ignoring the presidential race. Leslie Perry, the NAACP staffer from Washington, and Roy Wilkins presented a defeatist picture, arguing that the association had little influence over black voters and so ought to remain silent about both parties not living up to the declaration. [75]

William Hastie, backed by Thurgood Marshall and with a surprising endorsement from the normally conservative Channing Tobias, dissented. The Negro voters' declaration was important and had meaning; if they did nothing further in the aftermath of the two parties' near-complete disregard for the concerns of African Americans, the twenty-five organizations that signed the document "would lose prestige and effectiveness." Having "with our eyes open . . . gone out on a limb" and stated that the two parties faced repercussions if they did not act on the declaration, the NAACP now risked its credibility if it followed Wilkins's and Perry's advice. Thurgood Marshall said that the NAACP ought to threaten a boycott unless the candidates responded positively to African Americans' concerns.[76]

Arthur Spingarn, seconded by the secretary, tried hard to bend the association's traditional nonpartisanship into support for FDR. The New Deal was imperfect and the vanquished Wallace was superior to Truman, but the Democratic Party was all Negroes had, said Spingarn, echoing Frederick Douglass's earlier aphorism that the Republicans were the ship and all else the sea. The association, he urged, "should not do anything which will bring about the defeat of President Roosevelt." Their's became the association's position, and from then until the election, the secretary's weekly *Defender* column, when it discussed the presidential campaign, criticized Dewey, the Republicans, and the southern Democrats, while remaining nearly mute on the shortcomings of Roosevelt.[77]

In mid-December, with FDR and ER returned to the White House, the secretary left New York for four months in the South Pacific. In contrast to the earlier European jaunt, this trip was harder on White, physically and emotionally. Though he was regaled at its beginning and end, living conditions in the broad middle segment were more primitive. And perhaps because of the military's presence in colonial areas, the white enlisted men's and officers' attitude toward black soldiers was more feral.

White spent the first two weeks in Hawaii, resting and orienting himself to some of the realities of the Pacific war. The military, he said, had been exceedingly generous to him, allowing him access to several high-ranking officers and enlisted personnel. Ever the adventurer, he took a ride on an amphibious truck. He had the good fortune to meet up with John Hope's son, Edward, a navy lieutenant, and they went to a luau also attended by old comrades of the fighting 369th, the Harlem Hellcats. "Two 185-pound pigs baked over hot stones in a pit after being wrapped in ti-leaves (a palm like, aromatic leaf) was the main dish along with side dishes of raw fish, poi (a concoction like library paste which one eats by dipping one or more fingers in the dish), fresh pine-apple and a papaya and other tropical fruits," was the wide-eyed White's description to folks back home. Despite the presence of white Americans who packed Jim Crow in their steamer trunks beside their clothes, the mélange of races and ethnicities present on the island—the secretary catalogued whites, Hawaiians, Puerto Ricans, Japanese, Chinese, Portuguese, African Americans, and Filipinos—somehow mitigated racism's impact, he thought. He did not think discrimination here was as severe as what he found in Europe. In a public speech to black sailors and soldiers in Honolulu, the secretary said he believed the high command was sincere in its efforts to keep a lid on racism.[78]

And while he continued to have faith in the brass's good intentions, his probes uncovered a reality that was far grimmer than what he initially imagined. One incident in Hawaii was typical. As they had on other Pacific islands, black servicemen on Hawaii had performed heroic service constructing military installations. Black officers of one unit, however, complained that they were not being treated fairly by their superiors, because white officers were repeatedly promoted over them. The command's response to the formal complaint was to replace them with white officers. When they heard of this injustice, black enlisted men staged a brief work stoppage, after which they agreed to resume their jobs and make up for the lost time; still, seventy-four of the men were charged with mutiny, and courts-martial handed down stiff sentences. In another unit, a white officer wrote a friend that "I'm beginning to get an unholy pleasure out of sending those Eleanor's boys to the brig."[79]

The secretary arrived on Guam about one week after the arrest of forty four African American sailors for rioting on Christmas night. In the weeks leading up to this holiday violence, African American troops had been subjected to drive-by shootings and other acts of aggression; the day before Christmas, a group of black servicemen in the city of Agana were fired upon by a white marine. None of the white perpetrators had been punished. After their Christmas meal, black servicemen, despite their not having passes, took two trucks from camp and headed to town; white troops in a jeep shot at them. They returned fire, for which they were charged with rioting.[80]

The secretary was pressed into the role of defense counsel for the accused black servicemen. Most of Guam had been retaken from the Japanese, but there were still substantial pockets of resistance. For three weeks, White, who had no assistants, traveled frequently to forward areas to gather evidence. He worked seven days a week, often sixteen hours daily, though he did have time for an impromptu party with Ernie Pyle, whom White met in Italy, and other war correspondents.[81] Film writer-director Hal Kanter remembered the secretary from Guam and how once more his complexion helped him to get the full story:

> He arrived on Guam and it was my assignment to take him out to meet the commander of the troops. . . .
>
> We came out to see the colonel . . . I sat and they started to talk, and finally Mr. White said, "Now about this incident . . . Can you explain what that was all about?" He asked this question a lot better than I am repeating it now, incidentally. The colonel said, "Oh Mr. White. That was just a bunch of them damn niggers . . ." I thought I was going to go through the floor. Mr. White said, "Well thank you colonel. That about does it. Thank you very much." Then he said, "We can go now sergeant," and he got up.
>
> I followed him out and I could see when we got outside he was absolutely furious.[82]

The official board of inquiry heard more than 100 witnesses, some more than once, and the secretary was able to read into the record the daily provocation black servicemen faced. Perhaps because he was an outsider, the court-martial was conducted in an impartial manner; in any event, White thought so, and he held out hope not only for an acquittal but also for vigorous corrective action on the part of the military command. Authorities waited until the secretary left the area to render a verdict: all the accused were found guilty and received sentences ranging from four months to four years.[83]

Wherever he went in the Pacific—after Hawaii, he inspected the Mariana Islands, the Johnston atoll, the Marshall Islands, the Philippines, the Solomon Islands, and Australia—he found racist violence and a deliberate campaign to defame black uniformed personnel.[84] But he also found a high degree of political consciousness among blacks. His reports home and letters sent to the national office from African American troops stationed in the Pacific indicate both a growing impatience with military Jim Crow and a high level of respect for the secretary personally. He reported that it was "heartbreaking" to see the grateful response of black troops to the presence of an NAACP official; White knew that he could work around the clock for weeks and still not have the time to hear "half the folks who want to tell their stories." Bobbie Branche, his secretary in New York, reported on the reaction of one sailor to White's presence in the Pacific:

> A youngster I know just landed from the Phillipines [*sic*]. Of course the first question I asked him was did he see Mr. White. "Walter White," he asked. "No I didn't see him. I was sick in the hospital but that was alright. I didn't care whether I saw him or not. All I wanted to know was that he was *there. On the Spot.*" He went on to rave and rave.[85]

When he arrived on the island of Leyte, a group of servicemen began an NAACP membership drive and set a goal of sending the national office $5,000.

A black first lieutenant sent this report of his battalion's chance encounter with the NAACP secretary:

> Walter White, while on one of the recently liberated islands of the Philippines, was standing beside one of the Island's dusty roads, when by chance, a group of Negro Army Chaplains passed in a jeep.
>
> As fortune would have it, Mr. White was recognized by one of the Chaplains, thus they stopped and picked him up. . . .
>
> That night, as a movie was in progress, with hundreds of Negro soldiers as the audience, there was a hurried interruption. Immediately the lights flashed on and the Bn [battalion] Surgeon stepped upon the little improvised stage and said in words to this effect. "I have a surprise for you." Everything took on a quietness that was like the calm before the storm. It seemed as though everybody sensed that this was no ordinary surprise. "Do you know Walter White?" Hundreds yelled as one, Yes! "Well, he's here." At this the crowd of Negro soldiers went wild, they stomped the earth, they whistled, they threw their hats into the air; . . . Walter White, the War correspondent, . . . the voice of thirteen million, stepped upon the stage and spoke to a group of Negro soldiers . . . [86]

From the Philippines, the secretary made his way to Australia, where he was enjoying, he wrote to Arthur Spingarn, "staying in a hotel where there is a bed with a mattress on it and sheets and pillows, bathing in a tub with hot water, and eating at a table on which there is something else besides bully beef and Spam and C- or K-rations." His health had suffered some during his months in the jungle: he had lost more than twenty pounds, and he had been involved in a plane crash, which left him shaken and bruised.[87]

In Australia he not only became reacquainted with creature comforts, he reflected on what he had seen and done. After witnessing up close the valor of African American troops and the abuse to which they were subjected, he could hardly have been surprised to see the pattern repeated in Australia. Vice squads, he reported, roamed the streets breaking up interracial groups and couples. White Americans had done advance work. But he recognized that Australians, their British cousins, and other Asian-Pacific colonial powers harbored prejudices that were strikingly similar to the American-spread racial propaganda. His suspicions of the Allied war aims were confirmed as he found a stubborn unwillingness to liberate the people of the Asian-Pacific region from all forms of colonialism, not just the Japanese variety. "Apparently," he wrote with some sadness to the people at NAACP headquarters, "imperialism is to be continued, if the articulate element here has its way."[88]

As the war in Europe and the Pacific wound down, and as he returned to New York from a 36,000-mile journey, the secretary was losing hope of converting President Roosevelt's personal sentiments into a policy of decolonization; if the racist treatment black soldiers experienced during the war was one indication of this, another was his inability to find political-military leaders in the Pacific willing to commit to such a position. "Thousands of Americans have died and billions of American dollars have been spent in the Pacific to oust the Japanese—apparently only to restore the recaptured islands to the European powers which ruled and exploited these areas and their populations before the war," he said upon his return to the United States. He found it "disheartening to find everywhere calm acceptance of the fact that no other course is even thought of except to reestablish colonial empire." The government and people of the United States must wake up, he said, to the fact that a reestablishment of the old order "inevitably will breed another war."[89] On this note, an exhausted White staggered home to New York.

Chapter 10

The Making of
a Cold War Liberal

After a quick stop in New York to recover from the punishing regimen of a war correspondent, Walter White joined in the planning for the April 1945 founding conference of the United Nations in San Francisco. Preparations had been under way since before the secretary left for the Pacific. In September 1944, W.E.B. Du Bois returned to the NAACP staff as director of special research. He was to conduct wide-ranging research on the peoples of Africa and the African diaspora, with an initial focus on the anticipated peace conferences, at which he would promote efforts to ensure their proper status and progress in the postwar world. For this work, which he desired to pursue "in leisurely peace and financial security," Du Bois would receive $5,000 annually, a full-time assistant, and adequate office space. The inability—some would charge unwillingness—of the secretary to provide a commodious work environment would become a flashpoint between Du Bois and White, as the two resumed practically immediately their adversarial pas de deux. Conflict over allocations of office furniture emerged as a proxy for policy battles.[1]

The secretary needed Du Bois's expertise in international affairs, not to mention his contacts, especially in the Pan-African world. With White still abroad when the San Francisco conference was announced, Du Bois, because of his conversance with the international struggle for racial equality, his grasp of the impact of world affairs on black America, and his history of activism in the cause of world peace, was initially chosen to lead the NAACP's efforts in San Francisco.[2] In anticipation of this meeting, he developed position papers on the postwar world for the association's board of directors, organized the Harlem Colonial Conference, which brought together leaders of liberation movements in Africa, Asia, and Latin America, and solicited mandates from a panoply of African American organizations to be represented in San Francisco by the NAACP.[3]

Du Bois was encouraged by evidence of the late President Roosevelt's anti-imperialist convictions, but he had little faith in the direction of American foreign policy. Spending a lot of time buttonholing the American delegates was of questionable value, he felt, though he did present them and their consultants the NAACP's positions.[4] In contrast to White, who exuded optimism in *A Rising Wind* in America's openness (with some lobbying, of course) to push for decolonization after the war, Du Bois was highly suspicious that the United States would try to supplant the old colonial empires, especially in the Pacific.[5] His plan was to create public opinion for decolonization by organizing the collective voice of those who were excluded from or banished to the periphery of the conference deliberations. His principal exertions were directed toward establishing contacts with grassroots black organizations, colonial independence movements, and the Soviet Union.[6]

Du Bois's preparations for the San Francisco conference complemented the more extensive and protracted efforts to bring Africa before the American public and government by the Council on African Affairs (CAA). Founded as a clearinghouse in 1937 by Paul Robeson and Max Yergan, and soon after joined by Alphaeus Hunton, the CAA was by 1945 the most influential pro-Africa lobby in the United States, and it had, in one historian's words, "a definite stamp of ideological radicalism."[7] It combined research—its monthly newsletter *New Africa* was the best American source of information about the continent—with public mass meetings, conferences, and material aid drives for African labor and nationalist organizations, and it maintained ties with State Department and White House officials. In preparation for the U.N. founding conference, Yergan and Hunton briefed Assistant Secretary of State Archibald MacLeish; Yergan and CAA member Eslanda Robeson were among the observers in San Francisco. The CAA maintained pressure on American policy makers through not only regular contact with officials but also picket lines and demonstrations.

Upon his return from the Pacific, the secretary replaced Du Bois as head of the NAACP delegation to San Francisco; that position, White thought, rightfully belonged to the head of the association. The late addition of Mary McLeod Bethune rounded out the trio. As White boarded the special train that carried journalists and consultants to the American delegation westward, he was given a warm send-off by Roy Wilkins. Wilkins impressed on his boss the importance of this conference and pledged the entire membership's support and assistance. "The spotlight in Negro America will be upon us so that it will be up to us to interpret fairly, and to advance with skill and vigor the aspirations of colored people in this world crisis."[8] Fulfilling this charge would prove difficult, because of both personal animus between White and Bethune and strategic differences between the secretary and Du Bois.[9]

In White's estimate, passing most of each workday in the company of the other consultants and the delegates on the conference floor was the valuable and difficult work, and he prized his frank exchanges with American officials. Neither Du Bois nor Bethune were capable of conducting this work, he thought; when he had to leave San Francisco for a few days, he wired Roy Wilkins to come and take his place "because emergencies may arise think you should come out. Du Bois and Bethune haven't stamina to stand pounding job requires."[10] Rather than an issue of fortitude, however, it appears as if Du Bois at least had a different calculation of the value of politicking.

White's "quiet lobbying" of fellow consultants—from the American Bar Association and Chamber of Commerce on the right to the CIO on the left—equaled significant influence, he thought. "Little by little," he relayed to the NAACP leadership, "a sense of unity developed, on the basis of friendly relations formed by meeting day after day, some staying in the same hotels. . . ." He was able, he implied, to bring the consultants around to his view on decolonization.[11] So completely had the secretary convinced himself that upon his presence at the U.N. conference rested the postwar destinies of African Americans and colonial peoples that he deliberately neglected imperatives over which he had some control, such as building the association's membership. White had earlier committed to participate in the NAACP spring membership drive by embarking on an eight-city speaking tour, including some of the largest and most influential branches. When Daisy Lampkin reminded him not to forget the stop in Cleveland, he wired her his regrets: "But future of Negro at stake here. . . . Cannot possibly leave until those issues settled. . . . Hate do this to you, darling, but have no other alternative." White's histrionic description of the conference scene to Roy Wilkins argued that, with Du Bois's misguided departure, only he stood between the Negro and generations of disaster. The secretary told the board he would be "grateful" if it "would send an explanatory note and apology . . ." Determined efforts of his colleagues, especially Wilkins, brought the secretary around to a more realistic perspective, however, and White decided to keep his speaking engagements after all.[12]

The secretary clearly believed that he could, through his contacts with top government officials, alter the course of American policy on issues of human rights and freedom for people of color around the world. But his encounters with the highest levels of government belied his pluck, which usually stood him in good stead. On his final day in San Francisco, Secretary of State Stettinius, who headed the U.S. delegation, summoned White to a private meeting to get his assessment of the United States' performance at the U.N.'s founding. "Do you want the truth, or do you want to hear something pleasant?" White asked. He told Stettinius that the United States' equivocation on the issue of independence for colonies and dependent areas was hurting American stature in the world; two days later, Stettinius voted with Britain and France, who were trying to regain their empires. A few days later still, White told the same things to President Truman, with similar results. The new occupant of the White House told the secretary that his principal foreign policy concern was an alliance with Britain, France, and the Soviet Union, which favored decolonization in the U.N. votes; the fates of colonial and dependent peoples remained far down his list of priorities.[13]

The secretary also found the scramble for empire, especially Britain's, alarming and deserving of criticism. When Prime Minister Clement Attlee begged Washington for foreign aid, claiming that the stability of Western civilization was at stake, White responded with a blistering telegram. Attlee's government spoke of the need for decency in international relations but was responsible for the slaughter of Indonesian and Palestinian youth protesting continued foreign domination, the secretary said. What portion of the much-desired multibillion-dollar loan "will be used to perpetuate empire and to suppress by force of arms or otherwise the legitimate demands of colonial peoples that they too share in the fruits of victory which Allied arms have won[?]," he demanded to know. The prime minister's predecessor received similar treatment. Winston

Churchill's March 1946 "Iron Curtain" speech, which called for an Anglo-American coalition to fight Soviet influence in Europe and the dependent world and which launched the iconic image of the early cold war, was "beyond question one of the most dangerous and cynical made in contemporary history by a presumably responsible spokesman." The "Anglo-Saxon bloc" that Churchill proposed would "cause only shudders of apprehension" among colonial peoples and have the effect of drawing all Americans into the underwriting of empire. Although the secretary may have been far more comfortable telling this to a well-heeled set than to a group down-at-the-heels, he was unwilling to compromise with imperialism or a government that supported it.[14]

The secretary's quixotry was in sharp contrast to the hard-nosed realism of others. Percival Prattis, editor of the *Pittsburgh Courier*, thought *all* of the American consultants were ineffective simply because the U.S. did not want to consult them; Prattis implied—or so Thurgood Marshall thought—that the NAACP consultants were simply taking a vacation on the association expense accounts. Rayford Logan, who analyzed the proceedings also for the *Courier*, was of a similar opinion, absent the personal slaps. Before the deliberations in San Francisco had ended, Logan had already concluded that the deck had been heavily stacked against African Americans and dependent peoples around the world. Du Bois and the Council on African Affairs likewise understood that African Americans had been locked out of the decision-making process.[15]

Sharp as he was in plotting and anticipating politicians' moves, the secretary was simply over his head when it came to international issues and their effect on domestic politics. Certainly Du Bois thought so: American diplomats at the San Francisco conference "put over certain decisions on Walter by reason of his unfamiliarity with the broader implications." Rayford Logan believed that several of the secretary's questionable strategic and tactical decisions flowed directly from this same ignorance plus an inflated sense of his own personal influence.[16]

In the immediate postwar period, growing labor dissatisfaction and mobilization and heightened racial violence continued to focus White and the NAACP on progressive solutions to the nation's ailments. As the war drew to a close, workers once again began to feel the pinch of an economic downturn. In 1945 and 1946, the average number of hours worked per week declined, as did workers' average weekly pay. Unemployment jumped from 800,000 in August 1945 to 2.7 million in March 1946, while consumer prices surged. In the first three months of the postwar period alone, workers suffered a 15 percent decline in real income. The situation further worsened when wartime price controls expired in mid-1946. Organized labor, which had adhered to no-strike pledges during the war, was catapulted out of it by a pent-up energy and determination to defend its rapidly deteriorating standard of living. Nineteen forty-six was the most bellicose year in American history for union-management relations. There were more strikes (4,985), strikers (4.6 million), and lost workdays (116 million) in unionized establishments than in any other single year in the country's history.[17]

As African Americans constituted a significant percentage of the unionized workforce in key industries like automobile manufacturing, and as the CIO announced plans for Operation Dixie, a southern organizing drive, that promised to include black workers, the NAACP's historic distrust of organized labor melted.

White encouraged local branches to raise money for union strike funds, and he represented the NAACP at high-profile meetings designed to compel General Motors to negotiate in good faith with the UAW. When veteran board member and NAACP founder Oswald Garrison Villard objected to White's involvement in organized labor's issues, most others dismissed him, including Arthur Spingarn and Eleanor Roosevelt, who joined the board immediately after her husband's death. Hubert Delany, the New York jurist, and William Hastie simply said that Villard was out of step with what the association was trying to accomplish. In January 1946, Villard was removed as an association vice president because of his antilabor posture. As further proof of the stunning volte-face in the NAACP's labor policy, when the notoriously racist railroad brotherhoods struck in mid-1946 and President Truman threatened to break the strike by militarizing the industry, the secretary unhesitatingly backed the unions while calling on them to change their exclusionary practices.[18]

Labor was not the only area of American life that saw massive upheavals in the wake of the war. Much had changed in the South. The region was more urbanized and industrialized than it was in the thirties, and African Americans streamed to the cities. Public-works projects and the spread of radio had worked to lessen the South's isolation from the rest of the nation. Operation Dixie promised to take advantage of what appeared to be more favorable conditions for unionizing unorganized workers. But *plus ça change, plus c'est la même chose.* As at the end of World War I, the Bourbon South was hell-bent on maintaining white supremacy. It was particularly keen on thwarting returning African American veterans. Like their predecessors from the earlier conflict, demobilized black soldiers were internationally aware, had been told they were fighting for democracy, and were determined to seize rights for themselves and their race. They professed their refusal to return to the status quo antebellum, and as such presented a special challenge to the Jim Crow social order.

In response, a swell of racist violence crashed upon the South, hitting especially hard the black former GIs.[19] In Birmingham, police chief Eugene Connor, who would two decades hence earn national calumny for his obstruction of the freedom struggle, headed a force that was widely suspected of murdering a half-dozen black men in uniform in January and February 1946. On Lincoln's birthday that same year, Isaac Woodard received his discharge papers in Georgia—he had been more than a year in the Pacific—and, still in uniform, caught a bus to North Carolina to meet his wife. Soon after the bus entered South Carolina, he and the bus driver got into an argument over some detail of Jim Crow etiquette, which Woodard was not inclined to follow. The dispute continued for some time, and when Woodard debarked to use the facilities at the Aiken terminal, the bus driver called ahead to the next stop for police assistance. They resumed their shouting match until Batesburg, where the driver ordered Woodard off the bus. The local police chief and his deputy were waiting for him and beat him bloody. They gouged both his eyes with a billy club, which permanently blinded him, and then arrested him. So nakedly merciless and unprovoked was the assault, the local magistrate dropped all charges against Woodard.

Less than two weeks later came Columbia, Tennessee, a town of 5,000 whites and 3,000 blacks about forty-five miles from Nashville. On the morning of February 25, an African American woman, Gladys Stephenson, and her son James, a navy veteran, went to a downtown department store to pick up the radio they had earlier brought in for repair. Mrs. Stephenson got into an argument with a white clerk, who yelled at and then hit her. James Stephenson intervened and, after some wrestling, threw the clerk through a plate glass window. Mother and son were arrested, fined, released, and then rearrested after the clerk's father swore out a complaint. Late in the evening, they posted bail and went home. As night fell, a gathering mob of white men, drunk and armed, gathered downtown and made their way to Mink Slide, the black section of town; they were met by a picket of armed black veterans who shot at them when they refused to halt. Around 10:00 that evening a brigade of national guardsmen arrived; they swept through Mink Slide, shooting into and looting businesses, vandalizing homes, and arresting more than 100 African Americans.

The secretary and Thurgood Marshall arrived the next week to investigate what appeared to be an officially sanctioned riot. Also on the scene were investigators from the Southern Conference for Human Welfare (SCHW), founded in November 1938 by New Dealers, black and white middle-class reformers, and a sprinkling of leftists, including Communists. (Eleanor Roosevelt addressed the founding conference in Birmingham over the long Thanksgiving weekend, and Supreme Court Justice Hugo Black received a medal for his humanitarian work in the liberal spirit of Thomas Jefferson; White had endorsed its founding, and only the foggy weather that grounded his flight prevented him from attending.)[20] The secretary's investigation and the SCHW's somewhat more detailed report—compiled after three weekends on the scene—substantially confirmed what he called "one of the most serious episodes of its kind." White found official misconduct and hostility toward African Americans at the highest levels of state government, conditions he had found in practically every instance of violence he investigated since he joined the NAACP. His interview with the governor was terribly revealing, as he reported in his weekly *Defender* column. The governor's secretary ran the show, sitting at the head of the table, feet propped up, interrupting White and the two prominent black Nashvilleans who accompanied him. He resorted to undisguised racial contempt and belligerence whenever the three questioned him, and he boasted of illegal state-sponsored activity against Columbia's black population.[21]

Southern liberalism, he saw, also trod its well-worn path. Immediately after the riot, White initiated the Committee of 100 and then helped to form the National Committee against Mob Violence. Reactions from southerners were tepid at best. Guy Johnson, the University of North Carolina sociologist and officer of the Southern Regional Commission, the successor to the Commission for Interracial Cooperation, declined to endorse the SCHW's pamphlet or join the newly formed anti–mob violence committee. Professing a desire to work with the NAACP, Johnson claimed that the political momentum to respond to the Columbia riot was cluttered with "left-wing groups" who, he believed, "might try to horn in on the legal defense and create another Scottsboro." A Vanderbilt University professor and native Tennessean was more slippery—and typical. He touted his sympathy for Columbia blacks but nevertheless claimed that the incident had been distorted. Although not acquainted with Mrs. Stephenson, he was quite certain that she was rude to the department store clerk. And while white hostility and an inadequate black standard of living may have had something to do with the outbreak of violence, "there are a good many so-called 'bad' Negroes as one of the ministers in Columbia told me, in the Negro section hunting for trouble." [22]

If this had been 1936 instead of 1946, the secretary likely would have spent a disproportionate amount of time searching for common ground with the southern liberals. But the world war had germinated a sympathetic northern audience, and an aroused black electorate was emerging as a critical factor in national elections. White no longer felt that he had to pussyfoot with unreliable allies, and thus liberated, he pursued other avenues for organizing for civil rights. After the cold-blooded slaughter of two African American tenant-farmer couples in Georgia by their landlord in September, White arranged a meeting with President Truman. Accompanied by Leslie Perry and Channing Tobias, both NAACP officials, James Carey of the CIO, and Charles E. Wilson of General Electric—none residents of the South—the secretary insisted the president use his "bully pulpit" to protect the lives of African Americans. Truman responded by appointing the Presidential Committee on Civil Rights. Chaired by Wilson and with a membership of fifteen that included two African Americans (Tobias and Philadelphia attorney Sadie Alexander; White, whom Truman had asked to suggest members, could not very well nominate himself) and only two white southerners, this body produced *To Secure These Rights* (1947), which condemned segregation and proposed a series of measures to eliminate Jim Crow from national life. (Significantly, the southern members—Frank Porter Graham, certainly the best of the southern liberals, and Dorothy Tilly of the Southern Methodist church—declined to sign the final document, favoring the end of segregation but opposing a federal mandate to this end.) [23]

Yet neither was White tethered to the Truman administration. In early September, just two weeks after Truman dismissed Henry Wallace as commerce secretary for criticizing the administration's incipient cold war foreign policy, White signed the call for a Conference of Progressives; in this he joined representatives of seven labor and independent political organizations, including the National Citizens Political Action Committee (NCPAC), the SCHW, the CIO's Political Action Committee (CIO-PAC), the CIO, and the Independent Citizens Committee of the Arts Sciences. Held in Chicago at the end of September, it aimed to mobilize "independent" voters and put an end to the "reactionary coalition" of the dominant elements in the Democratic and Republican parties in Congress.[24]

For most of the New Deal, the secretary's endorsement of "independent" voting was the formal nod to official NAACP policy of nonpartisanship that masked a fairly consistent loyalty to Roosevelt's administration. But obeisance was no longer the order of the day, despite Truman's assembling of a civil rights commission. Bellicose rhetoric on international affairs, the two parties' collaborating to defeat a permanent fair employment practices committee, and Truman's moves against organized labor all begged for an aggressive response. From within the NAACP came a push to loosen its traditional nonpartisan stance and allow the association to endorse and work for candidates for office as well as pay back undesirable politicians.[25]

White's speech to the late-September gathering of progressives made clear that the black vote was not for sale and was beholden to no party. "No American was more shocked or disheartened" by Wallace's firing than was the secretary, he said. His was a feeling "shared by Negro Americans especially because Mr. Wallace has been the one member of the President's Cabinet who has spoken out without fear against discrimination and bigotry." African Americans, who were registering in ever larger numbers in the South and were participating in primary elections, were prepared to vote only for candidates who endorsed a democratic, anti-imperialist, and peaceful American foreign policy, a reduced military budget, and a domestic program that included the abolition of the poll tax, civil rights legislation, universal health care legislation, strict price and rent controls, and solidarity with organized labor.[26]

The secretary resisted taking sides in the emergent schism between those who leaned toward Henry Wallace and the cold war liberals of the Union for Democratic Action, who stressed anticommunism as much as social reforms. After all, the stampede that followed the rout of Wallace and the Progressive Party was only just organizing itself in 1946, and the secretary had not yet divined which side would be victorious. But he must have been chilled by Arthur Schlesinger, Jr.'s Communists-under-the-bed feature in *Life*. Illustrated with photographs of stoney-faced CP leaders and sprinkled with accusations of zealotry, fanaticism, and the duplicity of "lonely and frustrated people" seeking "social, intellectual, even sexual fulfillment," Schlesinger sought credibility for liberalism by embracing anticommunism. Most alarming to the secretary must have been Schlesinger's claims that the "Communists are working overtime to expand party influence, open and covert . . . among Negroes" and are "sinking tentacles into the National Association for the Advancement of Colored People." [27]

For the moment, however, the secretary reacted to libel without panic. His concern with Communist activity among African Americans was the same as it had always been: would it deplete NAACP resources? The multiplicity of organizations active on the civil rights front, including ones influenced by the CP, was a clear sign of a national awakening of African Americans. But their existence also challenged the hegemony of the NAACP. White directed branches to be careful when considering whether to join forces with these organizations and to safeguard the association's name and reputation. Especially in election years, they had to make certain they were not hoodwinked by politicians who recognized the power of the black vote but whose records did not match their rhetoric. Most important, they had to make certain that participation in local coalitions did not drain the NAACP of financial resources. He wanted aggressive action to maintain the primacy of the association in the civil rights movement, of course, but he was not yet ready to move to exclude the CPUSA from it. And as late as December 1947, he wrote in his syndicated column that appeared in the *New York Herald-Tribune* that while he cared not one whit for it, communism posed less of a threat to the NAACP and American democracy than did the professional anticommunists. [28]

With Arthur Schlesinger's ominous chatter as background noise, White turned his attention once again to airing the grievances of African Americans on a world stage by endorsing W.E.B. Du Bois's petition to United Nations, *An Appeal to the World*, and helping him to bring it before that world body. But the political terrain was once again changing in ways the secretary was slow to recognize. At the San Francisco conference American officials simply ignored most of White's and Du Bois's recommendations and criticisms. But by 1947, despite the publication of *To Secure These Rights*, official measures conspired to stifle all but a narrow range of public criticism of Jim Crow and colonialism. The witch-hunts that commenced in 1945 with the permanent establishment of the House Un-American Activities Committee (HUAC) frequently labeled civil rights activism (and even simple sympathy for the cause) subversive; federal employees who, by Truman's 1947 executive order, underwent loyalty checks were sometimes asked if they entertained blacks at home or protested the Red Cross policy of segregating blood or why they owned records by Paul Robeson. With Attorney General Tom Clark no less than J. Edgar Hoover campaigning against a red menace, white supremacy was a salient ingredient of the growing federal anticommunist crusade. Official pronouncements notwithstanding, the U.S. government viewed with hostility and suspicion calls for full equality for African Americans and criticism of the government's role in maintaining segregation. It viewed as particularly unwelcome the parading of these facts before international audiences.[29]

Du Bois crusaded to bring a petition before either the United Nations General Assembly or its Commission on Human Rights. The National Negro Congress had circulated a petition that Du Bois thought good but "deficient" in several respects. He believed that the NAACP, with its superior resources, ought to be able to produce a more detailed and better documented work.[30] White agreed. He secured the NAACP Committee on Administration's approval, and by the beginning of 1947 Du Bois and his collaborators had completed the first draft of *An Appeal to the World*. A collection of meticulously documented and reasoned essays, the petition at ninety-five pages was a compact statement of the historical oppression and continued exclusion and disfranchisement of people of African descent from American life.[31]

Writing the petition turned out to be the easier task, though several of the contributors wrote pieces that were overly technical and laced with indigestible prose and required revisions by Du Bois.[32] The exasperating and ultimately impossible part of the job was bringing the document before the United Nations. For several months Du Bois received a runaround that could have appeared in *Catch-22*. Even entreaties by both Du Bois and White to Eleanor Roosevelt, who was a delegate to the

U.N., were unavailing.[33] Du Bois charged ahead undeterred, and he tried to interest other countries in presenting the petition before the General Assembly. (India and Liberia indicated they would assist, but the United States blocked its consideration.)[34] He gave up appealing to the American government. The secretary, who in the past had not held his tongue in conversations with government officials, discovered that proximity to power increasingly came with a price. He now advocated cooperation with the government, almost at any cost, and this difference in approach led to heated controversy in 1947 and 1948.

Eleanor Roosevelt approached White for a memorandum to assist her in the work of drafting the Covenant on Human Rights. Assuming his recommendations would carry weight with the American delegation, White thought that what she had requested "may be one of the most important documents which the Association has ever prepared," and he asked Du Bois to draft it.[35] Unimpressed by her request, Du Bois's reply to White was characteristically curt: "I have no suggestions for Mrs. Roosevelt."[36] Incensed, White demanded that Du Bois deliver to him a specific statement on what the NAACP should recommend to ER.

Du Bois once again balked, though he did enlarge on his refusal. Grandiose statements of the kind Mrs. Roosevelt requested already existed in multiples. What was needed was not more of the same but their application when human rights were violated; in this regard, the Commission on Human Rights failed miserably, and the American government, including ER, had been of no help. "The fact is," Du Bois charged, "that the United States Department of State is determined that American Negroes shall have no chance to state their grievances before the world. Mrs. Roosevelt is following orders." If she had sincerely wanted the opinion of the NAACP, she would have asked for it months before; instead, she and the American delegation had in fact discouraged association participation. What Du Bois intuited but White refused to believe was that her request was an artifice designed in part to efface the *Appeal to the World*.[37]

White was not used to such insubordination, and he forced the issue again in 1948, as he prepared to attend the Paris sessions of the General Assembly as a consultant. Again Du Bois demurred, insisting that nothing productive would result from submitting his ideas to the American delegation. His refusal to participate in what he believed to be a charade was a factor in Du Bois's dismissal from the association later in September; he accused White of demanding complete obedience, something Du Bois could never give.[38]

To this charge White pleaded guilty. During a break in the U.N. deliberations in Paris, he penned a refreshingly candid letter to Poppy Cannon, whom he would marry a year later, confessing the extent to which he thought of the NAACP in proprietary terms and saw himself as single-handedly carrying on the struggle of the race:

> They are right in charging that I dominate the Association. But if I hadn't done so there wouldn't be any NAACP. I kept it alive during the terrible days of the Depression when nearly everybody else was ready to surrender to despair. I have built it up (only to you would I say this) to its present power. . . .
>
> And all this [controversy] descends on me here where I am waging almost a one-man battle against fear and cowardice and national opportunism to get something done about human rights and colonies.[39]

White summoned all his skill as an interracial emissary. Aboard the SS *America* bound for Havre, the American delegation met twice daily with its advisors, at 11:00 and 2:00 in the afternoon, to discuss such issues as atomic energy, human rights, and Palestine. The atmosphere was leavened with movies and rounds of cocktail parties hosted by various delegates. ER was the star guest at the affair White gave in his cabin to show off his new Dictaphone—which, unfortunately, did not work. Frank discussion over highballs was the order of the day. "I may be wrong," White wrote back to headquarters, "but I believe that the most effective job I can do on this trip is the one now being done under the relaxed conditions aboard ship."[40]

During informal gatherings and formal meetings, aboard ship and in Paris, White raised issues of central concern to African Americans in the postwar era: positive action on an expansive definition of human rights and the disposition of the colonies in Africa. He argued vigorously that the United States take the moral high ground. At a meeting of the delegation's advisors, White criticized the dominant official thinking: "I took the floor to ask why we always let Russia take moral leadership; why we couldn't demonstrate for a change that the democracies could really fight for freedom instead of letting our enemies get the jump on us in proving that there is some value in our way of life." The effect was "electric," he told Poppy Cannon, and his fellow consultants pledged support for a strong statement to the American delegation urging a "more courageous course" on the issue of colonies.[41]

He fought against powerful odds. The American government automatically opposed whatever the socialist bloc championed. The Soviet Union supported an accord on human rights that enumerated social and economic rights as well as political ones, and it encouraged emerging African nations in their efforts to break free of the Western empires. Thus, the United States vigorously opposed any binding statement of human rights that went beyond formal political rights. At the same time, it equivocated its opposition to colonies because it needed to retain the support of Britain and France. Further, because President Truman wanted to attract the Italian-American vote, the United States stood ready to support Italy's quest to regain its former colonies of Libya and Eritrea under the guise of trusteeship. White was regularly apprised of the direction of American foreign policy. He chose not to heed Du Bois's counsel, but Rayford Logan informed him in gloomy detail of the prospects for influencing the diplomatic establishment. Though White took it all in—and angered Logan in the process by using his ideas without attribution in his syndicated column—he continued in his romantic belief that he alone would be able to make an impact on foreign policy.[42]

But White eventually (and much later than Du Bois and Logan, who succeeded Du Bois as the NAACP foreign affairs expert) came to understand that while he might muster the support of his fellow consultants, he stood no chance of budging official American policy.[43] While still aboard the SS *America*, the secretary had written the NAACP that he felt it was within his power to shepherd through the U.N. an effective plan for decolonization: "The odds against our point of view prevailing are considerable but I believe we have a fighting chance." Having been on the job in Paris for several weeks, however, he now reported home that "the chief value, as I now see it, of our work here is in putting pressure on various nations, particularly our own, and in getting maximum publicity for our objectives which we seek."[44]

Not wanting to be pressured, American officials tried to silence White, alleging that a memorandum on colonial issues that he circulated among his fellow consultants and representatives of some nongovernmental organizations (NGOs) who also attended the General Assembly session was based on information provided in off-the-record briefings.

Using such phrases as *we are informed* and *we are advised*, the memo had discussed probable American positions and criticized the government's apparent support of the parceling of Italy's former colonies among Italy, Britain, and Ethiopia. Chester Williams, a high-ranking member of the delegation, attacked White for these "serious infringements of confidence," confiscated the outstanding copies of the memorandum, pressured at least two consultants who had initially agreed with White to change their minds, and threatened to end White's and the other advisors' access to off-the-record meetings.[45]

White denied he had breached any confidences and decried Williams's heavy-handedness. Information that America was leaning away from placing Libya and Eritrea under U.N. supervision and on the road to independence and toward, as White put it in a letter to ER, "dividing [them] as war booty" had been widely available since September, before the General Assembly convened. Logan, as consultant to the NAACP on U.N. affairs, had called this to White's attention, and the association had taken the shift into account as it planned its activities in Paris. Further, the secretary would have preferred to present his views to the American delegation in person, but the delegation would not carve out the time, thus making necessary the memo.[46]

He asked ER for her understanding, if not for her help: "I don't want you to do anything at all about the enclosed exchange of correspondence between Chet Williams and myself, but I do want you to have the facts. I would not want anyone, and especially yourself, to believe for a moment that I had violated a confidence."[47] Williams continued to isolate White among the consultants and the NGO representatives. When he had sufficiently cowed them, he offered White a carrot. Williams did what he had to do, he wrote White in a letter marked "personal and confidential"; White's memo had "produced difficulties for me . . . I had to take certain actions . . ." Williams hoped that the steps he took against White would "not affect our personal friendship in the slightest . . . I think this can close the matter."[48]

The two had reached an understanding: White would cease public criticism of American foreign policy, thus allowing him to continue to attend off-the-record briefings. The secretary must have thought that his concessions were part of a quid pro quo. The previous year, in June 1947, hadn't he arranged for President Truman to address the monster rally at the Lincoln Memorial that closed the NAACP annual convention? An unprecedented event, Truman's speech called for federal, state, and individual action against lynching, disfranchisement, and inequality in education and employment. Had he not also been invited to meet with America's corporate and political elite to plan the Freedom Train, which transported the United States' founding documents around the country for public display? Access to the nation's upper echelons, White reasoned, was crucial to the association's success because it symbolized the organization's legitimacy and acceptance.[49] He was right, of course, but he mistook symbol for substance. Gone were the reasonably politically fluid days when the secretary could lambaste government decisions and still enjoy access to its upper echelons. The foreign and domestic cold war made White's emphasis on lobbying obsolete because government officials were demanding conformity as the price of access.

From America's entry into World War II until about 1948, Walter White led the NAACP to place the predicament of Afro-America in a global context. Colonial peoples' problems—economic exploitation, political domination, violence—were remarkably similar to African Americans'. The war, White said, would not lead to world peace if its aim was simply to defeat the Axis powers. Lasting peace would come only if the doctrine and practice of racial superiority were defeated also in the Allied countries, and this meant the abolition both of empire and of Jim Crow. National liberation movements and the domestic civil rights movement were thus mutually beneficial, and White lent wholehearted support to anticolonial struggles. But after Truman's victory, White decoupled the domestic and international dimensions of race. Civil rights for African Americans now became an imperative in the worldwide fight against communism. Concessions to blacks' aspirations would win for the U.S. the loyalty of the third world, diminish Soviet influence in the developing countries, and preserve the practically unrestricted access to those countries' resources. But White also fought to suppress the African American left, which continued to link colonial oppression abroad with racial oppression at home.

The secretary's concessions on the international stage were accompanied by his extinguishing the brief flare-up of political independence within the NAACP, sending Du Bois into exile for a second time, and flexing his bureaucratic muscles to maneuver the association behind

Truman's election campaign. The alternatives in the 1948 elections could not have been more plain. Set against Truman's bold symbolic gestures was his preference for appointing southern Democrats to the federal bench, his waffling on the poll tax, his embrace of the cold war. By contrast, Progressive candidate Henry Wallace proposed a fresh start to the Soviet Union, a domestic economic policy that favored workers and organized labor, and a determined campaign against racial discrimination and segregation in the South. Where Truman decided it was best not to antagonize white southerners and so stayed out of the region during his campaign, Wallace twice toured the area, speaking only before integrated audiences and promising all who would listen to eliminate the poll tax and dismantle Jim Crow; his campaign established an energetic voter registration drive among southern blacks too.[50]

Progressives' dreams for a united campaign against cold war domestic and foreign policy were dashed by the injection of red-baiting. Liberals grouped around the Americans for Democratic Action—for whom anti-communism was an article of faith more important than the four freedoms articulated by FDR—attacked the Wallace campaign for being riddled with Communists and its followers for being unable to detect the radical threat. Important backers of the Progressive efforts backed away from Wallace. The new political wind blowing in from the right was more than a zephyr, they felt, and they decided to hunker down against its rhetoric and try to preserve the institutions they had built up during the Depression and New Deal. In 1946, the CIO restricted its constituent unions' political activities and forbade them from contributing to organizations with which they had previously cooperated, including the SCHW. In 1947, officials of the Textile Workers Union in North Carolina cut its ties with an organization that encouraged the participation of African Americans and established a competing chapter of the Americans for Democratic Action. Organized labor tried to dodge accusations of being "red," which the unions felt could ruin them. Fearing the inauguration of a Republican administration under Dewey, labor tried to find shelter under Truman's protective wing.

Walter White, always exceptionally sensitive to political currents, also appreciated the gathering strength of the cold war. He would never give an inch in the patriotism department to segregationists like Rankin of Mississippi or the extremists of the House Un-American Activities Committee, all of whom assiduously attacked the left. But to avoid the label of

Communist sympathizer, he began to extol the virtues of the cold war liberals. He explained his willingness to sacrifice principle to political expediency in his weekly syndicated column. A certain progressive acquaintance of his, herself not a Communist, refused to join the NAACP-initiated National Committee Against Mob Violence, which responded to the Columbia, Tennessee, riot, so long as Communists were excluded from it. "Technically and theoretically she had much on her side of the argument," the secretary rationalized. "But Mrs. Franklin D. Roosevelt, who was co-chairman of the national committee, took the position . . . that any participation by communists in the already difficult defense would needlessly complicate the case and play into the hands of those who were determined to convict the hapless defendants." To satisfy powerful friends, he was willing to dabble in a little opportunism.[51]

By the time of the 1948 presidential campaign, White had concluded that backing a winner and preserving the NAACP was more valuable than supporting the principled Henry Wallace and exposing the association to the punishing defeat that would almost certainly be the left's measure following the election. Having thus calculated, White moved with dispatch to discredit Wallace and trumpet Truman's virtues. He began in the summer of 1948. His first article of the party convention season claimed that certain Republicans were promoting Wallace's presidential bid as a means of splitting the Democratic vote. Perhaps fearing Du Bois's conviction that African Americans would vote either Republican or Progressive and shun Truman for his hesitation on civil rights, the secretary followed with critical analyses of the GOP's platform. In his report on the intense political discussion at the NAACP's annual convention, the secretary claimed that the Republican Party had no support. But White's anti-Republicanism was merely prelude to his real purpose: he claimed that delegates and onlookers alike "resented" the presence of Wallace supporters. More, Truman was the staunch defender of black rights and protector of the Democratic Party legacy in the internecine battle with the Dixiecrats at the party's nominating convention. In the several weeks before he departed for the Paris U.N. sessions, his denunciations of Wallace became more severe, his praise of Truman more lavish. Forgetting that just four years before he had ripped FDR for dumping Wallace as his running mate and that two years earlier he had condemned Truman for dismissing him, White now argued that the Progressive candidate promoted discrimination when he was in the Roosevelt administration. Truman, about whose foreign policy and predilection for playing it safe White had earlier held strong reservations, now was an "example of rare courage."[52]

Not everyone in the NAACP shared White's opportunism or his enthusiasm for Truman. The Wallace campaign captured the imagination of many people in the NAACP, locally and nationally. Branch leaders in Houston, Memphis, Greensboro, and Columbia, South Carolina, boarded the Wallace train. So did Daisy Bates, who with her husband published a weekly in Little Rock, Arkansas; a decade later, she would be a key organizer of the movement to desegregate Central High School. Palmer Weber, a veteran leftist, who joined the NAACP board of directors in 1946, became the codirector of Wallace's southern campaign. Du Bois heartily endorsed Wallace, and he was joined by Charles Houston, who saw in the candidate a commitment to "a democracy which works and embraces all people." Houston also refused to pay fealty to the cold war liberals: "Certainly there are Communists in the Wallace movement. So what? There are Fascists in the Democratic Party, such as Ellender, Eastland, Rankin and the whole crew of southern poll taxers and I do not see anybody trying to excommunicate them."[53]

Du Bois believed that during the 1948 election White had "loaded [the NAACP] on the Truman bandwagon" and had tied it to "the reactionary, war-mongering colonial imperialism of the present administration."[54] He said this not merely because the secretary appeared to abandon principle for political advantage. Rather, Du Bois objected to the duplicity the secretary used to maneuver the NAACP behind Truman while simultaneously denying other association members their rights to hold differing opinions and to campaign as individuals for the candidates of their choice.

Without doubt, the secretary used his syndicated column to boost Truman's fortunes. He asked board members to vet his weekly output "to insure that the Secretary as a columnist violates no principle of the Association," that is, nonpartisanship.[55] That his request was simply a patina on White's pronounced affinity for Truman would soon become clear. A few days later, when the board reaffirmed its traditional injunction against paid officers engaging in partisan political activities, Du Bois argued that such a prohibition did not prevent officials from acting on their convictions as private citizens, so long as they clearly distinguished themselves from the NAACP. Although Earl Dickerson of Chicago, and

Hubert Delany and John Hammond of New York, three of the most in-dependent board members, believed Du Bois's caveats were sound, the board chose to reject them.[56] The board also kept pace with the secre-tary's strategy of isolating the Wallace campaign. In practically all past elections, the NAACP presented its demands to the contesting parties and reported publicly on their responses; but only with the Progressive Party did the NAACP stipulate that it take "proper safeguards and care in participation with the third party platform" so as not even to hint at any approval.[57]

But as the campaign intensified, Du Bois, not surprisingly, would not censor himself. At a rally in Philadelphia, he called on people to vote for Wallace and Joseph Rainey, that branch's president and candidate for the U.S. House. White was highly irritated, accusing his rival of behaving in an unauthorized manner. But Du Bois was more so and hurriedly fired back this reply: board policy "has not forbidden an employee to hold po-litical views and to express them properly, as you are doing daily."[58] What had been simmering became a rolling boil in September, as Du Bois re-fused the secretary's request for advice on the imminent Paris U.N. ses-sion and then—after White continued his rant—released to the press his charge that White had hijacked the NAACP for Truman.

This was more than the board or the secretary could stand, and at its September meeting, with White in absentia and on his way to Paris, the board terminated Du Bois for a second time. It pretended to be even-handed by briefly entertaining a discussion about an alleged double stan-dard in measuring Du Bois's and the secretary's actions, but just as quickly the board decided that it would not be proper to question the propriety of White's writings while he was out of the country. A few weeks later, the Committee on Administration, which ran the association in between board meetings, absolved the secretary of any wrongdoing. It held that White's unabashedly pro-Truman articles were his own evaluation only, while, without explanation, finding Du Bois's support for Wallace suffi-cient grounds for dismissal.[59]

Exonerated, White took his final shots at Du Bois from a safe transat-lantic distance. The secretary did not seek an opportunity to greet Du Bois on the sidewalk, jauntily extending a hand and explaining that he harbored no hard feelings, as he did the first time Du Bois was dismissed. This time, his postscript was a fustian letter. He had taken pity on Du

Bois in 1944 when he was summarily dismissed from Atlanta University, White wrote. He insisted on rehiring Du Bois against all advice and common sense. But,

> knowing you as I did, I expected no gratitude nor did I want any . . . It is a matter of profound regret to me that, having attempted to give you freedom from worry and the opportunity to be of service and to utilize your knowledge and experience, you have chosen instead to wreck or, more accurately, to attempt to wreck the Association which came to your rescue in time of need.[60]

So ended the last serious challenge from the left to the secretary's stewardship of the NAACP. Du Bois was vanquished, and on the national scene Truman was triumphant, with Walter White having done his part to scare the black vote away from Wallace.

What the secretary discovered, however, was that remaining in good graces with Truman required additional championing of the president's foreign policy, with the added injunction of attacking those on the left who opposed it. The centerpiece of Truman's policy vis-à-vis the developing world was the Point Four foreign policy initiative. Unveiled during his first inaugural address and designed to win the loyalty of the world's nonwhite population, Point Four—Truman called it a "bold new program"—held out the promise of economic development as a way to stop the advance of leftist revolutionary movements. It was not to be a new Marshall Plan of massive government aid. Rather, it was to share technical knowledge to help the third world's transition to modernity and ease the way for private American investment; in large parts of Africa and Asia, which were still under colonial rule, oversight would remain in the hands of the imperial powers, while the indigenous people would have limited participation at best.[61]

The African American left, especially the Council on African Affairs led by Paul Robeson, denounced Point Four as double-talk, a way in which the United States could continue to prop up colonialism while simultaneously penetrating previously restricted markets in Africa and Asia. Other prominent blacks gave qualified endorsement to Point Four. Rayford Logan, for example, urged that government and not private capital be the rule, that the colonial peoples be fully represented, that labor have at least as much protection as capital, and that the selection of personnel be based as much on human-relations qualities as technical expertise.[62]

But the secretary enthusiastically supported Point Four and endorsed the crusade to stop international communism.[63] His efforts to goad Truman into providing famine assistance to India in 1949 reveals how sincerely he embraced anticommunism. White wrote to the president that America needed to alleviate India's hunger because it was creating conditions for communism to flourish. Should the government allow Nehru to fail, nothing in the region could prevent Communists from taking over all of Asia. "The United States will then be even more imperiled."[64] His considerable lobbying for food and other economic assistance for India, which ended only when the Congress authorized $190 million in loans in June 1951, were uniformly laced with anticommunism. (Always convinced of the power of public relations, White even tried to construct a coalition of organized labor and the farm-equipment manufacturers like Ford, Caterpillar, and International Harvester to donate money and machinery to India. A symbolic gift, he believed it would be a demonstration of American generosity and, with enough publicity, a prophylactic against Communist expansion.)[65] The State Department, no longer holding White at arm's length, asked him to tour the subcontinent for three months to publicize the importance of India in America's foreign policy and support anticommunism in that country.[66]

A major component of White's anticommunism was a commitment to stifling criticism of American race relations in international arenas. This is most clearly seen in his attempts to squelch the *We Charge Genocide* petition written by the Civil Rights Congress for presentation to the United Nations in 1951. Scrupulously researched and documented (much of the information was culled, as Roy Wilkins noted, from NAACP records[67]), *We Charge Genocide* reasoned that the discrimination to which African Americans were subjected, in part officially sanctioned, was so severe and pervasive as to constitute genocide under the terms of the Geneva Convention. Among the issues the petition raised were mob violence, assassination of race leaders, denial of the right to vote, extensive material deprivation, and mental harm.

The State Department called upon prominent African Americans to denounce the petition as so much Communist propaganda. Rayford Logan, representing the NAACP at the Paris U.N. sessions, refused. Though he felt that the association better represented the opinions of

African Americans than did the Civil Rights Congress, he believed that the arguments in *We Charge Genocide* were compelling and deserved to be aired; the United States could disprove the indictment by launching thorough investigations of the accusations. Delegation members Channing Tobias and Edith Sampson felt that it was unfair of the State Department to demand that blacks prove their loyalty by participating in a ritual repudiation of the petition, though each eventually agreed to make a statement "as an American, rather than as a Negro."[68]

In 1948 Walter White had been frustrated that the United States sacrificed an airing of the violation of African Americans' rights to its jockeying for position against the Soviet Union. In 1951 he agreed unhesitatingly to denounce the petition, though this caused some discomfort within the association. Just after the State Department requested that White issue a statement, the Voice of America claimed that the NAACP, having just learned of the "gross and subversive conspiracy" that was the petition, repudiated it in the strongest terms. The report gave Roy Wilkins pause: did the organization want to be associated with rightist attacks? Board member Hubert Delany also took exception to a denunciation of the petition. The charges were leveled at the United States government, and it, not the NAACP, ought to answer to it. By defending the government the NAACP was becoming a "pawn in the hands of the United States in attempting to justify the brutalities outlined in 'We Charge Genocide' . . ." White took issue; the NAACP ought to cooperate with the State Department and not worry about who else joined the attack.[69]

White's statement, while different in tenor from the Voice of America's, evaded the issues raised by *We Charge Genocide*, arguing that it "purposely paints only the gloomiest picture of American democracy and the race question." Yes, African American soldiers are subjected to gross injustices in the military, but these are being corrected. True, African Americans are disfranchised in the South, but the Supreme Court has outlawed grandfather clauses and white primaries. White sidestepped the surfeit of racial violence, stating simply that "measurable gains have been made in reducing racial bigotry." The abuses were the unfinished business of a democracy. In any event, such a petition would never have been tolerated by an "authoritarian government," and White taunted the sponsor of *We Charge Genocide* to submit a petition investigating allegations of human rights abuses in the Soviet Union.[70]

The secretary's statement was a digest of his cover article for the *Saturday Review of Literature*, "Time for a Progress Report." The piece was framed around a statement by a Hindu college professor who had recently returned to the United States after a decade-long absence: "I was startled, amazed, almost overwhelmed by the change in the American attitude toward the Negro and other dark-skinned people," the professor said. "It is a change I did not expect." White highlighted progress since the war in fifteen areas, including the abolition of the white primary, headway in the desegregation of higher education, the establishment of commissions on civil rights and fair employment practices, and unstereotyped representations of African Americans in films and television. This "bloodless revolution of attitudes" was making the country more hospitable.[71]

Yet America was not so open in 1951 that it was ready to hear White's message of interracial comity, and he knew as much. Outlining the NAACP's plan to counteract *We Charge Genocide*, he told the philanthropist Lessing Rosenwald that his publisher, Viking, wanted him to expand his article into a book of between 60,000 and 70,000 words for distribution in "key places." But a full accounting of the facts catches White fabricating a version of events to inflate his own importance as a writer, much as he did decades earlier with *Fire in the Flint*. Viking did not suggest the book; rather, the State Department did, and the key places for distribution were Asia, Africa, Latin America, and Europe—not the United States. Viking reluctantly agreed to dispense an inexpensive edition overseas, but it refused to do so in America, for it believed there would be no market for it. For the sake of fighting communism White was prepared, in the words of Hubert Delany, to state that African Americans were "making rapid progress and are satisfied with the progress we are making."[72]

Walter White had embraced America's cold war foreign policy and locked the NAACP into supporting it. In 1949 the association went on record in favor of the Marshall Plan; in 1951 it backed the Korean War and called for a struggle against the peace movement, which it called Communist-inspired; in 1954 it upheld the further militarization of the cold war by approving collective security pacts like NATO and SEATO. Whereas in the thirties the association was simply concerned with liberating Ethiopia from Italian Fascism (giving no thoughts to Haile Selassie's own politics), by 1954 it distinguished between "movements that really fight for national freedom" and those that were oriented toward what it labeled "the most savage imperialism of our time: the road of Moscow and Peiping." [73]

White's reversal—and, really, he did not stand alone, as Roy Wilkins, Mary McLeod Bethune, Adam Clayton Powell, Jr., and a host of other political and religious figures joined the patriotic and anticommunist chorus—bears upon both the cold war pressures on the black freedom struggle and White's strategic limitations. [74] The United States government successfully imposed a new arrangement on the African American leadership: limited and gradual embrace by the government of the goal of desegregation in exchange for that leadership's backing in the domestic and foreign cold war. The foreign policy community was becoming increasingly sensitive to the worldwide negative attention that Jim Crow was bringing to the United States. Repairing America's image abroad required concessions to African Americans' aspirations; the culmination of these cold war exigencies was the Supreme Court's *Brown* school segregation decision of 1954. At the same time, the potential fallout from such a politically expedient move had to be contained, and this meant the isolation of African American radicals like Du Bois and Robeson, who denounced American racism as fundamental to American capitalism and demanded far-reaching changes in the country's polity and economy. [75]

White could not help but sense America's direction as the cold war intensified following Truman's 1948 election. In 1949, the NAACP failed to get important legislation concerning housing passed. Southern congressmen opposed an amendment to the bill that forbade discrimination in public housing, of course; but they were unexpectedly joined even by sympathizers of the NAACP, notably board member Republican Senator Wayne Morse, who broke ranks with the association on the fundamental issue of provision of government services on a nonsegregated basis. [76] On a mass level, the government treated even expressions of sympathy for civil rights as potentially subversive. At the level of leadership, Paul Robeson's 1949 appearance in Peekskill, New York, was disrupted by anticommunist vigilantes, with the tacit endorsement of officials; the next year his passport was confiscated. In 1951, Du Bois was arrested on charges of being a foreign agent.

These attacks, combined with government threats to cut off his access to officials should he not cease his own criticism of American foreign policy, convinced Walter White that the survival of the NAACP as a respected and influential organization in the country's inner circle was at stake. To preserve the association's status, White took up cudgels against the black left, abandoned support for anticolonial struggles, and predicated his appeals for civil rights upon the need to improve America's image abroad as part of a fight against international communism. But, as historian of the cold war and civil rights Penny Von Eschen shows, at a time when the federal government—the *Brown* decision notwithstanding—was willing to concede very little by way of racial equality, "by acquiescing in a narrowed civil rights agenda, many civil rights leaders forfeited the means to address" the need for structural change.[77]

Certainly White's alarm at a potential loss of access was well placed. That he saw such access as the principal method of conducting the fight for equality, however, underscores the tenuous nature of his lifelong strategy and how dependent it was on the goodwill of government officials and other influential elites. The cold war simply magnified the secretary's dilemma. In earlier years he found it difficult, for example, to alter his methods to attain a federal antilynching law because he feared alienating Eleanor Roosevelt and a variety of New Dealers. Now at the start of the American century, anticommunism punctured the progressive chrysalis, and White sought protection for himself and his organization in the cold war.

Chapter 11

Looking for a
Larger Pond

For much of his adult life, Walter White faced violence and threats to his personal safety with a sui generis self-possession. He did not waver, nor did the carnage he saw cause him to shrink from his task of baring this human stain to the nation and purging it from the land. To the contrary, encounters with atrocity convinced him of the rightness of his cause; the omnipresent corporal and homicidal menaces energized him. He laughed in the face of danger and took deep personal satisfaction in out-witting lynchers and pogromists.

It is ironic, then, that having prepared psychologically for martyrdom, a heart attack should pivot a sweeping self-evaluation and proposals to alter his life and work. While vacationing in the Virgin Islands in February 1947, the secretary suffered what his physician and board chairman Louis Wright delicately termed in a letter to branch leaders "an attack which proves to be cardiac in origin." (White's own pronouncement was more distressing; he told Roy Wilkins that the episode was "severe" and required a six-day hospital stay.) His health, Wright more frankly told the board, was "not good," and he wanted to place White in a sanatorium for a six-week recuperation. The secretary would not agree to this arrangement, but at the board's behest he reduced his administrative and speaking responsibilities from April until September. Wilkins was not elevated to the position of acting secretary, but much of the business of oversight devolved to him.[1]

Hors de combat, White also gave signs of placing his interest in the organization on the sidelines. He became absorbed, for example, in trying to desegregate the legitimate theater in Baltimore and Washington; he met with New York playwrights and convinced them to refuse to allow their work to be produced in Jim Crow venues and embarked on negotiations with theater owners and Actors Equity to end the practice. He continued freely to dispense advice to Hollywood writers and producers. And he was certainly healthy enough to claim his place beside Harry Truman when the president addressed the monster rally at the Lincoln Memorial that closed the NAACP convention in June. He had always gravitated toward activities that promised a hefty publicity return, of course. But for a micromanager like Walter White, who was far from incapacitated and still visited the office regularly, his apparent indifference in the administration of the organization was a startling shift.[2]

White would once again mount himself in the saddle and even manage some spirited riding in the campaign to influence U.S. foreign policy with the *Appeal to the World* and in service to Truman during the 1948 election. But the intense clash with Du Bois that crowned their running battle drained him. He had once more to rethink whether he had the literal and metaphoric heart to continue at the controls of the NAACP. He decided he did not, and as he sailed to France for the Paris U.N. sessions, he asked the NAACP board of directors to grant him a year's leave of absence, to begin one month after his return.[3]

While his coronary condition—and lingering ailments from the plane crash in the Philippines, he added in his letter to the board—was responsible for the timing of his petition, he likely had been wearying of the NAACP regimen for several years. Board members, who usually were uninvolved in the daily routine, enjoyed working with and valued White, but the secretary's relations with his subordinates on the executive staff could tend toward the contentious. Du Bois was not the secretary's only headache. From the time he was hired in 1931, the ambitious Roy Wilkins had periodically irritated White too. The new assistant secretary made his entrance with a memorable faux pas when he signed on to Du Bois's accusations of the secretary's financial impropriety and imperious leadership. During the debate over the future plan and program, Wilkins sailed with whatever wind was prevailing at the moment, reinforcing the secretary's view that his assistant was an opportunist. Since that time, according to board member John Hammond, Wilkins had made known his dissatisfaction with the secretary's leadership. At one point, Hammond said, an alcohol-lubricated Wilkins complained loudly that he could run the association better than White. Though Wilkins categorically denied the charges, it was clear that the secretary was prepared to believe them or at least to doubt Wilkins's sincerity.[4]

White's relations with staff counsel Thurgood Marshall, while extraordinarily productive, were also abrasive. The two men were enormously competitive and liked to be in control of the direction of their work, recalled Mabel Smith, White's secretary in the mid- and late-forties, and a close friend of Marshall. Ever since he directed the successful appeal to the Supreme Court of *Moore* v. *Dempsey* in the twenties, White asserted a prerogative to be involved in the association's legal matters. The strength of his decision was that he brought his keen political instincts to forensic proceedings usually dominated by lawyers; White's decision to encourage the use of black attorneys in the association's legal pleadings and his determination to take up the salary-equalization suits are prime examples of his political acumen affecting the association's legal activity. But he was not an attorney, and because he had a healthy ego, he was known to offer expert advice when he was not an authority. What Marshall felt was meddling, White believed was legitimate oversight. In the secretary's opinion, Marshall was an employee of the organization of which he was the boss, and he would do whatever he thought was appropriate. Marshall's close relationship with Roy Wilkins, whom Marshall would have preferred as secretary, only exacerbated tensions, said NAACP labor secretary Herbert Hill.[5]

The infighting led the secretary to begin the spadework to move out of the NAACP ambit. In a bit of serendipity, Harold Oram approached White with a proposal to syndicate a weekly column for the white press. Oram was a professional fund-raiser for liberal and progressive causes— among his first clients was the Southern Tenant Farmers Union—who met White at an event to benefit the NAACP's legal defense of African Americans wrongly arrested during the 1943 Detroit riot. Oram had recently founded Graphic Syndicate, for which he envisioned a stable of progressive writers. He conceived the column as a "showpiece for promoting Walter White" and his new venture, he said. White was receptive. They approached the *New York Herald-Tribune*, which for $100 per column became White's flagship outlet. With Oram's nurturing—he said only luminaries like Walter Lippmann had self-sustaining columns—the secretary was picked up by dailies across the country.[6]

The weekly column gave the secretary unprecedented regular access to white liberal public opinion, for which he could interpret Afro-America's thoughts, desires, and actions. During its first two years, he used the column to preach the desirability of a black-Progressive alliance. As the domestic cold war constricted the acceptable boundaries of dissent it became his tribune to warn of the dangers of Wallace and declaim the virtues of Truman. White used syndication to reassure the cold war liberal establishment of Afro-America's fealty and reinforce his credentials as a legitimate African American spokesperson apart from the NAACP.

White alienated many of his colleagues and associates by writing this column. Carl Murphy, publisher of the *Afro-American* and an association board member, had long opposed the secretary's freelance activity; the *Defender* column placed his own paper at a competitive disadvantage, and the syndicated column put the entire black press in the position of trailing behind the dailies. Murphy was now joined by the *Pittsburgh Courier.* The grumbling became louder and more common as the secretary endorsed Truman's election in articles that violated the NAACP's policy of nonpartisanship. And it wasn't only the Communists who criticized White's hypocrisy in firing Du Bois while letting pro-Democrat ink flow from his pen. In the association, black Republicans, a not entirely extinct breed, complained of White's favoritism. But even the secretary's "best friends" on the board and executive staff, reported Thurgood Marshall, questioned White's flaunting of NAACP policy. Only his absence in Paris for the meeting of the United Nations prevented the board from censuring him. As White understood it, lumping all of his critics together, "They don't want me to earn a few measly extra dollars" writing a weekly column. But in fact they were dissatisfied with White's growing independence from the association.[7]

The coronary did more than aggravate the claustrophobia he felt inside the NAACP. It also triggered an epiphany: not only must he loosen his bonds to the NAACP, which he felt now straitened his career as a public figure, he needed radically to adjust his whole life. For the better part of two decades, his marriage to Gladys had been a charade. She had raised their children and made a home for them. In the process she had given up much, including a potential singing career and a chance of being—at least in her husband's eyes—anything other than Mrs. Walter White. She did this not because she enjoyed the public attention—she did not—but because she loved her husband and believed in his and the NAACP's mission.[8] She appears in his voluminous correspondence primarily as the dutiful fulfiller of the social obligations incumbent upon a major public figure's wife: hostessing intimate evenings in their apartment, accompanying him as he escorted literary and artistic giants about New York, taking her place on the dais next to Walter White, guest of honor.

He had married her, Mary White Ovington said he had told her, because "being excitable himself he has incurred the proper contrast." At some point, the patina of Gladys's subdued approach to life dulled in White's eyes. Having subsumed herself in the myriad tasks he expected her to fulfill, White now resented her devotion and expressed a desire to be alone. He no longer shared with her his legendary warmth and conviviality. Considering all the time he spent on the road, they wrote surprisingly little to each other. Only a few letters to her survive; a typical one, penned while she was out of town, assured her that Jane was cheerful in her absence. (Because he diligently saved all of his correspondence—incoming and outgoing—one can reasonably assume that most of it is extant.) Gladys's notes to "Dad" (her name for him) are as distant as the miles that separated them.[9]

By the late twenties, he started to direct his affections to Poppy Cannon. It was to her that he turned to find solace after his father's cruel death. Audaciously, they planned a summer weekend together, spouses in tow, at the Cannons' Connecticut home. In the middle of the Depression, at a time when unemployed actors were also unemployed waiters, White worked his network to find stage roles for her sister. In late 1933, the two began a project together—part cookbook, part culinary history—about the black contribution to American cuisine; when Cannon traveled South to collect recipes and historical anecdotes about food, White introduced her to his favorite sister, Madeline, in Atlanta—to facilitate the project, certainly, but also, one suspects, to win the approval of one important woman in his life from another. "She certainly fell in love with you; thinks you are the grandest person ever," he gushed to his youngest sister. "It is great to have my own opinion confirmed."[10]

There is nothing to intimate that White was anything but contented with this arrangement of his personal life throughout most of the Depression years. There is no evidence that he gave thought to ending his marriage. Perhaps he rationalized that leaving Gladys for Poppy would have had calamitous personal and political fallout. His young children would despise him, he feared. As he was embroiled in sequential challenges to his leadership of the NAACP during much of the thirties, a personal scandal would likely have led the association to dump him unceremoniously, especially when his first nemesis, Du Bois, had broadcast that Walter White preferred to associate with Caucasians. A public disclosure of his affair would undoubtedly have meant the destruction of the campaign for a federal antilynching law; not only would he have inflamed the Bourbon senators and representatives, it likely would have made his shaky white southern allies squeamish and confirmed in their minds nagging suspicions that "social equality" really was about sex.

Nor were they star-crossed lovers. Much as White preferred to have both a wife and a lover, Cannon too had her own life. When they began their affair, she was married and had an infant girl. She and her husband had divorced by 1936. For reasons now dimmed by both the passage of time and the secrecy in which they were enveloped, White and Cannon stopped seeing each other around the time of her divorce; she then married Alf Askland, a Swedish noble, and had another child, a boy, before she was widowed in 1939. She married a third time, to Claudius Phillippe in 1941, the maître d'hôtel of the Waldorf-Astoria, by whom she bore her third child (and second girl), divorcing him in 1949. In 1944 White and Cannon resumed their affair. Over time she had built a career as a food writer and in advertising and public relations. People who knew her remarked on her dedication to her work, and it is entirely plausible that she may have felt that making a public commitment to Walter White would have unduly complicated her life.[11]

The casual approach to their relationship was wiped away by White's heart attack. He likely was jolted into the realization that his remaining years were limited, and he wanted them to be happy. She too came to understand the depth of her feelings for him. Cannon's older daughter remembers that White suited her mother much better than any of her other husbands. There was, of course, an intense sexual attraction. But they also had a shared intellectual life, a love of literature, a strong commitment to human rights, and a passion for food and wine.[12] He developed relationships with Cannon's children and he took an interest in their upbringing. Theirs also was a professional partnership, as Cannon helped to develop the NAACP's fund-raising and assisted White's journalistic and public-speaking careers.

In 1948, as he steamed to the U.N. sessions in Paris, he began dropping public hints of his infatuation with Cannon. As he wrote her from aboard ship, "I'm sure I've turned the conversation a dozen times on this trip to some subject like Nan [Pandit, Nehru's sister, with whom Cannon and White worked to promote Indian independence] or cook books or writing so that I could say your name." If such actions seemed to White to be passionate declarations of his love, Cannon may have had her doubts. One of White's letters to her contained an oblique injunction to her not to let anything about his present marriage to Gladys "upset" her. A second letter delicately broke the news to her that he would be taking his wife to Truman's inaugural. He and Gladys would not be traveling together, and they would be going their separate ways immediately afterward. "It seems Truman wants me there to indicate further his attitude on the Negro issue. Please, Darling, don't let it disturb you," he begged. She may have had more reason to doubt his seriousness about her when he worried that his love letters to her would be intercepted by nosy mail clerks on her job at the Peter Hilton advertising agency. Other letters, in which he detailed his and Gladys's routine interactions, must have chafed, especially as he had promised to leave his wife for her.[13]

Cannon stiffened what she must have seen as White's flagging resolve. She told him that his wife was having an affair, and White, hoping he could foist upon Gladys responsibility for the dissolution of their marriage, confronted her. Gladys wept uncontrollably, Walter said, but then blasted him for his fecklessness:

> Now I realize your suspicious and difficult attitude all these years have been due to listening to lies about me. You certainly do not show much trust or faith in me.
>
> *I* also have heard stories during the past few years of our married life time which I would not think of letting touch me. . . . But I can now see you have harboured thoughts of distrust about me for years. I have never thought of divorce—but I can read between the lines that it is the thing you want. . . .
>
> . . . [I]f you had a little more faith in me you would not have the slightest doubt.[14]

Gladys White agreed to a divorce under the condition that he initiate it. He was pleased to be released from his marriage, but was plunged into guilt-induced paralysis and hand-wringing that must have tried Poppy Cannon's patience.

White planned to use his yearlong leave of absence, scheduled to begin in December, actively to consider a new career and make decisive changes in his personal life. But the NAACP board, anticipating a bruising fight for civil rights legislation, delayed the secretary's leave until sometime after the January opening of the Eighty-first Congress.

Following the example of organized labor, which mobilized for Truman because it could not stomach a Dewey victory and did not believe Wallace had a chance, the black vote had gone overwhelmingly for Truman after he had pledged support for civil rights. As NAACP staffer Henry Lee Moon presciently predicted, African Americans possessed the balance of power in a close contest. They provided Truman with the margin of victory in Illinois, Ohio, and California; had he lost any two of these states, Dewey would have won the presidency. Walter White had expended considerable capital within the association backing Truman; to make sure the president's nod to civil rights was not an election gambit, the secretary was determined to hold him and the Democratic Party to those promises.[15]

With the secretary's approval and the help of William Hastie, Leslie Perry of the NAACP Washington office developed an outline for congressional action. The NAACP wanted an omnibus civil rights act that contained antilynching and anti–poll tax provisions and banned discrimination in transportation and public accommodations; more, the association asked for a separate bill authorizing the Fair Employment Practices Commission. Anticipating the moderate Democrats' attempts to squirm out of supporting a full civil rights program, the association leadership declared that it would support no bill concerning housing, health, or education that did not explicitly forbid segregation. The NAACP tried to cement a coalition with civil liberties groups and organized labor. The AFL was reluctant, insisting that Congress's first agenda item be the repeal of the Taft-Hartley Act. The Brotherhood of Railway Trainmen went so far as to say that scrapping the antilabor Taft-Hartley was a "fight for freedom," while the NAACP's proposed program was "too controversial." Labor's nearly mute response to this statement—only the CIO committed itself to civil rights—spoke volumes. Still, both formally endorsed the formation of the Joint Committee on Civil Rights, an alliance of twenty religious, social action, liberal, and race-advancement organizations.[16]

Despite the president's clear declaration that he desired a full civil rights program, the legislative campaign proceeded slowly and indirectly for the first three months of the new Congress. Under Senate rules, a filibuster could not be ended until two-thirds of the upper house's members voted to invoke cloture, or a limitation on debate, after which would follow a floor vote on the legislation. Southern Democrats like Connally, Bilbo, Byrnes, and Black wielded this tool to defeat antilynching legislation in the thirties, and they could be counted on again to do the same to civil rights legislation. Under these circumstances, the joint committee and its senatorial backers decided first to attempt to modify the cloture rules.

The secretary spent considerable time in Washington between January and March, engaging senators in a shadow-boxing match. It was as if little had changed at the Capitol since White's dramatic appearances there more than a decade earlier. Republicans had initiated the first attempt to change Senate rules. But as members of the minority party, they knew they could not enact the changes and so were simply raising the point to embarrass the Democratic Party and split it north from south. Wayne Morse, Republican from Oregon and an NAACP board member, was an exception and handled with humor the race-baiting that was directed at him. He had told White "a funny story about the time he and [White] had breakfast together here at the Statler a week or so ago. A night or so later, Wayne says, he was greeted at a dinner party with the accusation, 'I hear, Senator Morse, that you invited a Negro to breakfast at the Statler.' To which Wayne retorted, 'You're wrong. A Negro invited ME to the Statler.' " As the secretary reported when parliamentary maneuvers started, "Both Democrats and Republicans were as deferential to the Southerners as though the Dixiecrats had won the election."[17]

The secretary expended lots of breath and ink prodding the Senate to amend its rules to allow a simple majority to invoke cloture. During a series of private encounters with Democratic senators just before a party-strategy session, the secretary confided to Poppy Cannon, one moaned that the Republicans were putting him and the others on his side of the aisle on the spot only to embarrass them and score political points. His reply was testy and unsympathetic: "You're damn right you're being put on the spot. And the only way you're going to get off the spot is by getting in there and fighting!" For backup, he pressed into service representatives of the other organizations from the joint committee, and conscripted the best representatives from NAACP branches in seventeen key states to travel to Washington and "talk turkey" to their senators. He exchanged letters with Philip Murray, which bound the CIO to finish the fight for cloture in exchange for the NAACP's pledge to support repeal of Taft-Hartley. Both his syndicated and *Defender* columns rang an urgent alarm—don't be intimidated by "loud-mouthed" southern Democrats, send telegrams, keep up the pressure—and threatened wavering senators with forced retirement in the 1950 and 1952 elections.[18]

The results were mostly predictable. Parliamentary skullduggery, northern Democratic cravenness, and an alliance between conservative Republicans and southern Democrats defeated the proposed change in the Senate rules in mid-March. Truman's and the NAACP's civil rights platform was doomed, at least for the duration of the Eighty-first Congress.[19] In his autopsy, the secretary assigned the cause of death variously to meticulous preparation by the filibusterers, the president's enemies capitalizing on his absence from Washington on vacation, and African Americans' complacency. "The greatest weakness visible during the fight," he informed his *Defender* readers, "was that too many Americans, especially Negroes, took a victory in amending the Senate rules for granted."

> Had not Harry Truman won on the basis of his civil rights stand? There was nothing to be done, most of us thought, except to sit down and wait for victory. We did not bother to telegraph, telephone, visit or even write a penny post card to our Senators urging them to get in there and fight and to refuse to compromise. As a result, senator after senator told me that he had seen no great interest in the civil rights program.

Finally, he said, civil rights were defeated for lack of money. "Unless we are willing to pay for victory as well as beg for it, we will suffer more defeats."[20]

But the secretary was being disingenuous, and his postmortem was little more than a rote recitation of reasons for past drubbings. Thurgood

Marshall complained that White's being stuck in a rut, not mass indifference, was a key reason for defeat. It was no longer sufficient for White alone to lobby Congress or ask sympathetic organizations and association branches to wire their representatives. Rather, said Marshall, the NAACP needed to bring members en masse to Washington to camp out in their legislators' offices. Marshall was advocating a return to the vigorous methods of previous campaigns, like the one against the Parker nomination. Board member Alfred Baker Lewis too criticized White's "inept leadership" for not sufficiently mobilizing other organizations as a cause of defeat.[21]

In truth, the secretary seemed distracted and not focused during the campaign. His desire to end his marriage and begin a new life with Poppy kept intruding on his political activity. Was he panicked or elated by her news that she might be pregnant? (She was not, it turned out.) In past lobbying efforts, White's time was consumed almost exclusively by strategy sessions. This time, however, personal disclosure assumed a prominence in conversation with his intimates. Bill Hastie was not surprised to hear White confess his affair; he had suspected as much for some time, but decided that it was none of his business. Nor was it anyone else's, Hastie said, though he believed the secretary needed to resign from the association before he changed his marital status. When he was not hounding senators or representatives, White used to be an attentive observer of congressional debates. Now, he sat impassively in the Senate gallery, composing letters to Poppy surreptitiously, because note-taking and writing were not allowed there. The impending legislative defeat was magnified by the imminent implosion of his marriage, making him ever more discouraged and plagued by insomnia. He had wanted a victory, not only for the sake of the race, but because a favorable outcome would allow him to retire from the association on a high note and avoid charges that he was abandoning the cause. That would not happen now, but Walter White, exhausted and disgusted, would leave anyway.[22]

A couple of days after accusing his wife of having an affair, he confessed to her his own infidelity and his desire to leave her. She would go to visit her sister, who lived in Mexico, and there obtain a divorce. Having thus devised his marital escape, he planned an exit from the association. In early April he informed the board that he had been invited to participate in a world tour sponsored by the *Town Meeting of the Air*, a wildly popular public affairs program on the NBC radio network. A predecessor to shows like *Face the Nation, Town Meeting* was hosted by George V. Denny, who moderated a panel discussion and then allowed a studio audience to question the guests. Denny planned to broadcast weekly from locations across Europe, North Africa, and Asia between June and September. The secretary asked for both permission to go and the NAACP to pick up the $3,750 price tag. Walter White thought of this as his grand send-off, but the board was losing its patience with him. Arthur Spingarn was unusually irascible. He doubted the publicity value of the junket, and he introduced a motion ordering the secretary to begin his leave of absence no later than June. The motion was tabled, and a substitute motion passed that permitted him to go, provided he could obtain funding independent of the NAACP. But the board was not happy with White's priorities or his attempts to saddle the association with the costs of his whims.[23]

White riposted with a stunning announcement that rather than beginning his leave of absence he would resign his post effective June 1. His health had been failing, he said, and the only way to lead the more sensible life that his heart specialist recommended was to leave the NAACP. And in the most direct signal yet that his interest in the association was flagging, he informed board members that "[he wanted] to devote the rest of [his] life to promotion of the cause of human liberty on a somewhat expanded basis." He made no mention of the pending divorce and looming marriage to Poppy as precipitating his decision, and the board, thus misled, refused to accept his resignation. Alfred Baker Lewis begged the secretary to reconsider and take the leave before deciding permanently to vacate his position. His sudden departure would damage morale and leave the association leaderless, as Roy Wilkins was not yet ready to assume the organization's helm. Staffers Wilkins and Henry Lee Moon agreed absolutely with Lewis's assessment. Other board members weighed in too, and after ruminating for two weeks, he notified the board that he deferred to its judgment and would evaluate his final disposition when he returned in June 1950.[24]

The black press reported the leave of absence and the possibility of its per-manence with a mixture of relief and regret. Louis Martin, who would become prominent in the Johnson administration, reported in the *Chicago Defender* that the secretary's request was symptomatic of the punishing regimen of a race leader and a harbinger of the graceful exuent of a generation's standard-bearers. Many of these were infirm or suffering chronic illnesses, and Martin, while thanking them for their unselfish service, warmed up the drumbeat for the younger squadron of black leaders, including Ralph Bunche, Adam Clayton Powell, and NAACP lawyer Oliver Hill—but not, oddly enough, Thurgood Marshall.[25]

Carl Murphy's *Afro-American*, which over the years had been a strong, but critical, supporter of White and the NAACP, hailed White too, but was less ambivalent about his passing from the scene. "It is remarkable," said the paper, that White kept at his race work as long as he had. He had achieved great victories, but had also suffered ringing defeats, which were "due to his own personality." He had an "exalted ego" and was a "prima donna." "For more than 25 years, the word of Walter White has been accepted as the voice of colored America," opined the *Afro*. "Much of the illusion of Mr. White's power was traced to his own ability to dramatize the activities of the NAACP. . . ." On balance the race owed him a debt of gratitude, but the big task now was to find "a successor to Moses."[26]

Meanwhile, White disclosed his intentions to his family. There is no record of brother George's reactions—probably because he lived at 409 Edgecomb and they communicated in person—but for sisters Alice, Helen, and Madeline, the news had the destructive power of a nuclear explosion. All three were distressed at the impact of their brother's decision on Gladys and Jane and Pidge. Walter, they agreed, was supremely selfish to abandon his wife. Gladys "sacrificed herself to stay in the background and hide away her charm and personality," Alice scolded him. "She made your life her life and had very few outside contacts," is how Madeline put it. She wondered whether her brother had used the darker and visually striking Gladys to inflate his racial credentials; one of the reasons black people so admired him, she said, was because he "fell in love with and married a person of Gladys' complexion." She took umbrage at the length of her brother's affair; why had he not told his wife about it years before, "so she could rearrange her life when she was younger?"[27]

As dismayed as they were about the treatment of their sister-in-law, niece, and nephew, they were still their brother's sisters, and their primary concern was blood relations. Marrying a white woman was a stain on the family, Alice said. "I am glad moma [*sic*] and papa are not here to suffer this disgrace. However it will make them both turn over in their graves . . . especially papa, who saw a great future for you and believed so in you." Helen begged her brother to reconsider: "[I]t will be the first scandal in our family. . . . Please, please don't be a fool. I know I will be so ashamed I will not want to face any of my friends." Divorce Gladys, if you must, they said, but do not marry a white woman.[28]

Of course, they were also concerned with the fallout on their brother's career and the fight for civil rights. When the public hears that Walter White has married a white woman, Madeline wrote, "the Ralph McGills [the liberal segregationist editor of the *Atlanta Constitution*], the Rankins and their ilk will go to town and the NAACP will suffer more than you will. Can you afford to destroy what you have been 31 years building up[?]" Helen warned that what was at stake was how people will remember him: "From the lowest to the highest, both races respect and envy you but if you take the step you plan to take, your name will be mud." But Alice was bluntest:

> [T]he selfishness is unbelievable[.] [I]n black and white you are saying to us I have gotten all the NAACP can offer me—now I am going to further myself and my ambition by marrying this white woman. . . .
>
> . . . Now you are telling . . . all the world that all this race pride and work for the Negroe [*sic*] race was only to advance your interest—and you had no real interest in them. You want a white woman to share the rest of your days.[29]

Their anguish and indignance was palpable. But their sentiments differed not at all from what coursed through some of the leadership of the NAACP, the black press, and much of Afro-America when his new nuptials became public. Still, White marched forward. On July 1, White's fifty-sixth birthday and one month after commencing his leave, he and Poppy gathered her three children and sent them to the Virgin Islands, where they would be under the care of the territory's finance commissioner and his wife, who were personal friends of the bride and groom, and be away from a prying press. Five days later, they were wed privately in a judge's chambers in Jersey City, New Jersey, and the following day, unencumbered by offspring, the newlyweds were jetting to London to take part in the *Town Meeting of the Air*.[30]

Reaction to White's divorce was calm enough, with two black weeklies with national editions raising eyebrows, but not much more. The *Defender* splashed the news across its front page in a short factual article; the next week, perhaps in an effort to keep tongues wagging, the paper printed Gladys White's denial of rumors that she was romantically linked to the actor Fredric March. The *Pittsburgh Courier,* likewise reported the divorce, with a hint that the secretary was involved with another woman, whom the paper did not identify by name. Interestingly, the *Afro* did not report the Whites' divorce at all when it occurred.[31]

But news of his remarriage to Poppy Cannon was a thunderclap. To be sure, some board members supported White: William Hastie, who thought it prudent for the secretary to resign before he changed his marital status, declined to ask for his resignation after White's remarriage became public knowledge, and Palmer Weber was an adamant defender of White's right to love whomever he desired. But there was strong sentiment to bounce White from leadership. Alfred Baker Lewis expressed it when he declared that he felt betrayed: the secretary had obtained his leave of absence on the pretext of ill health, when the real reason, now clear to everyone, was his desire to duck criticism of his marriage to a white woman. Carl Murphy said White must not return to the association and that his replacement must be chosen immediately. Board members and other association officials were free to take a spouse of another race, but not the chief executive of the most prominent civil rights organization in the country. In a letter to Weber, Murphy was plainspoken: White's marriage to Poppy "has so weakened his usefulness that the Association will assume a grave risk in attempting to keep him in office. . . . The public believes Mr. Walter White, as an outstanding leader of the country and as an executive of our Association, has done the wrong thing in marrying across racial lines. That bitterness is more pronounced among women than men."[32]

Murphy was more blunt, brutal even, in his *Afro-American.* With his marriage to Poppy Cannon, the secretary "tossed away" his thirty-five-year investment in the struggle for equality. Although "people are human beings first and members of a particular race second," and although White was only acting "as the creator intended" by selecting a mate to whom he was attracted, he "unwittingly placed in the hands of our most vocal opponents the very rebuttal they have attempted to use against our battle for freedom." The *Afro-American* wondered whether White could not have found his desired qualities in a woman of his own race. Murphy then sliced at the secretary's well-exposed Achilles' heel. One should not blame Walter White for wanting to marry a white woman; "the race itself is to blame for permitting a man who wanted to be white so bad to be their spokesman for so long. This error should not be repeated."[33]

The *Norfolk Journal and Guide* too was stinging in its rebuke of White. "Serious embarrassment, if not something worse, is likely to befall the National Association for the Advancement of Colored People as a result of the recent marriage of its executive secretary, Walter White, to a white divorcee," the paper editorialized. "It is not likely, however, that this gentleman, prone as he is to serving his selfish interests, will feel overly concerned about what happens to the NAACP, now that he has attained his latest ambition. . . ." It then called for his removal and replacement "by someone with more statesman-like perspective."[34]

The *Defender*'s reporter, Lillian Scott, dressed up Poppy Cannon's biographical information in vaguely salacious language that would have spiced mid-twentieth-century gossip. "It is reported," she informed readers, that Poppy had children by three different men, and she emphasized the great difference in the newlyweds' ages. But even the *Defender*, which maintained friendly relations with the secretary, was compelled to report the opposition to his marriage. It featured sharp criticism by C. C. Spaulding, the president of North Carolina Mutual Insurance, the largest black-owned business of its day. Spaulding prefaced a speech he made in Detroit with the disclaimer that he personally was not opposed to intermarriage. Still, White was guilty of "snatch[ing] at the rug of economic, social and political advancement upon which the feet of Negroes rest. . . . Moreover, he has given credence" to libelous statements that African American men's greatest ambition is "to invade the white race."[35]

Initial public opinion was somewhat more mixed than the African American opinion makers indicated. Typical was Lucille Miller, a veteran rank-and-file race woman, whose enlistment in the cause went back to the Niagara Movement, the NAACP's predecessor. She used to think that the secretary was a man of solid morals and great integrity; but now "it leaves me speechless to learn that Mr. White has been another one of those philandering husbands." While she appreciated his past accomplishments, she firmly opposed his return because "most certainly he cannot be trusted . . ."[36] But there were also those who supported the secretary's right to marry whom he wanted without having to sacrifice his career. The *Louisiana Weekly* of New Orleans printed a defense of White. "We don't get leaders like Walter White every day and it would make us as a group appear very ungrateful to throw him overboard for something that is his own personal and private business. . . . Let us not forget that the NAACP is an interracial organization, so now its executive secretary and his wife are an interracial couple." He received private encouragement too from African Americans. One letter in particular put the issue succinctly: "Race . . . bah! Another old wives' tale. 'The white race,' 'the black race,' 'the red race,' 'the yellow race,' 'his race,' 'your race,' and so on ad infinitum . . . ad nauseam. Absolutely correct you are. There's one and only one, <u>THE HUMAN RACE</u>."[37]

The initial roil did not wash over the newlyweds, because by design they were out of the country with the *Round the World Town Meeting of the Air*. For the summer they traversed parts of three continents, promoting American world leadership but also learning about the global significance of race. White wrote about encounters with citizens of Turkey, Egypt, Lebanon, Syria, Pakistan, and India; they admired the United States, but they also wondered how the country could talk so earnestly "about democracy and freedom while lynching and segregation continue in America." Certainly one objective of this trip was for White to establish connections with people who could facilitate a new career independent of the NAACP. But his desultory journalism and fact-finding expeditions seemed to take second place to other purposes. More important, the secretary-on-leave and the new Mrs. White were graciously received by other participants—bankers, representatives of organized labor, officials of the Lions and the Elks, academics, and other middle Americans. They were able to enjoy the group's conviviality, and they avoided the whorl that would consume them on their return to the United States.[38]

But the black public's reserves of goodwill or initial willingness to suspend judgment evaporated with *Look* magazine's publication of White's article "Has Science Conquered the Color Line?" at the end of August.[39] Dressed up as a straightforward report on the discovery of a chemical that could change skin color from black to white by removing melanin, it was an endorsement of "passing" as the way to overcome racial barriers. Scientists would have to conduct more experiments before they could ensure the chemical was safe for use on humans, he said,

> [b]ut consider what would happen if a means of racial transformation is made available at reasonable cost. The racial, social, economic and political consequences would be tremendous.

The compound "will provide a way to get the fair treatment [Negroes] have always wanted. The chemical will enable them to break the barriers that hem them in, let them live like other Americans and be judged on their own merits."

But did not cultural annihilation loom as a repercussion from somatic erasure? White gestured toward this position, quoting *Defender* editor John Sengstacke that "Negroes are proud of their heritage and do not want to lose it by merging with the white world." Blacks, the editor stated emphatically, wanted first-class citizenship *"as Negroes."* But acknowledgment of this concern, surely shared by the majority of African Americans, was a rhetorical device employed quickly to dismiss it. White quoted Lena Horne, more glamorous than Seng-stacke, as saying the chemical was "wonderful!" and "the greatest thing for world peace and race relations that has ever happened." (Did Horne even utter these words, and if so, in what context? In several communications in the spring 2001, Horne, through her personal assistant, refused to comment on the article or her quotation. But behind the assistant's "no comment" was a suggestion that Horne was not familiar with the article.) Racial obliteration would reduce racial friction, White implied, and the appearance of this chemical compound promised to enlarge "the range of human free choice."

Walter White had lobbed a grenade into a crowd, but the reaction of many was to pick it up and toss it back. African Americans were willing to limit their public criticism of White's union with Cannon to grumbling, said the *New York Amsterdam News*, for that, after all, was "just another development, or a private matter which was not Johnny Q's business." But they could hardly ignore White's *Look* article, and "the Negro public turned both barrels on the little NAACP chieftain" and his plan for racial harmony. The paper's query of black New Yorkers, not surprisingly, turned up only one person (who preferred not to give her name), who would use the chemical bleach; all others expressed comfort or satisfaction with their skin color and refused to demean themselves by changing their appearance to suit white society. The weekly also reported the opinions of Anita Lyons, a black journalist from St. Louis, who said that this latest incident rendered White unfit to lead the nation's African Americans, and William Patterson, the Communist lawyer and head of the Civil Rights Congress, who labeled White's article a "grievous insult" to both American Negroes and colonial peoples around the world.[40]

Lillian Scott at the *Defender* reported that race leaders far more moderate than Patterson were disassociating themselves from White. A.

Philip Randolph called the proposal "wholly fantastic," adding that "[he did] not share the faith of Mr. White in the virtue of a chemical solution to the Negro problem." Lester Granger of the Urban League termed White's article "something less than a valuable contribution to the discussion of the racial question." NAACP board member Channing Tobias opposed White's angle, and even Roy Wilkins had to disagree publicly with his boss. As had the *Amsterdam News*, the *Defender* found that regular black Chicagoans were more than satisfied with their complexions.[41]

The *Afro-American* was most withering in its coverage. It differed not at all from the other weeklies in its gauge of black public opinion, but it was by far the most bitter in its denunciation of White. Carl Murphy explicitly stated that White was isolated and distanced from the race. The secretary-on-leave, said the paper, "has solved his personal problem of the color line by marrying a white woman," and now proposes turning black people white as his contribution to solving the race problem. Alphaeus Hunton of the Council on African Affairs said it was "too silly for serious comment," while a minister in Florida termed it "frivolous to the point of absurdity." Summarizing the feeling of racial betrayal and of White's perceived irrelevance to the tasks at hand, Edith Alexander, a black New York City politician, said, "It's time that we get proud of being colored."[42]

The secretary-on-leave, back in the country soon after *Look* appeared with his article, feigned astonishment at its negative reception. Finding that his essay could not speak for itself, he wrote an apologia for the *Chicago Defender*, which the editor aptly headlined " 'You Got Me Wrong'— Walter White."[43] He commenced his defense with the claim that the near universal condemnation of his article was simply a huge misunderstanding, an example of "the old saying about shooting an arrow into the air and knowing not where it lands." All he had done was to report on scientific research that seemed to offer the potential to remove melanin from dark skin, yet people were accusing him of encouraging black people to embark on this chemical regimen. White implied that his *Look* article was satire; George Schuyler, he said, had written *Black No More*, which burlesqued both white racism and elitist race uplifters—including White, thinly disguised as voluntary Negro "Walter Williams"—and he was not lambasted for proposing instant "whitening" as the solution to the race problem. "You can imagine my surprise" instead to be vilified, he wrote.

But then he shifted his argument, portraying his critics as unreasonable. The "highly vocal individuals" responsible for the uproar "seem not to have read the article" or to have willingly misinterpreted it. They—he did not name them—"read with their emotions instead of their brains" when they "screamed" that he planned to erase the color line by extracting the color from dark peoples' skins. It was "sheer idiocy" to criticize him just for bringing scientific facts to the public's attention, he said. According to White, while the unnamed assail-ants were fleeing from reality, Leo Szilard, the nuclear physicist whose research was instrumental in laying the foundation for nuclear weapons, believed the melanin-leaching chemical was "a more explosive discovery than the atom bomb."

Having characterized his adversaries as unthinking and "ostrich-like" in their avoidance of facts, White again shifted direction. Confusion may have been caused by the *Look* editor's decision to pare the article to a third of its original size. A paragraph in the excised portion explained that a worldwide revolt against colonialism and white supremacy may make possession of a white skin less desirable, and scientists were also looking into a process whereby melanin could be added to one's skin. He then rested his defense with a plea for thicker skin, as he labeled his interlocutors "hypersensitive."

Walter White was clumsy in his disingenuousness. "Has Science Conquered the Color Line?" was not satire. He never wrote in that genre—though he did on occasion employ the closely related irony—*Look* did not publish satiric pieces, and none of his audience took it as such.[44] This exegesis is further undercut by his cross-complaint that, because he only reported the extant facts, his opponents were shooting the messenger. His plea that the editorial process had distorted his message is weakened by the absence of an unexpurgated version of the article and the fact that he approved the final copy. And his charge that his opponents censured him for simply writing about the chemical similarly rings hollow: how else but as an endorsement is one to read the article's concluding sentence that "the color line, the shame of the twentieth century, may go forever, as slavery did in the nineteenth"? His readers correctly interpreted what he wrote.

White's assertion that he was dumbfounded by the drubbing is not credible. He kept the impending changes in marital status from the NAACP board as it debated his resignation because enough board members viewed as apostasy his remarriage to a white woman. His close friend William Hastie had told him to leave his post before doing anything.

Thurgood Marshall, who, like Hastie, believed White had the indubitable right to marry whomever he wished provided she consented, was not at all certain that White ought to exercise that right; what may have been personally satisfying was sure to plunge the NAACP needlessly into damaging controversy.[45] If anything, the association leadership was more cosmopolitan and broad-minded than blacks' public opinion generally. He had to have known that "Has Science Conquered the Color Line?," incendiary in its own right, was, when piled atop his new domestic arrangement, certain to consume him in flames.

Illustrating just how far from good graces Walter White had fallen, a disappointed African American woman, of middle age at least, recalled that "a number of years ago when you were in field work for the NAACP and went on some perilous missions, I heard you speak at Mother Zion Church in New York, and you began your speech by saying, 'Unfortunately, I have a color that I can use on both sides of the fence.' I admired you for that; why the change?"[46]

It is tempting to conclude that White's gaffe was a public admission of what he had always privately believed. Accusations that he wanted to be white had followed him throughout his career, of course, most famously when Du Bois poked around in this fire, hoping to dislodge some embers and ignite a challenge to the secretary's leadership. And it was White's patron Joel Spingarn who observed that " 'Analyzing' Walter White isn't analyzing a Negro; but it wd. be something much more interesting and complicated."[47] Yet Du Bois had ulterior motives for uttering his charges, and, as has been noted in chapter three, one can reasonably conclude that Spingarn projected his own hibernating prejudices onto White. White could have decided early in life not to become involved in race work and could have easily passed over to the white world. Yet he did exactly the opposite, repeatedly making extra efforts to accentuate his solidarity and identification with the African American people. And though he had tired of the NAACP by the mid-forties, there is no evidence that he regretted devoting his adult life to it.

Rather than reading the *Look* article primarily as the product of a defective racial self-concept, this embarrassment in the twilight of his career is more fruitfully read against the background of White's reaction to his dicey health, a precarious household situation, late-in-life future plans, and intra-association bickering. Although the secretary hid his affair with Poppy Cannon as the proximate reason for his resignation, he was not entirely untruthful when he cited heath concerns for leaving the NAACP. He was clearly not disabled, but facing an uncertain future, he decided that he had to explore other professional avenues, the key to which was a partnership with his wife-to-be. As he wrote to Poppy one evening following an engagement on a radio program, "I thought of how indebted to you I am for the sense of direction and the channeling of action which you and you alone have given me since 1944." In a flourish of love-induced distortion of perspective, the secretary credited his collaboration with Poppy with what he considered the major accomplishments of the postwar years: Truman's establishment of the presidential civil rights committee and the derailing of the Wallace campaign and the Communists' bid to insinuate themselves into the political mainstream. And, he said, she was the chief inspirer of his newspaper columns and his muse while he wrote *A Man Called White*.[48]

Nor was this effusiveness sentiment without action. With her connections in the emerging television industry, Poppy tried to interest executives of that medium in broadcasting a weekly public affairs program hosted by White and based upon the *Meet the Press* formula. White and his soon-to-be wife made a firm decision to end the relationship with the NAACP and establish himself "solidly in the non-organizational world," especially as a public relations "consultant to the movies, radio, various industrial associations and a number of foreign governments." Within a short time after his and Poppy's return from the *Round the World* tour, he thought he would be making an annual salary of somewhere between $20,000 and $25,000.[49]

Everywhere, he believed, people stood in the way of his happiness. His supposed allies were arrayed against him. The black press, willingly and with measured relief at least, accepted his resignation; White could anticipate their vociferous opposition upon the breaking of the news of his marriage to Poppy. Other external foes, including leftists and segregationists, were poised to snatch the joy from his remaining years and threaten the social good that could come out of it. And within the association, he felt the hot breath of disapproval. Thurgood Marshall, he felt, was "obstreperous," and his wife Buster was "patronizing." The mean-spiritedness of the "Thurgoods and *Daily Workers* and *Rankins*" placed Poppy, her "kids and Jane and Pidge and the cause" in immediate danger. "The most perfect love in the world—threatened by those who would gleefully and savagely tear it to shreds, neither knowing nor caring that out of it came immense strides forward for human decency. . . . " [50]

White's intention not to return to the NAACP, his desire to establish a public profile that rather exploited his influence in the New Deal and Fair Deal, and above all his fury at those who opposed him—given these circumstances, it is highly likely that he was just mischievous enough to set off some fireworks on his departure. "Has Science Conquered the Color Line?" was just the journalistic effort to bollix up a raft of his tormentors on both sides of the color line. And it might also have the added benefit, he must have thought, of establishing him as a maverick, and thus someone whose opinion was valuable to solicit.

Upon his return from the *Round the World Town Meeting,* and after he had met the black press, defending to them his marriage, and giving them no inkling of his future with the NAACP, the secretary-on-leave avidly pursued career alternatives. He would try to fashion a place for himself in journalism, international affairs, and public speaking, drawing in nearly equal parts on his convictions, his experiences at various U.N. gatherings and his recent globe-trotting, and his attraction to glamour. His almost complete disengagement from and lack of interest in the NAACP's work can be gauged from a joke that made the rounds at association headquarters. According to Herbert Hill, staffers cracked that if one wanted to see Walter White, one had to make an appointment with U.N. secretary-general Trygve Lie. Hill has a vivid memory of White looking self-importantly at his watch and declaring that he had to run because he had a meeting with Lie in fifteen minutes. [51]

The NAACP was able to shrug off as irrelevant (or nonessential, at best) the secretary-on-leave's efforts to earn a livelihood as an international consultant; the sense of the board meeting that approved White's leave was that upon his return the secretary would enter into a semi-retirement similar to the one it envisioned for Du Bois when he rejoined the association in 1944. [52] While the board believed that White's emeritus status would be mutually advantageous, White acted as if the benefits of the arrangement flowed in one direction only. He thought nothing of using the resources of the NAACP and the prestige that accrued to him by his affiliation with it, while at the same time refusing to be obligated or accountable to it. White was identified in his column as the secretary of the NAACP. He signed with the Colston-Leigh agency, which, based upon the drawing power of his NAACP connection, offered him a per diem of $100 plus expenses for three speaking tours of the Northwest and Midwest in 1949 and 1950. At the same time, he balked at speaking at NAACP branch-sponsored events.[53]

But the ill will and embarrassment generated by the *Look* article caused the board to jettison its benign attitude toward his efforts to re-make himself as an independent journalist and public speaker. A commit-tee of four—Arthur Spingarn, Louis Wright, Channing Tobias, and Hubert Delany, all sympathetic to White—was formed to meet with him "for the purpose of clarifying his official relationship to the NAACP at this time in connection with any press conferences he might hold or any other activities in which he might engage." Though the board later de-cided this mission was too restrictive, its desire to maintain oversight of White remained strong, and he was compelled to remove from his syndi-cated column any mention of his position in the NAACP.[54]

White believed that his syndicated column would do the heavy lifting required to establish the other facets of his new career. He had written it for four years, when, in 1950 the *Herald-Tribune*, which had a conserva-tive readership, dropped him from its stable of columnists. White sus-pected that the editors had been unhappy with him since the 1948 presidential campaign when he criticized John Foster Dulles, then of the U.S. delegation to the U.N. General Assembly, of pandering to the Ital-ian-American vote by advocating the return of Italy's former colonies under the guise of a trusteeship. Poppy Cannon believed that the *Herald-Tribune*, which had expected White to express himself primarily on racial matters, tired of his dilations on international affairs and the gamut of na-tional politics. Harold Oram, whose Graphic Syndicate had distributed White's column, believed that the late forties and early fifties was too early for a black columnist to make a living. Until the *Herald-Tribune* can-celed him, White was the only one of Oram's clients to make a profit; but now, with Oram paying him 50 percent of the proceeds plus office ex-penses, even White was a financial drain. Oram decided to get out of the syndication business altogether, turning distribution over to White. But even with Poppy as a partner, White did not have the business knowledge to continue without Oram, and in mid-fifties White suspended for good his syndicated column.[55]

With the anticipated demise of this outlet to a broadly liberal white

audience also came the conclusion of White's attempts to separate completely from the NAACP, and he laid plans to retake the leadership of the
organization. On March 10, 1950, he sent the board of directors a letter
rescinding his previous letter of resignation. Continuing his lack of can-
dor by keeping mum about his divorce, remarriage, and unrequited desire to live beyond the NAACP as the principal reasons for his
resignation, White cited a changed health prognosis for his retraction.
". . . I have been informed by Dr. Arthur Master that my health has improved to such an extent that, although I have a coronary condition, my
present problem is more neurogenic than coronary. He states that if I will
lead a 'sensible life' so far as work is concerned I can count on a number of
years of continued active life." More, he missed the NAACP, he said: "I
have discovered also that I am heartbound to the Association." And placing the best face on the collapse of his job search, he said that he could
imagine doing work for none but the NAACP.[56]

He also portrayed his change of heart as salvific for the association.
The NAACP was rife with disunity, as the Communists tried to penetrate
the organization and take it over. (There were some left-leaning
branches—Richmond, California, in the San Francisco Bay area; New
York City; and Philadelphia, to name three. But much of the strife over
the previous two years had been caused by White's own stifling of support
for Wallace's Progressive presidential campaign and the final shunning of
Du Bois.) His implication was clear enough: He was a unifier, while Roy
Wilkins, the acting secretary, was divisive and incapable of ending the
dissension.

White's oblique references to the Communist threat were meant to
capitalize on Wilkins's leadership miscues. The February 14 edition of
the *New York World-Telegram and Sun* commented on power struggles
within the NAACP. Wilkins, it said, was being challenged not by White
trying to regain his position, but by Earl Dickerson, while Hubert Delany
was being groomed to replace the ailing Louis Wright as board chairman.
The article identified Dickerson as a close associate of the Communist
Party, and Delany as a "Republican and a friend of Paul Robeson" and an
executive board member of the "pro-Communist National Lawyers
Guild." When the article appeared White was on one of his speaking
tours, and Poppy provided him the latest news. Delany, she said, was furious. She spoke with Louis Wright, who told her he believed that Wilkins
had inspired the *World-Telegram and Sun* article as a way both to boost his

anticommunist credentials and to neutralize Delany, who was also a vocal critic of Wilkins.[57]

If Wilkins did plant the story—and he heatedly denied it—his plan backfired. The *Amsterdam News* followed the *World-Telegram and Sun* with an article that predicted that White would return to the NAACP's helm. Wilkins's anticommunism, the paper said, was causing dissension within the NAACP and was one reason for the steep decline in membership during the year he had been acting secretary. White, the article said, would better be able to " 'passify' progressive branches" that found him a more palatable leader. More, Dickerson and Delany denounced the "subtle innuendo"; Dickerson denied that he had ever been interested in White's or Wilkins's position and accused someone within the NAACP of scheming to "discredit" and render him and Delany "uninfluential board members." They were not silenced and continued to speak out on all issues before the board.[58]

Grousing by some branches about the vilification of the left within the association notwithstanding, the central issues in White's return were his marriage to Poppy and Wilkins's unwillingness to return to a subordinate position in the NAACP hierarchy. Outside the organization, the black weeklies continued to hammer at White's matrimonial status as his prime disqualification. The *Afro-American* and the *Journal and Guide* were joined by the *Dallas Express*, edited by the influential Carter Wesley, whose newspaper empire spread across Texas. The indictment was direct and stinging: "In the deep South nobody will be able to think of Walter again, or his actions or statements, as pure, unadulterated Negro thinking, acting, or feeling. . . . If Walter comes back now, [the NAACP] will have a Negro as secretary with a white covering."[59]

A notable exception to this trend against White was the *Chicago Defender*, which after initially roundly boxing his ears for his marital indiscretions and the *Look* article, now embraced him. The change was owed primarily to Lillian Scott, "whom Harlem," Poppy said, "is calling the W.W. campaign manager." The *Defender's* news coverage of White's climb back to the association's pinnacle was bland, but its editorials encouraged his return. According to Poppy, Scott's disposition was deliberately cultivated by White, and Wilkins thought the paper's favorable editorial slant was entirely owed to White leaking exclusives to it.[60]

Board members tried to prevent White from returning too. When

Washington bureau head Leslie Perry's affair with a white woman was exposed and board members flinched at the prospects of yet another interracial sex scandal, they redoubled the pressure to keep White out. Those concerned with bad publicity were joined by others who were affronted by White's drive to come back after several years of indifference to the central mission of the NAACP. Arthur Spingarn dismissed White's international travel as frivolous and believed him unwilling—or lacking in stamina—to devote energy to the association program. More, Spingarn said at the March board meeting that back in May 1949 both sides had agreed White would resign after his leave expired. Channing Tobias lost patience with White; he did not think that the secretary-on-leave "can blow in and out of the organization and then expect a decision to be made to accommodate his personal convenience."[61]

For two months, from mid-March to mid-May, the board took no action on White's resignation as sentiment on both sides surged. Then Eleanor Roosevelt threw her weight about. For several months she had been worried by steadily crescendoing criticism of Walter White. The previous November, she had tendered her resignation with the explanation that her schedule was too hectic for her to participate in NAACP business; but the *Amsterdam News* reported it was prompted by intra-association attacks on her friend. She denied this, though she allowed privately to White that her move was prompted in part "because I do not think Mr. Wilkins is in the least interested in consulting with me or would agree with my point of view on many things." Only White's intervention convinced her to withdraw her resignation.[62]

In March, however, her simmering resentment again boiled over. In a conversation with White she claimed to have received a letter from Wilkins that stated that White's leadership had been compromised by his remarriage and demanded she "take a stand" on it. White persuaded her not to act rashly and to wait until he had a chance to discuss matters with Wilkins. He denied, both to White and to Mrs. Roosevelt, writing such a letter. Mrs. Roosevelt gradually backed away from her accusation against Wilkins when she could not produce the letter in question and after White gently suggested to her that she must be mistaken. In a letter to Wilkins she grudged that the letter "may have been from someone else." To Wilkins, this was a barely acceptable explanation. He was nonplussed, angered even, at what he implied was Mrs. Roosevelt's irresponsibility or duplicity. "[S]he should have it in her files," Wilkins told the board, if it was explosive enough to have caused her to resign; he was "very disturbed over the matter" and said "the implications are not very pleasant ones." [63]

Yet ER remained mostly unapologetic, brushing aside Wilkins's irk. "I am sorry if I did Mr. Wilkins an injustice," she wrote White, but "my files are not in very good shape . . ." She thought she had received the letter from someone with the title of "acting secretary," though, in a comment that surely expressed her slight regard for Wilkins, "the name I would not particularly notice." Then she confessed what she had previously denied: the letter "certainly mentioned the fact that your marriage created a problem for the organization, and that was one of the reasons I felt I should resign." [64]

In the meantime, and in anticipation of White's possible return to the association, William Hastie had since January been chairing a board committee to reorganize the executive staff's responsibilities. Reflecting the close division of the board as a whole, the committee pitched and yawed toward an accommodation of the secretary-on-leave. It endorsed the idea of providing him with an "appropriate job description relevant to national and international public relations functions," wrote board member A. Maceo Smith of Texas confidentially to Roy Wilkins. A substantial number of board members, perhaps a majority, believed that "despite any past indiscreet acts on the part of Walter, he should not be completely sacrificed by the Board." [65]

Wilkins was not pleased by the apparent drift of the board. When White began his leave nearly a year before, Wilkins had been happy to hold his slot until he returned; he had in fact argued with White not to resign. But he quickly developed second thoughts. Wilkins asked his boss not to appear at the 1949 annual conference, fearing that White's presence would undermine his efforts to establish his own authority over the association. By the end of White's leave, Wilkins had become even more pugnacious. He became angry as he read Smith's words, promising a fight should he be denied what he thought was his rightful place in the NAACP. The secretary-on-leave and his supporters were trying to deny him:

> One aspect of this whole situation that has been most distasteful to me and has caused me (for the first time) to become actually angry has been the campaign to discredit me personally, to belittle my hard work and my ac-

tual accomplishments, to say that I am not trustworthy, etc. . . . The purpose, clearly, seems to have been to force me out altogether.[66]

The first order of business at the May board meeting was discussion and adoption of Hastie's proposed reorganization. Its thrust was to create nearly coequal executive positions: an executive secretary responsible for public relations and the appointment of the majority of the junior executive staff, excepting notably the second-in-command, and an administrator accountable for the daily running of the association, including supervision of the national office and oversight of the budget. Although the administrator would be subordinate to the executive secretary on the organization chart, both would report to the board of directors. It was the Hastie committee's clear intention to shear the executive secretary position of much of its authority, and the board adopted the report unanimously.[67]

The board meeting, which endured for more than four hours and from which White and Wilkins were excluded, then turned to the meaty issue of Walter White's return. Despite Hastie's plan to bring White back, a strong contingent of board members opposed White's leadership. Competing motions were introduced: Hubert Delany's that Walter White be appointed executive secretary, and North Carolinian Kelly Alexander's that Roy Wilkins assume that position. The minutes record only that by a vote of 16–10 White was named executive secretary and Wilkins administrator. But the *Afro-American* reported that debate was "hectic and bitter" and the division on the board much closer than the vote indicated. Eleanor Roosevelt led the fight for White, by some accounts threatening to resign should she not prevail. Arthur Spingarn and Alfred Baker Lewis held out until the end for retiring Walter White and elevating Wilkins. But fearing the potential for considerable fallout from her threat, the board decided to bring White back for an encore.[68]

The secretary embraced his reinstallation with an alloy of feelings. His pleasure at continuing his affiliation with the most significant civil rights organization of the day was tempered by his failure to stake his own position in American politics and an inkling that he was settling for second-best. Nor was he sure he could cede power to Wilkins: "Several newspapers, including the Amsterdam News, have asked me if I believe the new arrangement voted by the Board on Monday is workable," he told publicity director Henry Lee Moon. "Quite frankly I have ducked that one, saying that all of us will, of course, do everything possible to make it work." But White fumed when the board demanded that he give up his regular newspaper columns and speaking engagements, upon which the Hastie committee "specifically indicate[d] its disapproval."[69]

White believed this edict was onerous, especially since he wrote on his own time, usually on Sundays. Did the board, he wanted to know, plan to control its paid employees both on and off the job? By any fair standard, he continued, he ought to be allowed to speak to whatever audience he wanted without interference by the board. For more than three decades, he wrote to his friends Hastie, Wright, and Spingarn, he had spent countless overtime hours and weekends speaking for the NAACP, all without additional compensation; he had, he asserted, "devoted not only a full measure of regular office hours to the Association but a few more. . . . I had not thought the time would ever come when I would be forced to point this out to the Board," he lamented.[70]

Inasmuch as the board resolution was directed at him, it was not only a bad decision, but exhibited ingratitude for all he had done for the organization, White said. His journalistic and elocutionary exertions were not for his benefit alone. They resulted in substantial financial contributions to the association from affected readers and listeners and amounted to a public-relations bonanza for the NAACP, which according to a Madison Avenue friend could not have been purchased for less than one million dollars. Likening the NAACP to a business for which he was the most recognizable brand, he related to Hastie that the H. J. Heinz company had a multimillion-dollar advertising budget, but spent an additional substantial sum to keep the eponymous owner in the news "as a public spirited citizen." The company was smart enough to know that showing Heinz's concern for "starving children in Europe" helped to sell beans, and the NAACP board needed to be just as savvy.

More, the board's restrictions seemed to reflect jealousy of his success, he claimed. Rumors persisted that White was becoming wealthy from his extramural activities and was thus diverting most of his attention from the association. He said that several people on the board and the executive staff believed too that he was double-dipping, drawing a payment from the association and from outside sources for the same work. White admitted that his entertainment expense account was unusually large. Over the previous year or two, he had feted foreign dignitaries and American diplomats, bankers, publishers, and editors, and influential persons in Hollywood, but if he derived personal satisfaction from these soirees, a significant collateral effect was interesting his guests in the work of the association. So far as his writing and speaking padding his bank account, that was nonsense, he said. After paying alimony, child support, and Jane's and Pidge's college tuition, $175 remained from his monthly salary. As neither he nor Poppy were independently wealthy, he had to rely on outside income to meet his obligations to his new family.[71]

In one sense, White's umbrage was not only understandable but justified, and the board backed down, striking the restrictions in October. But as so often happens, this squabble about money masked another conflict. The board's plans for reorganization were its reactions to the multiple contusions the secretary had inflicted over the past couple of years. Turning down Walter White's volume was the board's ham-handed way of stoppering his periodic eruptions—like his *Look* article and his controversial stand on the *We Charge Genocide* petition—that were unnecessarily distracting the association. If the secretary was going to continue to neglect his primary job of superintending the NAACP program, the association board, unable for political reasons to get rid of him entirely, would try in other ways to regulate him.

What promised to be a running sore in White's relationship with the association in fact proved to be nothing more than a minor irritant. Rumor had persisted before he was reinstated that he would retire "after being 'vindicated'" at the board meeting to decide his future. This he heatedly denied, as well as the "wishful thinking in [Arthur Spingarn's] statement that I had only six or seven years of active life left."[72] For a moment, it appeared as if the feisty White of old had returned and a period of bruising was in order as he tried to wrest his former authority from the board. But it became swiftly obvious that he no longer had the constitution to be more than the titular head the board intended for him to be.[73]

What White wanted to do was ease into a semiretirement, with the liberty to choose his projects and the option to slough off organizational responsibilities that had become burdensome. He championed Indian friendship, by both lobbying administration and congressional officials on that nation's behalf and hosting visiting officials from the subcontinent. He and Poppy pursued her business interests in the Caribbean, try-ing, for example, to promote Haiti as a filming location for the movie in-dustry and improve its image in the United States.[74]

Only occasionally did he try to meddle in the running of the associa-tion, which, while unwanted, were more annoyance than impediment. Upon Eisenhower's inauguration, Thurgood Marshall began to meet with Herbert Brownell, the new attorney general. It was Marshall's esti-mate, he informed White, that the administration would be responsive to the NAACP legal campaign against segregation in education, which was proceeding apace. To make sure this interaction continued without com-plication, Marshall wrote to White, "I would appreciate that any matters concerning the Department of Justice be referred to this office." White was pleased with Marshall's progress, but he refused to designate Marshall as the point man for relations with the attorney general. "I want to make it clear," was White's reply, that he would talk with Brownell if he wanted to and would advise Marshall of any legal matters that arose in the conversation. White could still exasperate Marshall, but that was about all. The association's legal campaign was on a direct course for *Brown* under Marshall's guidance and without input from White. And when that decision was announced in May 1954, and the aging secretary pushed Marshall aside to monopolize the microphone at the NAACP's press con-ference, Marshall asked White in front of the assembled reporters from which law school he received his degree.[75]

The secretary wore his ceremonial crown with aplomb as he turned increasingly to family and friends for sustenance. He and Poppy were an exceptionally affectionate and devoted couple—to the point, thought White's college-age niece, that they could be oblivious to the needs of Poppy's three teens. At other times, perhaps in an attempt to make amends for his absence while his own children were growing up, White tried to become an involved stepparent. In Poppy's recollections, her hus-band was a presence in the home, dispensing paternal advice especially to her younger daughter, Claudia. He seemed to have a soft spot for her, taking her father to task for his neglect and physical abuse of her. And Claudia Philippe fondly remembers sitting on his lap and taking part in festivities when Eleanor Roosevelt and others visited.[76]

White made the effort not to allow his remarriage to become a reason for an estrangement with his sisters. He patched things up with Helen and Madeline and found a way to bring Poppy and her children into the family fold. If Helen's Christmas 1950 invitation to the still-newlywed Whites was simply a politeness one says after receiving a present, Walter and Poppy took them up on it the following summer, when they visited Atlanta for the NAACP's annual convention. The highlight of the meeting was the presentation of the Spingarn medal to Ralph Bunche, and Helen and Eugene Martin hosted a reception for him and the Walter Whites. One native black Atlantan who was then a teenager remembers his mother—a distant relative of White and very fond of him—going to the affair with the express purpose of laying eyes on Poppy. In 1952, Walter, Poppy and her children, and Madeline spent several weeks vacationing at a villa in Ocho Rios, Jamaica; daughters Cynthia and Claudia then left for home, while Madeline took son Alf to Atlanta for a few weeks to stay with Helen and Eugene Martin, allowing the couple some time alone. They returned the family favor the following year when the Martin family enjoyed the Whites' hospitality while on vacation and Rose Martin moved into the Whites' Manhattan apartment for several months while she settled into a life in New York.[77]

When Arthur Spingarn hurtfully speculated that the secretary had only a half-dozen good years left, White poignantly replied that "I may not live that long; it is also possible . . . that I may have even more than six years. It is my plan and hope to contribute what I can for as long as possible on the basis of the experience and knowledge which I may have acquired." The death of his close friend Charlie Houston, whose punishing regimen drastically shortened his life, weighed upon the secretary, and his relieving himself of administrative duties was his way of avoiding the famed attorney's far too early departure.[78] But White's good years were fewer than he anticipated.

The first signs of decline appeared in 1952. Just after the new year, White's heart acted up, and on Louis Wright's orders he was confined to his home and ordered to rest for more than two weeks. He resumed a tailored schedule, embarking on a West Coast speaking tour for the NAACP in April and attending the Democratic national convention in July. Increasingly, however, these exertions exhausted him, and he spent more time at home presiding over a succession of visitors who came to talk about politics and partake in meals created by Poppy Cannon, now a food writer. Mme. Pandit, Tennessee Senator Estes Kefauver, politically and socially ambitious young men from Africa and Asia, Eleanor Roosevelt, Averell and Pamela Harriman, Clare Booth Luce, and editor Helen Reid of the *Herald-Tribune* were some of the guests. In October, he felt a stab of mortality with the passing of Louis Wright, and he suffered another heart episode, which once more restricted him to bed.[79] It was around this time that he began his last book, *How Far the Promised Land?*, which was to be the final punctuation mark on his more than three decades' fight for civil rights. Further trimming his schedule allowed him more time to think and compose.

The denouement commenced in late 1954. That September he went to Atlantic City to address the national convention of the CIO. Past midnight, he experienced severe chest pain and was admitted to a local hospital. Over the next twenty-four hours he improved, and for a few more weeks he was able to pretend that he was returning to normal. But on Columbus Day, he suffered a severe coronary, which landed him in the hospital for nearly six weeks. White summoned the pluck that had seen him through his extraordinarily perilous lynching investigations. A letter of thanks to the NAACP staff illustrates his characteristic optimism and bonhomie:

> I've been trying to write this note for some time to thank all of you from the bottom of my heart for the cards, letters and other "get well" messages such as the beautiful flowers you've sent. But several things have interrupted. First they've kept me "sedated" to such a degree the dope problem in New York City ought to have been solved this past month—they gave it all to me. . . .
>
> . . . I didn't (and don't yet) have the energy to write each of you individually as I would very much like to do. They tell me I pulled through because I had a "fighting heart"—you folks helped give me that! Last Wednesday was a very wonderful day—I was permitted to "dangle" which means sitting on the side of the bed with my legs on a chair. Today I'm to be allowed to sit in a chair for a few minutes. What a prospect! Some folks want to climb Mount Everest, others to be president. Fine, right now, is to be allowed to walk to the bathroom to clean my teeth, shave, shower, etc, all by myself.[80]

In February 1955, White received word from his friend Mme. Pandit, whose diplomatic posting was now in London, that he and Poppy were the only two Americans officially to be invited to attend the Afro-Asian

Solidarity Conference, in Bandung, Indonesia. As a longtime opponent of colonialism in general and a steadfast proponent of independence for India, one of the prime movers of Bandung, White was anxious to observe firsthand the formation of the nonaligned movement. So much did it mean to him that he was prepared to violate his physicians' orders and make the journey.[81]

But even he must have realized that he could not withstand the rigors of intercontinental travel, and much to his regret he and Poppy declined the invitation. Opting instead for recuperation and rejuvenation, he and Poppy took a vacation—their final trip to the islands of Puerto Rico, Jamaica, and Hispaniola. He did some thinking about the upcoming 1956 elections and how to keep Henry Lee Moon from taking a more lucrative job, and he worked some on *How Far the Promised Land?* But "a combination of inertia caused by the sun and the slower tempo of the tropics, a continuation of the gastric but not, thank goodness, cardiac disturbances which are growing fewer but still wake me up three or four times a night, and engagements which could not be avoided," conspired to keep him from doing much else than rest.[82]

Their monthlong holiday seemed to do the trick, and when they returned, White fulfilled a couple of speaking engagements in Manhattan. But for a few weeks he avoided the office, knowing that the excitement of the place would do his heart no good. He also worked steadily at home on his unfinished manuscript, apparently completing a first draft. After lunch on Monday, March 21, with Poppy's consent, he went to NAACP headquarters—for an hour only, he promised, though he ended up staying until the end of the business day. He returned home electrified at all he had missed in the intervening months. But fatigued by the day, he went to the bedroom to lie down. When Poppy arrived home around 6:30, he eagerly related it all to her: he loved running into the doorman, the elevator operator, and the newspaper vendor after so long an absence; the clerical staff at the office was "swell" and indispensable; he would, after all, attend the Bandung conference in April and would next work on getting the doctors' consent.

Then, spying his book manuscript on the dresser, he apologized to Poppy for the clutter in the bedroom. Walter scooped it up to straighten up the room. While Poppy was in the dressing room to change out of her work clothes, Walter White, final project in hand, collapsed. Within minutes, he was dead.[83]

Chapter 12

"Mr. NAACP" Is Dead:
The Legacy of Walter White

If Walter White's funeral was not an official state affair, it came close in scale and recognition. For two days after his death, his body lay in state at St. Martin's Protestant Episcopal Church in the heart of Harlem; more than a thousand persons filed past the body, which, as the *New York Times* reported, "was laid out in a mahogany coffin, covered with white carnations, before an altar banked with hundreds of floral arrangements." President Eisenhower praised him as a "vigorous champion of justice and equality for all our citizens." Vice President Richard Nixon echoed his boss, adding, in an ironic twist the glad-hander par excellence surely would have appreciated, that he was privileged to know White "not only in his official capacity but also as a personal friend." They were joined in bipartisan mourning by Senators Hubert Humphrey of Minnesota, Leverett Saltonstall of Massachusetts, and Paul H. Douglas of Illinois. The day he was laid to rest, March 24, 1955, 1,800 people filled St. Martin's to capacity as the Reverend John H. Johnson led the services, assisted by an interracial and interdenominational group of eighteen clergymen. An overflow of thousands more lined Harlem's streets.[1]

Those who came to memorialize Walter White reflected, not surprisingly, the milieus he thrived in during his nearly four decades in public life. The civil rights establishment, of course, was foremost, as NAACP board members, leaders of other national organizations, and the distinguished cadre of African American lawyers that White helped to create lined up to say good-bye. Politicians were in evidence: New York Governor and Mrs. Averell Harriman were there, as was Jacob Javits, the state's attorney general and future U.S. senator, and Anna Hedgeman, who represented New York Mayor Robert Wagner and was his top African American advisor. The journalism world made an appearance, including the publishers of the *Pittsburgh Courier* and *New York Herald-Tribune* and the editor of the *Saturday Review*. Stage and screen were represented too, with Oscar Hammerstein II, who was an honorary pallbearer, and film producer Louis de Rochement. Paul Robeson put aside severe political disagreements that had of late estranged him from his longtime friend and joined mourners inside the church, providing more evidence that White's disputes with the left were not particularly over principles. Organized labor showed up in force, with representatives from both the AFL and the CIO and their constituent union.[2]

Ordinary people paid their respects too, as evidenced by the photos of Harlem residents packing their sidewalks and front stoops to hear the services and glimpse the funeral cortege. The major black papers all commented on the multi-class nature of the grievers, though all but one chose to focus exclusively on the luminaries present. The masses' reaction is to be found in a few column inches and sympathy notes in the association's archives. A columnist for the *Afro-American* told of answering the constantly ringing telephone at his desk the night the secretary died. The voice of an elderly woman, who asked whether the news was true, haunted him for "the tiredness, the grief, yes, the forlorn despair" that lingered long after he placed the receiver back on its cradle. That same paper also published "Walter White . . . Man in Street View," which conveyed the regrets of people of various stations in life. A condolence letter, one of many sent to the NAACP, suggests Walter White's impact on the lives of the majority of African Americans. Hallie Hahn, who lived in Kentucky, wrote to Roy Wilkins of how the late secretary saved him. In language that was ungrammatical yet clear, Hahn said he was arrested, beaten, and thrown in jail in 1940. Desperate for help, he wrote to White. As a matter of office routine, White's role in the affair was to deliver the request to the association lawyers, who did the work. But to Hahn, it was Walter White who set him free. Now that he had passed away, Hahn asked, would the NAACP please send him a photograph of the deceased to remember him by?[3]

The black press lionized him, mostly setting aside the controversy that dogged him in his last years and limiting comments about his complexion to his well-known incognito investigations of racial violence. The *Afro-American*, which had been among his fiercest critics, called him a "giant killer." Not only was he the "most energetic" of NAACP leaders, "He can be credited with revising the whole thinking and approach of the NAACP to the question of discrimination." To him the paper attributed an uncompromising opposition to the fallacy of "separate but equal" and an equally steadfast insistence on racial integration, which manifested itself in the association's New Deal and World War II agitation and especially in the legal campaign culminating in the *Brown* decision. Carl Murphy's paper replaced the ignominy it heaped on the living secretary with the accolade in death that "finding a successor to the militant man named White will be no easy task." The *Defender* took exception to comparisons of the late secretary with Booker T. Washington, because whereas the Wizard of Tuskegee was a Negro leader, White "grew to the stature of spokesman, not only for Negroes, but for all Americans who loved justice and for the great majority of the world's peoples who are colored."[4]

National black leaders who, like White, had their own newspaper columns, predictably praised him. Of them all, however, Lester Granger, head of the Urban League, captured not only White's substantial accomplishments, but also the flavor of his personality. "It was a good life that Walter White led, and a good death that claimed him at the end," for "up to the very moment of his death, Walter was doing the job that he loved and believed in—and was doing it in his own way at all times." White was "restless, energetic, 'cocky,' " or, in the words of his friend Louis Wright, "that damned little pony, always prancing around." He was opinionated, vain, and impulsive, and could engage in chicanery with the best. "His cocky aggressiveness stayed with him as long as he lived—as did his boyish vanity—but it was these very qualities that helped to make him the best lobbyist our race has ever produced, and one of the very best of any race."[5]

The most complete inventory of the late secretary's career, however, was—as befitted the master self-promoter—written in his own hand. *How Far the Promised Land?*, published posthumously, is, in the guise of a report on the progress toward the racially just society, a brief for his place in history. His final book assessed many of the vital issues the NAACP tackled during his tenure: education, employment, ending discrimination in the military and in the national defense program, segregation, the franchise, organized labor, communism, and lynching.

The chapter on unions was eyewash. To be fair, White did expose the sordid anti-Negroism of the nineteenth- and early-twentieth-century trade union movement. But he overlooked what he knew firsthand: white workers' role in fomenting much of the most serious urban violence in the years during and after World War I. Left out of the story too was AFL president William Green's extreme reluctance to join forces with the NAACP to fight disfranchisement and lynching in the twenties and thirties. In fact, White lauded the late Green for his "vigorous support for a fair-employment practices law," while applauding his successor for his strong support for civil rights and the abolition of Jim Crowism in his federation.[6] The AFL's practices, as White himself had much earlier exposed, were far more checkered than he here admitted; for much of the campaign for a federal antilynching law the AFL was absent, and it actively opposed provisions in the New Deal labor legislation that would have forbidden discrimination by unions. The CIO was far better on racial discrimination, but it too was far from the Valhalla White portrayed.

White's new spin reflected more the NAACP's cozy post-1948 relationship with the AFL and CIO (and their financial contributions) than the actual historical or contemporary labor movement. For as labor historian and former NAACP labor secretary Herbert Hill has detailed, organized labor, before and after the creation of the AFL-CIO, aggressively continued to discriminate against African American workers even while it tidied its image with donations to NAACP legal campaigns to eliminate segregation in education and Jim Crow public accommodations and transportation.[7]

Likewise, the chapter on blacks and the Communist Party and the prologue, which scores the countries of the socialist camp for what he considered their deliberate distortion of the condition of blacks in the United States, are more genuflections at the cold war altar than an honest rendering of his and the NAACP's differences with the CP over time. Relying heavily on the loaded lexicon of the day, White claimed the Communists were unprincipled sneaks. They were "subservient to Moscow," did what "the Kremlin ordered," and tried to hijack legitimate protest through "various segregated Communist subsidiary organizations . . . wherever . . . the creation of such units" was ordered.[8] He praised organized labor for its expulsion of Communist workers from its ranks, and expressed approval of the NAACP's determination to yank the charter of any branch in which Communists exerted any influence.

Significantly, as White wrote these words he was engaged in just such an act of duplicity of which he accused the Communists. New Dealer and racial equalitarian Aubrey Williams had returned to his native Alabama, there to lead the Southern Conference Education Fund (SCEF—the successor to the Southern Conference on Human Welfare) and publish the *Southern Farmer.* The government's red hunters had labeled practically any antisegregation activist a subversive, and the Senate Internal Security Committee, which was investigating the SCEF, had subpoenaed Williams. Williams asked White for assistance: would he please use his influence with the *New York Times, New York Herald-Tribune,* and *Washington Post* to publicize his fight and help defeat the witch-hunt? "This looks like a direct effort to silence the only group in the South—white— which has worked for abolition of segregation," he pleaded. "The fight for integration will be set back. For you have got to have some white help." White assured him that "we will do everything we can." He then raised the issue with the NAACP staff, which decided not to do anything because of insinuations of Communist participation in the SCEF. More, the staff moved against the Bessemer, Alabama, branch of the NAACP because it publicly resolved to support Williams. Bessemer's backing of the beleaguered New Dealer was, according to secretary of branches Gloster Current, "the first evidence we have had that the Branch is following the [Communist] party line." White had abandoned a friend and former ally for the sake of political expediency.[9]

In fact, White's incarnation as an anticommunist ideologue had been not more than ten years old, and his invective against radicalism in *How Far the Promised Land?* concealed two important facts: first, that he embraced the cold war only under government pressure, and second, that for most of his political career his attitude toward communism had been driven not by faith but by flinty calculation, particularly about money. Even his Communist opponents recognized this and respected it, despite not liking being on the business end of his fillips. The *Daily Worker* published an obituary and an account of the funeral that, because they were based on those from the black press, lauded White's leadership; and in an article describing protests against Jim Crow municipal transportation, columnist Abner Berry prominently praised the late secretary. But nothing illustrates this understanding better than a heartfelt sympathy note from black Communist leader Ben Davis to Roy Wilkins. "Dear Roy," wrote Davis, a native Atlantan and contemporary of White, from the Allegheny (Pennsylvania) County Jail where he was serving a sentence for contempt of court in connection with various Smith Act trials:

> I express my deep personal sorrow at the death of Walter White who made many outstanding contributions to Negro rights in America.
>
> Differences in our political philosophies were well-known. But this does not prevent me from appreciating his talented participation on the front of American democracy.
>
> Do me the courtesy of remembering me to his relatives in Atlanta, and to his immediate family.[10]

But apart from these peccadilloes, *How Far the Promised Land?* records the singular accomplishments of the preeminent civil rights organization during its zenith. The protracted struggle for desegregated and equal education for African Americans is narrated accurately and with relish, as White traced all its rivulets, from the breaking down of professional school barriers to eliminating the salary differential for black teachers to the final decision to attack segregation head-on. Perhaps he was overly optimistic—unwarrantedly so, in retrospect—about the immediate impact of *Brown*, giving a nod of thanks to what he said was a potent group of liberal-minded realists in the white South. This assortment of politicians, evangelical Protestant clergy, journalists, and ordinary citizens did not represent the will of all white southerners, he said. But he anticipated their presence would materially hasten the inevitable desegregation of public education. His generous estimate of the white South, while erroneous, certainly was consistent with his previous attempts, especially during the campaign for a federal antilynching law, to get them on board with the NAACP program. Yet White might be forgiven his untempered enthusiasm. He did, after all, issue his verdict before the Supreme Court handed down its infamous second *Brown* decision, which conjured the phrase *with all deliberate speed* that would guide the white liberal South in its decades-long procrastination of school integration. As the reviewer for the *Journal of Negro History* perceptively put it, "If his reassurances were premature in the light of current turmoil and unrest, they must have been consoling to a fighter who thought that he saw on the wane the evils and wrongs which he fought so relentlessly. That he was in error is not yet certain because the struggles in which White participated continue and their outcomes cannot be predicted."[11]

Chronicled here too is the struggle for the vote. The NAACP had considerable success in this area, with Supreme Court victories outlawing the grandfather clause (1915) and the white primary (1927 and 1944). And in 1930 the association, with White newly anointed as secretary, prevailed over John Parker, President Hoover's Supreme Court nominee who had been an avowed opponent of the franchise for blacks. White saw that access to the ballot was far from assured, especially in Mississippi and elsewhere in the deep South, but in relatively minor advances such as the election of African Americans to school boards in Atlanta, Knoxville, and Augusta, Georgia, and to city councils across North Carolina, White saw the harbinger of black political influence. A particular point of pride was his role in the creation of Truman's commission on civil rights, whose report *To Secure These Rights* called for immediate action to rid the nation of all impediments to the free exercise of the vote. He prized what he said was African Americans' political independence—within the confines, that is, of the Democrats and Republicans, frowning as he did on left and progressive challenges to the main parties—and relished the development of the black vote as the balance of power.

An especial source of satisfaction, White said, was the virtual elimination of lynching. He knew the danger of mob violence had not completely disappeared—as the lynchings of Emmett Till (1955) and Mack Parker (1959) would make amply clear—just as he knew other types of antiblack violence would continue so long as segregation in housing and the color bar in employment persisted. But the days of spectacle violence were gone, owed in large measure to his and the association's Herculean efforts to propagandize and agitate the issue. As he wrote in the final pages of *How Far the Promised Land?*, "as I am finishing this book, something seems to have been left out. It would have been impossible a quarter of a century ago, or, for that matter, a decade ago, to write a book on the status of the American Negro without devoting at least one voluminous chapter to lynching."[12]

The NAACP had earned favorable High Court decisions in other spheres of society as well, including one in 1948 invalidating restrictive covenants that prevented the sale of homes to racial and religious minorities and another in 1944 eliminating segregation on interstate buses. He knew that enforcement of rulings was not guaranteed, just as he could see that the obduracy of the real estate, construction, and banking industries—not to mention all manner of Bourbon politicians and their conservative Republican allies—would likely retard progress on most of the programmatic issues to which he devoted his life. At the same time it is clear he did not expect African Americans still to be fighting these same issues well into the sixties and certainly not into the next century.

For all his faults, African American pundits did not hesitate to call the late secretary a Moses. But like that prophet before him and Martin Luther King Jr. afterward, Walter White did not live to see the land of milk and honey, though he thought that he was able to glimpse it on the horizon. "Fifty years from today," the *Chicago Defender* eulogized White, "when the rivers flowing in the democracies have eddied into every area barren of democracy, men the world over will still be acknowledging Walter White as a poet of freedom, an author of justice." Given his effectiveness as a propagandist and salesman and the considerable record of accomplishment of the NAACP over the nearly forty years he either assisted or led it, this was hardly an outlandish claim, or a sentimental one uttered in grief.[13]

But it was a prediction that was not fulfilled. At some point soon after White's death, NAACP labor secretary Herbert Hill recalled, he realized not only that White was gone but that he was becoming but a dim recollection at association headquarters.[14] As the organization went about its business, Walter White was hardly mentioned at all. As the civil rights movement, that discrete period that he had done so much to usher onto the historical stage, unfolded after the *Brown* decision, White receded still further from memory. In the NAACP, after the expected obsequies, he was reduced to a decennial mention in *The Crisis*. With few exceptions, he was rarely alluded to otherwise. August Meier's and Elliott Rudwick's pathbreaking scholarship on the NAACP, of course, takes measure of White as a civil rights organizer, administrator, and politician. Robert Zangrando's *The NAACP Crusade against Lynching* is indispensable for White's storied career as an investigator and lobbyist. And some studies, most notably David Levering Lewis's *When Harlem Was in Vogue*, have elucidated his literary and cultural-political efforts. White's omission from a standard book in African American history courses, *Black Leaders of the Twentieth Century* (1982), was simply a recognition that scholars had let White slip from view: the editors of this outstanding volume, Meier and John Hope Franklin, had decided to include for scrutiny only those women and men who had already been treated to authoritative study and analysis.

How to account for Walter White's prolonged absence from history's stage, much like a stone dropped in a lake that briefly radiates ripples yet sinks to the bottom? Both immediate and long-term processes conspired to produce his erasure. As Herbert Hill's comments suggest, it is highly likely that Roy Wilkins was anxious to eliminate his former boss as an organizational reference. Wilkins had spent the better part of two decades laboring, frequently uneasily, in White's long shadow. He wanted to consign his predecessor to the museum—the way White did with Joel Spingarn upon his death—and mold the association according to his own image.

If organizational politics was dispatching the late secretary to evanescence, Rosa Parks's defiant act that precipitated the Montgomery bus boycott a little more than eight months after White's death hastened his departure as a guiding spirit. Occurring in the aftermath of the unsatisfactory second *Brown* decision, the boycott initiated direct action as the new strategic phase of the civil rights movement. The organizations that mustered to take part in this new era of civil rights—Martin Luther King's Southern Christian Leadership Conference; the Student Non-Violent Coordinating Committee; the Congress on Racial Equality; maverick branches of the NAACP and NAACP youth councils; and a bevy of local organizations of college and high school students of various states of permanence—were suspicious of the national NAACP's hegemonic tendencies and lacked patience for its strategy of litigation and lobbying, all of which were refined by White or under his supervision.

Generation and politics divided the new wave of activists from the civil rights establishment, of which White was an archetype. Mainly but not exclusively students, they were more apt to remember W.E.B. Du Bois, but even here recollection was likely to be selective. They felt keenly his observations of "double consciousness," knew of his polemics against Booker T. Washington, and perhaps later they familiarized themselves with his Pan-African activities; but they were unlikely to have been conversant with the "Old Man's" leftist sympathies after 1948, largely because these ideas were beyond the pale of the cold war consensus that dominated American politics. And Du Bois would not be able entirely to escape caricature as an elitist concerned only of the fate of the talented tenth. They drew inspiration instead from Gandhi, Niebuhr, and, somewhat later, Malcolm X and African independence movements. Though Dr. King was enormously popular and proclaimed the newest Moses by the U.S. press—this action in itself would have effaced White in the popular consciousness, as the media are loath to project more than one black leader at a time—many of the new activists rejected the installation of a single leader, working instead to develop a plethora of independent and self-reliant local leaders. As a new generation, neither would they allow themselves to be lashed to the mast of old tactics. They preferred to work matters out on their own, according to their own experiences, and as the struggle unfolded.

Of Walter White they had even less ken. As a theorist he was not edifying. If his novels were any longer read, they almost certainly would have been considered passé: a man's inner struggles with gradualism or a light-skinned woman's conflicted decision to pass for white were not considered relevant or fortifying to activists who already made the decision to face jail and mob and police violence to bring down segregation.

Walter White belonged to an earlier era whose activists' initial open-mindedness about strategy and the future organization of society—his expressed admiration of the Soviet experiment in the twenties was more than a pose—was trumped by the exigencies of building a movement for equality during an extended lull in mass activity. Racial violence in the North as well as the South; organized hostility from African Americans' reputed allies in the labor movement; indifference, obtuseness, and betrayal at the hands of white progressive and liberal friends; the collapse of the economy into the Great Depression, all contributed to the paralysis of African Americans in the political arena. He overcame these centrifugal forces with political acumen, the ability to select campaigns that would achieve material results (Judge Parker) or a tangible spike in favorable public opinion (antilynching legislation), outstanding lobbying skills, and an innate gift for schmoozing. He was most comfortable testifying before a congressional hearing he orchestrated or confronting a president in the name of so many hundreds of thousands of members of the NAACP. He was least at home with the prospects of independent mass action, which he almost without exception considered messy, unruly, and likely to harm his—the NAACP's—political influence. Faced with the prospects of a Montgomery bus boycott led by an upstart minister and local NAACP officers Rosa Parks and E. D. Nixon, or the sixties wave of sit-ins, whose most prominent leaders the fractious former NAACP field secretary Ella Baker mentored, White would likely have urged them to stand down and support his efforts to influence the three branches of government and punish recalcitrant legislators at the next general election.

In his deep skepticism, Walter White was not alone; others of his political generation—Thurgood Marshall is an excellent case in point—were just as dismissive of mass action. As head of the NAACP Legal Defense and Education Fund, Marshall paid the bills and put up the bail for civil rights demonstrators, but he resented their actions and publicly disagreed with civil disobedience.[15] In this cohort, Ella Baker was the exception in her ability to switch tactics and embrace new methods of political action as the situation demanded. But then, as a thoroughgoing advocate of intra-organizational democracy, she was a rare presence within the NAACP staff in the forties.

The movement of the sixties secured one victory upon another in its "lunch counter" phase, to use historian and King biographer David Lewis's classic expression, obtaining with the Civil Rights Act of 1964 and the Voting Rights Act of 1965 full formal equality. Alternative voices, which had in fact been present in the forties and fifties, were increasingly being heard within the movement questioning whether this new legal standing was sufficient to eradicate African Americans' oppression. These were once again positing pan-Africanist, nationalist, black power, and socialist solutions. Under these circumstances Walter White, taken as a complete bundle—the Euro-American looks, his inclination toward society's powerful and a strategy of obtaining civil rights by rallying enlightened elites, the passionate belief in integration with a whiff of assimilationism, and even amalgamation—must have seemed positively unredeemable.

Yet at his best, Walter White offered an expansive view of civil rights and an example of dedication and courage in service to the cause. His explosive exposés of lynchings awakened the nation's conscience to eradicate the barbaric practice, and his accompanying parody of the mob and its sympathizers as not only dangerous sociopaths but also ignorant yahoos and the best the Nordic race could produce, helped to dissipate African Americans' fear. The several campaigns he directed or oversaw projected African American political power onto a national stage and forced the political system to reckon with it. He preserved and expanded the single most important civil rights organization of the first half of the twentieth century.

His energy was boundless, his enthusiasm contagious, and apparently it had always been so. He began his adult life in Atlanta selling insurance for the Standard Life Insurance Company, the largest Negro business of its day. He trudged the countryside convincing poor sharecroppers to purchase a patrimony for their children. After a year or so, he moved on to help form a company subsidiary that concentrated on real estate, in which his job was to convince people to invest their money with him. In these endeavors he was marvelously successful. All was in preparation, however, for his switch to the NAACP. Here he sold a policy for the future. He aroused the support of African Americans and drew them into the work of the association, and he sold the American polity and a large part of the public on its compelling program of civil rights and its vision of racial equality.

Notes

ABBREVIATIONS KEY

ABS/LC—Arthur B. Spingarn Papers, Manuscript Division, Library of Congress.

B of D Minutes—Board of Directors Minutes.

ER/mf—Eleanor Roosevelt Papers, on microfilm. Followed by a reel and frame number.

JES/NYPL—Joel E. Spingarn Papers, New York Public Library.

JWJ—James Weldon Johnson.

JWJ/Yale—James Weldon Johnson Papers, Beinecke Rare Books and Manuscript Collection, Yale University, New Haven, Connecticut.

Logan Diary/LC—Rayford Logan Diary, Rayford W. Logan Papers, Manuscript Division, Library of Congress, Washington, D.C.

NAACP/LC—Papers of the National Association for the Advancement of Colored People, Manuscript Division, Library of Congress.

NAACP/mf—Papers of the National Association for the Advancement of Colored People, on microfilm. Followed by part, reel, and frame numbers.

RL/H—Rayford Logan Papers, Moorland-Spingarn Research Center, Howard University, Washington, D.C. Followed by a Roman numeral indicating first or second installation.

WEBD/mf—Papers of W.E.B. Du Bois, on microfilm. Followed by a reel number and in some cases a frame number.

WFW—Walter White.

WFW/PCW—Walter Francis White/Poppy Cannon White Papers, Beinecke Rare Books and Manuscript Collection, Yale University, New Haven, Connecticut.

Chapter 1: BECOMING BLACK

   1. WFW to Channing Tobias, 22 February 1955, NAACP/mf p17 r22 f958.
   2. Roy Wilkins to Carl Johnson, 28 March 1955, NAACP/mf p17 r19 f126.
   3. WFW to Roy Wilkins and Channing Tobias, memo, 21 March 1955, NAACP/mf

p16B r19 f300; the office secretary noted on this memo that it was *"the very last* item dictated by Mr. White."

4. The *New York Times,* 22 March 1955, p. 31.

5. Walter White, *A Man Called White* (New York: Viking, 1948), 240.

6. Walter White, "I Investigate Lynchings," *American Mercury* 16 (January 1929): 77–84; WFW to Carey B. Lewis, 5 November 1919, NAACP/LC I-C-5.

7. Constance Ridley Heslip to WFW (November 1931), NAACP/mf p2 r14 f485.

8. JES to WFW, memo, 10 January 1934, NAACP/mf p11A r30 f200.

9. Rose Palmer, interview by author, 15 January 1998, Atlanta, Georgia; Marie Elizabeth Harrison, handwritten note on family history (1919), Caroline Bond Day Papers, box 3 folder 1, Peabody Museum of Archaeology and Ethnology, Harvard University, Cambridge, Massachusetts; Lucile Bridges, Sarah Lane, Marguerite Spearman, edited by J. R. Jones, "Educational Progress of Negroes in Troup County," n.d. (circa 1930s), typescript, Troup County Archives, La Grange, GA.

10. Information on Joseph Poythress and Augustus Ware is extracted from the 1830, 1840, 1850, and 1860 censuses and compiled in Forrest Clark Johnson III, *People of Ante-Bellum Troup County, Georgia* (La Grange, GA: Sutherland-St. Dunstan Press, 1993), 107, 125, 259, 296, 425.

11. Glenda Majors and Forrest Clark Johnson III, *Treasures of Troup County: A Pictorial History* (La Grange, GA: Troup County Historical Society, 1993), 196.

12. Rose Palmer, interview by author, 15 January 1998, Atlanta, Georgia; Marie Elizabeth Harrison, handwritten note on family history (1919), Caroline Bond Day Papers; Kaye Lanning Minchew (Director of the Troup County [Georgia] Archives) to Kenneth Janken, e-mail, 12 June 1998, in author's possession; Forrest Clark Johnson III (Troup County Historian) to Kenneth Janken, e-mail, 12 June 1998, in author's possession; Augustus C. Ware, last will and testament, 10 August 1870, Troup County Archives, La Grange, GA.

13. "Educational Progress of Negroes in Troup County"; F. Clark Johnson to Kenneth Janken, e-mail, 12 June 1998; *Population schedules of the 9th census of the United States, 1870,* National Archives microfilm publication T, microcopy 593, reel 178, page 232. For a fictional treatment of the issue of concubinage, see Mildred D. Taylor, *The Land* (New York: Dial, 2001).

14. *La Grange (Georgia) Reporter,* 25 September 1879, p. 3; on the critical role of the generational transfer of wealth in the formation of the postbellum African American elite, see Mark R. Schultz, "Interracial Kinship Ties and the Emergence of a Rural Black Middle Class: Hancock County, Georgia, 1865–1920," in *Georgia in Black and White: Explorations in the Race Relations of a Southern State, 1865–1950,* ed. John C. Inscoe (Athens, GA: University of Georgia Press), 141–72.

15. Birth information on George White from *12th census of population, 1900,* National Archives microfilm publication T, microcopy 623 (Washington, D.C.: National Archives and Records Service, 1978?), reel 200, enumeration district 78, sheet number 11.

16. Ridgely Torrence, *The Story of John Hope* (New York: Macmillan, 1948), 54–73; Willard B. Gatewood, *Aristocrats of Color: The Black Elite, 1880–1920* (Bloomington, IN: Indiana University Press, 1993), 90–91. See also Helen Martin, interview by Robert N. Zangrando, 19 March 1975, transcript in author's possession, and also available at Trevor Arnett Library, Atlanta University, Atlanta, Georgia. Martin states that George White's first cousin was Levi White, who was a close friend of John Hope.

17. Karen L. Jefferson (Archivist, Atlanta University Center) to Kenneth Janken, e-mail, 15 July 1998, in author's possession, citing White's listing in the catalogue of the normal and preparatory departments of Atlanta University for 1874 through 1879; Helen Matthews (Reference Librarian, Atlanta History Center) to Kenneth Janken, 8 June

1998, in author's possession, citing George White's appearance in the Atlanta city directories, 1881–1899.

18. *A Man Called White*, 13–14; Kaye Lanning Minchew (Director of the Troup County [Georgia] Archives) to Kenneth Janken, e-mail, 12 June 1998, in author's possession; *Treasures of Troup County*, 76.

19. August Meier and David Lewis, "History of the Negro Upper Class in Atlanta, Georgia, 1890–1958," in August Meier, *A White Scholar and the Black Community, 1945–1965: Essays and Reflections* (Amherst, MA: University of Massachusetts Press, 1992), 103.

20. Homer C. McEwen, Sr., "First Congregational Church, Atlanta," *Atlanta Historical Society Bulletin* 21 (Spring 1977): 129–42; C. T. Wright, "The Development of Public Schools for Blacks in Atlanta, 1872–1900," *Atlanta Historical Society Bulletin* 21 (Spring 1977): 115–28; Kathleen Redding Adams Interview, *Black Women Oral History Project*, vol. 1 (Westport, CT: Meckler, 1991), 143–44.

21. Edwina Ford, interview by author, 28 January 1998, Savannah, Georgia.

22. Kathleen Redding Adams interview, *Black Women Oral History Project*, 1:144–45.

23. Michael Leroy Porter, "Black Atlanta: An Interdisciplinary Study of Blacks on the East Side of Atlanta, 1890–1930" (Ph.D. diss., Emory University, 1974), 89, 177 (Lucy Rucker Aiken quote); Helen Matthews (Reference Librarian, Atlanta History Center) to Kenneth Janken, 8 June 1998, in author's possession, citing George White's appearance in the Atlanta city directories, 1881–1899.

24. Porter, "Black Atlanta," 89, 92 (Jordan quote); *A Man Called White*, 5.

25. Kathleen Redding Adams interview, *Black Women Oral History Project*, 1:134; Rose Palmer to Kenneth Janken, 5 June 1998, in author's possession.

26. Kathleen Redding Adams interview, *Black Women Oral History Project*, 1:132; Rose Palmer interview.

27. Wright, "The Development of Public Schools for Blacks in Atlanta," 120–25.

28. Edwina Ford, interview by author; Helen Martin, interview by Robert Zangrando; Rose Palmer to author, 6 February 1998, in author's possession.

29. WFW to Eleanor Roosevelt, 28 July 1940, ER/mf r19 f657.

30. *A Man Called White*, 19–20.

31. The Rucker Sisters interview, *Black Women Oral History Project*, 8:281–82; Rose Palmer to Kenneth Janken, 5 June 1998, in author's possession.

32. *A Man Called White*, 21–22; Rose Palmer to Kenneth Janken, 5 June 1998.

33. Rose Palmer to Kenneth Janken, 5 June 1998; Kathleen Adams interview, "Living Atlanta" collection, Atlanta History Center, Atlanta, GA; Porter, "Black Atlanta," 20–22 (Amos quote on 20).

34. For accounts of the riot, see Charles Crowe, "Racial Massacre in Atlanta, September 22, 1906," *Journal of Negro History* 54 (1969): 150–73; Gregory Mixon, " 'Good Negro—Bad Negro': The Dynamics of Race and Class in Atlanta during the Era of the 1906 Riot," *Georgia Historical Quarterly* 81 (1997): 593–621; David Fort Godshalk, "In the wake of riot: Atlanta's struggle for order, 1899–1919" (Ph.D. diss., Yale University, 1992) 8–59; and Mark Bauerlein, *Negrophobia: A Race Riot in Atlanta, 1906* (San Francisco: Encounter Books, 2001).

35. This paragraph and the next draw heavily upon Gregory Lamont Mixon, "The Atlanta Riot of 1906" (Ph.D. diss., University of Cincinnati, 1989).

36. Tera W. Hunter, *To 'Joy My Freedom: Southern Black Women's Lives and Labors after the Civil War* (Cambridge: Harvard University Press, 1997); Lawrence C. Goodwyn, "Populist Dreams and Negro Rights: East Texas as a Case Study," *American Historical Review* 76 (1971): 1435–56; Lawrence C. Goodwyn, *Democratic Promise: The Populist Movement in America* (New York: Oxford University Press, 1976), 276–306.

37. On the Atlanta Compromise, see Louis R. Harlan, *Booker T. Washington: The Making of a Black Leader, 1856–1901* (New York: Oxford University Press, 1975), 204–28.

38. *Atlanta Journal*, 1 August 1906, cited in *A Man Called White*, 8.
39. *Atlanta Georgian*, 25 August 1906, cited in Godshalk, "In the wake of riot," 64; on how modernization exacerbated white racial animosoties, see Godshalk, "In the wake of riot," 60–66, and Dominic J. Capeci, Jr., *The Lynching of Cleo Wright* (Lexington, KY: University Press of Kentucky, 1998), 3–6, 10–12.
40. Godshalk, "In the wake of riot," 410–11; on Jim Crow racial etiquette, see Neil McMillan, *Dark Journey: Black Mississippians in the Age of Jim Crow* (Urbana, IL: University of Illinois Press, 1990), 23–28; *A Man Called White*, 11.
41. The Rucker Sisters Interview, *Black Women Oral History Project*, 8:283–85; David Levering Lewis, *W.E.B. Du Bois: Biography of a Race, 1868–1919* (New York: Henry Holt, 1993), 335; Ridgley Torrence, *The Story of John Hope* (New York: Macmillan, 1948), 153; Helen Martin, interview with Michael Leroy Porter, 30 March 1973, in Porter, "Black Atlanta," 17.
42. Walter White, *Flight* (New York: Knopf, 1926; reprinted Baton Rouge: Louisiana State University Press, 1998), 77–78.
43. On New Orleans's Creole society, see Willard B. Gatewood, *Aristocrats of Color: The Black Elite, 1880–1920* (Bloomington, IN: Indiana University Press, 1993), 82–89.
44. White, *Flight*, 74–77 ("there flashed through her mind . . . ," 74; "Mimi dated . . . her consciousness . . . ," 77).
45. *12th census of population, 1900*, National Archives microfilm publication T, microcopy 623 (Washington, D.C.: National Archives and Records Service, 1978?), reel 200, enumeration district 78, sheet number 11; Dr. Alexa Henderson and Dr. Eugene Walker, *Sweet Auburn: The Thriving Hub of Black Atlanta, 1900–1960* ([Atlanta]: U.S. Department of the Interior/National Park Service, [1984]), 9–10; Rose Palmer to Kenneth Janken, 5 June 1998.
46. *A Man Called White*, 10–12.
47. WFW to William Aspinwall Bradley, 2 February 1927, NAACP/mf p2 r10 f559.
48. Heywood Broun, "It Seems to Heywood Broun," *The Nation*, 21 May 1930, p. 591.
49. Alice Glenn to WFW, 1 October 1930, NAACP/mf p2 r13 f180.
50. WFW, untitled manuscript, 6 September 1934, NAACP/mf p11B r35 f832.
51. WFW to Madeline White, 8 September 1934, NAACP/mf p2 r17 f22.
52. WFW to Madeline White, 26 September 1934, NAACP/mf p2 r17 f57.
53. Madeline White to WFW, telegram 1 October 1934, NAACP/mf p2 r17 f102.
54. WFW to Madeline White, 3 October 1934, NAACP/mf p2 r17 f101. Helen Martin, Walter's younger sister, remembered the assault on their home in a way that involved no shooting by anyone: "I was about seven or eight years old. My father was a mail carrier, and he had a horse and buggy for transportation purposes. Walter would go with him to distribute the mail. They were coming home on that night when someone yelled out, 'Let's get that White nigger.' My father and Walter stood guard of our two-story home, from two windows within the house. The mob came down Houston Street and started in our gate. However, they saw a man with an ice wagon, and they decided to go and chase him. The man ran and hid under a house and stayed there all night. The next day the man told my father about it." Porter, "Black Atlanta," 17.
55. See Keven K. Gaines, *Uplifting the Race* (Chapel Hill: University of North Carolina Press, 1996), for a discussion of how the black elite lay claim to the race's humanity with a defense of the gender hierarchy.
56. Walter White, "Why I Remain a Negro," *The Saturday Review of Literature*, 11 October 1947, 13–14, 49–52.
57. L. B. Palmer to WFW, 25 January 1925, NAACP/mf p2 r8 f558.
58. Kathleen Redding Adams Interview, *Black Women Oral History Project*, 1:143–44.
59. The Rucker Sisters Interview, *Black Women Oral History Project*, 8:279.
60. Edwina Ford, interview by author.

61. Clarence A. Bacote, *The Story of Atlanta University: A Century of Service, 1865–1965* (Atlanta: Atlanta University, 1969), 239; Rucker Sisters interview, *Black Women Oral History Project*, 8:277, 279; Kathleen Redding Adams interview, *Black Women Oral History Project*, 1:138.

62. *A Man Called White*, 27.

63. Walter F. White's cumulative transcript, Atlanta University, copy in author's possession.

64. Frank Bell to WFW, 10 October 1930, NAACP/mf p2 r13 f333; Bacote, *The Story of Atlanta University*, 220–26 (quote is on 223).

65. *A Man Called White*, 26.

66. Bacote, *The Story of Atlanta University*, 213, 251; Kathleen Redding Adams interview, *Black Women Oral History Project*, 1:142.

67. Nancy MacLean, "The Leo Frank Case Reconsidered: Gender and Sexual Politics in the Making of Reactionary Populism," *Journal of American History* 78 (1991): 917–48.

68. *A Man Called White*, 28.

69. WFW to W.E.B. Du Bois, 7 September 1915, NAACP/mf p12A r9 f599; May Childs Nerney to WFW, 13 September 1915, NAACP/mf p12A r9 f598.

70. WFW to Roy Nash, 3 February 1917, cited in Edgar A. Toppin, "Walter White and the Atlanta NAACP's Fight for Equal Schools, 1916–1917," *History of Education Quarterly* 7 (1967): 8–9.

71. Ronald H. Bayor, *Race and the Shaping of Twentieth-Century Atlanta* (Chapel Hill: University of North Carolina Press, 1996), 199–202.

72. Bazoline Usher, quoted in Clifford M. Kuhn, Harlon E. Joyce, and E. Bernard West, *Living Atlanta: An Oral History of the City, 1914–1948* (Athens, GA: University of Georgia Press, 1990), 130.

73. WFW to Roy Nash, 16 December 1916, NAACP/mf p12A r9 f602.

74. Elliott Rudwick and August Meier, "The Rise of the Black Secretariat in the NAACP, 1909–35," in August Meier and Elliott Rudwick, *Along the Color Line: Explorations in the Black Experience* (Urbana, IL: University of Illinois Press, 1976), 104–105; Lewis, *W.E.B. Du Bois: Biography of a Race, 1868–1919*, 500.

75. JWJ to WFW, 21 December 1916, NAACP/mf p12A r9 f601; WFW to JWJ, 5 January 1917 [incorrectly dated 1916], NAACP/mf p12A r9 f592; JWJ to WFW 9 January 1917, WFW/PCW box 3 folder 105; James Weldon Johnson, *Along This Way: The Autobiography of James Weldon Johnson*, with an introduction by Sondra Kathryn Wilson (New York: Viking, 1933; rpt. New York: Penguin, 1990), 316.

76. WFW to JWJ, 22 February 1917 (first of two letters to JWJ of that date), NAACP/mf p12A r9 f588; WFW, first draft of statement on Lorenzo King's candidacy for House of Representatives, 20 October 1938, NAACP/mf p11B r24 f753.

77. WFW to JWJ, 22 February 1917 (first letter), NAACP/mf p12A r9 f588; WFW to Roy Nash, 3 March 1917, NAACP/mf p12A r9 f661 ("representatives of the best"); the Atlanta branch's memorial to the school board was published on the front page of the *Atlanta Independent*, 24 February 1917.

78. WFW to Roy Nash, 3 March 1917, NAACP/mf p12A r9 f661; WFW to JWJ, 22 February 1917 (second letter), NAACP/mf p12A r9 f590.

79. WFW to Roy Nash, 19 March 1917, NAACP/mf p12A r9 f630; WFW to JWJ, 27 March 1917, NAACP/mf p12A r9 f618.

80. WFW to Roy Nash, 19 March 1917, NAACP/mf p12A r9 f630; Atlanta Branch [probably written by WFW] to members, [March 1917], NAACP/mf p12A r9 f665.

81. WFW, "How the Double Sessions Do Injustice to Negro Population," letter to editor, *Atlanta Constitution*, 28 September 1917, p. 8.

82. Toppin, "Walter White and the Atlanta NAACP's Fight for Equal Schools," 13–15; WFW to JWJ, 27 September 1917, NAACP/mf p12A r9 f667; the *Atlanta Independent*,

10 February 1917, lends credence to White's view of the clergy, criticizing the city's black ministers for not supporting the NAACP campaign to preserve seventh grade.

83. Bayor, *Race and the Shaping of Twentieth Century Atlanta*, 202–205; Toppin, "Walter White and the Atlanta NAACP's Fight for Equal Schools," 15–16; *A Man Called White*, 33.

84. WFW to Roy Nash, 3 March 1917; JWJ, 22 February 1917 (first letter) ("other measures" and "Sounds big"); *A Man Called White*, 34. See the *Atlanta Independent*, 24 March 1917, for a report on Johnson's speech.

85. Johnson, *Along This Way*, 316.

86. JWJ to WFW, 7 October [1917], WFW/PCW box 3 folder 105.

87. WFW to Roy Nash, 9 May 1917, NAACP/mf p12A r9 f644.

88. *Atlanta Independent*, 22 April 1916.

89. Johnson, *Along This Way*, 316–17.

90. WFW to JWJ, 10 October 1917, WFW/PCW box 3 folder 105; JWJ to WFW, 15 December 1917, 6 January 1918, 15 January 1918, all in WFW/PCW box 3 folder 105; White's concerns about the draft were contained in a letter to Johnson dated 9 January 1918 and no longer extant, but which were alluded to in Johnson's letter of 15 January 1918.

91. JWJ to WFW, 15 January 1918, WFW/PCW box 3 folder 105.

92. WFW to Edgar Webster, 26 March 1931, NAACP/mf p2 r13 f530.

Chapter 2: WITNESS FOR THE PROSECUTION

1. Robert L. Zangrando, *The NAACP Crusade against Lynching, 1909–1950* (Philadelphia: Temple University Press, 1980), 26–31, 35.

2. Walter White, *A Man Called White* (New York: Viking, 1948), 40.

3. John R. Shillady to William English Walling, 19 July 1918, NAACP/mf p1 r23 f246.

4. WFW to John R. Shillady, 18 February 1918, NAACP/mf p7A r17 f821.

5. WFW to John R. Shillady, 18 February 1918, NAACP/mf p7A r17 f821.

6. Walter White, "The Burning of Jim McIlherron: An N.A.A.C.P. Investigation," *The Crisis*, May 1918, pp. 16–20.

7. Walter White, *Rope and Faggot: A Biography of Judge Lynch*, with a new introduction by Kenneth Robert Janken (New York: Knopf, 1929; reprinted Notre Dame, Indiana: University of Notre Dame Press, 2001), 40–53, 245–50.

8. White, "The Burning of Jim McIlherron."

9. White, "The Burning of Jim McIlherron."

10. WFW to Editor, *Cheyenne State Leader*, 20 February 1919, NAACP/mf p7A r1 f1343.

11. Walter White, "The Work of a Mob," *The Crisis*, September 1918, pp. 221–23.

12. White, "The Work of a Mob."

13. White, "The Work of a Mob"; WFW to C. P. Dam, memo, 19 November 1918, NAACP/mf p7A r10 f1140.

14. WFW to John R. Shillady, 9 July 1918, NAACP/mf p12A r9 f695.

15. WFW to John R. Shillady, telegram, 11 July 1918, NAACP/mf p12A r9 f697; Shillady to Mary White Ovington, 16 July 1918, NAACP/mf p1 r23 f244; Shillady to William English Walling, 19 July 1918, NAACP/mf p1 r23 f246; Shillady to WFW, 17 October 1918, NAACP/mf p10 r23 f187.

16. Summary of antilynching press coverage (January 1919), NAACP/mf p7A r1 f805; Zangrando, *The NAACP Crusade against Lynching*, 40; "Brief Summary of Anti-Lynching Work," *The Crisis*, February 1919, p. 182–84.

17. David Levering Lewis, *W.E.B. Du Bois: Biography of a Race, 1868–1919* (New York: Henry Holt, 1993), 536–37; W.E.B. Du Bois, "The Black Man and the Unions," *The Crisis*, March 1918, pp. 216–17.

18. On the Commission on Interracial Cooperation, see John Egerton, *Speak Now against*

the Day: The Generation before the Civil Rights Movement in the South (New York: Knopf, 1994; Chapel Hill: University of North Carolina Press, 1995), 47–51.

19. Zangrando, *The NAACP Crusade against Lynching*, 31.
20. Bolton Smith to W. R. Manier [secretary of the Commercial Club of Nashville], 12 March 1918, NAACP/mf p7A r1 f856 (first and second problems created by lynching). Many African American elites would have been otherwise predisposed to combating what they perceived as criminal—or at least immoral—activity among the lower classes. See Kevin K. Gaines, *Uplifting the Race* (Chapel Hill: University of North Carolina Press, 1996), 1–17, 152–78; Evelyn Brooks Higginbotham, *Righteous Discontent* (Cambridge: Harvard University Press, 1993), 185–229. Bolton Smith, article appearing in *Public*, reprinted in *The Crisis*, November 1918, pp. 26–27 (third problem created by lynching). Bolton Smith to John R. Shillady, cited in WFW to Shillady (June 1918), NAACP/mf p7A r1 f1024 ("jolly, care-free, and good natured").
21. James Hardy Dillard, letter to the editor, *New York Times*, 13 April 1919; Dillard to John R. Shillady, 3 July 1919, NAACP/mf p7A r2 f72; WFW, handwritten reply on Shillady to WFW, memo, 21 April 1919, NAACP/mf p7A r2 f69; WFW to JWJ, 15 April 1919, NAACP/mf p7A r2 f70.
22. George Chamlee "Is Lynching Ever Defensible?" *The Forum* 76 (1926): 811–17; James Weldon Johnson, "Letter to Editor," *The Forum* 77 (1927): 308–309; WFW to John R. Shillady, 17 January 1919, NAACP/mf p1 r24 f452; Bolton Smith to L. C. Dyer, 4 June 1918, NAACP/mf p7A r1 f1022.
23. John R. Shillady to William English Walling, 19 July 1918, NACP/mf p1 r23 f246.
24. WFW to John R. Shillady, 12 November 1918, NAACP/mf p7A r10 f1138; B of D Minutes, 9 December 1918, NAACP/mf p1 r1 f856.
25. C. P. Dam to Senator Knute Nelson, 20 November 1918, NAACP/mf p7A r1 f1145.
26. C. P. Dam to John R. Shillady, 16 November 1918, NAACP/mf p7A r10 f1136.
27. C. P. Dam to John R. Shillady, 16 November 1918, NAACP/mf p7A r10 f1136; WFW to C. P. Dam, memo, 19 November 1918, NAACP/mf p7A r10 f1140; WFW to John R. Shillady, memo, 12 November 1918, NAACP/mf p7A r10 f1138.
28. John R. Shillady to C. P. Dam, 19 December 1918, NAACP/mf p7A r10 f1157; Shillady to Archibald Grimke, 19 December 1918, NAACP/mf p7A r10 f1156; [Shillady] to Anti-Lynching Committee, memo, 7 May 1918, NAACP/mf p1 r23 f241.
29. C. P. Dam to John R. Shillady, 16 November 1918, NAACP/mf p7A r10 f1136.
30. C. P. Dam to John R. Shillady, 24 December 1918, NAACP/mf p7A r10 f1153.
31. Zangrando, *The NAACP Crusade against Lynching*, 45.
32. On "work or fight" and other forms of labor coercion see Gerald E. Shenk, "Race, Manhood, and Manpower: Mobilizing Rural Georgia for World War I," *Georgia Historical Quarterly* 81 (1997): 622–62; William Cohen, "Negro Involuntary Servitude in the South, 1865–1940: A Preliminary Analysis," *Journal of Southern History* 42 (1976): 31–60; Tera Hunter, *To 'Joy My Freedom: Southern Black Women's Lives and Labors after the Civil War* (Cambridge: Harvard University Press, 1997), 227–31. On African American entertainment locations and the crackdown on them, see Shenk; Hunter, chapters 7 and 8; and Gregory Mixon, " 'Good Negro–Bad Negro': The Dynamics of Race and Class in Atlanta during the Era of the 1906 Riot," *Georgia Historical Quarterly* 81 (1997): 593–621.
33. WFW to R. R. Church, 2 October 1918, NAACP/mf p10 r23 f157; WFW to A. L. Lewis [of Jacksonville, FL], 4 October 1918, NAACP/mf p10 r23 f159.
34. WFW to John R. Shillady, [17?] October 1918, NAACP/mf p10 r23 f190; see Albion Holsey to WFW, 10 July 1923, NAACP/mf p11B r30 f360, for an example of the relationship between the two.
35. WFW to John R. Shillady, [17?] October 1918, NAACP/mf p10 r23 f190; Ann. Bus. Mtg. Minutes, 6 January 1919, NAACP/mf p1 r4 f19.

36. WFW to John R. Shillady, 26 October 1918, NAACP/mf p10 r23 f194; Walter F. White, " 'Work or Fight' in the South," *The New Republic* 18 (1919): 144–46; an expanded version of this article is at NAACP/mf p10 r23 f283.

37. WFW to John R. Shillady, 14 November 1918, NAACP/mf p10 r23 f226.

38. WFW to John R. Shillady, 26 October 1918, NAACP/mf p10 r23 f194.

39. White, " 'Work or Fight' in the South"; WFW to John R. Shillady, 16 November 1918, NAACP/mf p10 r23 f231.

40. WFW to John R. Shillady, 14 November 1918, NAACP/mf p10 r23 f226; Ann. Bus. Mtg. Minutes, 6 January 1919, NAACP/mf p1 r4 f19.

41. WFW to John R. Shillady, 20 January 1919, NAACP/mf p7A r13 f1182.

42. WFW to John R. Shillady, 20 January 1919, NAACP/mf p7A r13 f1182; Report of the Special Investigator [WFW], 29 January 1919, NAACP/mf p7A r1 f1302; WFW, "An Example of Democracy," (February or March 1919), NAACP/mf p7A r1 f1350.

43. WFW to JWJ, 17 January 1919, NAACP/mf p1 r24 f452.

44. WFW to John R. Shillady, 20 January 1919, NAACP/mf p7A r13 f 1182; WFW to JWJ, 22 January 1919, NAACP/mf p7A r17 f1002.

45. [WFW], draft article on Tuscumbia County, Alabama, lynchings, NAACP/mf p1 r24 f454; an edited version appeared as "18 Indicted for Alabama Lynchings Finally Escape," *New York Evening Post*, 19 February 1919. John R. Shillady to Moorfield Storey, 15 February 1919, NAACP/mf p1 r23 f268.

46. WFW to Mary White Ovington, 30 July 1919, NAACP/mf p1 r24 f473.

47. WFW, speech to the annual conference of the NAACP, 28 June 1919, NAACP/mf p1 r8 f705.

48. *The Crisis*, November 1919, p. 339, in *A Documentary History of the Negro People in the United States*, volume 3 *1910–32*, ed. Herbert Aptheker (New York: Citadel Press, 1993), 278–79.

49. Walter F. White, "Chicago and Its Eight Reasons," *The Crisis*, September 1919, 293–97.

50. James R. Grossman, *Land of Hope: Chicago, Black Southerners, and the Great Migration* (Chicago: University of Chicago Press, 1988), 208–22; for the characterizations of unions as white job trusts, see Herbert Hill, "Lichtenstein's Fictions Revisited: Race and the New Labor History," *New Politics*, n.s. 7 (1999): 148–63.

51. William M. Tuttle, Jr., *Race Riot: Chicago in the Red Summer of 1919* (New York: Atheneum, 1985), 163, 173–74, 179–80; White, "Chicago and Its Eight Reasons."

52. Tuttle, *Race Riot: Chicago in the Red Summer of 1919*, 3–10, 32–66; Arthur I. Waskow, *From Race Riot to Sit-In, 1919 and the 1960s* (Garden City, NY: Doubleday & Co., 1966), 38–59; Herbert Shapiro, *White Violence and Black Response* (Amherst: University of Massachusetts Press 1988), 150–52.

53. Grossman, *Land of Hope*, 222–23.

54. WFW to Mary White Ovington, 7 August 1919, NAACP/mf p1 r24 f474.

55. *A Man Called White*, 45.

56. Christopher Robert Reed, *The Chicago NAACP and the Rise of Black Professional Leadership, 1910–1960* (Bloomington: Indiana University Press, 1997), 15, 32–34, 37–41, 45–47; Grossman, *Land of Hope*, 161.

57. WFW to Mary White Ovington, 7 August 1919, NAACP/mf p1 r24 f474.

58. Herbert J. Seligmann, "Report of the Activities of the National Office Re: Washington and Chicago," 14 August 1919 [excerpts and summary notes], John R. Shillady to Mary White Ovington, 4 August 1919 [copy]. Both of these documents were generously provided the author by Professor Michael Homel of Eastern Michigan University, with the gracious permission from Professor William R. Tuttle, Jr., of Kansas University, from whose research papers they come.

59. WFW to Mary White Ovington, 7 August 1919, NAACP/mf p1 r24 f474.

60. WFW to Mary White Ovington, 13 August 1919, NAACP/mf p1 r24 f476.

61. WFW to Mary White Ovington, 11 August 1919, NAACP/mf p1 r24 f475.

62. WFW to Mary White Ovington, 11 August 1919, NAACP/mf p1 r24 f475; WFW to Ovington, 13 August 1919, NAACP/mf p1 r24 f476; WFW to Ovington, 21 August 1919 [Home]; WFW to John R. Shillady, 26 August 1919, [Home]; WFW, "Memorandum re: Chicago Riots Situation," 8 September 1919, [Home].

63. John R. Shillady to Mary White Ovington, 20 August 1919, copy, in author's possession, from Michael Homel; Lewis, *W.E.B. Du Bois: Biography of a Race, 1868–1919*, 395–98, 402; Patricia A. Schechter, *Ida B. Wells-Barnett & American Social Reform, 1880–1930* (Chapel Hill: University of North Carolina Press, 2001), 4, 106–107, and chap. 4 passim. For more on White's disposition toward Wells-Barnett, see chapter 4 below.

64. Waskow, *From Race Riot to Sit-In*, 48, 50.

65. This summary is based upon Walter F. White, "Finds No 'Massacre Plot' in Arkansas," *Chicago Daily News*, 18 October 1919; Walter F. White, " 'Massacring Whites' in Arkansas," *The Nation*, 6 December 1919, 715–16; Walter F. White, "The Race Conflict in Arkansas," *Survey*, 13 December 1919, 233–34, in *A Documentary History of the Negro People in the United States*, volume III, 279–82; Waskow, *From Race Riot to Sit-In*, 121–42; Richard C. Cortner, *A Mob Intent on Death* (Middletown, CT: Wesleyan University Press, 1988), 5–23; and Grif Stockley, *Blood in Their Eyes: The Elaine Race Massacres of 1919* (Fayetteville: University of Arkansas Press, 2001).

66. Walter F. White, "Finds No 'Massacre Plot' in Arkansas," *Chicago Daily News*, 18 October 1919; Walter F. White, " 'Massacring Whites' in Arkansas," *The Nation*, 6 December 1919, 715–16 [quote].

67. Walter F. White, " 'Massacring Whites' in Arkansas"; Cortner, *A Mob Intent on Death*, 154.

68. WFW to John R. Shillady, 7 October 1919, Arthur I. Waskow Papers, State Historical Society of Wisconsin, Madison, Wisconsin. Most of the NAACP materials concerning the investigation of the Arkansas riot have been lost; however, Arthur Waskow, in preparation of his *From Race Riot to Sit-In, 1919 and the 1960s*, made copies of much of the correspondence and deposited this material in this archive.

69. WFW to Robert T. Scott (secretary to Attorney General Palmer), 9 October 1919, Waskow Papers.

70. *A Man Called White*, 49–50.

71. *A Man Called White*, 50–51.

72. WFW to Charles E. Bentley, 24 October 1919, Waskow Papers.

73. Anonymous [probably Walter White], report to *The Crisis*, no date, Waskow Papers. Here White contradicts his statement in *A Man Called White* that he talked to no African Americans in Helena. See *A Man Called White*, 50. Grif Stockley believes that White spent only a few hours in Helena (having gathered most of his information from the state capital of Little Rock). Stockley, *Blood in Their Eyes*, 98.

74. Walter White, "I Investigate Lynchings," *The American Mercury* 16 (1929): 77–84.

75. W. H. King to WFW, 25 November 1919, Waskow Papers; WFW to Carey B. Lewis, 5 November 1919, NAACP/LC I-C-5. In this letter to Lewis, White says, "In this particular instance, my sole success in the south was due to the fact that the persons whom I interviewed were of the opinion that I was not a colored man. By changing the wording in this story you have greatly jeopardized my own personal safety on future trips."

76. Cortner, *A Mob Intent on Death*, 1–2.

77. Secy. Monthly Report, 9 July 1923, NAACP/mf p1 r4 f405.

78. B of D Minutes, 10 November 1919, NAACP/mf p1 r1 f732; B of D Minutes, 11 October 1920, NAACP/mf p1 r1 f793; B of D Minutes, 12 October 1923, NAACP/mf

p1 r1 f976; Field Secy. Monthly Report, 3 March 1920, NAACP/mf p1 r4 f73; Secy. Monthly Report, 6 January 1921, NAACP/mf p1 r4 f129; Secy. Monthly Report, 9 May 1923, NAACP/mf p1 r4 f383; Cortner, *A Mob Intent on Death*, 106–30.
79. B of D Minutes, 12 January 1920, NAACP/mf p1 r1 f756.

Chapter 3: AMBITIONS
1. Secy. Monthly Rpt., 5 May 1920, NAACP/mf p1 r4 f85.
2. James Weldon Johnson, *Along This Way* (New York: Penguin, 1990), 343–44, 353–54, 356–57 (quote); Charles Flint Kellog, *NAACP: A History of the National Association for the Advancement of Colored People*, I, *1909–1920* (Baltimore: The Johns Hopkins Press, 1967), 245–46. Johnson's observation of Shillady's abundant moral courage but absence of physical courage refers to Shillady's encounter with a mob in Texas in the summer of 1919. Most accounts of this incident state that he was beaten on a main business thoroughfare in the capital of Austin when he tried to meet with the governor concerning the state's attempt to keep the NAACP out. But Arthur Spingarn disputed this account. Shillady had not faced the mob, Spingarn was certain; rather he was a "coward" who had fled. It was guilt rather than emotional trauma from a beating that led Shillady to resign as association secretary, an action that cleared the way for James Weldon Johnson to assume the leadership position. See Arthur Spingarn Oral History, 6 March 1968, Ralph J. Bunche Oral History Project, Moorland-Spingarn Research Center, Howard University, Washington, D.C.
3. Tentative program for NAACP conference, NAACP/mf p1 r8 f842; see also press release in advance of the conference, 18 May 1920, NAACP/mf p1 r8 f843, and press release, 12 June 1920, NAACP/mf p1 r8 f845, which summarized the conference.
4. Walter F. White, "Election by Terror in Florida," *The New Republic*, 12 January 1921, pp. 195–97.
5. WFW, summary of statements by witnesses of election day violence in Ocoee, Florida, n.d. [November 1920], NAACP/mf p11B r4 f708.
6. White, "Election by Terror in Florida."
7. Secy. Monthly Rpt., 8 December 1920, NAACP/mf p1 r4 f117.
8. Congress, House, Committee on the Census, *Hearings on H.R. 14498, H.R. 15021, H.R. 15158, and H.R. 15217 before the Committee on the Census*, 66th Cong., 3rd sess., 29 December 1920, 37–42.
9. *Hearings on H.R. 14498, H.R. 15021, H.R. 15158, and H.R. 15217 before the Committee on the Census*, 42–67.
10. *Hearings on H.R. 14498, H.R. 15021, H.R. 15158, and H.R. 15217 before the Committee on the Census*, 68–79.
11. B of D minutes, 10 January 1921, NAACP/mf p1 r1 f811.
12. N. B. Young to JWJ, 7 January 1921, NAACP/mf p11B r4 f894.
13. B of D minutes, 10 January 1921, NAACP/mf p1 r1 f811.
14. Secy. Monthly Rpt., 9 June 1921, *In Search of Democracy: The NAACP Writings of James Weldon Johnson, Walter White, and Roy Wilkins (1920–1977)*, ed. Sondra Kathryn Wilson (New York: Oxford University Press, 1999), 27.
15. Walter F. White, "The Eruption of Tulsa," *The Nation*, 29 June 1921, 909–910. The following account of the riot also draws upon Scott Ellsworth, *Death in the Promised Land: The Tulsa Race Riot of 1921*, foreword by John Hope Franklin (Baton Rouge: Louisiana State University Press, 1982), chap. 3. See also "Final Report of the Oklahoma Commission to Study the Tulsa Race Riot of 1921," 28 February 2001 (available at http://www.ok-history.mus.ok.us/trrc/freport.htm, accessed 14 January 2002).
16. *Washington Bee*, 10 June 1921.
17. W.E.B. Du Bois, "The Negro and Radical Thought," *The Crisis*, July 1921, 102–104,

Du Bois, "The Class Struggle," *The Crisis*, August 1921, 151–52, Du Bois, "Socialism and the Negro," *The Crisis*, October 1921, 245–47.

18. On the Pan-African Congress movement see Kenneth Robert Janken, *Rayford W. Logan and the Dilemma of the African-American Intellectual* (Amherst: University of Massachusetts Press, 1993), 47–61; Kenneth R. Janken, "African American and Francophone Black Intellectuals During the Harlem Renaissance," *The Historian* 60 (1998): 487–505; and David Levering Lewis, *W.E.B. Du Bois: The Fight for Equality and the American Century, 1919–1963* (New York: Henry Holt, 2000), chap. 2.

19. Universal Tour Company to W.E.B. Du Bois, 7 July 1921, NAACP/mf p11B r18 f124.

20. WFW to JWJ, 13 August 1921, NAACP/mf p11B r18 f260.

21. W.E.B. Du Bois to John Harris, 26 May 1921, WEBD/mf r9; Jessie Fauset, "Impressions of the Second Pan-African Congress," *The Crisis*, November 1921, 12.

22. John Harris to W.E.B. Du Bois, 6 May 1921, 10 June 1921, Du Bois to Harris, 8 July 1921, WEBD/mf r9; Wm. Roger Louis, "Great Britain and the African Peace Settlement of 1919," *American Historical Review* 71 (1966): 875–92; Paul B. Rich, *Race and Empire in British Politics* (Cambridge: Cambridge University Press, 1986), 37–41.

23. W.E.B. Du Bois to John Harris, 8 July 1921, WEBD/mf r9; WFW to Du Bois [August 1921], WEBD/mf r10.

24. WFW to JWJ, 28 August 1921, NAACP/mf p11B r18 f275 (quote); *A Man Called White*, 61.

25. W.E.B. Du Bois, "To the World (Manifesto of the Second Pan-African Congress)," *The Crisis*, November 1921, 5–10.

26. Fauset, "Impressions of the Second Pan-African Congress."

27. WFW to JWJ, 12 September 1921, NAACP/mf p11B r18 f282.

28. WFW to Board of Directors, 17 October 1921, NAACP/mf p1 r4 f208.

29. WFW to Mary White Ovington, 15 September 1921, NAACP/mf p11B r18 f285 ("elderly colored gentleman"), WFW to Board of Directors, 17 October 1921, NAACP/mf p1 r4 f208.

30. WFW to Mary White Ovington, 15 September 1921, NAACP/mf p11B r18 f285 ("cannibalistic orgy"), WFW to Board of Directors, 17 October 1921, NAACP/mf p1 r4 f208 ("proper persons" and "wrong angle"), *A Man Called White*, 61–62. White's prejudices are confirmed in a plea to Moorfield Storey to encourage his close friend, the philanthropist George Peabody, to resume his financial contributions to the NAACP. Peabody had been an annual donor, but recently became discouraged. It seems that he employed black labor in his home and encouraged his friends to do likewise; their labor was not satisfactory, and he thought they stole from him. Walter begged Peabody not to damn an entire race based on "migrants who had come north from states where they had always been denied even the simplest of human rights." WFW to Moorfield Storey, 5 December 1921, NAACP/mf p1 r24 f545.

31. JWJ to WFW, 26 September 1921, NAACP/mf p11B r18 f307 (quote), JWJ to WFW, 9 September 1921, NAACP/mf p11B r18 f278.

32. Mary White Ovington to Joel Spingarn, 11 January 1922, JES/NYPL box 9 folder 2.

33. Mabel Smith interview by author, 15 July 1997, New York City, recording and notes in author's possession.

34. Jane White Viazzi, interview by author, 18 July 1997, New York City, recording and notes in author's possession.

35. Eugene Levy, *James Weldon Johnson: Black Leader, Black Voice* (Chicago: University of Chicago Press, 1973), 239–43; Elliott Rudwick and August Meier, "The Rise of the Black Secretariat in the NAACP, 1909–35," August Meier and Elliott Rudwick, *Along the Color Line* (Urbana: University of Illinois Press, 1976), 94–127, esp. 111.

36. WFW to Bishop John Hurst, 25 November 1921, quoted in Levy, *James Weldon Johnson*, 246 ("treachery"); JWJ to WFW, 4 January 1922, NAACP/mf p1 r17 f393. When

the battle for Dyer ended, White had this to say about black opposition: "I share with you complete disgust at many of the venal Negro politicians whose souls can be bought for a few dollars. Right now, the NAACP and most of us as individuals are going through a campaign of calumny of the vilest sort. Every despicable method is being used to lie to the public but we do not have any fears—in the first place, we have kept the record of the NAACP absolutely clean (in marked contrast to some of our opponents) and as long as people see as straight as you do, we don't have any fears. If the great masses of colored people were of such a sort that they would believe the things which are being said and, worse, believe in those who will sell out the race for personal gain, then they don't deserve an organization like the NAACP." WFW to Frank Bell, 26 December 1924, NAACP/mf p2 r8 f389.

37. Levy, *James Weldon Johnson*, 247–48.
38. Secy. Monthly Rpt., February 1922, *In Search of Democracy: The NAACP Writings of James Weldon Johnson, Walter White, and Roy Wilkins (1920–1977)*, ed. Sondra Kathryn Wilson (New York: Oxford University Press, 1999), 42–43.
39. Secy. Monthly Rept., 31 July 1922, NAACP/mf p1 r4 f297, Secy. Monthly Rept., 6 April 1922, NAACP/mf p1 r4 f266, Secy. Monthly Rept., 11 November 1922, NAACP/mf p1 r4 f324, WFW to Moorfield Storey, 21 August 1922, NAACP/mf p1 r24 f575.
40. WFW to Moorfield Storey, 29 November 1922, NAACP/mf p1 r24 f599 ("unfortunately the Negro vote"); for another postelection analysis, see WFW to Nathan Strauss, Jr., 11 November 1922, NAACP/mf p11B r19 f873, in which he discusses the factors that "make efforts as yet to educate the colored people of [parts of Manhattan] out of their blindness and senseless allegiance to the Republican Party abortive ones." Levy, *James Weldon Johnson*, 258–61.
41. Ronald H. Bayor, *Race and the Shaping of Twentieth Century Atlanta* (Chapel Hill: University of North Carolina Press, 1996), 53–58.
42. WFW to JWJ, 16 September 1925, NAACP/mf p5 r2 f943; Sidney Fine, *Frank Murphy: The Detroit Years* (Ann Arbor: University of Michigan Press, 1975), 146–47.
43. WFW to JWJ, 16 September 1925, NAACP/mf p5 r2 f943; Sidney Fine, *Frank Murphy: The Detroit Years* (Ann Arbor: University of Michigan Press, 1975), 148–51; Moses L. Walker to JWJ, 12 September 1925, NAACP/mf p5 r2 f931.
44. Moses L. Walker to JWJ, 12 September 1925, NAACP/mf p5 r2 f931; B of D Minutes, 14 September 1925, NAACP/mf p1 r2 f42.
45. *A Man Called White*, 74; WFW to JWJ, 17 September 1925, NAACP/mf p5 r2 f1031.
46. WFW to JWJ, 16 September 1925, NAACP/mf p5 r2 f943; *Detroit Free Press*, 16 September 1925, clipping in NAACP/mf p5 r2 f942; W.E.B. Du Bois, "The Challenge of Detroit," *The Crisis*, November 1925, 7.
47. WFW, undated handwritten note, NAACP/mf p5 r2 f960.
48. WFW to JWJ, 16 September 1925, NAACP/mf p5 r2 f943; Richard Kluger, *Simple Justice* (New York: Vintage: 1977), 125–31.
49. *Pittsburgh Courier*, 31 October 1925, in NAACP/mf p5 r2 f1023; WFW to Oscar W. Baker, 25 October 1925, NAACP/mf p5 r2 f1115.
50. WFW to Mose Walker, 21 September 1925, NAACP/mf p5 r2 f1055.
51. WFW and Arthur Spingarn, memo, NAACP/mf p5 r2 f1097; Otis Sweet and others to W.E.B. Du Bois, 29 September 1925, NAACP/mf p5 r2 f1088.
52. JWJ to Clarence Darrow, telegram, 7 October 1925, NAACP/mf p5 r2 f1137; WFW to JWJ, telegram, 14 October 1925, NAACP/mf p5 r2 f1183.
53. Arthur Garfield Hays, "NAACP Legal Victories and Civil Liberties," speech to the annual convention of the NAACP, 20 June 1940, Philadelphia, Pennsylvania, NAACP/mf p1 r10 f997.
54. Mose Walker to WFW, 27 October 1925, NAACP/mf p5 r3 f26; WFW to JWJ [31

October 1925], NAACP/mf p5 r3 f64 ("asked me to have luncheon" and "He's eating out of my hand"); WFW to JWJ, 7 November 1925, NAACP/mf p5 r3 f65 ("My flimsy connection").

55. WFW to JWJ, 7 November 1925, NAACP/mf p5 r3 f65; WFW to JWJ, 9 November 1925, NAACP/mf p5 r3 f71; B of D minutes, 9 November 1925, NAACP/mf p1 r2 f52; *The Crisis*, February 1926, 187.

56. *The Crisis*, February 1926, 185; WFW to Ira Jayne, 22 October 1925, NAACP/mf p3 f2 ("solves our problems"); WFW to JWJ, 13 November 1925, NAACP/mf p5 r3 f82 ("the very worst thing"); WFW to JWJ, 1 February 1926, NAACP/mf p5 r3 f427; WFW to Arthur Spingarn, 16 December 1925, NAACP/mf p5 r3 f288.

57. Robert Bagnall to JWJ, 18 February 1926, NAACP/mf p5 r3 f447; WFW, memo, 18 February 1926, NAACP/mf p5 r3 f451; JWJ to Mose Walker, 20 February 1926, NAACP/mf p5 r3 f452.

58. W.E.B. Du Bois, "The Reward," *The Crisis*, February 1926, 166; Andrew Buni, *Robert L. Vann of the* Pittsburgh Courier: *Politics and Black Journalism* (Pittsburgh, PA: University of Pittsburgh Press, 1974), 149–61; Lewis, *W.E.B. Du Bois: The Fight for Equality and the American Century*, 212–14.

59. Jane White Viazzi, interview by author, 18 July 1997, New York City, recording and notes in author's possession; WFW to Jane and Pidge, 1 August 1934, NAACP/mf p2 r16 f716; WFW to Jane and Pidge, 7 August 1934, NAACP/mf p2 r16 f717.

60. WFW to Bessie Stillman, 9 October 1925, NAACP/mf p2 r9 f238 ("considerable financial sacrifices"); B of D Minutes, 14 January 1924, NAACP/mf p1 r1 f992; B of D Minutes, 8 December 1924, NAACP/mf p1 r1 f1049; WFW to John B. Nail, 31 January 1927, NAACP/mf p2 r10 f547; Jane White Viazzi, interview by author, 18 July 1997.

61. Two examples of the largesse bestowed upon him are the use of Mary White Ovington's summer cottage "Riverbank" and Smith College president Ralph Harlow's inviting White and his family to spend the summer at his home in western Massachusetts. See Jane White Viazzi, interview by author, 18 July 1997, New York City.

62. See, for example, Alice Glenn to WFW, 6 April 1926, NAACP/mf p2 r9 f665; George White (father) to WFW, 6 April 1925, NAACP/mf p2 r8 f687; Alice Glenn to WFW, 21 June 1926, NAACP/mf p2 r10 f178; WFW to parents, 14 May 1927, NAACP/mf p2 r10 f726; Alonzo Glenn to WFW, 7 December 1926, NAACP/mf p2 r10 f451; WFW to Alonzo Glenn, 14 December 1926, NAACP/mf p2 r10 f450.

63. George White (brother) to WFW, 30 October 1924, NAACP/mf p2 r8 f211.

64. John M. Barry, *Rising Tide: The Great Mississippi Flood of 1927 and How It Changed America* (New York: Simon & Schuster, 1997), 312–13. My recounting of the 1927 flood follows Barry's, which also was my starting point for the relevant primary documents in the Herbert Hoover Papers, cited below.

65. Barry, *Rising Tide*, 307–11.

66. B of D Minutes, 9 May 1927, NAACP/mf p1 r2 f143; WFW to JWJ, 17 May 1927, NAACP/mf p1 r24 f697; WFW to JWJ, 16 May 1927, NAACP/mf p1 r24 f695.

67. WFW, "The Negro and the Flood," NAACP/mf p10 r13 f491.

68. WFW, "The Negro and the Flood," NAACP/mf p10 r13 f491.

69. WFW to Herbert Hoover, 14 June 1927, Herbert Hoover Papers, Commerce Papers subgroup, Mississippi Valley Flood-Relief Work, Telegrams—Office & Akerson, 1927 June–July and undated, Herbert Hoover Library, West Branch, Iowa.

70. Will Irwin to Laurence Richey, quoted in Richey to George Akerson, telegram, 9 June 1927, Herbert Hoover Papers, Commerce papers subgroup, Mississippi Valley Flood-Relief Work, Telegrams—Office & Akerson, 1927 June–July and undated, Herbert Hoover Library, West Branch, Iowa.

71. Herbert Hoover to WFW, 21 June 1927, Hoover papers, Commerce Papers subgroup,

Mississippi Valley Flood-Relief Work Negroes ("no responsibility" and list of committee members); Hoover to Will Irwin, 10 June 1927, Hoover papers, Commerce Papers subgroup, Mississippi Valley Flood-Relief Work Negroes ("appointed a general investigative committee.")

72. Associated Negro Press release, 14 June 1927, Hoover papers, Commerce Papers subgroup, Mississippi Valley Flood-Relief Work Negroes; Claude Barnett to Herbert Hoover, 10 June 1927, Hoover papers, Commerce Papers subgroup, Mississippi Valley Flood-Relief Work Negroes 1927 June 1–15; Barry, *Rising Tide*, 388–91.

73. WFW to Ruby Edwards, 27 May 1927, NAACP/mf p2 r11 f37.

74. Louis Marshall, speech to the NAACP annual business meeting, 2 January 1927, NAACP/mf p1 r13 f870.

75. Poppy Cannon, tape-recorded interview by David Levering Lewis, March 1970, Voices from the Renaissance Collection, 1974–1977, Schomburg Center for Research in Black Culture, New York Public Library, New York, New York.

76. WFW to Roland Hayes, 2 December 1924, NAACP/mf p2 r8 f304.

77. WFW to Roland Hayes, 4 December 1924, NAACP/mf p2 r8 f320 ("bitterness or venom"); WFW to Hayes, 13 December 1924, NAACP/mf p2 r8 f351 ("different field of literature"); Hayes to WFW, 18 December 1924, NAACP/mf p2 r8 f375.

78. WFW to Sinclair Lewis, 20 October 1926, NAACP/mf p2 r10 f337; Joel Spingarn to WFW, 23 October 1926, NAACP/mf p2 r10 f371.

79. Joel Spingarn to Amy Spingarn, 22 November 1926, Joel E. Spingarn papers, collection 95, box 15 folder 584, Moorland-Spingarn Research Center, Howard University, Washington, D.C. Thanks much to David Levering Lewis for sharing with me this most remarkable document.

80. L. B. Palmer to WFW, 25 January 1925, NAACP/mf p2 r8 f558; N. B. Young to WFW, 22 December 1925, NAACP/mf p2 r9 f376; Mary Talbert to WFW, 25 July 1921, NAACP/mf p11B r18 f208. For Talbert's antilynching activities, see Rosalyn Terborg-Penn, "African-American Women's Networks in the Anti-Lynching Crusade," in *Gender, Class, Race, and Reform in the Progressive Era*, eds. Noralee Frankel and Nancy S. Dye (Lexington, KY: University Press of Kentucky, 1991), 157–58.

81. WFW to L. B. Palmer, 18 February 1925, NAACP/mf p2 r8 f558.

82. Anna Strunsky to Louis Kaplan, 30 June 1962, William English Walling papers, reel 2 frame 59–66 (quotes on frame 61–63), State Historical Society of Wisconsin, Madison, Wisconsin, microfilm. Many thanks to Leon Fink, now of the University of Illinois, Chicago, for making me aware of this revealing document.

83. Bishop John Hurst to WFW, 31 March 1927, NAACP/mf p2 r10 f686.

84. WFW to Henry Allen Moe, 10 March 1927, NAACP/mf p2 r10 f636; WFW to Carl Roberts, 12 May 1927, NAACP/mf p2 r11 f23; WFW to George White, 20 June 1927, NAACP/mf p2 r11 f55; WFW to Sinclair Lewis, 6 July 1920, NAACP/mf p2 r11 f64.

Chapter 4: SOCIALIZING AND CIVIL RIGHTS IN THE
HARLEM RENAISSANCE

1. Alain Locke, "The New Negro," *The New Negro*, ed. Alain Locke (New York: Albert & Charles Boni, 1925; repr., New York: Atheneum, 1992), 3; Langston Hughes, "The Negro Artist and the Racial Mountain," *The Nation*, 26 June 1926, in *The Portable Harlem Renaissance Reader*, ed. David Levering Lewis (New York: Penguin, 1995), 95.

2. JWJ to WFW, 13 April 1923, NAACP/mf p2 r7 f364. David Levering Lewis, *When Harlem Was in Vogue* (New York: Vintage, 1982). Scholarship on the Harlem Renaissance is voluminous, but some useful works are Thadious Davis, *Nella Larsen, Novelist of the Harlem Renaissance* (Baton Rouge: Louisiana State University Press, 1994); Arnold Rampersad, *The Life of Langston Hughes* I, *1902–1941: I, Too Sing America* (New York: Oxford University Press, 1986); Cheryl A. Wall, *Women of the Harlem Renaissance*

(Bloomington, IN: Indiana University Press, 1995); Nathan I. Huggins, *The Harlem Renaissance* (New York: Oxford University Press, 1971); George Hutchinson, *The Harlem Renaissance in Black and White* (Cambridge: Harvard University Press, 1995); Langston Hughes, *The Big Sea* (New York: Knopf, 1940); James Weldon Johnson, *Black Manhattan* (New York: Viking, 1930); Sheila Tully Boyle and Andrew Bunie, *Paul Robeson: The Years of Promise and Achievement* (Amherst, Mass.: University of Massachusetts Press, 2001).

3. David Levering Lewis, introduction to *The Portable Harlem Renaissance Reader*, xlii.
4. WFW to F. E. DeFrantz, 10 March 1923, NAACP/mf p2 r7 f356.
5. Alain Locke to WFW, 10 March 1923, NAACP/mf p2 r7 f360.
6. Alain Locke to WFW, memo (10 March 1923), NAACP/mf p7 f366 ("something in the nature" and "opinion that no foundation"; Locke to WFW, 10 March 1923, NAACP/mf p2 r7 f360 ("by men of the race").
7. WFW to Herman Lieber, 28 January 1924, NAACP/mf p2 r7 f525; Lieber to WFW, 26 February 1924, NAACP/mf p2 r7 f528.
8. Alain Locke to WFW (January 1924), NAACP/mf p2 r7 f522; WFW to William Stuart Nelson, 15 January 1924, NAACP/mf p2 r7 f503; WFW to Locke, 28 January 1924, NAACP/mf p2 r7 f525; WFW to Locke, 7 April 1924, NAACP/mf p2 r7 f573; WFW to Locke, 9 April 1924, NAACP/mf p2 r7 f577; Roger Baldwin to WFW, 29 May 1924, NAACP/mf p2 r7 f641.
9. "Aaron Douglass Chats about the Harlem Renaissance," in *The Portable Harlem Renaissance Reader*, 119; Langston Hughes, *The Big Sea* (New York: Knopf, 1940; repr., New York: Hill & Wang, 1993), 228 ("ordinary Negroes"), 227 ("It was a period").
10. Charles S. Johnson, "The Negro Renaissance and Its Significance," in *The Portable Harlem Renaissance Reader*, 214 ("one of the most significant").
11. David Levering Lewis, *When Harlem Was in Vogue*, 93–94 (*Opportunity* dinner program); WFW to Albert Barnes, 24 March 1924, NAACP/mf p2 r7 f570 (seating arrangements); Charles S. Johnson to WFW, 26 March 1924, NAACP/mf p2 r7 f581 ("shown itself in frequent"); Johnson, "The Negro Renaissance and Its Significance," 215 ("as soon as he finished"); WFW to Countee Cullen, 14 April 1924, NAACP/mf p2 r7 f592, WFW to Carl Van Doren, 16 April 1924, NAACP/mf p2 r7 f594, WFW to Horace Liveright, 25 April 1924, NAACP/mf p2 r7 f599, Liveright to WFW, 2 May 1924, NAACP/mf p2 r7 f601, WFW to Cullen 3 May 1924, NAACP/mf p2 r7 f602 (on White's promotion of Cullen's poetry). Walter White was remarkably consistent about what ought to be most important to the New Negro author. Five years after being introduced at the first *Opportunity* dinner, he spoke before an audience at the Harlem branch of the New York Public Library on "Where Is Negro Literature Going?" He expressed some concern that novelists were restricting themselves to a few dominant themes, including passing, "very nice" colored people, and lowlifes, and he once again called on black authors to cease pandering to white stereotypes. But he had no objection "to dirt if done well." Doing it well was the challenge. At the same time, and contrary to Du Bois's insistence, "Publishers will bring out Negro novels not devoted to rent parties, seductions, gin orgies, prostitutes,—if books are good enough." WFW, notes to lecture on "Where Is Negro Literature Going?" 27 February 1929, NAACP/mf p2 r15 f12.
12. Arthur Spingarn to Joel Spingarn, 6 April 1924, JES/NYPL box 13 no folder number.
13. WFW to Moorfield Storey, 26 October 1921, NAACP/mf p1 r24 f542; B of D minutes, 11 February 1924, NAACP/mf p1 r1 f1000.
14. WFW to Miguel Covarrubias, 2 March 1931, NAACP/mf p2 r13 f448.
15. Arthur Spingarn Oral History, 6 March 1968, Ralph J. Bunche Oral History Project, Moorland-Spingarn Research Center, Howard University, Washington, D.C. (on Studin's parties). On Poppy Cannon's early life, see Cynthia White, telephone inter-

view with author, 19 October 2000, notes in author's possession; Cynthia White (née Cannon) is Poppy Cannon's daughter. On Poppy Cannon's and Walter White's early relationship, see Poppy Cannon, tape-recorded interview by David Levering Lewis, March 1970, Voices from the Renaissance Collection, 1974–1977, Schomburg Center for Research in Black Culture, New York Public Library, New York, New York; Poppy Cannon to Gladys White, Monday (June 1936), NAACP/mf p2 r15 f309; WFW to Poppy Cannon, 30 June 1932, NAACP/mf p2 r15 f308; WFW to Madeline White, 15 March 1934, NAACP/mf p2 r16 f516; and Poppy Cannon, *A Gentle Knight: My Husband Walter White* (New York: Rinehart & Co., 1956), 3–9.

16. Jane White Viazzi, interview by author, 18 July 1997, New York City, recording and notes in author's possession.

17. WFW to Roland Hayes, 5 January 1925, NAACP/mf p2 r8 f421.

18. WFW to Sinclair Lewis, 8 October 1925, NAACP/mf p2 r9 f234.

19. WFW to Aline and Arthur Garfield Hays, 2 January 1926, NAACP/mf p2 r9 f392.

20. WFW to Carl Van Doren, 26 January 1924, NAACP/mf p2 r9 f478, White to Alain Locke, 28 January 1924, NAACP/mf p2 r7 f525, Konrad Bercovici to White, 28 January 1924, NAACP/mf p2 r7 f531; WFW to Bercovici, 29 January 1924, NAACP/mf p2 r7 f530.

21. Oswald Garrison Villard to WFW, 28 October 1925, NAACP/mf p2 r9 f297.

22. WFW to Rudolph Fisher, 12 March 1925, NAACP/mf p2 r8 f624 ("writing about Negro life").

23. WFW to H. L. Mencken, 22 November 1920, NAACP/mf p2 r7 f326. See also Charles Scruggs, *The Sage in Harlem: H. L. Mencken and the Black Writers of the 1920s* (Baltimore: The Johns Hopkins University Press, 1984).

24. David Levering Lewis, *When Harlem Was in Vogue*, 87–88.

25. W.E.B. Du Bois, "The Criteria of Negro Art" (1926), in *The Portable Harlem Renaissance Reader*, 103, 104.

26. WFW to Carl Van Doren (14 December 1923), NAACP/mf p2 r7 f471 ("artstically"); H. L. Mencken, quoted in Fred Hobson, *Mencken: A Life* (New York: Random House, 1994), 142 ("well fed"); James Weldon Johnson, preface to the original edition of *The Book of American Negro Poetry*, ed. James Weldon Johnson, rev. ed. (New York: Harcourt, Brace & World, 1931), 21–22. Mencken's editorial orientation quoted here was stated for *Smart Set*, the publication he edited before *American Mercury*, which emulated its predecessor.

27. WFW to Carl Van Doren (14 December 1923), NAACP/mf p2 r7 f471; Van Doren to WFW, 18 December 1923, NAACP/mf p2 r7 f476.

28. WFW to Albert Barnes, 24 March 1924, NAACP/mf p2 r7 f570 ("meagre"); Barnes to WFW, 25 March 1924, NAACP/mf p2 r7 f571; Barnes to WFW, 11 April 1924, NAACP/mf p2 r7 f586 ("cheap"). On Barnes and the Harlem Renaissance, see George Hutchinson, *The Harlem Renaissance in Black and White*, 45–46, 185, 425–27; *The Barnes Bond Connection*, ed. Niara Sudarkasa (Lincoln University, PA: Lincoln University Press, 1995).

29. WFW to Rudolph Fisher, 3 February 1925, NAACP/mf p2 r8 f499; WFW to Fisher, 5 February 1925, NAACP/mf p2 r8 f515 ("I was talking with him").

30. WFW to Fisher, 12 March 1925, NAACP/mf p2 r8 f624. As the career of Roland Hayes (discussed shortly) demonstrates, White did not limit his assistance to writers, and he strived to help virtual unknowns. In 1924 Carl Van Vechten alerted his friend White of the Sabbath Glee Club of Richmond, Virginia; Van Vechten had heard no other group sing spirituals so well. White immediately contacted the Victor Talking Machine Company to see if it had an interest in recording the club. More, upon hearing of discord among glee-club members, he asked Maggie Walker, the Richmond businesswoman and founder of that city's largest African American bank, to

intervene; whatever differences might exist, White told Walker, they were insignificant compared to the recognition that sponsorship by Van Vechten was sure to bring. See WFW to Victor Talking Machine Company, 23 September 1924, NAACP/mf p2 r8 f93; WFW to Walker, 23 September 1924, NAACP/mf p2 r8 f95; WFW to E. T. King, 7 October 1924, NAACP/mf p2 r8 f146; WFW to Walker, 7 October 1924, NAACP/mf p2 r8 f146; WFW to Julia Sully, 7 October 1924, NAACP/mf p2 r8 f147. On the history of the Sabbath Glee Club, see Sully to WFW 18 October 1924, NAACP/mf p2 r8 f159.

31. Hubert H. Harrison, "White People versus Negroes," *Negro World,* 7 January 1922; Claude McKay to WFW, 3 February 1922, NAACP/mf p2 r7 f350 ("NAACP crowd"); McKay to Hubert Harrison, 7 January 1922, NAACP/mf p2 r7 f351 ("lionized at lunch" and "pseudo-intellectuals"); WFW to McKay, 6 February 1922, NAACP/mf p2 r7 f350.

32. McKay to WFW, 8 July 1923, NAACP/mf p2 r7 f403.

33. McKay to WFW, 4 December 1924, NAACP/mf p2 r8 f525; McKay to WFW (4 August 1925), NAACP/mf p2 r9 f178; McKay to WFW, 7 September 1925, NAACP/mf p2 r9 f193; WFW to McKay, 25 September 1925, NAACP/mf p2 r9 f220; McKay to WFW, 25 November 1925, NAACP/mf p2 r9 f319; WFW to Joel Spingarn, 24 January 1924, NAACP/mf p2 r7 f513; WFW to Arthur Spingarn, 24 January 1924, NAACP/mf p2 r7 f517; WFW to McKay, 26 January 1924, NAACP/mf p2 r7 f519; WFW to McKay, 20 May 1925, NAACP/mf p2 r9 f21; WFW to Viking Press, 22 May 1925, NAACP/mf p2 r9 f29; McKay to WFW, 15 June 1925, NAACP/mf p2 r9 f74; WFW to McKay, 28 August 1925, NAACP/mf p2 r9 f178; Max Eastman to McKay, undated ("bourgeois philanthropist" and "very hard person to help"), enclosed in McKay to Joel Spingarn, 18 December 1934, McKay to Spingarn, 24 December 1934, McKay to Spingarn, 12 March 1937, all in JES/NYPL box 7 folder 1.

34. Claude McKay to Joel Spingarn, 9 January 1917, JES/NYPL box 7 folder 1.

35. WFW to McKay, 6 November 1924, NAACP/mf p2 r8 f230; McKay to WFW, 4 December 1924, NAACP/mf p2 r8 f325.

36. McKay to WFW, 7 September 1925, NAACP/mf p2 r9 f193 ("make himself the instrument"); McKay to WFW, 4 August 1925, NAACP/mf p2 r9 f179 ("that the white literati"); McKay to Arthur Schomburg, 17 July 1925, quoted in David Levering Lewis, *When Harlem Was in Vogue,* 141 ("that may run contrary").

37. WFW to McKay, 20 May 1925, NAACP/mf p2 r9 f21 (all quotes in paragraph); WFW to McKay, 28 August 1925, NAACP/mf p2 r9 f178

38. WFW to George Judd, 11 January 1924, NAACP/mf p2 r7 f500; WFW to Roland Hayes, 21 January 1924, NAACP/mf p2 r7 f512 ("I do not know").

39. WFW to Roland Hayes, 13 June 1924, NAACP/mf p2 r7 f654; see also Allen Keiler, *Marian Anderson* (New York: Scribner, 2000), 60–61. For information on Jules Bledsoe's stage and film career, see *Dictionary of American Negro Biography,* s.v. "Bledsoe, Jule [Julius, Jules]," by Raymond Lemeiux.

40. WFW to Sol Hurok, 26 May 1925, NAACP/mf p2 r9 f43; see also WFW to Hurok, 29 May 1925, NAACP/mf p2 r9 f48.

41. Julius Bledsoe to Sol Hurok, [n.d.], NAACP/mf p2 r9 f100; WFW to Arthur Spingarn, 28 September 1925, NAACP/mf p2 r9 f266.

42. WFW to NAACP Board of Directors, memo, 8 December 1938, NAACP/mf p11A r7 f191 ("From what we know"); WFW to Hubert Delany, 9 December 1938, NAACP/mf p11A r7 f198. See also Keiler, *Marian Anderson,* 256–60.

43. *A Man Called White,* 66. See also, WFW to Claude McKay, 15 August 1924, NAACP/mf p2 r7, f721.

44. Walter White, *The Fire in the Flint,* foreword by R. Baxter Miller (Athens: University of Georgia Press, 1996), 28.

45. Ibid., 53, 46 ("Jus' do like your daddy . . . ," 53; "the Booker T. Washington nostrum . . . ," 46).

46. Ibid., 279, 295 ("You've murdered my brother . . . ," 279; ". . . before I go I'm going to take a few along . . . ," 295).

47. Lee W. Formwalt, "Southwest Georgia: A Garden of Irony and Diversity," *The New Georgia Guide* (Athens: University of Georgia Press, 1996) 497–536, esp. 506–508; WFW to Eugene Saxton, 23 August 1923, NAACP/mf, p2 r7 f406; *Dictionary of American Negro Biography*, s.v. "Wright, Louis Tompkins," by Rayford W. Logan.

48. White, *The Fire in the Flint*, 32.

49. W.E.B. Du Bois, *The Souls of Black Folk*, in Eric J. Sundquist, ed., *The Oxford W.E.B. Du Bois Reader* (New York: Oxford University Press, 1996), 158.

50. Du Bois, *The Souls of Black Folk*, chaps. 7–8, in ibid. For a photographic record of Du Bois's journey, see Lee W. Formwalt, " 'Corner-Stone of the Cotton Kingdom': W.E.B. Du Bois's 1898 View of Dougherty County," *Georgia Historical Quarterly* 71 (1987): 693–700.

51. White, *The Fire in the Flint*, 25–26.

52. Claude McKay to WFW, 15 December 1924, NAACP/mf p2 r8 f355.

53. WFW to Claude McKay, 6 November 1924, NAACP/mf p2 r8 f230.

54. Du Bois, *Souls of Black Folk*, in *The Oxford W.E.B. Du Bois Reader*, 219–30, esp. 228–30.

55. Walter White, *Rope and Faggot: A Biography of Judge Lynch*, with a new introduction by Kenneth Robert Janken (New York: Knopf, 1929; repr. Notre Dame, In.: University of Notre Dame Press, 2001), 78–79; John Dittmer, *Black Georgia in the Progressive Era, 1900–1920* (Urbana: University of Illinois Press, 1977), 136–37.

56. WFW to Robert T. Kerlin, 26 December 1923, NAACP/mf p2 r7 f463; see also White to Claude McKay, 15 August 1924, NAACP/mf p2 r7 f721, and *A Man Called White*, 65–67. The publishing history of *The Fire in the Flint* with Doran can be traced in the following correspondence: White to Eugene Saxton, 17 July 1923, NAACP/mf p2 r7 f396, White to Saxton, 23 August 1923, NAACP/mf p2 r7 f406, White to Saxton, 19 August 1923, NAACP/mf p2 r7 f412, White to Saxton, 23 August 1923, NAACP/mf p2 r7 f416, Saxton to White, 8 June 1923, NAACP/mf p2 r7 f374, Saxton to White, 23 July 1923, NAACP/mf p2 r7 f401, Saxton to White, 16 August 1923, NAACP/mf p2 r7 f411, Saxton to White, 21 August 1923, NAACP/mf p2 r7 f416, Saxton to Will W. Alexander, 30 August 1923, NAACP/mf p2 r7 f426, Saxton to White, 8 October 1923, NAACP/mf p2 r7 f444. See also Edward E. Walrond, *Walter White and the Harlem Renaissance* (Port Washington, NY: Kennikat Press, 1978) 47–55, Charles W. Scruggs, "Alain Locke and Walter White: Their Struggle for Control of the Harlem Renaissance," *Black American Literature Forum* 14 (1980): 91–99, esp. 92, and David Levering Lewis, *When Harlem Was in Vogue*, 132–36.

57. WFW to Arthur Spingarn, 22 August 1923, NAACP/mf p2 r7 f421, White to Joel Spingarn, 22 August 1923, NAACP/mf p2 r7 f422, Eugene Saxton to Will W. Alexander, 30 August 1923, NAACP/mf p2 r7 f426, Alexander to White, 1 October 1923, NAACP/mf p2 r7 f438, White to Saxton, 23 August 1923, NAACP/mf p2 r7 f416.

58. Eugene Saxton to WFW, 8 October 1923, NAACP/mf p2 r7 f444.

59. WFW to Eugene Saxton, 23 August 1923, NAACP/mf p2 r7 f406, emphasis added.

60. WFW to Alfred A. Knopf, 17 October 1923, NAACP/mf p2 r7 f454, White to Blanche Knopf, 18 December 1923, NAACP/mf p2 r7 f478, White to Blanche Knopf, 21 April 1924, NAACP/mf p2 r7 f597. For two among a large number of examples of White's distribution work, see White to E. R. Merrick, 8 May 1924, NAACP/mf p2 r7 f621, and Bishop John Hurst to White, 5 September 1924, NAACP/mf p2 r8 f20.

61. Eugene O'Neill to WFW, 12 October 1924, NAACP/mf p2 r8 f368, O'Neill to White,

24 October 1924, NAACP/mf pr 28 f367, Konrad Bercovici to White, 28 February 1924, NAACP/mf p2 r7 f553, Carl Van Doren to White, 24 December 1923, NAACP/mf p2 r7 f477.

62. Jacob Billikopf to WFW, 25 September 1924, NAACP/mf p2 r8 f115, White to Billikopf, 26 September 1924, NAACP/mf p2 r8 f114. White wrote a less cordial missive to the *Boston Independent*, which, in its book review, charged him with the same sin. See WFW to the *Boston Independent*, 26 September 1924, NAACP/mf p2 r8 f113.

63. A. S. Frissell to Alfred Knopf, 17 September 1924, NAACP/mf p2 r8 f80.

64. WFW to A. S. Frissell, 20 September 1924, NAACP/mf p2 r8 f80.

65. WFW to George S. Oppenheimer, 20 September 1924, NAACP/mf p2 r8 f87, A. S. Frissell to WFW, 29 September 1924, NAACP/mf p2 r8 f134. White was gracious in receiving this admission; see WFW to Frissell, 6 October 1924, NAACP/mf, p2 r8 f134.

66. Annie Bridgman to WFW, 5 November 1924, NAACP/mf p2 r8 f237, WFW to Bridgman, 8 November 1924, NAACP/mf p2 r8 f236.

67. WFW to Blanche Knopf, 17 March 1925, NAACP/mf p2 r8 f641; Edward E. Waldron, *Walter White and the Harlem Renaissance*, 76–77; W.E.B. Du Bois, review of *The Fire in the Flint*, by Walter White, in *The Crisis* 29 (November 1924): 25; Charles S. Johnson, review of *The Fire in the Flint*, by Walter White, in *Opportunity* 2 (November 1924): 344–45.

68. Joel E. Spingarn to WFW, 2 October 1923, NAACP/mf p2 r7 f442.

69. Sinclair Lewis to Joel E. Spingarn, 6 September 1924, NAACP/mf p2 r8 f46; Charles F. Cooney, "Walter White and Sinclair Lewis: The History of a Literary Friendship," *Prospects* 1 (1975): 63–75.

70. H. G. Wells to WFW, 3 July 1924, NAACP/mf p2 r7 f560.

71. *Savannah Press* and *Macon Telegraph* quoted in "Southerners at Odds over 'The Fire in the Flint,'" press release, 28 November 1924, NAACP/mf p2 r8 f299. Josephus Daniels, Jr., review of *The Fire in the Flint*, by Walter White, *News and Observer*, 10 October 1924.

72. WFW to Sinclair Lewis, 15 October 1924, NAACP/mf p2 r8 f168.

73. WFW to Jim Tully, 7 May 1926, NAACP/mf p2 r10 f18.

74. WFW to Tully, telegram, 26 May 1926, NAACP/mf p2 r10 f66.

75. Richard Halliday to WFW, 30 June 1926, NAACP/mf p2 r10 f132; Halliday to WFW, 7 July 1926, NAACP/mf p2 r10 f132.

76. Alain Locke to WFW (May 1923), NAACP/mf p2 r9 f53; WFW to Alain Locke, 3 June 1925, Alain Locke Papers, box 164–92, folder 53, Moorland-Spingarn Research Center, Howard University, Washington, D.C.; Melville J. Herskovits, "The Color Line," *American Mercury* 6 (1926): 204–208.

77. WFW to Amy Spingarn, 8 September 1924, NAACP/mf p2 r8 f13.

78. Walter White, *Flight* (New York: Knopf, 1926; repr. Baton Rouge: Louisiana State University Press, 1998), 300.

79. Carl Van Vechten, review of *Flight* by Walter White, in *New York Herald-Tribune Books* 11 April 1926, p. 3; review of *Flight* by Walter White, *The New Republic*, 1 September 1926, p. 53; review of *Flight* by Walter White, *The New York Times*, 11 April 1926, p. 9; review of *Flight* by Walter White, *Independent*, 8 May 1926, p. 555; Edward E. Waldron, *Walter White and the Harlem Renaissance*, 94–95; Sinclair Lewis, letter contributed to symposium "The Negro in Art," *The Crisis*, May 1926, p. 36.

80. Jessie Fauset to WFW, 14 April 1926, NAACP/mf p2 r9 f695; Nora E. Waring, review of *Flight* by Walter White, *Crisis*, July 1926, 142; Frank Horne, review of *Flight* by Walter White, *Opportunity*, July 1926, 227; WFW to Charles Johnson, 6 July 1926,

NAACP/mf p2 r10 f134; Johnson to WFW, 22 July 1926, NAACP/mf p2 r10 f192; WFW to Johnson, 28 July 1926, NAACP/mf p2 r10 f191; Johnson to WFW, 5 August 1926, NAACP/mf p2 r10 f212; Nella Imes, letter to editor, *Opportunity*, September 1926, 295; Frank Horne, letter to editor, *Opportunity*, October 1926, 326.

81. Walter White, letter to editor, *Opportunity*, December 1926, 397.

82. WFW to George E. Haynes, 6 January 1930, NAACP/mf p2 r12 f329; Joel Spingarn to WFW, 9 January 1930, NAACP/mf p2 r12 f339; WFW to Haynes, 5 February 1930, NAACP/mf p2 r12 f425.

83. WFW to Countee Cullen, 14 June 1927, NAACP/mf p2 r11 f51; on refusal to use his son's name, see *A Man Called White*, 92; WFW to Sinclair Lewis, 6 July 1927, NAACP/mf p2 r11 f64; and WFW to William Aspinwall Bradley, 6 July 1927, NAACP/mf p2 r11 f60. On middle name of Darrow, see WFW to Lewis, 6 July 1927, NAACP/mf p2 r11 f64. On naming the child Carl, see WFW to Carl Roberts, 12 May 1927, NAACP/mf p2 r11 f23. On naming the child Walter, see WFW to Roberts, 12 May 1927, NAACP/mf p2 r11 f23 (Gladys "was rather set on"), WFW to Roberts, 9 July 1927, NAACP/mf p2 r11 f69, and WFW to George White (brother), 20 June 1927, NAACP/mf p2 r11 f55. At least one of their friends thought White's habit of not using his son's name was odd. According to Dorothy Peterson, Nella Larsen acidly commented that "he dedicated his first book to Gladys, his second to Jane his daughter, but . . . he feared to dedicate the third to his son, because we would discover what the infant's name really is." Thadious Davis, *Nella Larsen, Novelist of the Harlem Renaissance* (Baton Rouge: Louisiana State University Press, 1994), 250n29.

84. On the provenance of the name Carl, see Jane White Viazzi, interview by author, 18 July 1997; and Langston Hughes to Carl Van Vechten, 15 July 1927, in *Remember Me to Harlem: The Letters of Langston Hughes and Carl Van Vechten*, ed. Emily Bernard (New York: Knopf, 2001), 54. A 1948 *New Yorker* profile of White stated his son was named for three Carls—Roberts, Van Vechten, and Van Doren. E. J. Kahn, Jr., "Profiles: The Frontal Attack—II," *The New Yorker*, 11 September 1948, 44. On Van Vechten's novel and his role as a Harlem Renaissance patron, see Lewis, *When Harlem Was in Vogue*, 180–89; and Emily Bernard, introduction to *Remember Me to Harlem*.

85. W.E.B. Du Bois, "Critique of Carl Van Vechten's *Nigger Heaven*" (1926), in *The Portable Harlem Renaissance Reader*, 106 ("blow in the face"); see also James Weldon Johnson's 1933 assessment of *Nigger Heaven* in *The Portable Harlem Renaissance Reader*, 108–109. WFW to W.E.B. Du Bois, 26 November 1926, NAACP/mf p2 r10 f425 ("will be read by people").

86. WFW to William Aspinwall Bradley, 20 June 1927, NAACP/mf p2 r11 f54; B of D Minutes, 14 March 1927, NAACP/mf p1 r2 f134. On Villefranche and securing domestic help, see WFW to JWJ, 16 August 1927, JWJ/Yale series 1 folder 539; WFW to Arthur Spingarn, 16 August 1927, Arthur Spingarn Papers/HU box 948 folder 175; W.E.B. Du Bois to Loulouse Chapoteau, 7 July 1927, Du Bois papers r21 f1073; WFW to Bradley, 6 July 1927, NAACP/mf p2 r11 f60; WFW to JWJ, 1 January 1928, NAACP/mf p2 r11 f146. On Pidge, see *A Man Called White*, 175–76, and Jane Viazzi, interview with author. Viazzi dissents vigorously from this interpretation of Pidge's name change. Sometime after the interview, she said his name change was for professional reasons; as a classically trained and accomplished musician living and performing in Europe, he found it advantageous to be known as "Carl Darrow." But Rose Palmer, White's niece, drew a connection between the divorce and the name change. Though he attended his father's funeral, he cut off contact with Palmer and her family, she believed, because of their support for White after the divorce. Rose Palmer to author, e-mail, 5 February 2001. On relocation to Avignon and contact with Anglophone writers, see WFW to Arthur Spingarn, 9 January 1928, Arthur Spingarn Papers/HU box

948 folder 175; WFW to JWJ, 21 February 1928, JWJ/Yale series 1 folder 539; WFW to JWJ, 13 October 1927, NAACP/mf p1 r24 f705; WFW to JWJ, 1 January 1928, NAACP/mf p2 r11 f146.

87. Walter White, *Rope and Faggot: A Biography of Judge Lynch* (New York: Knopf, 1929; repr. Notre Dame, IN: University of Notre Dame Press, 2001), 58.

88. Jacqueline Jones Royster, introduction to *Southern Horrors and Other Writings: The Anti-Lynching Campaign of Ida B. Wells, 1892–1900* by Ida B. Wells (Boston: Bedford, 1997), 20.

89. White, *Rope*, 67.

90. Ibid., 66–68. For an outstanding discussion of the psychosexual dimensions of lynching, see Trudier Harris, *Exorcizing Blackness: Historical and Literary Lynching and Burning Rituals* (Bloomington, IN: Indiana University Press, 1984). See also, Donald G. Mathews, "The Southern Rite of Human Sacrifice," *Journal of Southern Religion* (Online) 3 (2000), section three, available at http://jsr.as.wvu.edu/mathews.htm (accessed 29 November 2000).

91. White, *Rope*, 76–77.

92. Ibid., 92.

93. Eric Foner, *Reconstruction: America's Unfinished Revolution, 1863–1877* (New York: Harper & Row, 1988), 119–23, 425–44.

94. Walter White, "The Work of a Mob," *The Crisis*, September 1918, pp. 221–23; Grace Elizabeth Hale, *Making Whiteness* (New York: Pantheon, 1998), 201, 202; W. Fitzhugh Brundage, *Lynching in the New South* (Urbana: University of Illinois Press, 1993), 62–63, 111–113.

95. White, *Rope*, 9.

96. Hale, *Making Whiteness*, chap. 5.

97. White, *Rope*, 44–45.

98. Ibid., 44.

99. John Egerton, *Speak Now against the Day* (Chapel Hill: University of North Carolina Press, 1995).

100. Ida B. Wells-Barnett's principal writings on lynching are collected in *Southern Horrors and Other Writings: The Anti-Lynching Campaign of Ida B. Wells, 1892–1900*, edited and with an introduction by Jacqueline Jones Royster (Boston: Bedford/St. Martin's, 1997); an insightful analysis of the campaign is Gail Bederman, " 'Civilization,' the Decline of Middle-Class Manliness, and Ida B. Wells's Antilynching Campaign (1892–94)," *Radical History Review* no. 52 (1992): 5–30.

101. On Ida B. Wells-Barnett and the NAACP, see Paula Giddings, *When and Where I Enter* (New York: William Morrow, 1984), 180–81; Patricia A. Schechter, *Ida B. Wells-Barnett & American Social Reform, 1880–1930* (Chapel Hill: University of North Carolina Press, 2001), 135–37, 141–42.

102. Patricia A. Schechter, "Unsettled Business: Ida B. Wells against Lynching, or, How Antilynching Got Its Gender," in *Under Sentence of Death: Lynching in the South*, ed. W. Fitzhugh Brundage (Chapel Hill: University of North Carolina Press, 1997), 308, 309. See also, Deborah Gray White, "The Cost of Club Work, the Price of Black Feminism," in *Visible Women: New Essays on American Activism*, eds. Nancy A. Hewitt and Suzanne Lebsock (Urbana and Chicago: University of Illinois Press, 1993), 247–69; and Dorothy Salem, *To Better Our World: Black Women in Organized Reform, 1890–1920* (Brooklyn, NY: Carlson, 1990), 145–79; and Rosalyn Terborg-Penn, "African-American Women's Networks in the Anti-Lynching Crusade," in *Gender, Class, Race, and Reform in the Progressive Era*, eds. Noralee Frankel and Nancy S. Dye (Lexington, KY: University Press of Kentucky, 1991), 148–61. On the Anti-Lynching Crusaders, see B of D minutes for 11 September 1922, NAACP/mf p1 r1 f903, 13 November

1922, NAACP/mf p1 r1 f913, 11 December 1922, NAACP/mf p1 r1 f917, and 8 January 1923, NAACP/mf p1 r1 f923.

103. On White's plagiarizing Du Bois: WFW to Du Bois, memo, 19 April 1945, NAACP/mf p14 r19 f62 and Du Bois's reply on same document, and WFW to William Agar, 11 April 1945, NAACP/mf p14 r19 f61, in which he passes on Du Bois's statement with the note that "Dr. Du Bois joins me in this recommendation." On White's plagiarizing of Logan, see Logan Diary/LC, 30 January 1949.

104. Ernestine Rose to WFW, 6 February 1929, NAACP/mf p2 r11 f491; WFW to Henry Block, 8 February 1929, NAACP/mf p2 r11 f495; WFW to Rayford Logan, 31 October 1951, NAACP/mf p14 r8 f180.

105. White, *Rope*, 76.

106. Stewart E. Tolnay and E. M. Beck, *A Festival of Violence: An Analysis of Southern Lynchings, 1882–1930* (Urbana and Chicago: University of Illinois Press, 1995), 255.

107. Orlando Patterson, *Rituals of Blood: Consequences of Slavery in Two American Centuries* (Washington, D.C.: Civitas/Counterpoint, 1998), 175. Chapter two of Patterson's study is a penetrating study of the Protestant fundamentalist religious dimensions of lynching.

108. Hale, *Making Whiteness*, 227.

109. Donald G. Mathews, "The Southern Rite of Human Sacrifice," *Journal of Southern Religion* (Online) 3 (2000), section three, available at http://jsr.as.wvu.edu/mathews.htm (accessed 29 November 2000).

110. H. L. Mencken to WFW, 23 December 1929, and WFW, "The Technique of Lynching," both in NAACP Papers, group II series L box 21, "H. L. Mencken 1920–29," Manuscript Division, Library of Congress, Washington, D.C.

111. Letters to the editor, *Time*, 8 July 1929; WFW to Aaron Bernd, 6 July 1929, NAACP/mf p2 r12 f101.

112. Arthur Raper, *The Tragedy of Lynching* (Chapel Hill: University of North Carolina Press, 1933), 38.

113. Will Alexander to WFW, 8 April 1935, NAACP/mf p7B r8 f51; George Fort Milton to WFW, 31 January 1935, NAACP/mf p7B r7 f381; Virginius Dabney, 2 January 1935, NAACP/mf p7B r6 f1226.

114. On fund-raising: WFW to JWJ, 1 March 1928, NAACP/mf p2 r11 f118, and WFW to JWJ, 5 March 1928, NAACP/mf p2 r11 f117.

115. WFW to William Aspinwall Bradley, 21 June 1929, NAACP/mf p2 r12 f82, reports how much of the novel he wrote in France; in WFW to Blanche Knopf, 18 March 1928, quoted in Jon Christian Suggs, " 'Blackjack': Walter White and Modernism in An Unknown Boxing Novel," *Michigan Quarterly Review* 38 (1999): 522, White states that "the prizefighting novel is shaping up." The unfinished manuscript of *Blackjack* is in the Walter White Papers, Manuscripts, Archives, and Rare Books Division, Schomburg Center for Research in Black Culture, New York Public Library, New York, New York.

116. Charles Studin to WFW, 21 February 1928, NAACP/mf p2 r11 f109; WFW to Studin, 7 March 1928, NAACP/mf p2 r11 f112; WFW to Studin 26 March 1928, NAACP/mf p2 r11 f125.

Chapter 5: A CROOKED PATH TO POWER

1. Charles Studin to WFW, 21 February 1928, NAACP/mf p2 r11 f109.
2. B of D Minutes, 13 September 1920, NAACP/mf p1 r1 f787.
3. WFW to Shelby Davidson, 9 August 1923, NAACP/mf p11B r30 f494. On the Tuskegee veteran's hospital incident, see Pete Daniel, "Black Power in the 1920s: The Case of the Tuskegee Veterans Hospital," *Journal of Southern History* 36 (1970): 368–88; and Desmond King, "A Strong or Weak State? Race and the US Federal Government in the 1920s," *Ethnic and Racial Studies* 21 (1998): 21–47.

4. WFW to JWJ, memo, 7 July 1923, NAACP/mf p11B r30 f421. White's mission to Washington reveals something of the assistant secretary's trademark style and persistence. In this memo, he reports that he had gone to the capital to talk with an assistant attorney general with whom he had had past dealings. He planned to walk in unannounced. While in later years he would be known to keep up with contacts and work a network, this time White arrived to find out to his "great shock" that the person he wanted to see had been dead since the previous September. Not to be denied a hearing, White turned to Theodore Roosevelt, Jr., an NAACP board member and assistant secretary of the navy, for advice. Roosevelt put him in touch with Hoover. When Hoover stonewalled, White left and found the assistant attorney general who had taken his contact's place and extracted a commitment from him to order Hoover to conduct an investigation.

5. WFW, letter to editors of the *New York Times* and other New York papers, 14 May 1923, NAACP/mf p11B r30 f372; see also Daniel, "Black Power in the 1920s: The Case of Tuskegee Veterans Hospital."

6. William E. Leuchtenberg, *The Perils of Prosperity, 1914–32*, 2d ed. (Chicago: University of Chicago Press, 1993), 132–36 (on Democratic and Republican nominees); B of D Minutes, 14 July 1924, NAACP/mf p1 r1 f1022 (on Progressive Party convention). For more on African Americans and the 1924 elections, see W.E.B. Du Bois, "In Philadelphia" and "La Follette," *The Crisis*, August 1924, 151–54, both reprinted in *Writings in Periodicals Edited by W.E.B. Du Bois: Selections from* The Crisis, I, *1911–1925*, comp. and ed. Hebert Aptheker (Millwood, NY: Kraus-Thomson, 1983), 406–408, 410; A. Philip Randolph, "The Political Situation and the Negro: Coolidge, Davis or La Follette" (1924), in *A Documentary History of the Negro People in the United States*, III, *From the NAACP to the New Deal*, ed. Herbert Aptheker (New York: Citadel Press, 1993), 471–83.

7. WFW to Charles Studin, 7 March 1928, NAACP/mf p2 r11 f112.

8. WFW to John Hurst, 20 July 1928, NAACP/mf p2 r11 f135.

9. [WFW], "Suggested Program of Work" (1928), NAACP/mf p2 r11 f141.

10. [WFW], "Analysis of Possible Effect of Negro Vote in the 1928 Election," NAACP/mf p2 r11 f139; see also Henry Lee Moon, *Balance of Power: The Negro Vote* (Garden City, NY: Doubleday, 1948). White acknowledged a debt to Du Bois for his research on the balance of power, which was subsequently published as "The Negro Voter," *The Crisis*, August 1928, 275–76, and "The Possibility for Democracy in America," published in the September and October 1928 issues of *The Crisis*, and reprinted in *Writings in Periodicals Edited by W.E.B. Du Bois: Selections from* The Crisis, II, *1926–1934*, ed. Herbert Aptheker (Millwood, NY: Kraus-Thomson, 1983), 520–29.

11. Moorfield Storey to WFW, 25 July 1928, NAACP/mf p2 r11 f152. See also Storey to JWJ, 25 July 1928, NAACP/mf p2 r11 f153. On the fact that the NAACP board was divided, see WFW to Storey, 22 July 1928, NAACP/mf p2 r11 f134.

12. WFW to Bishop John Hurst, 20 July 1928, NAACP/mf p2 r11 f135; Hurst to WFW, 21 July 1928, NAACP/mf p2 r11 f138. White must have misunderstood Du Bois's objections. It is possible that Du Bois believed that lending the association's secretary to Smith's presidential bid was a partisan act that would harm the NAACP. But his objection was not that the endorsement of Smith by White was impermissibly partisan. Du Bois, while railing against both Smith and Hoover, endorsed Socialist candidate Norman Thomas and provided favorable coverage in *The Crisis* to the Communists. See, inter alia, W.E.B. Du Bois, "As the Crow Flies," *The Crisis*, August 1928, 257; Du Bois, "Thomas," *The Crisis*, November 1928, 368, 386; Du Bois, "Communists," *The Crisis*, September 1928, 320–21.

13. JWJ to Storey, 24 July 1928, JWJ ser. 1 folder 465 ("doubtful about the wisdom," "quite definitely opposed," and "irretrievable harm"); JWJ to Storey, 31 July 1928, JWJ/Yale

series 1 folder 465; the goings-on in Houston, see also W.E.B. Du Bois, "Houston," *The Crisis* September 1928, 312.

14. WFW to Storey, 31 July 1928, NAACP/mf p2 r11 f150.

15. WFW to William H. Lewis, 18 September 1928, NAACP/mf p2 r11 f225 ("Smith [does not know] very much about Negroes"); WFW to Lewis, 4 August 1928, NAACP/mf p2 r11 f165; WFW to Bishop John Hurst, 9 August 1928, NAACP/mf p2 r11 f172; WFW to Hurst, 16 August 1928, NAACP/mf p2 r11 f277; WFW to William Gaston, 20 August 1928, NAACP/mf p2 r11 f175.

16. "An Appeal to America [The 1928 Elections]," in *A Documentary History of the Negro People in the United States*, III, 580–84.

17. Walter White, "For Whom Shall the Negro Vote?" *Harlem: A Forum of Negro Life*, November 1928, 5–6, 45.

18. W.E.B. Du Bois, "The Campaign of 1928," *The Crisis*, December 1928, 418.

19. Some of the conference presentations and summaries of some of the discussions are in Charles S. Johnson, *The Negro in American Civilization* (New York: Henry Holt, 1930).

20. W.E.B. Du Bois, "The National Interracial Conference," *The Crisis*, February 1929, 47, 69–70; Du Bois, "The Negro Citizen," *The Crisis*, May 1929, 154–56, 171–73; Walter White, "Solving America's Race Problem," *The Nation*, 9 January 1929, 42–43.

21. On White's attitude toward Howard, see "For Whom Shall the Negro Vote?" See also W.E.B. Du Bois, "Howard," *The Crisis*, September 1928, 312. On Hoover's racial attitudes, and in particular his drive against Howard and in support of the lily-white Republicans, see Donald J. Lisio, *Hoover, Blacks, and Lily-Whites* (Chapel Hill: University of North Carolina Press, 1985).

22. See Elliott Thurston to WFW, 19 March 1930, NAACP/mf p11B r26 f280. This letter from the Washington correspondent for the *New York World*, which responded to a nonextant inquiry from White as to whom Hoover favored nominating; it is written in such a way as to confirm that White was preparing to launch a drive against any person Hoover would propose.

23. WFW to A. M. Rivera, 22 March 1930, NAACP/mf p11B r26 f282; Rivera to WFW, 24 March 1930, NAACP/mf p11B r26 f284; WFW to NAACP Branches, 28 March 1930, NAACP/mf p11B r26 f288.

24. Lucille Black Oral History, Ralph J. Bunche Oral History Project, Moorland-Spingarn Center, Howard University, Washington, D.C., 1 November 1967.

25. Arthur Spingarn Oral History, Ralph J. Bunche Oral History Project, 6 March 1968.

26. B of D Minutes, 9 September 1929, NAACP/mf p1 r2 f264.

27. B of D Minutes, 8 April 1929, NAACP/mf p1 r2 f244 and B of D Minutes, 13 May 1929, NAACP/mf p1 r2 f251 (on Pickens's vacation); Robert Bagnall and William Pickens to Budget Committee, 14 October 1929, and Bagnall and Pickens to Board of Directors, memo, 23 December 1929, both in Arthur B. Spingarn Papers, box 9, folder "August–December 1929," Manuscript Division, Library of Congress, Washington, D.C. (on pay raises); Mary White Ovington to WFW, (October 1929), NAACP/mf p2 r12 f239; WFW to JWJ, 3 November 1928, NAACP/mf p1 r25 f17 (on Marshall's fund-raising prowess); WFW to Eugene Martin, 17 September 1929, NAACP/mf p2 r12 f172 (on financial distress).

28. Acting Secy. Report to COA, 28 October 1929, NAACP/mf p16A r5 f36; Leonard Baker, *Brandeis and Frankfurter: A Dual Biography* (New York: Harper & Row, 1984), 473.

29. WFW to Jacob Billikopf, 22 November 1929, NAACP/mf p1 r25 f88; WFW to Billikopf, 4 December 1929, NAACP/mf p1 r25 f100; WFW to Billikopf 12 December 1929, NAACP/mf p1 r25 f99; WFW to Billikopf, 14 December 1929, NAACP/mf p1 r25 f99; Acting Secy. Monthly Rpt., 6 February 1930, NAACP/mf p1 r5 f139; Supple-

ment to Acting Secy. Monthly Rpt., 10 February 1930, NAACP/mf p1 r5 f146; Acting Secy. Monthly Rpt., 4 June 1930, NAACP/mf p1 r5 f209. On Edsel Ford, see *A Man Called White*, 213.

30. WFW to Eugene Martin, 17 September 1929, NAACP/mf p2 r12 f172; Billikopf to WFW, 26 December 1930, NAACP/mf p2 r13 f355, WFW to Billikopf, 30 December 1930, NAACP/mf p2 r13 f355.

31. WFW to William Pickens and Robert Bagnall, 2 October 1929, NAACP/mf p1 r25 f48.

32. On Lampkin's ideas and qualifications see [WFW], memo to Board of Directors, 14 October 1929, NAACP/mf p1 r18 f190, Daisy Lampkin to WFW, 19 October 1929, NAACP/mf p1 r18 f191, and Lampkin to WFW, 23 October 1929, NAACP/mf p1 r18 f191 ("Where women are weak"); WFW to COA, memo, 4 November 1929, NAACP/mf p16A r5 f43 ("dwell not so much").

33. *A Man Called White*, 106; Walter White, "The Negro and the Supreme Court," *Harper's* 157 (January 1931), reprinted in *In Search of Democracy: The NAACP Writings of James Weldon Johnson, Walter White, and Roy Wilkins (1920–1977)*, ed. Sondra Kathryn Wilson (New York: Oxford University Press, 1999) 239; Congress, Senate, Subcommittee of the Committe on the Judiciary, *Hearing before the Subcommittee of the Committee on the Judiciary United States Senate on the Confirmation of Hon. John J. Parker to Be An Associate Justice of the Supreme Court of the United States*, 71st Cong., 2nd sess., 5 April 1930.

34. WFW to Ernest Gruening, 7 April 1930, NAACP/mf p11B r26 f420; NAACP press release, 25 April 1930, NAACP/mf p11B r26 f1023; Kenneth W. Goings, *"The NAACP Comes of Age": The Defeat of Judge John J. Parker* (Bloomington: Indiana University Press, 1990), 32.

35. WFW, memo, 18 April 1930, NAACP/mf p11B r26 f778 (Ludwell Denny); WFW to Harry Davis, 16 April 1930, NAACP/mf p11B r26 f628; Goings, *"The NAACP Comes of Age,"* 30; Lisio, *Hoover, Blacks, and Lily-Whites*, 216–18, 222.

36. Clara Cox to WFW, 25 April 1930, NAACP/mf p11B r26 f1025.

37. Lisio, *Hoover, Blacks, and Lily-Whites*, 213–15.

38. WFW, memo, 21 April 1930, NAACP/mf p11B r26 f843; WFW to Harry Davis, 21 April 1930, NAACP/mf p11B r26 f832 ("would have been disastrous").

39. Acting Secy. Monthly Rpt., (8 May 1930), NAACP/mf p1 r5 f193. See also Goings, *"The NAACP Comes of Age,"* 48–49. In his highly readable and useful account of the Parker fight, Goings emphasizes that it is difficult to identify a single reason for Parker's defeat, but that the NAACP's influence was considerably more than the American Federation of Labor's.

40. Acting Secy. Monthly Rpt., (8 May 1930), NAACP/mf p1 r5 f193; Daisy Lampkin to WFW, 9 May 1930, NAACP/mf p1 r18 f245; Lampkin to WFW, 24 April 1930, NAACP/mf p1 r18 f239.

41. Lampkin to WFW, 1 April 1930, NAACP/mf p1 r18 f232 (on Toledo women's auxiliary); Lampkin to WFW, 5 May [1930], NAACP/mf p1 r18 f242 (on Indiana and Ohio branches).

42. On the Kansas campaign, see Goings, *"The NAACP Comes of Age,"* 59–62.

43. [WFW to Board of Directors], digest of opinions on the Ohio senatorial election, 3 September 1930, NAACP/mf p11B r25 f311.

44. WFW to Harry Davis, 27 August 1930, NAACP/mf p11B r25 f296 ("The future attitude"); [WFW to Board of Directors], digest of opinions on the Ohio senatorial election, 3 September 1930, NAACP/mf p11B r25 f311; Lampkin to WFW, 17 September 1930, NAACP/mf p11B r25 f351 ("It seems to be taken for granted"); B of D Minutes, 13 October 1930, NAACP/mf p1 r2 f332 (on continued opposition to political involvement); Du Bois to WFW, memo, 11 October 1930, NAACP/mf p11B r25 f528.

45. Memo of conference on Ohio political situation, 17 September 1930, NAACP/mf p11B r25 f360; WFW to editors of the colored press, 24 September 1930, NAACP/mf p11B r25 f418; WFW to Arthur B. Spingarn, 17 September 1930, NAACP/mf p11B r25 f365 ("if in advising Negroes"); Acting Secy. Monthly Rpt., 8 October 1930, NAACP/mf p1 r5 f254; *Cleveland Gazette,* 11 October 1930 (on White's meeting with Bulkley and on the ostensibly nonpartisan nature of the proposed anti-McCulloch campaign); Goings, *"The NAACP Comes of Age,"* 66; Leslie J. Stegh, "A Paradox of Prohibition: Election of Robert J. Bulkley as Senator from Ohio, 1930," *Ohio History* 83 (1974): 180–81.

46. WFW to Robert Bagnall, William Pickens, and W.E.B. Du Bois, 9 October 1930, NAACP/mf p11B r25 f514 ("friendly letter"); WFW to Herbert Seligmann, 28 October 1930, NAACP/mf p11B r25 f679 ("paid political hireling"). The Republicans also activated local black supporters; see WFW to Ohio Branches, 17 October 1930, NAACP/mf p11B r25 f588.

47. Geraldyne Freeland to Daisy Lampkin, 5 November 1930, NAACP/mf p11B r25 f718.

48. Acting Secy. Monthly Rpt., 6 November 1930, NAACP/mf p1 r5 f269; Harry Davis to WFW, 7 November 1930, NAACP/mf p11B r25 f744; Goings, *"The NAACP Comes of Age,"* 67. The *Cleveland Gazette,* a Republican-oriented black weekly, offered a similar analysis in its 8, 15, and 22 November 1930 editions.

49. Goings, *"The NAACP Comes of Age,"* 52–53. As the NAACP—both the national leadership and a majority of the membership—became more receptive to the overtures from organized labor and New Dealers, black Republicans within the association continued to question the propriety of becoming involved in electoral politics; for an excellent example of this debate, see the minutes of the discussion at the annual conference, May 1932, NAACP/mf p1 r9 f218.

50. Constance Ridley Heslip to WFW (November 1931), NAACP/mf p2 r14 f485.

51. WFW to P. A. Stephens, 20 April 1931, NAACP/mf p6 r2 f653.

52. B of D Minutes, 13 April 1931, NAACP/mf p1 r2 f367; WFW, handwritten interview notes, 1 May 1931, NAACP/mf p6 r2 f787.

53. WFW to Robert Bagnall and Herbert Seligmann, 3 May 1931, NAACP/mf p6 r2 f825 ("ignorance and stupidity" and "our chief mistake"); WFW to Herbert Turner, 11 May 1931, NAACP/mf p6 r2 f920 ("illiterate," flattery and flamboyance, and "the type of Negro"). See also WFW to William Pickens, 27 May 1931, NAACP/mf p6 r3 f141: "I think I ought to warn you in advance that you have probably never before encountered such ignorance as you will find here."

54. *Baltimore Afro-American,* 16 May 1931, copy found at NAACP/mf p6 r2 f1032; *Washington World,* 24 July 1931, copy found at NAACP/mf p6 r3 f908; WFW to William Pickens, telegram, 12 June 1931, NAACP/mf p6 r3 f484; WFW to N.K. McGill, 23 October 1931, NAACP/mf p6 r4 f679.

55. WFW to H. B. Webber, 23 April 1931, NAACP/mf p6 r2 f696; NAACP press release, 1 May 1931, NAACP/mf p6 r2 f798; WFW to Editors of the Colored Press, 8 May 1931, NAACP/mf p6 r2 f902; WFW to Carl Murphy, 16 May 1931, NAACP/mf p6 r2 f1038; WFW to Eugene Davidson, 27 July 1931, NAACP/mf p6 r3 f930. See also WFW to P. A. Stephens, 20 April 1931, NAACP/mf p6 r2 f653, for a statement that the NAACP "is interested solely in saving the lives of these boys if innocent and of securing a fairer and more impartial trial than was the case at Scottsboro even if they are guilty."

56. WFW to Jeanne S. Scott, 20 April 1931, NAACP/mf p6 r2 f655; for a sample of the grassroots criticism, see John Wilder Syphax, 30 April 1931, NAACP/mf p6 r2 f770. For more evidence that White was aware of the membership's dissatisfaction with the way he was conducting the Scottsboro campaign and their readiness to engage in active

support work, see WFW to Mary White Ovington, 21 May 1931, NAACP/mf p1 r25 f393.

57. *Daily Worker,* 24 April 1931; B of D Minutes, 11 May 1931, NAACP/mf p1 r2 f374; Mary White Ovington to William Pickens, 30 April 1931, NAACP/mf p6 r2 f761; WFW to Pickens, 12 May 1931, NAACP/mf p6 r2 f947. See also Pickens to Ovington, 2 May, 3 May 1931, JES/NYPL box 9 folder 4; Pickens to WFW, 6 May 1931, NAACP/mf p6 r2 f863.

58. Roy Wilkins to WFW, 7 May 1931, NAACP/mf p6 r2 f889; WFW to Wilkins, 13 May 1931, NAACP/mf p6 r2 f973.

59. Mark Solomon, *The Cry Was Unity* (Jackson: University Press of Mississippi, 1998), 197.

60. The CP scattered its attacks on White and the NAACP throughout its publications and rallies. For one instance that captures the outlandish flavor of the CP accusations, see Cecil Hope [secretary of the Scottsboro Defense Committee] to WFW, 2 January 1932, NAACP/mf p6 r5 f167.

61. James Goodman, *Stories of Scottsboro* (New York: Vintage, 1995), 37–38; NAACP press release 1 May 1931, NAACP/mf p6 r2 f798; WFW to JWJ, 15 January 1932, NAACP/mf p1 r25 f535, and WFW to Floyd Calvin [columnist for the *Pittsburgh Courier*], 15 January 1932, NAACP/mf p6 r5 f336; JWJ to WFW, 25 January 1932, JWJ/Yale series 1 folder 541. See also Floyd Calvin to WFW, n.d., NAACP/mf p6 r5 f339; Calvin takes issue with White's proposition that the CP loses whether the defendants are executed or set free. On the contrary, Calvin wrote, if the defendants are executed, the CP has a new set of martyrs, and if they are freed, the CP wins enormous prestige.

62. Hollace Ransdell, report on Scottsboro, 27 May 1931, NAACP/mf p6 r3 f150.

63. Secy. Monthly Rpt., 5 June 1931, NAACP/mf p1 r5 f361.

64. Will Alexander to WFW, 7 January 1932, WFW/PCW box 1 folder 1.

65. William Pickens to WFW, 6 June 1931, NAACP/mf p6 r3 f355.

66. Howard Kester to Dear Friend, 15 August 1931, Howard Kester Papers, ser. I folder 5, Southern Historical Collection, University of North Carolina, Chapel Hill, NC.

67. Roderick Beddow to WFW, 19 November 1931, NAACP/mf p6 r4 f818; Godfrey Cabot to WFW, 1 August 1939, NAACP/mf p11A r13 f487.

68. WFW to W. A. Domingo, 16 January 1923, NAACP/mf p11A r35 f811.

69. W.E.B. Du Bois, "Marxism and the Negro Problem," *The Crisis,* May 1933, 103–104, 118, reprinted in *Writings in Periodicals Edited by W.E.B. Du Bois: Selections from* The Crisis, II, 695–99; Ralph J. Bunche, "A Critical Analysis of the Tactics and Programs of Minority Groups," *Journal of Negro Education* 4 (1935): 308–20; Ralph J. Bunche, "A Critique of New Deal Social Planning as it Affects Negroes," *Journal of Negro Education* 5 (1936): 59–65; James Weldon Johnson, *Negro Americans, What Now?* (New York: Viking, 1934); W.E.B. Du Bois, "Colored Editors on Communism," *The Crisis,* June 1932, 190–91, reprinted in *Writings in Periodicals Edited by W.E.B. Du Bois: Selections from* The Crisis II, 660–61.

70. G. F. Lamb to Frank Burke, 28 October 1919, *Federal Surveillance of Afro-Americans (1917–1925: The First World War, the Red Scare, and the Garvey Movement* (Bethesda, MD: University Publications of America, 1986), microfilm, reel 11, frame 125; Theodore Kornweibel, Jr., *"Seeing Red": Federal Campaigns against Black Militancy, 1919–1925* (Bloomington: Indiana University Press, 1998), 62. I wish to thank Professor Kornweibel of the Department of Africana Studies at San Diego State University for his assistance in locating this early material on White.

71. On McKay, see chapter 4. On Cullen, see, for example, WFW to Countee Cullen, 3 December 1932, NAACP/mf p2 r15 f618. On Hughes, see, for example, Langston

Hughes, profile of WFW (August 1933), NAACP/mf p2 r16 f215, WFW to Hughes, 15 January 1935, and Hughes to WFW, 21 January 1935, Langston Hughes Papers, box 166, Beinecke Library, Yale University, New Haven, Connecticut.

72. Lydia Gibson Minor to WFW (February 1925), NAACP/mf p2 r8 f522. See also Lydia Minor to WFW, 27 July [1925], p2 r9 f124, and Minor to WFW [received 23 October 1925], p2 r9 f125. WFW to Minor, 26 October 1925, p2 r9 f290.

73. Sylvia Feningston to WFW, 29 May 1930, NAACP/mf p10 r9 f282; Feningston to WFW, 24 June 1930, NAACP/mf p10 r9 f282; Will Alexander to WFW, 27 June 1930, NAACP/mf p10 r9 f269; Walter Wilson to ACLU [Roger Baldwin], 13 July 1930, NAACP/mf p10 r9 f276; Feningston to Arthur B. Spingarn, 24 June 1930, NAACP/mf p10 r9 f280 (quote); WFW to Albert Mayer, 17 September 1930, NAACP/mf p10 r9 f200; WFW to JWJ, 9 June 1930, NAACP/mf p10 r9 f264; WFW to Arthur B. Spingarn, 26 August 1930, NAACP/mf p10 r9 f278. On the Atlanta Six, see Solomon, *The Cry Was Unity*, 126–27; and Charles H. Martin, *The Angelo Herndon Case and Southern Justice* (Baton Rouge: Louisiana State University Press, 1976), 22–27.

74. Minutes of the One Hundredth Meeting of the Board of Directors of the American Fund for Public Service, Inc., 28 May 1930, box 6, American Fund for Public Service Papers, Manuscript Division, New York Public Library, New York, NY. I would like to thank William Jelani Cobb for sharing this document with me.

75. See, for example, these articles in the *Daily Worker:* James Ford, "Negro Workers of South Africa and American Negro Misleaders," 20 January 1930; "TUUL Negro Organizing Conference Scores Misleaders," 4 February 1930; "Negro Masses are Unemployed," and "200 in Chicago Negro Organizing Meeting Cheer TUUL Program," 8 February 1930. See also Solomon, *The Cry Was Unity*, 330n24.

76. WFW to Morris Ernst, 6 November 1929, NAACP/mf p3A r1 f244.

77. WFW to Morris Ernst, 6 November 1929, NAACP/mf p3A r1 f244; JWJ to Roger Baldwin, 6 January 1930, NAACP/mf p3A r1 f315.

78. Certainly Walter White dated the attacks from then. See WFW to Will Alexander, 12 May 1931, NAACP/mf p6 r2 f944; WFW to Alexander, 16 August 1932, JWJ/Yale, series 1 folder 541; Herbert Seligmann to Daisy Lampkin, 20 May 1931, NAACP/mf p1 r23 f213; WFW to William Pickens, 28 May 1931, NAACP/mf p6 r3 f182; WFW to P. B. Young, 18 January 1932, NAACP/mf p6 r5 f387. The record appears to back him up. After several months during which the *Daily Worker*'s coverage of lynching and race in the South focused on the Communist Party's activities, beginning in late May there appeared in the party newspaper renewed criticism of the NAACP. See, for example, "Down with Lynching!" *Daily Worker*, 29 May 1930, and B. D. Amis, "ANLC as Mass Organization of Negro Workers," *Daily Worker*, 13 June 1930.

79. Congress, House of Representatives, Special Committee to Investigate Communist Activities in the United States, *Investigation of Communist Propaganda*, part 3, volume 4, 71st Cong., 2nd sess., 26 and 27 September 1930, 199–204; B of D Minutes, 11 May 1931, NAACP/mf p1 r2 f386.

80. Forrest Bailey to WFW, 6 October 1931, NAACP/mf p2 r14 f404.

81. Walter White, "The Negro and the Communists," *Harper's Magazine* 164 (December 1931): 62–72. For how White saw the development of the Scottsboro campaign, see WFW to Floyd Calvin, 15 January 1932, NAACP/mf p6 r5 f336; WFW to JWJ, 15 January 1932, NAACP/mf p1 r25 f535; JWJ to WFW, 25 January 1932, JWJ/Yale, series 1 folder 541. For White's continued attack on the CP and his belief that the party threatened the NAACP's financial health, see WFW to Roger Baldwin, 7 February 1933, JWJ/Yale, series 1 folder 542; WFW to JWJ, 7 February 1933, JWJ/Yale, series 1 folder 542; WFW to Will Alexander, 16 August 1932, JWJ/Yale, series 1 folder 541; Herbert J. Seligmann to Daisy Lampkin, 20 May 1931, NAACP/mf p1 r23 f213; WFW to P. B. Young, 18 January 1932, NAACP/mf p6 r5 f387.

82. See, for example, WFW to L. H. King [pastor of St. Mark's M.E. Church in Harlem], 13 October 1931, NAACP/mf p6 r4 f603; King to WFW, telephone message, 14 October 1931, NAACP/mf p6 r4 f616; Goodman, *Stories of Scottsboro*, 67–68; Robert Bagnall to WFW, memo, 19 August 1931, NAACP/mf p1 r25 f441; WFW to Bagnall, 22 August 1931, NAACP/mf p1 r25 f445 ("an outstanding instance").

83. NAACP press release, 5 February 1932, NAACP/mf p6 r5 f515; Secy. Monthly Rpt., 7 June 1932, NAACP/mf p1 r5 f516; [WFW], memorandum re: luncheon conference at the Lawyers' Club between Arthur B. Spingarn, Walter Pollak, Thomas I. Emerson of Mr. Pollak's office, and Walter White, 29 June 1932, NAACP/mf p6 r5 f909; *Baltimore Afro-American*, 30 July 1932 (clipping of ILD statement found at NAACP/mf p6 r5 f930); Roy Wilkins to WFW, confidential memo, 14 January 1935, NAACP/mf p2 r17 f291 (NAACP's Scottsboro funds).

84. The crack Birmingham legal firm of Beddow, Fort, and Ray, which White had hired for a couple of defendants, was ineffective in the short time it was on the case, and White could not create conditions conducive to Clarence Darrow's involvement.

85. Mary White Ovington to Joel Spingarn, 15 December (1931), JES/NYPL box 9 folder 2 (on board support for the secretary). See also, Robert Zangrando, interview with Alfred Baker Lewis [former NAACP treasurer and board member], 27 September 1973, University of Akron, Akron, OH, tape-recorded notes in author's possession. I am indebted to Professor Zangrando for sharing with me this and several other interviews he has conducted over the past four decades for his own work on Walter White.

86. See Secy. Monthly Rpt., 4 May 1933, NAACP/mf p1 r5 f686, in which White, discussing the association's next big criminal defense, states that "the Communists would not be able to 'snatch the case from the Association' as was done at Scottsboro."

Chapter 6: A HARD DECADE

1. JWJ, speech to the NAACP annual business meeting, 4 January 1931, NAACP/mf p1 r13 f1216.

2. Description of staff size is an estimate based on the following sources: Carolyn Wedin, *Inheritors of the Spirit: Mary White Ovington and the Founding of the NAACP* (New York: John Wiley & Sons, 1998), 145 (photo at bottom); Roy Wilkins to WFW, 17 February 1945, NAACP/mf p14 r13 f169 (on office space); B of D Minutes, 14 December 1931, NAACP/mf p1 r2 f409; B of D Minutes, 11 April 1932, NAACP/mf p1 r2 f448; financial statements contained in the *NAACP Annual Report* between 1928 and 1932; Mabel Smith, telephone interview by author, 24 January 2002; and Mildred Roxborough, telephone interview by author, 30 January 2002. Smith worked at NAACP headquarters in the forties, after it had moved from 69 Fifth Avenue to the Wendell Wilkie Memorial Building at 20 West Fortieth Street; I am reading back from her description of the physical organization of the workforce. Roxborough began with the NAACP in the fifties and is the association's longest-serving employee; she estimated that the NAACP employed between fifteen and twenty clerical workers in the thirties.

3. Richetta Randolph to JWJ, 10 October 1930, JWJ/Yale series 1 folder 387. On Johnson's and White's contrasting styles, see Elliott Rudwick and August Meier, "The Rise of the Black Secretariat in the NAACP, 1909–35," in August Meier and Elliott Rudwick, *Along the Color Line* (Urbana: University of Illinois Press, 1976), 94–127.

4. Richetta Randolph to Mary White Ovington, 19 January 1931, JWJ/Yale series 1 folder 387; WFW to Staff, memo, 4 September 1930, NAACP/mf p1 r25 f250 ("rigidly adhere"); WFW to staff, memo, 1 October 1930, NAACP/mf p1 r25 f271; WFW to staff, memo, 15 September 1930, NAACP/mf p1 r25 f257; Catherine T. Freeland to WFW, memo, 23 September 1930, NAACP/mf p1 r25 f257; WFW to Clerical Staff, 30 March 1936, NAACP/mf p1 r26 f519; WFW to staff, memo, 29 January 1936, NAACP/mf p1 r26 f484 ("demonstrate the proper spirit").

5. WFW to Robert Bagnall, memo, 7 October 1930, 10:45 A.M., NAACP/mf p1 r25 f281; WFW to Juanita Jackson, 5 October 1936, NAACP/mf p1 r26 f628; WFW to Herbert Seligmann, 16 November 1931, NAACP/mf p1 r25 f478; WFW to Daisy Lampkin, 18 January 1933, NAACP/mf p1 r25 f695.

6. W.E.B. Du Bois to Roy Wilkins, 27 February 1930, WEBD/mf r34 f333; Du Bois to Wilkins, 28 March 1930, WEBD/mf r34 f336; Wilkins to Du Bois, 9 July 1930, WEBD/mf r34 f341; David Levering Lewis, *W.E.B. Du Bois: The Fight for Equality and the American Century, 1919–1963* (New York: Henry Holt, 2000), 279–80. My discussion of Walter White's efforts to exert control over *The Crisis* is also influenced by Lewis, *W.E.B. Du Bois: The Fight for Equality*, 279–86. But see also discussion of the same conflict from the perspective of another participant: B. Joyce Ross, *J. E. Spingarn and the Rise of the NAACP, 1911–1939* (New York: Atheneum, 1972), 139–43.

7. Du Bois to White and Bagnall, 24 March 1930, NAACP/mf p1 r25 f169; WFW to Arthur Spingarn, 27 March 1930, NAACP/mf p1 r25 f168; WFW to Edwin Embree, 3 June 1930, NAACP/mf p2 r12 f673; Embree to WFW 11 June 1930, NAACP/mf p2 r12 f700; Acting Secy. Monthly Rpt., 4 June 1930, NAACP/mf p1 r5 f209; Du Bois to WFW, memo, 10 June 1930, NAACP/mf p3A r1 f420; WFW to Du Bois, memo, 12 June 1930, NAACP/mf p3A r1 f421.

8. B of D Minutes, 14 July 1930, NAACP/mf p1 r2 f318; B of D Minutes, 8 September 1930, NAACP/mf p1 r2 f327; WFW to Arthur Spingarn 22 August 1930, NAACP/mf p2 r13 f105.

9. W.E.B. Du Bois to Arthur Spingarn, 7 February 1930, WEBD/mf r35 f330 (May 1929 resolution and "drastic"); Robert Bagnall to Du Bois, 23 January 1931, WEBD/mf r35 f312; B of D Minutes, 9 February 1930, NAACP/mf p1 r2 f355.

10. B of D Minutes, 14 December 1931, NAACP/mf p1 r2 f409.

11. W.E.B. Du Bois, Herbert Seligmann, William Pickens, Robert Bagnall, and Roy Wilkins to Board of Directors, 21 December 1931, JES/NYPL box 9 folder 4. There likely was no collusion in this instance between White and Ovington. After the board meeting that prompted this collective polemic, Ovington wrote to Joel Spingarn about her discouragement and her desire to resign as chairwoman. Walter White, she said, was nice enough, and she believed the two liked each other, but he wanted her out of the way, and he encouraged her to resign and assume the largely honorary post of treasurer; she had, she said, long since ceased to offer him advice on organizational policy. See Mary White Ovington to Joel Spingarn, 15 December (1931), JES/NYPL box 9 folder 2. White received some small comfort when Richetta Randolph, the senior person on the clerical staff and one of the most influential persons in the national office, wrote to Du Bois and the other protesters that she did not know whom the signers classified as clerks, "but I do want you to know that I personally do not subscribe to the above statement." See Richetta Randolph to Du Bois, Seligmann, Pickens, Bagnall, and Wilkins, memo, 22 December 1931, WEBD/mf r35 f464.

12. WFW to Eugene Martin, 16 November 1931, NAACP/mf p2 r14 f501. The sequence of events in the immediate aftermath of the accident is murky. White's account in his autobiography is completely unreliable, as will be discussed shortly. This reconstruction is based upon Edwina Ford (daughter of Will and Olive Westmoreland), interview by author, 28 January 1998, Savannah, Georgia; WFW to George White (brother), 4 October 1934, NAACP/mf p2 r17 f105 (which contains Walter White's summary of Madeline White's remembrances of the accident); and Madeline White to WFW, 6 October 1934, NAACP/mf p2 r17 f115. On conditions at Grady Hospital, see Ronald Bayor, *Race and the Shaping of Twentieth-Century Atlanta* (Chapel Hill: University of North Carolina Press, 1996), 155–58.

13. WFW, untitled article on his father's death and life, 6 September 1934, NAACP/mf

p11B r35 f832; only the discovery of his father as a Negro and his transfer to the Jim Crow ward is related in *A Man Called White*, 135–36.

14. NAACP press release, 11 December 1931, NAACP/mf p11A r20 f870. On Juliette Derricotte, see also David Levering Lewis, *W.E.B. Du Bois: The Fight for Equality and the American Century, 1919–1963*, 297–99.

15. Spencie Love, *One Blood: The Death and Resurrection of Charles R. Drew* (Chapel Hill: University of North Carolina Press, 1996), 41.

16. Madeline White to WFW, 6 October 1934, NAACP/mf p2 r17 f115.

17. *A Man Called White*, 136.

18. WFW to Madeline White, 26 September 1934, NAACP/mf p2 r17 f57; WFW to George White, 4 October 1934, NAACP/mf p2 r17 f105.

19. WFW to Madeline White, 15 March 1934, NAACP/mf p2 r16 f516 ("get"; the full quote reads, "A lot of effort is now being put into a plan to 'get' me because Du Bois has not been able to have his way without question."). Du Bois did in fact claim the secretary was unfit to lead the NAACP because of his complexion. See below and W.E.B. Du Bois, "Segregation in the North," *The Crisis*, April 1934, 115–17.

20. WFW to George White, 29 October 1929, NAACP/mf p2 r12 f234 (relating letter from Olive Westmoreland about their father's illness); Helen Martin to WFW, 3 December 1929, WFW/PCW box 4 folder 131; WFW to Helen Martin, 16 December 1929, NAACP/mf p2 r12 f303; George White to WFW, 5 March 1930, NAACP/mf p2 r12 f509 (reporting on positive family reaction to meeting Gladys).

21. Bishop John Hurst to WFW, 5 September 1924, NAACP/mf p2 r8 f20 (on *Fire in the Flint* publicity); Bishop John Hurst to WFW, 31 March 1927, NAACP/mf p2 r10 f686 ("Bertha and I"). Biographical information on Hurst is in Richard R. Wright, Jr., *The Bishops of the African Methodist Episcopal Church* (Nashville, Tenn.: A.M.E. Sunday School Union, 1963), 232–33.

22. WFW, funeral eulogy for Bishop John Hurst, 8 May 1930, NAACP/mf p16A r3 f183.

23. WFW to General Manager, Southern Railway System, 8 December 1931, NAACP/mf p2 r14 f546; Poppy Cannon, *A Gentle Knight: My Husband Walter White* (New York: Rinehart, 1956), 3–9 (on the White-Cannon reunion); Poppy Cannon, tape-recorded interview by David Levering Lewis, March 1970, Voices from the Renaissance Collection, 1974–1977, Schomburg Center for Research in Black Culture, New York Public Library, New York, New York (on the White-Cannon reunion); Eugene Martin to WFW, 12 December 1931, NAACP/mf p2 r14 f585 (on accident settlement); WFW to Martin, 15 December 1931, NAACP/mf p2 r14 f584 (on accident settlement); George White to WFW and siblings, 10 December 1931, NAACP/mf p2 r14 f569 (on support for their mother). Poppy Cannon's account of White's train ride home from Atlanta, included in both her memoirs and the Lewis interview, is inaccurate. She claims that White rode the Jim Crow day coach home from Atlanta because the Southern Railway would not provide African Americans a Pullman berth and White never passed for convenience. The effect of this story is to increase the level of White's psychic discomfort. In fact, White did occupy a Pullman berth. See WFW to General Manager, Southern Railway System, 8 December 1931, NAACP/mf p2 r14 f546. What is not clear is whether White told Cannon he went day coach or whether Cannon invented this detail for dramatic purposes.

24. Joel Spingarn to WFW, 4 December 1931, NAACP/mf p2 r14 f533. Langston Hughes to WFW, 8 December 1931, NAACP/mf p2 r14 f540.

25. Mary White Ovington to Arthur Spingarn (22 December 1931), ABS/LC box 10 folder "November–December 1931"; Joel Spingarn to Du Bois, 6 January 1932, WEBD/mf r37 f293.

26. Du Bois to Joel Spingarn, 31 December 1931, JES/NYPL box 9 folder 4; Roy Wilkins

to WFW, 22 December 1931, ABS/LC box 10 folder "November–December 1931"; William Pickens to WFW, 22 December 1931, WEBD/mf r35 f463; Pickens to Du Bois, 22 January 1932, WEBD/mf r37 f300; Herbert Seligmann to WFW, 22 December 1931, WEBD/mf r35 f464; Robert Bagnall to Du Bois, 22 December 1931, WEBD/mf r35 f463. In his memoirs Wilkins disingenuously tried to exculpate himself by claiming he didn't know that he was signing an attack on Walter White. Roy Wilkins with Tom Mathews, *Standing Fast: The Autobiography of Roy Wilkins* (New York: Viking, 1982), 117.

27. [Joel Spingarn to Board of Directors] (January 1932), JES/NYPL box 4 folder 2.
28. Mary White Ovington to Joel Spingarn, 12 April 1932, NAACP/mf p16A r3 f560.
29. B of D Minutes, 29 March 1932, NAACP/mf p1 r2 f443; B of D Minutes, 11 April 1932, NAACP/mf p1 r2 f448; WFW to John Haynes Holmes, 21 June 1932, NAACP/mf p2 r15 f186; Holmes to WFW, 12 May 1932, NAACP/mf p2 r15 f186.
30. On Communist activity, see Robin D.G. Kelley, *Hammer and Hoe: Alabama Communists during the Great Depression* (Chapel Hill: University of North Carolina Press, 1990); and Mark Solomon, *The Cry Was Unity: Communists and African Americans, 1917–1936* (Jackson: University Press of Mississippi, 1998).
31. B of D Minutes, 11 April 1932, NAACP/mf p1 r2 f448; B of D Minutes, 9 May 1932, NAACP/mf p1 r2 f458.
32. Minutes of roundtable discussion on "The NAACP and Politics," NAACP annual convention (May 1932), NAACP/mf p1 r9 f218; WFW, speech to NAACP annual convention 22 May 1932, NAACP/mf p1 r9 f154.
33. W.E.B. Du Bois, "What Is Wrong with the NAACP," speech to the NAACP annual convention, May 1932, NAACP/mf p1 r9 f52.
34. WFW, speech to NAACP annual convention, 22 May 1932, NAACP/mf p1 r9 f154. The conference gave a boost to White's leadership—something he was desperate to see happen—and helped to smooth over many of the rough spots that had developed, as he acknowledged in a letter to James Weldon Johnson, "during this period when everybody is hypercritical." WFW to JWJ, 27 May 1932, JWJ/Yale series 1 folder 541. He was given an assist by association vice president and veteran clubwoman Addie Hunton. In a featured tribute to White, Hunton fondly recalled his attempt to disguise himself before he conducted one of his numerous incognito investigations by growing a mustache. She told the audience that Arthur Spingarn told White, who was nicknamed "Fuzzy," that "Nobody will know you have it except you and your wife." This was merely prelude to her more serious point, that White was completely dedicated to the cause of race advancement, and that in his zeal he was like the apostle Paul. Said she, "Like Paul, he is willing to give his life to the cause that he serves, and this ought to be a wonderful inspiration for the young men of our race at this particular time, when we so much need the strength of our youth in formulating the policies which shall make for progress in the life of the race." Addie Hunton, speech to the NAACP annual convention, 17 May 1932, NAACP/mf p1 r9 f45.
35. Secy. Monthly Rpt. (May 1932), NAACP/mf p1 r5 f499; Secy. Monthly Rpt., 7 July 1932, NAACP/mf p1 r5 f538; Secy. Monthly Rpt., 15 August 1932, NAACP/mf p1 r5 f553; Secy. Monthly Rpt., 8 October 1932, NAACP/mf p1 r5 f577; Secy. Monthly Rpt., 7 June 1933, NAACP/mf p1 r5 f697; Donald J. Lisio, *Hoover, Blacks, and Lily-Whites* (Chapel Hill: University of North Carolina Press, 1985), 270–71.
36. Helen Boardman to WFW, 27 June 1932, NAACP/mf p10 r13 f679; Secy. Monthly Rpt., 8 September 1932, NAACP/mf p1 r5 f561; Will W. Alexander to WFW, 5 October 1932, WFW/PCW, box 1 folder 1; Roy Wilkins to WFW, 5 January 1933, NAACP/mf p10 r14 f639; Secy. Monthly Rpt., 10 November 1932, NAACP/mf p1 r5 f601; WFW to Robert Bagnall, memo, 7 September 1932, NAACP/mf p10 r13 f816 ("form the basis"); Secy. Monthly Rpt., 8 October 1932, NAACP/mf p1 r5 f577; Secy.

Monthly Rpt., 8 December 1932, NAACP/mf p1 r5 f617; Secy. Monthly Rpt., 7 June 1933, NAACP/mf p1 r5 f697; Lisio, *Hoover, Blacks, and Lily-Whites*, 270.

37. Chicago branch to Roy Wilkins (received 24 May 1933), NAACP/mf p1 r9 f374. See also Beth Tompkins Bates, "A New Crowd Challenges the Agenda of the Old Guard of the NAACP, 1933–1941," *American Historical Review* 102 (1997): 340–77.

38. Earl Dickerson, speech to the NAACP annual convention, 29 June 1933, NAACP/mf p1 r9 f435.

39. Roundtable discussion on tactics, NAACP annual convention, 1 July 1933, NAACP/mf p1 r9 f487. On MacPherson, see Kelley, *Hammer and Hoe*, 83–90.

40. Charles Houston, speech to the NAACP annual convention, 2 July 1933, NAACP/mf p1 r9 f547.

41. WFW to Robert Bagnall and William Pickens, memo, 9 September 1932, NAACP/mf p10 r13 f826 (on stimulating branches); WFW, speech to the NAACP annual convention (2 July 1933), NAACP/mf p1 r9 f556; NAACP press release, 19 May 1933, NAACP/mf p1 r9 f367 and WFW to Joel Spingarn, 22 June 1933, NAACP/mf p1 r26 f13 (on pivotal nature of the convention).

42. B of D Minutes, 14 March 1933, NAACP/mf p1 r2 f520.

43. Joel Spingarn to Mary White Ovington, 28 March 1933, JES/NYPL box 9 folder 2.

44. WFW to Joel Spingarn, 14 March 1933, NAACP/mf p1 r25 f718.

45. B of D Minutes, 14 April 1933, NAACP/mf p1 r2 f520; W.E.B. Du Bois to Lillian Alexander, 23 June 1933, WEBD/mf r39 f531 ("Walter did nothing"); WFW to JWJ, 3 April 1933, JWJ/Yale series 1 folder 542.

46. My account of the Amenia Conference is influenced by David Levering Lewis, *W.E.B. Du Bois: The Fight for Equality and the American Century, 1919–1963*, 315–25; W.E.B. Du Bois to Joel Spingarn, 10 April 1930, WEBD/mf r40 f652 ("without the slightest").

47. List of persons invited to the Amenia Conference, August 18–21, 1933, NAACP/mf p11A r18 f277.

48. Joel Spingarn, "Important Notice number 3," end of July 1933, NAACP/mf p11A r18 f341 (conference schedule); Frances Williams to WFW, 23 August 1933, NAACP/mf p11A r18 f281; WFW to Joel Spingarn, 8 September 1933, NAACP/mf p11A r18 f324 (reporting Emmet Dorsey's reactions); Louis Redding to Roy Wilkins, 2 September 1933, NAACP/mf p11A r18 f310.

49. Louis Redding to Roy Wilkins, 2 September 1933, NAACP/mf p11A r18 f310.

50. "Findings" (1 September 1933), NAACP/mf p11A r18 f275.

51. "Findings" (1 September 1933), NAACP/mf p11A r18 f275; E. Franklin Frazier to WFW, 17 May 1934, ABS/LC box 12 folder "May–June 1934."

52. Preliminary Report of the Committee on Future Plan and Program of the NAACP, (1934), NAACP/mf p16A r4 f272.

53. This account of Hocutt's suit draws heavily upon Richard Kluger, *Simple Justice* (New York: Vintage, 1977), 155–58.

54. Secy. Monthly Rpt., 6 April 1933, NAACP/mf p1 r5 f672; WFW to E.R. Merrick, 27 May 1933, NAACP/mf p12A r18 f203.

55. The *News & Observer* of Raleigh, North Carolina, for 23 May 1933, carried a sympathetic front-page article titled "Asks Equality in Negro Education" on White's stop at Shaw University in Raleigh. WFW to Ralph Harlow, 29 May 1933, NAACP/mf p2 r16 f134; WFW to JWJ, 6 June 1933, JWJ/Yale series 1 folder 542; WFW to Charles Houston, 14 October 1933, NAACP/mf p7A r8 f159. In October 1933 he returned to North Carolina for the meeting of the state conference of branches. In his speech closing the meeting, according to the *Greensboro Daily News* of 30 October 1933 (clipping of which is in NAACP/mf p12A r17 f997), he proclaimed the birth of "a new white man and a new negro [*sic*]" in the state, proof of which was his invitation to dine with a "fine southern white man" and in the company of white women.

56. Walter White, "George Crawford—Symbol," *The Crisis*, January 1934, 15. Genna Rae McNeil, *Groundwork: Charles Hamilton Houston and the Struggle for Civil Rights* (Philadelphia: University of Pennsylvania Press, 1983), 89–94; Kluger, *Simple Justice*, 147–54. So charged was the atmosphere in Loudon County that White and Houston had to stay in Washington, D.C., and commute to court each day. None of the hotels in the county seat of Leesburg catered to African Americans, and Negro residents of the city were afraid to house them. WFW to Drew Pearson, 18 December 1933, NAACP/mf p7B r4 f183.

57. WFW to Arthur Spingarn, 25 March 1933, NAACP/mf p1 r25 f728; Secy. Monthly Rpt., 4 May 1933, NAACP/mf p1 r5 f686; Martha Gruening, "The Truth About the Crawford Case," *New Masses*, 8 January 1935, 9–15; Helen Boardman and Martha Gruening, "Is the NAACP Retreating?" *The Nation*, 27 June 1934, 730–32; W.E.B. Du Bois, "The Crawford Case," *The Crisis*, June 1934, 149. See also the accusations contained in Martha Gruening, "An Open Letter to Walter White" (after January 1934), WEBD/mf r42 f351, which the *Norfolk Journal and Guide*, a black weekly, declined to publish. Gruening, whose ties to Du Bois went back to 1917 when she investigated the East St. Louis riot with him, believed that "there is dynamite enough in the stuff we have to retire Walter—and possibly Houston, too—to private life for ever . . ." Martha Gruening to W.E.B. Du Bois, 14 May 1934, WEBD/mf r42 f350.

58. WFW to Daisy Lampkin, 26 December 1933, NAACP/mf p1 r26 f65; WFW, Report of the Secretary to the NAACP Annual Business Meeting, 8 January 1934, NAACP/mf p1 r14 f263; and August Meier and Elliott Rudwick, "Attorneys Black and White: A Case Study of Race Relations within the NAACP," in August Meier and Elliott Rudwick, *Along the Color Line* (Urbana: University of Illinois Press, 1976), 128–173, and McNeil, *Groundwork*, part II (development of a cadre of black lawyers); WFW to Charles Houston, 16 January 1935, NAACP/mf p1 r26 f254 (on Crawford case and white liberals).

59. W.E.B. Du Bois, "Segregation," *The Crisis*, January 1934, reprinted in *Writings in Periodicals Edited by W.E.B. Du Bois: Selections from The Crisis*, II, *1926–1934*, ed. Herbert Aptheker (Millwood, NY: Kraus-Thomson, 1983), 727–28.

60. WFW to W.E.B. Du Bois, telegram, 11 January 1934, NAACP/mf p11A r30 f193; Du Bois to WFW, 11 January 1934, NAACP/mf p11A r30 f192. On the Arthurdale colony, see Blanche Weisen Cook, *Eleanor Roosevelt*, II, *1933–1938* (New York: Viking, 1999), 133–52. Clarence Pickett, the director of the subsistence homestead program for the Department of the Interior, welcomed Du Bois's endorsement of voluntary segregation, as did the southern white liberal Will Alexander, in *The Crisis* symposium on segregation. See *The Crisis*, March 1934, 82.

61. Joel Spingarn to WFW, 10 January 1934, NAACP/mf p11A r30 f200.

62. WFW to Joel Spingarn, 15 January 1934, NAACP/mf p11A r30 f218; Walter White, "On Segregation," *The Crisis*, March 1934, reprinted in *In Search of Democracy: The NAACP Writings of James Weldon Johnson, Walter White, and Roy Wilkins (1920–1977)*, ed. Sondra Kathryn Wilson (New York: Oxford University Press, 1999), 63–65, and also found at NAACP/mf p11A r30 f226.

63. W.E.B. Du Bois, "Subsistence Homestead Colonies," *The Crisis*, March 1934, reprinted in *Selections from The Crisis*, II, *1926–1934*, 735–39.

64. W.E.B. Du Bois, "Segregation in the North," *The Crisis*, March 1934, reprinted in *Selections from The Crisis*, II, *1926–1934*, 745–50.

65. Joel Spingarn to W.E.B. Du Bois, 27 March 1934, WEBD/mf r42 f888; Lewis, *W.E.B. Du Bois: The Fight for Equality and the American Century*, 341–42 ("letters flooded"). For other reaction to Du Bois's editorials, see C. A. Hansberry to Board of Directors, 8 May 1934, NAACP/mf p11A r30 f259; Irvin Mollison [for the Illinois Conference of

Branches] to Board of Directors, 11 May 1934, NAACP/mf p11A r30 f259; Montgomery (WV) Branch to Board of Directors, 13 May 1934, NAACP/mf p11A r30 f262.
On board support for the secretary, see, Ross, *J. E. Spingarn*, 195; Mary White Ovington to Charles Houston, 7 May 1934, NAACP/mf p2 r16 f579; JWJ to WFW, 14 May
1934, JWJ/Yale series 1 folder 543; Isadore Martin, 4 April 1934, NAACP/mf p16A r3
f897; Carl Murphy to Board of Directors, 17 June 1934, NAACP/mf p11A r30 f265.
On the board debate and resolution on segregation, see Ross, *J. E. Spingarn*, 192–98;
Lewis, *W.E.B. Du Bois: The Fight for Equality and the American Century*, 341–43.

66. Bruised as he was, White nevertheless took the high road by trying to reconcile with
Du Bois and thereby revealing essential features of both men's characters. On advice
from board member and black Republican from Memphis Robert Church, the secretary made a special trip to Atlanta to see Du Bois. Motoring to his quarters on the Atlanta University campus with his brother-in-law, White saw the former editor walking
down the street. "I alighted and followed Dr. Du Bois and spoke to him. We shook
hands and he remarked: 'You are looking thin.' At this juncture several people came up
to speak and Dr. Du Bois moved away." WFW to Robert Church, 9 July 1934,
NAACP/mf p11A r30 f356.

67. Frances Williams to WFW, 12 June (1934), NAACP/mf p2 r16 f620.

68. B of D Minutes, 9 July 1934, NAACP/mf p1 r2 f605; WFW to Joel Spingarn, 11 July
1934, NAACP/mf p11A r30 f359.

69. Joel Spingarn to WFW, 12 July 1934, NAACP/mf p2 r16 f682.

70. WFW to Abram Harris, 13 July 1934, NAACP/mf p16A r4 f145 ("I would like to suggest"); Mary White Ovington to WFW, 2 September 1934, NAACP/mf p16A r8 f703
("Some interesting"); Harris to WFW, 17 September 1934, NAACP/mf p16A r8 f736.

71. Mary White Ovington to Joel Spingarn, 23 September 1934, NAACP/mf p16A r8
f751; William Hastie to WFW, 24 September 1934, NAACP/mf p16A r8 f757; B of D
Minutes, 25 September 1934, NAACP/mf p1 r2 f624.

72. Proposed resolutions for the annual conference (June 1935), NAACP/mf p1 r9 f847;
Notes for NAACP press release, 25 June (1935), NAACP/mf p1 r9 f693 (on J. L.
LeFlore and Chicago branch); NAACP Press Release, 30 June 1935, NAACP/mf p1 r9
f691 (Walter White's speech).

73. Joel E. Spingarn, speech to NAACP annual convention, 25 June 1935, St. Louis, Missouri, NAACP/mf p1 r9 f703.

74. WFW to Eleanor Roosevelt, 6 June 1935, NAACP/mf p1 r26 f380; B of D Minutes 10
June 1935, NAACP/mf p1 r2 f672. According to the revisions to the new program affirmed in the 10 June 1935 board meeting, the secretary was now "the central coordinating agency of the Association's activities to be hereafter distinguished as Economic;
Legal and Political; Educational; Publicity, Research and Investigations; and Financial;
that responsibility be definitely placed upon him for integrating the work of these various divisions; that much of the present detail work of an almost purely administrative
character be shifted to other members of the staff; and that, in addition to the continu-
ance of his personal direction of the Association's activities, the Secretary be requested
to assume the added responsibility of personally directing the educational activities as
proposed in section V of this Plan and Program."

75. WFW to Will Jones, 11 June 1935, NAACP/mf p7B r8 f749; Jones to WFW, 5 June
1935, NAACP/mf p7B r8 f746.

76. Howard Kester to WFW, 30 July 1935, NAACP/mf p1 r26 f407. See also the following
correspondence that tracks the NAACP's standing among white leftists sympathetic to
the NAACP: Francis Henson to Howard Kester, 17 July 1935, Kester to Henson, 21
July 1935, and Henson to Kester, 3 August 1935, all in Howard Kester Papers, #3834,
folder 17, Southern Historical Collection, Library of the University of North Carolina

at Chapel Hill, Chapel Hill, NC. On Kester, see John Egerton, *Speak Now against the Day* (New York: Knopf, 1994); on the Southern Tenant Farmers Union, see Howard Kester, *Revolt among the Sharecroppers* (New York : Covici, Friede, [1936]).

77. Mary White Ovington to William Hastie, 7 May 1934, NAACP/mf p2 r16 f579.

78. Elliott Rudwick and August Meier, "The Rise of the Black Secretariat in the NAACP, 1909–35," in August Meier and Elliott Rudwick, *Along the Color Line* (Urbana: University of Illinois Press, 1976), 117–19.

79. Arthur Spingarn Oral History, 6 March 1968, Ralph J. Bunche Oral History Project, Moorland-Spingarn Research Center, Howard University, Washington, D.C. (on White's lack of appreciation for Joel Spingarn); WFW, statement on Joel Spingarn's death, 26 July 1939, NAACP/mf p1 r27 f448; WFW to Nannie Helen Burroughs, 16 August 1939, NAACP/mf p1 r27 f455 (on lawyers answering the call of Spingarn's death). In an ironic twist, Senator Arthur Capper of Kansas, who also served on the NAACP board, wrote White a sympathy note on Spingarn's death: "It goes without saying that he was one of the foremost members of your race and one of the most useful Americans of our time." Capper to WFW, 27 July 1939, NAACP/mf p1 r16 f16. The secretary thanked Capper: "I am certain that no tribute to Mr. Spingarn would have pleased him more than the one you unwittingly paid him in your letter of July 27—that he was a Negro—in that your believing him such showed how completely he had identified himself with the cause to which he devoted himself so unselfishly for more than thirty years." WFW to Capper, 28 July 1939, NAACP/mf p1 r27 f449.

Chapter 7: WALTER, ELEANOR, AND FRANKLIN: THE FEDERAL ANTILYNCHING CAMPAIGN, 1933–1940

1. Acting Secy. Monthly Rpt., 8 October 1930, NAACP/mf p1 r5 f254 (statistics); WFW to JWJ, 22 August 1930, JWJ/Yale series 1 folder 540 (reasons for increase in lynchings); NAACP press release, 18 July 1930, NAACP/mf p7A r3 f1016 (statements by Blease and Heflin). The acting secretary's report includes an incident that illustrates Walter White's skills as a publicist. Ludwell Denny of the Scripps-Howard newspaper chain asked White to prepare a memo on lynching in America. Denny did not plan to publish it, but he assured White that he would put it to good use and for the benefit of blacks. On White's analysis of the economic causes of lynching in *Rope and Faggot*, see chapter 4.

2. News story from unidentified newspaper (7 August 1930), NAACP/mf p7A r11 f502; W.E.B. Du Bois, "Marion," *The Crisis*, October 1930, 353; Mrs. F. K. Bailey to WFW, 8 August 1930, NAACP/mf p7A r11 f517; Walter White, "Sheriff's Fears Permitted Indiana Lynching," *New York World*, 24 August 1930.

3. WFW to James Ogden [Indiana state attorney], 22 August 1930, NAACP/mf p7A r11 f577; White, "Sheriff's Fears Permitted Indiana Lynching," *New York World*, 24 August 1930; Acting Secy. Monthly Rpt., 5 March 1931, NAACP/mf p1 r5 f317; Mrs. F. K. Bailey to WFW, 29 December 1930, NAACP/mf p7A r11 f667; William Pickens, "Aftermath of a Lynching," *The Nation*, 15 April 1931, 406–407. The International Labor Defense conducted its own investigation and reported that it was the sheriff who fomented the rumors that the white woman had been raped, and that in preparation for the lynching he had sent the town's black officers home. International Labor Defense press release, 11 September 1930, NAACP/mf p7A r11 f644.

4. WFW to JWJ, 22 August 1930, JWJ/Yale series 1 folder 540. See also, Robert Zangrando, *The NAACP Crusade against Lynching, 1909–1950* (Philadelphia: Temple University Press, 1980), 98–99.

5. Addie Hunton to Hannah Hull, 6 April 1933, NAACP/mf p7B r4 f901. Hunton here was reporting on her conversation with White; WFW to Hunton, 14 April 1933,

NAACP/mf p7B r4 f900, calls Hunton's letter to Hull "a superb statement—infinitely better than I could have summarized our conversation."

6. Roy Wilkins to B. M. Miller, telegram, 14 August 1933, NAACP/mf p7A r8 f109; Charles Houston to WFW, 30 August 1933, NAACP/mf p7A r8 f121; Leon Ransom, Edward Lovett, Charles Houston to ILD, ACLU, NAACP, 13 October 1933, NAACP/mf p7A r8 f144; Houston to WFW, 6 September 1933, NAACP/mf p7A r8 f135. According to Genna Rae McNeil's excellent biography of Charles Houston, Houston first tried to see President Roosevelt. He and his associate were told to return the next morning, which they did. After waiting for more than an hour, they were rudely turned away by a receptionist who demanded, "What do you boys want?" Genna Rae McNeil, *Groundwork: Charles Hamilton Houston and the Struggle for Civil Rights* (Philadelphia: University of Pennsylvania Press, 1983), 88–89.

7. Secy. Monthly Rpt. (November 1933), NAACP/mf p1 r5 f747; Robert L. Zangrando, *The NAACP Crusade against Lynching, 1909–1950*, 103–104; *The Great Depression*, pt. 6, *To Be Somebody*, produced by Henry Hampton, 57 min., Blackside, Inc., in association with BBC-2, 1993, videocassette, contains testimony of witnesses to the lynching; Statement of the Hon. William Preston Lane, Jr., Congress, Senate, Subcommittee of the Committee on the Judiciary, *Punishment for the Crime of Lynching: Hearings before a Subcommittee of the Committee on the Judiciary United States Senate*, 73rd Cong., 2nd sess, 20 and 21 February, 1934, 111–28.

8. Secy. Monthly Rpt. (November 1933), NAACP/mf p1 r5 f747; WFW to Edward Costigan, 19 December 1933, NAACP/mf p7B r4 f997; WFW to NAACP Branches, 29 November 1933, NAACP/mf p7B r4 f948.

9. WFW to NAACP Branches, 29 November 1933, NAACP/mf p7B r4 f948; WFW to James H. Dillard, 6 December 1933, NAACP/mf p7A r4 f365.

10. *Punishment for the Crime of Lynching*, iii, 3 (witness list and "limited to its proponents"); WFW to William Pickens, 26 February 1934, NAACP/mf p1 r26 f88 (broadcast of hearings and appearances by Ford and Ades); on the AFL, see WFW to William Green, 1 February 1934, NAACP/mf p7B r5 f90, and Green to WFW, 5 February 1934, NAACP/mf p7B r5 f178.

11. *Punishment for the Crime of Lynching*, 73–75, 62–67, 38–49. White had asked Clarence Darrow to endorse the bill, but he regretfully declined, citing his distrust of the federal government as a defender of personal liberty. See Clarence Darrow to WFW, telegram, 15 February 1934, NAACP/mf p7B r5 f433.

12. *Punishment for the Crime of Lynching*, 77–78.

13. *Punishment for the Crime of Lynching*, 82–93.

14. *Punishment for the Crime of Lynching*, 14 ("extend their activities"), 15 ("No longer is the Negro"), 17–35 (texts of editorials).

15. *Punishment for the Crime of Lynching*, 79–82.

16. *Punishment for the Crime of Lynching*, 49–58; Albert Barnett to WFW, 29 December 1933, NAACP/mf p7B r4 f1034; Barnett to WFW, 1 January 1934, NAACP/mf p7B r4 f1039; Barnett to WFW, 12 February 1934, NAACP/mf p7B r5 f447; Barnett to WFW, 2 January 1934, NAACP/mf p7B r4 f1208; Barnett to Will Alexander, 2 January 1934, NAACP/mf p7B r4 f1209.

17. Jacqueline Dowd Hall, *Revolt against Chivalry: Jessie Daniel Ames and the Women's Campaign against Lynching* (New York: Columbia University Press, 1979), 129–30, 159 (quote).

18. Commission on Interracial Cooperation press release, 8 December 1933, NAACP/mf p7B r4 f993; "South's Women Ask U.S. Aid to Stop Lynching," *New York Herald-Tribune*, 9 January 1934, typewritten copy in NAACP/mf p7B r4 f1245; WFW to Jessie Daniel Ames, 12 January 1934, NAACP/mf p7A r4 f465; WFW to Ames, 18 January

1934, NAACP/mf p7A r4 f471; Ames to WFW, 22 January 1934, NAACP/mf p7A r4 f472.

19. Jacqueline Dowd Hall, *Revolt against Chivalry: Jessie Daniel Ames and the Women's Campaign against Lynching,* rev. ed. (New York: Columbia University Press, 1993), 223–36 ("ingenious use" on 223), 248–49. For another detailed examination of southern female reform, see Glenda Elizabeth Gilmore, *Gender and Jim Crow* (Chapel Hill: University of North Carolina Press, 1996).

20. Charles Houston to WFW 14 October 1933, NAACP/mf p7A r8 f147, in which Houston echoes White's opinion about the CIC.

21. Albert Barnett to WFW, 27 January 1934, NAACP/mf p7B r5 f146; *Punishment for the Crime of Lynching,* 181; Will Alexander to WFW, 23 January 1934, NAACP/mf p7B r4 f1421.

22. Julian Harris to WFW, 6 January 1934, NAACP/mf p7B r5 f6.

23. John T. Kneebone, *Southern Liberal Journalists and the Issue of Race, 1920–1944* (Chapel Hill: University of North Carolina Press, 1985), 77–84; George Fort Milton to WFW, 30 January 1934, NAACP/mf p7B r4 f1475; WFW to Milton, 2 February 1934, NAACP/mf p7B r5 f103 ("one of the finest"); Milton to WFW, 12 February 1934, NAACP/mf p7B r5 f350. Fear of communism was a thread that often bound southern white liberals to each other. More than once anticommunism led Will Alexander to compromise with the Jim Crow order. A case in point is the case of the Atlanta Six, who in 1930 were charged with insurrection. Rather than pursue an aggressive defense, he urged the accused to hire the state's ex-governor and promised a small contribution to the cause if the six followed his advice. At a meeting called to organize a legal and extralegal defense, Alexander pontificated that "the communists really deserved no help because they were foolish enough to talk Negro social equality in the South." He tried to broker a deal in which the defendants would leave town immediately if they were released, and he tried to squash a sympathetic statement organized by other Atlanta-area liberals; finally, in a fit of pique, Alexander removed himself from the Atlanta Six's defense. See Walter Wilson [southern representative of the American Civil Liberties Union] to [Roger Baldwin], 13 July 1930, NAACP/mf p10 r9 f276.

24. WFW to Charles Houston, 16 February 1934, NAACP/mf p7B r5 f505.

25. Clarence Pickett to WFW, 2 March 1934, NAACP/mf p2 r16 f499; WFW to Albert Barnett, 20 March 1934, NAACP/mf p7B r5 f985 ("told her to inform me"). On President Roosevelt's willingness to sacrifice black advancement for his other programs, see, among other works, Harvard Sitkoff, *A New Deal for Blacks* (New York: Oxford University Press, 1981), 43–45.

Of course White was not the only one talking with ER. If Will Alexander and his journalist confreres maintained a paralytic neutrality—they said they would neither endorse nor oppose Costigan-Wagner—Jessie Daniel Ames took action to derail the bill. Invited to lunch with ER, Ames tried to persuade her that the legislation would stiffen the South's resistance and urge to lynch. Eleanor Roosevelt apparently had not made up her mind, and she in turn invited the secretary to meet with her, both to inform him of her husband's desires concerning the bill and to relate her conversation with Ames and get his opinion. The first point should have put the secretary at ease, not so much because she said the president wished to see antilynching legislation passed, but because of the manner in which the message was delivered. As White reported the conversation to his confidant Charles Houston, ER had referred to the president as "Frank," indicating a level of comfort and intimacy between the secretary and first lady that boded well for continued access to the White House. WFW to Charles Houston, 20 April 1934, NAACP/mf p7B r5 f1248.

But White, fearful of losing ground, wrote ER a long letter—he apologized for penning three pages—rebutting Ames's stock arguments. It was his coalition that had the

momentum, he said; even some of the state branches of the women's antilynching association and the largest organization of Southern Methodist women had deserted Ames.
Her belief that the bill would make matters worse for blacks was a baseless evasion, he
said. "The plight of the Negro in the areas where lynchings are most frequent is so terrible that it could hardly be worse." This was one skirmish that White won; ER
promptly wrote to Ames urging her, unsuccessfully it turned out, to reconsider her opposition to Costigan-Wagner. WFW to Eleanor Roosevelt, 20 April 1934, ER/mf r18
f932; Blanche Weisen Cook, *Eleanor Roosevelt*, II, *1933–1938* (New York: Viking, 1999),
178–79.

26. Eleanor Roosevelt to WFW, 2 May 1934, ER/mf r18 f931. White's meeting with ER
and the president took place the following Sunday, which was May 6, 1934; at various
times, however, White mistakenly dated the meeting May 7, and this very minor but
potentially confusing error, given all parties' busy schedules, has entered the historical
record.

27. Secondary accounts of White's meeting with FDR are *A Man Called White*, 168–69 (incorrectly placing the meeting in 1935), and Cook, *Eleanor Roosevelt*, II, 181. Primary
sources that touch on this meeting are WFW, statement of meeting with the president
(6 or 7 May 1934?), NAACP/mf p2 r16 f587; WFW to Edward Costigan, 8 May 1934,
NAACP/mf p7B r6 f2; Secy. Monthly Rpt., 9 May 1934, NAACP/mf p1 r5 f826;
WFW to Daisy Lampkin, 11 May 1934, NAACP/mf p1 r26 f126; WFW to Eleanor
Roosevelt, 14 May 1934, ER/mf r18 f946.

28. NAACP press release, 1 June 1934, NAACP/mf p7B r6 f248; WFW to Eleanor Roosevelt, 29 May 1934, NAACP/mf p1 r26 f131. For a sampling of Republican sentiment
on the antilynching bill, see Hamilton Kean to Roy Wilkins, 11 June 1934, NAACP/mf
p7B r6 f307; Roscoe Patterson to Roy Wilkinson [*sic*], 11 June 1934, NAACP/mf p7B
r6 f309; Frederick Steiwer to Roy Wilkins, 11 June 1934, NAACP/mf p7B r6 f318.

29. WFW to Eleanor Roosevelt, 29 May 1934, NAACP/mf p1 r26 f131; Secy. Monthly
Rpt., 6 June 1934, NAACP/mf p1 r5 f835; WFW to Edward Costigan, 8 June 1934,
NAACP/mf p7B r6 f303.

30. There were specific factors too that led to Jewish officialdom's reluctance to support
antilynching. It wrongly interpreted the growing friction between African Americans
and the Jewish merchants and landlords situated in ghetto communities as a wave of
black anti-Semitism. Whatever the nationalistic rhetorical excesses there were in the
mid-thirties' "don't buy where you can't work" boycotts of Jewish-owned businesses in
Harlem and elsewhere, African Americans' fundamental complaint was with discriminatory practices by merchants who happened to be Jewish, not the presence of Jews in
itself. Jewish leaders were also slow to recognize the connection between fascism in
Germany and racism in the United States. While they were quick to seek NAACP support for a boycott of the Berlin Olympics—a position the association had independently taken—on the sound theory that "we minorities must stick together," they were
unwilling to unite with African Americans on issues that did not touch Jewish life. Walter White, who appears initially to have mistaken the interest in black causes by specific
Jewish elites for that of the Jewish establishment, complained bitterly about the lack of
reciprocity. He scored leading Jews' silence on discriminatory practices by Jewish merchants as well as their refusal to support the NAACP's legal challenge to racially restrictive real-estate covenants in the thirties. See WFW to Joel Spingarn, 28 November
1935, NAACP/mf p1 r26 f454; WFW to A. C. MacNeal, 16 December 1935,
NAACP/mf p11A r1 f383; Irvin Mollison to WFW, 17 December 1935, NAACP/mf
p11A r1 f384; WFW to Jacob Billikopf, 9 January 1936, NAACP/mf p1 r26 f472;
Emanuel Celler to WFW, 31 March 1936, NAACP/mf p7B r17 f597; WFW to Celler,
6 April 1936, NAACP/mf p7B r17 f613; WFW to Lewis Strauss, 14 April 1936,
NAACP/mf p7B r10 f128; WFW to Charles Edward Russell, 18 January 1937,

NAACP/mf p16A r4 f371 ("we minorities"). See also additional correspondence between WFW and Lewis Strauss, in Lewis Strauss Papers, Name and Subject File I, box 51E Accretions, folders "White, W., April–Dec. 1936," and "White, W., January–March 1936," Herbert Hoover Presidential Library, West Branch, Iowa. On the "don't buy where you can't work" boycotts, see August Meier and Elliott Rudwick, "The Origins of Nonviolent Direct Action in Afro-American Protest: A Note on Historical Discontinuities," in August Meier and Elliott Rudwick, *Along the Color Line* (Urbana: University of Illinois Press, 1976), 307–404.

31. August Meier and John H. Bracey, Jr., "The NAACP as a Reform Movement, 1909–1965: 'To reach the conscience of America,'" *Journal of Southern History* 69 (1993): 23–24; David Levering Lewis, "Parallels and Divergencies: Assimilationist Strategies of Afro-American and Jewish Elites from 1910 to the Early 1930s," *Journal of American History* 71 (1984): 543–64; WFW to Jacob Billikopf, 9 April 1934, NAACP/mf p7B r5 f1173; WFW to Stephen Wise, 17 May 1934, NAACP/mf p7B r6 f138; WFW to Wise, 12 May 1934, NAACP/mf p7B r6 f71.

32. Wilton Steinberg to WFW, 28 November 1934, NAACP/mf p7B r6 f858; Joshua Goldberg to WFW, 12 December 1934, NAACP/mf p7B r6 f930; Morris Waldman to WFW, 11 December 1934, NAACP/mf p7B r6 f932; WFW and others to William Green, telegram, 30 April 1935, NAACP/mf p7B r8 f390; Gertrude Stone to WFW, 9 September 1935, NAACP/mf p7B r8 f917; NAACP press release, 28 February 1936, NAACP/mf p7B r9 f742. See Hasia R. Diner, *In the Almost Promised Land: American Jews and Blacks, 1915–1935* (Westport, CT: Greenwood Press, 1977), chap. 4, for a detailed discussion of Jewish relations with the NAACP. But see also Lewis, "Parallels and Divergencies"; Cheryl Greenberg, "Negotiating Coalitions: Black and Jewish Civil Rights Agencies in the Twentieth Century," and Nancy Weiss, "Long-Distance Runners of the Civil Rights Movement: The Contribution of Jews to the NAACP and the National Urban League in the Early Twentieth Century," both in *Struggles in the Promised Land*, eds. Jack Salzman and Cornel West (New York: Oxford University Press, 1997), 123–75.

33. Secy. Monthly Rpt., 9 November 1934, NAACP/mf p1 r5 f881; WFW to Edward Costigan and Robert Wagner, 30 January 1935, NAACP/mf p7B r7 f388; Secy. Monthly Rpt., 6 February 1935, NAACP/mf p1 r6 f9; WFW to Mike Flynn, 20 January 1936, NAACP/mf p7B r9 f523.

34. On the lynching of Claude Neal, see [Howard Kester] to WFW, 7 November 1934, NAACP/mf p7A r4 f635, and Secy. Monthly Rpt., 9 November 1934, NAACP/mf p1 r5 f881. Kester, who investigated the lynching at White's behest, wrote a final report on the lynching, which was substantially the same as his letter to White; it is reprinted in *African Americans in the Industrial Age: A Documentary History, 1915–1945*, eds. Joe W. Trotter and Earl Lewis (Boston: Northeastern University Press, 1996), 209–17. See also James R. McGovern, *Anatomy of a Lynching: The Killing of Claude Neal* (Baton Rouge: Louisiana State University Press, 1982).

35. WFW to Eleanor Roosevelt, 8 November 1934, ER/mf r18 f1006 (includes both White's requests and Eleanor Roosevelt's handwritten replies); Cook, *Eleanor Roosevelt*, II, 243 ("this is dynamite"); Eleanor Roosevelt to WFW, 23 November 1934, NAACP/mf p1 r22 f616 ("I talked with the President yesterday").

36. L. C. Dyer to WFW, 28 January 1935, NAACP/mf p7B r7 f318; WFW to Dyer, 2 February 1935, NAACP/mf p7B r7 f447; WFW to Eleanor Roosevelt, 1 February 1935, ER/mf r19 f22.

37. WFW to Eleanor Roosevelt, 10 January 1935, NAACP/mf p1 r26 f248; WFW to Eleanor Roosevelt, 12 January 1935, NAACP/mf p1 r26 f250 ("is going to grow speedily"); Eleanor Roosevelt to WFW, 22 January 1935, NAACP/mf p1 r22 f619.

38. Margaret Rose Vendryes, "Hanging on Their Walls: *An Art Commentary on Lynching, the Forgotten 1935 Art Exhibition,*" in *Race Consciousness: African-American Studies for the New Century,* eds. Judith Jackson Fossett and Jeffrey A. Tucker (New York: New York University Press, 1997), 153–76.

39. WFW to Langston Hughes, 15 January 1935, Langston Hughes Papers/Yale box 166, leaves 42–43; Hughes to WFW, Langston Hughes Papers/Yale, box 166 leaf 44. In a less guarded commentary on the flap with the Communist Party over the Art Commentary, White told his brother that "the Communists tried to break this up because they were sore that they had not thought of the idea themselves." WFW to George White, 26 February 1935, NAACP/mf p2 r17 f354. Hughes did not become one, but the list of patrons was a distinguished one, including "the playwrights Sherwood Anderson, Sidney Howard, and Elmer Rice; the novelists Faith Baldwin, Pearl Buck, Erskine Caldwell, and Fannie Hurst; the actresses Ina Claire, Molly Picon, and Blanche Yurka; the writers and critics Charles A. Beard, Robert Benchley, Heywood Broun, Clifton Fadiman, Douglas S. Freeman, George Jean Nathan, Dorothy Parker, Carl Van Doren, and Carl Van Vechten; the poets Stephen Vincent Benét, Countee Cullen, and James Weldon Johnson; the politicians Edward P. Costigan, Herbert Lehman, and Robert F. Wagner; the socially prominent Mrs. Thomas Watson; the musician George Gershwin; the art-world figures Alfred Barr, Jr., Edward Bruce, Rene d'Harnoncourt, Lloyd Goodrich, Suzanne LaFollette, Dr. Alain Locke, and Audrey McMahon; the educator Dr. Alvin Johnson; the social worker Mrs. Mary M.K. Simkhovitch; the NAACP leaders Mary White Ovington, Arthur B. and J. E. Spingarn, Oswald Garrison Villard, White himself, and Roy Wilkins; and the bibliophile Arthur A. Schomburg." Marlene Park, "Lynching and Antilynching: Art and Politics in the 1930s," *Prospects* 18 (1993): 328–29.

The CP's exhibit, "The Struggle for Negro Rights," opened about two weeks later, on March 2, 1935. Although there was some overlap in artists, the CP's show notably lacked the religious emphasis and self-consciously promoted "fighting pictures" that "carry the fight to a higher political level," rather than simply evoke sympathy and pity for African Americans. Park, "Lynching and Antilynching," 338–44.

40. WFW to Eleanor Roosevelt, telegram, 8 February 1935, ER/mf r19 f26 (White's invitation and Eleanor Roosevelt's acceptance, which was handwritten at the bottom of the telegram); WFW to ER, 12 February 1935, ER/mf r19 f28 (Seligmann Galleries' cancellation); Park, "Lynching and Antilynching," 326–28.

41. Eleanor Roosevelt to WFW (before 23 February 1935) NAACP/mf p1 r22 f630.

42. Eleanor Roosevelt to WFW, 20 February 1935, ER/mf r19 f30.

43. Roy Wilkins to WFW, 21 November 1934, NAACP/mf p7B r4 f528; WFW to Wilkins, 28 November 1934, NAACP/mf p7B r4 f536.

44. WFW to Roy Wilkins, memo, 6 December 1934, NAACP/mf p7B r4 f543; Wilkins to WFW, telegram, 7 December 1934, NAACP/mf p7B r4 f544; WFW to Wilkins, telegram, 7 December 1934, NAACP/mf p7B r4 f546; Charles Houston to NAACP, telegram, 14 December 1934, NAACP/mf p7B r4 f595; *Washington News,* 11 December 1934, p. 1, clipping at NAACP/mf p7B r4 f654; WFW to Boake Carter, 13 December 1934, NAACP/mf p7B r4 f592; Wilkins to Houston, 19 December 1934, NAACP/mf p7B r4 f616. See also Roy Wilkins with Tom Mathews, *Standing Fast: The Autobiography of Roy Wilkins* (New York: Viking, 1982), 132–36.

45. WFW to Charles Houston, 14 November 1934, NAACP/mf p7B r6 f657 (reporting on WFW's conversations with Katherine Gardner and Gardner's conversations with Will Alexander); WFW to Eleanor Roosevelt, 20 November 1934, NAACP/mf p1 r26 f221 and ER to WFW, 23 November 1934, NAACP/mf p1 r22 f616 (on finding out whether FDR in fact opposed the bill). Based on what Gardner had told him, the secre-

tary reluctantly came to the conclusion that Alexander's opposition was largely based upon "personal and organizational jealousy. I believed him superior to such emotions." WFW to William Hastie, 15 November 1934, NAACP/mf p7B r6 f659.

46. On efforts to put white southern liberals on the spot, see Edward Costigan to WFW, 23 February 1935, NAACP/mf p7B r7 f685; WFW to Costigan, 25 February 1935, NAACP/mf p7B r7 f684; WFW to Albert Barnett, 19 March 1935, NAACP/mf p7B r7 f959; WFW to Will Alexander (19 March 1935), NAACP/mf p7B r7 f975. George Fort Milton to WFW, 31 January 1935, NAACP/mf p7B r7 f381; WFW to Aaron Bernd, 13 December 1934, NAACP/mf p7B r6 f925; Virginius Dabney to WFW, 2 January 1935, NAACP/mf p7B r6 f1226; Jessie Daniel Ames to Katherine Gardner, 14 February 1935, NAACP/mf p7B r7 f619.

47. Charles Houston to WFW, telegram, 21 February 1935, NAACP/mf p7B r7 f669; WFW to George White, 26 February 1935, NAACP/mf p2 r17 f354; Wilkins to WFW, memo, 2 February 1935, NAACP/mf p7B r7 f459; WFW to Eleanor Roosevelt, 8 March 1935, ER/mf r19 f46.

48. The following sequence of letters illustrates the access Walter White had to Eleanor Roosevelt. "For the reasons we discussed in New York it seems to me wiser not to seek this interview through the regular channels," he wrote to her in WFW to Eleanor Roosevelt, 8 March 1935, ER/mf r19 f46. She handed the request to the president's secretary, Marvin McIntyre, who denied it. Explained McIntyre to ER, "Confidentially, also, this is a very delicate situation and it does not seem advisable to draw the President into any more than we have to." Marvin McIntyre to Mrs. Scheider [Eleanor Roosevelt's secretary], 14 March 1935, ER/mf r19 f45. Undeterred, White pressed his case again, asking ER to make him an appointment before the president left for Florida. WFW to Eleanor Roosevelt, 14 March 1935, ER/mf r19 f44. This time, she bypassed his staff, forwarding White's letter to her husband with the following note appended to it: "FDR—I think you could see him *here* & help him on tasks with advice. This ought to go through."

49. Richetta Randolph to JWJ, 19 April 1935, NAACP/mf p7B r8 f226; NAACP press release, 20 April 1935, NAACP/mf p7B r8 f252 (list of lobbyists).

50. White's eyewitness reports from the Senate gallery are in Secy. Monthly Rpt., 4 April 1935, NAACP/mf p1 r5 f914; WFW to George Schuyler (April 1935), NAACP/mf p1 r26 f336; WFW to John Hope, 6 May 1935, NAACP/mf p7B r8 f470. Secy. Monthly Rpt., 6 May 1935, NAACP/mf p1 r5 f931; Richetta Randolph to WFW, telegram, 30 April 1935, NAACP/mf p7B r8 f384 (demonstrations at black colleges); WFW to Madeline White and mother, 6 May 1935, NAACP/mf p2 r17 f454; Zangrando, *The NAACP Crusade against Lynching*, 128–29.

51. WFW to Franklin Roosevelt, 6 May 1935, NAACP/mf p1 r26 f347; Stephen Early to Malvina Schneider, 5 August 1935, ER/mf r19 f176.

52. Will Alexander to WFW, 14 August 1931, NAACP/mf p6 r4 f121; Roger K. Newman, *Hugo Black: A Biography* (New York: Pantheon, 1994), 146; WFW to William Pickens, 14 March 1933, NAACP/mf p1 r25 f719.

53. Newman, *Hugo Black*, 13–14, 42–44.

54. Newman, *Hugo Black*, 42, 43.

55. On Black's refusal to vote for explicitly antidiscriminatory legislation, see WFW to J. E. Chappelle [editor of the *Birmingham News*], 25 May 1937, NAACP/mf p7B r21 f761, and Newman, *Hugo Black*, 225. See also C[harles] H. T[hompson], "Editorial Comment: The Harrison-Black-Fletcher Bill Makes Its Debut," *Journal of Negro Education* 6 (1937): 129–33, on the reluctance of Black and other white liberals to include specific antidiscriminatory wording in pioneering legislation authorizing federal aid to education.

56. Newman, *Hugo Black*, 57 (racial epithets), 69 (Black's financial comfort), 71–88 (murder case), 89–100 (Klan membership), 128–29 (Senate record).
57. WFW to Hugo Black, 6 May 1935, NAACP/mf p7B r8 f450.
58. Newman, *Hugo Black*, 236; B of D Minutes, 13 September 1937, NAACP/mf p1 r2 f832.
59. WFW to Franklin Roosevelt, memo, 2 January 1936, NAACP/mf p7B r9 f385; WFW, "Memorandum of interview of the Secretary of the N.A.A.C.P. with the President at the White House on January 2, 1936, from 12:15 to 12:50," 3 January 1936, NAACP/mf p2 r18 f103; WFW to William Illig, 3 January 1936, NAACP/mf p7B r30 f204.
60. WFW to Frederick Van Nuys, 4 January 1936, NAACP/mf p7B r9 f422; Zangrando, *NAACP Crusade against Lynching*, 133.
61. WFW to Joseph Gavagan, 8 April 1936, NAACP/mf p7B r17 f647; WFW to Thomas Ford, 26 March 1936; WFW to Eleanor Roosevelt, 5 April 1936, NAACP/mf p7B r10 f32.
62. John Dingell to WFW, 8 June 1936, NAACP/mf p7B r17 f899; Lowell Mellett to WFW, 25 May 1936, handwritten reply appended to bottom of WFW to Mellett, 23 May 1936, NAACP/mf p7B r10 f406.
63. James Byrnes and Theodore Bilbo, quoted in Zangrando, *The NAACP Crusade against Lynching*, 150. For an account of the filibuster, see *Time*, 24 January 1938, 8–10. For biographical sketches of the Bourbons in the Senate, see John Egerton, *Speak Now against the Day* (Chapel Hill: University of North Carolina Press, 1995).
64. Zangrando, *The NAACP Crusade against Lynching*, 148; George C. Rable, "The South and the Politics of Antilynching Legislation, 1920–1940," *Journal of Southern History* 51 (1985): 215–19; WFW to Mr. Ellis, 16 September 1938, NAACP/mf p2 r19 f335 (Hay-Adams Hotel); Hall, *Revolt against Chivalry*, 245–47. For more on the fracture within the liberal camp, see WFW to Victor Weybright, 3 June 1939, NAACP/mf p7A r5 f744; Monroe Work to WFW, 4 November 1938, NAACP/mf p7A r5 f691; Work to Jessie Daniel Ames, 4 November 1938, NAACP/mf p7A r5 f689; Ames to WFW, 17 November 1938, NAACP/mf p7A r5 f696; Thurgood Marshall to WFW, memo, 14 November 1938, NAACP/mf p7A r5 f692.

Walter White's scraps with liberals were not confined to the southern type; he had his hands full with white liberals in his own organization as well. In 1939, Joe Rodgers was lynched in Canton, Mississippi. Buck Kester investigated for the NAACP and concluded that "lynching is entering a new phase and one much more difficult to deal with than the open mob. I was told that after the exposure of the double lynching at Duck Hill that word was passed that all further trouble would be handled by a 'small number of men' designated by the mob to do the job for them." Howard Kester to WFW, 20 September 1939, Howard Kester Papers, series I folder 76, Southern Historical Collection, University of North Carolina, Chapel Hill, NC. In another letter, Kester wrote that "Lynchings, in my judgment are not declining as the Tuskegee reports suggest, but they are not getting into the newspapers. The lynching of Joe Rodgers in Canton went completely unreported by the press. . . . I ran across what appeared to be four other lynchings in the vicinity of Cleveland, Mississippi when I was down there the other day." Kester to Elisabeth Gilman, 20 October 1939, Kester papers, series I folder 77. Despite these shocking developments, however, the secretary had a most difficult time publicizing them. First, Jessie Daniel Ames refused to allow ASWPL material to be used in the report that the NAACP prepared based on Kester's report. Jessie Daniel Ames to WFW, 25 October 1939, Kester papers, series I folder 77. Then, when White sought money to print and broadcast the report from association vice president Godfrey Cabot, Cabot hedged, saying that he thought it better in criminal cases to win in court rather than agitate outside. WFW to Godfrey Cabot, 29 November 1939, NAACP/mf p7A r21 f891. When the secretary reminded Cabot that the standard procedure in these cases was to agitate and expose wrongdoing, Cabot agreed to provide money for printing, but only if the secretary could get a "representative committee of whites" to endorse Kester's report and only "after careful revision by men of political experience." Cabot to WFW, telegram, 19 December 1939, NAACP/mf p7A r21 f894.

65. WFW to Gertrude Stone, 31 July 1939, NAACP/mf p7B r20 f554.

66. Elizabeth Eastman wrote to White that "It has occurred to me that we may be unrealistic in this matter. What chance has our anti-lynching bill,—to face the cold facts? The agitation for it and public education is what we get out of all our efforts, but absolutely no chance of passing the bill, for many reasons." Elizabeth Eastman to WFW, 30 December 1936, NAACP/mf p7B r11 f150. More than two years earlier, as the first Costigan-Wagner bill was bottled up in committee, Mary White Ovington worried in a letter to William Hastie that failure to win solid—not only moral—victories would damage the association's reputation. Mary White Ovington to William Hastie, 7 May 1934, NAACP/mf p2 r16 f579. Charles Houston was typically more direct. Recognizing that organized labor and other progressives were lukewarm to an antilynching bill, Houston nevertheless saw great opportunity to push for the full inclusion of African Americans in the New Deal and win labor's support. "What I fear," Houston wrote to White, "is that with the activity of the national office centering so much around the anti-lynching bill, there are not enough irons in the fire, and that the success of the [Roosevelt] administration may tend to be judged on one issue alone. From my view this is bad strategy. There should be a three-ringed fight going on at all times. Further lots of us feel that a fight for anti-lynching legislation without just as vigorous a battle for economic independence is to fight the manifestation of the evil and ignore its cause." Charles Houston to WFW, 9 February 1935, quoted in Richard Kluger, *Simple Justice* (New York: Vintage, 1977), 162–63.

67. On the McDuffies, see WFW to William Hastie, 7 October 1935, NAACP/mf p2 r17 f691; and *Time*, 24 January 1938, 10.

68. WFW to Clarence Darrow, 26 August 1932, NAACP/mf p6 r6 f26 (voting for Thomas); WFW to Joel Spingarn, 17 January 1933, NAACP/mf p1 r25 f696; Secy. Monthly Rpt., 9 February 1934, NAACP/mf p1 r5 f789; Eleanor Roosevelt to WFW (1935), NAACP/mf p1 r22 f630 (telephone number). On the New Deal's early attention to black concerns, see these standard works: John B. Kirby, *Black Americans in the Roosevelt Era* (Knoxville: University of Tennessee Press, 1980), Patricia Sullivan, *Days of Hope: Race and Democracy in the New Deal Era* (Chapel Hill: University of North Carolina Press, 1996), and Harvard Sitkoff, *A New Deal for Blacks* (New York: Oxford University Press, 1978).

69. B of D Minutes 13 September 1937, NAACP/mf p1 r2 f832; WFW to NAACP Branches, 16 September 1937, NAACP/mf p11A r9 f515; John Haynes Holmes to WFW, 18 September 1937, NAACP/mf p11A r9 f527; WFW to Holmes, 20 September 1937, NAACP/mf p11A r9 f532; Holmes to WFW 21 September 1937, NAACP/mf p11A r9 f528; WFW to Franklin Roosevelt, 22 January 1938, NAACP/mf p7B r4 f665 (earlier draft containing political threat is WFW to Roosevelt, January 1938, NAACP/mf p7B r4 f668). For some time White had been in a minority within the NAACP leadership when it came to dealing with the president. For example, when the Gavagan bill passed the House and was to be considered in the Senate, White drafted a letter, which he planned to have signed by prominent whites, imploring Roosevelt to support the bill. Charles Houston thought the letter excellent, but he believed that the only way to get the president's attention was to have a large number of black signers as a way of threatening him with the loss of African American votes. See WFW to Franklin Roosevelt, 11 May 1937 (draft), NAACP/mf p7B r21 f692; Charles Hous-

ton to WFW, Roy Wilkins, Thurgood Marshall, and Juanita Jackson, memo, 13 may 1937, NAACP/mf p7B r21 f715. In the planning for a meeting of prominent blacks with Roosevelt in the wake of the 1938 filibuster, NAACP leaders were unanimous in their opinion that the president be apprised of the prospects of a black defection from Roosevelt in the 1938 elections should he not come around on antilynching legislation; significantly, White was silent in this meeting. But when the delegation met with FDR, White, who was the spokesperson, only told him how "bitterly disappointed" blacks were in Roosevelt. "Suggestions from the Board re: Conference with the President," 11 April 1938, NAACP/mf p7B r4 f754; WFW to Board of Directors, 12 April 1938, NAACP/mf p1 r6 f274.

70. John P. Davis to WFW, 20 January 1936, NAACP/mf p11B r16 f940; B of D Minutes 9 December 1935, NAACP/mf p1 r2 f702; B of D minutes, 6 January 1936, NAACP/mf p1 r2 f712.

71. Charles Houston to [WFW], 31 January 1936, NAACP/mf p11B r16 f955.

72. WFW to A. Philip Randolph, 3 February 1936, NAACP/mf p11B r16 f961; Charles Houston to WFW, 29 February 1936, NAACP/mf p11B r16 f980.

73. John P. Davis to WFW, 15 January 1937, NAACP/mf p11B r17 f7; WFW to Davis 9 April 1937, NAACP/mf p11B r17 f21; Roy Wilkins to Henry Lee Moon, 2 February 1937, NAACP/mf p7B r21 f278; Gertrude Stone to WFW, telegram, 24 January 1936, NAACP/mf p7B r9 f534; WFW to Stone, 24 January 1936, NAACP/mf p7B r9 f532; B of D Minutes, 1 July 1937, NAACP/mf p1 r2 f825; Davis to WFW, 20 July 1937, NAACP/mf p11B r17 f23; Davis to WFW, 12 August 1937, NAACP/mf p11B r17 f29; WFW to Davis, 18 August 1937, NAACP/mf p11B r17 f28.

74. WFW to ER, 28 February 1936, ER/mf r19 f228 (with ER's notations).

75. Elizabeth Eastman to WFW, 30 December 1936, NAACP/mf p7B r11 f150.

76. Roy Wilkins to Board of Directors, 9 March 1936, NAACP/mf p11B r16 f983.

77. John P. Davis to WFW, 24 February 1938, NAACP/mf p11B r17 f61; WFW to Davis, 26 February 1938, NAACP/mf p11B r17 f60; Davis to WFW, 28 February 1938, NAACP/mf p11B r17 f62; WFW to Davis, 1 March 1938, NAACP/mf p11B r17 f64; Davis to WFW, 7 March 1938, NAACP/mf p11B r17 f68; WFW to Davis, 8 March 1938, NAACP/mf p11B r17 f70; WFW to Roy Wilkins and Charles Houston, memo, 8 March 1938, NAACP/mf p11B r17 f72; Elizabeth Eastman to Henrietta Roelofs, 15 March 1938, NAACP/mf p10 r15 f526; Gertrude Stone to WFW, memo, 23 March 1938, NAACP/mf p11B r17 f90; WFW to William Hastie, 30 March 1938, NAACP/mf p1 r27 f115; WFW to Davis, 1 April 1938, NAACP/mf p11B r17 f115.

Chapter 8: RADICALS, LIBERALS, AND LABOR: THE NAACP IN THE NEW DEAL AND THE GREAT DEPRESSION

1. B of D Minutes, 14 October 1924, NAACP/MF p1 r1 f1036.

2. Secy. Monthly Rpt., 15 August 1921, NAACP/mf p1 r4 f191; Roy Lancaster to WFW, 4 February 1926, NAACP/mf p2 r9 f504; B of D Minutes, 12 December 1927, NAACP/mf p1 r2 f171; William H. Harris, *The Harder We Run: Black Workers since the Civil War* (New York: Oxford University Press, 1982), 82; William H. Harris, *Keeping the Faith: A. Philip Randolph, Milton P. Webster, and the Brotherhood of Sleeping Car Porters, 1925–37* (Urbana: University of Illinois Press, 1977), 165, notes the NAACP's endorsement of the BSCP and appointment of A. Philip Randolph as labor consultant to the association, but calls that support "superficial." Beth Tompkins Bates, *Pullman Porters and the Rise of Protest Politics in Black America, 1925–1945* (Chapel Hill: University of North Carolina Press, 2001), 108–109, makes this same point, also calling the NAACP's support "lukewarm." While Harris and Bates are correct to point out that the association's support for the BSCP did not translate into a general endorsement of organized labor, which the NAACP still viewed suspiciously, the NAACP's early back-

ing of the Pullman porters' union was both an important and a welcome action. That there was no impermeable barrier between the NAACP's civil liberties and civil rights activities and the business of organizing black workers is clear from the collaboration of White, the BSCP, and the network of agents for the Atlanta Life Insurance Company, of which White's brother-in-law Eugene Martin was an officer, to investigate the lynching of a Pullman porter and lobby—without success—the federal government to take action. See WFW to Eugene Martin, 8 April 1930, NAACP/mf p7A r3 f947; A. Philip Randolph to WFW, 27 May 1930, NAACP/mf p7A r3 f988.

3. Frank Crosswaith to NAACP, 31 October 1929, NAACP/mf p10 r7 f500; Crosswaith to WFW, 19 December 1929, NAACP/mf p10 r7 f543; WFW to Abram Harris, 25 January 1930, NAACP/mf p10 r7 f566; Abram Harris, "A Brief Description of the Power of the American Federation of Labor," n.d., NAACP/mf p10 r7 f573; William Kohn to WFW, 8 February 1930, NAACP/mf p10 r7 f581 ("making an issue"); WFW to William Green, 14 February 1930, NAACP/mf p10 r7 f600; Kohn to WFW, 28 February 1930, NAACP/mf p10 r7 f611; J. H. Jones to WFW, 13 June 1930, NAACP/mf p10 r7 f650; Acting Secy. Monthly Rpt., 6 December 1929, NAACP/mf p1 r5 f117; Acting Secy. Monthly Rpt., 5 March 1930, NAACP/mf p1 r5 f159; B of D Minutes, 10 February 1930, NAACP/mf p1 r2 f291. On Frank Crosswaith, see *Dictionary of American Negro Biography*, s.v. "Crosswaith, Frank R." Significantly, one of the reasons that White thought the NAACP ought to take up Jones's grievance was Norman Thomas's interest in it, inasmuch as Thomas sat on the board of the Garland Fund, before which the NAACP had a grant proposal. WFW to William T. Andrews, memo, 20 November 1929, NAACP/mf p10 r7 f505.

4. Committee on Negro Work, "Memorandum to the Directors of the American Fund for Public Service," 28 May 1930, NAACP/mf p3A r1 f360 (on the efficacy of labor organizing and "to put money"); A. Philip Randolph to WFW, 27 September 1930, American Fund for Public Service Papers, box 54, Manuscript Division, New York Public Library, New York, New York (on White's support for the BSCP); WFW, comparison of programs of the American Negro Labor Congress and the NAACP (January 1930), NAACP/mf p3A r1 f273. Du Bois concurred with White and Johnson; see W.E.B. Du Bois, "Programs of Emancipation," *The Crisis*, April 1930, 137. Thanks very much to William Jelani Cobb, a graduate student in history at Rutgers University for sharing with me several documents from the AFPS papers.

5. Patricia Sullivan, *Days of Hope* (Chapel Hill: University of North Carolina Press, 1996), 46–48. An evocative portrait of Davis's family life in early-twentieth-century black Washington can be found in Hilmar Ludvig Jensen, "The Rise of an African American Left: John P. Davis and the National Negro Congress" (Ph.D. diss., Cornell University, 1997), 26–70. On Davis, Weaver, and the Harvard poker sessions, see Jensen, "The Rise of the African American Left," 298–308.

6. Sullivan, *Days of Hope*, 48; Raymond Wolters, *Negroes and the Great Depression* (Westport, CT: Greenwood Publishing, 1970), 3–55.

7. John Kirby, *Black Americans in the Roosevelt Era: Liberalism and Race* (Knoxville: University of Tennessee Press, 1980), 156–57; Secy. Monthly Rpt., 6 September 1933, NAACP/mf p1 r5 f783; B of D Minutes, 8 October 1934, NAACP/mf p1 r2 f628. Hilmar Jensen offers a different account of the formation of the NIL. Almost on a lark, Davis attended the first of the code hearings (on the textile industry) and was incensed at the extent of orchestration by industry leaders and the almost total lack of interest by black organizations. At the end of the first day of hearings, Davis importuned upon an NRA official for a slot on the witness list as head of the NIL, an organization whose name he made up on the spot and to which he appointed himself head. He then went home and dragooned Robert Weaver into service. Jensen, "The Rise of an African American Left," 312–14.

8. Sullivan, *Days of Hope*, 50–52; Wolters, *Negroes and the Great Depression*, 98–168.

9. Secy. Monthly Rpt., 6 September 1933, NAACP/mf p1 r5 f783; Sullivan, *Days of Hope*, 53. Weaver's appointment was not without controversy. Rayford Logan, history professor at Atlanta University and at the time director of education for the Alpha Phi Alpha fraternity, believed Weaver insufficiently militant, and established black leaders felt he was inexperienced. See Sullivan, *Days of Hope*, 53; and Kenneth Robert Janken, *Rayford W. Logan and the Dilemma of the African-American Intellectual* (Amherst: University of Massachusetts Press, 1993), 101–102.

10. Mark Solomon, *The Cry Was Unity: Communists and African Americans, 1917–1936* (Jackson: University Press of Mississippi, 1998), 236 ("became increasingly committed"), 237; Sullivan, *Days of Hope*, 49 ("typified the new" and "dynamic"); Keith Griffler, *What Price Alliance? Black Radicals Confront White Labor, 1918–1938* (New York: Garland, 1995), 231–32n40 (Davis's political transformations).

11. WFW to George E. Haynes, 14 September 1933, NAACP/mf p10 r9 f425; WFW to Abram Harris, 14 September 1934, NAACP/mf p16A r8 f737.

12. B of D Minutes, 25 September 1934, NAACP/mf p1 r2 f624; B of D Minutes, 8 October 1934, NAACP/mf p1 r2 f628; B of D Minutes, 13 November 1934, NAACP/mf p1 r2 f635 ("shall have the privelege").

13. WFW to Charles Houston, 16 March 1935, NAACP/mf p1 r26 f296. White's skittishness concerning the possibility of Davis contacting witnesses and officials was prompted by a typical Davis action a few years earlier. Davis had gotten wind of a December 1933 meeting between NRA officials and moderate black leaders, which he suspected was called to have these blacks ratify the discriminatory wage differential. Davis wrangled an invitation and spoke to the gathering of fifty at Howard University, bringing to their attention minutes of a meeting of several important New Dealers in which NRA head Hugh Johnston expressed the opinion that Negro leaders were clamorous and only seeking government appointments and could be easily dismissed. When Davis leaked the minutes to the press, an indignant Harold Ickes ordered an investigation into how Davis came to have the minutes. Ickes's minion called on Davis, hoping to intimidate him into a confession. But in what looked to be a scene from a Marx Brothers movie, Davis hid a stenographer in an adjoining room during the interview, in which Davis made his adversary out to be a buffoon. He then provided this transcript to the press too. Walter White expressed grudging respect for Davis's boldness, but he was also irritated at the damage Davis could do to black leaders' relations with the Roosevelt administration. See Jensen, "The Rise of an African American Left," 385–98.

14. The Howard conference is nicely chronicled and perceptively analyzed in Griffler, *What Price Alliance?*, 139–51; WFW to Charles Houston, 22 May 1935, NAACP/mf p1 r26 f363; WFW to William Hastie, 7 October 1935, NAACP/mf p2 r17 f691; B of D Minutes 11 November 1935, NAACP/mf p1 r2 f693; B of D Minutes, 6 January 1936, NAACP/mf p1 r2 f712.

15. WFW to James Couzens, 11 April 1934, NAACP/mf p10 r4 f1002.

16. Griffler, *What Price Alliance?*, 115–16; Lizabeth Cohen, *Making a New Deal: Industrial Workers in Chicago, 1919–1939* (New York: Cambridge University Press, 1990) ("moral capitalism").

17. WFW to William Hastie, 28 March 1934, NAACP/mf p10 r4 f983; Secy. Monthly Rpt. (April 1934), NAACP/mf p1 r5 f814; WFW to Bertha Rhodes, 14 April 1934, NAACP/mf p7B r5 f1194; Wolters, *Negroes and the Great Depression*, 182–87; Harris, *Keeping the Faith*, 198–99; Herbert Hill, *Black Labor and the American Legal System: Race, Work, and the Law* (Washington, D.C.: The Bureau of National Affairs, 1977), 104–106; Robert Wagner to WFW, telegram, 16 April 1934, NAACP/mf p10 r4 f1005; James Couzens to WFW, 18 April 1934, NAACP/mf p10 r4 f1014.

18. Secy. Monthly Rpt., 13 May 1940, NAACP/mf p1 r2 f1048; WFW to Sidney Red-

mond, 1 May 1940, NAACP/mf p13B r23 f722; Redmond to WFW, 2 May 1940, NAACP/mf p13B r23 f723; WFW, speech to annual conference of the NAACP, 23 June 1940, NAACP/mf p1 r10 f1042.

19. The Tampa shipyard disturbances are discussed in the following documents: Secy. Monthly Rpt., 7 September 1939, NAACP/mf p1 r6 f377; Secy. Monthly Rept., 5 October 1939, NAACP/mf p1 r6 f391; Secy. Monthly Rpt. (November 1939), NAACP/mf p1 r6 f401; WFW to Eleanor Roosevelt, 18 August 1939, ER/mf r19 f488; Eleanor Roosevelt to WFW, 19 August 1939, ER/mf r19 f486; Eleanor Roosevelt to WFW, 29 August 1939, ER/mf r19 f589; William H. Hastie, memo of conference with officials from the Justice Department, 23 August 1939, ER/mf r19 f591; B of D Minutes, 13 May 1940, NAACP/mf p1 r2 f1048; Digest of correspondence with Department of Justice, 4 September 1940, NAACP/mf p18C r1 f4. See also, Herbert Hill, "The Racial Practices of Organized Labor—The Age of Gompers and After," *Employment, Race, and Poverty*, eds. Arthur M. Ross and Herbert Hill (New York: Harcourt, Brace & World, 1967), 395.

20. Secy. Monthly Rpt., 6 May 1937, NAACP/mf p1 r6 f162; August Meier and Elliott Rudwick, *Black Detroit and the Rise of the UAW* (New York: Oxford University Press, 1981), 38; Secy. Monthly Rpt., 4 November 1937, NAACP/mf p1 r6 f213; WFW to Board of Directors, memo, 19 March 1940, NAACP/mf p13B r23 f649.

21. Meier and Rudwick, *Black Detroit and the Rise of the UAW,* chaps. 1 and 2.

22. NAACP press release, 18 June 1937, NAACP/mf p1 r9 f1079; John P. Davis, speech to the NAACP annual conference, 30 June 1937, NAACP/mf p1 r9 f1165; Homer Martin, speech to the NAACP annual conference, 30 June 1937, NAACP/mf p1 r9 f1177; Frances Williams to Howard Kester, 10 August 1937, Howard Kester Papers, series I folder 34, Southern Historical Collection, University of North Carolina, Chapel Hill, North Carolina; Meier and Rudwick, *Black Detroit and the Rise of the UAW,* 56–61; WFW, speech to the NAACP annual conference, 4 July, NAACP/mf p1 r9 f1186.

23. Griffler, *What Price Alliance?*, 139–81.

24. Griffler, *What Price Alliance?*, 169. In his speech to the 1937 annual convention of the NAACP, Davis extolled the benefits of organized labor by saying that the CIO in particular could be an important ally in the campaign for a federal antilynching law. John P. Davis, speech to the NAACP annual conference, 30 June 1937, NAACP/mf p1 r9 f1165.

25. Three accounts of the concert controversy are Walter White, *A Man Called White* (New York: Viking, 1948), 180–85; Scott A. Sandage, "A Marble House Divided: The Lincoln Memorial, the Civil Rights Movement, and the Politics of Memory, 1939–1963," *Journal of American History* 80 (1993): 135–67; Allan Keiler, *Marian Anderson: A Singer's Journey* (New York: Scribner, 2000), 181–217. Unless noted otherwise, this account draws upon the three mentioned above.

26. WFW to Charles Houston, 21 March 1939, NAACP/mf p1 r27 f384. The secretary's derision betrayed a fractious history between White and Hurok and other managers of black talent. It was only with great effort that the secretary twisted Hurok's arm hard enough to get him to contribute a portion of his profits from Anderson's performances to the NAACP and other black advancement organizations. Similarly, Joe Louis's promoter, Mike Jacobs, used his star's fame to raise money for a variety of causes, but refused to give to the NAACP, despite Louis's and his black manager John Roxborough's wishes. In the secretary's view, white managers and promoters exploited African American talent that had been nurtured by the black community long before it had been recognized by the white mainstream. Without Joe Louis, said White, Jacobs "would still be a third-rate prize-fight promoter instead of the czar of the industry." WFW to Board of Directors, memo, 8 December 1938, NAACP/mf p11A r7 f191; WFW, memo on Marian Anderson benefit concert, 25 January 1939, NAACP/mf p11A r7

f206; WFW to Hubert Delany, 9 December 1938, NAACP/mf p11A r7 f198 ("third-rate").

27. WFW to Charles Houston, 21 March 1939, NAACP/mf p1 r27 f384. "What I have in mind is the possibility of some arrangement with Hurok by which the Association would probably benefit from the concert," White wrote to Houston. Apparently, however, the propaganda value of a free and well-attended open-air concert outweighed the monetary benefits—and the chance to put the screws to Hurok. "The NAACP originally suggested, as you know, that the concert be held at the Memorial to the Great Emancipator," White reported to a board member. "Our suggestion that Miss Anderson lead in the singing of 'America' has been accepted. This will have ironic implications which will not be lost, I think, upon either the crowd or the radio listeners." WFW to Godfrey Cabot, 31 March 1939, NAACP/mf p11A r13 f425.

28. WFW to Charles Houston, 11 April 1939, ER/mf r19 f470 ("pathetic old ladies"); Eleanor Roosevelt to WFW, 12 April 1939, ER/mf r19 f465 ("to use your influence"); Sandage, "A Marble House Divided," 136 ("format for mass politics").

29. Rayford W. Logan, "The Negro Studies War Some More," *Norfolk Journal & Guide*, 28 June 1935. This article was reprinted under different titles in black weeklies throughout the country in that year's summer and fall.

30. "Objectives of the Committee on Participation of Negroes in the National Defense Program," NAACP/LC group II, series A, box 333, "LABOR, Discrimination in National Defense Industries, General 1940–41"; Logan Diary/LC, 4, 6, 14 September 1940; Ulysses Lee, *The Employment of Negro Troops*, United States Army in World War II, Special Studies (Washington, D.C.: Office of the Chief of Military History, United States Army, 1966), 72. For Logan's activity in the CPNNDP, see Kenneth Robert Janken, *Rayford W. Logan and the Dilemma of the African-American Intellectual* (Amherst: University of Massachusetts Press, 1993), 116–30.

31. Janken, *Rayford W. Logan*, 120–21; Roy Wilkins to WFW, 16 September 1940, NAACP/LC group II, series A box 441, "National Defense, General, 1940–41."

32. Meier and Rudwick, *Black Detroit and the Rise of the UAW*, 82–107; B of D Minutes, 14 April 1941, NAACP/mf p1 r3 f24.

33. *A Man Called White*, 211–19.

34. Meier and Rudwick, *Black Detroit and the Rise of the UAW*, 100–102; WFW to James McClendon, 11 April 1941, NAACP/mf p13A r3 f800; WFW to McClendon, 12 August 1941, NAACP/mf p13A r3 f801.

35. Secy. Monthly Rpt., 5 December 1940, NAACP/mf p1 r6 f498. To glimpse White at his affable Hollywood best, see WFW to Melvyn Douglas, 12 December 1940, NAACP/mf p18B r20 f49. Douglas could not attend the lunch, but his wife Helen Gahagan did, and the secretary "had a grand time talking with her. You and I solved all the economic problems the day before while she and I settled all the political ones at the luncheon. Now, if only the three of us could get the world to accept our point of view!"

36. B of D Minutes, 9 December 1940, NAACP/mf p1 r2 f1099; WFW to Board of Directors, 6 December 1940, NAACP/mf p16B r5 f615; WFW to Staff Executives, memo, 19 December 1940, NAACP/mf p13B r23 f804.

37. *Pittsburgh Courier*, 30 November 1940, p. 1; Charles Houston to J. Henry Scattergood, 29 November 1940, NAACP/LC group II, series A, box 442, "National Defense, Participation of Negroes in, Conference, 1940–41"; Roy Wilkins to WFW, memo, 5 December 1940, NAACP/LC group II, series A, box 442, "National Defense, Participation of Negroes in, Conference, 1940–41"; Rayford Logan, speech to a meeting of the CPNNDP (9 March 1941), RL/H-I, box 15, "Colored Reserve Officers" ("asleep at the switch").

38. "Join Now!—Organize!," *Pittsburgh Courier*, 13 December 1940, p. 13; Janken, *Rayford W. Logan*, 119–25.

39. John H. Bracey, Jr., and August Meier, "Allies or Adversaries?: The NAACP, A. Philip Randolph and the 1941 March on Washington," *Georgia Historical Quarterly* 75 (1991): 7–8; B of D Minutes, 14 April 1940, NAACP/mf p1 r3 f24; B of D Minutes of 12 May 1941, NAACP/mf p1 r3 f31; WFW to All Branches, 12 May 1941, NAACP/mf p13B r22 f500.
40. A. Philip Randolph to WFW, 19 May 1941, NAACP/mf p13B r23 f48.
41. WFW to A. Philip Randolph, 13 May 1941, NAACP/mf p13B r23 f62; Charles Houston to A. Philip Randolph, 20 May 1941, NAACP/mf p13B r22 f508.
42. WFW to William Hastie, 20 May 1941, NAACP/mf p13B r22 f512; NAACP press release, 20 June 1941, NAACP/mf p1 r10 f1105.
43. Minutes of Local Unit of Negro March-on-Washington Committee, 14 June 1941, NAACP/LC group II, series A, box 416, "March on Washington, General, 1940–41"; Eleanor Roosevelt to A. Philip Randolph, 10 June 1941, ER/mf r15 f4; Eleanor Roosevelt to Assistant Secretary of War Robert Patterson, n.d., ER/mf r15 f5.
44. Minutes of Local Unit of Negro March-on-Washington Committee, 14 June 1941, NAACP/LC group II, series A, box 416, "March on Washington, General, 1940–41." A copy of this document can also be found at NAACP/mf p13B r22 f536.
45. Eugene Davidson, "The Birth of Executive Order #8802," n.d., Eugene Davidson Papers, box 91–2, folder 43, Moorland-Spingarn Research Center, Howard University, Washington, D.C.; Logan Diary/LC, 24 June 1941; Janken, *Rayford W. Logan*, 128–129; Bracey and Meier, "Adverseries or Allies?," 11–15. Davidson's and Logan's accounts are the only ones written by participants in the final negotiations; they are identical in practically every detail. Logan was the only one of the MOWM negotiators not pleased with Davidson's compromise. He believed it was worthless to recognize the wrongness of government discrimination in the first part but then do nothing about it in the second.
46. WFW to Eleanor Roosevelt, telegram, 21 July 1941, NAACP/mf p17 r20 f377; WFW, speech to annual meeting of the NAACP, 27 June 1941, NAACP/mf p1 r10 f1261.
47. Logan Diary/LC, 25 October 1940.
48. Rayford Logan, speech to the American Teachers Association (before 4 August 1941), RL/H-I, box 2, "CPNNDP."
49. Roy Wilkins to WFW, 24 June 1942, NAACP/mf p13B r23 f158; Wilkins to WFW, memo, 1 September 1942, NAACP/mf p13B r23 f174. White's attitude toward a permanent MOWM can be traced in WFW to A. Philip Randolph, 2 September 1942, NAACP/mf p13B r23 f185; Randolph to WFW, 9 September 1942, NAACP/mf p13B r23 f195; B of D Minutes, 14 September 1942, NAACP/mf p1 r3 f160; WFW to Alfred Baker Lewis, 21 September 1942, NAACP/mf p13B r23 f197; B of D Minutes, 8 February 1943, NAACP/mf p1 r3 f216; B of D Minutes, 12 April 1943, NAACP/mf p1 r3 f234; Wilkins to WFW, 21 May 1943, NAACP/mf p13B r22 f984; WFW, handwritten note at bottom of Milton Konvitz to WFW and Wilkins, memo, 9 June 1943, NAACP/mf p13B r22 f986.
50. [WFW], handwritten notes for a speech, (1942?), NAACP/LC, group II, series A, box 416, "March on Washington, General, 1940–41." This document is unsigned but in Walter White's own hand. It is undated, but references in it to his recent speeches at MOWM meetings in Chicago and New York place it sometime shortly after late June 1942.
51. Roy Wilkins to WFW, 24 June 1942, NAACP/mf p13B r23 f158 ("traditional NAACP attitude"); WFW to Wilkins, memo, 11 August 1942, NAACP/mf p13B r23 f168 ("some people").

Chapter 9: LIVE FROM THE WAR ZONES: HOLLYWOOD, HARLEM, EUROPE, AND THE PACIFIC

1. Secy. Monthly Rpt. (September 1941), NAACP/mf p1 r6 f596; Merl E. Reed, *Seedtime for the Modern Civil Rights Movement: The President's Committee on Fair Employment Practices, 1941–46* (Baton Rouge: Louisiana State University Press, 1991), 34–35, 155; *NAACP Annual Report for 1941* (New York: National Association for the Advancement of Colored People, n.d.), 4–7.

2. *NAACP Annual Report for 1941*, 35–37; *NAACP Annual Report for 1942* (New York: National Association for the Advancement of Colored People, n.d.), 36–37.

3. Dept. of Branches Monthly Rpt., December 1941, NAACP/mf p1 r6 f649.

4. Roy Wilkins to WFW, 25 September 1941, NAACP/mf p17 r29 f190; WFW to Wilkins, 27 September 1941, NAACP/mf p17 r29 f186; Ann. Bus. Mtg. Minutes, 6 January 1941, NAACP/mf p1 r6 f512 (White's salary).

5. Dept. of Branches Monthly Rpt., 10 November 1941, NAACP/mf p1 r6 f634; Dept. of Branches Monthly Rpt., December 1941, NAACP/mf p1 r6 f649; *NAACP Annual Report for 1940*, 9–12; *NAACP Annual Report for 1941*, 18–20; *NAACP Annual Report for 1942*, 16–17. The *Alston* case is discussed in detail in Earl Lewis, *In Their Own Interests: Race, Class, and Power in Twentieth-Century Norfolk, Virginia* (Berkeley: University of California Press, 1991), 155–65.

6. Charles Houston to WFW, memo, 18 April 1938, NAACP/mf p11A r13 f440. The standard history of the legal campaign to abolish segregated education, culminating in the 1954 and 1955 *Brown* decisions, is Richard Kluger, *Simple Justice* (New York: Vintage, 1977). But see also *Brown v. Board of Education: A Brief History with Documents*, ed. Waldo E. Martin Jr. (Boston: Bedford, 1998).

7. WFW to John W. Davis, 7 March 1939, NAACP/mf p11A r20 f140; Secy. Monthly Rpt., 9 March 1939, NAACP/mf p1 r6 f331; WFW to James Ryan, 24 May 1939, NAACP/mf p7B r30 f556; Adam Fairclough, " 'Being in the Field of Education and Also Being a Negro . . . Seems . . . Tragic': Black Teachers in the Jim Crow South," *Journal of American History* 87 (2000): 65–91.

8. B of D Minutes, 9 June 1941, NAACP/mf p1 r3 f41; Fairclough, " 'Being in the Field'," 84–85. According to Lewis, *In Their Own Interests*, 157, White's estimation of the conservative stranglehold on the majority of teachers was shared by Thurgood Marshall. For additional insight into the NAACP's campaign for salary equalization, see Lewis, *In Their Own Interests*, 155–65; Adam Fairclough, *Teaching Equality: Black Schools in the Age of Jim Crow* (Athens: University of Georgia Press, 2000), 56–63; and Mark V. Tushnet, *The NAACP's Legal Strategy against Segregated Education, 1925–1950* (Chapel Hill: University of North Carolina Press, 1987), 58–65, 77–81, 88–104.

9. Coordinator of Branches Monthly Rpt., May 1940, NAACP/mf p1 r6 f455.

10. Dept. of Branches Monthly Rpt., December 1941, NAACP/mf p1 r6 f649; Youth Director Report, January 1942, NAACP/mf p1 r6 f658. For two perspectives on one such branch, Baltimore, see Joanne Grant, *Ella Baker: Freedom Bound* (New York: John Wiley, 1998), 75–76, and Genna Rae McNeil, "Youth Initiative in the African American Struggle for Racial Justice and Constitutional Rights: The City-Wide Young People's Forum of Baltimore, 1931–1941," in *African Americans and the Living Constitution*, eds. John Hope Franklin and Genna Rae McNeil (Washington, D.C.: Smithsonian Institution Press, 1995), 56–80.

11. Herbert Hill, interview with author, 12, 13 August 1997, Madison, Wisconsin. The board of directors was for the most part comfortable with the direction set by the secretary. Whereas a decade previous the board had reservations about White's judgment and established oversight mechanisms like the Committee on Administration, it now

had none. In 1941 the board explicitly recognized White's power to hire and fire executive staff and handed him carte blanche to weed out dead and inactive branches. See B of D Minutes, 5 January 1942, NAACP/mf p1 r3 f98; Secy. Monthly Rpt., 5 February 1942, NAACP/mf p1 r6 f662; and B of D Minutes, 9 February 1942, NAACP/mf p1 r3 f109.

12. Thomas Cripps, *Making Movies Black* (New York: Oxford University Press, 1993), 3–34; the term *structured absence* is explained on page 8. On Paul Robeson's film career, see Sheila Tully Boyle and Andrew Bunie, *Paul Robeson: The Years of Promise and Achievement* (Amherst, MA: University of Massachusetts Press, 2001).

13. WFW to Joseph Breen, 27 July 1942, NAACP/mf p18B r15 f473. Breen was head of the Production Code Administration, the film industry's own censorship board.

14. WFW to Arthur Spingarn, 27 November 1937, NAACP/mf p11A r1 f394.

15. On the work of black consultants on *Gone With the Wind* and black public opinion to the film, see Cripps, *Making Movies Black*, 18–23. On the Office of War Information, see Clayton R. Koppes and Gregory D. Black, *Hollywood Goes to War* (New York: Free Press, 1987). On White and the film, see WFW to David O. Selznick, 7 June 1938, WEBD/mf r49 f310; Selznick to WFW, 20 June 1938, WEBD/mf r49 f310; WFW to Selznick, 28 June 1938, WEBD/mf r49 f311; WFW to Selznick, 26 March 1940, NAACP/mf p18B r20 f681; Selznick to WFW, 2 April 1940, NAACP/mf p18B r20 f686. On Selznick's financial contributions, see Selznick to WFW, 2 April 1940, NAACP/mf p18B r20 f686; Frances Ingless [secretary to David O. Selznick] to WFW, 14 October 1941, NAACP/mf p18B r20 f688; Selznick to WFW, 29 December 1942, NAACP/mf p18B r20 f699; Lillian Browne [secretary to David O. Selznick] to WFW, 27 July 1944, NAACP/mf p18B r20 f701. On White's consulting on other projects, see WFW to Sara Boynoff, 1 April 1942, NAACP/mf p18B r15 f31; WFW to Louis B. Mayer, 3 August 1942, NAACP/mf p18B r18 f258; WFW to Lowell Mellett, 17 August 1942, NAACP/mf p18B r18 f264; WFW to Marc Connelly, 21 November 1942, NAACP/mf p18B r15 f68; WFW to Selznick, 16 April 1946, NAACP/mf p18B r15 f145; WFW to Darryl Zanuck, 5 September 1948, NAACP/mf p18B r19 f750. Early in his dealings with Hollywood, White also floated his own film ideas, including an unnamed epic that anticipated the blockbuster *Roots*. The first part of the film would be "that of a benevolent chief of a tribe in Africa who is betrayed by members of another tribe, seized and sold to English slavetraders, and transported to the United States. This chieftain would be the possessor of a voice and a figure like Paul Robeson." The second part of the film would highlight the son of that chief, who grew up in slavery and through him show how the spirituals came into being. The third part would focus on the grandchild of the chief, who became a concert artist at Carnegie Hall. See WFW to Jonathan Daniels, 11 April 1940, NAACP/mf p18B r15 f269.

16. *A Man Called White*, 198–200; WFW to Kyle Crichton, 6 April 1942, NAACP/mf p18B r20 f14; Secy. Monthly Rpt., April 1942, NAACP/mf p1 r6 f691; Minutes of luncheon meeting concerning establishment of a Hollywood Bureau, 17 October 1945, NAACP/mf p18B r17 f421; Eleanor Roosevelt to To Whom it May Concern, 17 February 1942, NAACP/mf p18B r15 f417.

17. WFW to Roy Wilkins, 23 February 1942, NAACP/mf p17 r20 f432.

18. WFW to Sara Boynoff, 16 March 1942, NAACP/mf p18B r15 f27; Secy. Monthly Rpt., April 1942, NAACP/mf p1 r6 f691 ("and pledged").

19. Lena Horne and Richard Schickel, *Lena* (Garden City, N.Y.: Doubleday, 1965), 132, 134–39 (on Lena Horne in Hollywood); Secy. Monthly Rpt., September 1942, NAACP/mf p1 r6 f747 ("that he did not"); Darryl Zanuck to E. J. Mannix, 21 July 1942, NAACP/mf p18B r15 f472 ("simple and direct" and "committed myself").

White's and Willkie's initiative received extensive coverage in the magazine of the Screen Actors Guild. See *Screen Actor*, August 1942, pp. 21–23.

20. *Variety* 17 June 1942, clipping in NAACP/mf p18B r15 f445 (on improved roles for blacks); *Los Angeles Tribune*, 29 March 1942, clipping in NAACP/mf p18B r20 f7.

21. WFW to Louis B. Mayer, 3 August 1942, NAACP/mf p18B r18 f258; *Daily Worker*, 2 August 1942, clipping in NAACP/mf p18B r18 f254; Mayer to WFW, 19 August 1942, NAACP/mf p18B r18 f267; WFW to Lowell Mellett, 17 August 1942, NAACP/mf p18B r18 f264.

22. Nelson Poynter to WFW, 28 August 1942, NAACP/mf p18B r18 f281; Lowell Mellett to Louis B. Mayer, 26 November 1942, NAACP/mf p18B r18 f323. On *Tennessee Johnson*, see also Koppes and Black, *Hollywood Goes to War*, 87–90.

23. WFW to Almena Davis, 28 April 1942, NAACP/mf p18B r20 f10.

24. *Pittsburgh Courier*, 12 September 1942, clipping in NAACP/mf p18B r18 f675.

25. WFW to Walter Wanger, 26 February 1943, NAACP/mf p14 r1 f180 ("would not materially effect"); WFW to Marc Connelly, 16 June 1943, NAACP/mf p18B r15 f142 (plans for meeting film industry personnel); Thomas Griffith to WFW, 14 September 1943, NAACP/mf p18B r17 f730, and WFW to Griffith, 2 September 1943, NAACP/mf p18B r17 f729 (on living arrangements while in Hollywood); WFW to Lena Horne, 27 May 1943, NAACP/mf p18B r17 f664 ("not in the least bothered"); Peter Furst to WFW, 31 May 1943, NAACP/mf p18B r17 f661 (advice from *PM* critic); Norman Houston to WFW, 16 September 1943, NAACP/mf p18B r20 f257 ("Naturally, a person"); WFW to Norman Houston, 23 September 1943, NAACP/mf p18B r20 f260; on the Fair Play Committee, see Carlton Jackson, *Hattie: The Life of Hattie McDaniel* (Lanham, Md.: Madison Books, 1990), 100, 101, 103. Carlton Moss, then a young African American scriptwriter, argued that black Hollywood veterans viewed Horne, because of her complexion and her roots outside Hollywood, as an interloper and an upstart. See Jackson, *Hattie: The Life of Hattie McDaniel*, 104–105; and Horne and Schickel, *Lena*, 134–39.

26. Franklin Williams to WFW, 5 August 1947, NAACP/mf p18B r20 f397 (McDaniel's comment about Walter White's lack of leadership bona fides); *Baltimore Afro-American*, 9 February 1946, clipping in NAACP/mf p18B r17 f435; *Chicago Defender*, 23 February 1946, clipping in NAACP/mf p18B r17 f437. See also *Pittsburgh Courier*, 23 February 1946, clipping in NAACP/mf p18B r17 f438; *People's Voice*, 9 February 1946, clipping in NAACP/mf p18B r17 f640. On the establishment of the Hollywood bureau, see, for example, minutes of luncheon meeting concerning establishment of a Hollywood Bureau, 17 October 1945, NAACP/mf p18B r17 f421; Secy. Monthly Rpt., November 1945, NAACP/mf p1 r7 f99; WFW to Roy Wilkins and Office, 25 January 1946 (incorrectly dated 1945), NAACP/mf p18B r17 f427; [WFW], "Draft Statement Regarding the NAACP's Establishment of Hollywood Bureau" (18 February 1946), NAACP/mf p18B r17 f428.

27. WFW to Joseph Breen, 27 July 1942, NAACP/mf p18B r15 f473 (six-month relocation); WFW to Walter Wanger, 26 February 1943, NAACP/mf p14 r1 f180 (Eboué); WFW to Marc Connelly, 16 June 1943, NAACP/mf p18B r15 f142; and Clarence Muse to WFW, n.d. [received 22 March 1944], NAACP/mf p18B r15 f728 (being available for script reading); WFW to David O. Selznick, 16 April 1946, NAACP/mf p18B r15 f145 (George Washington Carver film).

28. *Pittsburgh Courier*, 9 February 1946, clipping in NAACP/mf p18B r15 f1014; *An Oral History with Carlton Moss*, interviewed by Barbara Hall, Academy of Motion Picture Arts and Sciences, 1996, pp. 125, 126.

29. Michael Rogin, *Blackface, White Noise: Jewish Immigrants in the Hollywood Melting Pot* (Berkeley: University of California Press, 1996), 3–15, 159–208.

30. Bruce Nelson, "Organized Labor and the Struggle for Black Equality in Mobile during World War II," *Journal of American History* 80 (1993): 952–88.

31. August Meier and Elliott Rudwick, *Black Detroit and the Rise of the UAW* (New York: Oxford University Press, 1981), 176–79, 162–74.

32. WFW, "Keynote Address of Emergency Conference on the Status of the Negro in the War for Freedom," NAACP/mf p1 r11 f1218.

33. WFW, "Keynote Address of Emergency Conference on the Status of the Negro in the War for Freedom," NAACP/mf p1 r11 f1218.

34. Secy. Monthly Rpt., July 1943, NAACP/mf p1 r6 f853; Secy. Monthly Rpt., September 1943, NAACP/mf p1 r6 f864; Walter White, "What Caused the Detroit Riot," NAACP/mf p18C r27 f25. See also *A Man Called White*, 224–32; Meier and Rudwick, *Black Detroit*, 192–97; Herbert Shapiro, *White Violence and Black Response* (Amherst: University of Massachusetts Press, 1988), 310–30; Dominic J. Capeci, Jr., and Martha Wilkerson, *Layered Violence: The Detroit Rioters of 1943* (Jackson: University of Mississippi Press, 1991), 3–31. The quoted phrase "lawlessness and racial hatred" is from the *Detroit Free Press*, 22 June 1943, and is cited in Meier and Rudwick, *Black Detroit*, 194. But as Meier and Rudwick suggest, one reason for the absence of violence in the plants is that black absenteeism during the riot was high, between 50 and 90 percent; white absenteeism reached up to 30 percent, and presumably many of them participated in the riots. Meier and Rudwick, *Black Detroit*, 194n.

35. Walter White, "Behind the Harlem Riot," *The New Republic*, 16 August 1943, 220–22; the secretary's reflections on the late appearance of looters is in *A Man Called White*, 235–36.

36. White, "Behind the Harlem Riot"; *A Man Called White*, 233–41; Dominic J. Capeci, Jr., *The Harlem Riot of 1943* (Philadelphia: Temple University Press, 1977), 99–108; Shapiro, *White Violence and Black Response*, 330–37.

37. White, "Behind the Harlem Riot"; Secy. Monthly Rpt., September 1943, NAACP/mf p1 r6 f864 ("unchecked, unpunished").

38. Capeci, *The Harlem Riot*, 169–184, esp. 171–76 ("resentment over" on 176); Shapiro, *White Violence and Black Response*, 334–37.

39. Mary McLeod Bethune, " 'Certain Inalienable Rights,' " in *What the Negro Wants*, ed. Rayford W. Logan (orig. published 1944, rept. with a new introduction by Kenneth Robert Janken, Notre Dame, In.: University of Notre Dame Press, 2001), 249–50.

40. White, "Behind the Harlem Riot"; see also White's patronizing description of the "toothless old woman" stuffing booty in the "two grimy pillow cases which apparently she had snatched from the bed in which she had been sleeping," in *A Man Called White*, 238.

41. Gary R. Hess, *America Encounters India, 1941–1947* (Baltimore and London: The Johns Hopkins University Press, 1971), 29–40; Sundarshan Kapur, *Raising up a Prophet: The African-American Encounter with Gandhi* (Boston: Beacon Press, 1992).

42. WFW, confidential memo of interview with Lord Halifax, 24 April 1942, NAACP/mf p14 r9 f17. See also WFW to R. O'Hara Lanier, 28 April 1942, NAACP/mf p14 r9 f25; according to a list, NAACP/mf p14 r9 f53, identical letters were sent to Carl Murphy, A. Philip Randolph, W.E.B. Du Bois, John W. Davis, Elmer Anderson Carter, Rayford W. Logan, and Roy Wilkins.

   White's missive updated his correspondents on his efforts and asked for their frank opinion on the merits of his commission proposal, their suggestions for specific actions Roosevelt could take to demonstrate his opposition to discrimination, and their permission to be nominated to the commission. By his tone he indicated that he could sway the president. John W. Davis of West Virginia State College sent a detailed endorsement of White's plan. So did R. O'Hara Lanier of the Hampton Institute. W.E.B. Du Bois's reply, however, was terse and studied in its avoidance of White's request for fresh ideas: "Any duty which the President of the United States may lay upon me," Du Bois wrote, "I will be glad to perform to the best of my ability." W.E.B. Du Bois to WFW, 2 May 1942, NAACP/mf p14 r9 f46. Though its brusqueness may have betrayed lingering ill feelings toward the secretary, it is equally likely that Du Bois was simply cool to the merits, feasibility, and approach of White's plan. Du Bois, the man with a lifetime of fighting the great powers' foreign policies, may have viewed the secretary's plan as a gimmick, the exertions of a man for whom international affairs held only a passing interest.

43. Brenda Gayle Plummer, *Rising Wind: Black Americans and U.S. Foreign Affairs, 1935–1960* (Chapel Hill: University of North Carolina Press, 1996), 16–22. On the competition between the NAACP and the UNIA, see David Levering Lewis, *W.E.B. Du Bois: The Fight for Equality and the American Century, 1919–1963* (New York: Henry Holt, 2000), chap. 2.

44. The *Crisis* was not unique in this regard; during the thirties, especially in the Ethiopian crisis and the Spanish civil war, the black press continually informed its readers about the stakes for blacks in these international conflicts. See Plummer, *Rising Wind*, 24–27, 58–64.

45. William R. Scott, *The Sons of Sheba's Race* (Bloomington: Indiana University Press, 1993), 38–43, 105, 121; Mark Naison, *Communists in Harlem during the Depression* (New York: Grove Press, 1984), 155–58, 174–76, 195–96.

46. WFW to Rayford Logan, 18 July 1935, RL/H-I, box 15, "Walter White."

47. WFW to Franklin D. Roosevelt, 4 May 1942, NAACP/mf p14 r9 f50. White's call for a "Pacific Charter" echoed the statements of Sun Fo, Sun Yat-sen's son and a leading Chinese government official. Hess, *America Encounters India*, 43.

48. WFW to Eleanor Roosevelt, 24 April 1942, NAACP/mf p14 r9 f19; WFW to Eleanor Roosevelt, 30 June 1942, NAACP/mf p14 r9 f183; M. H. McIntyre [secretary to President Roosevelt] to WFW, 26 June 1942, NAACP/mf p14 r9 f182; WFW to McIntyre, 1 July 1942, NAACP/mf p14 r9 f181.

49. WFW to Du Bois, 12 May 1942, Du Bois Papers r54 f3; WFW to Du Bois, 5 June 1942, Du Bois Papers r54 f6; see also Thomas Borstlemann, *Apartheid's Reluctant Uncle: The United States and Southern Africa in the Early Cold War* (New York: Oxford University Press, 1993), 12–16, esp. 15; Franklin Roosevelt to Winston Churchill, 10 March 1942, quoted in Hess, *America Encounters India*, 39–40.

50. Alan Murray [of the Office of War Information] to WFW, 3 August 1942, NAACP/mf p14 r9 f193; [WFW, prepared broadcast message to Japanese people], NAACP/mf p14 r9 f189; WFW to Murray, telegram, 10 August 1942, NAACP/mf p14 r9 f201; WFW to President Roosevelt, telegram, 10 August 1942, NAACP/mf p14 r9 f203. White's dismay and reduced desire to cooperate with his government was not unique and was shared by fellow leaders like A. Philip Randolph. The two shared an exchange on the Indian situation, Randolph agreeing with his friend's assessment and then adding that he didn't "want to become involved in any program to bolster the morale of the Negro unless the Government does something fundamental about racial discrimination." See A. Philip Randolph to WFW, 14 May 1942, NAACP/mf p14 r9 f115.

51. Memo from the secretary, 9 June 1942, NAACP/mf p14 r9 f170. Quotations in this paragraph and the next are from this memo.

52. In WFW to Editors [of the black press], December 1943, NAACP/mf p17 r17 f799, White writes that he sought accreditation with a white daily because the black correspondents' pool was filled, and if he waited for an opening, his trip would be delayed. See also Roy Wilkins to WFW, memo, 21 December 1943, NAACP/mf p17 r17 f794, in which Wilkins argues against saying anything to the black press at all, and WFW to Wilkins, memo, 21 December 1943, NAACP/mf p17 r17 f793. See also WFW to Board of Directors, 29 December 1943, NAACP/mf p17 r17 f804, for White's arrange-

ments with major national news outlets. On the secretary's bids for official sponsorship, see WFW to Hugo Black, 13 September 1943, NAACP/mf p17 r17 f712; WFW to Eleanor Roosevelt, 1 November 1943, NAACP/mf p17 r17 f743; ER to WFW, 3 November 1943, NAACP/mf p17 r17 f746; WFW to ER, 29 November 1943, NAACP/mf p17 r17 f763; ER to WFW, 1 December 1943, NAACP/mf p17 r17 f766; WFW to Lord Halifax, 18 November 1943, NAACP/mf p17 r17 f760.

53. Viscount Halifax to Foreign Office, 9 December 1943, F.O. 371/38609, *British Foreign Office United States: Correspondence, 1938–1945* (Wilmington, Del.: Scholarly Resources, 1979, 1981), reel 25, microfilm. All subsequent references to F.O. 371/38609 are on reel 25 of this collection. A. D. Surles to John J. McCloy, 6 September 1943, NAACP/mf p17 r17 f1011; Walter White, *A Rising Wind* (Garden City, N.Y.: Doubleday, Doran, 1945), 14. On the importance of domestic politics in the government's allowing White to travel, see the comments of an official in the British Foreign Office: "With the negro [*sic*] and liberal vote so important in the election, this solicitude for WW is not surprising." J. Foster (of Foreign Office), minute, 24 January 1944, attached to Viscount Halifax to Foreign Office, 21 January 1944, F. O. 371/38609.

54. White's investigation of conditions in Britain are ably discussed in Thomas Hachey, "Walter White and the American Negro Soldier in World War II: A Diplomatic Dilemma for Britain," *Phylon* 39 (1978): 241–49; for a different perspective, see Marika Sherwood, "Walter White and the British: A Lost Opportunity," *Contributions in Black Studies* 9/10 (1990–1992): 215–26. I was alerted to the relevant British foreign office correspondence collection cited in this chapter by these two articles.

55. Walter White, quoted in N. M. Butler (Foreign Office) to R. T. Peel (India Office), 14 January 1944, F.O. 371/38609 ("it appears that Negroes"); handwritten minute attached to Mr. Cruikshank (Ministry of Information) to Mr. Butler (Foreign Office), 18 January 1944, F.O. 371/38609 ("nigger in the woodpile"); N[evile] B[utler], minute, 11 January 1944, F.O. 371/38609; Nevile Butler to R. J. Cruikshank, 28 January 1944, F.O. 371/38609.

56. Viscount Halifax to Foreign Office, 20 November 1943, F.O. 371/38609.

57. R. J. Cruikshank (Ministry of Information) to Nevile Butler (Foreign Office), 18 January 1944, F. O. 371/38609.

58. WFW to Dear Folks [at the NAACP], 15 January 1944, NAACP/mf p17 r17 f825; WFW to Roy Wilkins (and the Office), 22 January 1944, NAACP/mf p17 r17 f827; Nevile Butler, Foreign Office, to Sir Ronald Campbell, British Embassy, Washington, 14 March 1944, British Foreign Office collection 371/38609, quoted in Thomas Hachey, "Walter White and the American Negro Soldier in World War II: A Diplomatic Dilemma for Britain," *Phylon* 39 (1978): 248.

59. WFW to Paul Tierney [managing editor of the *New York Post*], 23 May 1944, NAACP/mf p17 r18 f21; *New York Post*, 31 May 1944, copy of article in NAACP/mf p17 r18 f222; *New York Post*, 1 June 1944, copy of article in NAACP/mf p17 r18 f224; *Chicago Defender*, 4 March 1944, p. 15; *Chicago Defender*, 11 March 1944, p. 15.

60. Kenneth R. Janken, "African American and Francophone Black Intellectuals during the Harlem Renaissance," *The Historian* 60 (1998): 499–504.

61. *A Rising Wind*, 71, 31, 53–55.

62. WFW to Board of Directors, 21 April 1944, NAACP/mf p17 r18 f98 ("in various ways"); WFW, recommendations on race relations in the European Theater of Operations, 11 February 1944, NAACP/mf p17 r18 f246; WFW, Report to General Eisenhower and the War Department, 11 February 1944, NAACP/mf p17 r18 f249. Other summaries of White's report and recommendation are in *A Rising Wind*, 62–67, and *A Man Called White*, 247–48; B of D Minutes, 8 May 1944, NAACP/mf p1 r3 f349 and Secy. Monthly Rpt., May 1944, NAACP/mf p1 r6 f927 (Eisenhower's acceptance of White's report); Lt. Gen. John C. H. Lee to WFW, 3 April 1944, NAACP/mf p17 r18

f318; Inspector General's Office, Report of Investigation of Racial Relations in the United Kingdom, NAACP/mf p17 r18 f298.

63. B of D Minutes 8 May 1944, NAACP/mf p1 r3 f349; B of D Minutes, 8 November 1943, NAACP/mf p1 r3 f286 ("Walter ought to"). Outside the association, some black papers took the secretary to task for leaving his post in the U.S. See George Nesbitt to Abe Noel, 27 March 1944, NAACP/mf p17 r17 f928.

64. Program of testimonial dinner honoring Walter White, 25 May 1944, NAACP/mf p17 r24 f843; Edwin Embree to WFW, 1 June 1944, NAACP/mf p17 r24 f957.

65. Program of testimonial dinner honoring Walter White, 25 May 1944, NAACP/mf p17 r24 f843.

66. "A Declaration by Negro Voters," June 1944, in *A Documentary History of the Negro People of the United States, IV, 1933–1945*, ed. Herbert Aptheker (New York: Citadel Press, 1992), 465–70.

67. *Chicago Defender*, 8 July 1944, p. 15.

68. WFW, speech closing the NAACP annual convention in Chicago, 16 July 1944, NAACP/mf p1 r11 f431 (also in *A Documentary History of the Negro People of the United States, IV, 1933–45*, 474–86); WFW to Eleanor Roosevelt, 19 July 1944, ER/mf r19 f1013; Patricia A. Sullivan, *Days of Hope* (Chapel Hill: University of North Carolina Press, 1996), 181–82.

69. WFW, speech closing the NAACP annual convention in Chicago, 16 July 1944, NAACP/mf p1 r11 f431.

70. WFW to Eleanor Roosevelt, 19 July 1944, ER/mf r19 f1013.

71. *Chicago Defender*, 29 July 1944, p. 15.

72. Eleanor Roosevelt to WFW, 3 August 1944, ER/mf r19 f1010.

73. WFW to Eleanor Roosevelt, 9 August 1944, ER/mf r19 f1034.

74. WFW, *Chicago Defender*, 5 August 1944, p. 15.

75. B of D Minutes, 31 July 1944, NAACP/mf p1 r11 f471.

76. B of D Minutes, 31 July 1944, NAACP/mf p1 r11 f471.

77. B of D Minutes, 31 July 1944, NAACP/mf p1 r11 f471; see White's columns in the *Chicago Defender* for 26 August, 16 September, 7 October, and 4 November 1944.

78. WFW to Dear Folks, 18 December 1944, NAACP/mf p17 r24 f480; WFW to Dear Roy and all the Folks, 26 December 1944, NAACP/mf p17 r24 f490; *Honolulu Advertiser*, 20 December 1944, clipping in NAACP/mf p17 r24 f497.

79. "Walter White Bares Discrimination at U.S. Pacific Bases," *New York Post*, 8 February 1945, p. 10, copy in NAACP/mf p17 r18 f218.

80. WFW, draft of article for *New York Post*, 20 January 1945, NAACP/mf p17 r17 f1082.

81. WFW to Roy Wilkins, 25 January 1945, NAACP/mf p17 r24 f502; WFW to Pvt. Artie Shumake, 31 July 1945, NAACP/mf p17 r24 f617; WFW, draft of article for *New York Post*, 20 January 1945, NAACP/mf p17 r17 f1082.

82. *An Oral History with Hal Kanter*, interviewed by Douglas Bell, Academy of Motion Picture Arts and Sciences Library, 1995 pp. 101–102. It should be noted that while Kanter's recollection of White himself is vivid, his recounting of the events immediately preceding the alleged riot by black troops is substantially different from what White himself wrote.

83. WFW to Roy Wilkins, 25 January 1945, NAACP/mf p17 r24 f502; Secy. Monthly Rpt. [August] 1945 (incorrectly dated July), NAACP/mf p1 r7 f66.

84. "White Finds GIs Draw No Color Line for Filipinos," *New York Post*, 16 February 1945, clipping in NAACP/mf p17 r18 f220; WFW to President Roosevelt, memo, 12 February 1945, NAACP/mf p14 r13 f155.

85. Bobbie Branche to WFW, n.d. [1945], NAACP/mf p17 r17 f1070.

86. Curtis B. Todd, report on Walter White's visit to Philippines base, 14 March 1945 [received], NAACP/mf p17 r24 f552.

87. WFW to Arthur Spingarn, 23 March 1945, Arthur Spingarn Papers box 948 folder 181, Moorland-Spingarn Research Center, Howard University, Washington, D.C.

88. WFW to Dear Folks, 23 March 1945, NAACP/mf p14 r13 f190.

89. "Walter White Warns U.S. Must Wake up to Happenings in Pacific: Restoration of Colonial Systems Will Lead to World War III," press release, 12 April 1945, NAACP/mf p14 r13 f227.

Chapter 10: THE MAKING OF A COLD WAR LIBERAL

1. B of D Minutes, 14 July 1944, NAACP/mf p1 r3 f371; W.E.B. Du Bois to Arthur Spingarn and Louis T. Wright, memo, 1 June 1944 ("leisurely peace"), Du Bois to WFW, 23 June 1944, Du Bois to WFW, 5 July 1944, WFW to Du Bois, 21 July 1944, all in *The Correspondence of W.E.B. Du Bois*, II, *Selections 1934–1944*, ed. Herbert Aptheker (Amherst: University of Massachusetts Press, 1976), 410–15; B of D Minutes, 13 November 1944, NAACP/mf p1 r3 f410 (conflict over space and furniture).

2. Wilkins to Clark Eichelberger, 30 March 1945, NAACP/mf p14 r19 f17, Wilkins to WFW, 26 March 1945, NAACP/mf p14 r13 f199, NAACP press release, 10 March 1945, NAACP/mf p14 r18 f526.

3. [NAACP Board of Directors to the President of the United States], 9 April 1945, NAACP/mf p14 r18 f4, [W.E.B. Du Bois], "Proposed Resolution for Meeting of Board of Directors, NAACP, March 12, 1945," NAACP/mf p14 r19 f15. On the Harlem Colonial Conference, see Kenneth Robert Janken, *Rayford W. Logan and the Dilemma of the African-American Intellectual* (Amherst: University of Massachusetts Press, 1993), 175–76, and David Levering Lewis, *W.E.B. Du Bois: The Fight for Equality and the American Century, 1919–1963* (New York: Henry Holt, 2000), 500–502.

4. Du Bois to the American Delegation, U.N. Conference on International Organization, 16 May 1945, NAACP/mf p14 r18 f331.

5. See, for example, W.E.B. Du Bois, "Japan, Color, and Afro-Americans," *Chicago Defender*, 25 August 1945, in *W.E.B. Du Bois: A Reader*, ed. David Levering Lewis (New York: Henry Holt, 1995), 86–87, and W.E.B. Du Bois, "The Realities in Africa," *Foreign Affairs* 21 (1943), in *The Oxford W.E.B. Du Bois Reader*, ed. Eric Sundquist (New York: Oxford University Press, 1996), 653–63. Du Bois's statement of America's war aims are put squarely in his 1945 book, *Color and Democracy: Colonies and Peace:* "Insofar as such efforts [to bring to a successful conclusion to World War II] leave practically untouched the present imperial ownership of disfranchised colonies, and in this and other ways proceed as if the majority of men can be regarded mainly as sources of profit for Europe and North America, in just so far we are planning not peace but war, not democracy but the continued oligarchical control of civilization by the white race." In *A Documentary History of the Negro People in the United States*, volume 5 *From the End of the Second World War to the Korean War*, 53.

6. WFW to Board of the NAACP, 9 May 1945, NAACP/mf p14 r18 f58; WFW, "Memorandum on Mrs. Bethune and the United Nations Conference on International Organization at San Francisco and other matters related to the Conference," NAACP/mf p14 r17 f757. For a sampling of the variety of black organizations that sent representatives to San Francisco, see P. B. Young, "Sidelights on Historic Frisco Conference," *Norfolk Journal and Guide*, national edition, 5 May 1945, p. 8.

7. Hollis R. Lynch, *Black American Radicals and the Liberation of Africa: The Council on African Affairs, 1937–1955*, with an introduction by St. Clair Drake (Ithaca, New York: Africana Studies and Research Center, 1978), 22. This paragraph on the Council on African Affairs draws on Lynch's monograph.

8. Roy Wilkins to WFW, 20 April 1945, NAACP/mf p14 r18 f130.

9. Largely because of the secretary's connections to Eleanor Roosevelt, the NAACP had been selected as one of forty-two consulting organizations to the United States' dele-

gation; under this arrangement the State Department covered travel and accommodation expenses for two representatives of organizations thus recognized. Bethune, who in addition to being an association vice president also headed the National Council of Negro Women (NCNW), protested to Archibald MacLeish, the assistant secretary of state who was in charge of doling out the invitations, no African American women were designated to be present at the conference in an official capacity, and she urged him to correct this serious oversight by inviting the NCNW to send a consultant. MacLeish demurred but then telephoned the secretary and asked him if he could see his way to adding Bethune to the NAACP delegation. White agreed, but the matter of financing her trip was left murky. Bethune had initially told MacLeish that the NCNW could sponsor her; White said MacLeish told him the State Department would pay. But when Bethune accepted the NAACP's invitation and asked who would fund her trip, White informed her that the State Department expected the NCNW to do so. Pressed by her supporters, White placed her on the NAACP tab, but the secretary clearly believed Bethune was double-dipping. He was not alone: Daisy Lampkin thought Bethune was simply "mercenary" for submitting an expense statement exceeding $700 for five weeks in San Francisco.

Some of her actions at the conference too rankled White and even Du Bois. At a mass meeting, for example, at which the NAACP representatives met with representatives of African American organizations not recognized by the State Department, she distanced herself from her colleagues; filliping Du Bois and White, she said she didn't have a "string of degrees" after her name and hadn't much international experience but she lacked fear and had the courage to represent "the people." She also irritated the secretary when, following the conference, she organized a meeting to discuss its results without coordinating with her fellow NAACP consultants. "Memorandum on Mrs. Bethune and the United Nations Conference on International Organization at San Francisco and other Matters Relating to the Conference Prepared by the Secretary," 13 June 1945, NAACP/mf p14 r17 f757, documents most of White's spat with Bethune. But see also WFW to Roy Wilkins, 28 April 1945, NAACP/mf p14 r17 f763; Wilkins to WFW, 27 May 1945, NAACP/mf p14 r18 f244; WFW to Wilkins, 31 May 1945, NAACP/mf p14 r17 f768; WFW to Wilkins, 15 June 1945, NAACP/mf p14 r17 f775; Mary McLeod Bethune to WFW, telegram, 22 May 1945, NAACP/mf p14 r17 f743; Daisy Lampkin to WFW, 28 June 1945, NAACP/mf p14 r17 f791.

10. WFW to Wilkins, telegram, 13 May 1945, NAACP/mf p14 r18 f202.
11. [Minutes of the Meeting of the Committee on Administration], 28 May 1945, NAACP/mf p14 r18 f340.
12. WFW to Daisy Lampkin, telegram, 10 May 1945, NAACP/mf p14 r18 f191, WFW to Wilkins, telegram, 10 May 1945, NAACP/mf p14 r18 f194, WFW to NAACP Board, 9 May 1945, NAACP/mf p14 r18 f58; Wilkins to WFW, telegram, 11 May 1945, NAACP/mf p14 r18 f197.
13. [Minutes of the Meeting of the Committee on Administration], 28 May 1945, NAACP/mf p14 r18 f340; "Memorandum to Mr. Stettinius from Mr. Walter White," 15 May 1945, NAACP/mf p14 r18 f332.
14. WFW to Clement Attlee, 15 November 1945, NAACP/mf p14 r13 f293; "Comment by NAACP on Ex–Prime Minister Winston Churchill's Address on March 5th at Westminister College, Fulton, Missouri," 7 March 1946, NAACP/mf p14 r13 f313; Walter White, "People, Politics, and Places," *Chicago Defender,* 16 March 1946, p. 19.
15. *Pittsburgh Courier* 10 May 1945, copy in NAACP/mf p14 r19 f265; Thurgood Marshall to P. L. Prattis, 18 May 1945, NAACP/mf p14 r19 f262; Prattis to Marshall, May 25, 1945, NAACP/mf p14 r19 f265; Dr. Rayford W. Logan, "The 'Little Man' Just Isn't Here," *Pittsburgh Courier,* 5 May 1945; W.E.B. Du Bois to Lawrence E. Spivak, 22 May 1945, *The Correspondence of W.E.B. Du Bois,* volume III, *Selections, 1944–1963,* ed. Her-

bert Aptheker (Amherst: University of Massachusetts Press, 1978), 13; Lynch, *Black American Radicals*, 29–30.

16. W.E.B. Du Bois to Arthur Spingarn, 30 May 1945, *The Correspondence of W.E.B. Du Bois*, volume III, 14; Rayford W. Logan, speech to the American Teachers Association (before 4 August 1941), RL/H-I, box 2, "CPNNDP."

17. Michael Goldfield, *The Color of Politics: Race and the Mainsprings of American Politics* (New York: New Press, 1997), 235–36, 238.

18. B of D Minutes, 10 December 1945, NAACP/mf p1 r3 f545 and Walter White, "People, Politics, and Places," *Chicago Defender*, 16 February 1946, p. 15 (on General Motors strike, White's involvement in it, and Villard's statement); B of D minutes 9 January 1946, NAACP/mf p1 r3 f555 (on Villard's dismissal and Delaney's and Hastie's comments); Secy. Monthly Rpt., 8 March 1946, NAACP/mf p1 r7 f177 and B of D Minutes, 11 March 1946, NAACP/mf p1 r3 f572 (on NAACP's reactions to strike wave; the NAACP contributed $500 to the CIO strike fund); Secy. Monthly Rpt., 6 June 1946, NAACP/mf p1 r7 f229 (on railroad brotherhoods). On the NAACP and the UAW in 1945–1946, see August Meier and Elliott Rudwick, *Black Detroit and the Rise of the UAW* (New York: Oxford University Press, 1981), 215–19. On Operation Dixie, see Patricia Sullivan, *Days of Hope* (Chapel Hill: University of North Carolina Press, 1996), 207–10. For another discussion of labor and the civil rights movement in the immediate postwar period, see Robert Korstad and Nelson Lichtenstein, "Opportunities Found and Lost: Labor, Radicals, and the Early Civil Rights Movement," *Journal of American History* 75 (1988): 786–811. But see also Goldfield, *The Color of Politics*, chap. 7.

19. This paragraph and the next are based on John Egerton, *Speak Now against the Day* (Chapel Hill: University of North Carolina Press, 1995), 361–65.

20. On the origins of the SCHW, see Egerton, *Speak Now against the Day*, 167–97; and Sullivan, *Days of Hope*, 98–101. On White's absence, which has largely and incorrectly been interpreted as disapproval of the venture, see WFW to Mary McLeod Bethune, 30 October 1938, NAACP/mf p1 r27 f217; and WFW to Mercer Cook, 23 November 1938, NAACP/mf p2 r19 f439.

21. Secy. Monthly Rpt., 8 March 1946, NAACP/mf p1 r7 f177 ("one of the most serious"); Southern Conference for Human Welfare, *The Truth about Columbia, Tennessee Cases* (Nashville: The Conference, [1946?]); Walter White, "People, Politics, and Places," *Chicago Defender*, 13 April 1946, p. 19.

22. Guy Johnson to WFW, 19 April 1946, NAACP/mf p7A r21 f1010; Smiley Blanton to Carl Van Doren, 2 May 1946, NAACP/mf p7A r21 f1025 ("there are a good many"); White, whose prejudices about the deportment of ordinary African Americans have been well documented in previous chapters, had met Mrs. Stephenson and had this to say in reply to Blanton: she was "one of the quietest and best behaved persons I have met in a long time." WFW to Blanton, 7 May 1946, NAACP/mf p7A r21 f1032. For other expressions of southern liberal sentiment, see Herman Jones to Van Doren, 14 May 1946, NAACP/mf p7A r21 f1057; and Peyton R. Williams to WFW, 28 July 1946, NAACP/mf p7A r22 f19.

23. On the background of the president's committee, see Secy. Monthly Rpt., 11 October 1946, NAACP/mf p1 r7 f270; B of D Minutes, 9 December 1946, NAACP/mf p1 r3 f643; Secy. Monthly Rpt., November 1947, NAACP/mf p1 r7 f497; Summary Minutes of the 39th Annual Conference, 26 June 1948, NAACP/mf p1 r12 f315; Egerton, *Speak Now against the Day*, 413–16.

24. Summary Release of Conference of Progressives, September 28–29, NAACP/mf p18C r25 f76 ("reactionary coalition"); Sullivan, *Days of Hope*, 226–29.

25. Charles Toney to WFW, 15 May 1946, NAACP/mf p18C r15 f776; B of D Minutes, 27 June 1946, NAACP/mf p1 r3 f607; WFW to Philip Murray, 25 July 1946, NAACP/mf

p18C r15 f846; Minutes of Political Action Committee, 27 August 1946, NAACP/mf p18C r15 f852.

26. Summary Release of Conference of Progressives, NAACP/mf p18C r25 f76; WFW, speech to Conference of Progressives, 28 September 1946, NAACP/mf p18C r25 f35. The secretary devoted two of his *Defender* columns to the achievements of this "historic" gathering, defending it against charges that it was a Communist front. In the first instance, said White, the Conference of Progressives had the potential "to stop the headlong plunge of America into the slough of reaction and defeatism." In contrast to past progressive meetings, it was notable for its attitude toward African Americans. White paternalism was conspicuously absent; blacks were "regarded wholly as an equal and a most important factor in the framework of the bitter struggle ahead to preserve political democracy in the United States." Walter White, "People, Politics, and Places," *Chicago Defender*, 12 October 1946, p. 17. Was the NAACP being used by Communists? Emphatically not, declared the secretary. That cant emanated from the "forces of conservatism and organized greed [that] steadily increase their dominance over a war-weary, ideal-weary people." While he was by no means predisposed toward the Communists, he was unwilling to join the red-baiters. "Every indication I have seen to date is that any political group—whether it be Communist or Democratic or Republican—which attempts to influence or control policy will have its ears pinned back with vigor and promptness," he wrote. Walter White, "People, Politics, and Places," *Chicago Defender*, 2 November 1946, p. 19.

27. Arthur M. Schlesinger, Jr., "The U.S. Communist Party," *Life*, 29 July 1946, 84–85, 87–88, 90, 93–94, 96. Quotes appear on 84 and 90.

28. Edward Dudley to WFW, memo, 4 June 1945, NAACP/mf p18C r16 f78, outlines the growth of civil rights organizations in the immediate postwar years and recommends a response; WFW to Dudley, 5 June 1945, NAACP/mf p18C r16 f77, endorses Dudley's memo; WFW to NAACP branches, 7 May 1946, NAACP/mf p18C r16 f90; Gloster Current to WFW, 2 May 1946, NAACP/mf p18C r7 f11; Marian Wynn Perry to WFW, 7 May 1946, NAACP/mf p18C r7 f43; Current to WFW, 14 June 1946, NAACP/mf p18C r16 f595; WFW to Alfred Baker Lewis, 14 October 1946, NAACP/mf p18C r16 f102; Current to WFW, 20 September 1946, NAACP/mf p18C r10 f402; Walter White, "Reported Red Plot to 'Take Over' the NAACP Is Discounted," *New York Herald Tribune*, 21 December 1947, sec. II, p. 2.

29. Egerton, *Speak Now against the Day*, 448–60.

30. Du Bois to WFW, 1 August 1946, NAACP/mf p14 r16 f244. The NNC's petition is excerpted in *A Documentary History of the Negro People in the United States*, volume 5, *1945–1951*, 135–41.

31. WFW to Committee on Administration, memo, 28 August 1948, NAACP/mf p14 r16 f247.

32. Du Bois to WFW, memo 15 January 1947, NAACP/mf p14 r16 f386, Du Bois to Arthur Spingarn, 16 January 1947, NAACP/mf p14 r16 f388.

33. Du Bois to WFW, memo, 29 January 1947, NAACP/mf p14 r16 f411, John P. Humphrey to Arthur Spingarn, 19 February 1947, NAACP/mf p14 r16 f527, William H. Stoneman to Du Bois, 29 September 1947, NAACP/mf p14 r16 f408, Du Bois to Stoneman, 16 October 1947, NAACP/mf p14 r16 f397, Warren Austin to Du Bois, 21 October 1947 NAACP/mf p14 r16 f406.

34. Vijaya Pandit to Du Bois, 25 September 1947, NAACP/mf p14 r16 f402, Gabriel L. Dennis to Hugh H. Smythe, 10 October 1947, NAACP/mf p14 r16 f463.

35. WFW to Du Bois, memo, 12 November 1947, NAACP/mf p14 r16 f736.

36. Du Bois to WFW, memo, 13 November 1947, NAACP/mf p14 r15 f174.

37. Du Bois to WFW, memo, 24 November 1947, NAACP/mf p14 r14 f422; WFW to

Arthur Spingarn and Louis T. Wright, memo, 16 December 1947, NAACP/mf p14 r16 f629.

38. W.E.B. Du Bois, *The Autobiography of W.E.B. Du Bois* (New York: International Publishers, 1968), 336. White's version of the events that precipitated Du Bois's dismissal are contained in a letter he wrote to Du Bois from Paris; see WFW to Du Bois, 5 October 1948, NAACP/mf p14 r15 f499.

39. WFW to Poppy Cannon, 11 October 1948, WFW/PCW box 12 folder 111.

40. WFW to [NAACP] Office, 17 September 1948, NAACP/mf p14 r15 f382, WFW to Poppy Cannon, 20 September 1948, WFW/PCW box 12 folder 111.

41. WFW to Poppy Cannon, 10 October 1948, WFW/PCW box 12 folder 111. See also WFW to NAACP, memo (received) 11 October 1948, NAACP/mf p14 r15 f440; WFW to Colonel Ray, 11 October 1948, NAACP/mf p14 r15 f433.

42. Rayford Logan to WFW, memo (March 1948), NAACP/mf p14 r15 f345; Rayford Logan, statement on behalf of twenty-two organizations represented at the United Nations General Assembly by Walter White (August 1948), NAACP/mf p14 r15 f346; Logan Diary/LC, 5, 10 September 1948, 30 January 1949.

43. For Logan's understanding of the nuances of the development of American policy on human rights and colonialism and his suggestions for action, see "Problems Concerning Human Rights for Discussion at Meeting September 7th in Mr. White's Office," memo, 7 September 1948, NAACP/mf p14 r15 f338; Rayford Logan to WFW, memo (March 1948), NAACP/mf p14 r15 f345.

44. WFW to NAACP, 17 September 1948, NAACP/mf p14 r15 f382; WFW to NAACP, memo, [received] 11 October 1948, NAACP/mf p14 r15 f440.

45. Chester Williams to WFW, 22 October 1948, NAACP/mf p14 r15 f523, Williams to WFW, 22 October 1948, NAACP/mf p14 r15 f527, Williams to WFW, 29 October 1948, NAACP/mf p14. r15 f546.

46. WFW to Williams, 25 October 1948, NAACP/mf p14 r15 f521, WFW to Williams, 26 October 1948, NAACP/mf p14 r15 f526, WFW to Rayford Logan, 25 October 1948, NAACP/mf p14 r15 f521, WFW to Eleanor Roosevelt, 26 October 1948, NAACP/mf p14 r15 f529.

47. WFW to Eleanor Roosevelt, 26 October 1948, NAACP/mf p14 r15 f529.

48. Williams to WFW, 29 October 1948, NAACP/mf p14 r15 f547.

49. *A Man Called White*, 347–52.

50. On the 1948 presidential campaign, see Sullivan, *Days of Hope*, 249–75; Alonzo Hamby, *Beyond the New Deal: Harry S. Truman and American Liberalism* (New York: Columbia University Press, 1973), 195–265.

51. Walter White, "House Committee's Red Charge on Eve of Wallace Talk Assailed," *New York Herald-Tribune*, 22 June 1947, sec. II, p. 4; see also Walter White, "Communism Is Called Obstacle to Unified Liberal Movement," *New York Herald-Tribune*, 2 March 1947, sec. II, p. 4. But see also Walter White, "Censure of Communist Attack on Freedom Train Is Disputed," *New York Herald-Tribune*, 12 October 1947, sec. II, p. 9, in which White simply declares the CP made public-relations blunders rather than continuing to charge them with malevolent intent.

52. Walter White, "Some Republicans Said to Back Wallace to Cut Democratic Vote," *New York Herald-Tribune*, 13 June 1948, sec. II, p. 8; Walter White, "Republicans Called Weak on Negro Rights," *New York Herald-Tribune*, 27 June 1948, sec. II, p. 8; Walter White, "NAACP Parley Held Symbol of a New Negro, Politically Free," *New York Herald-Tribune*, 4 July 1948, sec. II, p. 2; Walter White, "Democrat Stand for Civil Rights Called the Only Hope for Party," *New York Herald-Tribune*, 11 July 1948, sec. II, p. 2; Walter White, "Walter White Views the Session as Opportunity for Republicans," *New York Herald-Tribune*, 25 July 1948, sec. II, p. 2; Walter White, "Truman Praised for Courage in Fight against Discrimination," *New York Herald-Tribune*, 1 August 1948, sec.

II, p. 2; Walter White, "Walter White Assails Wallace for His Record on Civil Rights," *New York Herald-Tribune*, 12 September 1948, sec. II, p. 2; Walter White, "Walter White Criticizes Dewey for His Record on Civil Rights," *New York Herald-Tribune*, 19 September 1948, sec. II, p. 2; Walter White, "Truman's Stand on Civil Rights Held Example of Rare Courage," *New York Herald-Tribune*, 26 September 1948, sec. II, p. 2.

53. Sullivan, *Days of Hope*, 249–75, 258 ("a democracy" and "Certainly there are Communists").

54. Du Bois to Secretary and Board of Directors of the NAACP, memo, 7 September 1948, NAACP/mf p14 r15 f331.

55. WFW to Board of Directors, 3 March 1948, NAACP/mf p18C r15 f928.

56. B of D Minutes, 8 March 1948, NAACP/mf p1 r3 f790.

57. B of D Minutes, 14 June 1948, NAACP/mf p1 r3 f826.

58. WFW to Du Bois, memo, 9 July 1948, NAACP/mf p16B r5 f259; Du Bois to WFW, memo, 9 July 1948, NAACP/mf p16B r5 f260.

59. B of D Minutes, 13 September 1948, NAACP/mf p1 r3 f839; Committee on Administration Minutes, 27 September 1948, NAACP/mf p16B r5 f264; Thurgood Marshall to Hubert Delany, Grace Fenderson, John Hammond, Arthur Spingarn, Charles Toney, and Louis Wright, memo, 6 October 1948, NAACP/mf p16B r5 f268.

60. WFW to Du Bois, 5 October 1948, NAACP/mf p14 r15 f499.

61. Borstlemann, *Apartheid's Reluctant Uncle*, 109–11; Michael H. Hunt, *Ideology and U.S. Foreign Policy* (New Haven: Yale University Press, 1987), 159–61.

62. "Truman's Bold New Program," *New Africa*, July–August 1949, pp. 1, 3–4; Rayford Logan to WFW, 21 March 1949, NAACP/LC, Group II, Series A, box 404, "Rayford Logan, 1948–49"; Logan to Roy Wilkins, 9 June 1949, RL/H-I, box 15, "Walter White"; Logan, "Draft of Resolutions on International Affairs, 1950," Logan to Roy Wilkins, 2 January 1950, NAACP/LC, Group II, Series A, box 404, "Rayford Logan II, 1950–51"; Logan, "Bold New Program *or* Old Imperialism," *New Times and Ethiopian News*, 11 June 1949.

63. WFW to Dean Acheson, 31 January 1949, WFW/PCW, folder 1, box 2.

64. WFW to Harry Truman, 23 August 1949, NAACP/mf p14 r8 f609.

65. WFW to Victor Reuther, 22 December 1949, Victor Reuther to WFW, 1 February 1950, WFW to Victor Reuther, 10 February 1950, WFW to Victor Reuther and Walter Reuther, 16 February 1950, WFW/PCW box 6 folder 175; WFW to Mme. Pandit, 21 December 1949, WFW/PCW box 5 folder 157; WFW to Henry Ford II, 11 February 1950, WFW/PCW box 2 folder 66; WFW to Eleanor Roosevelt, 14 March 1950, WFW/PCW box 6 folder 179; WFW to Walter Reuther, 19 June 1951, NAACP/mf p14 r8 f860.

66. Reed Harris to WFW, 28 October 1952, NAACP/mf p14 r9 f636. White declined the invitation, saying he was being kept busy fighting for civil rights, and that since his marriage to Poppy Cannon and the concomitant support of more children, money was in short supply. See WFW to Chester Bowles, 30 October 1952, NAACP/mf p14 r9 f653.

67. Wilkins to WFW, memo, 22 November 1951, NAACP/mf p14 r16 f86.

68. Rayford W. Logan, untitled autobiographical manuscript (hereinafter cited as Logan autobiography), vol. 2, chap. 1, RL/H-II box 5.

69. Voice of America broadcast statement, 16 November 1951, NAACP/mf p14 r16 f96, Wilkins to WFW, memo, 20 November 1951, NAACP/mf p14 r16 f65, WFW to Wilkins, memo, 23 November 1951, NAACP/mf p14 r16 f85, Hubert T. Delany to WFW, 23 November 1951, NAACP/mf p14 r16 f90.

70. WFW statement on *We Charge Genocide* (20 November 1951), NAACP/mf p14 r16 f66.

71. Walter White, "Time for a Progress Report," *The Saturday Review of Literature*, September 22, 1951, pp. 9–10, 38–41.

72. WFW to Lessing Rosenwald, 30 November 1951, NAACP/mf p14 r16 f77; WFW to Channing Tobias, 12 December 1951, NAACP/mf p14 r16 f75; Delany to WFW, 23 November 1951, NAACP/mf p14 r16 f90.

73. Herbert Hill to Roy Wilkins, memo, 9 December 1954, NAACP/mf p14 r6 f1012.

74. Martin Bauml Duberman, *Paul Robeson* (New York: Knopf, 1988), 343–49; Charles V. Hamilton, *Adam Clayton Powell, Jr.: The Political Biography of an American Dilemma* (New York: Collier, 1991), 237–48.

75. Mary Louise Dudziak, "Cold War Civil Rights: The Relationship between Civil Rights and Foreign Affairs in the Truman Administration" (Ph.D. diss., Yale University, 1992); Penny M. Von Eschen, *Race against Empire : Black Americans and Anticolonialism, 1937–1957* (Ithaca, New York: Cornell University Press, 1997), 145–66.

76. Board of Directors minutes, 9 May 1949, NAACP/mf p1 r3 f929.

77. Von Eschen, *Race against Empire*, 149.

Chapter 11: LOOKING FOR A LARGER POND

1. Louis Wright to Branch Officers, 11 April 1947, NAACP/mf p17 r23 f191 ("an attack"); WFW to Roy Wilkins, 8 March 1947, quoted in Roy Wilkins with Tom Mathews, *Standing Fast: The Autobiography of Roy Wilkins* (New York: Viking, 1982), 196–97 ("severe"); B of D Minutes, 10 March 1947, NAACP/mf p1 r3 f668 ("not good"). White discussed aspects of his Virgin Islands activities in his newspaper columns. See Walter White, "People, Politics and Places," *Chicago Defender*, 22 March 1947, p. 19, and 3 May 1947, p. 19; Walter White, "Virgin Islands' Regime Praised As Race-Relations Experiment," *New York Herald-Tribune*, 30 March 1947, section II, p. 10.

2. Secy. Monthly Rpt., March 1947, NAACP/mf p1 r7 f385; B of D Minutes, 13 October 1947, NAACP/mf p1 r3 f726; Laura Veiller to WFW, 11 April 1947, NAACP/mf p18B r16 f79; WFW to Veiller, 21 April 1947, NAACP/mf p18B r16 f75. Gloster Current, who joined the NAACP executive staff in 1946, confirms this interpretation, when he commented that once assignments were made, White did not closely scrutinize staff members' implementation; that job was left to Roy Wilkins. Gloster Current, interview by Robert L. Zangrando, 14 March 1978, New York, New York, tape-recording of Zangrando's notes in author's possession.

3. WFW to Board of Directors, 7 September 1948, NAACP/mf p1 r7 f634.

4. On board members' affection for White, see Alfred Baker Lewis, interview by Robert L. Zangrando, 27 September 1973, Akron, Ohio, tape-recorded notes in author's possession. On Wilkins's role in the 1931 protest against White by executive officers of the association, see chapter 6. C. A. Franklin to Roy Wilkins, 26 January 1935, NAACP/mf p7B r7 f311, is a patronizing and demagogic letter about the NAACP that Wilkins fully endorses in Wilkins to WFW, memo, 31 January 1935, NAACP/mf p7B r7 f417. On Wilkins's disruptive ambition in the forties, see Wilkins to John Hammond, 25 September 1943, NAACP/mf p17 r27 f3; Wilkins to Arthur Spingarn, 25 September 1943, NAACP/mf p17 r27 f5; Wilkins to Hubert Delany, 28 September 1943, NAACP/mf p17 r27 f12; Wilkins to WFW, memo, 27 September 1943, NAACP/mf p17 r27 f15; Wilkins to Daisy Lampkin, 28 September 1943, NAACP/mf p17 r27 f24; Hammond to Wilkins, 8 October 1943, NAACP/mf p17 r27 f22; Wilkins to Hammond, 9 October 1943, NAACP/mf p17 r27 f29; Hammond to Wilkins, 19 October 1943, NAACP/mf p17 r27 f39. Herbert Hill, who joined the NAACP national staff in 1947 and who soon thereafter became the association's labor secretary, said that because of the way decisions were made at NAACP headquarters—White huddled with Louis Wright and whoever else they felt was necessary and determined the organization's actions before board meetings—he had no specific evidence of differences between White and Wilkins; at the same time, he said, one could not help but be aware of the tension between the two. Herbert Hill, interview by author, 13–14 August 1997, Madi-

son, Wisconsin, tape-recording in author's possession. Judge Jane Bolin, a board member in the forties, noted—and vehemently objected to—White's practice of usurping the board's functions. See Jane Bolin to Arthur Spingarn, 9 March 1950, NAACP/mf p16B r1 f603.

5. Mabel Smith, interview by author, 15 September 1997, New York, tape-recording and additional notes in author's possession; "The Reminiscences of Thurgood Marshall," in the Oral History Collection of Columbia University, New York, New York, reprinted in *Thurgood Marshall: His Speeches, Writings, Arguments, Opinions, and Reminiscences*, ed. Mark V. Tushnet (Chicago: Lawrence Hill Books, 2001), 503; Herbert Hill, interview by author, 13–14 August 1997, Madison, Wisconsin, tape-recording in author's possession. Hill's recollection is corroborated by Gloster Current. Like Hill, Current said he was too junior for the first few years at NAACP headquarters to be privy to specific disagreements among the senior staff. Gloster Current, interview by Robert L. Zangrando, 14 March 1978, New York, New York, tape-recording of Zangrando's notes in author's possession. See also Carl T. Rowan, *Dream Makers, Dream Breakers: The World of Thurgood Marshall* (Boston: Little, Brown, 1993), 129, 227.

6. Harold Oram, interview by Robert L. Zangrando, 23 August 1982, Yorktown, New York, tape-recording of Zangrando's notes in author's possession; Harold Oram to WFW, 18 October 1948, WFW/PCW box 2 folder 73.

7. Val J. Washington to Louis T. Wright, September 27, 1948, WFW/PCW box 12 folder 111; Thurgood Marshall to WFW, 7 October 1948, WFW/PCW box 4 folder 130 ("best friends"); WFW to [NAACP Board?], 11 October 1948, NAACP/mf p14 r15 f510; Committee on Administration Minutes, 27 September 1948, NAACP/mf p16B r5 f264; Thurgood Marshall to Hubert Delany, Grace Fenderson, John Hammond, Arthur Spingarn, Charles Toney, and Louis Wright, memo, 6 October 1948, NAACP/mf p16B r5 f268; Abner Berry, "As We See It," *Daily Worker*, 20 September 1948; WFW to Poppy Cannon, 11 October 1948, WFW/PCW box 12 folder 111 ("They don't want me").

8. Gladys White to Dear Family [Helen Martin, Madeline White, and Olive Westmoreland], 25 May (1949), copy in author's possession courtesy Rose Palmer.

9. Mary White Ovington to Joel Spingarn, 11 January 1922, JES/NYPL box 9 folder 2; Gladys White to Dear Family, 25 May (1949), copy in author's possession courtesy Rose Palmer (desire to be alone); WFW to Gladys White, 18 August 1926, NAACP/mf p2 r10 f262; Gladys White to WFW, 28 April (1938) and 30 December (1944), WFW/PCW box 7 folder 221; Gladys White to WFW, 5 March 1945, NAACP/mf p17 r17 f1069.

10. Poppy Cannon to Gladys White (June 1932), NAACP/mf p2 r15 f309, and WFW to Poppy Cannon, 30 June 1932, NAACP/mf p2 r15 f308 (weekend in Connecticut); WFW to Fania Marinoff, 26 March 1932, NAACP/mf p2 r15 f73, WFW to Lawrence Langner, 29 March 1932, NAACP/mf p2 r15 f81, and WFW to Cherryl Crawford, 29 March 1932, NAACP/mf p2 r15 f83 (on finding Mina Ruskin a job); WFW to H. L. Mencken, 12 September 1933, NAACP/mf p2 r16 f232, WFW to Madeline White, 15 March 1934, NAACP/mf p2 r16 f516, and WFW to Madeline White, 2 May 1934, NAACP/mf p2 r16 f569 (on Poppy Cannon's southern trip).

11. According to Poppy Cannon, White broke off their affair without a word of explanation in spring 1934 shortly after she returned from her recipe-gathering tour of the South; she said he did not telephone her, refused to take her calls, returned the advance on the cookbook from Knopf, and ceased work on it. Poppy Cannon, *A Gentle Knight: My Husband, Walter White* (New York: Rinehart, 1956), 22–25. Yet her memory is frequently plagued by omission and distortion as to make it generally unreliable. Casting more doubt on Cannon's version of events is White's statement to Mary White Ovington a year after he supposedly put the cookbook project aside that he was still working

on it, and a later letter to Cannon herself that indicated that the hiatus in their affair was mutual. See WFW to Mary White Ovington, 21 September 1935, NAACP/mf p2 r17 f656; WFW to Poppy Cannon, 6 February (1949), WFW/PCW box 12 folder 112. The year of the resumption of their affair is inferred from WFW to Cannon, 3 February 1949, WFW/PCW box 12 folder 112. On Poppy's concentration on her work, see Rose Palmer, interview by author, 15 January 1998, Atlanta, Georgia, tape-recording in author's possession. For dates of Poppy Cannon's marriages, see Cynthia White to Kenneth Janken, e-mail, 20 October 2001, and 23 October 2001, in author's possession.

12. Cynthia White, telephone interview by author, 19 October 2000, notes in author's possession.

13. WFW to Poppy Cannon, 20 September 1948, WFW/PCW box 12 folder 111; WFW to Cannon, 17 January (1949), WFW/PCW box 12 folder 112; WFW to Cannon, 18 January (1949), WFW/PCW box 12 folder 112.

14. Gladys White to WFW, n.d., quoted in WFW to Poppy Cannon, 6 February (1949), WFW/PCW box 12 folder 112.

15. B of D minutes, 3 January 1949, NAACP/mf p1 r3 f881; Henry Lee Moon, *Balance of Power: The Negro Vote* (Garden City, New York: Doubleday & Co., 1948); Walter White, "Walter White Says Negro Vote Swung Pivotal States to Truman," *New York Herald-Tribune*, 14 November 1948, section II, p. 10; William C. Berman, *The Politics of Civil Rights in the Truman Administration* (Columbus, Ohio: Ohio State University Press, 1970), 128–33.

16. B of D minutes, 3 January 1949, NAACP/mf p1 r3 f881; Leslie Perry to WFW, 18 January 1949, NAACP/mf p13B r8 f303; Perry to WFW, memo, 8 December 1948, NAACP/mf p13B r8 f281; Secy. Monthly Rpt., February 1949, NAACP/mf p1 r7 f698.

17. WFW to Poppy Cannon, 25 January (1949), WFW/PCW box 12 folder 112.

18. WFW to Poppy Cannon, 4 February (1949) ("You're damn right") and 6 February (1949) ("talk turkey"), WFW/PCW box 12 folder 112; WFW to Poppy Cannon, 4 March 1949, WFW/PCW box 12 folder 113 (exchange of letters with CIO); Walter White, "Three Things to Watch for in This Congress," *Chicago Defender*, 15 January 1949, p. 7; Walter White, "Watch Your Congressman on Civil Rights Issue," *Chicago Defender*, 29 January 1949, p. 7; Walter White, "Who Does Lucas Think Won, the Dixiecrats?" *Chicago Defender*, 26 February 1949, p. 7; Walter White, "Citizens Should Ignore Anti-Cloture Arguments," *Chicago Defender*, 5 March 1949, p. 7; Walter White, "The Civil Rights Ball Is on Five-Yard Marker," *Chicago Defender*, 12 March 1949, p. 7 ("loud-mouthed"); Walter White, " '97th Senator' Ready to Steer Truman's Program past Shoals," *New York Herald-Tribune*, 9 January 1949, section II, p. 4; Walter White, "Filibuster Seen as a Threat to Civil Rights," *New York Herald-Tribune*, 23 January 1949, section II, p. 2; Walter White, "Parties Warned of Voters' Ire If They Fail to Bar Filibuster," *New York Herald-Tribune*, 6 February 1949, section II, p. 2; Walter White, "Fates of Democrats in 1950 Seen Hanging on Stand on Civil Rights," *New York Herald-Tribune*, 20 February 1949, section II, p. 2; Walter White, "Leaders of the Senate Filibuster," *New York Herald-Tribune*, 13 March 1949, section II, p. 8.

19. On the fight for cloture and the fate of civil rights in the 81st Congress, see Donald R. McCoy and Richard T. Ruetten, *Quest and Response: Minority Rights and the Truman Administration* (Lawrence, Kansas: University Press of Kansas, 1973), 171–204; Berman, *The Politics of Civil Rights in the Truman Administration*, 137–81; Hubert H. Humphrey, "Notes and Memoranda: The Senate on Trial," *American Political Science Review* 44 (1950): 650–60; Oliver C. Cox, "The Programs of Negro Civil Rights Organizations," *Journal of Negro Education* 20 (1951): 354–66; B. R. Brazeal, "The Present Status and Programs of Fair Employment Practices Commissions—Federal, State, and Municipal," *Journal of Negro Education* 20 (1951): 378–97.

20. Walter White, "Champions or Quitters, Civil Rights Will Tell," *Chicago Defender,* 26 March 1949, p. 7; see also Walter White, "The Civil Rights Fight," *New York Herald-Tribune,* 27 March 1949, section II, p. 2.

21. Thurgood Marshall to WFW, 16 February 1949, NAACP/mf p13B r8 f101; Alfred Baker Lewis to Arthur Spingarn, 31 March 1949, quoted in McCoy and Ruetten, *Quest and Response,* 175.

22. WFW to Poppy Cannon, 6 February (1949), 7 February (1949), and 10 February (1949) (possible pregnancy), WFW/PCW box 12 folder 112; WFW to Cannon, 1 March (1949), WFW/PCW box 12 folder 113 (reporting on White's conversation with Hastie).

23. WFW to Poppy Cannon, 20 February (1949), WFW/PCW box 12 folder 113 (divorce); B of D Minutes, 11 April 1949, NAACP/mf p1 r3 f915.

24. B of D Minutes, 9 May 1949, NAACP/mf p1 r3 f929 ("I want to devote"); Arthur Master to Louis Wright, 9 May 1949, NAACP/mf p17 r23 f142 (White's heart specialist's opinions); Alfred Baker Lewis to WFW, 10 May 1949, NAACP/mf p17 r23 f909; WFW to NAACP Branches, 11 May 1949, NAACP/mf p17 r23 f989; WFW to Board of Directors, 24 May 1949, NAACP/mf p17 r23 f905; B of D minutes, 13 June 1949, NAACP/mf p1 r3 f943; Mabel Smith interview by Kenneth Janken, 15 July 1997, New York City, tape-recording in author's possession.

25. *Chicago Defender,* national edition, 21 May 1949, p. 1.

26. *Washington Afro-American,* 21 May 1949, p. 2.

27. Alice Glenn to WFW (postmarked 20 May 1949), WFW/PCW box 2 folder 72A; Madeline White to WFW, 20 May 1949, WFW/PCW box 7 folder 225.

28. Alice Glenn to WFW (postmarked 20 May 1949), WFW/PCW box 2 folder 72A; Helen Martin to WFW, 20 May 1949, WFW/PCW box 4 folder 131.

29. Madeline White to WFW, 20 May 1949, WFW/PCW box 7 folder 225; Helen Martin to WFW, 20 May 1949, WFW/PCW box 4 folder 131; Alice Glenn to WFW (postmarked 7 June 1949), WFW/PCW box 2 folder 72A.

30. Cannon, *A Gentle Knight,* 10–11, 47.

31. *Chicago Defender,* national edition, 16 July 1949, 23 July 1949; *Pittsburgh Courier,* 16 July 1949.

32. William Hastie to Carl Murphy, 3 October 1949, NAACP/mf p17 r24 f128; Palmer Weber to Carl Murphy, 1 September 1949, NAACP/mf p17 r23 f927; Alfred Baker Lewis to Carl Murphy, 30 August 1949, NAACP/mf p17 r23 f922; Carl Murphy to Palmer Weber, 31 August 1949, NAACP/mf p17 r23 f925.

33. "Mr. White's Marriage," *Washington Afro-American,* 30 July 1949, p. 20.

34. *Norfolk Journal and Guide,* 6 August 1949, quoted in Rowan, *Dream Makers, Dream Breakers,* 173.

35. Lillian Scott, "Walter White, New Wife Now in Europe," *Chicago Defender,* national edition, 30 July 1949, p. 1; "C. C. Spaulding Chides Walter White for His Recent Marriage," *Chicago Defender,* national edition, 3 September 1949, p. 1.

36. Lucille Miller to Louis T. Wright, 2 August 1949, NAACP/mf p17 r24 f114.

37. C. C. Dejoie, Jr., article in *Louisiana Weekly,* 10 September 1949, typescript copy in WFW/PCW box 2 folder 45; James A. Atkins, 3 October 1949, WFW/PCW box 1 folder 7 (ellipses in original).

38. Walter White, "Foreign Peoples Curious about U.S. Race Question," *Chicago Defender,* national edition, 10 September 1949, p. 7 ("about democracy"). In addition to White's *Defender* columns in August and September 1949, and his *Herald-Tribune* columns between the end of July and October 1949, see Cannon, *A Gentle Knight,* 59–150; Mary Bell Decker, *The World We Saw with Town Hall* (New York: Richard R. Smith, 1950); and George Wilson, *Farmer to Farmer around the World* (Stockton, Calif.: n.p., 1987), 163–89, for participant accounts of the *Round the World Town Meeting of the Air.*

39. Walter White, "Has Science Conquered the Color Line?" *Look*, 30 August 1949, 94–95.
40. *New York Amsterdam News*, 27 August 1949, p. 2.
41. *Chicago Defender*, national edition, 27 August 1949, p. 27.
42. *Baltimore Afro-American*, 27 August 1949, photocopy of article in author's possession. Thanks to Brent Staples for sending me a copy of this article. The edition of the *Afro-American* that has been microfilmed was the *Washington Afro-American*, and this article does not appear in it.
43. *Chicago Defender*, national edition, 24 September 1949, p. 1.
44. Thanks to Brent Staples for bringing this to my attention in our dialogue on White's article.
45. Rowan, *Dream Makers, Dream Breakers*, 170–71, 172.
46. Letter to the editor, *New York Amsterdam News*, 17 September 1949, p. 18.
47. Joel Spingarn to Amy Spingarn, 22 November 1926, Joel E. Spingarn Papers, box 15 folder 584, Moorland-Spingarn Research Center, Howard University, Washington, D.C.
48. WFW to Poppy Cannon, 3 February 1949, WFW/PCW box 12 folder 112.
49. WFW to Poppy Cannon, 1 February 1949, NAACP/mf p17 r21 f673; Harold Oram to John Rich, memo, 1 June 1949, WFW/PCW box 2 folder 73 ("of establishing himself" and "consultant to"); Oram to WFW, memo, 23 June 1949, WFW/PCW box 2 folder 73; WFW to Cannon, 22 February (1949), WFW/PCW box 12 folder 113. See also WFW to William Hastie, 24 March 1949, NAACP/mf p17 r21 f692, in which White describes the thrust of the program by listing the guests he would like to have: Ralph Bunche, Mme. Pandit, former governor Ellis Arnall of Georgia, Eric Johnston of the Motion Picture Producers Association, Pearl Buck, Tallulah Bankhead, Frank Porter Graham, and Larry Doby, the second black major-league baseball player. White went about publicizing his show in typical fashion: he approached potential guests by proclaiming the program as a fait accompli; in fact, however, it never was, and the major networks declined to produce it. See Vera Eikel to WFW, 4 April 1949, NAACP/mf p17 r21 f704; Eikel was White's agent.
50. WFW to Poppy Cannon, 10 February (1949), WFW/PCW box 12 folder 112 ("obstreperous"); WFW to Cannon, 29 January 1949, WFW/PCW box 12 folder 112 ("patronizing"); WFW to Cannon, 3 February 1949, WFW/PCW box 12 folder 112 ("Thurgoods and Daily Workers" and "The most perfect love").
51. Herbert Hill interview by author, 13–14 August 1997, Madison, Wisconsin.
52. B of D minutes, 9 May 1949, NAACP/mf p1 r3 f929.
53. WFW to Poppy Cannon, 22 February (1949), WFW/PCW box 12 folder, 113; WFW to Colston Leigh, 27 May 1949, NAACP/mf p17 r21 f717; WFW to newspaper editors, 28 October 1949, WFW/PCW box 2 folder 73; Beatrice R. Grant to WFW, 14 April 1950, NAACP/mf p17 r18 f762; WFW to Gloster Current, 31 October 1949, NAACP/mf p17 r21 f769. In this letter to Current, White begs off of speaking at branch functions: "Wherever I can fit it in to so tight a schedule, I will try to meet at least with the executive committees. A number of these branches, as you know, have asked me to speak for them but, unfortunately, I have had to decline because of lack of time." For White's 1949 itinerary, see several letters between November 1949 and January 1950 from Elizabeth Curtis to WFW, WFW/PCW box 1 folder 44.
54. B of D minutes, 12 September 1949, NAACP/mf p1 r3 f961 ("for the purpose"); B of D minutes, 10 October 1949, NAACP/mf p1 r3 f970; WFW to Harold Oram, 21 September 1949, WFW/PCW box 2 folder 73. In this letter to Oram, White declines to state the reasons for removing mention of his NAACP connections, but tells him that "it is imperative that it be done."
55. WFW to F. E. de Frantz, 7 March 1950, WFW/PCW box 2 folder 45; Cannon, *A Gentle Knight*, 220; Harold Oram, interview by Robert L. Zangrando, 23 August 1982,

Yorktown, New York, tape-recording of Zangrando's notes in author's possession; Oram to WFW, 28 March 1950, NAACP/mf p17 r18 f751; Poppy Cannon to Elizabeth Curtis, 10 April 1950, WFW/PCW box 1 folder 44.

56. WFW to Board of Directors, 10 March 1950, NAACP/mf p17 r24 f41.

57. *New York World-Telegram and Sun*, 14 February 1950, quoted in B of D minutes, 13 March 1950, NAACP/mf p1 r3 f1039; Poppy Cannon to WFW, 18 February 1950 (postmarked), WFW/PCW box 8 folder 230; Cannon to WFW, 21 February 1950 (postmarked), WFW/PCW box 8 folder 230.

58. B of D minutes, 13 March 1950, NAACP/mf p1 r3 f1039.

59. *Dallas Express*, 8 April 1950, quoted in Carl Murphy to Roy Wilkins, 4 May 1950, NAACP/mf p17 r29 f239.

60. Poppy Cannon to WFW, 18 February 1950 (postmarked), WFW/PCW box 8 folder 230 ("whom Harlem"); *Chicago Defender*, national edition, 6 May 1950, p. 6; *Chicago Defender*, national edition, 13 May 1950, p. 1; *Chicago Defender*, national edition, 20 May 1950, pp. 1, 6; Roy Wilkins to Daisy Lampkin, 24 March 1950, NAACP/mf p17 r24 f25.

61. Palmer Weber to WFW, 1 March 1950, WFW/PCW box 7 folder 211; WFW to Arthur Spingarn (2 May 1950), WFW/PCW box 6 folder 195; B of D minutes, 13 March 1950, NAACP/mf p1 r3 f1039 ("can blow in"); Nathan K. Christopher to WFW, 1 April 1950, WFW/PCW box 1 folder 39.

62. Roy Wilkins to Eleanor Roosevelt, 5 December 1949, WFW/PCW box 6 folder 179; WFW to Roosevelt, 9 December 1949, WFW/PCW box 6 folder 179; *Amsterdam News*, 10 December 1949, clipping in WFW/PCW box 6 folder 179; Roosevelt to WFW, 15 December 1949, WFW/PCW box 6 folder 179 ("because I do not think"); WFW to Roosevelt, 19 December 1949, WFW/PCW box 6 folder 179.

63. Eleanor Roosevelt to Roy Wilkins, 4 April 1950, quoted in B of D minutes, 10 April 1950, NAACP/mf p1 r3 f1055; Wilkins's comments in this paragraph also come from these board minutes.

64. Eleanor Roosevelt to WFW, 29 March 1950, WFW/PCW, box 6 folder 179.

65. A. Maceo Smith to Roy Wilkins, 21 April 1950, NAACP/mf p17 r29 f514.

66. Roy Wilkins to A. Maceo Smith, 2 May 1950, NAACP/mf p17 r29 f512.

67. Report of the Special Committee on Top Level Staff Organization (May 1950), NAACP/mf p1 r7 f897; B of D minutes, 8 May 1950, NAACP/mf p1 r3 f1073; *Washington Afro-American*, 13 May 1950, p. 1.

68. B of D minutes, 8 May 1950, NAACP/mf p1 r3 f1073; *Washington Afro-American*, 13 May 1950, p. 1; Mabel Smith interview by Kenneth Janken, 15 July 1997, New York City, tape-recording in author's possession; *Standing Fast: The Autobiography of Roy Wilkins*, 212. As historian Patricia Sullivan pointed out to me in one of many conversations, in Eleanor Roosevelt's actions, one can see either exceptional loyalty to a friend or an expression of political bossism.

69. WFW to Henry Lee Moon, 9 May 1950, NAACP/mf p17 r22 f57; Report of the Special Committee on Top Level Staff Organization (May 1950), NAACP/mf p1 r7 f897.

70. WFW to William Hastie (with copies to Louis T. Wright and Arthur B. Spingarn), 20 July 1950, NAACP/mf p17 r22 f183.

71. In addition to WFW to William Hastie (with copies to Louis T. Wright and Arthur B. Spingarn), 20 July 1950, NAACP/mf p17 r22 f183, see WFW to Arthur Spingarn (2 May 1950), WFW/PCW box 6 folder 195; on double-dipping, see WFW to Poppy Cannon, 3 February 1949, WFW/PCW box 12 folder 112.

72. WFW to Arthur Spingarn (2 May 1950), WFW/PCW box 6 folder 195.

73. For example, he asked the board at its October 1950 meeting for permission to travel to military bases and report on the armed forces' progress on racial integration. Channing Tobias was opposed; someone of lesser rank should make the investigation and turn the

information over to White so he could write the report. Bill Hastie said White should concentrate his diminished energy on raising money for the association. But two of White's staunchest supporters, Hubert Delany and Lillie Jackson of Baltimore, felt that the board should not restrain him from doing what he wanted to do, and they acceded to his request. B of D Minutes, 9 October 1950, NAACP/mf p1 r3 f1116.

74. Poppy Cannon to Luc Foch, memo, 6 September 1950, NAACP/mf p14 r8 f44; WFW to Paul Magloire, 18 February 1952, WFW/PCW box 4 folder 128. The Whites also organized a conference on improving the United States' image in that island nation. Held at their Breakneck Hill home in West Redding, Connecticut, among the individual participants were people remarkably accomplished in their fields: Ralph Bunche, Eleanor Roosevelt, Victor Reuther, federal judge Waties Waring, Admiral Chester Nimitz, the pollster Elmo Roper, and representatives of William Paley of CBS, the secretary of state, and the president. But the composition of the roster was eclectic, and with many conferees bringing along their spouses, the meeting took on the flavor more of a day in the country than an earnest policy-proposing gathering, and—not surprisingly—its lasting effects were nil. See minutes of conference held at Breakneck Hill, West Redding, Conn., 16 September 1950, NAACP/mf p17 r18 f819.

75. Thurgood Marshall to WFW, memo, 2 April 1953, NAACP/mf p18C r1 f76 ("I would appreciate"); WFW to Marshall, memo, 7 April 1953, NAACP/mf p18C r1 f77 ("I want to make it clear"); Marshall to WFW, memo, 22 April 1953, NAACP/mf p18C r1 f74; WFW to Marshall, memo, 28 April 1953, NAACP/mf p18C r1 f73; Mabel Smith interview by Kenneth Janken, 15 July 1997, New York City, tape-recording in author's possession (Marshall's reaction to White's performance at the press conference). See also "The Reminiscences of Thurgood Marshall," 438, 503.

76. Rose Palmer interview by Kenneth Janken, Atlanta, Georgia, 15 January 1998; Cannon, *A Gentle Knight*, 154–58, 221–22; WFW to C. C. Philippe, 22 September 1952, NAACP/mf p17 r22 f504; Kenneth Janken's recollections of telephone conversation with Claudia Philippe, n.d.

77. Helen Martin to WFW and Poppy Cannon, 30 December 1950, WFW/PCW box 4 folder 131; Cannon, *A Gentle Knight*, 204–12, and David Levering Lewis to Kenneth Janken, e-mail, 14 November 2001, in author's possession (Atlanta visit); Poppy Cannon to Madeline White, Alf Askland, Cynthia Cannon, and Claudia Philippe, WFW/PCW box 7 folder 225; Cannon to Helen and Eugene Martin, 20 October 1952, WFW/PCW box 4 folder 131; Eugene Martin to Cannon and WFW, 2 August 1953, WFW/PCW box 4 folder 131; Rose Palmer, interview by Kenneth Janken, Atlanta, Georgia, 15 January 1998.

78. WFW to Arthur Spingarn (2 May 1950), WFW/PCW box 6 folder 195.

79. NAACP press release, 24 January 1952, NAACP/mf p17 r22 f452; Franklin H. Williams to WFW, 16 April 1952, NAACP/mf p17 r22 f461; Poppy Cannon to Madeline White, Alf Askland, Cynthia Cannon, and Claudia Philippe, 20 August 1952, WFW/PCW box 7 folder 225; Cannon, *A Gentle Knight*, 225–31; Poppy Cannon to Helen and Eugene Martin, 20 October 1952, WFW/PCW box 4 folder 131; Jane Wright to WFW, 12 November 1952, NAACP/mf p17 r23 f150.

80. Herbert Hill interview by author, 13–14 August 1997, Madison, Wisconsin; Cannon, *A Gentle Knight*, 255–61; WFW to Dear Folks (at NAACP headquarters), 14 November 1954, NAACP/mf p17 r23 f157.

81. Nan Pandit to WFW, 18 February 1955, NAACP/mf p14 r6 f199; WFW to Jawaharlal Nehru, 5 January 1955, NAACP/mf p14 r9 f742. On the Bandung conference, see the Council on African Affairs journal *Spotlight on Africa*, May 1955, p. 17; Penny M. Von Eschen, *Race against Empire: Black Americans and Anti-Colonialism* (Ithaca, New York: Cornell University Press, 1997), 168–73; and Richard Wright, *The Color Curtain: A Report on the Bandung Conference* (Cleveland: World Publishing Company, 1956).

82. WFW to Channing Tobias, 22 February 1955, NAACP/mf p17 r22 f958.
83. Cannon, *A Gentle Knight*, 271–76.

Chapter 12: "MR. NAACP" IS DEAD: THE LEGACY OF WALTER WHITE

1. *New York Times*, 25 March 1955, p. 31 ("was laid out"); *New York Times*, 23 March 1955 ("vigorous champion"); *Washington Afro-American*, 26 March 1955 (Nixon quote). Estimates of the size of the crowd varied widely. At the low end was the *New York Times* for 25 March 1955, which put the number at 3,000 total—1,500 inside and a similar number outside. The *New York Amsterdam News*, 2 April 1955, said 1,800 mourners packed the church and 3,000 more were on the streets. The *Washington Afro-American*, 26 March 1955, estimated a crowd of 9,000; while the *Chicago Defender*, 2 April 1955, said 10,000 people paid their respects at the funeral.

2. *Washington Afro-American*, 26 March 1955, 2 April 1955; *Chicago Defender*, 2 April 1955.

3. Hallie Hahn to Roy Wilkins, 4 April 1955, NAACP/mf p17 r19 f113.

4. *Washington Afro-American*, 26 March 1955, p. 4; *Chicago Defender*, 2 April 1955.

5. Lester B. Granger, "Manhattan and Beyond," *Amsterdam News*, 2 April 1955.

6. Walter White, *How Far the Promised Land?* (New York: Viking, 1955), 191.

7. Herbert Hill, "The Problem of Race in American Labor History," *Reviews in American History* 24 (1996): 189–208; Herbert Hill, *"Lichtenstein's Fictions:* Meany, Reuther and the 1964 Civil Rights Act," *New Politics*, n.s., 7 (1998): 82–107; Herbert Hill, *"Lichtenstein's Fictions Revisited:* Race and the New Labor History," *New Politics*, n.s., 7 (1999): 148–63.

8. White, *How Far the Promised Land?*, 213, 214, 218.

9. Aubrey Williams to WFW, 7 March 1954, NAACP/mf p18C r10 f254; WFW to Williams, 16 March 1954, NAACP/mf p18C r10 f253; Gloster Current to Clarence Mitchell, 14 May 1954, NAACP/mf p18C r10 f277; William Thomas [president of Bessemer branch] to WFW, 7 May 1954, NAACP/mf p18C r10 f278. For more on White's attitude toward the SCEF, see Roy Wilkins to Carl Johnson, 1 May 1954, NAACP/mf p18C r10 f241.

10. *Daily Worker*, 23 March 1955, 25 March 1955, 29 March 1955; Benjamin J. Davis to Roy Wilkins, 25 March 1955, NAACP/mf p17 r19 f87. To show his dislike for Wilkins and his abrasive anticommunism, Davis added this postscript: "While I'm at it, I wish to let you know that I read your lurid and false article about the Communists in the American Magazine ('51 or '52) while I was in the U.S. penitentiary in Terre Haute. And your statement in that article that I had 'heckled' speakers at NAACP convention was just a plain damn lie."

11. W. M. Brewer, review of *How Far the Promised Land?* by Walter White, *Journal of Negro History* 41 (1956): 359. William H. Chafe, *Civilities and Civil Rights* (New York: Oxford University Press, 1981), and David S. Cecelski, *Along Freedom Road: Hyde County, North Carolina, and the Fate of Black Schools in the South* (Chapel Hill: University of North Carolina Press, 1994), are two excellent studies of white intransigence to school desegregation.

12. White, *How Far the Promised Land?*, 229.

13. *Chicago Defender*, 2 April 1955.

14. Herbert Hill, interview by author, 13–14 August 1997, Madison, Wisconsin, tape-recording in author's possession.

15. "The Reminiscences of Thurgood Marshall," in the Oral History Collection of Columbia University, New York, New York, reprinted in *Thurgood Marshall: His Speeches, Writings, Arguments, Opinions, and Reminiscences*, ed. Mark V. Tushnet (Chicago: Lawrence Hill Books, 2001), 471, 476, 478–79, 503–504.

Bibliography

Manuscript Collections

British Foreign Office United States: Correspondence, 1938–1945, reel 25, file F.O. 371/38609. Wilmington, Del.: Scholarly Resources, 1979, 1981. Microfilm.

W.E.B. Du Bois Papers. Special Collections and Archives, University of Massachusetts, Amherst, Massachusetts; Sanford, NC: Microfilming Corporation of America, 1980–1981. Microfilm.

Frank Porter Graham Papers. Southern Historical Collection, Libraries of the University of North Carolina, Chapel Hill, North Carolina.

Herbert Hoover Papers, Commerce Papers subgroup. Herbert Hoover Library, West Branch, Iowa.

Langston Hughes Papers. Beinecke Rare Books and Manuscript Library, Yale University, New Haven, Connecticut.

James Weldon Johnson Papers. Beinecke Rare Books and Manuscript Library, Yale University, New Haven, Connecticut.

Howard Kester Papers. Southern Historical Collection, Libraries of the University of North Carolina, Chapel Hill, North Carolina.

Rayford W. Logan Papers. Manuscript Division, Library of Congress, Washington, D.C.

Rayford W. Logan Papers. Unprocessed manuscript collection. Moorland-Spingarn Research Center, Howard University, Washington, D.C.

August Meier Papers. Schomburg Center for Research in Black Culture, New York Public Library, New York, New York.

National Association for the Advancement of Colored People Papers. Manuscript Division, Library of Congress, Washington, D.C.; Frederick, MD: University Publications of America, Inc., 1982–. Microfilm.

Arthur Raper Papers. Southern Historical Collection, Libraries of the University of North Carolina, Chapel Hill, North Carolina.

Eleanor Roosevelt Papers. Franklin Delano Roosevelt Library, Hyde Park, New York; Frederick, MD: University Publications of America, Inc., 1986. Microfilm.

Arthur B. Spingarn Papers. Manuscript Division, Library of Congress, Washington, D.C.

Arthur B. Spingarn Papers. Moorland-Spingarn Research Center, Howard University, Washington, D.C.

Joel E. Spingarn Papers. Manuscripts and Archives Division, New York Public Library, New York, New York.

Joel Spingarn Papers. Moorland-Spingarn Research Center, Howard University, Washington, D.C.

Lewis L. Strauss Papers, Name and Subject File I: Accretions. Herbert Hoover Library, West Branch, Iowa.

Arthur I. Waskow Papers, State Historical Society of Wisconsin, Madison, Wisconsin.

Walter Francis White and Poppy Cannon White Papers. Beinecke Rare Books and Manuscript Library, Yale University, New Haven, Connecticut.

Walter White Bio File. Archives, Atlanta University Center, Robert W. Woodruff Library, Atlanta, Georgia.

Interviews Conducted by Author

Edwinna Ford
Herbert Hill
Rose Palmer
Mildred Roxborough
Mabel D. Jackson Smith
Chuck Stone
Jane White Viazzi
Cynthia Cannon White

Interviews Conducted by Others

Black Women Oral History Project. Schlesinger Library, Harvard University, Cambridge, Massachusetts; Westport, CT: Meckler, 1991–.
Kathleen Adams interview
Rucker Sisters interview

Voices from the Renaissance, 1974–1977. Summaries of interviews and tape-recorded interviews by David Levering Lewis. Schomburg Center for Research in Black Culture, New York Public Library, New York, New York.
Wilhemina Adams
Poppy Cannon
Owen Dodson
Pearl and Ivy Fisher
Bruce Nugent
Amy Spingarn
Charles Wesley
Corrine Wright

Columbia University Oral History Project
Will Alexander
W.E.B. Du Bois
Joseph Gavagan
Thurgood Marshall
George Schuyler
Roy Wilkins

Ralph J. Bunche Oral History Project. Moorland-Spingarn Research Center, Howard University, Washington, D.C.
Lucille Black
Arthur Spingarn
Roy Wilkins

Interviews by Robert Zangrando

Raymond Pace Alexander
Allan Knight Chalmers
Gloster Current
Morris Ernst
Eustace Gay
Lester Granger
Daisy Lampkin
Alfred Baker Lewis
Helen Martin
H. L. Mitchell
E. Frederic Morrow
Jean Muir
Carl Murphy
Harold Oram
C. A. Scott
Theodore Spaulding
Norman Thomas

Periodicals

Amsterdam News
Baltimore Afro-American
Chicago Defender
The Crisis
Daily Worker
Norfolk Journal and Guide
Opportunity
Pittsburgh Courier

Government Documents

U.S. Congress. House. Committee on the Census. *Hearings on H.R. 14498, H.R. 15021, H.R. 15158, and H.R. 15217 before the Committee on the Census.* 66th Cong., 3rd sess., 29 December 1920.

U.S. Congress. House. Special Committee to Investigate Communist Activities in the United States. *Investigation of Communist Propaganda,* part 3, volume 4, 71st Cong., 2nd sess., 26 and 27 September 1930.

U.S. Congress. Senate. Subcommittee of the Committee on the Judiciary. *Hearing before the Subcommittee of the Committee on the Judiciary United States Senate on the Confirmation of Hon. John J. Parker to Be an Associate Justice of the Supreme Court of the United States.* 71st Cong., 2nd sess., 5 April 1930.

U.S. Congress. Senate. Subcommittee of the Committee on the Judiciary. *Punishment for the Crime of Lynching: Hearings before a Subcommittee of the Committee on the Judiciary United States Senate,* 73rd Cong., 2nd sess, 20 and 21 February 1934.

Other Collections of Primary Documents

Aptheker, Herbert, ed. *A Documentary History of the Negro People in the United States.* Vol. 3, *From the NAACP to the New Deal.* New York: Citadel Press, 1993.

———, ed. *A Documentary History of the Negro People in the United States.* Vol. 4, *From the New Deal to the End of World War II.* New York: Citadel Press, 1992.

———, ed. *A Documentary History of the Negro People in the United States.* Vol. 5, *From the Second World War to the Korean War.* New York: Citadel Press, 1993.

Bernard, Emily, ed. *Remember Me to Harlem: The Letters of Langston Hughes and Carl Van Vechten*. New York: Knopf, 2001.

Kuhn, Clifford M., Harlon E. Joyce, and E. Bernard West. *Living Atlanta: An Oral History of the City, 1914–1948*. Athens, GA: University of Georgia Press, 1990.

Wilson, Sondra Kathryn, ed. *In Search of Democracy: The NAACP Writings of James Weldon Johnson, Walter White, and Roy Wilkins (1920–1977)*. New York: Oxford University Press, 1999.

Selected Published Writings by Walter White

"18 Indicted for Alabama Lynchings Finally Escape." *New York Evening Post*, 19 February 1919.

A Man Called White. New York: Viking, 1948.

"Behind the Harlem Riot." *The New Republic*, 16 August 1943, 220–22.

"The Burning of Jim McIlherron: An N.A.A.C.P. Investigation." *The Crisis*, May 1918, 16–20.

"Chicago and Its Eight Reasons." *The Crisis*, September 1919, 293–97.

Column in the *Chicago Defender*, 1942–1955.

Column in the *New York Herald-Tribune*, 1946–1950.

"Election by Terror in Florida." *The New Republic*, 12 January 1921, 195–97.

"The Eruption of Tulsa." *The Nation*, 29 June 1921, 909–910.

"Finds No 'Massacre Plot' in Arkansas." *Chicago Daily News*, 18 October 1919.

The Fire in the Flint. New York: Knopf, 1924; reprinted with a foreword by R. Baxter Miller, Athens: University of Georgia Press, 1996.

Flight. New York: Knopf, 1926; reprinted Baton Rouge: Louisiana State University Press, 1998.

"For Whom Shall the Negro Vote?" *Harlem: A Forum of Negro Life*, November 1928, 5–6, 45.

"George Crawford—Symbol." *The Crisis*, January 1934, 15.

"Has Science Conquered the Color Line?" *Look*, 30 August 1949, 94–95.

How Far the Promised Land? New York: Viking, 1955.

"How the Double Sessions Do Injustice to Negro Population." Letter to editor, *Atlanta Constitution*, 28 September 1917, 8.

"I Investigate Lynchings." *American Mercury* 16 (January 1929): 77–84.

" 'Massacring Whites' in Arkansas." *The Nation*, 6 December 1919, 715–16.

"The Negro and the Communists." *Harper's Magazine* 164 (December 1931): 62–72.

"The Negro and the Supreme Court." *Harper's* 157 (January 1931). Reprinted in Sondra Kathryn Wilson, ed. *In Search of Democracy: The NAACP Writings of James Weldon Johnson, Walter White, and Roy Wilkins (1920–1977)*, 237–46. New York: Oxford University Press, 1999.

"On Segregation." *The Crisis*, March 1934. Reprinted in Sondra Kathryn Wilson, ed. *In Search of Democracy: The NAACP Writings of James Weldon Johnson, Walter White, and Roy Wilkins (1920–1977)*, 263–65. New York: Oxford University Press, 1999.

"The Race Conflict in Arkansas." *Survey*, 13 December 1919, 233–34.

A Rising Wind. Garden City, N.Y.: Doubleday, Doran, 1945.

Rope and Faggot: A Biography of Judge Lynch. With a new introduction by Kenneth Robert Janken. New York: Knopf, 1929; reprinted Notre Dame, Indiana: University of Notre Dame Press, 2001.

"Sheriff's Fears Permitted Indiana Lynching." *New York World*, 24 August 1930.

"Solving America's Race Problem." *The Nation*, 9 January 1929, 42–43.

"Time for a Progress Report." *The Saturday Review of Literature*, September 22, 1951, 9–10, 38–41.

"Why I Remain a Negro." *The Saturday Review of Literature*, 11 October 1947, 13–14, 49–52.

"The Work of a Mob." *The Crisis,* September 1918, 221–23.

" 'Work or Fight' in the South." *The New Republic* 18 (1919): 144–46.

Books and Articles

Bacote, Clarence A. *The Story of Atlanta University: A Century of Service, 1865–1965*. Atlanta: Atlanta University, 1969.

Baker, Leonard. *Brandeis and Frankfurter: A Dual Biography*. New York: Harper & Row, 1984.

Barry, John M. *Rising Tide: The Great Mississippi Flood of 1927 and How It Changed America*. New York: Simon & Schuster, 1997.

Bates, Beth Tompkins. "A New Crowd Challenges the Agenda of the Old Guard of the NAACP, 1933–1941." *American Historical Review* 102 (1997): 340–77.

———. *Pullman Porters and the Rise of Protest Politics in Black America, 1925–1945*. Chapel Hill: University of North Carolina Press, 2001.

Bauerlein, Mark. *Negrophobia: A Race Riot in Atlanta, 1906*. San Francisco: Encounter Books, 2001.

Bayor, Ronald H. *Race and the Shaping of Twentieth-Century Atlanta*. Chapel Hill: University of North Carolina Press, 1996.

Bederman, Gail. " 'Civilization,' the Decline of Middle-Class Manliness, and Ida B. Wells's Antilynching Campaign (1892–94)." *Radical History Review* no. 52 (1992): 5–30.

Berman, William C. *The Politics of Civil Rights in the Truman Administration*. Columbus, Ohio: Ohio State University Press, 1970.

Boardman, Helen and Martha Gruening. "Is the NAACP Retreating?" *The Nation*, 27 June 1934, 730–32.

Borstlemann, Thomas. *Apartheid's Reluctant Uncle: The United States and Southern Africa in the Early Cold War*. New York: Oxford University Press, 1993.

Boyle, Sheila Tully and Andrew Bunie. *Paul Robeson: The Years of Promise and Achievement*. Amherst, Mass.: University of Massachusetts Press, 2001.

Bracey, John H., Jr. and August Meier. "Allies or Adversaries?: The NAACP, A. Philip Randolph and the 1941 March on Washington." *Georgia Historical Quarterly* 75 (1991): 1–17.

Brazeal, B. R. "The Present Status and Programs of Fair Employment Practices Commissions—Federal, State, and Municipal." *Journal of Negro Education* 20 (1951): 378–97.

Broun, Heywood. "It Seems to Heywood Broun." *The Nation,* 21 May 1930, 591.

Brundage, W. Fitzhugh. *Lynching in the New South*. Urbana: University of Illinois Press, 1993.

Bunche, Ralph J. "A Critical Analysis of the Tactics and Programs of Minority Groups." *Journal of Negro Education* 4 (1935): 308–20.

——— "A Critique of New Deal Social Planning as it Affects Negroes." *Journal of Negro Education* 5 (1936): 59–65.

Buni, Andrew. *Robert L. Vann of the* Pittsburgh Courier: *Politics and Black Journalism*. Pittsburgh, PA: University of Pittsburgh Press, 1974.

Cannon, Poppy. *A Gentle Knight: My Husband Walter White*. New York: Rinehart & Co., 1956.

Capeci, Dominic J., Jr. *The Harlem Riot of 1943*. Philadelphia: Temple University Press, 1977.

———. *The Lynching of Cleo Wright*. Lexington, KY: University Press of Kentucky, 1998.

Capeci, Dominic J., Jr. and Martha Wilkerson. *Layered Violence: The Detroit Rioters of 1943*. Jackson: University of Mississippi Press, 1991.

Carter, Dan T. *Scottsboro: A Tragedy of the American South*. Rev. ed. Baton Rouge: Louisiana State University Press, 1979.

Chamlee, George. "Is Lynching Ever Defensible?" *The Forum* 76 (1926): 811–17.

Cohen, William. "Negro Involuntary Servitude in the South, 1865–1940: A Preliminary Analysis." *Journal of Southern History* 42 (1976): 31–60.

Cook, Blanche Weisen. *Eleanor Roosevelt*. Vol. II, *1933–1938*. New York: Viking, 1999.

Cooney, Charles F. "Mencken's Midwifery." *Menckeniana: A Quarterly Review* 43 (1972): 1–16.

———. "Walter White and Sinclair Lewis: The History of a Literary Friendship." *Prospects* 1 (1975): 63–75.

———. "Walter White and the Harlem Renaissance." *Journal of Negro History* 57 (1972): 231–40.

Cortner, Richard C. *A Mob Intent on Death*. Middletown, CT: Wesleyan University Press, 1988.

Cox, Oliver C. "The Programs of Negro Civil Rights Organizations." *Journal of Negro Education* 20 (1951): 354–66.

Cripps, Thomas. *Making Movies Black*. New York: Oxford University Press, 1993.

Crowe, Charles. "Racial Massacre in Atlanta, September 22, 1906." *Journal of Negro History* 54 (1969): 150–73.

Daniel, Pete. "Black Power in the 1920s: The Case of the Tuskegee Veterans Hospital." *Journal of Southern History* 36 (1970): 368–88.

Davis, Thadious. *Nella Larsen, Novelist of the Harlem Renaissance*. Baton Rouge: Louisiana State University Press, 1994.

Decker, Mary Bell. *The World We Saw with Town Hall*. New York: Richard R. Smith, 1950.

Diner, Hasia R. *In the Almost Promised Land: American Jews and Blacks, 1915–1935*. Westport, CT: Greenwood Press, 1977.

Dittmer, John. *Black Georgia in the Progressive Era, 1900–1920*. Urbana: University of Illinois Press, 1977.

Douglass, Aaron. "Aaron Douglass Chats about the Harlem Renaissance." In *The Portable Harlem Renaissance Reader*, ed. David Levering Lewis, 118–27. New York: Penguin, 1995.

Duberman, Martin Bauml. *Paul Robeson*. New York: Knopf, 1988.

Du Bois, W.E.B. *The Autobiography of W.E.B. Du Bois*. New York: International Publishers, 1968.

———. "The Criteria of Negro Art" (1926). In *The Portable Harlem Renaissance Reader*, ed. David Levering Lewis, 100–105. New York: Penguin, 1994.

———. *The Souls of Black Folk* (1903). In *The Oxford W.E.B. Du Bois Reader*, ed. Eric J. Sundquist. New York: Oxford University Press, 1996.

———. *Writings in Periodicals Edited by W.E.B. Du Bois: Selections from The Crisis*, ed. Herbert Aptheker. Vol. I, *1911–1925*. Vol. II, *1926–1934*. Millwood, NY: Kraus-Thomson, 1983.

Egerton, John. *Speak Now Against the Day: The Generation Before the Civil Rights Movement in the South*. New York: Knopf, 1994; reprinted Chapel Hill: University of North Carolina Press, 1995.

Ellsworth, Scott. *Death in the Promised Land: The Tulsa Race Riot of 1921*. With a foreword by John Hope Franklin. Baton Rouge: Louisiana State University Press, 1982.

Fairclough, Adam. " 'Being in the Field of Education and Also Being a Negro . . . Seems . . . Tragic': Black Teachers in the Jim Crow South." *Journal of American History* 87 (2000): 65–91.

———. *Teaching Equality: Black Schools in the Age of Jim Crow*. Athens: University of Georgia Press, 2000.

Fauset, Jessie. "Impressions of the Second Pan-African Congress." *The Crisis*, November 1921, 12–18.

Fine, Sidney. *Frank Murphy: The Detroit Years*. Ann Arbor: University of Michigan Press, 1975.

Foner, Eric. *Reconstruction: America's Unfinished Revolution, 1863–1877*. New York: Harper & Row, 1988.

Formwalt, Lee W. " 'Corner-Stone of the Cotton Kingdom': W.E.B. Du Bois's 1898 View of Dougherty County." *Georgia Historical Quarterly* 71 (1987): 693–700.

———. "Southwest Georgia: A Garden of Irony and Diversity." In *The New Georgia Guide*. Athens: University of Georgia Press, 1996.

Gaines, Kevin K. *Uplifting the Race*. Chapel Hill: University of North Carolina Press, 1996.

Gatewood, Willard B. *Aristocrats of Color: The Black Elite, 1880–1920*. Bloomington: Indiana University Press, 1993.

Genizi, Haim. "V. F. Calverton, a Radical Magazinist for Black Intellectuals, 1920–1940." *Journal of Negro History* 57 (1972): 241–53.

Giddings, Paula. *When and Where I Enter*. New York: William Morrow, 1984.

Gilmore, Glenda Elizabeth. *Gender and Jim Crow*. Chapel Hill: University of North Carolina Press, 1996.

Goldfield, Michael. *The Color of Politics: Race and the Mainsprings of American Politics*. New York: New Press, 1997.

Goings, Kenneth W. *"The NAACP Comes of Age": The Defeat of Judge John J. Parker*. Bloomington: Indiana University Press, 1990.

Goodman, James. *Stories of Scottsboro*. New York: Vintage, 1995.

Goodwyn, Lawrence C. *Democratic Promise: The Populist Movement in America*. New York: Oxford University Press, 1976.

———. "Populist Dreams and Negro Rights: East Texas as a Case Study." *American Historical Review* 76 (1971): 1435–456.

Grant, Joanne. *Ella Baker: Freedom Bound*. New York: John Wiley, 1998.

Griffler, Keith. *What Price Alliance? Black Radicals Confront White Labor, 1918–1938*. New York: Garland, 1995.

Grossman, James R. *Land of Hope: Chicago, Black Southerners, and the Great Migration*. Chicago: University of Chicago Press, 1988.

Gruening, Martha. "The Truth About the Crawford Case." *New Masses*, 8 January 1935, 9–15.

Hachey, Thomas. "Walter White and the American Negro Soldier in World War II: A Diplomatic Dilemma for Britain." *Phylon* 39 (1978): 241–49.

Hale, Grace Elizabeth. *Making Whiteness*. New York: Pantheon, 1998.

Hall, Jacqueline Dowd. *Revolt against Chivalry: Jessie Daniel Ames and the Women's Campaign against Lynching*. New York: Columbia University Press, 1979.

Hamby, Alonzo. *Beyond the New Deal: Harry S. Truman and American Liberalism*. New York: Columbia University Press, 1973.

Hamilton, Charles V. *Adam Clayton Powell, Jr.: The Political Biography of an American Dilemma*. New York: Collier, 1991.

Harlan, Louis R. *Booker T. Washington: The Making of a Black Leader, 1856–1901*. New York: Oxford University Press, 1975.

Harris, Trudier. *Exorcizing Blackness: Historical and Literary Lynching and Burning Rituals*. Bloomington: Indiana University Press, 1984.

Harris, William H. *The Harder We Run: Black Workers since the Civil War*. New York: Oxford University Press, 1982.

———. *Keeping the Faith: A. Philip Randolph, Milton P. Webster, and the Brotherhood of Sleeping Car Porters, 1925–37*. Urbana: University of Illinois Press, 1977.

Henderson, Dr. Alexa and Dr. Eugene Walker. *Sweet Auburn: The Thriving Hub of Black Atlanta, 1900–1960*. Atlanta: U.S. Department of the Interior/National Park Service, 1984.

Herskovits, Melville J. "The Color Line." *American Mercury* 6 (1926): 204–208.

Hess, Gary R. *America Encounters India, 1941–1947.* Baltimore: The Johns Hopkins University Press, 1971.

Higginbotham, Evelyn Brooks. *Righteous Discontent.* Cambridge: Harvard University Press, 1993.

Hill, Herbert. *Black Labor and the American Legal System: Race, Work, and the Law.* Washington, D.C.: The Bureau of National Affairs, 1977.

———. "Lichtenstein's Fictions: Meany, Reuther and the 1964 Civil Rights Act." *New Politics*, n.s., 7 (1998): 82–107.

———. "Lichtenstein's Fictions Revisited: Race and the New Labor History." *New Politics*, n.s., 7 (1999): 148–63.

———. "The Problem of Race in American Labor History." *Reviews in American History* 24 (1996): 189–208.

Hobson, Fred. *Mencken: A Life.* New York: Random House, 1994.

Horne, Gerald. *Black and Red: W.E.B. Du Bois and the Afro-American Response to the Cold War, 1944–1961.* Albany, NY: State University of New York Press, 1986.

Horne, Lena and Richard Schickel. *Lena.* Garden City, N. Y.: Doubleday, 1965.

Huggins, Nathan I. *The Harlem Renaissance.* New York: Oxford University Press, 1971.

Hughes, Langston. "The Negro Artist and the Racial Mountain" (1926). In *The Portable Harlem Renaissance Reader,* ed. David Levering Lewis, 91–95. New York: Penguin, 1995.

Hughes, Langston. *The Big Sea.* New York: Knopf, 1940.

Humphrey, Hubert H. "Notes and Memoranda: The Senate on Trial." *American Political Science Review* 44 (1950): 650–60.

Hunt, Michael H. *Ideology and U.S. Foreign Policy.* New Haven: Yale University Press, 1987.

Hunter, Tera W. *To 'Joy My Freedom: Southern Black Women's Lives and Labors after the Civil War.* Cambridge: Harvard University Press, 1997.

Hutchinson, George. *The Harlem Renaissance in Black and White.* Cambridge: Harvard University Press, 1995.

Jackson, Carlton. *Hattie: The Life of Hattie McDaniel.* Lanham, Md.: Madison Books, 1990.

Janken, Kenneth R. "African American and Francophone Black Intellectuals During the Harlem Renaissance." *The Historian* 60 (1998): 487–505.

———. "Civil Rights and Socializing in the Harlem Renaissance: Walter White and the Fictionalization of the 'New Negro' in Georgia." *Georgia Historical Quarterly* 80 (1996): 818–34.

———. "From Colonial Liberation to Cold War Liberalism: Walter White, the NAACP, and Foreign Affairs, 1941–1955." *Ethnic and Racial Studies* 21 (1998): 1074–1095.

Janken, Kenneth Robert. *Rayford W. Logan and the Dilemma of the African-American Intellectual.* Amherst: University of Massachusetts Press, 1993.

Johnson, Charles S. *The Negro in American Civilization.* New York: Henry Holt, 1930.

———. "The Negro Renaissance and Its Significance." In *The Portable Harlem Renaissance Reader,* ed. David Levering Lewis, 206–18. New York: Penguin, 1995.

Johnson, Forrest Clark III. *People of Ante-Bellum Troup County, Georgia.* La Grange, GA: Sutherland-St. Dunstan Press, 1993.

Johnson, James Weldon. *Along This Way: The Autobiography of James Weldon Johnson.* With an introduction by Sondra Kathryn Wilson. New York: Viking, 1933; reprinted New York: Penguin, 1990.

———. *Black Manhattan.* New York: Viking, 1930.

———. *Negro Americans, What Now?* New York: Viking, 1934.

————. Preface to the original edition of *The Book of American Negro Poetry*, ed. James Weldon Johnson. Rev. ed. New York: Harcourt, Brace & World, 1931.

Kapur, Sundarshan. *Raising up a Prophet: The African-American Encounter with Gandhi.* Boston: Beacon Press, 1992.

Keiler, Allen. *Marian Anderson: A Singer's Journey.* New York: Scribner, 2000.

Kelley, Robin D. G. *Hammer and Hoe: Alabama Communists during the Great Depression.* Chapel Hill: University of North Carolina Press, 1990.

Kellog, Charles Flint. *NAACP: A History of the National Association for the Advancement of Colored People.* Baltimore: The Johns Hopkins Press, 1967.

Kester, Howard. *Revolt among the Sharecroppers.* New York: Covici, Friede, 1936.

King, Desmond. "A Strong or Weak State? Race and the U.S. Federal Government in the 1920s." *Ethnic and Racial Studies* 21 (1998): 21–47.

Kirby, John B. *Black Americans in the Roosevelt Era.* Knoxville: University of Tennessee Press, 1980.

Korstad, Robert and Nelson Lichtenstein. "Opportunities Found and Lost: Labor, Radicals, and the Early Civil Rights Movement." *Journal of American History* 75 (1988): 786–811.

Kluger, Richard. *Simple Justice.* New York: Vintage, 1977.

Kneebone, John T. *Southern Liberal Journalists and the Issue of Race, 1920–1944.* Chapel Hill: University of North Carolina Press, 1985.

Koppes, Clayton R. and Gregory D. Black. *Hollywood Goes to War.* New York: Free Press, 1987.

Kornweibel, Theodore, Jr. *"Seeing Red": Federal Campaigns against Black Militancy, 1919–1925.* Bloomington: Indiana University Press, 1998.

Leuchtenberg, William E. *The Perils of Prosperity, 1914–32.* 2d ed. Chicago: University of Chicago Press, 1993.

Levy, Eugene. *James Weldon Johnson: Black Leader, Black Voice.* Chicago: University of Chicago Press, 1973.

Lewis, David Levering. Introduction to *The Portable Harlem Renaissance Reader,* ed. David Levering Lewis, xv–xliii. New York: Penguin, 1995.

————. "Parallels and Divergencies: Assimilationist Strategies of Afro-American and Jewish Elites from 1910 to the Early 1930s." *Journal of American History* 71 (1984): 543–64.

————. *W.E.B. Du Bois: Biography of a Race, 1868–1919.* New York: Henry Holt, 1993.

————. *W.E.B. Du Bois: The Fight for Equality and the American Century, 1919–1963.* New York: Henry Holt, 2000.

————. *When Harlem Was in Vogue.* New York: Vintage, 1982.

Lewis, Earl. *In Their Own Interests. Race, Class, and Power in Twentieth-Century Norfolk, Virginia.* Berkeley: University of California Press, 1991.

Lisio, Donald J. *Hoover, Blacks, and Lily-Whites.* Chapel Hill: University of North Carolina Press, 1985.

Locke, Alain. "The New Negro." In *The New Negro,* ed. Alain Locke, 3–16. New York: Albert & Charles Boni, 1925; reprinted New York: Atheneum, 1992.

Logan, Rayford W. "The 'Little Man' Just Isn't Here." *Pittsburgh Courier,* 5 May 1945.

————. "The Negro Studies War Some More." *Norfolk Journal & Guide,* 28 June 1935.

————, ed. *What the Negro Wants.* Chapel Hill: University of North Carolina Press, 1944. Reprinted with a new introduction by Kenneth Robert Janken. Notre Dame, In: University of Notre Dame Press, 2001.

Louis, Wm. Roger. "Great Britain and the African Peace Settlement of 1919." *American Historical Review* 71 (1966): 875–92.

Love, Spencie. *One Blood: The Death and Resurrection of Charles R. Drew.* Chapel Hill: University of North Carolina Press, 1996.

Lynch, Hollis R. *Black American Radicals and the Liberation of Africa: The Council on African*

Affairs, 1937–1955. With an introduction by St. Clair Drake. Ithaca, NY: Africana Studies and Research Center, 1978.

MacLean, Nancy. "The Leo Frank Case Reconsidered: Gender and Sexual Politics in the Making of Reactionary Populism." *Journal of American History* 78 (1991): 917–48.

Majors, Glenda and Forrest Clark Johnson III. *Treasures of Troup County: A Pictorial History.* La Grange, GA: Troup County Historical Society, 1993.

Martin, Charles H. *The Angelo Herndon Case and Southern Justice.* Baton Rouge: Louisiana State University Press, 1976.

Martin, Waldo E., Jr., ed. *Brown v. Board of Education: A Brief History with Documents.* With an introduction by the editor. Boston: Bedford, 1998.

Mathews, Donald G. "The Southern Rite of Human Sacrifice." *Journal of Southern Religion* [Online] 3 (2000), available at http://jsr.as.wvu.edu/mathews.htm [accessed 29 November 2000].

McCoy, Donald R. and Richard T. Ruetten. *Quest and Response: Minority Rights and the Truman Administration.* Lawrence, Kansas: University Press of Kansas, 1973.

McEwen, Homer C., Sr. "First Congregational Church, Atlanta." *Atlanta Historical Society Bulletin* 21 (Spring 1977): 129–42.

McGovern, James R. *Anatomy of a Lynching: The Killing of Claude Neal.* Baton Rouge: Louisiana State University Press, 1982.

McMillan, Neil. *Dark Journey: Black Mississippians in the Age of Jim Crow.* Urbana, IL: University of Illinois Press, 1990.

McNeil, Genna Rae. *Groundwork: Charles Hamilton Houston and the Struggle for Civil Rights.* Philadelphia: University of Pennsylvania Press, 1983.

———. "Youth Initiative in the African American Struggle for Racial Justice and Constitutional Rights: The City-Wide Young People's Forum of Baltimore, 1931–1941." In John Hope Franklin and Genna Rae McNeil, eds. *African Americans and the Living Constitution*, 56–80. Washington, D.C.: Smithsonian Institution Press, 1995.

Meier, August and John H. Bracey, Jr. "The NAACP as a Reform Movement, 1909–1965: 'To reach the conscience of America.' " *Journal of Southern History* 69 (1993): 3–30.

Meier, August and David Lewis. "History of the Negro Upper Class in Atlanta, Georgia, 1890–1958." In August Meier, *A White Scholar and the Black Community, 1945–1965: Essays and Reflections.* Amherst, MA: University of Massachusetts Press, 1992.

Meier, August and Elliott Rudwick. *Along the Color Line: Explorations in the Black Experience.* Urbana, IL: University of Illinois Press, 1976.

Meier, August and Elliott Rudwick. *Black Detroit and the Rise of the UAW.* New York: Oxford University Press, 1979.

Mencken, H. L. "Sahara of the Bozart." In *The American Scene: A Reader.* Selected and edited and with an introduction and commentary by Huntington Cairns, 157–68. New York: Knopf, 1965.

Mixon, Gregory. " 'Good Negro—Bad Negro': The Dynamics of Race and Class in Atlanta during the Era of the 1906 Riot." *Georgia Historical Quarterly* 81 (1997): 593–621.

Moon, Henry Lee. *Balance of Power: The Negro Vote.* Garden City, NY: Doubleday, 1948.

Naison, Mark. *Communists in Harlem during the Depression.* New York: Grove Press, 1984.

Nelson, Bruce. "Organized Labor and the Struggle for Black Equality in Mobile during World War II." *Journal of American History* 80 (1993): 952–88.

Newman, Roger K. *Hugo Black: A Biography.* New York: Pantheon, 1994.

Park, Marlene. "Lynching and Antilynching: Art and Politics in the 1930s." *Prospects* 18 (1993): 328–29.

Patterson, Orlando. *Rituals of Blood: Consequences of Slavery in Two American Centuries.* Washington, D.C.: Civitas/Counterpoint, 1998.

Plummer, Brenda Gayle. *Rising Wind: Black Americans and U.S. Foreign Affairs, 1935–1960.* Chapel Hill: University of North Carolina Press, 1996.

Rable, George C. "The South and the Politics of Antilynching Legislation, 1920–1940" *Journal of Southern History* 51 (1985): 201–20.

Rampersad, Arnold. *The Life of Langston Hughes.* Vol. I, *1902–1941: I, Too Sing America.* New York: Oxford University Press, 1986.

Raper, Arthur. *The Tragedy of Lynching.* Chapel Hill: University of North Carolina Press, 1933.

Reed, Christopher Robert. *The Chicago NAACP and the Rise of Black Professional Leadership, 1910–1960.* Bloomington: Indiana University Press, 1997.

Reed, Merl E. *Seedtime for the Modern Civil Rights Movement: The President's Committee on Fair Employment Practices, 1941–46.* Baton Rouge: Louisiana State University Press, 1991.

Rich, Paul B. *Race and Empire in British Politics.* Cambridge: Cambridge University Press, 1986.

Rogin, Michael. *Blackface, White Noise: Jewish Immigrants in the Hollywood Melting Pot.* Berkeley: University of California Press, 1996.

Ross, B. Joyce. *J. E. Spingarn and the Rise of the NAACP, 1911–1939.* New York: Atheneum, 1972.

Rowan, Carl T. *Dream Makers, Dream Breakers: The World of Thurgood Marshall.* Boston: Little, Brown, 1993.

Salem, Dorothy. *To Better Our World: Black Women in Organized Reform, 1890–1920.* Brooklyn, NY: Carlson, 1990.

Salzman, Jack and Cornel West, eds. *Struggles in the Promised Land: Toward a History of Black-Jewish Relations in the United States.* New York: Oxford University Press, 1997.

Sandage, Scott A. "A Marble House Divided: The Lincoln Memorial, the Civil Rights Movement, and the Politics of Memory, 1939–1963." *Journal of American History* 80 (1993): 135–67.

Schechter, Patricia A. *Ida B. Wells-Barnett & American Social Reform, 1880–1930.* Chapel Hill: University of North Carolina Press, 2001.

———. "Unsettled Business: Ida B. Wells against Lynching, or, How Antilynching Got Its Gender." In *Under Sentence of Death: Lynching in the South,* ed. W. Fitzhugh Brundage. Chapel Hill: University of North Carolina Press, 1997.

Schlesinger, Arthur M., Jr. "The U.S. Communist Party." *Life,* 29 July 1946, 84–85, 87–88, 90, 93–94, 96.

Schultz, Mark R. "Interracial Kinship Ties and the Emergence of a Rural Black Middle Class: Hancock County, Georgia, 1865–1920." In *Georgia in Black and White: Explorations in the Race Relations of a Southern State, 1865–1950,* ed. John C. Inscoe, 141–72. Athens, GA: University of Georgia Press, 1994.

Scruggs, Charles W. "Alain Locke and Walter White: Their Struggle for Control of the Harlem Renaissance." *Black American Literature Forum* 14 (1980): 91–99.

———. *The Sage in Harlem: H. L. Mencken and the Black Writers of the 1920s.* Baltimore: The Johns Hopkins University Press, 1984.

Shapiro, Herbert. *White Violence and Black Response.* Amherst: University of Massachusetts Press, 1988.

Shenk, Gerald E. "Race, Manhood, and Manpower: Mobilizing Rural Georgia for World War I." *Georgia Historical Quarterly* 81 (1997): 622–62.

Sherwood, Marika. "Walter White and the British: A Lost Opportunity." *Contributions in Black Studies* 9/10 (1990–1992): 215–26.

Sitkoff, Harvard. *A New Deal for Blacks.* New York: Oxford University Press, 1981.

Solomon, Mark. *The Cry Was Unity: Communists and African Americans, 1917–1936.* Jackson: University Press of Mississippi, 1998.

Southern Conference for Human Welfare. *The Truth about Columbia, Tennessee Cases.* Nashville: The Conference, [1946?].

Stegh, Leslie J. "A Paradox of Prohibition: Election of Robert J. Bulkley as Senator from Ohio, 1930." *Ohio History* 83 (1974): 170–82.

Stockley, Grif. *Blood in Their Eyes: The Elaine Race Massacres of 1919.* Fayetteville: University of Arkansas Press, 2001.

Sudarkasa, Niara, ed. *The Barnes Bond Connection.* Lincoln University, PA: Lincoln University Press, 1995.

Suggs, Jon Christian. " 'Blackjack': Walter White and Modernism in An Unknown Boxing Novel." *Michigan Quarterly Review* 38 (1999): 515–40.

Sullivan, Patricia. *Days of Hope: Race and Democracy in the New Deal Era.* Chapel Hill: University of North Carolina Press, 1996.

Terborg-Penn, Rosalyn. "African-American Women's Networks in the Anti-Lynching Crusade." In *Gender, Class, Race, and Reform in the Progressive Era,* ed. Noralee Frankel and Nancy S. Dye, 148–61. Lexington, KY: University Press of Kentucky, 1991.

[Thompson, Charles H.] "Editorial Comment: The Harrison-Black-Fletcher Bill Makes Its Debut." *Journal of Negro Education* 6 (1937): 129–33.

Tolnay, Stewart E. and E. M. Beck. *A Festival of Violence: An Analysis of Southern Lynchings, 1882–1930.* Urbana and Chicago: University of Illinois Press, 1995.

Toppin, Edgar A. "Walter White and the Atlanta NAACP's Fight for Equal Schools, 1916–1917." *History of Education Quarterly* 7 (1967): 3–21.

Torrence, Ridgely. *The Story of John Hope.* New York: Macmillan, 1948.

Tushnet, Mark V. *The NAACP's Legal Strategy Against Segregated Education, 1925–1950.* Chapel Hill: University of North Carolina Press, 1987.

Tuttle, William M., Jr. *Race Riot: Chicago in the Red Summer of 1919.* New York: Atheneum, 1985.

Vendryes, Margaret Rose. "Hanging on Their Walls: *An Art Commentary on Lynching,* the Forgotten 1935 Art Exhibition." In *Race Consciousness: African-American Studies for the New Century,* eds. Judith Jackson Fossett and Jeffrey A. Tucker, 153–76. New York: New York University Press, 1997.

Von Eschen, Penny M. *Race Against Empire: Black Americans and Anticolonialism, 1937–1957.* Ithaca, NY: Cornell University Press, 1997.

Wall, Cheryl A. *Women of the Harlem Renaissance.* Bloomington: Indiana University Press, 1995.

Walrond, Edward E. *Walter White and the Harlem Renaissance.* Port Washington, NY: Kennikat Press, 1978.

Waskow, Arthur I. *From Race Riot to Sit-In, 1919 and the 1960s.* Garden City, NY: Doubleday & Co., 1966.

Wedin, Carolyn. *Inheritors of the Spirit: Mary White Ovington and the Founding of the NAACP.* New York: John Wiley & Sons, 1998.

Wells-Barnett, Ida B. *Southern Horrors and Other Writings: The Anti-Lynching Campaign of Ida B. Wells, 1892–1900.* Edited and with an introduction by Jacqueline Jones Royster. Boston: Bedford, 1997.

White, Deborah Gray. "The Cost of Club Work, the Price of Black Feminism." In *Visible Women: New Essays on American Activism,* eds. Nancy A. Hewitt and Suzanne Lebsock, 247–69. Urbana and Chicago: University of Illinois Press, 1993.

Wilkins, Roy with Tom Mathews. *Standing Fast: The Autobiography of Roy Wilkins.* New York: Viking, 1982.

Wilson, George. *Farmer to Farmer around the World.* [Stockton, Calif.]: Privately printed, 1987.

Wolters, Raymond. *Negroes and the Great Depression.* Westport, CT: Greenwood Publishing, 1970.

Wright, C. T. "The Development of Public Schools for Blacks in Atlanta, 1872–1900." *Atlanta Historical Society Bulletin* 21 (1977): 115–28.

Wright, Richard. *The Color Curtain: A Report on the Bandung Conference.* Cleveland: World Publishing Company, 1956.

Wright, Richard R., Jr. *The Bishops of the African Methodist Episcopal Church.* Nashville, Tenn.: A.M.E. Sunday School Union, 1963.

Zangrando, Robert L. *The NAACP Crusade against Lynching, 1909–1950.* Philadelphia: Temple University Press, 1980.

Unpublished Works

Bridges, Lucile, Sarah Lane, and Marguerite Spearman. "Educational Progress of Negroes in Troup County." Edited by J. R. Jones. Not dated [circa 1930s], Troup County Archives, La Grange, GA. Typescript.

Dudziak, Mary Louise. "Cold War Civil Rights: The Relationship between Civil Rights and Foreign Affairs in the Truman Administration." Ph.D. diss., Yale University, 1992.

Godshalk, David Fort. "In the wake of riot: Atlanta's struggle for order, 1899–1919." Ph.D. diss., Yale University, 1992.

Jensen, Hilmar Ludvig. "The Rise of an African American Left: John P. Davis and the National Negro Congress." Ph.D. diss., Cornell University, 1997.

Mixon, Gregory Lamont. "The Atlanta Riot of 1906." Ph.D. diss., University of Cincinnati, 1989.

Porter, Michael Leroy. "Black Atlanta: An Interdisciplinary Study of Blacks on the East Side of Atlanta, 1890–1930." Ph.D. diss., Emory University, 1974.

Index